FreeBSD®

UNLEASHED

Second Edition

Brian Tiemann
Michael C. Urban

SAMS   201 West 103rd Street, Indianapolis, Indiana 46290

FreeBSD® Unleashed

Second Edition

Copyright © 2003 by Sams Publishing

International Standard Book Number: 0-672-32456-3

Library of Congress Catalog Card Number: 2002106458

Printed in the United States of America

First Printing: April 2003

04   03   4   3   2   1

Trademarks

Warning and Disclaimer

Acquisitions Editor
Katie Purdum

Development Editor
Lorna Gentry

Managing Editor
Charlotte Clapp

Project Editor
Andy Beaster

Copy Editor
Bart Reed

Indexer
Becky Hornyak

Proofreader
Jessica McCarty

Technical Editor
Michael Watson

Team Coordinator
Vanessa Evans

Media Developer
Dan Scherf

Interior Designer
Gary Adair

Cover Designer
Aren Howell

Page Layout
Cheryl Lynch

Contents at a Glance

Table of Contents

About the Authors

Michael Urban is a biology student at the University of Minnesota. His current work on research projects involving African lions for the Lion Research Center includes programming projects with Java and C++. Michael has worked with various forms of Unix for several years, including FreeBSD, Linux, and Solaris. He has also worked as a technical analyst and is the author of *Teach Yourself FreeBSD in 24 Hours*, also from Sams Publishing. In his free time, which is very sparse these days between exams and research projects, he enjoys reading and is also starting to pursue wildlife photography.

Brian Tiemann has been a constant user of FreeBSD since his student days at Caltech, where he used it to build a movie fan Web site that continues to grow and sustain an ever-increasing load. Born in Ukiah, California, Brian has remained in the state all his life; he currently lives in San Jose and works in the networking appliance field. Aside from FreeBSD, his other interests include Macintoshes, motorcycles, and animation, topics about which he writes frequently.

Dedication

To my parents, Chris and Bonnie, and my sister, Beth. And to the
Serengeti lions. I hope my work helps contribute to the difference that
the Lion Research Center is making for them.

—Michael C. Urban

I dedicate this book to my parents, Keith and Ann, and to my
brother, Mike. And to Douglas Adams, wherever in the Galaxy
you are.

—Brian Tiemann

Acknowledgments

Several people need to be thanked for making this second edition of *FreeBSD Unleashed* possible. To begin, we would like to thank the entire staff at Sams Publishing for the opportunity to write a second edition of this book. Of course, the second edition would not exist without the support of readers, so we would also like to thank everyone who bought the first edition of *FreeBSD Unleashed*. We also thank those who sent us comments and suggestions on the first edition. We have incorporated many of these into the second edition, and we hope our readers will continue to send comments and suggestions so we can make future improvements.

A project of this magnitude would not have been possible without the efforts of a lot of people. We would like to thank the staff at Sams Publishing who worked with us on this book, including Kathryn Purdum, Andrew Beaster, and Dan Scherf. We would also like to thank Lorna Gentry for developing this second edition and Michael Watson for his thorough technical review of the manuscript. In addition, we would like to thank the rest of the staff who worked on this book for putting up with our frequent changes as we wrote for FreeBSD 5.0, which was a moving target that was still in development at the time.

Of course, without the efforts of the FreeBSD developers, this book would not exist. We would like to thank all the volunteer FreeBSD developers all over the world who donate their personal time toward making FreeBSD an operating system that is better than similar commercial operating systems that cost hundreds or even thousands of dollars. FreeBSD 5.0 is a major accomplishment and contains new technologies that most commercial operating systems don't even have yet. It is a great example of what volunteers with dedication and hard work can accomplish.

Michael Urban: I would like to thank Dr. Craig Packer and Peyton West—who as of January 31, 2003 is now Dr. Peyton West. Congratulations, Peyton :)—of the Lion Research Center, located at the University of Minnesota, for providing some of the photographs used in this book. (Please give the Lion Research Center's Web site a visit at www.lionresearch.org.) I would also like to thank my co-author, Brian Tiemann, because I would not have been able to write this book alone.

Brian Tiemann: I would like to thank Paul Summers for his untiring efforts doing all the hard and expensive site-admin work while I philosophize and hack and rant from afar; Lance, Kris, Chris, Brian D., David, Drew, Zjonni, Gerrit, Marcus, Matt, Trent, and the rest of my friends who have helped me solidify my opinions and passions about operating systems and software; James, Steven, Mike, Mike, and everyone else who has seen fit to read my daily online writing, supply encouragement, and keep me honest; Adam, Ian, Jarrod, and Sean for inspiration; and Cirque du Soleil and Brak for the music to write by. Finally, I thank all the members of the TLK-L and Lionking.org for supporting me so steadfastly all these years and making me feel as if I know what I'm talking about. Maybe a copy of this book will find its way into the γδβ library, as would be appropriate.

Tell Us What You Think!

As the reader of this book, *you* are our most important critic and commentator. We value your opinion and want to know what we're doing right, what we could do better, what areas you'd like to see us publish in, and any other words of wisdom you're willing to pass our way.

You can e-mail or write me directly to let me know what you did or didn't like about this book—as well as what we can do to make our books stronger.

Please note that I cannot help you with technical problems related to the topic of this book, and that due to the high volume of mail I receive, I might not be able to reply to every message.

When you write, please be sure to include this book's title and author as well as your name and phone or e-mail address. I will carefully review your comments and share them with the author and editors who worked on the book.

E-mail: opensource@samspublishing.com

Mail: Mark Taber
            Associate Publisher
            Sams Publishing
            201 West 103rd Street
            Indianapolis, IN 46290 USA

Reader Services

For more information about this book or others from Sams Publishing, visit our Web site at www.samspublishing.com. Type the ISBN (excluding hyphens) or the title of the book in the Search box to find the book you're looking for.

Introduction

Twenty years ago, when the first personal computers were being sold, could anyone have accurately predicted what they would be used for at the turn of the century? Could anyone have guessed that Microsoft would become as omnipresent a force in the computer industry as IBM was at that time? Was there any indication to predict the rise of open-source software and its contention against Microsoft for market share?

Even today, it's not necessarily any easier to tell what the picture is like, thanks to the fast pace of technology development. Even so, some trends seem clear: Commercial Unix operating systems are chosen less frequently for use as Internet servers, Microsoft Windows versions are a more popular choice, and open-source Unix systems or workalikes are even more popular. Chief among these open-source alternatives in the industry news headlines is Linux in its myriad forms.

However, a frequently overlooked fact is that Linux is not Unix; it's properly called "Unix-like," in that it performs the same functions as most commercially sold Unix variants do but was developed entirely by its user community. The guiding principles of the project are embodied in the GPL, the GNU General Public License, which states in part that any code developed under it must be made freely available. This extends to commercial software development bodies who must re-release as freely available source any software that they develop from earlier materials.

If there is any single strong point of contention between the supporters of open-source and those of commercial software, it is this seemingly innocent license. The problem is that many companies are unwilling to abide by its terms because to them, giving away the source code that they develop is tantamount to publishing trade secrets as soon as they're conceived. GPL-based software embodies an ideal: the notion of software written by the people, for the people, owned by nobody, and leveraged by nobody. It is the absolute antithesis of commercial, closed-source software that is sold in compiled, executable form from only one supplier. Linux adheres to that ideal in a number of important ways, but the unattractiveness of the spirit of the GPL to businesses that otherwise would have bought into it has slowed down its progress.

Enter FreeBSD, another freely available Unix-based operating system that has been around for as long as GNU/Linux has, and whose roots go back even further.

FreeBSD Versus Linux

FreeBSD is open-source with a twist. It is not based on software developed under the GPL but instead favors the BSD (Berkeley Software Design) open-source license that allows code developed privately or commercially to be used in current software development, whether the results are published in source form or not. The BSD license is friendlier to commercial software developers than is the GPL. It strikes a balance that encourages grassroots contributions from users but does not place undue restrictions on companies with the resources to develop BSD-licensed software into truly great products. This is part of the reason why Apple chose the freely available BSD operating system core to form the platform that became Mac OS X. Microsoft also appears to favor FreeBSD over Linux in maneuvers, such as its announcement of plans to port the C# programming environment to FreeBSD, and the widely publicized scandal over its anti-Unix "We Have the Way Out" Web site, which was quickly revealed to be running on a FreeBSD server.

Naturally, one might assume that Linux and FreeBSD are rivals. In part, or at least in some people's estimation, they are. The percentage of open-source operating systems currently in use that are not Linux is dominated by FreeBSD, but that "domination" currently corresponds only to about 15 percent of a segment of the market that is by no means the only major one. Even if FreeBSD has a number of high-profile reference installations to help it wave its flag—such as Yahoo!, The Apache Project, and Walnut Creek CD-ROM—these installations don't exist in such numbers as to give FreeBSD the high profile that Linux enjoys, for better or for worse.

Perhaps one of the biggest differences between FreeBSD and Linux is that of advocacy. FreeBSD has very little of it by comparison. The voices that aggressively promote Linux do not have comparable analogs in the FreeBSD world. In a way, this makes sense; Linux is a more "extreme" example of the open-source ideal, and FreeBSD is a moderate compromise between open-source enthusiasm and corporate accountability. The vibrancy of Linux contributes to its higher visibility, but also means it's a more chaotic platform and community. FreeBSD attempts to be more attractive to traditionalists, and so it's not as flashy, but it's in many ways more sturdy and predictable. FreeBSD is a true Unix, with original commercial Unix code that has the same stability as traditional "big-iron" Unix variants. It's hard to say whether Linux or FreeBSD is more "cutting edge" or has the more modern features, but in many ways FreeBSD trails Linux as a "showcase" platform for the newest Windows-challenging features that attempt to bring open-source to the desktop. That's really not where FreeBSD is targeted.

The Benefits of FreeBSD—and the Benefits of *FreeBSD Unleashed*

If you're reading this book, it might well be because you're a Linux user who wants to try a less-volatile platform for what has to be a reliable corporate network server; it might be because you're a commercial Unix user who wants to build a familiar-to-use but inexpensive server or workstation; or it might be because you're a Windows administrator who wants an alternative to the completely closed and welded-shut status quo of Microsoft's server offerings. In all these capacities, FreeBSD is an excellent choice.

I had my first exposure to FreeBSD in 1997, with release version 2.2.2. What attracted me was the fact that even at this early point in its development, Yahoo! had given it the nod as the platform of choice rather than Linux. Also, Hotmail (before it was taken over by Microsoft) used it side-by-side with Solaris machines to handle its already extraordinary load of "Web-mail" users. (Microsoft in 2000 finally was able to migrate most of Hotmail onto Windows 2000, but FreeBSD is known still to be in wide use there for many major functions.) I considered these to be strong testimonials, and the convenient floppy-based "net install" feature sealed the deal.

Since that time, FreeBSD has undergone a massive evolution. The layout of the system has become more and more organized; the security model has been tightened and enhanced over and over; the revolutionary "ports collection" has been successful enough though it has been ported to NetBSD, OpenBSD, and Mac OS X; and a Linux binary compatibility module allows software that is commercially developed for Linux, such as RealPlayer and StarOffice, to run on FreeBSD. Centralized configuration files and a tightly controlled filesystem structure lend to the platform's predictability and easy administration, perhaps more so than any other widely used Unix. Although FreeBSD doesn't enjoy the notoriety of Linux or suffer from the backlash against that notoriety, it does provide nearly all the meaningful benefits one can have by running Linux—and many that are uniquely its own.

When it comes to open-source operating systems, Linux has the spotlight—and probably will continue to have it for the foreseeable future. However, FreeBSD continues to gain in popularity, simply by being there as a sane alternative for companies that want out of the Microsoft hegemony but are put off by the politics or distribution-proliferation of Linux. Other BSD-licensed operating systems keep a firm grasp on their respective corners of the market: OpenBSD is focused on being the most secure OS available, and NetBSD has bragging rights for being able to run on a vast number of different hardware platforms, from Intel's x86 architecture, to the Motorola PowerPC, to the Sega Dreamcast. FreeBSD's appeal is more general; it excels in the role that's so important in this age where anybody with a few hundred dollars can launch a Web site or a home network to write software, run a small business, or simply share thoughts with the world—the role of a full-featured Internet server or workstation. It does so without excessive specialization and without being so politically charged as to alienate all-important corporate finance managers. It holds to a course that runs squarely between the extremes, and in the coming years it's likely to gain in popularity and reputation as more and more users discover what it can do for them.

Twenty, or ten, or even five years ago, the current state of the computer industry could hardly have been accurately predicted. We can't hope to imagine what the next decade or two will bring, but if FreeBSD's thus-far successful history is any indication, it will be with us as long as the open-source movement is relevant. Someday, the compromise between open-source and commercial assurance that FreeBSD represents might well be the only kind of platform anyone can imagine.

FreeBSD Unleashed is written with the computer-savvy, technologically curious reader in mind. Our goal is to provide a thorough education in how to leverage whatever level of computer knowledge you might already have (whether in Windows or in Unix) to get the most possible benefit out of a move to FreeBSD. Anybody can set up a FreeBSD box to use as a hobbyist machine or something casual to tinker with; this book gives you the know-how you need to replace your existing high-profile servers or workstations with smoothly running FreeBSD machines.

How This Book Is Organized

If you read straight through this book from cover to cover, you will get a tour of FreeBSD, from the first installation procedures to the most high-level administration details and techniques. Depending on how experienced you are with computers or with FreeBSD, you might want to start at a chapter in the middle of the book that's pertinent to your needs. However, to get the fullest understanding of what makes FreeBSD unique as an operating system and of the ideas behind its design, we encourage you to start at the beginning and with a fresh, guided installation of FreeBSD.

Whether you're reading *FreeBSD Unleashed* from cover to cover or searching for information on a specific task or topic, you'll appreciate the logical organization of this book's information:

- Part I, "Introduction to FreeBSD," deals with installing FreeBSD for the first time. If this is your first FreeBSD installation, or if you need a refresher on how it's done, you should begin with this section.

- Part II, "Using FreeBSD," acclimates you to FreeBSD's user-level working environment. Beginning with tours of the boot sequence, the Gnome environment, and X-Windows applications, this part of the book introduces you to FreeBSD, with information that's tailored to readers who are familiar with working in Windows. You also learn about working with the Unix shell—the primary means of interfacing with Unix.

- Part III, "Administering FreeBSD," delves deeper into the details of customizing FreeBSD for your specific purposes. You learn how FreeBSD's filesystem is laid out, how users and permissions work, and how to configure and monitor the system's operation. You also learn how to work efficiently in the shell and how to write shell programs and Perl scripts to automate common tasks. This part of the book teaches you how to install and upgrade third-party software and FreeBSD itself, how to configure printing, and how to add more hard disk space configured exactly as you need it. Finally, you'll get a "FreeBSD Survival Guide"—a quick reference chapter that gives you some of the most important tips and tricks necessary for successfully administering a FreeBSD system, including tips on how to tune your FreeBSD machine for maximum performance. Many of the tricks you learn here have taken Unix gurus years of painful first-hand experience to learn.

- Part IV, "FreeBSD Networking," prepares you for the daunting task of turning your FreeBSD machine into a world-class Internet server platform. The tour begins with background information on TCP/IP networking and how to set it up in FreeBSD. Then it proceeds step-by-step through setting up e-mail, Web, databases, FTP, and routing services, as well as DNS, Windows file sharing, and NFS. Network security is an extremely critical topic for anyone interested in running a network server, and one you should not miss.

- Part V, "X-Windows," guides you through the mysteries of the X Window System— the graphical interface layer that FreeBSD, like most Unixes, uses in order to present a friendly windowing user environment. Nobody ever said that configuring X-Windows was easy; these chapters will give you the knowledge you'll need in order to tame it.

- Part VI, "Appendixes," contains collections of information that are useful for reference regardless of your level of expertise. You'll find Unix command definitions, listings of compatible hardware, troubleshooting guides, and a set of further sources for information that pick up where this book's usefulness leaves off—at which point you'll presumably be an expert.

Conventions Used in This Book

Features in this book include the following:

> **NOTE**
>
> Notes give you comments and asides about the topic at hand, as well as full explanations of certain topics.

> **TIP**
>
> Tips provide great shortcuts and hints on how to program more effectively in FreeBSD.

> **CAUTION**
>
> Cautions warn you against making your life miserable and help you avoid pitfalls in programming.

In addition, you'll find the following typographic conventions throughout this book:

- Commands, variables, directories, and files appear in a `monospaced` font.
- Commands and such that you type appear in **boldface** type.

- Placeholders in syntax descriptions appear in *monospaced italic* type. This indicates that you should replace the placeholder with the actual filename, parameter, or other element that it represents.

PART I

Introduction to FreeBSD

IN THIS PART

CHAPTER **1**

What Is FreeBSD?

n a nutshell, FreeBSD is similar to a Unix operating system. runs on Intel *x*86 and Alpha architectures, although efforts re underway to create Sparc and PowerPC ports. Volunteers om all over the world develop FreeBSD, and the source code or the system is available free of charge to anyone who ants it.

his chapter introduces some of FreeBSD's most important atures and some of the benefits of using the FreeBSD ystem. From this chapter, you gain a basic understanding of hat FreeBSD is, and what you can do with it. You also learn bit of the history of FreeBSD and how it got to be where it today. Finally, the chapter looks at some other operating ystems and how they compare with FreeBSD.

Vhy Use FreeBSD?

here are probably as many reasons to use FreeBSD as there re the number of people who use it. Perhaps the most bvious reason is that FreeBSD is free, and there are no xpensive licensing fees. You can install a single copy of reeBSD on as many computers as you want without paying a ime. Unlike some commercial network operating systems, nere are also no "per-connection" or "per-user" fees for using reeBSD on a server. But just because FreeBSD is free does not nean it is of low quality. Here are some other very convinc-ng reasons to look into using FreeBSD:

- **It is extremely stable.** FreeBSD servers have been known to run for over three years without being rebooted.

- **It's trusted by some of the largest companies and busiest sites in the world.** Some of the compa-nies and sites running FreeBSD include Sony, Yahoo!, and The Apache Project.

- **It's open source.** The entire source tree for the operating system is available to you. You can change it, perform security audits on it, or do whatever else you like.

- **Thousands of free software packages are available.** FreeBSD users can take advantage of the thousands of free software packages available for Unix for everything from playing chess to simulating the division of cells and bacteria growth, word processing, image editing, and Web serving on the most popular Web server software in the world.

What Can You Do with FreeBSD?

Because FreeBSD comes with compilers for multiple programming languages, what you can do with FreeBSD is really limited only by your imagination and your hardware's technical capabilities. Various organizations are using FreeBSD for everything from low-end file sharing on an old 486 to creating high-end special effects and computer-generated animation rendering for motion pictures on multiprocessor FreeBSD systems linked together in powerful clusters.

> **NOTE**
>
> The special effects for the Warner Brothers motion picture *The Matrix* were rendered on a cluster of FreeBSD systems.

The following list provides some of the more common uses for FreeBSD that don't require any programming skill or custom software:

- **Economical file and print sharing**—You can create an economical file- and print-sharing solution. The freely available Samba software (covered in Chapter 33, "File and Print Sharing with Microsoft Windows") allows file and print sharing with Windows-based computers. Using Samba, FreeBSD can even serve as a primary domain controller (PDC) for a Windows network.

- **Web serving**—As mentioned previously, FreeBSD powers some of the busiest Web sites in the world. Even if you aren't setting up a Web site for the Internet, FreeBSD can make a great intranet server for your business.

- **E-mail services**—You can set up an e-mail server for your company with FreeBSD. Even an old 486 will perform quite well in this role.

- **Routing, DNS services, and Internet sharing**—Once again, you can turn even a low-end 486 into a very serviceable router, DNS server, or a gateway for sharing a single Internet connection with multiple computers.

- **Economical database solutions**—Using FreeBSD and one of the several freely available SQL databases for it, you can create a database solution for free that could easily cost tens of thousands of dollars to implement with commercial software. If the freely available databases don't have enough horsepower for your needs, you can run the Linux version of Oracle on FreeBSD because FreeBSD can run most Linux applications as well as (and sometimes even better than) Linux itself.

- **Economical custom solutions**—FreeBSD has a very liberal license agreement that allows you to use its code in other applications free of royalties. This makes it a perfect solution if you are an embedded systems designer. There are many other applications in which you might want to use BSD code as well. Apple's OS X uses a lot of BSD code, for example.

FreeBSD: It's Not Just for Servers Anymore

"Well, that's all well and good," you might be saying. "But I don't need any of that stuff. I'm not setting up a server or anything."

Well, don't put this book back on the shelf quite yet. There are plenty of workstation uses for FreeBSD that you might also be interested in:

- **Developing and testing Web sites**—The days of Web pages that display static HTML content are history. These days, Web pages use server-side technologies such as CGI, embedded scripting, and database back ends to display content that is dynamic and interactive. This means that testing your Web site by loading the pages into your browser from your hard drive are also history. To design a Web site of any complexity these days, you need to have a Web server available for development and testing. Even if you will not be running a Web server for public use, you can still use Apache, PHP, and one of the free SQL databases on a FreeBSD workstation to do Web site development and testing offline, without uploading any pages to your hosting service for testing. This can save you a lot of time and money.

- **Developing and testing databases offline**—This kind of ties in with the first point. FreeBSD can allow you to develop and test a database for your Web site entirely offline. When you finish, simply upload the database to your hosting service (assuming that your hosting service supports the database you use for development).

- **Learning software development or programming**—If you ever wanted to learn a programming language, you might be happy to know that using FreeBSD doesn't require you to spend hundreds of dollars on compilers and debuggers. All the software you need to learn programming and write powerful applications is already there, waiting for you to learn how to use it.

- **Learning about OS design and/or Unix**—If you are a computer science student and need to learn the ins and outs of operating system design, having access to all the source code for a real Unix operating system can be a great help. Suppose that you need to learn Unix for your job or for a course you are taking in college. FreeBSD can help you learn at home on your own time, instead of having to spend all your time in the Unix terminal lab.

- **Using free software to run an inexpensive workstation**—With all the free software available, FreeBSD can make a very powerful and inexpensive workstation for just about anything you might want to do. Some of the free applications available for FreeBSD include e-mail programs, Web browsers, word processors, spreadsheets, databases, CAD programs, and image editors. And, yes, there is a Winamp clone for FreeBSD and your MP3 collection.

Chances are, you found something in the previous list that whets your appetite to learn more about FreeBSD, and maybe even try it out. The next section gives you some history of FreeBSD and Unix, in general, and also explains some of the excellent design philosophies behind Unix that have kept it a driving force in computers today—more then 30 years after it was written.

A Brief History of FreeBSD and Unix

The original Unix operating system was developed at AT&T Bell Laboratories. Two men named Ken Thompson and Dennis Ritchie were the main driving forces behind Unix.

The origins of Unix can probably be traced to the spring of 1969. It was an offshoot of a largely unsuccessful effort by a conglomeration of companies to develop a time-sharing operating system. This operating system was called MULTICS. Although it was developed, it was never very successful.

Unix was originally written in assembly language for the DEC PDP-7 and was then ported to the DEC PDP-11. Then, an entirely new language called "C" was written for the purpose of rewriting the Unix operating system. The Unix operating system was then rewritten in C. The C programming language and Unix are two of the most important developments in the history of the computer. The C programming language was the first portable language that allowed applications (written in C) to be ported to other types of computer platforms relatively easily. Because Unix was written in C, it was also portable and could be made to run on other types of computer platforms relatively easily. This is one of the many points that made Unix so popular.

BSD Is Born

Because AT&T Bell Laboratories was not really in the business of selling computer operating systems, it licensed the Unix operating system and its source code to various academic institutions relatively cheaply. One of the institutions that did a lot of early work on Unix was the Computer Systems Research Group (CSRG) at the University of California at Berkeley. The CSRG at Berkeley made some very important contributions to Unix, including the development of the Unix File System (UFS) and adding TCP/IP networking to Unix. Eventually, the CSRG made so many changes to Unix that it released its own version, known as the *Berkeley Software Distribution*. Contrary to popular belief, CSRG did not do the first port of Unix to the DEC VAX. The first VAX port was done at AT&T Bell

Laboratories. But the port that Bell Labs had done did not support the VAX's virtual memory system. So, CSRG ported BSD to the VAX and added support for the VAX's virtual memory system.

CSRG made much of the BSD source code available to the public for free, and a man named Bill Jolitz ported BSD to the Intel *x86* platform in 1991. The port was called 386/BSD. In addition, a commercial spin-off company of CSRG named Berkeley Software Distribution, Incorporated, sold a commercial version of BSD for the *x86* platform that included source code.

FreeBSD Is Born

In 1993, it became apparent that because of full-time jobs and such, Bill Jolitz was no longer going to enhance 386/BSD. Two different groups decided that the project was worth doing though. Therefore, two spin-off projects were formed. The first was NetBSD, which seemed to focus on universal availability. If it's a platform, chances are there is a version of NetBSD that runs on it. The second was FreeBSD, which focused on making the system easier to use for nontechnical users and also focused primarily on Intel *x86* hardware (although, as mentioned previously, FreeBSD is now available for Alpha as well). Today, FreeBSD is the most popular of the BSD-based, Unix-like operating systems.

There are several more interesting events in the history of FreeBSD and Unix, such as the lawsuits over the Net/2 Tape, and more on the development of Unix. If you are interested in learning more about the history of FreeBSD and Unix, I recommend the following links:

- `http://www.bell-labs.com/history/unix/`—Contains a detailed history of the development of Unix at Bell Labs, including some rare photographs.

- `http://daemonz.org/bugs/history.html`—Contains a detailed history of the Berkeley Software Distribution.

- `http://www.freebsd.org/handbook/history.html`—Contains more history of FreeBSD in particular.

The Design Philosophy of Unix

Several things have kept Unix going strong even after 30 years. One of these is its portability, as mentioned previously. In my opinion, however, the most important thing that has kept Unix on the cutting edge, when most other software that old is considered obsolete, is its design philosophy about how an operating system should work.

Many people tend to think of Unix as an extremely complicated, complex, and confusing operating system. But in my opinion, Unix is the ultimate example of the KISS (Keep It Simple, Stupid) design in an operating system. One of the amazing things about Unix is that it is both simple and extremely powerful at the same time. Here is how the designers of Unix did it.

The Unix design philosophy is made up of a lot of small programs that do relatively simple tasks—and do them well. But the designers of Unix had a brilliant idea—that these programs should be able to be combined together by the user to do things that a single program could not do by itself.

> **NOTE**
>
> This combination concept is known as *piping*. Doug McIlroy of Bell Labs is credited with coming up with the idea. Thompson implemented it in Unix. (We cover pipes in detail when you learn about working with the shell in Chapter 7, "Working with the Shell.")

Here is an example of the way pipes work. Suppose that you have a plain-text file that serves as a simple address book. It uses one line per person and contains names, addresses, phone numbers, e-mail addresses, and so on. Fields in this file are separated by a tilde (~). A few sample lines from the file might look like these:

```
Doe, John~505 Some Street~Anytown~NY~55555~505-555-1212~jdoe@email.com
Doe, Jane~121 Any Street~Sometown~NY~12121~121-555-1212~jadoe@isp.com
Bar, Foo~501 Some Street~Anytown~NY 55555~505-123-4567~foobar@email.com
```

This file could contain 50 names or 500 names—it really doesn't matter. In this case, however, you want to get a list of all the people that live in Anytown, just their names and phone numbers, the list sorted alphabetically, and to create a hard copy of the list.

There is no single command that will do everything you want, but you can combine several commands together in a pipe to do what you want. Here is one of several ways that this task could be accomplished:

```
awk 'BEGIN {FS="~"} $3 == "Anytown" {print "%s\t%s\n",$1,$6}'\
address.txt | sort | lp
```

Don't worry if you don't understand exactly what this code does; it's explained in Chapter 12, "Shell Programming." In simple terms, the code sets the field separator to the tilde, selects lines where the third field (the field that contains the city name) is equal to Anytown, and then prints the first and sixth fields (the name and phone number) of these lines, separated by tabs (\t), with a new line at the end of each line (\n). The file it gets the information from is address.txt. The output is then piped to the sort command, which sorts it in alphabetical order. It is then piped to the lp command, which will print the output on the default printer. Here is what the output looks like using our simple three-record data file:

```
Bar, Foo     505-123-4567
Doe, John    505-555-1212
```

Although this command string may seem somewhat arcane right now, it is really quite amazing. Basically, the preceding single line of code creates a simple database that can search by any field and present output in any form you want.

Just so you can see how powerful this single line of code can be, here is a second example that modifies the previous example slightly to print a simple mailing list:

```
awk 'BEGIN {FS="~"} $3 == "Anytown"\
{printf "%s\n%s\n$s, $s $s\n\n",$1,$2,$3,$4,$5}' address.txt | lp
```

The output of the previous code is as follows:

```
Doe, John
505 Some Street
Anytown, NY 55555

Bar, Foo
501 Some Street
Anytown, NY 55555
```

For those who are willing to learn, Unix is about as close to an infinitely customizable and flexible operating system as you can get. Immense power is locked up inside Unix (and therefore FreeBSD) that can be unleashed and used to do things you probably didn't even know your computer could do without you buying expensive software. This book will teach you how to unleash that power (hence the name of the book).

It is this design philosophy that has kept Unix from becoming obsolete and falling by the wayside, as so many other programs have done.

How FreeBSD Compares to Other Operating Systems

When determining how FreeBSD compares to other operating systems, it's important to consider major systems such as Windows 2000/XP and Linux. This section explores these comparisons, in addition to those of other BSD-based operating systems.

Windows 2000/XP

Microsoft has done a good job of listening to what its customers want in an operating system. Windows 2000/XP doesn't allow you to "get under the hood" much. It is designed to work reasonably well for a wide variety of tasks without the user having to learn about the internals of the system. It does this at the expense of some performance and efficiency. Windows 2000/XP has relatively steep hardware requirements, but many users are willing to accept this in exchange for ease of use. In addition, because of the graphical design of Windows 2000/XP, "power users" can easily hit limits. There is only so much that can be done from a graphical user interface. The following list provides some of the important differences between FreeBSD and Windows 2000/XP:

- **The Windows 2000/XP kernel cannot be customized.** The kernel is the core of the operating system; it controls virtually every other aspect of how the system works. FreeBSD allows you to build a new kernel for the operating system that is customized for your specific system. This can increase performance and reduce memory usage. Windows 2000/XP does not allow you to rebuild the kernel. This is one of the areas where Windows 2000/XP sacrifices some efficiency and performance for ease of use.

- **Windows 2000/XP uses a GUI (graphical user interface) for almost all tasks, whereas FreeBSD relies much more on the command line.** The GUI in Windows 2000/XP is laid out so that things are easy to find and tasks are easy to perform. For example, setting up a network in Windows 2000/XP is done from a network control panel, and there are "wizards" that walk you through the process. FreeBSD, on the other hand, uses text-based configuration files for network configuration. Setting up the network involves editing one or more configuration files by hand.

- **The Windows 2000/XP GUI is always running; the GUI in FreeBSD is optional.** Although a GUI can make a workstation easier to use, it is wasteful overhead on a backroom server because no one ever sees its screen anyway. FreeBSD gives you the option of turning off the GUI or not using it at all.

- **Windows 2000/XP requires special software for remote administration.** Because everything in FreeBSD can be done from the command line, it is very easy to administer remotely. In FreeBSD, all system-administration tasks can be done from the command line. This makes remote administration easy. It can be done from any terminal—even a terminal that cannot display graphics. It can also be done from any type of system that is capable of running a terminal emulator. FreeBSD can be administered from another Unix-like system, a Windows system, a Macintosh, and so on. Windows 2000/XP, on the other hand, requires the GUI to do many tasks. Although remote administration is possible on Windows 2000/XP, special software is required to do it. Also, most of this software is available only for Windows. Because of this, most remote-administration tasks for Windows can be done only from another Windows system.

- **By nature, any GUI (including that of Windows 2000/XP) has limits that are not present in a command-line interface.** Only so many features can be crammed into a GUI. Sooner or later, a "power user" will want to do something that the operating system designers didn't think about. For example, the simple address book database demonstrated in the previous section could not be done with the software that is included with Windows. A similar system would require third-party software in Windows. The mailing list example could not be done with the software included with Windows, either. Although third-party GUI software is available for simple tasks like this, after you get familiar with the command line, you will actually find that you can type the command line much faster than you can go through the menus in a GUI-based system.

Linux

Unless you have been living in a cave for the last few years, you have at least heard of Linux, even if you don't know what it is. Linux is a clone of Unix that has become rather popular in recent years. Like FreeBSD, it is open source and developed by volunteers. Unlike FreeBSD, there is no single controlling authority for Linux, and there are well over 30 different distributions of Linux.

More similarities than differences exist between FreeBSD and Linux. Both are excellent operating systems, and both can serve the needs of most users quite well. Although more software is available for Linux than for FreeBSD, FreeBSD can run almost all Linux software that is available, so this is not really an issue. When running Linux software under FreeBSD, performance is not really an issue, either, because FreeBSD actually runs some Linux software faster than Linux itself does.

Here are some of the most important differences between FreeBSD and Linux:

- **FreeBSD has only one distribution, whereas Linux has more than 30 distributions.** FreeBSD will work the same way on all systems in which it is installed. This is not true with Linux. Each Linux distribution has a slightly different way of doing things. For example, Slackware Linux uses BSD-type run control scripts. Debian Linux uses Sys V run control scripts, and Red Hat Linux uses Sys V run control scripts but stores them in a different location than standard Sys V Unix does. This can be confusing for users who move from one distribution of Linux to another, because things may not work the same way in the other distribution.

- **FreeBSD is a complete operating system maintained by a core team; Linux is a kernel maintained by Linus Torvalds.** Linux is not a complete operating system. It is a kernel. As mentioned in the section on Windows, the kernel is the core of the operating system. It controls virtually all aspects of the operating system. The various companies that sell Linux distributions take the Linux kernel and package it with a bunch of other programs designed to work with Linux. Because each company has its own idea about what should be included in a distribution, you may find that a program you had available on one Linux system does not exist on another Linux system (although you could download and install it). This fact can also cause dependency problems when upgrading Linux. For example, you may upgrade your Linux kernel, only to find out that you need to upgrade several other packages as well. Because FreeBSD is a complete operating system, upgrades are generally easier to do because any dependencies are upgraded at the same time.

- **Anyone can contribute code to Linux; contributions to FreeBSD must be reviewed and accepted by the core team.** Although anyone can contribute to the FreeBSD project, it is much more of a coordinated effort than Linux is. Contributions to the FreeBSD source code need to be approved by the core team before they will be merged into FreeBSD. This is good for most users because you can be sure that the code has been checked for problems by people who know what they are doing. It also helps to ensure that the code will not cause problems with other code that already exists. This is sometimes a common problem with Linux, which is why many Linux distributions seem to come with at least some part "broken" out of the box. Because there is only one base of FreeBSD code (commonly known as a *source tree*), this is far less of a problem with FreeBSD.

These are some of the most important differences between Linux and FreeBSD. Because FreeBSD has a single source tree that is controlled by a core team, it tends to be more stable than Linux—and therefore is often more suitable for a production environment. The main drawback to this is that new features are not always implemented as quickly in FreeBSD as in Linux. There is a tradeoff here. Do you want stability for a production environment? Or, do you want the latest gizmos and gadgets to play with at the expense of performance and stability?

NetBSD

NetBSD's claim to fame is the sheer number of platforms that it runs on. NetBSD has been ported to everything from PDAs to gaming consoles such as the Sony PS2. It has also, of course, been ported to *x*86 hardware. The main drawbacks of NetBSD are that it is not as user friendly as FreeBSD and it doesn't have the number of applications ported to it that FreeBSD does. Because of this, new users who have *x*86 hardware are probably better off with FreeBSD.

OpenBSD

Like NetBSD, OpenBSD has been ported to quite a few platforms, although not nearly as many as FreeBSD. OpenBSD's main selling point is its security. Although much of this security comes from the default configuration, which can be mimicked in FreeBSD, some of it comes from OpenBSD features, such as the ability to encrypt that swap file. However, like NetBSD, OpenBSD is not nearly as user friendly as FreeBSD, and it also doesn't have nearly the number of ported applications that FreeBSD has. So once again, new users with *x*86 hardware are probably better off with FreeBSD.

FreeBSD Mascot

A quick word on the FreeBSD mascot is probably in order here because it is often a source of confusion for new users. Sometimes, people even get offended at the FreeBSD mascot. Well, the FreeBSD mascot is not a reference to a satanic cult or anything like that. It is a joking reference to background processes in Unix systems that handle various tasks. These background processes are called *daemons*, which is pronounced "demons." Daemons are actually wonderfully helpful things. If you've ever sent an e-mail or visited a Web page, you have used the services of a daemon without even knowing it. Windows 2000 also has daemons. They just aren't called that. Microsoft calls them "services" instead.

So, what about the pitchfork? That is a reference to an important system called "fork." You will learn more about forking later in the book, but for now, simply know that a fork causes a program to make a copy of itself in memory and then run that copy. Once again, if you have ever visited a Web page, you have used the services of the fork system without even knowing it. Without fork, the Web server could only handle one visitor at a time—and you can imagine how much fun that would be. You would get a lot of errors about the site being too busy.

Installing FreeBSD

Before you can use FreeBSD, you need to install it on your system's hard disk. This is a relatively painless process, and you shouldn't have any problems if you follow the directions in this chapter carefully. Depending on how fast your system and your CD-ROM drive run, the installation process will take anywhere from about 20 minutes to an hour or more. Most of this time is spent copying files, so you will not always have to sit in front of your computer.

I strongly suggest that you read this entire chapter before beginning the install. Mistakes in the install can result in losing some or possibly even all the existing data on your hard disk. Poor planning can also result in an install that has to be redone because the decisions you made don't work for the environment in which you will use FreeBSD. Read this whole chapter (and also Chapter 3, "Advanced Installation Issues," if necessary) before beginning the install. The information in these chapters will help you make the best decisions possible during the installation, because you will know what to expect.

CAUTION

Make sure to pick a time to do the installation when you will not be distracted. You will be performing actions during the installation that are potentially hazardous to existing data on your system if you make mistakes.

TIP

Now is a good time to look over the hardware compatibility list in Appendix B, "Hardware Compatibility Lists," to make sure your hardware is supported. You won't want to continue the install if you find out a key piece of hardware in your system is not supported by FreeBSD.

Checking Your Hardware

Before you begin the installation, you should have available some information about your hardware. Here is a list of the hardware information you will need during the FreeBSD installation:

- The type of video card and the amount of video RAM installed.
- The manual for your monitor. You need to know the horizontal and vertical refresh rates for setting up X-Windows.
- If you have a modem, the COM port and IRQ it is using.
- The type of mouse you have (serial, PS/2, or bus) and what port it uses.
- If you have a network card, the address and IRQ it uses.
- If you are connected to a network, you will also need to gather certain network information, such as your hostname, IP address, DNS server, gateway, and such. If you are unsure of these values, ask your network administrator for this information.

If you don't have this information available and you currently have Microsoft Windows installed on your system, you can often get it from the Device Manager in the Windows Control Panel. See your Microsoft Windows documentation or Windows Help for information on how to do this.

> **CAUTION**
>
> Users moving from FreeBSD 4 to FreeBSD 5 should be aware that the "Binary Upgrade" option in Sysinstall is broken when trying to make a major version jump like this. If you want to upgrade from FreeBSD 4 to FreeBSD 5, you must use a source upgrade instead. This is relatively easy to do. Chapter 17, "Keeping Up to Date with FreeBSD," discusses upgrading from source in detail.

Creating Boot Disks

The FreeBSD CD-ROM included with this book is bootable. If you plan to install on a system that supports booting from the CD-ROM drive, you can probably skip this section. If your CD-ROM does not support booting or if you plan to install from some method other than from the CD-ROM (such as installing over a network), read on.

If you're installing over a network or if your system doesn't support booting from a CD, you need to create two boot disks.

You can download the boot floppies from the FreeBSD FTP server at `ftp.freebsd.org`. They are located in `/pub/FreeBSD/releases/5.0-RELEASE/floppies`—assuming that 5.0 is the RELEASE version of FreeBSD. If it isn't, replace 5.0 with whatever the current RELEASE version is. The two files you need to download are `kern.flp` and `mfsroot.flp`. If you create the floppies on a DOS or Windows system, you also need the `fdimage.exe` program located in the `/pub/FreeBSD/tools` directory on the FTP server.

> **TIP**
>
> For better response time and also to cut down on the traffic load on the main FTP server, you might want to try downloading the boot floppies from one of the mirrors. In many of the mirrors, `ftp` is simply followed by a number (for example, `ftp1.freebsd.org` or `ftp2.freebsd.org`). Using a mirror can speed up the transfer.

The boot floppy files cannot simply be copied to a floppy disk. They have to be written to floppies using one of the procedures described in the following subsections. These subsections show you how to create the boot floppies in various environments. To begin any of the methods described next, you need two blank 1.44MB formatted floppies.

> **TIP**
>
> Use brand-new floppies to create the boot disks. The boot disks write raw data to the floppies with no regard for the format of the floppies. There can't be even one bad sector on the floppies because bad sectors can make tracking down installation problems difficult. Save yourself the headache and just use brand-new floppies.

Creating the Boot Floppies from a DOS or Windows System

Before creating the boot floppies from a Windows system, you should boot into plain DOS mode. Trying to create the boot floppies from a DOS window while Windows is running could cause problems.

Change to whatever directory you copied `fdimage.exe`, `boot.flp`, and `mfsroot.flp` to. Type the following commands at the DOS prompt, replacing the directory `temp` with whatever directory you copied the files to:

```
C:\> cd temp
```

```
C:\TEMP> fdimage boot.flp a:
```

When the program finishes running, remove the first floppy from the drive and insert the second one. Then type the following at the DOS prompt:

```
C:\TEMP> fdimage mfsroot.flp a:
```

Creating the Boot Floppies from Another FreeBSD or Unix System

If you are creating the floppies from another FreeBSD or Unix system, you do not need the `fdimage.exe` program. (You still need the `boot.flp` and the `mfsroot.flp` programs, though.)

Use the Unix dd utility to write the files to the floppies. On a FreeBSD system, it looks like this:

```
dd if=boot.flp of=/dev/rfd0
```

When the copy finishes, remove the first floppy from the drive and insert the second one. Once again, use dd to create the second floppy. On a FreeBSD system, it would look something like this:

```
dd if=mfsroot.flp of=/dev/rfd0
```

Note that for the previous commands to work, you must have write access to the raw floppy device. Also, on other versions of Unix, the device name may be different. See the documentation for your version of Unix to find out the name of the floppy device.

Now that you have created the installation disks, you are ready to begin the installation.

Booting into the Install Program

> **CAUTION**
>
> If you are installing on a system that already has Windows or some other operating system on it and you don't want to lose that operating system and all its data, stop here and read "Potential Problems with and Limitations of Dual Boot Systems" in Chapter 3. *It is very important that you read this first*. Failure to follow the instructions in that section could result in the loss of all data on your hard disk!

The next few sections assume that you either plan to wipe out everything currently on your hard disk to install FreeBSD, that you are installing on a new disk, or that you have already followed the instructions in Chapter 3 to create space for FreeBSD on a system that already has another operating system installed on it. These sections also assume that you are installing from the included CD-ROM. If this is not the case, stop here and read the relevant sections in Chapter 3 on NFS installs, FTP installs, or floppy installs. After you do that, come back and continue with the instructions given here.

When you are ready to begin the installation, insert the included CD-ROM into your CD-ROM drive. If you need to boot from floppy disks, also insert the floppy disk on which you installed boot.flp into your A drive. Reboot your system. If necessary, enter your BIOS setup program and enable booting from the CD-ROM drive. Some BIOSs also have a security feature that prevents booting from the floppy drive. If you have to boot from the floppy drive, you might need to check for this option and set it to allow booting from the A drive. See your system documentation for the way to configure the BIOS settings to control boot devices.

As the system boots, you should see some messages on your screen. You should also see a "twirling baton." As long as the baton keeps twirling, the system is doing something. If the baton stops twirling for a long period of time, it probably means your system is hanging. If that happens, refer to Appendix C, "Troubleshooting Installation and Boot Problems." The system will load a few items, and then you should see a message like this:

```
FreeBSD/i386 bootstrap loader, Revision 0.8
  (jkh@bento.freebsd.org, Mon Nov 20 11:41:23 GMT 2000)
  |
  Hit [Enter] to boot immediately, or any other key for command prompt.
  Booting [kernel] in 9 seconds... _
```

Go ahead and press Enter to continue. At some point during this process, you will also be asked to remove the boot floppy and insert the mfsroot floppy. When this happens, simply proceed as instructed and then press Enter so the kernel will finish booting. A flurry of messages will go past your screen as the kernel detects and initializes the hardware in your system. If your system hangs at any point during this period, see Appendix C for help on troubleshooting installation problems.

Navigating the Sysinstall Program

After the kernel has finished booting (and assuming you didn't run into any problems), you will be placed into the FreeBSD Sysinstall program. The first screen you see looks like Figure 2.1.

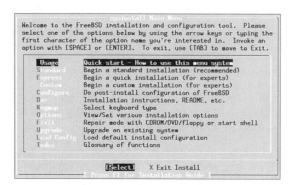

FIGURE 2.1   The main Sysinstall menu.

You can't use the mouse in Sysinstall, but the program is easy to navigate. Table 2.1 lists the navigation keys you can use in Sysinstall.

TABLE 2.1   Navigation Keys

Navigation Key	Command
Up arrow	Moves up to the previous option in the menu.
Down arrow	Moves down to the next option in the menu.
Left/right arrow	Toggles between the choices at the bottom of the menu. For example, on the main menu the left and right arrow keys toggle between Select and Exit Install.
Spacebar	In menus where multiple options can be selected, the spacebar toggles the current highlighted option on and off.
Tab key	Has the same effect as the left and right arrows in menus. You can tab between fields in screens in which you need to fill in blanks.

In addition, you can also select most options by typing their highlighted letter—usually the first letter in the option name.

If you want to read more about using Sysinstall, you can press Enter on the highlighted option Usage, but because it will all be explained here, I suggest you press the down arrow to move to the second option and then select it to begin a standard install.

After you select the Standard option, a message will inform you that you need to set up a DOS-style (fdisk) partitioning scheme for your hard disk. After you read this message, simply press Enter to continue.

Creating Partitions and Assigning Mount Points

After you press Enter on the informational message telling you about creating a DOS-style (fdisk) partitioning scheme, one of two things will happen:

- If you have only one hard disk in your system, you will be placed directly into the FreeBSD Partition Editor. In this case, you can skip the next section, "Selecting Hard Disks," and continue with "Partitioning the Disk(s)."

- If you have more than one hard disk in your system, you will be given a menu to select on which hard disk or disks you want to install FreeBSD. If this is the case, read the next section, "Selecting Hard Disks."

CAUTION

Creating partitions and assigning mount points are areas in which a mistake can cause the loss of all data on your hard disk. If your hard disk contains anything you want to keep, make sure you back it up first. Also, read Chapter 3 if you will be installing FreeBSD on a drive that already has another operating system on it.

Selecting Hard Disks

If you have multiple hard disks on your system, you will see a menu that looks similar to Figure 2.2.

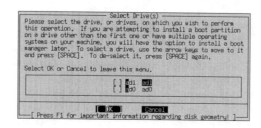

FIGURE 2.2   Selecting the hard disks on which to install FreeBSD.

Your menu might not look exactly like the one shown in the figure. Table 2.2 lists some of the values you might see in the menu and what they mean.

TABLE 2.2   Menu Values

Value	Meaning
ad0	The first physical ATA hard disk on the system. This is the master drive on the primary IDE controller. If you have DOS or Windows installed on your system, it will be located on this drive.
da0	Similar to ad0, except that it indicates an SCSI disk instead of an ATA disk. Once again, this would be the first SCSI disk on your system. If you have only SCSI drives on your system and you have DOS or Windows installed, it will be located on this drive.
ad1	The second ATA disk on the system. Depending on how your system is set up, this can be either a slave disk on the primary controller or a primary disk on the secondary controller.
da1	The second SCSI disk on the system.

You might also have ad2 and ad3 in your list—or da2, da3, and so on. Just remember that the number represents the number of the drive in your system and that FreeBSD starts numbering the drives at zero instead of one.

Use the spacebar to select which disk or disks you want to use for FreeBSD. You can select more than one disk for the FreeBSD installation. This is fairly common, and the end result is transparent for everyday operation. In other words, even if FreeBSD is installed across multiple disks, it appears to the end user that everything is on a single disk. You will see in the next section, "Partitioning the Disk(s)," why it might be advantageous to install on multiple disks.

When you select a disk from this menu, you are placed in the FreeBSD Partition Editor, where you can edit the partition table for that disk. After you finish editing the partition table for the disk and leave the Partition Editor, you are placed back at this menu. You can then select another disk to edit or press Enter to leave the menu and continue with the installation. After you finish editing disks, you are placed into the FreeBSD Disk Label Editor (more on that after the next section, which explains the Partition Editor).

CAUTION

If you're going to install FreeBSD on a second hard disk, you have another operating system on the first hard disk, and you don't plan to make any changes to the first hard disk, you need to install a boot manager so that you can choose which operating system you want to boot at system startup. FreeBSD will give you the option of installing the boot manager later in the process. However, the boot manager *must* be installed on the first disk in your system. In order for this to happen, you *must* select the first drive in this menu. If you do not want to make any changes to the first disk, simply select it in the menu and then exit the Partition Editor without making any changes to the disk. You can then select a different disk in the menu and partition it for use with FreeBSD. This allows FreeBSD to install the boot manager on the first disk. If you do not do this, the boot manager will not be installed on the first disk, and you will not be able to boot FreeBSD after the installation is finished.

Partitioning the Disk(s)

Here is what the Partition Editor looks like:

```
Disk name:      ad0                                      FDISK Partition Editor
DISK Geometry:  29795 cyls/16 heads/63 sectors = 30033360 sectors (14664MB)

Offset        Size(ST)         End     Name  PType       Desc  Subtype    Flags


        0          63          62       -      12      unused        0
       63    30033297    30033359     ad0s1      8     freebsd      165
```

```
The following commands are supported (in upper or lower case):


A = Use Entire Disk    G = set Drive Geometry    C = Create Slice    F = `DD' mode
D = Delete Slice       Z = Toggle Size Units     S = Set Bootable    | = Wizard m.
T = Change Type        U = Undo All Changes      W = Write Changes


Use F1 or ? to get more help, arrow keys to select.
```

In this case, the first line tells you that you are working on the disk ad0, which, as mentioned previously, is the first ATA disk in the system. The second line gives you information about the geometry of this disk. (See Chapter 18, "Understanding Hard Disks and Filesystems," if you need help with this. It's not important that you understand the geometry of your disk unless FreeBSD is having trouble detecting it.) The next several lines give you information about each currently defined partition on the system. If this is a new disk, or if you deleted all the partitions on it before installing FreeBSD, there will be only one partition with the description "unused" that takes up the entire disk. Table 2.3 explains what each column of information means.

> **NOTE**
>
> If you are unfamiliar with the terms used in the next section (such as *sectors*), see Chapter 18, which provides an introduction to hard disks and the terminology related to them.

TABLE 2.3 Partition Table Information

Column	Information
Offset	The starting sector of the partition.
Size (ST)	The size of the partition in sectors.
End	The last sector in the partition.
Name	The FreeBSD-assigned device name of this partition (if known).
Ptype	A number representing the partition type.
Descr	The type of partition.
Subtype	More information about the partition type.
Flags	The following symbols can appear in this column:
	= The slice is properly aligned.
	> The slice extends past the 1,024th cylinder on the hard disk. This becomes an issue later on when you create the disk labels, because boot partitions that extend past the 1,024th cylinder can cause problems on some systems (this is a BIOS limitation, not a limitation of FreeBSD).
	R The slice contains the root filesystem, which is the top-level filesystem on the FreeBSD system.
	B The slice uses BAD144 bad-spot handling.
	C The slice is a FreeBSD partition.
	A The slice is the active partition (that is, the slice is the bootable slice).

> **TIP**
>
> Press Z to toggle the display units between sectors, kilobytes, and megabytes.

To assign all available space on this hard disk to FreeBSD, simply select A for "Use Entire Disk." After this, you should see a line that shows a single partition of subtype 165 with the description freebsd. You will also see a line with the description unused. Don't worry about this because it's normal, even when you're selecting the entire disk for use. Press Q to exit the Partition Editor. Do not press W (Write Changes) first, because that option is intended only for making changes to existing filesystems, not for initial installs.

CAUTION

Selecting the entire disk for use deletes everything currently on the disk. Make sure you have backed up any information you want to keep from the disk. If you don't want to delete everything on this disk, see Chapter 3 before you proceed with the install.

NOTE

Unlike with Linux, you do not create multiple partitions on a single disk for FreeBSD, even if you will probably be creating more than one partition on the disk to hold your FreeBSD filesystems. You use the Disk Label Editor to create the separate areas for your different filesystems.

If you have only a single hard disk on your system, you will receive a message that tells you to create BSD partitions inside the fdisk partition(s) just created. Go ahead and press Enter to go to the Disk Label Editor. If you have multiple disks, go back to the disk selection menu.

If you want to spread your FreeBSD installation out across more than one disk (either because you don't have enough space on one disk for a complete install or for performance reasons), select any other disks you want to use for FreeBSD, repeating the previous steps outlined in this section. When you have partitioned all the disks you want to use for FreeBSD, make sure OK is highlighted and then press the Enter key.

FreeBSD will then ask whether you want to install the FreeBSD boot manager. If you are installing FreeBSD on a drive other than the first one, select the BootMgr option. You also select this option if you are installing more than one operating system on this drive. If FreeBSD is the only operating system to be installed and it will be installed on the primary drive, you can select the Standard option.

Once you have finished installing the boot manager, you will receive a message about creating BSD partitions inside the fdisk partition(s) just created. Press Enter again, and you go to the Disk Label Editor.

The Disk Label Editor

The Disk Label Editor is where you will actually create the filesystems that will hold the FreeBSD installation. When you first enter the editor, it will look like this:

```
                    FreeBSD Disklabel Editor

Disk: ad0       Partition name: ad0s1   Free: 0 blocks (0MB)


Part      Mount           Size Newfs  Part      Mount           Size Newfs
----      -----           ---- -----  ----      -----           ---- -----



The following commands are valid here (upper or lower case):
C = Create       D = Delete   M = Mount pt.           W = Write
N = Newfs Opts   Q = Finish   S = Toggle SoftUpdates  Z = Custom Newfs
T = Toggle Newfs U = Undo     A = Auto Defaults       R = Delete+Merge

Use F1 or ? to get more help, arrow keys to select.
```

Your system may have one or more disks listed here. It depends on how many disks you selected to use with FreeBSD.

Beginning with FreeBSD 5.0, the Auto Defaults option provides reasonable defaults that will work for most purposes. If you aren't sure about partitioning (explained in the next section), you should probably choose the Auto Defaults option and then press Q to quit the editor and move on to "Selecting a Canned Distribution Set," later in this chapter. If you use more than one disk, you need to manually set up the partitions. If you need to manually create your partitions or if you aren't sure whether you need to create custom partitions, read on.

Manual Partitioning

At a bare minimum, you need to create two partitions: a root filesystem and a swap partition. This is not the best way to do things, however. You might be tempted to do this because it ensures you won't end up in a situation in which you run out of space on a partition where you need it and have 150 zillion gigabytes of free space on a different partition that you can't use for what you need. In fact, there is at least one well-known Linux distribution that encourages putting everything in the root filesystem. This is a dangerous way to live for two reasons.

First of all, FreeBSD and all other versions of Unix are powerful multitasking operating systems. They are almost always doing something—especially on a busy server. These systems usually have several files open at the same time, and they often write to the disk. If the system crashes, a power failure occurs, or the janitor runs the vacuum cleaner over the server's power cord while a write is in progress, the filesystem can be damaged. Depending on what was being written when the crash occurred, the damage can be severe enough to destroy the filesystem. Filesystem damage is far less likely to occur if the filesystem is not being written to when the crash or power failure occurs.

This is why it is a good idea to use multiple filesystems. It not only helps to restrict damage to one area—instead of the entire system—it also helps protect the all-important root filesystem. In a properly laid-out filesystem, the root partition is almost never written to.

The second reason why having everything in one partition is dangerous is that it opens a server to various Denial of Service (DoS) attacks. Whether these attacks are intentional or not, they can occur. For example, on a system in which user disk quotas are not enforced, a user could either intentionally or accidentally (through the misuse of the command that copies files) create a file that fills up the entire partition where the home directory is located. If all the filesystems are located on that same partition, this would do far more than prevent users from saving files in the home directory. Other fallout from this event could include denial of mail service, because there is no room in the mail spool directory, and denial of print service, because there is no room to queue print jobs. Also, the Web server could stop serving because it can't write its log file. `syslogd` (the program that logs system messages) will be unable to record important messages, which could allow crackers to enter your system undetected. Any programs that need to write temp files will fail because no room is left in the `tmp` filesystem.

Unfortunately, predicting when you'll run out of space on all filesystems is difficult. Regardless, running out of space is never a good situation. Therefore, I recommend a minimum of four partitions: One for the root filesystem (`/`), one for the swap space, one for the user filesystem (`/usr`), and one for the var (`/var`) filesystem. Some people recommend placing the `/var` filesystem in the same partition as `/usr` because it is difficult to judge how much space to give `/var`. I don't recommend doing this, however, because it subjects your system to various possible Denial of Service attacks—especially if users' home directories are also located in the same partition as the `/usr` filesystem.

> **NOTE**
>
> FreeBSD has the capability to use more memory than is actually installed in the system. This memory is called *virtual memory*. To use virtual memory, FreeBSD moves to the disk any memory pages that are not currently in use. That frees up room in memory for memory pages that are currently needed. When a memory page that was moved out to disk is needed again, FreeBSD moves it back into memory and, if necessary, moves something else in memory out to the disk to make room. These operations are known as *swapping*, and the area of the disk that the swapped-out memory pages are stored in is called the *swap partition*.

To help you better decide what filesystems you want to put on each partition, Table 2.4 describes some of the directories in FreeBSD and what they are used for. Note that this is not a complete list; it has only the directories for which you might want to have separate partitions. For a complete list of all directories and their purposes, see Chapter 8, "The FreeBSD Filesystem."

TABLE 2.4   FreeBSD Directories and Their Purposes

Directory	Purpose
/	This is the root filesystem. It is the directory under which all other filesystems will appear (even if they are located on different partitions, different disks, or even different computers on different continents). The root filesystem needs to have a partition. 120MB should be enough for this partition. If you are really tight on space, you could probably get away with 100, but don't go any lower than that. Note that FreeBSD will give you a warning if you set root to less than 118MB.
/boot	Beginning with FreeBSD 5.0, the kernel and other files required to start the operating system are now located in the boot directory instead of the root directory. You can now have a root partition that extends past the 1,024th cylinder by putting /boot on its own partition. (Note that /boot has to be contained completely in the first 1,024 cylinders.)
/usr	The /usr filesystem contains most of the utilities and programs that will be accessed by normal users. /usr should definitely have its own partition.
/usr/local	This is where third-party software that is not part of the operating system is installed (such as Web servers and database programs). Some people like to put /usr/local on its own partition, separate from the /usr partition. Personally, I don't recommend this for normal operations. The only time I would recommend this is if you have multiple disks and need to split /usr for space reasons.
/var	This is where the system stores files that have a variable size. I like to put /var on its own partition. Some of the things stored in /var include incoming mail, system logs, Web server logs, and jobs queued for the printer. The size you need to make /var depends on whether you will be running a print server, mail server, or Web server. Note that on a busy Web server, log files can easily grow to more than 100MB in only a couple of days. If you are going to be running a busy Web server, either give /var a lot of space or make sure you rotate your logs often. If you expect to receive a lot of mail, you will also want to make /var quite large.
/tmp	This is where programs and users can write temporary files. This directory is usually cleaned out at each reboot. Properly behaved programs that need to write very large temp files should not use this directory; they should use /usr/tmp or /var/tmp instead. You can either give /tmp its own partition or link it to a place in /usr. Also, note that if a particular operation requires more temp space than is available, you can temporarily change the location where temp files are written for that one operation.
/home	This is where users' home directories are located. It is often placed under the /usr partition. If you are going to have a lot of users and you expect them to have a lot of files, you might want to put /home in its own partition or even give /home an entire disk.

> **TIP**
>
> If you have more than one hard disk on your system, you can optimize your system's perfor-mance by carefully dividing up disk-intensive tasks between multiple hard disks. For example, if you run a Usenet news server (which is rather disk intensive) and a Web server (also quite disk intensive), you should put the news directory and the directory where the Web server keeps its pages on separate disks.

The Root Partition

If you aren't using a /boot partition, the first partition on your drive should be the root partition (/). To create the root partition, use the up or down arrow key to highlight the disk at the top of the Disk Label Editor that you want to put the root partition on. Then press C for Create Partition.

You then see a dialog box that asks you for the size of the partition (see Figure 2.3).

FIGURE 2.3   Setting the size of the partition.

As mentioned previously, 120MB should be sufficient for the root partition. If you are not pressed for space, this is the size I recommend. As the dialog box says, you can specify a size in megabytes by adding an "M" to the end of the number. So, assuming you want to make your root partition 120MB in size, enter **120M** at the prompt and then press Enter. You are then asked to choose a partition type for this partition. Because this will hold the root filesystem, select the "FS   A filesystem" option and press Enter. You are then asked to specify a mount point for this partition. The *mount point* is the directory under which the filesystem will be available. Because this is the root filesystem, enter / in this box and press Enter.

Your screen should now look similar to this:

```
                         FreeBSD Disklabel Editor

Disk: ad1        Partition name: ad1s1   Free: 29828560 blocks (14564MB)

Part        Mount          Size Newfs   Part      Mount           Size Newfs
----        -----          ---- -----   ----      -----           ---- -----
ad1s1a      /              100MB UFS Y
```

```
The following commands are valid here (upper or lower case):
C = Create        D = Delete   M = Mount pt.   W = Write
N = Newfs Opts    Q = Finish   S = Toggle SoftUpdates
T = Toggle Newfs  U = Undo     A = Auto Defaults

Use F1 or ? to get more help, arrow keys to select.
```

This code shows that we now have a filesystem at ad1s1a (the device name and slice entry that FreeBSD uses to refer to this filesystem), it is mounted on /, the size is 100MB, and it is of type UFS (the standard filesystem for FreeBSD). Next, we deal with the swap partition.

The Swap Partition

FreeBSD is a virtual memory operating system; it can use more memory than it has available in physical RAM. It does this by swapping memory pages of programs that are not currently being used out to the hard disk. When those pages are needed again, FreeBSD swaps them back into memory from the hard disk and, if necessary, swaps something else out to the hard disk to make room for the pages it is bringing in. Of course, accessing something from the hard disk is many times slower than accessing something from RAM, so swap space is no alternative for having enough RAM in a system. But still, swap space is often very useful, especially on busy servers that have many processes running at the same time.

The proper (or improper) placement of your swap partition can have a significant impact on the performance of your system. Here are some guidelines for choosing where to put your swap partition:

- Put the swap partition as close to the beginning of the disk as possible. Lower-numbered cylinders on the disk can be accessed slightly faster than higher-numbered cylinders.

- If you have multiple drives in your system, as a general rule, you should put the swap partition on the fastest drive in your system.

- If the fastest drive on your system is also the most heavily accessed by users, Web servers, mail transfer agents, and so on, you will probably want to violate the previous point and put the swap partition on the least-accessed drive in your system. Not only does this allow more time for the drive to access the swap space instead of accessing other things, but it also increases the chances that the hard disk heads will already be positioned within the swap partition when swapping is needed. Little things like the time it takes the hard disk heads to cross the disk to where the swap partition is located really make a difference during high loads and heavy swapping.

So, how much space should you give your swap partition? Long ago, when RAM was an expensive commodity and most users made do with 4MB to 16MB of RAM, the rule of thumb was to have 2.5 times as much swap space as you had RAM. But today, RAM is cheap and affordable. A high-end workstation with 512MB of RAM and servers with 1GB or more of RAM are not uncommon these days. Today, the average user can afford to have more RAM than he actually needs. So with that in mind, if your workstation has 512MB of RAM, it probably doesn't make much sense to create a 1.2GB swap partition. More than likely, this would just be a huge waste of disk space because a workstation with 512MB of RAM will rarely need to swap at all, much less need anything close to 1.2GB of swap space.

256MB of swap space is a nice number to use if you have 256MB of RAM or less and you aren't really pressed for disk space. If at all possible, you should try to have at least as much swap space as you have RAM. If you plan to do development or track the FreeBSD CURRENT branch, this is practically a necessity. Here is why.

Occasionally, something happens that the operating system's kernel doesn't know how to handle. When such an event occurs, the kernel gives up, panics (you get a message that reads "Kernel panic"), and then reboots the system. If configured to do so, however, the panicked kernel attempts to dump the contents of RAM into the swap partition before it reboots. The contents of RAM when the panic occurred are essential to programmers for debugging what is causing the panics. One of two things happens if there is more information in RAM than can fit in the swap space:

- The kernel will refuse to dump the RAM contents. This is the most likely scenario. In this case, no debugging information will be available for diagnosing the cause of the panic.

- If the panic was caused by some state of confusion in the kernel over something regarding the filesystems, it's conceivable that the kernel could dump the RAM contents to the swap partition and keep right on going when it hits the end boundary of the swap partition. The result would likely be irreparable damage to whatever filesystem came after the swap partition on the disk.

Kernel panics don't happen often in FreeBSD. When they do happen, it's nice to be able to use the RAM dump feature so that you or someone else can examine the contents of RAM when the panic occurred and attempt to figure out what is causing the panic. Therefore, try to make your swap partition at least as big as the amount of RAM you have in your system.

> **NOTE**
>
> Unix kernel panics are similar to the infamous BSOD (Blue Screen of Death) errors in Windows NT/2000. If you are used to working with Windows NT/2000, you can breathe a sigh of relief. You won't be seeing nearly as many kernel panics with FreeBSD as you see blue screens in Windows NT/2000. I've personally only had one kernel panic on my FreeBSD workstation in nearly seven years of working with FreeBSD.

After you decide on a size for your swap partition, create it just like you created the root partition, except this time select Swap when prompted for the filesystem type. The swap partition does not get a directory mount point, so you will not be asked the question about where you want to mount the partition when you are creating a swap partition.

Creating the Rest of the Partitions

After you create the root (and possibly boot) partition and the swap partition, create the rest of the partitions as filesystems, give them the size you decided on earlier, and set the mount points to the proper directories when asked (for example, /usr or /var). Don't forget to include the leading slash.

If you have more than one hard disk on your system and you need to switch between them, use the up and down arrow keys to move the highlighted line over the disk at the top of the screen on which you want to create the partition.

Here is an example of what a final result might look like:

```
                         FreeBSD Disklabel Editor

Disk: ad0        Partition name: ad0s1   Free: 0 blocks (0MB)
Disk: ad1        Partition name: ad1s1   Free: 0 blocks (0MB)

Part      Mount           Size Newfs  Part      Mount          Size Newfs
----      -----           ---- -----  ----      -----          ---- -----
ad0s1a    /               100MB UFS  Y
ad0s1b    swap            256MB SWAP
ad0s1e    /var            200MB UFS  Y
ad0s1f    /tmp            100MB UFS  Y
ad0s1g    /usr          18817MB UFS  Y
ad1s1e    /home         14664MB UFS  Y




The following commands are valid here (upper or lower case):
C = Create        D = Delete    M = Mount pt.    W = Write
N = Newfs Opts    Q = Finish    S = Toggle SoftUpdates
T = Toggle Newfs  U = Undo      A = Auto Defaults

Use F1 or ? to get more help, arrow keys to select.
```

This example has two hard disks in the system, and the /home directory is on a partition in the second hard disk that takes up the entire disk.

> **NOTE**
>
> When creating a partition, if you get an error message at the bottom of your screen that reads "You can only do this in a master partition (see top of screen)," it means that you have to highlight one of the filesystem partitions. Use the up arrow until the highlight is on the main disk at the top of the screen on which you want to create the partition and then try again to create the partition.

Notes on Soft Updates

Starting with FreeBSD 5.0, Soft Updates are enabled by default on most filesystems (except for /). You learn more about Soft Updates in Chapter 8, but for now simply know that they can greatly increase the performance of most filesystems, so you probably want to leave them enabled. To enable Soft Updates on a filesystem, move the highlight over the filesystem you want and press S to toggle Soft Updates on or off. A filesystem that has Soft Updates enabled will have "+S" following the filesystem type (for example, UFS1+S).

After you finish creating partitions, press Q to leave the Partition Editor. Once again, do not use the W option, because this is intended for making changes to existing filesystems, not for installing new ones. The next screen will ask you what you want to install.

Selecting a Canned Distribution Set

Figure 2.4 shows the Choose Distributions menu.

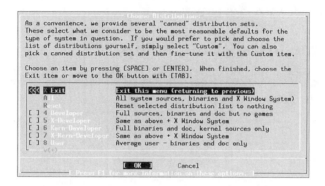

FIGURE 2.4   Selecting the distribution.

If you have the space, I suggest that you select the All option. If you are running a server and you are sure you will not need the X-Windows system, you can select the Developer option instead. If you select an option that doesn't include the source code, you cannot build a new kernel or upgrade the system through cvsup (unless you download all the sources while running cvsup, which negates the space-savings of not installing the sources here). If you select an option that only installs the kernel sources but not the rest of the sources, you will be able to build a new kernel, but you still can't upgrade the system with cvsup. If you are a new user, you probably won't know what most of these packages are for. Therefore, I suggest you stick to one of the canned distributions—preferably, the All distribution.

> **NOTE**
>
> cvsup is a system that automatically updates the FreeBSD operating system by connecting to servers and determining what has changed since the last time you ran cvsup. Any changes are automatically downloaded from the server and applied to the FreeBSD source code. This is much faster than downloading the entire source tree. With cvsup, only the things that have changed need to be downloaded. cvsup is covered in detail in Chapter 17.

To select a distribution, highlight the one you want and press the spacebar. If you selected the All distribution, you will then be asked whether you want to install the FreeBSD ports collection. You really should install the ports collection if you can afford the space because it provides an easy way to download and install additional software for your FreeBSD system and handles most of the dirty work for you. Installing additional software is a breeze if you have the ports collection installed. Use the Tab key to select the option you want and then press Enter.

Next, you return to the Choose Distributions menu. Don't worry if it looks like nothing is selected here. If you selected the All option previously, it is still selected. Use the up arrow to go to the Exit option and then press Enter.

Choosing the Installation Media

The next screen asks you to choose the installation media (see Figure 2.5).

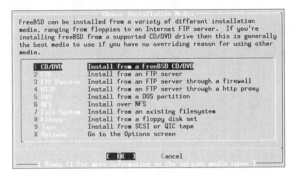

FIGURE 2.5   Choosing the installation media.

This chapter assumes that you are installing from the CD-ROM included with this book (or from an official CD-ROM set). If this is not the case and you need to perform an installation from a network, tape, or floppy, or if you are installing from an existing filesystem, see the relevant sections of Chapter 3 before continuing.

Assuming that you are installing from a CD-ROM, make sure the CD/DVD option is highlighted and press Enter.

The system will then print the following warning message:

```
                    User Confirmation Requested

  Last Chance! Are you SURE you want to continue the installation?

  If you're running this on a disk with data you wish to save then WE
  STRONGLY ENCOURAGE YOU TO MAKE PROPER BACKUPS before proceeding!

We can take no responsibility for lost disk contents!
```

> **CAUTION**
>
> Up to this point, no changes have actually been made to your hard disk. This is your last chance to back out of the installation. After you select Yes, the partitions you created will be formatted and the installation will begin. Any existing data on the partitions you selected to use will be lost!

Assuming you are happy with the installation choices you made, select Yes. The system then prints a message telling you it is starting an emergency holographic shell on vty4. It then proceeds to format the partitions. After partition formatting is done, Sysinstall will begin copying files to your hard disk(s).

Post-installation Configuration and Customization

When the file-copying process is complete, you will see a screen that congratulates you for making it to this point. The screen also informs you that Sysinstall will now move on to the final configuration questions. In addition to configuring the network in this post-installation phase, you will set the time; configure the mouse; choose the desktop, software packages, and users you want to assign to your system; and set the root password. Select OK to continue.

Configuring the Network

Next, you are asked if you want to configure any Ethernet or SLIP/PPP network devices. If you have the values from your system administrator, you can go ahead and set these up now. If you don't have the values available or if you are setting up a new network and are unfamiliar with networking, you can always re-enter this utility later after you have read the chapters on networking.

> **CAUTION**
>
> If you are on a network and you do not configure the network device(s) now, be aware that when the system reboots, you cannot access the network until you configure the network devices to work with your network. With that said, if you don't have a network or you don't know what values should go in the fields for the network configuration, go ahead and skip this section and come back to it later after you have read the networking chapters.

If you don't want to configure any network devices now, simply select No and move on to the next section of this chapter. If you do want to configure network devices at this time, select Yes. You should now see a screen like the one shown in Figure 2.6.

Select the network device you wish to configure from the list and then press Enter. Note that depending on the make and model of your Ethernet adapter, it may have various names. It will usually have the number zero, though, if it is the first Ethernet adapter in the system.

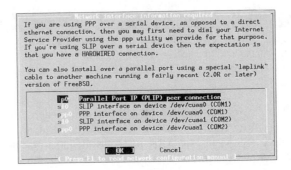

FIGURE 2.6   Selecting the network interface to configure.

After you select the network device you want to configure, you are asked if you want to try the IPv6 configuration of the interface. Unless you are sure your network has an IPv6 server on it that is set up to send you configuration information, you should select No.

The next question asks you the same thing about the DHCP configuration of the interface. If your network has a DHCP server on it, FreeBSD will attempt to contact that server and obtain its network information. If your network does not have a DHCP server, you should select No.

The next screen allows you to enter the information about your network. This will be covered in much more detail in Chapters 21, "Networking with FreeBSD," and 22, "Configuring Basic Networking Services," but here are a few guidelines to get you started.

Figure 2.7 shows the Network Configuration screen; Table 2.5 lists what the fields in this screen are for.

```
┌──────────────────── Network Configuration ────────────────────┐
│ Host:                          Domain:                         │
│ ┌──────────────────────────┐   ┌──────────────────────────┐   │
│ │ kiara.lionresearch.org   │   │ lionresearch.org         │   │
│ └──────────────────────────┘   └──────────────────────────┘   │
│ IPv4 Gateway:                  Name server:                    │
│ ┌──────────────────────────┐   ┌──────────────────────────┐   │
│ │                          │   │                          │   │
│ └──────────────────────────┘   └──────────────────────────┘   │
│  ┌────────── Configuration for Interface ppp0 ──────────┐      │
│  │ IPv4 Address:              Netmask:                   │      │
│  │ ┌──────────────────┐       ┌──────────────────┐       │      │
│  │ │                  │       │ 255.255.255.0    │       │      │
│  │ └──────────────────┘       └──────────────────┘       │      │
│  │ Extra options to ifconfig:                            │      │
│  │ ┌──────────────────────────────────────────┐         │      │
│  │ │                                          │         │      │
│  │ └──────────────────────────────────────────┘         │      │
│  └───────────────────────────────────────────────────────┘      │
│        ┌──────────┐            ┌──────────┐                     │
│        │    OK    │            │  CANCEL  │                     │
│        └──────────┘            └──────────┘                     │
└────────────────────────────────────────────────────────────────┘
```

FIGURE 2.7   Configuring the network interface.

TABLE 2.5   Network Configuration Fields

Field	Description
General Network Options for This System	
Host	The hostname and domain name of your system go here (in this example, `kiara.lionresearch.org`).
Domain	The name of the domain name where your system is located (in this example, `lionresearch.org`).
IPv4 Gateway	If your system will use another host to access nonlocal network resources (the Internet), put the address of that host here. If this system has direct Internet access, this field should be left blank.
Name server	The IP address of your DNS server, which is the server that resolves network names into IP addresses.
Network Options Specific to This Network Interface	
IPv4 Address	The IP address of this system.
Netmask	The netmask value for the network that this interface accesses.
Extra Options to ifconfig	Any extra options you need to pass to the network configuration should go here.

If you are unclear about any of these concepts, you should read Chapters 21 and 22 before configuring the network.

> **CAUTION**
>
> If you aren't sure what numbers or names should go in the Network Configuration screen, ask someone who will know. Never simply fill in random numbers or names if your system is on a network. If your system is connected to a network, simply inserting random numbers in the IPv4 Address field or a random hostname in the Host field is a sure way to get on the bad side of the network administrators as well as other network users. If you select an IP address that conflicts with an existing system on the network, bad things will happen, including possible denial of service to an important network resource if your IP address conflicts with that of a major server.

Use the Tab or Enter key to move between fields. When you are done, select OK to leave the configuration screen.

Depending on the type of network interface you set up, you may now be asked if you wish to bring the interface up right now. Select No, because you are almost done with the install and will be rebooting the system soon anyway.

Sysinstall will then ask you a series of questions about the network:

- **Will this machine be a leaf node (for example, will it not forward packets between interfaces)?**

  Unless this machine will be a gateway that other systems on the network will use to get to the Internet, or a router that will handle network traffic intended for other systems, you should select Yes.

- **Do you want to grant only normal users FTP access to this host (for example, no anonymous FTP connections)?**

  I suggest you select Yes unless you have already read the chapters on networking. You can always configure anonymous FTP access later on.

- **Do you want to configure this machine as an NFS server?**

  The NFS server allows you to share directories on your hard disk so that users on other systems can mount them and read and/or write files to them. Once again, unless you have read Chapter 32, "The Network Filesystem (NFS)," I suggest you select No for now, even if you know that you will need this service. NFS can be a security problem if it's not set up properly. After you read Chapter 32, you can come back and set this up.

- **Do you want to configure this machine as an NFS client?**

  If you need to mount filesystems on your drive that are located on other systems, you need to set up the NFS client. Once again, see Chapter 32 for more information on configuring NFS.

- **Do you want to select a default security profile for this host (select No for medium security)?**

  Unless high security is absolutely critical in your environment, I suggest you select No. Later, you can customize the security settings by editing the system configuration files. These settings are very easy to change in the system configuration files.

After you select No for the last option, you see a message that tells you about the services that will be enabled in this profile. The "high" security profile will disable services such as X, so you can't even start the X-Server on your local machine. Therefore, I suggest using the default "medium" security profile for now unless you will be running the server in an environment where security is critical. After you read this message, press Enter to continue.

Customizing the Console

Next, you have the opportunity to customize the FreeBSD console settings. You can use these settings to customize the behavior of your keyboard, to choose which font will be used on the screen display, and to select which screensaver to use. If you select Yes to the question asking you whether you want to customize your console setting, you see a menu like the one shown in Figure 2.8.

Most of the options here are self-explanatory. Simply select any options you need to configure and then follow the onscreen instructions.

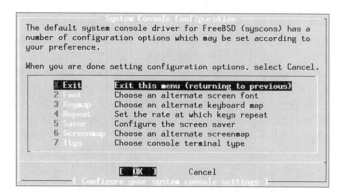

FIGURE 2.8   Customizing the console settings.

Setting the Time Zone

Next, Sysinstall asks whether you want to set the system's time zone. Select Yes. The next screen will ask whether your system's clock is set to UTC (known also as Coordinated Universal Time, Greenwich Mean Time, and Zulu Time). It probably isn't, so unless you are sure your clock is set to UTC, select No. The next menu asks you to select your region, your country, and other information about where you are located. After you provide Sysinstall with all this information, it shows you a three-letter abbreviation for your time zone and asks whether this abbreviation looks reasonable. If it looks correct, select Yes. If it doesn't, select No. You can always do it again.

Linux Compatibility

The next question asks whether you would like to enable Linux binary compatibility. If you select Yes, Sysinstall will install a "mini-Linux filesystem" in your /usr partition that includes the Linux share libraries and other necessary programs for Linux to run on FreeBSD. Unless you are sure you will not be running any Linux programs, I suggest you select Yes. This can be a very useful option. (In fact, I wrote much of the manuscript for this book on StarOffice for Linux, which I ran on my FreeBSD workstation.)

> **NOTE**
>
> Your first thought might be that you don't want to do this. If you worked with emulators under other operating systems, you know how slow they can be. With FreeBSD, however, this is not the case. Linux support in FreeBSD is not done through an emulator but rather is implemented at the kernel level. FreeBSD's Linux support is so good that it runs most Linux applications as fast as native Linux. In fact, FreeBSD will even run some Linux applications faster than Linux itself runs them!

Configuring the Mouse

FreeBSD comes with a console mouse daemon that allows you to cut and paste text from the console using the mouse. The next question asks whether you have a non-USB mouse attached to your system. If you do, select Yes, and you will see the mouse configuration menu (see Figure 2.9). If you plan to use X-Windows (the FreeBSD graphical interface) most of the time, I suggest you skip this option by selecting Yes at the prompt and then choosing Disable from the next menu. This will allow X-Windows to access the mouse directly.

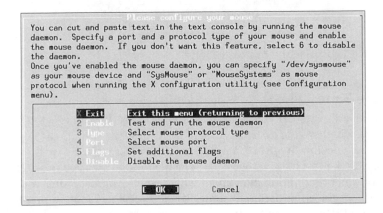

FIGURE 2.9   Configuring the mouse.

Use the menu options to select the type of mouse you have and the port it is connected to. Read the instructions at the top of each menu to help you determine which protocol and port to select.

X-Windows makes use of all three buttons on a standard mouse. If you have a mouse with only two buttons on it, you need to emulate a three-button mouse by telling the mouse driver to interpret the clicking of both buttons at the same time as the third button. You can do this by selecting the Flags option on the menu and typing **-3** in the dialog that pops up. Another useful option you might want to put in here is -r high to make the pointer move faster or -r low if the pointer moves too fast and you want to slow it down. If you need both options, you can use -3 -r high, for example.

After you finish configuring the mouse settings, select the Enable option to test and run the mouse daemon. If the mouse is set up correctly, you should now be able to move the mouse pointer around on the screen. When you are done testing the mouse, select Yes if the mouse worked (note that the mouse still doesn't work in the menu; you still need to use the arrows and the Tab key) or choose No if it didn't.

You are then returned to the mouse configuration menu. Assuming that the mouse worked, select the Exit option.

Configuring the X-Server

Assuming that you installed the X-Windows system, you are now asked if you want to configure the X-Server. Select Yes. You see a menu like the one shown in Figure 2.10.

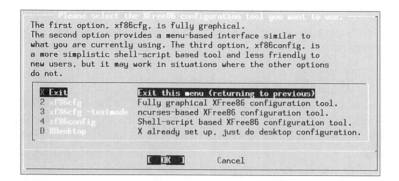

```
┌─── Please select the XFree86 configuration tool you want to use. ───┐
│ The first option, xf86cfg, is fully graphical.                       │
│ The second option provides a menu-based interface similar to         │
│ what you are currently using. The third option, xf86config, is       │
│ a more simplistic shell-script based tool and less friendly to       │
│ new users, but it may work in situations where the other options     │
│ do not.                                                              │
│ ┌──────────────────────────────────────────────────────────────┐   │
│ │ X Exit              Exit this menu (returning to previous)     │   │
│ │ 2 xf86cfg           Fully graphical XFree86 configuration tool.│   │
│ │ 3 xf86cfg -textmode ncurses-based XFree86 configuration tool.  │   │
│ │ 4 xf86config        Shell-script based XFree86 configuration tool. │
│ │ D XDesktop          X already set up, just do desktop configuration. │
│ └──────────────────────────────────────────────────────────────┘   │
│                                                                      │
│               [  OK  ]        Cancel                                 │
└──────────────────────────────────────────────────────────────────────┘
```

FIGURE 2.10   Selecting the X-Server configuration method.

In FreeBSD 5.0, one of the options available in this menu is xf86cfg. This is a graphical interface that helps you configure the X-Server. However, xf86cfg is a user interface nightmare, and it is easier to just configure the X-Server using the shell script prompts. Therefore, this section does not cover xf86cfg. Instead, go to Chapter 35, "Advanced X-Windows Configuration," and read the section "Configuring X-Windows with the xf86config Script." After you have finished with the xf86config script, return to this chapter and continue with the next section.

> **CAUTION**
>
> If you decide to try using xf86cfg anyway, you should be aware that improper refresh rate settings can cause damage to your monitor. Therefore, make sure you do not use settings your monitor is not capable of supporting. This is discussed in more detail in Chapter 35.

Selecting the Default Desktop

Now you are back to the familiar text-based Sysinstall program, and you can no longer use the mouse. Instead, you must go back to using the arrow, Tab, spacebar, and Enter keys to navigate screens and choose options.

In the next screen, you can select which desktop you want to use as your default FreeBSD desktop in X-Windows. Unlike Microsoft Windows, FreeBSD allows you a wide choice of desktops with different features, looks, and so on. Far more desktops are available than are in this list, and they are very easy to change.

If you are an old Linux guru and you already know which desktop you want to use, select it here. If you have never worked with X-Windows before, I suggest you select the WindowMaker option because this desktop is fairly easy for new users to work with, and it is the one used in the next few chapters. If you later decide you don't like the desktop, you can always change it to a different one.

After you make your selection, the packages for your chosen desktop will be loaded onto your system.

Installing Additional Software Packages

Select Yes to answer the question about whether you want to browse the FreeBSD package collection. From this menu, you can install some additional software that will be useful in the next couple chapters. Feel free to browse through the collection as long as you want, only to see what is available. For now, however, I don't recommend that you install a ton of software at this point because it is very easy to add more later. There are a few packages that I recommend you install for use in the next few chapters, however.

If you are asked where you want to install the packages in the Choosing Installation Media menu, select CDROM, assuming you are installing FreeBSD from the included CD-ROM.

Figure 2.11 shows the main menu for the package installation system.

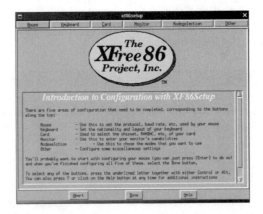

FIGURE 2.11   Installing additional packages.

To navigate through the package installation system, use the arrow keys to move between packages and categories. Use the spacebar or Enter key to select or unselect a package. When you have finished selecting packages in a category, use the Tab key to highlight the OK option and press Enter to get back to the main selection menu (where you can select the category you want to browse). Packages that are already installed will have an *X* next to them; unselecting these packages causes them to be uninstalled. Packages that have a *D* by them are *dependencies*, meaning that they are required by some other package currently installed. At the bottom of the screen is a short description of the currently highlighted package.

2

> **NOTE**
>
> By the time this book goes to press, some of the version numbers on the software listed may have changed. In this case, select the option that appears closest to what I list here. For example, I list Bash-2.05. If your menu has Bash-2.07 instead, select it.

I suggest that you choose the Bash-2.05 package in the Shells category. This is a very powerful and easy-to-use shell for the FreeBSD command-line interface. Linux users will be familiar with this shell because it is the default shell on almost all Linux distributions.

Unix gurus can also install any other shell in this list that they want to have available.

Adding a User

When the package installation is complete, you are asked whether you want to add any user accounts to the system. Select Yes to create a normal user account for yourself. It is dangerous to use the root account for normal operations because root has no restrictions and can damage or destroy important system files if you make a mistake. Using your normal user account for most operations prevents this.

On the Help screen, shown in Figure 2.12, select User to add a new user to the system.

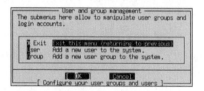

FIGURE 2.12   Adding users and groups to the system.

You are then taken to a form you need to fill out to add the new user (see Figure 2.13).

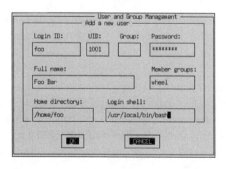

FIGURE 2.13   The Add a New User form.

Not all the fields on this form have to be filled in. Actually, you should leave some of them blank so the system can make a default choice for you. Use the Tab key to move between the various fields. The following sections describe each of these fields and make recommendations for adding values to them.

Login ID

Login ID is the name you use to identify yourself to the system when you sign in. The ID you type in this field should not be more than eight characters long. Common conventions are to use initials, nicknames, or combinations of initials and first or last name. For example, I might use mikeu, murban, or mcu as my login name. Each user on the system must have a unique login name. Names are case sensitive and, by convention, use all lowercase letters.

UID

UID is a numeric ID that the system uses to keep track of users. You should leave this field alone and let the system pick the number for you.

Group

This field refers to the primary group you will be a member of. Once again, leave this field alone and let the system pick for you.

Password

In this field, you type the password you will use to log in. Passwords are case sensitive. Here are some guidelines for choosing good passwords that crackers (commonly known as *hackers*, although this is not the correct term for people who illegally break into computer systems) can't figure out:

- Use at least eight characters. Short passwords are easier for programs designed to try random combinations of letters and numbers to crack.

- Use a combination of uppercase and lowercase letters, numbers, and at least one special character, such as $ or !.

- Don't use words found in a dictionary. Password-cracking programs exist that go through the dictionary trying various words until they hit one that works.

- Don't use things that other people know about you or can easily find out about you. In other words, the name of your child, your cat, or the city you were born in does not make a good password.

At the same time, it's good to pick something you can remember easily. Some techniques for doing this include combining parts of various words together (remembering, of course, to include both uppercase and lowercase letters and to stick a few numbers and at least one special character in somewhere). You can also use what I call *keyboard substitution*—a technique where you pick a word that means something to you (but that others will not know) and then substitute the character to the upper-left, upper-right, lower-left, or lower-right as the actual character in the password.

After you decide on a password, enter it carefully because you will not be asked to verify it. (The password will show up on the screen as asterisks (*). If you mistype it, you will not be able to log in (if you accidentally do mistype the password, you can read how to fix it in Appendix C).

After you decide on your password, do not write it down anywhere. Do not write it on the bottom of your desk. Do not write it down in your appointment book. Do not have it tattooed on your arm. And whatever you do, do not write it on a Post-It note and stick it on your monitor. (I know that seems like stating the obvious, but you would be surprised how many users do just that.) Also, do not tell your password to anybody, including your coworkers, your spouse, or your children.

Full Name
You can either type your name in this field or leave it blank (remove "User &" if you intend to leave it blank). Note that some programs, such as the Unix mail program, will use this field to determine what to put in the From field of the e-mail you send. Therefore, it is probably a good idea to enter your name here.

Member Groups
I suggest you type **wheel** in this field. This will make you a member of the group "wheel," which will allow you to assume the identity of the root user (super-user or system administrator) without having to log out and log back in as a different user (although you still need to supply the root password to do this).

Home Directory
This field lists the place where your home directory will be located on the hard disk. You should leave this field alone and let the system choose for you.

Login Shell
The login shell is the default command-line shell you will be placed in after you log in. Assuming you installed the Bash shell, as suggested earlier, I suggest you type **/usr/local/bin/bash** in this field (including the slashes). If you later decide you do not like the Bash shell, it is easy to change your default shell to a different one.

After you finish entering the information, tab over to the OK button and press Enter. The user account will be created for you, and you will be returned to the menu shown earlier in Figure 2.12. Select the Exit option.

Setting the Root Password
Press Enter when you see the message about setting the system manager's password. You are then given a prompt at the bottom of the screen that asks you to enter a root password. It looks like this:

```
Changing local password for root.
New password :
```

All the guidelines you read earlier for choosing and protecting your normal user password are doubly important here. Anyone who knows your root password (or can find it out) can access anything on your entire system and can do anything to your entire system as well. He will have access to read confidential information, e-mail it to other places, destroy data on your system, change data on your system, and do whatever other evil things he decides to do.

After you decide on a root password, enter it at the prompt. Notice that it will not show up onscreen as you type it. This prevents someone from looking over your shoulder as you type and reading your password. After you enter the password, press Enter. You will be asked to verify it. Type it again and press Enter. Assuming that you typed it the same way both times, the installation will ask whether you want to visit the general configuration menu for a chance to set any last options. Select No. You are then returned to the main menu.

Exiting the Install Program and Rebooting the System

At the main menu, tab over to Exit Install and press Enter. The system asks you to confirm that you wish to exit. It then asks you to remove any CD-ROMs or floppies from the drives on your system. After you remove them, select Yes. The system will then reboot.

NOTE

You may find that you've pressed the Eject button on your CD-ROM drive but nothing happened. Don't worry. FreeBSD didn't break your CD-ROM drive; it just locked it to ensure you couldn't accidentally eject the CD-ROM in the middle of the install. If you can't open your CD-ROM drive, select Yes anyway and wait until just after your system has started to reboot (when it is counting the memory and such). Then, press the Eject button on your CD-ROM drive. It should now open and you can remove the FreeBSD CD-ROM.

TIP

When the system reboots, you might want to go into your BIOS setup utility right away and configure the system so that it will not try to boot from the CD-ROM anymore. Some systems can hang for a long time while trying to boot from CD-ROM if there is no bootable CD-ROM in the drive (or no CD-ROM at all). Although most systems will eventually give up and boot from the hard disk, it can sometimes take as long as a minute or more before the system decides it can't boot from the CD-ROM and goes to the hard disk instead. Disable CD-ROM booting in the BIOS to avoid this problem. (See your hardware documentation for information on how to configure your system BIOS settings.)

Booting FreeBSD for the First Time

When your system restarts, one of two things should happen: Either you get a boot menu asking you which operating system you want to boot or, if FreeBSD is the only operating system on the drive, the system begins to boot straight into FreeBSD. If this is not the case, and your system either hangs or boots right into some other operating system without giving you the option of starting FreeBSD, see Appendix C.

Assuming that the restart is successful, you should get a flurry of messages going past your screen as the kernel finds and initializes your system hardware. Kernel messages are in a bright white color. After the kernel is finished, it will pass control to a program called init, which starts up various other processes and programs in the system. These messages have a light gray color. There will be a short pause the first time the system boots as it generates RSA and DSA encryption keys for your system (which are used for secure communication across networks or the Internet). Eventually, after init is finished, you should be left with the following:

```
FreeBSD/i386 (simba.samplenet.org) (ttyv0)
login:
```

Your display, of course, will have the name of your host and network instead of (simba.samplenet.org). If you didn't set up the network, it will have the system default hostname, which will probably be Amnesiac.

Log in using the name root. After pressing Enter, type in the password you gave to root (once again, the password will not display on the screen).

Assuming you type the username and password correctly, you will see a welcome message that tells you a little bit about FreeBSD and where you can get help (as well as how you can change this message or get rid of it) and then you are left with a shell prompt, which will look something like this:

```
Copyright (c) 1980, 1983, 1986, 1988, 1990, 1991, 1993, 1994
        The Regents of the University of California.  All rights reserved.

FreeBSD 5.0-RELEASE (GENERIC) #0: Mon Jan 20 00:47:09 CST 2003

#
```

Here, # is the command prompt, and it means the shell is waiting for you to give it something to do.

Shutting Down FreeBSD

FreeBSD (like other versions of Unix) is a multitasking, multiuser operating system. It is constantly doing something and usually has many files open at the same time. Because of this, you can simply turn off the power when you want to shut down a FreeBSD system. First, you have to tell FreeBSD to shut itself down so that it can terminate any programs it is running and save any files it has open in an orderly fashion. The proper way to do this right now is with the following command:

```
shutdown -h now
```

This tells FreeBSD to perform a system shutdown, to halt after the shutdown is complete (as opposed to rebooting or going into single-user mode), and that you want the shutdown to happen now instead of five minutes from now, for example. (Usually you put a delay here so that users will get a warning of the upcoming shutdown and have time to save whatever files they are working on.)

Type **shutdown -h now** at the prompt and press Enter.

You'll see a few messages on your screen, including Broadcast message from root and various status messages from some processes as they shut down.

Look for the following message:

```
System halted
Please press any key to reboot
```

Then, and only then, is it safe to turn off your computer.

CAUTION

Never shut down a FreeBSD system or any other Unix system by simply turning off the power. Doing so can cause serious damage to the filesystems. You should always issue a proper shutdown first.

CHAPTER **3**

Advanced Installation Issues

Chapter 2, "Installing FreeBSD," discussed a standard installation with a few complicating factors, such as dual-boot disk configurations and coexistence with other operating systems. It also assumed that you were installing FreeBSD from a CD-ROM rather than via one of the many different alternate installation media available.

This chapter serves mostly as a supplement to Chapter 2, by explaining a number of essential preinstallation tasks for those whose systems don't fit the previously mentioned assumptions. If you are installing FreeBSD on a system with another operating system previously installed, or if you aren't using a CD-ROM to install FreeBSD, you'll want to read this chapter before performing the installation. After you have completed the necessary preinstallation tasks you learn here, you should return to Chapter 2 and proceed with the normal installation.

Most people install FreeBSD on a workstation that is already running Windows. This chapter shows how to prepare for a FreeBSD installation that will enable the two systems to operate side by side. We'll also look briefly at installing FreeBSD on a system that is running Linux. After reading this chapter, you will know how to install FreeBSD in such a way that you can choose to boot your computer into FreeBSD or into Windows or Linux.

In addition, we'll briefly cover NFS and FTP network installs for situations where an installation CD is not available.

Backing Up an Existing Windows or Linux Filesystem

Before you go any further, back up any existing Windows or Linux filesystem you want to maintain. Although the next section shows you how to nondestructively create space for FreeBSD, mistakes can still happen, and programs can cause errors. It is best to have a backup of anything you want to keep.

Media that can be used for backup purposes include recordable CDs, Zip or Jaz disks, tape drives, or even floppy disks, if the amount of data you need to save is small. Backing up the operating system and installed programs, such as word processing programs, is not necessary because they can be easily reinstalled. The primary things to worry about are your files containing data that cannot easily be replaced.

If you do not have an actual backup program, you can use an archiving program such as WinZip to help you compress data for backup and also to place that data onto disks.

> **NOTE**
>
> The exact procedures for doing a system backup are beyond the scope of this book. Therefore, see the documentation for the backup program you plan to use for information on how to complete the backup.

Once you have backed up any existing files that you wish to keep, you will need to free up some space on your hard disk for installing FreeBSD. There are a few ways that this can be done:

- *Simply delete the partitions and start over.* This causes you to lose all the existing data on your system, and you will have to reinstall everything that is currently on your system once you have re-created the partitions. This is a desirable option when you don't really care what's on the disk, or if you don't have a nondestructive partitioning program such as Partition Magic—*and* if you aren't daunted by the idea of reinstalling Windows or Linux after you have made space for FreeBSD and installed it.

- *Use a commercial partitioning program such as Partition Magic.* If you have PowerQuest's Partition Magic, by all means use it. This solution is the "best of both worlds," allowing you to nondestructively reallocate the space on your hard disk for a FreeBSD installation without losing any of your data or configurations. A discussion of how to use this commercial program is beyond the scope of this book. See the Partition Magic documentation for instructions. Partition Magic's Web site is http://www.powerquest.com/partitionmagic/.

- *Use the FIPS utility.* This freely available program allows you to split an existing partition to create free space. FIPS is included on the CD with this book, and it is the method we'll discuss in this chapter. It's not as polished a solution as Partition Magic, but it's free and can give you similar results.

Nondestructive Hard Disk Partitioning with FIPS

FIPS, which stands for *First (nondestructive) Interactive Partition Splitting*, is a partitioning program designed to run under DOS or Windows in DOS mode. It splits an existing DOS partition into two at the point you specify. You can then use the new partition it creates as the space for FreeBSD. Note that FIPS works only with DOS-style partitions (FAT16 or FAT32). FIPS does not work with Windows NT/2000/XP NTFS partitions, nor does it work with Linux Ext2FS partitions. Finally, those running OS/2 need to be aware that FIPS does not work with HPFS partitions, either.

FIPS has a couple of limitations:

- *It cannot split an extended DOS partition, only a primary one.* Extended DOS partitions are a form of second-level partitioning in common use in the DOS/Windows and Linux worlds; they allow a disk to contain more than the BIOS-supported four partitions by subdividing them and then providing access to them as though they were regular partitions. (FreeBSD doesn't use extended partitions; instead, it has the concept of *slices* and *BSD partitions*, which we will cover in Chapter 18, "Understanding Hard Disks and Filesystems.") If you are like most people running Windows 95 OSR2 or Windows 98, this will not be a problem because you likely have one primary partition that takes up the entire disk.

- *You cannot currently have more than three partitions on your disk.* FIPS creates a new primary partition with the free space it is assigned. Because you can only have four partition entries on a disk, you can have no more than three existing partitions when you run FIPS.

If neither of these issues applies to you, and assuming you have made a backup, you are ready to begin the partitioning process.

> **CAUTION**
>
> Windows XP partitions are often formatted as NTFS. Because of this, FIPS may not work with Windows XP at all, even for Windows XP Home Edition. If you're using Windows XP or NT/2000 with an NTFS filesystem, you will need to look into the commercial Partition Magic for nondestructive disk partitioning.

Running ScanDisk and the Defragmenter

Before you use FIPS, you should run DOS or Windows ScanDisk to fix any problems on the disk. After ScanDisk has finished running, you need to run the disk defragmenter.

FIPS needs contiguous free space at the end of the drive in order to split the partition. It cannot split before the last sector on the disk containing data. Running the disk defragmenter moves all the data to the beginning of the disk without leaving holes in the middle.

> **CAUTION**
>
> Be aware that the defragmenter in Windows 2000 and XP often fails to move all files into a contiguous chunk; the NTFS filesystem tends to prevent this from working correctly, and defragmenting tools often leave large holes in the midst of the used disk space. Again, Partition Magic may be the best solution for these platforms if FIPS fails to find enough contiguous free space.

Depending on the speed of your computer, the size of your hard disk, how fast the disk is, and how badly fragmented it is, the defragmentation process could take anywhere from a few minutes to several hours.

Obtaining FIPS and Creating a Boot Disk

Once the defragmentation process is finished, you are ready to start FIPS. FIPS is located on this book's CD in the TOOLS directory with the name FIPS.EXE. You also want the files named RESTORRB.EXE and ERRORS.TXT from the CD. You can also download FIPS from the FreeBSD FTP server at ftp.freebsd.org or one of its mirror sites in the directory /pub/FreeBSD/tools/fips.exe. You can download restorrb.exe from the same directory.

You should create a bootable floppy and copy the three files mentioned previously to it. In DOS or Windows, you can create a bootable floppy from a DOS prompt with the command format a: /s, assuming that you have a blank floppy in drive A. The following is a sample procedure for creating the boot disk:

```
C:\> format a: /s
Insert new diskette in drive A:
and press ENTER when ready...

Checking existing disk format.
Verifying 1.44M
Format complete.
System transferred

Volume label (11 characters, ENTER for none)?

    1,457,664 bytes total disk space
      388,608 bytes used by system
    1,069,056 bytes available on disk

        512 bytes in each allocation unit.
      2,088 allocation units available on disk.

Volume Serial Number is 031B-0831
```

```
Format another (Y/N)? n

C:\>d:
D:\>cd tools
D:\TOOLS>copy fips.exe a:\
    1 file(s) copied
d:\TOOLS>copy restorerb.exe a:\
    1 file(s) copied
D:\TOOLS>copy errors.txt a:\
    1 file(S) copied
D:\TOOLS>
```

> **NOTE**
>
> You cannot use `format a: /s` to create a bootable floppy under Windows 2000 or XP. You will need to use Windows 95 or 98 for this task.

When you've created the bootable floppy, use it to reboot your system. After the system has finished booting, type **fips** at the DOS prompt to start the FIPS program.

Working with FIPS

When FIPS first starts, it gives you a warning about not using it in a multitasking environment, among other things. Once you have read all the information, press any key to continue. If you have more than one hard disk in your system, FIPS will ask you which one you want to work on. Select the disk you want. FIPS will then show you the partition table of your disk. It will look something like the following:

```
      |         |      Start       |      |      End         | Start  |Number of|
Part. |bootable|Head Cyl. Sector|System|Head Cyl. Sector| Sector |Sectors  |  MB
------+--------+----------------+------+----------------+--------+---------+----
1     |   yes  |  1   0      1|  06h|  12  983      32|    32|  409312| 199
2     |   no   |  0   0      0|  00h|   0   0       0|     0|       0|   0
3     |   no   |  0   0      0|  00h|   0   0       0|     0|       0|   0
4     |   no   |  0   0      0|  00h|   0   0       0|     0|       0|   0

Checking root sector ... OK

Press any Key
```

If you have more than one partition on your disk, FIPS asks you to select which one you want to split. If you only have one partition on your disk, you are asked to press any key, as in the preceding example. After you have selected a partition or pressed a key to continue, FIPS reads the boot sector and presents some more information on the disk:

```
Bytes per sector: 512
Sectors per cluster: 8
Reserved sectors: 1
Number of FATs: 2
Number of rootdirectory entries: 512
Number of sectors (short): 0
Media descriptor byte: f8h
Sectors per FAT: 200
Sectors per track: 32
Drive heads: 13
Hidden sectors: 32
Number of sectors (long): 409312
Physical drive number: 80h
Signature: 29h
```

When FIPS has finished presenting information, it asks you to choose the starting cylinder for the new partition. The size of the new partition and the size of the old partition are presented. Use the left- or right-arrow key to decrease or increase the number the new partition will start on. In addition, you can use the up- or down-arrow key to increase or decrease the size of the new partition in increments of 10 cylinders. You can use the "Start" and "End" numbers of heads, cylinders, and sectors to gauge how you want to divide up your disk; you can decrease the size of the existing partition(s) until the remaining space is big enough for your FreeBSD installation (use the Size column to determine how big it is). Note that, as we'll discuss shortly, a FreeBSD boot partition must exist entirely within the first 1,024 cylinders of the disk. When you have finished, press Enter to continue.

> **TIP**
>
> Write down the starting cylinder information for the new partition you create. This will help you verify later on during the FreeBSD installation that you have selected the correct partition on which to install FreeBSD.

Once you have pressed Enter, FIPS shows you what the new partition table will look like. It then gives you the option to re-edit the partition table or continue. If you select Continue, FIPS asks you one last time if you are sure you want to write the changes to the partition table. Be careful at this point! Selecting Y will cause FIPS to write the changes and then exit. This is an irrevocable change; if you write the changes, you won't be able to revert back to the old configuration. After you commit the changes and exit FIPS, you need to reboot your system immediately.

## 3

If FIPS exits with any errors, see the README file included with FIPS for more information.

> **CAUTION**
>
> It is very important that after you exit FIPS, you do *not* create any new data on the hard disk until after you have rebooted. Doing so could corrupt the disk because DOS will not be aware that the partition table has changed until the system has been rebooted.

Once you have rebooted, you should run FIPS again with the -t option. This will check to make sure the partition was split correctly. If errors are reported, restore the previous partition table by running RESTORRB.EXE and then reboot again.

> **CAUTION**
>
> Once you have made *any* changes to the filesystems on the disk, you can no longer use RESTORRB.EXE to restore the old partition table. Therefore, it is very important that you run fips with the -t option after you reboot before you do anything else.

If fips -t doesn't report any errors, remove the floppy from the drive and then reboot again. When Windows or DOS has finished restarting, you should run ScanDisk on the partition you split to check for any errors.

Potential Problems with and Limitations of Dual-Boot Systems

It is possible to have a dual-boot system in which you have two (or even more) operating systems on the hard disk, and you can select which one you want at each system boot. This is a very useful configuration in many circumstances; if you only have one computer, and you want to use FreeBSD for programming and Windows for gaming, dual-booting is an ideal solution. Working with dual-boot systems can present some problems, however, if you don't take steps to avoid and/or deal with them.

First, be aware that all the information necessary to boot FreeBSD must be located within the first 1,024 cylinders of the hard disk. This is necessary for the FreeBSD boot manager to work; it means that when you partition the disk for FreeBSD using FIPS, either the root partition must be completely located within the first 1,024 cylinders or you can use a separate boot partition that is completely located in the first 1,024 cylinders. Use the "Start" and "End" cylinder readouts in FIPS to determine where your partitions start and end. If you choose the latter option, the root partition does not have to be completely located in the first 1,024 cylinders. Note that "completely located" means that the partition has to both start and end below the 1,024th cylinder. Simply starting below the 1,024th cylinder is not good enough.

If you need more space for Windows or DOS than is available below 1,024 cylinders, you can use FIPS again to split the Windows or DOS partition into two partitions, giving you a C drive and a D drive in Windows or DOS. In between these C and D drives, you need to put a small partition for FreeBSD to boot from. This partition will be used as /boot later on during the install (30MB should be more than enough for this partition).

Second, when you reinstall programs after partitioning, be certain to install DOS or Windows before you install FreeBSD. DOS and Windows assume that they are the only operating system on the hard drive and will overwrite the master boot record without asking. If you install FreeBSD first, installing DOS or Windows later will clobber FreeBSD's boot manager, and you will no longer be able to boot into FreeBSD. This problem is easily fixed, but save yourself the headaches and just install DOS or Windows first.

Dual-Booting with DOS, Windows 95, Windows 98, Windows Me, or Windows XP

FreeBSD comes with a boot manager that allows you to dual-boot with various operating systems. If you already have DOS, Windows 95, Windows 98, or Windows Me installed, it is easy to set up the boot manager. You are given the option to install it during the FreeBSD installation. DOS, Windows 95, Windows 98, or Windows Me is automatically added to the boot menu.

Dual-Booting with Linux

If you want to dual-boot with Linux and load Linux from the FreeBSD boot manager, install LILO (the Linux boot manager) at the beginning of your Linux boot partition rather than in the master boot record (MBR). See the LILO documentation for instructions on how to do this. After you have installed LILO, you can boot Linux from the FreeBSD boot manager. If you want to boot FreeBSD from LILO, see the section later in this chapter titled "Booting FreeBSD from LILO."

The FreeBSD Boot Manager

You can install the FreeBSD boot manager during the FreeBSD installation to enable booting of multiple operating systems. After the install, you can configure the boot manager with the boot0cfg program.

boot0cfg -B will install the boot manager onto the hard disk's MBR. This is one way to restore the boot manager if Windows should wipe it out (if, for example, you install Windows after you install FreeBSD). Of course, you would have to boot from a FreeBSD boot disk to use boot0cfg -B if the boot manager has been wiped out. In addition, if you wish to make changes to the boot manager configuration, you will need to reinstall it using this command, followed by the changes you wish to make.

boot0cfg is command-line driven. Fortunately, you probably do not need to be concerned with most of the options, although you might be interested in a few of them. The list of options shown in Table 3.1 is supported for making changes to the boot manager configuration.

TABLE 3.1   Boot Manager Configuration Options

Option	Description
-v	boot0cfg will be more verbose about what it is doing.
-b *image*	Here, *image* is the name of the boot image to use. The default is /boot/boot0.
-d *drive*	Here, *drive* is the drive number used by the PC's BIOS for referencing the disk. Usually this is 0x80 for the first drive, 0x81 for the second, and so on.
-f *file*	Here, *file* is the name of a file that the original MBR should be backed up to in case there are problems. If the file already exists, it will be truncated.

The -o option is also supported, and it allows a comma-separated list of arguments, whose meanings are listed in Table 3.2.

TABLE 3.2   Arguments for boot0cfg -o

Argument	Description
packet	If the PC's BIOS supports it, this will tell boot0cfg to use int 0x13 extensions instead of CHS for disk I/O. This will get around the 1,024 cylinder boot limit described previously. However, if the PC's BIOS does not support this option, it may cause the system to hang on the next reboot.
setdrv	Forces boot0cfg to use the drive number specified in the –d option to reference the drive you're working with.
noupdate	By default, the boot manager can write to the MBR and update it (to set the active flag and so on). This can cause problems if you have hardware antivirus support enabled that prevents writing to the MBR and such. The noupdate option will prevent the boot manager from attempting to write to the MBR.

boot0cfg also supports the -s *n* option, where *n* is a number from 1 to 5 that specifies the default slice (commonly referred to as a *partition* in MS-DOS/Windows) to boot if no selection is made. The -t *n* option is also supported, where *n* is a number representing the number of "ticks" to wait before booting the default operating system. There are approximately 18.2 ticks in a second.

Booting FreeBSD from LILO

If you're running Linux and want to boot FreeBSD from Linux's LILO, it is fairly easy to do. In Linux, edit the file /etc/lilo.conf and add the following lines:

```
other=/dev/hda2
   table=/dev/hda
   label=FreeBSD
```

Change the line beginning with `other=` to reflect whatever device Linux recognizes your FreeBSD drive as.

After you have changed the configuration file, reinstall LILO by typing **lilo** as the root user.

Alternate Installation Methods

If you can't or (for whatever reason) don't want to install FreeBSD from the CD included with this book, you have several other options available. These include network installs with FTP or NFS. Installation over the network is especially convenient when you are in a location with a lot of bandwidth and don't have the CD-ROM handy, or if the machine doesn't have a working CD-ROM drive. For many servers or workstations in enterprise environments, installing from a network source is the quickest and most efficient way to get FreeBSD installed.

Installing FreeBSD over FTP

FTP stands for *File Transfer Protocol*. It is one of the earliest methods of transferring files over the Internet, from one system to another. FTP is still widely used; it's the backbone of file transfers on the Internet, as we will discuss in Chapter 26, "Configuring an FTP Server."

You can install FreeBSD directly from an FTP server, but you should have a full-time, fast Internet connection available in order to do so. Performing an FTP install over a modem will take a *very* long time.

If you are installing FreeBSD from the FreeBSD sites or one of the official mirrors, you can log in as "anonymous." In this case, you can skip the next section. If, however, you are installing from an FTP server that does not allow anonymous logins (such as an internal FTP server on a LAN), you will need to follow the procedures in the next section to config-ure the username first.

Configuring the Username

From the `sysinstall` main menu, shown in Figure 3.1, arrow down to Options and press Enter. In the Options menu, shown in Figure 3.2, you can set the FTP login name.

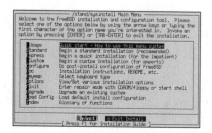

FIGURE 3.1   The FreeBSD `sysinstall` main menu. From here, select the Options menu item.

FIGURE 3.2   The Options menu, in which you can set the FTP login name (among other installation preferences).

Arrow down to the option that reads FTP Username and press the spacebar. A dialog asks you to enter the username for FTP access; the administrator of the FTP server you will be using should furnish you with a username and password that will let you into the server. Enter the username and press Enter. You are asked to supply a password. Enter the password you need to use and press Enter again.

After you have finished, press Q to quit, and you will be returned to the Main `sysinstall` menu.

Selecting an FTP Install
After you have set the FTP username and password (if necessary), follow the instructions in Chapter 2, found in the "Creating Partitions and Assigning Mount Points" and "Selecting a Canned Distribution Set" sections, until you get to the screen where you are asked to choose the installation media. From this screen, select FTP or FTP Passive if the server you intend to install from is behind a firewall (ask your system administrator if you are not sure). You will then be asked to select a distribution site (see Figure 3.3).

FIGURE 3.3 The list of available FTP servers from which you can install FreeBSD. Choose the public server closest to you or choose a private server.

If you are installing from one of the FreeBSD mirror sites, you can select the site from the list, using whichever server is listed as being geographically closest to you (to maximize download speed). Otherwise, select URL to specify an FTP server manually. In the dialog that comes up (see Figure 3.4), you will be asked to specify the name of the FTP server as well as the path to where the FreeBSD installation files are located. Figure 3.4 shows an example for an FTP site with the hostname `lion` located on the network `samplenet.org`, with the FreeBSD files located in the `/FreeBSD` directory.

FIGURE 3.4 Specifying a custom FTP server location by URL.

Once you have configured the FTP server you wish to install from, you will need to configure the network (see Figure 3.5). Follow the procedure in the "Configuring the Network" section of Chapter 2 to complete this configuration. This step only needs to be completed once; after your network has been configured, you can return to `sysinstall` and perform other post-installation tasks without having to configure the network again. The `sysinstall` program gives you the option to skip that step or re-enter other network data.

Once you have finished configuring the network, the various distribution sets will download to your computer and install themselves. This process will probably take a long time; you may want to turn your attention to something else for the next few hours. When files have finished copying, you can go ahead with the instructions offered in the "Post-Installation" section of Chapter 2. Because you have already configured the network to do the installation, you can skip the network-configuration portion of those instructions.

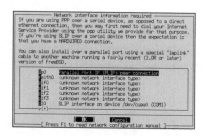

FIGURE 3.5 Configuring the TCP/IP networking parameters. This information is stored as the system's TCP/IP configuration.

Note that this chapter has covered only how to install FreeBSD from an FTP server. If you want to set up an "installation server" that can be used by clients to install FreeBSD, see Chapter 26. Once you have an FTP server set up and the FreeBSD installation files available on it, you can have other systems install from it using the procedures in this chapter.

Performing an NFS Install

NFS stands for *Network File System*. It provides a way for filesystems located on a server elsewhere on the network to be mounted into your own computer's directory structure, and the files in it to be made accessible as though they were on your own hard disk. File sharing with NFS is fully covered in Chapter 32, "The Network Filesystem (NFS)." FreeBSD can be installed over NFS, assuming that there is an NFS server on your network that has the installation files available.

If your NFS server will work only on a secure port (or if you have a slow Ethernet adapter), follow the procedure in the following section. Otherwise, you can skip immediately ahead to "Selecting an NFS Install."

Configuring sysinstall for a Secure Port or Slow Connection

At the sysinstall main menu (shown previously in Figure 3.1), select Options and press Enter. The first listing in the Options menu is NFS Secure. If your NFS server only works on a secure port (ask your system administrator if you're not sure), press the spacebar to toggle this to Yes. The second option (NFS Slow) should be toggled to Yes if you have a slow PC (something from the 386 era) or an Ethernet card with very poor performance. This is almost certainly unnecessary; the only cases where an Ethernet card would be slow enough to necessitate this option is if your own computer's filesystem is being remotely accessed, as from yet another NFS server, instead of being locally mounted. Once you have made these changes, press Q to return to the sysinstall main menu.

Installation then continues, as discussed in Chapter 2, up to the point where you are asked to choose installation media.

Selecting an NFS Install

At the Choose Installation Media screen, select NFS. You will then be asked to enter the name of the NFS server followed by the path where the FreeBSD installation files are located. In the example in Figure 3.6, the server is lion and the installation directory is install/FreeBSD.

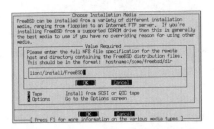

FIGURE 3.6   Specifying the NFS location of the remote FreeBSD installation files.

Once you have entered this information, you will need to configure the network (shown previously in Figure 3.5). Follow the procedure shown in Chapter 2 under the "Configuring the Network" heading for instructions on how to do this.

Once you have finished configuring the network, the various distribution sets will be downloaded from the remote server and installed. This will naturally take longer than installing from a CD-ROM, but it will likely be faster than an FTP installation. When files have finished copying, you can go ahead with the "Post-Installation" section of Chapter 2. Because you have already configured the network to do the installation, you can skip the network-configuration portion.

Note that this chapter has covered only how to install FreeBSD from an NFS server. If you want to set up an installation server that can be used by clients to install FreeBSD over NFS, see Chapter 32. Once you have an NFS server set up and the FreeBSD installation files available on it, you can have other systems install from it using the procedures discussed in this chapter.

PART II

Using FreeBSD

IN THIS PART

Your First Session with FreeBSD

If you're a Windows user, you'll discover some of the differences of working with FreeBSD during your first session. Unlike with Windows, when you first start up FreeBSD, you are given a text mode command prompt (you can change this prompt, as you'll learn in Chapter 36, "Customizing the X-Windows System"). If you're accustomed to working in older versions of Windows, FreeBSD's system login will be new to you, as well. In this chapter, you become acquainted with FreeBSD through a first working session. You learn how to log in to FreeBSD and start the X-Windows system. You also get some experience working with the FreeBSD filesystem. The chapter also helps you become acquainted with the Gnome Desktop Environment, FreeBSD's graphical user interface, which is the equivalent of Windows, before teaching you how to log out of the FreeBSD system and shut it down safely.

FreeBSD Startup Process

When you first start FreeBSD, it prints a flurry of messages on your screen from the kernel and also from the various processes starting up. We won't go into detail about what all these messages mean right now (a complete discussion of the FreeBSD startup procedure and how to control it can be found in Chapter 10, "System Configuration and Startup Scripts"), but the following sections give a quick rundown of what you will be seeing while you wait for the command prompt.

> **NOTE**
>
> The following sections apply only to FreeBSD running on *x86* (Intel) hardware. Although the startup process on Alpha systems is similar, some of the details are slightly different.

The Power-On Self Test (POST) and BIOS

The first thing your computer does when you turn it on is run the POST, which stands for *Power-On Self Test*. During this phase, your computer's BIOS, which stands for *Basic Input/Output System*, checks out all its hardware and makes sure everything is working.

The BIOS is a small piece of software on a ROM or EPROM chip on your computer's system board. Among other things, the BIOS is responsible for testing hardware when the computer is first turned on. The BIOS also finds and tests the first part of the operating system off the hard drive. Then, it counts RAM and probes PnP (Plug and Play) devices to see what resources they can use. At that point, the POST is completed.

The Bootstrap

After the POST is complete, the BIOS searches for a device on your system that it can boot from. The system normally boots from the first bootable device it finds. The specific devices the BIOS searches for and the order in which it searches for them are both determined by the configuration you have specified in your BIOS setup program, as will be discussed more fully in Chapter 10.

Typically, the BIOS boots from the first hard disk in the system, but other possible devices include the floppy drive and the CD-ROM drive. The BIOS can even boot from the network card on systems that have no hard disk and support loading the operating system over the network from a server. (In this latter case, the network card trumps the boot order—a card with "wake" capabilities will boot the system before the BIOS can even poll any local storage devices.) After a bootable device is found (in this case, we'll assume it is the hard disk), the BIOS begins the *bootstrap* procedure—a multistage process, comprising several "boot blocks" (small programs that pull successively larger and larger pieces of the operating system into memory), as will be discussed in more detail in Chapter 10.

Selecting the Bootable Slice (boot0)

After the BIOS finds a bootable hard disk, it reads whatever is in sector 0 of the hard disk. Sector 0 is also known as the *master boot record* (MBR). The program located in the MBR can be only 512 bytes long. Therefore, it is a very simple program that knows just enough about the disk to be able to present a menu of the slices that can be booted from. Here is an example of a screen that might be produced by boot0:

```
F1 DOS
F2 FreeBSD
F3 Drive 1


Default: F2
```

Here, you can use the function keys to select which slice you want to boot from—and thus which operating system you want to start. (A *slice* is what other operating systems refer to as a *partition* or a *BIOS partition*, as we will discuss in Chapter 10.) After you make a selection, boot0 finds and loads whatever is in the boot sector of the slice you selected. If FreeBSD is the only operating system on your hard disk, you will not see this menu, and the boot sector will be loaded immediately.

The loader Menu and the Kernel

The boot1 and boot2 boot blocks lead to the loader program, whose job is to give you an interface with which to control the *kernel*. As you will see, the kernel is literally the heart of the operating system, and it is loaded only after all the infrastructure of a bootable disk partition has been loaded into memory. The loader menu, which is covered in more detail in Chapter 10 along with fuller details on the disk partitioning structure that underlies the startup process, gives you the ability to pass options manually to the kernel, such as -s (to boot the system in single-user mode), or to load kernel modules (such as the IPFW firewall, the Linux compatibility module, or various external filesystem types) to enhance its capabilities.

In the simplest and most common case, you will simply press Enter during the 10-second countdown that the loader gives you, or you can wait until it expires. The kernel will then load, completing the bootstrap process.

The Kernel

The standard kernel is normally located at /boot/kernel and is started by the loader. As mentioned before, the kernel is the core of the operating system. It controls all access to hardware resources from both programs and users.

Most of the lines that you see on the screen at this point are shown in bold white text, instead of the dimmer light-gray style of the normal screen text. These are status messages from the kernel that it emits for your information as it finds and initializes your hardware. Most of these messages will go by too fast for you to read, but after you log in to the system, you can use the command dmesg | more to view them one screen at a time, using the spacebar to advance to the next screen.

You may be interested in the kernel startup messages for a variety of reasons (for instance, to troubleshoot misbehaving hardware or to determine what device name FreeBSD has assigned to a particular component). Let's look at some sample messages from the kernel. This first example gives you an idea of the kind of messages you will see and what they mean (note that your messages might be different, depending on the type of hardware in your system):

```
Copyright (c) 1992-2002 The FreeBSD Project.
Copyright (c) 1979, 1980, 1983, 1986, 1988, 1989, 1991, 1992, 1993, 1994
        The Regents of the University of California. All rights reserved.
```

```
FreeBSD 5.0-RELEASE #0: Sun Dec 8 15:17:26 CDT 2002
   murray@builder.freebsdmall.com:/usr/src/sys/compile/GENERIC/i386
```

The first three lines are simply copyright information. Line 4 gives the operating system and the version of the kernel (the kernel version number will increase by one each time you rebuild the kernel). It also tells the date and time the kernel was built.

The first part of line 5 gives the username and local e-mail address of the person who built the kernel. In this case, the GENERIC kernel was built by murray@builder.freebsdmall.com, and that kernel was then copied to the system during installation. If you compile your own kernel, which you will learn how to do in Chapter 16, "Kernel Configuration," the line shown here will reflect your own e-mail address and your machine's hostname. The second part of line 5 tells where the directory is that this kernel was built in. (For you C-programming gurus, this is where you will find some of the C source files, the header files, and the object files that this kernel was built from—as well as the makefile for the kernel.)

In the next message, the kernel has detected the CPU type, and it is simply printing out some information about the CPU type and the features it supports:

```
Timecounter "i8254"  frequency 1193182 Hz
CPU: AMD-K6(tm) 3D+ Processor (400.91-MHz 586-class CPU)
  Origin = "AuthenticAMD"  Id = 0x591  Stepping = 1
  Features=0x8021bf<FPU,VME,DE,PSE,TSC,MSR,MCE,CX8,PGE,MMX>
  AMD Features=0x80000800<SYSCALL,3DNow!>
```

Here, the kernel has found the mouse and has detected that it is a PS/2-type mouse. It has assigned the device psm0 to refer to this mouse for future reference:

```
psm0: <PS/2 Mouse> irq 12 on atkbdc0
psm0: model Generic PS/2 mouse, device ID 0
fdc0: <NEC 72065B or clone> at port 0x3f0-0x3f5,0x3f7 irq 6 drq 2 on isa0
fdc0: FIFO enabled, 8 bytes threshold
fd0: <1440-KB 3.5" drive> on fdc0 drive 0
```

The kernel has also found the floppy controller and the floppy drive. fdc0 is the device name of the floppy controller, and fd0 is the device name of the floppy drive itself. (fd0 is analogous to A: in Windows/DOS. It is the device name you use when you want to access this device.)

The next message shows that the kernel has found the SoundBlaster AWE 64 sound card, and it gives information about the resources the card is using:

```
sbc0: <Creative SB AWE64> at port 0x220-0x22f,0x330-0x331,0x388-0x38b
➥irq 5 drq 1,5 on isa0
pcm1: <SB16 DSP 4.16> on sbc0
```

Note that in this case, sbc0 is actually the name for a group of devices related to the sound card. The sound card uses several devices, depending on what features you want to access, including dsp, which is where output such as WAV and MP3 files go, and mixer, which controls the levels of various audio devices.

You may also see some of the following lines on your startup message:

```
unknown: <PNP0303> can't assign resources
unknown: <PNP0f13> can't assign resources
unknown: <PNP0501> can't assign resources
unknown: <PNP0700> can't assign resources
unknown: <PNP0401> can't assign resources
unknown: <PNP0501> can't assign resources
```

These lines indicate that the kernel has found some "Plug and Play" (often abbreviated to PnP) devices in the system, but it doesn't know anything about them, and it can't assign resources for them. These messages are harmless. If you don't like seeing them, then note that, as the FreeBSD FAQ says, "the FreeBSD project will happily accept driver contributions via send-pr." (This is for you C gurus who are good at writing device drivers.)

The next message shows that the kernel has found the hard drives, and it provides various information about the drives, including device name, size, manufacturer and model, geometry, and what controller the drive is located on:

```
ad0: 19473MB <Maxtor 92049U6> [39566/16/63] at ata0-master UDMA33
ad1: 14664MB <IBM-DJNA-351520> [29795/16/63] at ata0-slave UDMA33
```

It also tells what access mode the drive is using. In this case, both of the drives are using Ultra DMA 33. (This will be covered in more detail in Chapter 18, "Understanding Hard Disks and Filesystems.")

The final message shows that the kernel has mounted the root filesystem:

```
Mounting root from ufs:/dev/ad0s1a
```

After the root filesystem is mounted, the kernel passes control to a process called init. The messages in light gray are triggered by events that occur during the init stage. You can differentiate kernel messages from non-kernel messages by color. Kernel messages appear in white; non-kernel messages appear in light gray.

init

The init program is the first actual process that runs under the operating system, and as such its process ID is 1. init is responsible for starting up all the rest of the processes that constitute a completely functional operating system; to do that, though, it must first determine whether the disks are in suitable shape.

When a FreeBSD system is properly shut down, it runs a program called `sync` on each disk to ensure that all data is written out, dismounts the filesystems, and then sets the "clean" flag on the filesystems. This is similar to the process that Windows goes through when it shuts down. If a FreeBSD system is not properly shut down, the clean flag will not be set.

Filesystem Consistency Check

One of the first things that `init` does is to check whether the clean flag is set. If it is, `init` mounts the filesystem for use. If it isn't, `init` first runs the `fsck` program on the filesystem to make sure it isn't damaged. This program repairs any damage it finds that it knows how to repair. `fsck` is similar to the Scandisk program in Windows, and this process is similar to the "Your system was not properly shut down" procedure you see on a Windows reboot following an improper shutdown. If `fsck` encounters an error it cannot fix at this point, it drops the system into single-user mode so the system administrator (which is probably you, if you are reading this book) can make the necessary repairs manually.

Assuming that the clean flag was set, or that `fsck` was able to repair the damage if the flag was not set, `init` then proceeds to mount each filesystem listed in the `/etc/fstab` file that has the `mount at boot` flag set (see "Understanding the `/etc/fstab` File," in Chapter 8, "The FreeBSD Filesystem").

> **TIP**
>
> If you need to, you can also run `fsck` manually. More information on `fsck` and its various options can be found in Chapter 8. Starting with FreeBSD 5.0, the filesystem consistency check will be run in the background, so you no longer have to wait until this is finished before you can use the system.

System Configuration Scripts

After the filesystems are mounted, `init` reads the system-configuration scripts (known alternately as *Run Control or Resource Configuration* scripts, abbreviated to *rc* scripts) located in `/etc` and `/etc/defaults`. In addition, `init` checks the `/usr/local/etc/rc.d` directory for any additional scripts it should run at boot (these might be scripts to start Web servers, database servers, or any other program you want to run automatically at startup). If you are familiar with Windows and/or DOS, this part of the boot process is similar to `config.sys`, `autoexec.bat`, `system.ini`, and the parts of the Windows Registry that control Windows startup options.

> **NOTE**
>
> The term *rc scripts* actually originates from RunCom, or "run commands," a facility from the CTSS system at MIT, circa 1965. While the acronym *rc* has been reassigned to numerous different meanings since then, its general application remains the same: a set of commands stored in a file and run in a batch. In typical Unix parlance, the meaning of *rc* by itself is clear enough that it is unnecessary to know what it stands for, and most people don't.
>
> This book will refer to *Run Control* for Sun-style run levels and *Resource Configuration* when it comes to FreeBSD's own startup scripts.

NOTE

For the sake of completeness, it should be mentioned that `init` also checks for and reads a file called `/etc/rc.local`, which can be used to start programs such as Web servers. However, this file is deprecated and may not be supported in future versions of FreeBSD. Therefore, it is recommended that you put your startup scripts in the `/usr/local/etc/rc.d` directory instead of in the `/etc/rc.local` file.

BSD Versus Sys V Run Control

If you come from a Sys V Unix background, you may be a little bit confused after that last section. So, here is a clarification: In BSD `init`, the concept of run levels doesn't really exist. You pretty much have single-user mode and a multiuser mode with network support. There is no multiuser mode without network support, as there is in Sys V run levels. Also, there is no `inittab` file in BSD, as there is in Sys V. In addition, startup options are mostly controlled by a single file called `rc.conf`. There aren't separate files to start most services with links in different run-level directories, as there are in Sys V. (You'll learn much more about `init` in Chapter 10.)

`getty` **and** `login`

After reading the run control scripts, `init` starts a program on the console (and several virtual terminals). This program is normally the `getty` program, but it doesn't have to be. Another common program used in place of `getty` is `xdm`, which starts a graphical login session for the X-Windows system immediately after system boot (similar to an NT login session). The program that is started is defined in the file `/etc/ttys`. For the purposes of this discussion, we'll assume it's the `getty` program.

The `getty` program initializes the terminal (or console), and it controls various security options and terminal-type options. Once again, these options and their values are defined in `/etc/ttys`. The `getty` program then starts the login program to validate your login name and password.

Logging In to FreeBSD

After all the startup processes are complete, you see a screen that looks something like this:

```
FreeBSD/i386 (amnesiac) (ttyp0)

login:
```

Assuming you didn't configure any network information during the installation, the default hostname for your system is "amnesiac." Enter the login name of the normal user (not the root user) that you created for yourself during the installation. Press Enter and then, when prompted, enter the password you gave yourself. Note that the password will not be displayed onscreen. Actually, nothing will be displayed onscreen. Don't worry, though. Your password is being read.

After you enter the password, the login program checks the password database for a match. If it finds one, you get a screen that looks something like this:

```
Last login: Tue Apr 10 15:19:17 on ttyp0
Copyright (c) 1980, 1983, 1986, 1988, 1990, 1991, 1993, 1994
        The Regents of the University of California.  All rights reserved.

FreeBSD 5.0-RELEASE (GENERIC) #0: Sun Dec  8 15:17:26 CDT 2002

>
```

If this is the first time you log in with your normal user account, you probably won't see the first line, `Last login`. In the future when you log in, however, this line will be present.

CAUTION

It's a good idea to pay attention to the "last login" information. If, for example, FreeBSD says your last login was

`Sat Sept 15 14:05:29`

and you know you didn't log in to the system on that day, then someone else has logged in to your account. If something like this ever happens, you need to change your password *immediately* (use the `passwd` command and follow the instructions it gives). Also, be sure to notify your system administrator of the security breach (assuming you are not the system administrator). If you are the system administrator, see Chapter 29, "Network Security," for further information on what to do if you think your network has been compromised.

The rest of the screen shows copyright information as well as information about the kernel and when it was built. The final line is the shell prompt. When you see the shell prompt, FreeBSD is waiting for you to give it something to do.

CAUTION

Notice the difference between the command prompt you get this time and the command prompt you got last time (when you logged in as the root user). The root user's login prompt is the pound sign (#). A normal user's login prompt will usually be either $ for Bourne-style shells or % or > for C-style shells. The default shell in FreeBSD is `tcsh`, which is a C-style shell. Either way, the type of prompt you have serves as a constant reminder of whether you are logged in as root. If you are, be extra careful when issuing potentially dangerous commands.

If you mistype either the login name or the password, FreeBSD will respond with the following message:

```
Login incorrect
login:
```

If this happens, simply try again, starting with your login name.

TIP

If you mistype your login name or password three times in a row, it may appear that the system has hung because it looks as if nothing is happening. Don't worry. The system isn't hung. This delay is a security feature built in to the kernel that helps reduce the effectiveness of password-cracking programs that simply try random words as passwords to break into an account. The delay may get progressively longer on each mistype after three. Wait several seconds, though, and the login prompt will reappear.

Logging Out of FreeBSD

When you are finished using FreeBSD (or you need to leave your computer for a while), you should log out of the system. That prevents anyone from using your computer or terminal to access your account during your absence. To log out of FreeBSD, simply type **exit** at the command prompt. This should return you to the login prompt, as you saw when FreeBSD first finished booting.

TIP

If you were working on something that you don't want others to see when they walk past your screen, you can clear the screen before logging out by typing **clear** at a command prompt. After that, you can log out of the system as described earlier.

Shutting Down the FreeBSD System

As mentioned in Chapter 2, it is very important that you always shut down a FreeBSD system (or any other Unix system) properly before turning off the power. Failure to do so can result in serious damage to the filesystem. Disks in Unix are treated as though they contain filesystems that are maintained in a very orderly fashion; if you shut down Windows abruptly by pulling the power cord, the disks will have some fragmented files lying around after it reboots, but the system can cope with them. However, FreeBSD—like most Unix systems—writes data to the disk in such a way that fragmentation is kept to an almost insignificant level, but an abrupt loss of power can cause the system to actually lose data that was active at the time. FreeBSD has a mechanism called Soft Updates to help combat this problem; see Chapter 8 for more details on using Soft Updates.

Using the `shutdown` **Command**

The normal way to shut down the system is with the `shutdown` command, which you first read about in Chapter 2 in the section titled "Shutting Down FreeBSD." Before you actually shut down the system, however, take a moment to learn about several other options for using this command.

The basic syntax of the `shutdown` command is as follows:

```
shutdown [option] [when] [broadcast message]
```

The first argument tells `shutdown` what to do, the second argument tells `shutdown` when to do it, and the third argument tells `shutdown` the message it should send to all logged-in users. Table 4.1 lists the options that can be used for [option] in `shutdown` and what they do.

TABLE 4.1   The Options for `shutdown`

Option	Result
Nothing	Kicks everybody off the system and brings the system down to single-user mode with no network support. This is rude to the users, but quick and efficient.
-h	Halts the system.
-p	Halts the system and turns off the power (if the system supports automatic power-off and the kernel is configured to support power management).
-r	Reboots the system.
-k	Kicks everybody off the system and disables any further logins (except from the root user). This option leaves the system in multiuser mode and connected to the network, though. This is useful for occasions when you need to do emergency maintenance but require network access while you do it.
-o	Shuts down without sending a signal to `init`. This is not usually a good idea because it prevents program-specific shutdown scripts from running.
-n	If the -o option has also been specified, this option prevents the filesystem cache from being flushed before the shutdown. This is probably never a good idea because it can cause data loss.

The "when" part of shutdown can be specified in several ways. As you learned in Chapter 2, the keyword now tells `shutdown` to perform the action immediately. `shutdown` also recognizes the format +*n*, where *n* is the number of minutes `shutdown` should wait before performing the action (this gives users time to save their files and close their programs). You can use the format yymmhhmm to specify an exact time when the action should be performed. In this case, *yy* is the year, *mm* is the month, *hh* is the hour (in a 24-hour format), and *mm* is the minute. If the year and month parts are eliminated, `shutdown` assumes that the shutdown should happen today. If you specify a time that has already passed, `shutdown` will complain.

The "broadcast message" option enables you to enter a shutdown-notification message that will be broadcast at regular intervals to all logged-in users. This message starts to appear 10 minutes before the impending shutdown and is broadcast more frequently as the shutdown time gets closer.

The following is a step-by-step walkthrough of a typical shutdown process that, in this case, uses a 10-minute delay (don't enter this command now if you don't want to wait 10 minutes for the system to shut down):

```
# shutdown -h +10 Hard disk needs to be replaced
```

This starts the shutdown command and runs it in the background. The system will halt in 10 minutes. In addition, the following broadcast message is displayed on all users' terminals:

```
*** System shutdown message from root@simba.samplenet.org ***
System going down in 10 minutes

Hard disk needs to be replaced
```

Five minutes before the impending shutdown, a file called /var/run/nologin will be created automatically by the shutdown program. This file disables any further logins and displays the shutdown message contents when someone attempts to log in. The shutdown command places the time of the shutdown and the broadcast message in this file. For example, in this case, anyone who attempts to log in will see the following:

```
NO LOGINS: System going down at 17:57

Hard disk needs to be replaced
```

When the countdown clock runs out, the following actions are performed:

- A TERM signal is sent to init, which ceases creating any new processes.

- init reads the file /etc/rc.shutdown and runs any program-specific shutdown scripts it contains.

- All processes are sent a TERM signal and given time to terminate themselves gracefully.

- Any processes that did not respond to the TERM signal in a reasonable amount of time are sent a KILL signal, which cannot be ignored. This will force the processes to terminate ungracefully.

- Cache data is written out to the filesystems with the sync command, the filesystems are dismounted, and the clean flag is set.

- The kernel is halted.

In addition, `shutdown` writes an entry in the system log noting the time of the shutdown and who performed the shutdown.

> **NOTE**
>
> You need to be the root user to shut down the system—either by logging in directly as root or by using the su command to become root.

To shut down your system now, type **su** and press Enter. Then, enter the root password when prompted. If you receive a message complaining that you are not in the proper group to use su, log out and then log back in as root. Then, assuming there are no other users logged in to the system, issue the following command:

```
shutdown -h now
```

As mentioned in Chapter 2, on a multiuser system, you would not normally shut down the system like this. Instead, you would give users some warning about the impending shutdown.

After the shutdown has completed, you will see the following message:

```
System halted
Please press any key to reboot
```

Then, and only then, is it safe to turn off your system.

Notes on `halt` and `reboot`

Two other commands can be used to halt and reboot the system: `halt` and `reboot`, respectively. However, I do not recommend that you get in the habit of using them. Neither of these commands runs the `rc.shutdown` script, which can cause some programs to terminate improperly. Also, neither of these programs allows you to specify a delay, and neither gives users any warning about the impending shutdown. Therefore, you should always use the `shutdown` command to halt the system.

However, these two programs do have their uses. You can use `halt` to make the system 100-percent safe to power down after you have shut down all multiuser processes through the `shutdown` command. The `reboot` command is also handy if you're working in single-user mode; it simply kills all running processes with a SIGKILL (a nonignorable signal) and reboots immediately. These commands are helpful for saving time when it's safe to use them, but those occasions are rare.

NOTE

If you've used DOS and/or Windows in the past, you might be in the habit of using the Ctrl+Alt+Delete combination to reboot a system. By default, FreeBSD will trap the signal sent by this combination and perform the equivalent of running the `reboot` command. This can be a problem when normal users have access to the server's keyboard, because it allows them to reboot the system without being root. In Chapter 10, you will see how to configure FreeBSD to trap the Ctrl+Alt+Delete sequence to prevent it from rebooting the system.

4

Working with X-Windows

Chapter 4, "Your First Session with FreeBSD," briefly introduced the X-Windows system. In this chapter, we will look at X-Windows in more detail. The X-Windows system basically has two parts—the X-Server and the window manager. The X-Server runs on your system and provides a graphical framework for applications to use. The window manager determines how X-Windows looks and feels. In this chapter, you learn about these parts of the system in more detail and how to work with and customize the WindowMaker window manager.

The X-Server

The X-Server is the underlying framework that allows graphical applications to run. By itself, the X-Server is not very useful because it contains no window-management functions. Figure 5.1 shows an X-Server running with no window manager.

Several applications are running in the X-Windows session shown in Figure 5.1: an xterm, a clock, a calculator, and the GIMP image-processing program used to take this screenshot. Notice that the windows have no title bars and borders. They are not resizable or movable, and they cannot be minimized or maximized. Obviously, this lack of flexibility makes for a pretty useless graphical user interface. This is where the window manager comes in.

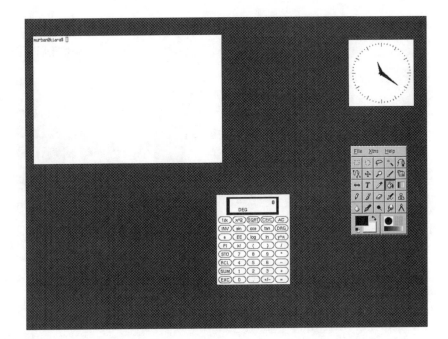

FIGURE 5.1   Here you see a very bland and rather useless X session.

Window Managers

The window manager controls how the graphical environment looks and works. Dozens of different window managers are available for X-Windows, so it is almost infinitely customizable. If you don't like the way X-Windows looks or feels, you can either customize your existing window manager or switch to a completely different window manager.

Figure 5.2 shows the same session as Figure 5.1, but this time it is running under the WindowMaker window manager.

In Figure 5.2 you see that each of the application windows now has a title bar with controls to maximize and close it. In addition, you can resize a window in a window manager interface. On the right side of the desktop is a menu from which you can launch applications by clicking an icon. Right-clicking the mouse on the desktop brings up another menu from which you can select various options or launch applications.

If the WindowMaker desktop isn't your cup of tea, you can use a different one. Figures 5.3 and 5.4 show just two of the window managers available to you—GNOME and Blackbox, respectively. You learn how to choose an alternative window manager later in this chapter. These figures simply give you an idea how customizable X-Windows is.

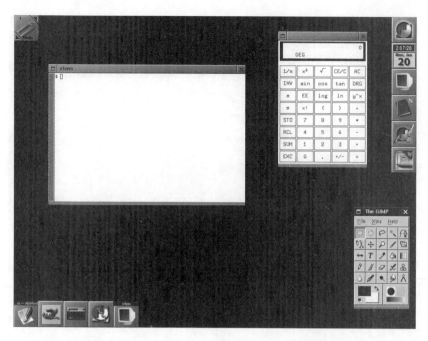

FIGURE 5.2   WindowMaker is a much more useful interface to X-Windows.

FIGURE 5.3   The GNOME Desktop Environment rivals the Microsoft and Apple desktops' ease of use and features. However, this desktop also rivals Microsoft's for heavy resource usage.

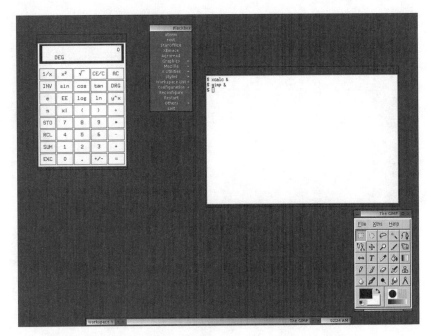

FIGURE 5.4   Blackbox is a no-frills window manager that stays out of the way and uses very few resources. It's a good choice for servers and older laptops.

This chapter focuses on WindowMaker for a couple reasons. For one, I am adamantly biased toward WindowMaker; it happens to be my favorite X-Windows desktop. But aside from my personal bias, WindowMaker does a good job of balancing ease of use and low resource requirements. Because of this, WindowMaker makes a good desktop for either a workstation or a server. It strikes a middle ground between the easy-to-use-but-resource-gobbling GNOME and the resource-light-but-not-so-easy-to-use Blackbox. (Both GNOME and Blackbox are available in the ports collection under the wm category. See Chapter 14, "Installing Additional Software," for more information on installing software from the ports collection.

The WindowMaker Window Manager

WindowMaker is a clone of the now defunct desktop for the NeXTSTEP operating system. This desktop is perhaps one of the most useful and functional desktops ever designed. Figure 5.5 shows a WindowMaker desktop.

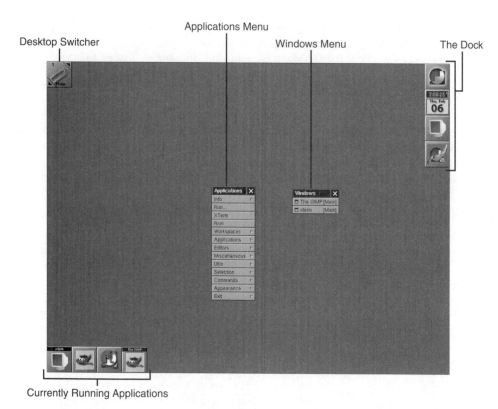

Desktop Switcher

Applications Menu

Windows Menu

The Dock

Currently Running Applications

FIGURE 5.5 The WindowMaker desktop contains a number of easy-to-use features.

The following list describes the main features of the WindowMaker desktop:

- The column of buttons along the right side of the desktop is known as the *dock*. Although you can't arbitrarily place icons on the WindowMaker desktop like you can in Windows, you can place buttons to launch commonly used applications onto the dock. The main advantage the dock offers over arbitrary icons is that it is never covered up, even when windows are maximized. Therefore, your application buttons are always available. In addition to application launchers, you can also place "mini-programs" on the dock. The calendar/clock shown in the figure is an example of one of these mini-programs. You learn more about the dock in "Working with the Dock," later in this chapter.

- You can think of the icons for currently running applications as being similar to the Windows taskbar. Double-clicking an icon, for example, will restore a window that has been minimized.

- The Applications menu is similar to the Start menu in Windows. This menu is accessed by right-clicking a blank area of the desktop.

- The Windows menu brings up a list of currently running windows. Clicking an entry will bring that window to the foreground and also make it the active one. This menu is accessed by clicking the middle mouse button on a blank area of the desktop. (For those with two-button mice, the Windows menu is accessed by clicking the left and right buttons at the same time.)

- The Desktop Switcher in WindowMaker allows you to move between multiple virtual desktops that are active at the same time, and all these desktops can be displaying different windows and applications. Clicking the arrows on the Desktop Switcher button allows you to "page" back and forth between the various desktops.

Working with Windows

If you are coming from a Microsoft Windows or Apple Macintosh background, you will find that WindowMaker windows are a bit different. Figure 5.6 shows a typical WindowMaker window.

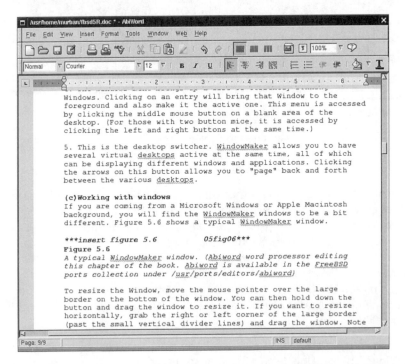

FIGURE 5.6   The AbiWord word processor demonstrates a typical WindowMaker window. AbiWord is available in the FreeBSD ports collection under /usr/ports/editors/abiword.

To resize the window, move the mouse pointer over the large border at the bottom of the window. You can then hold down the mouse button and drag the window to resize it. If you want to resize horizontally, grab the right or left end of the border (past the small vertical divider lines) and drag the window. Note that you cannot resize the window by grabbing the sides or the top of the window.

Clicking the icon at the left end of the title bar will minimize the window to an icon at the bottom of the screen. (You double-click the minimized icon to restore the window.) Clicking the × icon at the right end of the title bar closes the window. Double-clicking the title bar itself will roll up the window so that only the title bar is displayed. You can double-click the title bar again to restore the window. If you want to maximize the window or perform various other functions on the window, you can right-click the title bar to bring up a menu of options.

TIP

Notice the Close and Kill options when you right-click the title bar. What is the difference? The Close option closes the window normally. It performs the same function as clicking the × icon at the right end of the title bar. The Kill option, however, sends a kill signal to the window. This can be useful for terminating a misbehaving application that is not responding to the Close command. However, Kill should only be used if Close has failed. Close terminates the application gracefully and allows it to do all of its normal tasks before closing (such as ask whether you want to save any files that have been edited). Kill simply squashes the application immediately. This can sometimes result in lost data because applications can't perform their normal shutdown tasks. That's why Kill should be used only if Close has failed.

WindowMaker Menus

As mentioned previously, WindowMaker menus can be accessed by clicking a blank area of the desktop. Right-clicking brings up the Applications menu, whereas middle-clicking (or clicking both the left and right buttons on a two-button mouse) brings up the Windows menu. If you bring up a menu and then decide you don't want to select any of its options, you can close the menu by clicking the same mouse button somewhere on a blank spot of the desktop.

Normally, the menu will disappear after you have made a selection from it. However, if you want the menu to stay on the desktop, you can left-click its title bar. When you have done this, the × icon will appear at the right end of the title bar, which allows you to close the menu. Both main menus and submenus can be "pinned" to the desktop by left-clicking their title bars.

Working with the Dock

The WindowMaker dock is the bar of buttons along the right side of the screen. One of the functions of the dock is for placing application launchers on it. This is quite easy to do. A running application will have an icon placed at the lower-left part of the screen. To add this icon to the dock, simply hold down the left mouse button and drag the icon below the last button currently on the dock. When you have it in the correct location, a white border will appear around the icon. Release the mouse button and a new button will be created in the dock. Double-clicking this new button will launch the application. If you later decide you don't want the launcher anymore, simply click and hold down the left button and drag the launcher off the dock to a blank area of the desktop. Release the mouse button, and the launcher will disappear.

You can rearrange the order of the buttons on the dock by dragging them around. Note that you should only drag them up or down, though. Dragging a button to the left will result in that launcher being removed.

Changing Application Launcher Button Properties

To change the properties of a launcher button on the dock, right-click it and hold down the mouse button to bring up a pop-up menu. Move the mouse to the Settings menu option and then release the mouse button. This will bring up the Docked Application Settings dialog, as shown in Figure 5.7. You can use the options in this dialog to customize the launcher's look and functions.

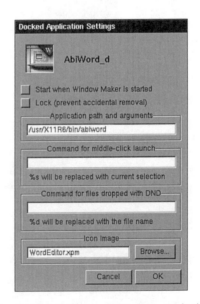

FIGURE 5.7   The Docked Application Settings dialog lets you lock a launcher button so you can't accidentally drag it off the dock.

Choosing the first option, Start when WindowMaker is Started, will cause the application to be automatically loaded each time WindowMaker is stated. For application launchers, you generally won't want to do this. However, you might want to do this for applications specifically created to run in the dock (such as clock and calendar applications). You learn more about these in the section titled "Installing and Using Dock Applications," later in this chapter.

Choosing the Lock option will prevent the application from being dragged off the dock and accidentally deleted. While a launcher button is locked, it will move back onto the dock when you drag it away and release the mouse button.

You can use the Icon Image field to change the icon shown in the button. Click the Browse button to see the available icons. WindowMaker has a large collection of prein-stalled icons, as shown in Figure 5.8. When you select a directory, a list of icons in that directory appears in the icons pane. Click one of the listed icons to see a preview of it. You can download additional icons if you can't find any that suit your taste in the default libraries.

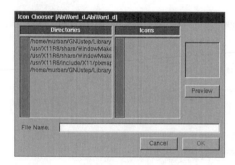

FIGURE 5.8   You can select a new icon for a launcher button.

Moving the Dock

If you want to move the dock to a different location on the screen, simply click and hold down the left mouse button on the top button of the dock and then drag. This action moves the entire dock. You can move the dock up and down the right side of the screen, or you can move it to the left side of the screen, if you prefer.

Installing and Using Dock Applications

A number of applications are designed specifically for running in the WindowMaker dock. These applications include a clock/calendar, network traffic monitors, system performance monitors, and a CD player. Figure 5.9 shows an example of a dock application.

FIGURE 5.9   The clock/calendar is an example of an application specifically designed for running in the dock.

A large number of dock applications are available in the FreeBSD ports collection (see Chapter 14 for information on installing software from the FreeBSD ports collection). Unfortunately, there is no ports category for WindowMaker dock apps, so finding them directly in the ports collection is not easy. However, you can visit the FreeBSD Web site at www.freebsd.org, click the "Ported Applications" link, and then scroll down and click the "WindowMaker" link. This brings up a list of applications available for WindowMaker, including the dock applications (see Figure 5.10).

FIGURE 5.10   A section of the Web page showing ported applications available for the WindowMaker dock.

If you find one that interests you, note the line that reads "Also listed in." For example, in Figure 5.10, wmsun-1.03 is shown at the top of the page. The description of this application tells you that wmsun-1.03 is also listed in Astro. It turns out that the category Astro is in the FreeBSD ports collection, and this is where you can find the wmsun-1.03 application.

WindowMaker dock applications can be installed like any other application (see Chapter 14 for information on how to do this). Once a dock application has been installed, you can start it by right-clicking the desktop to bring up the Applications menu and then selecting the Run option. This brings up the Run dialog shown in Figure 5.11.

In the Run dialog, type the name of the application you want to start and click OK. The dock application will start as a minimized icon that appears at the bottom of the desktop. To move the application onto the dock, move the mouse pointer over the border of the application, hold down the left mouse button, and drag the application over to the dock until a white border appears around it. Release the mouse button and the application will stay in the dock.

FIGURE 5.11   The Run dialog allows you to start an application by entering its name.

Once you have the application installed in the dock, you can configure it so that it starts automatically each time you start WindowMaker. To do this, produce the Docked Application Settings dialog, using the technique you learned in "Changing Application Launcher Button Properties," earlier in this chapter. Select the Start When WindowMaker Is Started option and then choose OK to close the dialog. From now on, the dock application will start automatically each time you start WindowMaker.

TIP

Many dock applications have customizations available that are dependent on the individual applications. Often these are in the form of options supplied to a program when it is started. Many dock apps will install manual pages. To access them, type **man** at the console command prompt, followed by the name of the command.

Customizing WindowMaker

You can customize various aspects of WindowMaker to your liking. For example, you can change the desktop background, the color scheme, and so on. The following sections explain how to perform these and other customizations in WindowMaker.

Changing the Desktop Theme

The desktop theme affects the color scheme as well as the desktop background. To change the theme, right-click the desktop to bring up the Applications menu and then select Appearance. From the Appearance menu, choose Themes to produce a list of available installed themes. To apply a new theme, simply click it in the list.

Changing the Style

You can also change the color scheme used for window borders, title bars, and menus as well as the dock. This is referred to as the *style*. To change the style, right-click the desktop to bring up the Applications menu. Then click Appearance and then Styles. WindowMaker has many available styles.

Customizing the Desktop Background

You can customize the desktop background in several ways. For example, you can select one of several solid colors, a color gradient, or an image that you want to use as the desktop background. If you have a custom image that you want to use as a background, you should place it in your home directory under the following subdirectory:

```
GNUstep/Library/WindowMaker/Backgrounds
```

After you have placed the image in this subdirectory, right-click the desktop to bring up the Applications menu. Then click Appearance and then Background to bring up a list of possible backgrounds. The custom image you added to the subdirectory will appear in the Backgrounds list. (See Chapter 7, "Working with the Shell," if you need help with copying or moving files.)

TIP

If the image you select is too small to cover your entire desktop, WindowMaker will tile it. Of course, if your image is a scanned photograph, tiling is probably not desirable. To avoid this, you should make sure the image is the same size as your desktop resolution. For example, if your desktop resolution is set to 1024×768, you should use the same size for the photograph. You can use any photo-editing program to resize the image. If you don't have a photo-editing program, a powerful one called the GIMP is available for free in the Graphics category of the ports collection.

The Preferences Utility

You can use the Preferences utility to make further configuration changes in WindowMaker. To access the Preferences utility, double-click the utility's dock button, as shown in Figure 5.12.

At the top of the Preferences utility window is a row of buttons you can click to access configuration preferences settings. Use the scroll bar beneath this row to display the remaining buttons. In the bottom-left corner of the WindowMaker Preferences utility window is a check box labeled Balloon Help. Check this box and then move your pointer over the various buttons to see pop-up descriptions of what configuration options are available for each button. In some cases, the picture on a button might not help you much if you aren't familiar with WindowMaker.

Configuring WindowMaker Preferences

To start configuring some aspect of WindowMaker, click the button representing what you want to configure. For example, scroll to the right to display the button with a drawing of a mouse on it. Click that button to open the Mouse Preferences dialog, shown in Figure 5.13, which allows you to configure your mouse.

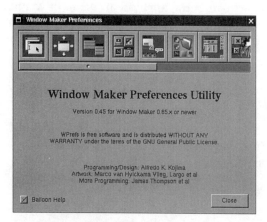

FIGURE 5.12   Click the utility's launcher button to open the Window Maker Preferences utility.

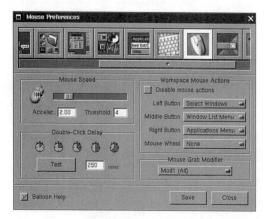

FIGURE 5.13   Configure the mouse in this dialog. Among other things, you can set the speed of the mouse and how much delay is allowed between double-clicks.

Here's another option you might be interested in: Click the button that looks like the title bar of a window (shown to the right of the Mouse Preferences button in Figure 5.13). Here, you can create a custom color scheme in case none of the default schemes suit your taste.

Customizing the Applications Menu

You can customize the Applications menu from within the Preferences utility. To do so, click the button that shows part of the Applications menu (if you have the Balloon Help box checked, the pop-up description for this button reads "Edit the menu for launching applications"). This will bring up the dialog shown in Figure 5.14.

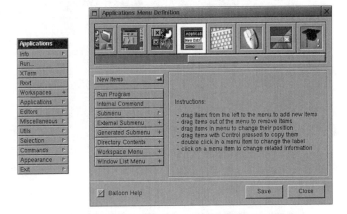

FIGURE 5.14   Click the Applications Menu button (outlined in white when selected) to open the Applications Menu Definitions dialog. Use the options in this window to configure the Applications menu.

This process is fairly straightforward and is explained in the Instructions list in the right pane of the dialog. You can drag items from the New Items list in the dialog and drop them where you want them on the Applications menu. A dialog will open asking you to specify the name of the item, the program to load, and so on. If you want to remove an item from the Applications menu, you can drag it off the menu.

# CHAPTER 6

Working with Applications

A computer that can't do any work isn't very useful, and neither is an operating system that doesn't have any applications. Thousands of applications are available for use with FreeBSD, ranging from scientific applications that do biological modeling, to office packages, to games. All the applications covered in this chapter are available for free.

In addition to the thousands of native FreeBSD applications, FreeBSD can also run most Linux applications. This gives you a very wide variety of applications to choose from for virtually any purpose.

Of course, this chapter cannot even begin to cover all the applications available for FreeBSD, but it does give a good sampling of some of the more popular applications within a range of categories.

> **NOTE**
>
> This chapter covers applications for workstation use. It does not cover server applications such as Web servers, FTP servers, and e-mail servers. If you are looking for information on setting up services such as these, you should read the appropriate chapters in Part IV of the book, "FreeBSD Networking," that cover the services you are interested in configuring.

> **TIP**
>
> Although this chapter will tell you where to obtain the applications it covers, it will not explain the procedure for *installing* the software. If you are unsure about how to install software on FreeBSD, see Chapter 14, "Installing Additional Software," for information on this topic.

Working with Text

Text editors are among the most common—and essential—applications.

Unlike a word processor, a text editor simply works on plain-text files. It does not have the ability to store font changes, margins, or any other such information in the document. Here are some common uses of a text editor:

- **Editing system configuration files**—FreeBSD, like most other versions of Unix, relies heavily on text-based configuration files to control system behavior. To edit these files, you will need a text editor that can write a plain-text file. Using a word processor on these configuration files would ruin them because the operating system would not understand the strange formatting that the word processor saves with the document. This will have unpredictable results, which could even render the system unbootable. (The system configuration files and how to configure them will be covered in Chapter 10, "System Configuration and Startup Scripts.")

- **Creating or modifying programming source code**—You will use a text editor to write the code that tells the computer what you want it to do. Although in many languages this code will be converted to machine language by a program called a *compiler*, your original instructions are still written in plain text. These instructions are called *source code*. Chapter 12, "Shell Programming," and Chapter 20, "Introduction to Perl Programming," introduce two popular programming languages in FreeBSD in which you would use a text editor to write the code.

- **Creating or modifying Web pages**—Web pages are written in HTML, which stands for *Hypertext Markup Language*. Although there are many GUI-based, WYSIWYG (What You See Is What You Get) programs available for designing Web pages, the end result is still a plain-text file with formatting control tags that the Web browser understands. Many people still choose to write Web pages by hand in a plain-text editor because it gives them total control over all the features of HTML. In addition, you would use a text editor to write PHP code, JavaScript, and other such extended features of Web design that allow you to give your pages interactive content.

- **Sophisticated typesetting**—Some very sophisticated typesetting languages are available for FreeBSD. Like HTML, typesetting languages generally use plain-text files with special formatting tags in them to control the layout and appearance of text. Although the word processor has largely replaced these languages (the word processor is easier to work with, and it shows you what the output will actually look like), there are still situations in which you might want to use a typesetting language. TeX and its extended macro package LaTeX might interest you if you are a scientist or engineer because of their extremely sophisticated mathematical equation-formatting capabilities.

In the following sections, you learn about a couple of the GUI-based editors available for the X-Windows system. These editors may seem familiar to you if you have a Windows or Macintosh background. After that, the chapter looks at some of the text-based editors available for FreeBSD.

Using ee (Easy Editor)

ee (Easy Editor) is installed by default along with FreeBSD. As its name indicates, the Easy Editor is a basic text editor that is designed to be easier to work with than some other traditional Unix text editors.

ee can be invoked either by simply typing **ee** at the command line or by typing **ee** followed by the name of a file you wish to edit. Figure 6.1 shows a sample ee session with a blank document.

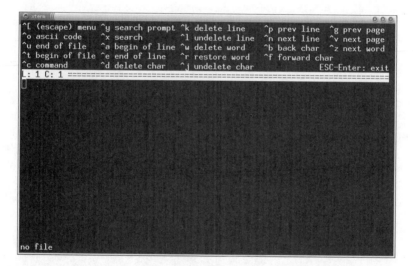

FIGURE 6.1   A sample ee session. You can use the key combinations shown at the top of the screen to access various features.

Using ee Key Combinations

The carat (^) in the options menu means the Ctrl key. Most of the options in the menu are self-explanatory, but there are a few that deserve greater discussion. Table 6.1 shows these options and their meanings.

TABLE 6.1   Ctrl Key Options in ee

Key Combination	Action
Ctrl+o	Brings up a prompt where you can enter an ASCII value. Useful for inserting special characters that do not exist on the keyboard and require their ASCII values to be entered directly.
Ctrl+c	Changes the top menu and also brings up a prompt at the bottom of the screen where you can type one of the commands listed at the top. Simply press Enter to leave the prompt without entering a command.
Ctrl+y	Brings up a search prompt. Here, you can type an expression to search for in the file. When you press Enter, the first occurrence of the expression after the current location of the cursor will be found.
Ctrl+x	Repeats the previous search done with Ctrl+y, causing ee to find the next occurrence of the expression.
Ctrl+g and Ctrl+v	As the menu says, these will move forward and backward one page at a time. You can also use the Page Up and Page Down keys on your keyboard to accomplish the same thing. Ctrl+g and Ctrl+v exist in case you are on a terminal that does not have Page Up and Page Down keys.

Setup and Configuration of ee

If a file called .init.ee exists in your home directory, ee will read the configuration options in this file each time it starts. You can create this file by hand, or you can choose setup options from the ee setup options list. To access this list, press Esc in ee to bring up the main menu, shown in Figure 6.2. Press e to select the Settings menu item or use the down arrow to highlight the settings option in the menu and then press Enter to open the Modes menu (see Figure 6.3).

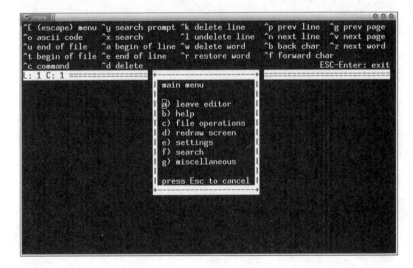

FIGURE 6.2   The main menu in ee.

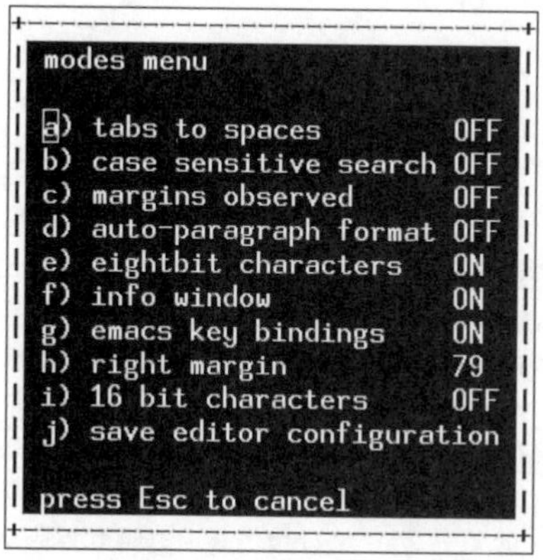

FIGURE 6.3   If you choose the Settings option from the ee main menu, you open this list of setup options.

In the Modes menu, shown in Figure 6.3, you can toggle an option on or off by pressing the letter corresponding to the option, or by using the arrow keys to highlight the desired option and then pressing Enter.

Table 6.2 shows the various setup options and what they do.

TABLE 6.2   The ee Setup Options

Option	Description
Tabs to Spaces	Off by default. This converts hard tabs into the equivalent number of spaces. It is useful for some programming languages, where whitespace is important (for example, Python and FORTRAN).
Case-Sensitive Search	Off by default. This controls whether searches are case sensitive.
Margins Observed	Off by default. When this option is on, ee wraps at the right margin and starts a new line automatically. When it is off, wrapping does not occur unless a new line is inserted manually.
Auto Paragraph Format	Off by default. When this option is on, ee tries to reformat the paragraph automatically when text is being inserted into the middle, similarly to the way a word processor behaves. When it is off, no reformatting is attempted. Note that turning this option on automatically turns the Margins Observed option on as well. Turning off the Margins Observed option automatically turns this option off, too.
Eight-Bit Characters	On by default. When this option is on, eight-bit extended ASCII characters are displayed. When it is off, those characters are not displayed.
Info Window	On by default. When this option is on, the top part of the screen shows the menu/help window. When it is off, this window is not displayed. You should probably leave this option on until you are familiar with the various key commands.

TABLE 6.2   Continued

Option	Description
Emacs Key Bindings	On by default. When this option is on, the Ctrl key sequences behave similarly to Ctrl key sequences in the Emacs editor. Even if you do not know what this is, you probably shouldn't change this option. If you do, some of the key bindings will change and will no longer work the way they are described here.
Right Margin	The column at which the right margin is set. By default, it is set for the width of a standard 80-column terminal display.
16-Bit Characters	This controls how 16-bit characters are handled (whether they are handled as two 8-bit characters or one 16-bit character). You shouldn't have to worry about this option unless you are using a Chinese character set or something similar.

The final option in the menu, Save Editor Configuration, writes the configuration information to the file .init.ee. If that file already exists, it will be overwritten.

When you choose to save the configuration information, you will be asked whether you want to write the configuration file to the current directory or to your home directory. If you write it to your home directory, the configuration will be the default configuration for all files you create and open in ee. If you write it to the current directory, the settings will override the default settings from the configuration file in the home directory any time ee is started from this directory.

The vi Editor

vi was one of the first editors developed for Unix-like operating systems. To this day, it is still one of the most powerful editors available, and it comes standard on virtually every Unix-like operating system. It has also been ported to several non-Unix systems, including Microsoft Windows and OS/2. Unfortunately, vi also has a reputation among newbies for being notoriously arcane and difficult to learn. This is because there are no menus, for example. Everything must be done by keystrokes and combinations of special keypresses that take some time to learn.

So why learn vi? There are two primary reasons, really. The first is that you can be virtually assured that vi will be available on any Unix-like system you might ever have to work on. Because of this, vi is a very nice thing to know if you may have to work on other Unix-like systems, because it might be the only editor you will have available.

The second reason for learning vi is that once you have learned its various keystrokes and commands, it is a very powerful editor. If you are a touch typist, it is also an extremely fast way to work because you do not have to remove your hands from the home keys to access most vi commands.

To start vi with an empty file, type **vi**. To start vi and load a file for editing, type **vi** followed by the filename. If the filename you specify doesn't already exist, vi will assume that this is a new file. Figure 6.4 shows a vi session with a new file ready for editing.

/tmp/vi.q5eZ1ftepA: new file: line 1

FIGURE 6.4   The vi editor, ready to edit a new file. The status line at the bottom of the screen gives information about the file being edited.

Looks rather plain and boring, doesn't it? One of the first things you may notice if you start trying to type text is that vi does nothing except beep at you; it doesn't insert any of the text you are typing. You may also hit certain keys and see strange-looking messages on the status line at the bottom of the screen. This is because vi has different modes of operation.

When vi first starts, it is in *command* mode. In command mode, keypresses are interpreted as commands to the editor rather than as text to be inserted into the document. To switch into the mode in which you can enter text into the document, you must press the a, i, or o key, depending on where you want the text to appear in the document:

- The a command stands for *append*. In this mode, the text you type will be inserted after whatever character the cursor is currently on.

- The i command stands for *insert*. In this mode, the text you type will be inserted before whatever character the cursor is currently on.

- Finally, the o command stands for *open*. This will cause a new line to be inserted after the line the cursor is currently on. Then, the cursor will move to the new line, and vi will enter insert mode, allowing you to enter text on the new line.

Some other text-entry mode commands are available, although they're less commonly used. These commands are 0, which adds a blank line above the current line, and A, which begins inserting text at the end of the current line.

If you wish to get back into command mode after entering text-entry mode, press the Escape key. By default, vi will beep when entering command mode.

TIP

Remember that if you are trying to enter text and vi simply keeps beeping at you or doing other strange things, you are probably in command mode. Press a, i, or o to enter text mode. Also, if you are ever unsure what mode you are in, simply press Escape to move into command mode (if you are already in command mode, it will have no effect). You can then press a, i, or o to enter text-entry mode.

Moving Around in vi

In text-entry mode, you can usually use the arrow keys and the Page Up/Page Down keys to move around. However, these may not always work while on a terminal. Also, some terminals don't have arrow keys or Page Up/Page Down keys. In this case, you can use other keys in command mode to move around in a document. Several command mode keys can be used to move in ways that cannot be done with the arrow keys and the Page Up/Page Down keys.

To use the movement keys, press Escape to get into command mode. You can then use the h, j, k, and l keys on the keyboard to move the cursor left, down, up, and right, respectively. The following four tips may help you remember which key moves the cursor in which direction.

- The l key is the farthest to the right, and it moves the cursor right.

- The j key looks somewhat like a downward-pointing arrow. It moves the cursor down.

- The h key is the farthest to the left, and it moves the cursor left.

- The remaining key, k, moves the cursor up.

Several other movement keys are available in command mode. Table 6.3 shows the various keys and their functions.

TABLE 6.3   The Movement Keys Available from vi's Command Mode

Key	Action
h	Moves the cursor left one character
j	Moves the cursor down one character
k	Moves the cursor up one character
l	Moves the cursor right one character

TABLE 6.3   Continued

Key	Action
w	Moves the cursor forward one word
b	Moves the cursor back one word
e	Moves the cursor to the end of the next word
0	Moves to the beginning of the line
$	Moves to the end of the line
)	Moves to the beginning of the next sentence
(	Moves to the beginning of the previous sentence
}	Moves to the beginning of the next paragraph
{	Moves to the beginning of the previous paragraph
G	Moves to the bottom of the current document
^	Moves to the first character in the line that is not a space
H	Moves the cursor to the first line on the screen
L	Moves the cursor to the last line on the screen

Note that each of the commands in the table (with the exception of G) uses the unit of one, by default. The command j moves the cursor down one line, k moves it up one line, w moves one word to the right, and so on. You can modify the default behavior by typing a number before the command. For example, the following line causes the cursor to move down five lines instead of one line:

5j

The following line causes the cursor to move to the 75th line in the current file that is being edited:

75G

The following line causes the cursor to move to the line that is five lines up from the bottom of the screen:

5L

This syntax works for all of the commands in Table 6.3, except for the ^ command, which moves to the first non-space character in the document.

> **TIP**
>
> If you enter a number followed by one of the previous commands, and vi seems to do nothing except beep, it probably means you entered a number out of range. For example, if you enter **560G** to move to line 560, and the document has only 557 lines, vi will simply beep at you—indicating that the number you entered is out of range. Unfortunately, no error message will be printed telling you what is wrong.

Other Movement Keys

In addition to the cursor-movement keys described previously, there are also some key combinations that are related to scrolling the screen (Table 6.4 lists them).

TABLE 6.4   Scrolling in vi

Key Combination	Action
z then Enter	Moves the line the cursor is on to the top of the screen
z then -	Moves the line the cursor is on to the bottom of the screen
z then .	Moves the line the cursor is on to the center of the screen
Ctrl+u	Scrolls up one-half screen
Ctrl+d	Scrolls down one-half screen
Ctrl+f	Scrolls forward one full screen
Ctrl+b	Scrolls backward one full screen
Ctrl+e	Scrolls down one line
Ctrl+y	Scrolls up one line

Text-Editing Commands

The Backspace and Delete keys will not do what you expect in vi. Instead, you will have to use various keystrokes from vi's command mode in order to delete text, and so on. Table 6.5 lists the various text-editing commands available in vi.

TABLE 6.5   Commands for Text Editing in vi

Command	Action
D	Deletes the text from the cursor position to the end of the line.
dd	Deletes the entire current line.
ndd	Here, n is the number of lines you wish to delete. For example, 5dd will delete the current line, as well as the next four lines.
rc	Here, c is a character. This will replace the character under the cursor with the character that follows r.
R	The text typed after R will overwrite the current text, starting at the cursor position until Esc is pressed to get back into command mode.
S	Deletes the current line and begins inserting text in the now-blank line.
x	Deletes the character under the cursor and moves the character to the right over to close the gap.
X	Deletes the character before the cursor and moves the characters on the right to close the gap.
~	Changes the case of the letter under the cursor.
J	Joins the current line with the previous line and removes the resulting blank line.

File Operations and Exiting vi

Several vi commands are related to loading and saving files. Table 6.6 shows the various commands available for these actions.

TABLE 6.6   File Operations in vi

Command	Action
ZZ	Saves changes to the current file and then exits.
:wq	Saves changes to the current file and then exits (the same as ZZ).
:w	Saves changes to the current file.
:w!	Saves changes to the current file, overwriting a file of the same name if it already exists.
:q	Quits vi. If there are unsaved changes, vi complains and does not quit.
:q!	Quits vi even if there are unsaved changes. All unsaved changes will be lost.
:e *filename*	Loads the specified file into vi for editing. If the specified file does not exist, a new file will be created.
:e!	Loses all changes and reloads the saved file from the disk.

CAUTION

Note that the ! option on the end of several of the commands in Table 6.6 forces the action to take place. You will not be prompted before the action is taken if you have unsaved changes in your document. For example, :q! will exit vi immediately without asking first whether you want to save any changes. Use the ! option with care.

Searching and Replacing Text in vi

Several commands are available for performing a search-and-replace operation in vi. Table 6.7 lists these commands and their actions.

TABLE 6.7   Search and Replace Commands in vi

Command	Action
/*pattern*	Here, *pattern* is what to search for. vi searches forward in the file for the first occurrence of the specified pattern.
/	Repeats the last search, finding the next occurrence of the pattern in the file.
?*pattern*	Here, *pattern* is what to search for. vi searches backward in the file for the first occurrence of the specified pattern.
?	Repeats the last search, finding the previous occurrence of the pattern in the file.
%	Moves to the matching parenthesis or brace for the one that the cursor is currently on. This is useful to programmers.
:s/*pattern1*/*pattern2*	Replaces each occurrence of *pattern1* with *pattern2* on the current line.
:%s/*pattern1*/*pattern2*	Replaces every occurrence of *pattern1* with *pattern2* in the entire file.

This table doesn't include a few other search-and-replace functions that aren't often used. The operations listed in the table are the ones you will probably use most often.

Copying, Cutting, and Pasting Text in vi

To copy text to a buffer in vi, use the y command. y is short for yank, and it basically "yanks" text into the buffer. Table 6.8 shows the various ways the yank command can be used.

TABLE 6.8   yank Commands in vi

Command	Action
yw	Yanks the word that the cursor is currently on into the buffer.
y$	Yanks from the current cursor position up to the end of the current line into the buffer.
yy	Yanks the entire current line into the buffer.
nyy	Here, n is the number of lines you wish to yank into the buffer. For example, 5yy yanks the current line, as well as the next four lines, into the buffer.

Once you have yanked text into the buffer, you can paste it into any location in the document by moving to the correct location in the document and then using p or P to "put" the text. The p command places the text into the document after the cursor, whereas P places the text into the document before the cursor. After you have "put" the text, it continues to remain in the buffer. You can use p or P again to copy the text to another location in the document.

If you want to cut instead of copy, use one of the deletion commands. For example, 5dd will cut the current line as well as the next four lines. They can than be pasted into the document in another location by using p or P.

> **CAUTION**
>
> vi stores only the last text that was yanked or deleted. In other words, if you use dd to delete a line of text, and you later use yy to copy a line of text, the text from the dd operation will be replaced with the text from the yy operation. This means the text from the dd operation will no longer be available, nor will you be able to undo the delete.

vi has many more powerful features that cannot be covered here due to lack of space. Once you get to know vi, you recognize it as a very powerful editor that offers a fast way to edit documents. If you would like to learn more about vi, a few books are available on the subject, including *Learning the vi Editor* and *vi Editor Pocket Reference*, both available from O'Reilly.

Creating Graphics and Editing Images with GIMP

Several graphics programs and image-editing programs are available for FreeBSD, including GIMP for image editing and Xfig for drawing figures and illustrations. GIMP is available for free in the FreeBSD ports collection.

GIMP stands for GNU Image Manipulation Program. It is a freely available and open-source image-editing program maintained by the GNU project. It has many advanced features, such as layers and filters. If you have worked with a program such as Adobe Photoshop before, most of GIMP's features will be familiar to you. Getting used to the layout of GIMP, however, may take some time.

GIMP recognizes most image formats, including BMP, GIF, JPEG, PNG, PCX, and TIFF. GIMP can also read PostScript files.

GIMP is available in the FreeBSD ports collection under the graphics directory. Once you have installed GIMP, you can simply type **gimp** from a terminal in X-Windows, or you can use the Run dialog box and type **gimp** in it. See Chapter 5, "Working with X-Windows," for more information on how to start applications from within X-Windows.

Figure 6.5 shows the main control panel for GIMP.

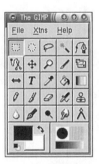

FIGURE 6.5   The main control panel for GIMP enables you to select the various tools available in GIMP, as well as load and save files.

The File option from the menu bar is usually your starting point for GIMP. Here, you can open an existing file, create a new file, or acquire an image—either from a screen shot or from a supported scanner, if installed.

Figure 6.6 shows the File, Open dialog box in GIMP.

> **TIP**
>
> The main sticking point for users of Windows image-editing software when converting to GIMP is that most of GIMP's editing functions are accessed by right-clicking the image window. Keep this in mind when working with GIMP and the transition will go a lot smoother.

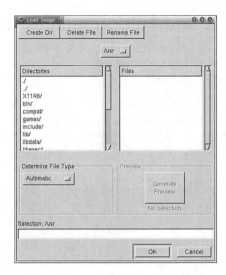

FIGURE 6.6   Opening a file in GIMP. Notice that there is a primitive file manager built in to it.

Working with Multimedia

The multimedia support in FreeBSD has become quite good in a rather short period of time. If you have any one of the common sound cards, chances are good that FreeBSD supports it natively. Even if FreeBSD does not have native support for your sound card, the commercial sound drivers from a company called 4Front Technologies might support your sound card. If you would like to look into the commercial drivers, the Web site for 4Front's sound drivers is located at www.opensound.com. Free trial versions are available, so you can try the drivers before purchasing them.

Checking for Sound Support

Before you can use any of the multimedia applications presented in this section, you will need to make sure you have sound support available in FreeBSD.

To see whether the PCM driver is loaded, examine your kernel configuration file for the line device pcm. If this line exists, sound support is compiled into the kernel. If you have not built a custom kernel, the kernel-configuration file will be located in /sys/i386/conf/GENERIC. If this line doesn't exist, you will need to add it and rebuild the kernel. This is not as scary as it sounds. See Chapter 16, "Kernel Configuration," for information on rebuilding the kernel.

Once you have verified that the kernel contains the PCM driver, type **dmesg | more** to check the dmesg output from the kernel. Look for information indicating that your sound card was correctly detected on system boot. For example, the dmesg output on my system contains the following lines:

```
sbc0: <Creative SB AWE64> at port 0x220-0x22f,0x330-0x331,0x388-0x38b irq 5 drq
1,5 on isa0
pcm1: <SB16 DSP 4.16> on sbc0
```

This output shows that FreeBSD detected a SoundBlaster AWE 64 as well as gives the addresses the sound card is on.

If FreeBSD doesn't seem to find your sound card, you might want to try to get sound working using the 4Front sound drivers. Once again, they can be obtained at www.opensound.com.

Note that if you decide to try using the 4Front drivers, you will probably need to remove or comment out the device pcm line from your kernel-configuration file and then rebuild the kernel. Otherwise, you may have problems with the kernel sound driver and the 4Front driver conflicting.

For complete instructions on kernel configuration and kernel building, see Chapter 16.

The Mixer

Once the device links have been created, you should be able to access the FreeBSD mixer from the command line. From a shell prompt or X-terminal window, type the command **mixer** and press Enter. Your system will output something similar to the following:

```
Mixer vol      is currently set to   75:75
Mixer bass     is currently set to   50:50
Mixer treble   is currently set to   50:50
Mixer synth    is currently set to   75:75
Mixer pcm      is currently set to   75:75
Mixer speaker  is currently set to   75:75
Mixer line     is currently set to   75:75
Mixer mic      is currently set to    0:0
Mixer cd       is currently set to   75:75
Mixer igain    is currently set to    0:0
Mixer ogain    is currently set to   50:50
```

This shows what levels (in percentage values ranging from 0 to 100) each audio device in the system is set to. As you would expect, the number on the left of the colon indicates the level for the left audio channel, and the number on the right of the colon indicates the level for the right audio channel.

Most of the items in the list are self-explanatory, but a few of them deserve some more attention:

- Mixer vol is the master volume for all the audio devices.

- Mixer pcm is the device through which most audio is played. This will control the volume of WAV files, MP3s, Real Audio files, and so on.

9

- `Mixer synth` controls the volume of the synthesizer. This generally affects MIDI files.

- `Mixer cd` controls the volume of audio CDs.

- `Mixer line` controls the volume of a device connected to the line in the jack on a sound card.

- `Mixer igain` controls the input gain level.

- `Mixer ogain` controls the output gain level.

To make changes to any one of the levels, you can type **mixer**, followed by the name of the device and the desired level. For example, the following will set the `cd` volume to 90 percent on both the left and right channels:

```
mixer cd 90
```

If you want to set the left and right channels to different values, you need to include both values, separated by a colon. For example, the following will set the `cd` volume to 100 percent for the left channel and 80 percent for the right channel:

```
mixer cd 100:80
```

At system boot, most of the mixer values will default to 75 percent. If you wish to have different default values at system boot, there are two ways to accomplish this.

The first way is by creating a startup file in `/usr/local/etc/rc.d`. In the file, simply include a list of the desired mixer commands. You can name the file anything you want. For example, you might call the file `mixerset`. Here is an example of what the file might contain:

```
mixer vol 80:80
mixer cd 90:90
mixer pcm 50:50
```

As root, create this file in the directory `/usr/local/etc/rc.d` and save it as `mixerset`, for example. Next, make the file executable by issuing the following command:

```
chmod u+x mixerset
```

The commands inside this file will now be run at each system boot and cause the mixer to be set to the desired values.

> **TIP**
>
> If the previous steps are unclear to you, see Chapter 7, "Working with the Shell," and Chapter 10, "System Configuration and Startup Scripts," for more information on these topics.

The second way you can change the default mixer values is by adding commands to your login profile to change the desired values. If you are using a Bourne-compatible shell, the file you will want to add these commands to is .profile. If you are using a C-type shell, the file you will want to add these commands to is .login. Both of these files are located in your home directory. If this is unclear to you, see Chapter 11, "Customizing the Shell," for further details.

Basically, what you want to do is open either .profile or .login in your favorite text editor and add the mixer commands that you want to set. For example, you might want to add the following lines to the file:

```
mixer vol 80:80
mixer cd 50:50
mixer pcm 90:90
```

Unlike the changes made to the startup file, these do not need to be made as root, and they also will not take effect at system boot. They will take effect as soon as you log in to the system. The benefit of this method is that if more than one person uses this system, each person can create his own customized set of mixer settings to suit his listening preferences. Each time that user logs in to the system, his custom mixer settings will be applied.

MP3 with XMMS

Now that you have the audio device configured properly, you will probably want to play something with it. Yes, your MP3 collection will work with FreeBSD. XMMS is a Winamp clone for FreeBSD and other Unix-like systems. It is available in the FreeBSD ports collection under the audio directory.

Once you have XMMS installed, you can start it with the command xmms. Like the other programs in this chapter, the command to start XMMS can be issued from either an X-terminal or the Run dialog box, or you can create menu entries or desktop shortcuts for the program.

Figure 6.7 shows XMMS with the mixer and playlist windows also open.

Yes, it even supports Winamp skins—and you don't even have to unzip them first. Simply place your zipped Winamp skins in the directory .xmms/Skins located in your home directory. Click the icon at the very upper-left corner of XMMS; then select Options, Skin Browser from the pull-down menu. This will bring up a dialog box in which you can select the desired skin.

TIP

In order for you to be able to use zipped skins, you will have to have the unzip program installed. It can be installed from the FreeBSD ports collection and is located in the archivers directory.

FIGURE 6.7   The XMMS MP3 player. Windows users who have used Winamp will be quite comfortable with XMMS because its controls are virtually identical.

In addition to Winamp skins, a large number of XMMS skins are available at www.xmms.org/skins.html. Like the Winamp skins, they can simply be copied into the .xmms/Skins directory and do not need to be unzipped first.

XMMS skins are normally distributed as gzipped tar files with a .tar.gz extension. This is a popular archive format for Unix-like systems that is similar to ZIP files.

XMMS also supports various visualization and audio effect plug-ins. Many of these are available as FreeBSD ports in the audio directory.

MP3 with mpg123

If you aren't running X-Windows but still want to be able to play your MP3 files, you have several command-line MP3 players available to you. One of the best and most popular is a program called mpg123. It is available in the FreeBSD ports collection under the audio directory.

In its most basic form, mpg123 is started by typing **mpg123** *filename*, where *filename* is the name of the MP3 file that you wish to play. It supports wildcards (see Chapter 7). For example, mpg123 *.mp3 will play every file in the current directory that ends in .mp3. You can also supply a list of files on the command line that you want mpg123 to play. The -z option will cause the files to play in random order. You can also use the -@ option followed by the name of a text file. mpg123 will then treat the contents of the text file as a list of MP3 files to play. The text file should contain the list of MP3s, one on each line.

mpg123 has many more options. For a complete list of all the features, type **man mpg123** to read the manual page for the program.

X-Based Mixers

If you are not keen on the idea of controlling the mixer from the command line, as described previously in this chapter, several X-Windows-based interfaces to the mixer are available. This section covers xmixer, which is available in the FreeBSD ports collection under the audio directory.

xmixer can be started using one of two commands; the command you use determines the appearance of the mixer. The first way to invoke xmixer is simply by typing **xmixer** at an X-terminal or in the Run dialog box (or by creating a desktop shortcut or menu entry for it). xmixer uses the Athena toolkit (a programmer's toolkit for designing graphical interfaces). Figure 6.8 shows what xmixer looks like when invoked by this method.

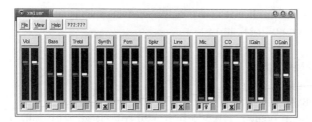

FIGURE 6.8   xmixer when invoked using the xmixer command. This version uses the Athena toolkit (a programmer's toolkit for creating graphical user interfaces).

The sliders in the mixer can be moved up and down by dragging them with your mouse (left-click the slider and then hold the left mouse button down as you move the slider up and down with the mouse). At the bottom of each slider are three buttons. The one on the left locks the sliders so that the left and right levels are changed at the same time and kept synchronized. Clicking this button will cause the black box inside of it to disappear, and now the left and right levels can be adjusted individually.

The right button controls whether the device is on or off. When it is green, the device is on. When it is red, its level is set to zero, thus cutting it out of the mix.

The middle button turns recording on and off for input devices such as the microphone and the line in. This is disabled on devices that are output only.

The second way xmixer can be invoked is with the command 1. This invokes the GTK version of the program, known as xgmixer. The GTK version is exactly the same as xmixer. The only difference is that the use of the GTK toolkit instead of the Athena toolkit gives it a different appearance. Figure 6.9 shows xgmixer.

Several other audio applications are available for FreeBSD, including various CD players, more MP3 players, the Real Audio player, and tools for ripping CD audio tracks to MP3. Browse through the audio category in the FreeBSD ports tree to see what is available.

FIGURE 6.9   xmixer when invoked with the 1 command as xgmixer. The functionality remains the same, but the appearance is different because this version uses the GTK toolkit instead of the Athena toolkit.

Networking Applications

Numerous networking applications are available for FreeBSD. This section will concentrate on Web browsers, e-mail, FTP, and so on.

Configuring Netscape

The Netscape Communicator Web browser is available for FreeBSD. The latest version available for FreeBSD is 4.8. If you want to run Netscape 7, you will need to run the Linux version of Netscape in FreeBSD. In addition, you will also need to run the Linux version if you want to use most plug-ins, such as Flash and Shockwave. These plug-ins are available only for Linux versions of Netscape. Running the Linux version of Netscape in FreeBSD allows you to use these plug-ins.

All the Netscape browsers, including the Linux versions, are available as ports in the www directory. This allows you to install and run the Linux versions just like they were normal FreeBSD applications.

Once Netscape has been installed, you can start it with the command netscape for Netscape 4.8 or with the command netscape7 for Netscape 7. This section will cover Netscape 4.8, but Netscape 7 is similar.

Most users have probably used Netscape before, and the configuration in FreeBSD is the same as the configuration in Windows. To change Netscape options, click Edit in the menu bar and then click Preferences. This brings up a configuration dialog box like the one in Figure 6.10.

To configure the various Netscape settings, click the plus sign (+) by the desired category of options to expand it. Then, click the item you wish to configure to bring up its configuration dialog box in the right side of the window.

Lynx Web Browser

Lynx is a Web browser that runs in text mode and has no graphical capabilities. Although it can still be used, it is getting more and more difficult to navigate the Web with Lynx because it does not support images, frames, or Java. Because many sites are using images as links and not making use of ALT tags, this can cause navigational problems in Lynx that are difficult or impossible to get around. Figure 6.11 shows Lynx with the FreeBSD Web site loaded into it.

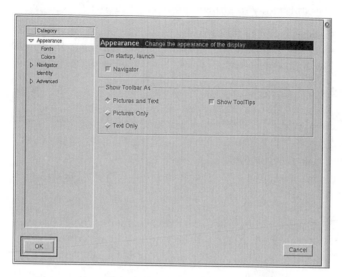

FIGURE 6.10   The configuration dialog box for Netscape. It is similar to configuring Netscape in Windows.

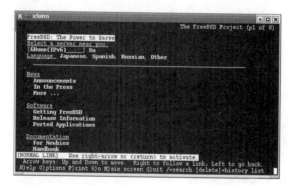

FIGURE 6.11   The FreeBSD Web site in Lynx.

Lynx can still work on quite a few sites, although navigation is not always easy. Use the arrow keys to move between links in the browser window. The spacebar will advance to the next page. Type **G** to change to a different Web site. You will be asked to enter a URL after typing G. Q quits Lynx after asking whether you are sure you want to quit.

For more information on Lynx, including customization options, see the Lynx man page by typing **man lynx**.

FTP

FTP (File Transfer Protocol) is a method of transferring files between systems. Although it is not commonly used directly anymore (often, files are downloaded from FTP by clicking Web site links), it is still handy to know if you need to move files to another server.

To start an FTP session, type **ftp** followed by the name of the server you wish to connect to at the shell prompt or X-terminal. For example, to connect to the FreeBSD FTP server, you would type the following:

```
ftp ftp.freebsd.org
```

Once you have done this, and assuming the connection is successful, you will eventually see something like the following:

```
Connected to ftp.beastie.tdk.net.
220 ftp.beastie.tdk.net FTP server (Version DG-4.1.73 983302105) ready.
Name (ftp.freebsd.org:murban):
```

At the Name prompt, you need to enter your login name for the FTP server. If your login name is the same as your login name for the system you are currently on, you can simply press Enter without entering a name here, and your local login name will be used.

If you do not have a login name for the system, you can log in to public FTP servers with the name anonymous. For example, this is how you would log in to the FreeBSD FTP server. Once you have entered anonymous as the username and pressed Enter, the remote host will respond with something like the following:

```
331 Guest login ok, send your e-mail address as password.
Password:
```

Simply do what it says, and enter your e-mail address as your password. Note that the password will not echo to your screen.

After you have logged in, you may get a welcome message and finally something that looks similar to the following:

```
Remote system type is UNIX.
Using binary mode to transfer files.
ftp>
```

At the prompt, you can use many of the same shell commands that you use at your local shell to navigate through the FTP server. See Chapter 7 for details on how to work with shell commands. Table 6.9 provides a list of some of the most commonly used commands in an FTP session.

TABLE 6.9   Commonly Used FTP Commands

Command	Action
ls	Lists the directory contents of the remote host.
cd	Changes the directory on the remote host.
pwd	Displays the current directory you are in on the remote host.
lcd	Changes the directory on the local host.
binary	Transfers files in binary mode (this mode should be used for anything other than plain-text).
ascii	Transfers files in ASCII mode (this mode should be used *only* for plain-text). Note that plain-text can also be transferred in binary mode, in most cases, with no problems.
put *filename*	Copies *filename* to the remote host. *filename* is assumed to be in the current directory unless a path is specified. If no destination file is specified, the file will be placed in the current directory in the remote host and have the same name as the local file. (This command works only if you have permission to write to the directory on the remote machine.)
mput *file1 file2*	Copies multiple files in a list to the remote host. The files will be placed in the current directory on the remote host. (This command works only if you have permission to write to the directory on the remote machine.)
get *filename*	Copies a file from the remote host to the local system. If no path is specified, the file is assumed to be located on the current directory on the remote host. If no destination file is specified, the file will be copied to the local system using the same filename.
mget *file1 file2*	Gets multiple files in a list from the remote host. The files will be placed in the current directory on the local system.
mkdir *dirname*	Creates a directory called *dirname* on the remote machine (assuming you have permission to do so).
rmdir *dirname* or rm *dirname*	Removes the directory called *dirname* on the remote machine (assuming you have permission to do so).
del *filename*	Deletes the file *filename* from the remote machine (assuming you have permission to do so).
bye or quit	Closes the connection with the remote host and quits the FTP program, returning you to the shell prompt.

You can also type **help** at the ftp> prompt to get a list of available commands. Type **help** followed by one of the commands in the list to get a short description of what that command does. Here's an example:

```
ftp> help
Commands may be abbreviated.   Commands are:

!                disconnect     mdelete        preserve       runique
$                edit           mdir           progress       send
account          exit           mget           prompt         sendport
append           form           mkdir          proxy          site
ascii            ftp            mls            put            size
bell             get            mode           pwd            status
binary           gate           modtime        quit           struct
bye              glob           more           quote          sunique
case             hash           mput           recv           system
cd               help           msend          reget          tenex
cdup             idle           newer          rename         trace
chmod            image          nlist          reset          type
close            lcd            nmap           restart        umask
cr               less           ntrans         restrict       user
debug            lpwd           open           rhelp          verbose
delete           ls             page           rmdir          ?
dir              macdef         passive        rstatus
ftp> help mdir
mdir            list contents of multiple remote directories
ftp>
```

For more information on using FTP, read the manual page for FTP by typing **man ftp** at the shell prompt. You might also want to read the sections in Chapter 7 on file-manipulation commands because the commands used in FTP are similar.

The following shows what a sample FTP session might look like:

```
bash$ ftp ftp.freebsd.org
Connected to ftp.beastie.tdk.net.
220 ftp.beastie.tdk.net FTP server (Version DG-4.1.73 983302105) ready.
Name (ftp.freebsd.org:murban): anonymous
331 Guest login ok, send your e-mail address as password.
Password:
230 Guest login ok, access restrictions apply.
Remote system type is UNIX.
Using binary mode to transfer files.
ftp> ls
227 Entering Passive Mode (62,243,72,50,88,26)
150 Opening ASCII mode data connection for 'file list'.
total 2
```

```
dr-xr-xr-x  2 root   wheel   512 May 15 18:30 etc
drwxr-xr-x  3 root   wheel   512 May 13 15:26 pub
226 Transfer complete.
ftp> cd pub/FreeBSD/tools
ftp> get gunzip.exe
local: gunzip.exe remote: gunzip.exe
227 Entering Passive Mode (62,243,72,50,89,241)
150 Opening BINARY mode data connection for 'gunzip.exe' (37178 bytes).
100% |**************************************************| 37178        00:00 ETA
226 Transfer complete.
37178 bytes received in 9.55 seconds (3.80 KB/s)
ftp> bye
221 Goodbye!
bash$
```

If you would rather work with a graphical FTP client in X-Windows, several graphical FTP client ports are available in the `ftp` directory.

E-mail Applications

E-mail was one of the first applications of the Internet, and it is still the most popular use of the Internet. There is no shortage of e-mail clients available for FreeBSD. Clients are available for text mode shell use, and also graphical clients are available for X-Windows. This section will look at some of the more popular e-mail clients available for both the shell and for X-Windows.

> **TIP**
>
> In addition to having an Internet connection configured and working properly, you will also need to have a mail transfer agent such as Sendmail configured and working properly before you can use some of these e-mail clients. In addition, if you need to retrieve your mail from a POP3 or IMAP server at your ISP, you will also need to have Fetchmail configured and working properly. Not all the clients listed here will require this because some can transfer mail on their own. It is better to use the mail transfer agent / `Fetchmail setup`, though. This allows much greater flexibility in dealing with e-mail because it uses FreeBSD's native mail-handling system. This will allow the shell to notify you when you have new e-mail, as well as allow mail-checking utilities for X-Windows, such as `xbiff`, to notify you of new mail. These features will not work if you use the mail client's built-in mail-handing functions. See Chapter 24, "Configuring E-mail Services," for details on how to set up and configure FreeBSD to send and receive e-mail.

Pine

Pine is a text-based e-mail and news client that was designed with the nontechnical user in mind. It is menu driven and is designed to be intuitive and easy to use for the average computer user. Pine is available in the FreeBSD ports collection under the `mail` directory. Figure 6.12 shows the main menu of Pine.

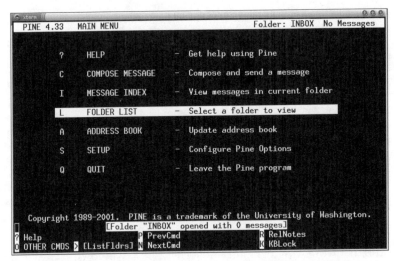

FIGURE 6.12   Pine is menu driven and can be navigated with the arrow keys or by pressing the letter in front of the menu entry.

Pine is very popular with end users because of its ease of use. Because it is text based, it also allows e-mail to be checked remotely over a dumb terminal.

Unfortunately, Pine has a reputation of being poorly programmed and having a lot of security problems. Although all the known problems have currently been fixed, many security experts believe that there are many more security holes in Pine that have not yet been discovered. Some even place the likely number of undiscovered holes in the thousands. You will also be warned of these potential security issues with Pine when you install the port.

If you do decide to make Pine available to your users, you should make sure your users are aware of the potential security hazards involved in using Pine.

If security is a high-level concern on your system (for example, if you have confidential data on the system that these users have access to), it is probably best to forbid the use of Pine altogether (in other words, don't install Pine, or uninstall it if it is already installed). Your users may have fits, but in some situations, security may be more important than user convenience. Other mail programs are available that your users can use (one popular alternative, Mutt, is discussed in the next section). Although they may not be as easy to use as Pine, these programs are generally much more secure.

CAUTION

Although it is generally a bad idea to open any e-mail while logged in as root, it is even more so with Pine. This is because of the nature of some of the potential holes in Pine that might allow someone to execute arbitrary code on your system as the user running Pine simply by sending a bad e-mail header. It is a much better idea to forward root's mail to a normal user account and then read the e-mail using that account instead. Instructions on e-mail forwarding can be found in Chapter 24.

Mutt

Mutt is another text-based e-mail client for FreeBSD and other Unix-like operating systems. It is available in the FreeBSD ports collection under the `mail` directory. Figure 6.13 shows the main screen of Mutt.

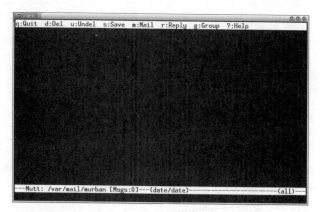

FIGURE 6.13   Although it does not have the simple menu-driven interface of Pine, Mutt is much more secure than Pine and is also more configurable.

Mutt got its name because it is known as "the mongrel of mail clients." This is because it is a relatively new mail client that attempts to combine the best features of Elm (a very old e-mail client that is not widely used anymore) and Pine (which was designed to be much easier to use than Elm). Mutt has many users who would agree that the client successfully fulfills these goals.

Mutt is a very complex program with a rich set of features. Its use and configuration is beyond the scope of this book. The Mutt Web site, located at www.mutt.org, has very good online documentation and reference manuals that explain the use and configuration of this powerful program.

uuencode and uudecode

A brief word on uuencode and uudecode is in order here. uuencode is basically a method of sending binary files as plain-text so that they can be sent through e-mail. Often, the e-mail client will handle encoding and decoding of the attachments automatically. However, this is not always the case. Sometimes, you may receive an e-mail that has an attachment, and the attachment may appear as several hundred lines of what appears to be garbage text. It will look something like the following:

```
begin 644 gunzip.exe
M35HZ`4D`````"`.I6____/6```.`,`,4('`````$Q`M8"#9"`.`/M&&
M``'_XKM\.#'`E"&X09+[F&E&.!5/$/#$,N$O3.O@`0B@,$J@&^,0;Y<&.0ZX@^^?=&
M>;._^\\7X#AP1%H@@?@%(G&L_H/('&88/.,-<--.""-C&#>X((&#@(?W
```

```
MBP<F"T<"==2+Y5W+D/V4`U-KD/U8SV*0^!%HD/@/E/@1=*<6E/@?N'C>@J/X
M$8BC^`\H]7#NGONEY/@.$+C>ML'N^`X(N,_N^!#A[O@0Z^[X$/)=_^[X$/CN
M^!`#".[X#E[U"E=6QT;Z$!!`107?C48(%L-'^P;[FE(#QP4&",,,@WB"C/B&)
```

These are what the first several lines of a uuencoded file may look like. The begin line contains the name of the file that this file will be saved to when uudecoded.

To decode the file, save the attachment (and/or e-mail message that contains the garbage text) to a file in the directory where you want to decode it. For example, suppose you save the file as program.txt. You can now use the following command to decode the file:

```
uudecode program.txt
```

This will decode the file and write the contents to whatever filename is given in the encoding. In the previous example, this would write an output file called gunzip.exe.

If you need to encode a file, you can do so with a command like the following (assume that the file you want to encode is called gunzip.exe):

```
uuencode gunzip.exe gunzip.exe > gunzip.txt
```

The three arguments in the previous command are the name of the file you want to encode (in this case gunzip.exe), the name of the output file that should be produced when the file is decoded (usually this will be the same as the input file, as in this example), and a redirect of the output to a file called gunzip.txt, which will contain the encoded file. The > character tells the command to redirect the output to whatever is on the right side of it. If we do not do this, the output will be sent to the screen instead. This allows the output to be piped directly into a mail program, for example, if you wish to send the encoded file to someone.

See Chapter 7 for more information on input/output redirection and pipes.

Working with Java Applications

Until recently, the latest Java runtime engine (JRE) available for FreeBSD was version 1.1.8. Of course, this version is very outdated and lacks many features of the newer runtime engines. Fortunately, the FreeBSD project was recently given Sun's blessing to develop a native port of a more recent version of the Java runtime engine. At this time, the most recent stable JRE for FreeBSD is 1.3, although 1.4 may be available by the time this book is printed.

> **NOTE**
>
> The Java compiler is actually written in Java. Therefore, once the Java Runtime Environment has been ported to a platform, the Java compiler will also run on that platform. Because this is the case with FreeBSD, you can also develop Java applications on FreeBSD and compile them on FreeBSD with the Java compiler.

The latest FreeBSD Java Development Kit (which also includes the Java runtime engine) is available in the ports collection under the `devel` category. See Chapter 14 for more information on installing ports.

Installing Java Applications

Many Java applications do not have a port. However, because Java applications are portable, you can install and run in FreeBSD any application written in Java. Installation procedures vary depending on the application, so refer to the `readme` files and other documentation that came with the application for instructions.

Java applications sometimes come as compressed Java archives. These archives have a `.jar` extension. You can uncompress Java archives by typing **java -jar** followed by the name of the compressed file.

Running Java Applications

Java applications need to be run with the aid of the Java runtime engine. To start a Java application, invoke the Java program followed by the name of a Java class file. Many applications contain multiple class files, but the documentation that comes with the application will tell you which class file to start. Java class files have a `.class` extension.

Sometimes Java applications come in a compressed format. These applications can be run in their compressed form and uncompressed on the fly. In this situation, the Java interpreter should be invoked with the `-jar` option.

> **NOTE**
>
> A detailed discussion of Java is beyond the scope of this book. For more information on Java, visit the Java Web site at `java.sun.com`. If you are interested in learning Java programming, many good books are available on the market today, including *Sams Teach Yourself Java 2 in 21 Days*.

Working with the Shell

Up to this point, you have worked mostly with the graphical user interface (GUI) in X-Windows and Gnome. Although this is the easiest way to work with an operating system, the real power of FreeBSD can be unleashed only if you learn how to work with the shell. The design philosophy behind the Unix command line and shells has helped Unix remain one of the most powerful operating systems available for more than 30 years. This chapter introduces several shells available for FreeBSD, gives a feature comparison of the various shells, and then shows how to work with the shell.

Introducing the Shell

The Unix shell is the command-line interface between the user and the operating system kernel. If you have worked with MS-DOS, you can think of the shell as being similar to the DOS prompt. In a looser sense, you could also think of the Windows or Macintosh desktop as being a shell. The shell acts as a translator, rendering human language into machine language that the kernel can understand. The shell also translates machine language from the kernel into language that humans can understand. Figure 7.1 shows the relationship between the system hardware, the kernel, and the shell.

You learn about the role of the kernel in detail in Chapter 16, "Kernel Configuration." For now, simply be aware that the *kernel* is a special piece of software that controls and regulates all the interactions of other software (and the actions of users) with the computer's hardware. Normally, you do not need to concern yourself with the kernel because it is transparent to the user, does its job in the background, and is "out of sight, out of mind."

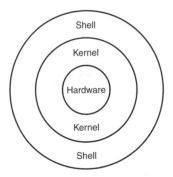

FIGURE 7.1　Relationship between the hardware, kernel, and shell.

Choosing a Shell for FreeBSD

A lot of different shells are available for FreeBSD, ranging from bare-bones models to some that are loaded with features. Some shells are very terse in the command syntax they accept, and insist that you type everything correctly; other shells allow you to repeat and edit previously used commands and automatically expand command lines with the Tab key. This chapter doesn't cover all shells but rather looks at some of the more popular ones. All shells listed here can be installed from the ports (in /usr/ports/shells) or packages, as described in Chapter 14, "Installing Additional Software."

The Bourne Shell (sh) and POSIX

The earliest shell still in common use is the Bourne shell, commonly known as sh. The original Bourne shell was developed at Bell Labs by Steven Bourne for the AT&T UNIX operating system. FreeBSD, like many other versions of Unix, has replaced the Bourne shell with an enhanced version called the POSIX shell. POSIX supports command-line editing, command history, and aliases—all things that the original Bourne shell did not support. You learn more about command-line editing and command history later in this chapter.

The C Shell (csh)

The C shell is the traditional BSD shell. The researchers at Berkeley saw all the limitations the original Bourne shell had, so they created their own shell for the BSD operating system. The C shell is so named because it has a syntax that looks a lot like the C programming language. The C shell has many enhancements over the Bourne shell because of its interactive use, including job control and command history. It also has a logout configuration file, which is something most Bourne shells (sh and its descendants) don't have. The C shell also supports a configuration file that gets read every time a new subshell that is not a login shell is started (the original Bourne shell does not support this).

The C shell is the opposite of the Bourne shell in that it is great for interactive use but absolutely terrible for shell programming. Some programmers insist on writing shell programs in the C shell, but because of its more cryptic and demanding syntax, this can be an exercise in frustration and futility.

Although the C shell is great for interactive use and has been very popular, it is somewhat dated, and better choices are available for an interactive shell.

> **NOTE**
>
> Modern versions of FreeBSD have replaced the original C shell with the tcsh shell. In fact, the C shell (csh) is often just a link to the tcsh shell. More on that shell later in this section.

The Korn Shell (ksh or pdksh)

This shell is my personal favorite. Not to be outdone by Berkeley, AT&T released the Korn shell in 1986. This shell was written by David Korn, and it was AT&T's answer to the C shell. The Korn shell is backward-compatible with the Bourne shell. Like the C shell, it supports job control, command history, command aliases, and a configuration file for subshells. The Korn shell goes even further, though, by supporting vi and Emacs-style history editing (the capability to recall a previous command and edit it before running it again). It also includes a number of very useful enhancements for shell programmers, such as extensibility with new commands and syntax compatibility with many other shells and command interpreters. The Korn shell has been very popular and is included with most commercial versions of Unix these days.

pdksh is a public domain version of the Korn shell. This is the version you can get for FreeBSD by installing it from the ports collection, as you'll learn in Chapter 14.

Users who are familiar with vi and Emacs will like the Korn shell, but users new to Unix will probably prefer the bash shell (discussed next) because vi and Emacs editing commands are not exactly intuitive.

The Bourne Again Shell (bash)

The Bourne Again shell is a Bourne-compatible shell developed by the Free Software Foundation (FSF). The bash shell is the default shell on virtually all Linux distributions. It is similar to the Korn shell but adds even more features, including built-in help, intuitive command-line editing and history editing that uses the arrow keys, extremely powerful history functions, and more environment variables than you can shake a stick at.

The only real problem with bash is that it is not standard software on most commercial Unix versions. Because of this, shell programs written specifically for bash can be less portable across different versions of Unix than programs written for the Bourne shell.

The tcsh Shell

The tcsh shell is an enhanced version of the C shell. (What does the *t* stand for? It refers to TENEX, an operating system for the DEC PDP-10, whose command-line behavior tcsh originally was intended to mimic.) It adds many new features to the C shell, including filename completion and command-line editing with intuitive editing controls like in bash (it uses the arrow keys). tcsh also has some nice features that even bash doesn't support, including the capability to watch your back for you by recognizing potentially dangerous commands and then asking whether you're sure you want to continue (for example, "Are you sure you want to delete ALL files?").

tcsh is a great shell for interactive use. In many ways, it is even better than bash. Unfortunately, it is still plagued by many of the problems of the C shell when it comes to shell programming. Although some of the problems have been fixed, you should still write your shell programs for a Bourne-style shell and avoid C shell programming like the plague.

Which Shell to Choose?

So, which shell should you choose? For most of this chapter, it doesn't really matter. Most of the standard FreeBSD commands work the same way under all shells. It is only when you want to start performing advanced tasks, such as changing shell variables, setting aliases, and shell programming, that the differences between the shells really become apparent.

If you don't plan to do any shell programming, pick Korn, bash, or tcsh as your shell. If you are interested in learning shell programming, pick Korn or bash because you won't have to unlearn anything when you start programming, and all the commands you learn for operating within the shell can be applied directly to programming within it.

Changing Your Shell

For most of this chapter, you'll use the bash shell because it is the easiest shell for new users to work with. To see what shell you are currently running, type the following command, where foo is your logon name and # is the command prompt:

```
# grep foo /etc/passwd
```

Don't worry if you don't know what this command line means. You'll understand it and far more before you are done with this chapter. The command returns a line that looks something like the following:

```
foo:*:1001:1001::Foo Bar:/home/foo:/usr/local/bin/ksh
```

The line on your screen will probably be different from this one. For now, all you need to worry about is the last field (the one that reads /usr/local/bin/ksh in the example). This is your default shell—in this case, the Korn shell. Your shell will probably have one of the following values:

- /bin/sh—The POSIX Bourne shell.

- /bin/csh—The C shell, which is now actually a hard link to the tcsh shell. Therefore, if your shell is /bin/csh, you are actually running the tcsh shell.

- /bin/tcsh—The tcsh shell.

- /usr/local/bin/ksh—The Korn shell.

- /usr/local/bin/bash—The bash shell.

To install bash, choose it from the Packages on the CD or build it from the ports, as described in Chapter 14. After it has been installed, log out and back in to register that bash is now a command that you can run.

To run the bash shell, simply type **bash** at the command prompt to change to the bash shell. In Chapter 11, "Customizing the Shell," you'll see how to permanently change your shell.

CAUTION

Unlike DOS, Windows, and VMS, Unix and FreeBSD *are* case sensitive. For example, the names Grep, grep, and greP are completely unrelated to each other as far as FreeBSD is concerned. This is a common source of errors for newcomers. If you are getting No such file or directory errors when you type commands in this chapter, make sure you are using the correct case.

Getting Help in the Shell

This chapter can't even begin to cover all the commands available from the shell; nor can it even cover all the options available for the commands that it does cover. Fortunately, FreeBSD includes an extensive set of online manuals that document each command and its various options. To access the manual page for a command, type **man** *commandname*. For example, to read the manual page for the man command itself, type **man man**.

You can use the spacebar, the arrow keys, and the Page Up/Page Down keys to review the contents of the manual page.

Searching for Manual Pages

Sometimes, you might know what you want to do, but you are not sure of the name of the command to use. In this case, you can use the -k option to the man command. Sometimes, you have to be fairly creative about what you search for in order for man -k to return the results you want. For example, suppose you want to find out about commands that can search text files for certain words or phrases, and you want to show each place in the text file where a certain word or phrase occurs. You would likely assume that such commands would have "search" in their names or their descriptions. First, you might try the man -k search command, as shown in Listing 7.1. The output of this command is a list of all the relevant entries in the whatis database, a dictionary of programs and their descriptions.

LISTING 7.1   Using man -k

```
# man -k search
apropos(1), whatis(1) - search the whatis database
bios(9), bios_sigsearch(9), bios32_SDlookup(9), bios32(9) - Interact
with PC BIO
S
bsearch(3)                - binary search of a sorted table
devclass_find(9)          - search for a devclass
device_find_child(9)      - search for a child of a device
lkbib(1)                  - search bibliographic databases
lookbib(1)                - search bibliographic databases
lsearch(3), lfind(3)      - linear searching routines
manpath(1)                - determine user's search path for man pages
res_query(3), res_search(3), res_mkquery(3), res_send(3), res_init(3),
dn_comp(3
), dn_expand(3) - resolver routines
tsearch(3), tfind(3), tdelete(3), twalk(3) - manipulate binary search
trees
Search::Dict(3), look(3) - search for key in dictionary file
bash$
```

Probably not what you had in mind. The results seem to be geared toward search routines for programmers using C. For your next attempt, you try searching for the keyword *pattern*, as shown in Listing 7.2, because you want a command that finds patterns in text files.

LISTING 7.2   Another Attempt with man -k

```
# man -k pattern
gawk(1) - pattern scanning and processing language
glob(3), globfree(3)      - generate pathnames matching a pattern
grep(1), egrep(1), fgrep(1), zgrep(1) - print lines matching a pattern
lptest(1)                 - generate lineprinter ripple pattern
menu_pattern(3)           - get and set a menu's pattern buffer
bash$
```

Now *that* looks more useful—especially the grep series of commands. These seem to be tools for searching for patterns within files, as you hoped. You could now type **man grep** to read the man page for grep, and you would find that indeed this command does what you need.

Command Summaries

At other times, you might know the name of a command but are not sure what it does (if you are poking around in /usr/bin or /usr/games, for example). You can use the -f option to man to get a short, one-line description of a command. For example, suppose you find the command pom in the /usr/games directory, and you want to know what it does:

```
# man -f pom
pom(6) - display the phase of the moon
bash$
```

The (6) at the end of the command name is the section of the manual that the command comes from.

Manual Sections

The online manuals are divided into nine sections, as detailed in Table 7.1.

TABLE 7.1   Manual Sections

Section	Description
1: User Commands	Information on user commands such as ls, rm, cp, and grep. This is the section you will probably use most often while working with and learning FreeBSD.
2: System Calls	Contains information on various APIs for FreeBSD. This section is primarily of interest to C programmers.
3: Subroutines	This section contains information on subroutines, also known as *library functions*. Once again, mostly of interest to C programmers.
4: Devices	More stuff for C programmers. Contains information on interfacing with device drivers in FreeBSD.
5: File Formats	Contains information on the formats of various system configuration files, such as the crontab files for the scheduling of regular jobs and the rc files for controlling system startup.
6: Games	The most important section of the manual. This section contains instructions for playing the various games and other amusements that come with FreeBSD.
7: Miscellaneous	If your topic doesn't fit anywhere else, it will be found here.
8: System Administration	Contains information on commands related to system administration, such as fsck, for checking filesystems.
9: Kernel Interfaces	More information for programmers. This section contains information on interfacing with the kernel in C.

7

Some commands have more then one entry. For example, the crontab entry has an entry in Section 1 for the crontab command and also an entry in Section 5 for the format of the crontab file. By default, you get the first entry that man comes to, which, in the case of crontab, means that you get the entry for Section 1. If you want to see the entry for Section 5, use man 5 crontab. If you want to specify only certain sections of the manuals when doing a search, use the -S option with a colon-separated list of section numbers.

Basic Shell File Manipulation

At the heart of working with any operating system is the ability to work with files—copying, moving, renaming, creating, and deleting them. Modern graphical operating systems have sophisticated visual metaphors for these tasks, such as dragging files in and out of folders. However, on the command line, such file operations require the use of specific commands.

Most of FreeBSD's file-manipulation tools are analogous to similar tools in MS-DOS. If you've worked with MS-DOS before, most of this chapter will come fairly easily to you. If you haven't worked with MS-DOS before, some background information is necessary.

How FreeBSD Stores Files

Like most other modern operating systems, FreeBSD stores files in a hierarchal tree structure. You can think of the FreeBSD filesystem as a system of filing cabinets in an office, and you can think of the hard disk as a group of filing cabinets. FreeBSD is organized into multiple directories. You can think of these directories as individual filing cabinets within the group of cabinets. Directories can contain files as well as other directories. These directories and files are analogous to the folders and papers in a filing cabinet. Windows and Macintosh systems both use this same type of filing system. The only real difference is that in Windows and Macintosh systems, you see a graphical representation of folders and files from a graphical file manager. From the FreeBSD command line, see a textual representation.

In Windows or DOS, you are usually placed at the top directory when you log in. This is not true with FreeBSD. When you log in to FreeBSD, you are placed in your home directory, which is located a few levels down from the top directory. You'll learn the details of directory structures in Chapter 8, "The FreeBSD Filesystem." For now, you need only be concerned with your home directory.

Each user on a Unix system (with certain exceptions) has his own home directory. Your home directory is like your own filing cabinet or your own private "virtual hard disk." Here, you can create and delete files, copy files, move files, and create and remove directories. Your home directory is your personal space on the FreeBSD system. Being able to manage the files and directories in your home directory is an important skill. The next few sections take a look at the various commands available to manage your files and directories.

Listing Directory Contents

Use the `ls` command to list the contents of the directory you are in. With no options, the `ls` command produces output similar to the following:

```
# ls
Mail      letter-to-boss      program      proposal-draft
fbu       mail                program.c
```

By itself, this output is not very useful because it tells us nothing about the contents of the files—or even whether they are files or directories. `ls` supports several options to modify its default behavior. One of the most useful is the `-F` option, which provides you with more information on the type of each file in the list. Here's an example:

```
# ls -F
Mail/     letter-to-boss      program*      proposal-draft
fbu@      mail/               program.c
```

Now you know a little bit more about the entries in the list. Here is what each symbol following the various files means:

Symbol	Description
/	The item is a subdirectory of the current directory.
*	The item is an executable binary file or script.
@	The item is a link to another location on the hard disk. This is analogous to shortcuts in Windows or to aliases in Mac OS.

Notice the executable file `program`. Unlike Windows, FreeBSD does not require a file to have a `.com`, `.exe`, or `.bat` extension to denote it as being executable. Whether a file is executable is a "permissions" bit that is stored in the file's i-node entry. You will almost never see an executable FreeBSD file with an `.exe` or `.com` extension.

This list does not include all the symbols. Type **man ls** and look at the `-F` option for a complete list.

Modern versions of the `ls` command also support the `-G` option, which tells `ls` to use different colors to denote different types of files. Not all terminals can display colors, though, and as a general rule, an xterm cannot display colors unless it is configured as a color xterm.

By default, `ls` does not display hidden files, also known as *dotfiles*, because they begin with a period. To display hidden files, use `ls` with the `-a` option:

```
# ls -a
.                .forward     .mailrc          ..profile       Mail
..               .hushlogin   .mysql_history   .project        fbu
.addressbook     .login       .rhosts          .login.conf     mail
.muttrc          .sh-history  .cshrc           .mail_aliases
```

Most of these hidden files are configuration files that store various types of information, such as profile information on how you want your shell set up, your address book for the mail program, and a list of the commands you have typed for the history functions of the shell. There are two main benefits to having these files hidden and begin with a period:

- They don't clutter up the directory during normal operation (because they are not shown).

- It's more difficult to accidentally delete important configuration files because dotfiles are not matched by shell wildcard operators when used by themselves.

If you want more detail about the files and directories in the list, use the -l option, as shown in Listing 7.3.

LISTING 7.3   Sample Output of ls -l

```
# ls -l
total 3
drwx------ 2 murban murban    512 Feb 15 16:04 Mail
lrwxr-xr-x 1 murban murban     15 Mar 20 06:55 fbu ->
/home/murban/documents/books/fbu
-rw-r--r-- 1 murban murban    782 Mar 15 09:21 letter-to-boss
drwx------ 2 murban murban    512 Mar 24 15:12 mail
-rwx------ 1 murban murban  15221 Feb 21 18:11 program
-rw-r--r-- 1 murban murban   1571 Feb 21 17:51 program.c
-rw-r--r-- 1 murban murban   2521 Feb 25 18:51 proposal-draft
```

Each entry has seven different fields of information. From left to right, they are as follows:

- **Permissions and other file attributes**—The first field in the ls -l listing tells you the permissions and attributes of the file. This field is covered in detail in the section titled "File Ownership," in Chapter 10, "Users, Groups, and Permissions." For now, simply be aware that the information in this field tells you who has read, write, and execute permissions on each file or directory.

- **Number of links**—This field contains the number of links that exist to the file. Every regular file contains at least one link, which is to itself, and every directory contains at least two links—one to itself and one to its parent.

- **Username of the file's owner**—This field and the next are covered in detail in Chapter 10. For now, be aware that these fields tell you who the owner of the file is and what group the file belongs to.

- **Name of the group the file belongs to**—See the previous field.

- **Size of the file**—This is the size of the file in bytes.

- **Date and time of the last modification of the file**—This is the time the file was last modified.

- **Name of the file**—This is the name of the file. Files that look like the following are links:

```
fbu -> /home/murban/documents/books/fbu
```

In this case, the entry `fbu` is actually a link to `/home/murban/documents/books/fbu`. I can use this link any time I want to reference the directory rather than having to type the entire pathname of the directory.

The `ls` command can take numerous different options at once. For example, combine `-l` (long listing), `-t` (sort by last-modified time), and `-r` (sort in reverse order) to get a listing of the files in the directory sorted so that you can easily tell which files have been modified most recently:

```
# ls -lrt /var/spool/mqueue/
total 180
-rw------- 1 root daemon 131913 Apr 19 00:18 dfg3J6hRq61454
-rw------- 1 root daemon   4436 Sep 25 18:16 dfg8Q1GmF96201
-rw------- 1 root daemon   2922 Sep 27 08:05 dfg8RF56F87464
-rw------- 1 root daemon    283 Sep 27 20:54 dfg8S3s6p77032
-rw------- 1 root daemon    336 Sep 28 07:09 dfg8SE98Z23923
-rw------- 1 root daemon    320 Sep 28 11:59 dfg8SIxUv57877
-rw------- 1 root daemon    344 Sep 29 07:37 dfg8TEbE365707
-rw------- 1 root daemon    360 Sep 29 10:22 dfg8THMim85609
-rw------- 1 root daemon    306 Sep 29 11:00 dfg8TI07g90919
-rw------- 1 root daemon    246 Sep 29 13:34 dfg8TKYvp14024
```

Moving Around the Filesystem

The `cd` command is used to change from one directory to another in the filesystem. You can give it directory names in several forms, as shown in Table 7.2.

TABLE 7.2   Usage of the cd Command

Command	Result
cd	Instantly takes you to your home directory from anywhere else.
cd /	Directories that begin with / are known as *absolute paths*. They always start at the root directory of the system (which is the very top directory). A / by itself takes you to the root directory.
cd /usr/local/bin	Takes you to the directory bin, located under the directory local, which is located under the directory usr, which is located under the root (top) directory.
cd bin	Takes you to the bin directory (if there is one) located directly under whatever directory you currently happen to be in. If there is no such directory, cd returns an error. Directory or filenames that do not begin with / are relative to the current directory you are in.
cd ../	The special "../" notation means the parent directory of the directory you are currently in. This takes you to the directory one level above where you are right now. The trailing slash is not required.
cd ../bin	Takes you to the directory bin, if one is located in the parent directory of the directory you are currently in.
cd ../../bin	Takes you to the directory bin, located two levels above the directory you are currently in.

Lost in the Filesystem?

Sometimes, it's easy to forget where you are in the filesystem hierarchy. The pwd command prints the current directory on your screen. Use it whenever you need to refresh your memory about where you are. (Yes, you can set your shell prompt to show you where you are. You'll learn how in Chapter 11.)

Copying Files and Directories

Use the cp command to copy files from one place to another. It takes as its arguments a list of files to copy, followed by where to copy the files. If you specify more then one file to copy or use a wildcard, the destination must be a directory. A few examples are shown in Table 7.3.

TABLE 7.3   Usage of the cp Command

Command	Result
cp file1 file2	Copies an existing file called file1 to a new file called file2.
cp file1/archive	Copies file1 to the directory archive, which is a subdirectory of the root directory.
cp file1 mystuff/newfile	Copies file1 to the directory mystuff in the current directory. If newfile is a subdirectory, file1 will be copied to the subdirectory newfile under mystuff. If newfile is not a subdirectory, file1 will be copied to the subdirectory mystuff and given the name newfile.
cp file1 file 2 /archive	Copies file1 and file2 to the directory archive, located under the root directory.

> **CAUTION**
>
> By default, the cp command simply overwrites the contents of an existing file if you accidentally copy a file to a filename that already exists. For example, cp file1 file2 overwrites file2 with the contents of file1 if file2 already exists. You can use the -i (interactive) option with cp to cause it to ask you before overwriting any existing files.

If you want to recursively copy a directory and everything under it, including subdirectories, to another location, use the -R option to cp. Here's an example:

```
# cp -R dir1 /dir2
```

This copies everything under dir1 to a new directory called dir2. If dir2 already exists, a new directory is created under dir2 called dir1, and the contents are placed there. If dir1 already exists in dir2, the contents of dir1 in the current directory are added to the dir1 directory under the dir2 directory. Any files in the directory that have the same name are overwritten by the copies, so be careful when using the -R option (or combine it with the -i option so that you are warned before overwriting anything). Also note that the newly copied files will have the same permissions as the originals, as long as you own them. The cp -R command ignores your umask, or the default permissions that are used to create new files.

> **CAUTION**
>
> Be careful that you do not do something like the following when using cp -R:
>
> ```
> # cp -R /* /old
> ```
>
> This command recursively copies everything in the root directory to a subdirectory called old, which is also in the root directory. Of course, this also means that the contents of old are copied into a subdirectory in old called "old." The result is a loop that copies the contents of old indefinitely. On a fast hard disk, this can quickly fill up the entire disk.

Moving and Renaming Files and Directories

The mv command can be used to move or rename files and directories. Some examples are shown in Table 7.4.

TABLE 7.4   Usage of the mv Command

Command	Result
mv file1 file2	Renames file1 to file2.
mv /dir1 /dir2	Renames dir1 to dir2. Generates an error message if dir2 already exists and is not empty.
mv file1 /dir2	Moves file1 to dir2, which is located under the root directory.
mv file1 /dir2/file2	If file2 is a directory, file1 is moved into the directory /dir2/file2. If file2 does not exist, file1 is moved into the /dir2 directory and renamed file2.

Deleting Files and Directories

To delete files, use the `rm` command. With no options, `rm` deletes the list of files it is given on its command line. It does not delete directories. If you want to delete a directory and everything under that directory, use the `-R` option with `rm`. Table 7.5 shows some examples of using the `rm` command.

TABLE 7.5   Usage of the `rm` Command

Command	Result
`rm file1`	Deletes `file1`
`rm file1 file2`	Deletes `file1` and `file2`
`rm -R dir1`	Deletes directory `dir1` and everything under it

Table 7.6 shows a list of some (but not all) of the other options supported by the `rm` command.

TABLE 7.6   Options for Use with the `rm` Command

Option	Result
`-f`	Causes `rm` to force the deletion without asking questions, even if the file is marked read-only. Use this option with care.
`-i`	Prompts before deleting each file. Useful when using `rm` with wildcards (more on that later) or with the `-R` option.
`-P`	Overwrites files three times with patterns of bytes before deleting. This is useful for deleting sensitive files because it reduces the chance that they can be recovered with the `-W` option.
`-W`	Attempts to undelete a file that was previously deleted with the `rm` command.

Removing Directories

Use the `rmdir` command to remove directories. `rmdir` will only remove a directory if it is empty. Used with the `-p` option, it removes a directory and its subdirectories, provided that the subdirectories are also empty. If you need to remove directories that have files in them, use the `rm  -R` command instead.

Creating Directories

The `mkdir` command is used to create a directory. If you don't specify a path on the command line, `mkdir` will assume that the directory should be created as a subdirectory of the current directory. For example, `# mkdir workdocs` will create a new directory called `workdocs` in whatever directory you are currently in.

The `touch` **Command**

The `touch` command serves two primary purposes: It can be used to create an empty file, and it can be used to modify the last access or last modification time of an existing file. Its basic format is

```
touch filename
```

where `filename` is the name of the file you wish to create or modify.

The `touch` command supports a few options that control how the last accessed or last modified times are set. See the man page for `touch` for full details.

Creating Links

As mentioned briefly, you can create links that point to other places in the filesystem. This is useful to avoid having to type long pathnames or having to navigate through many sublevels of folders from the GUI. You can think of links as being similar to shortcuts in Windows. There are a few important differences, though, which we will look at in the following sections. The two kinds of links are hard links and soft links. Let's look at hard links first.

Hard Links

A *hard link* is a directory entry that points to the same i-node (physical location on the hard disk) as another file. There is actually only one file, but two or more directory entries point to the same physical data on the hard disk.

By default, the `ln` command creates hard links. Here's an example:

```
# ln /home/foo/documents/books/fbsd/file1.txt ./file.txt
```

This creates an entry in the current directory called `file1.txt` that points to the same location on the hard disk as `/home/foo/documents/books/fbsd/file1.txt`. I can now access the same file by using either directory entry (presumably I would create a link like this so I only have to type `vi file1.txt` after I log in to edit this file rather than `vi documents/books/fbsd/file1.txt`). If I now use `ls -l` on this link, it will look something like the following:

```
-rw------- 2 foo bar 26896 Mar 25 19:18 file.txt
```

This looks like any other plain-old file, right? That's because it *is* a plain-old normal file, for all practical purposes. The only visual cue we have that this is a link is seeing the number 2 after the permissions. This indicates that two directory entries are pointing to this i-node (physical location) on the hard disk. Any changes I make to this file or its directory entry will affect the other directory entries that point to this same location. For example, if I change the permissions on this entry, the original directory entry in `/home/foo/documents/books/fbsd/file1.txt` will reflect the changes as well. The modification time here reflects the same modification time as the original directory entry. The size also reflects the size of the original directory entry.

If I delete the original directory entry in `/home/foo/documents/books/fbsd/file1.txt`, the directory entry will be removed, and the link count will be decremented by one to show the change. However, the file still exists because there is another link pointing to that same location on the hard disk (the link we created). The file will not actually be deleted until all its hard links have been removed, and the link count is decremented to zero.

Hard links have two important limitations:

- They cannot be used to link directories.

- They cannot cross filesystem boundaries.

If you need to link a directory or cross a filesystem boundary, you will have to use a soft link.

Soft Links

Soft links (also called *symbolic links* or *symlinks*) are virtually identical to shortcuts in Windows. Unlike hard links, a soft link is a separate file that has its own i-node on the hard disk. The soft link is simply a file that contains a pointer to another file. Use the `-s` option with `ln` to create a soft link. Here's an example:

```
# ln -s /home/foo/documents/books/fbsd/file1.txt file.txt
```

If you use `ls -l` on this file, it will look something like this:

```
lrwxr-xr-x 1 foo bar 31 Mar 25 19:56 file.txt ->
➥/home/foo/documents/books/fbsd/file1.txt
```

Notice the differences between this version and the hard link:

- The permissions do not indicate the permissions of the actual file. Also, you cannot change the attributes of a soft link (permissions, owner, or group). You must do this from the actual file.

- The link count is only one instead of two. This is because the soft link is an actual file that points to the other file. It is not simply a directory entry that points to a location on the hard disk (as a hard link is).

- The file size is lying to us. The size listed here is the size of the file containing the link—not the size of the actual file it points to.

- The file modification is also deceiving. It tells us the time the link was last modified, but it tells us nothing about the time the actual file the link points to was last modified.

- The filename tells us the name of the file that this file points to (after `->`).

Also, unlike with a hard link, if you delete the original file that a soft link points to, the file's data blocks are removed and the link becomes an orphan that no longer works. However, if you delete the link with rm, the original file remains untouched.

TIP

If are trying to access a file and you keep getting No such file or directory errors, and yet when you do an ls, the file is clearly there, you are probably trying to use a soft link that has become an orphan, meaning that its target (or parent) no longer exists. Use the -l option to ls and see whether the file is a soft link. If it is, check to see whether the file it points to actually exists. Note that deleting or even simply moving a file can cause its soft links to become orphans.

As a general rule of thumb, use hard links if you are pointing to a file located on the same filesystem as the one you are currently on. Hard links have the advantages of providing you with information about the actual files and of not becoming orphans if the original files are deleted or moved. However, if you need to link to a directory or link to a file that is located on a different filesystem, you must use soft links.

NOTE

Hard links also have one other advantage over soft links: They don't take up an i-node. This may not seem like a huge issue, but there's a fixed number of i-nodes available on the hard disk. It is possible to run out of i-nodes if you have a lot of very small files on the disk, even if you have a lot of space left on the hard disk. When you run out of i-nodes, no more files can be created until you have deleted some files and thus freed up some i-nodes.

Universal Options

Most (but not all) of the commands mentioned in this section support the options shown in Table 7.7.

TABLE 7.7   Universal Options for Most Shell Commands

Option	Result
-i	Runs in interactive mode, prompting you before taking action on each file if that action would cause damage to an existing file.
-v	Is verbose about what the command is doing. In other words, this option prints messages on the screen for each operation as the command performs it.
-f	Forces the action without asking, even if the file permissions prohibit the action (for example, this action could be used to delete a file without asking whether the file is set to read-only, assuming that you have write privileges in the directory where the file is located).

> **CAUTION**
>
> As you may have noticed, most Unix commands that deal with file and directory manipulation will pretty much do whatever you tell them to do without asking any questions, even if the action will destroy existing files. Unix doesn't hold your hand like Windows or DOS does. Unix assumes you know what you are doing when you tell it to do something. Because of this, if you aren't completely sure of what you are doing (for example, you aren't sure whether there might be existing files of the same name in a directory you are copying another directory to), it's often a good idea to use the -i option with many of these commands. This way, you will be prompted before the command does anything that will damage existing files.

Meta-characters and Wildcard Operators

All the previous commands also support meta-characters and wildcards. These allow you to match one or more unknown characters.

> **CAUTION**
>
> DOS users: Before you get any ideas of skipping this section because you think you know all about wildcards, remember that Unix and FreeBSD wildcards do *not* behave like DOS wildcards. Part of this is because the period is just another character in a filename as far as Unix is concerned. Unix gives no special treatment to the period like DOS does. This means that although del * would do virtually nothing in DOS, it will delete *every file* in the current directory in Unix! Be careful with Unix wildcards, especially if you are used to wildcards in DOS.

You can use three primary wildcard operators in FreeBSD. These wildcard operators are shown in Table 7.8.

TABLE 7.8   Wildcard Operators

Operator	Meaning
?	Matches any single unknown character. For example, file?.txt will match the files file1.txt, file2.txt, and fileA.txt. However, it will not match file10.txt or fileAB.txt.
*	Matches any number of unknown characters. For example, f* will match the files f, foo, file, file1.txt, file2.txt, fileA.txt, file10.txt, and fileAB.txt.
[]	Matches a range of characters. (This operator is explained in the following section because it requires more detail than can fit well in this table.)

Matching Ranges of Characters

You can match ranges of characters by enclosing them in brackets. For example, file[1-3] will match file1, file2, and file3, but not file4. This also works with characters: file[a-c] will match filea, fileb, and filec.

When dealing with ranges of characters, it is important to remember that the matching is based on the ASCII number value of the character. For example, file[A-b] will match fileA and fileb, but it will also match fileB, fileC, fileD, fileE, and so on—all the way up to fileZ. This is because uppercase letters come before lowercase letters in the ASCII chart. Therefore, any time you specify an uppercase letter as the starting point for the match and a lowercase letter as the ending point, all the uppercase letters between the one you specify and the letter *Z* will also be matched.

You can also match one of several characters simply by including them in a list. For example, file[1234]* will match any file beginning with file1, file2, file3, or file4, no matter what follows it. Notice that this example combines two wildcard operators, which is perfectly legal.

Finally, you can use the logical NOT operator with wildcards. For example, file[!1234]* will match all files that do *not* begin with file1, file2, file3, or file4.

Be extremely careful when using wildcards with commands such as rm because it is easy to make disastrous mistakes. For example, suppose you accidentally type rm note * when you meant to type rm note*. The shell interprets the space as an argument separator. Therefore, this simple typo of putting a space between note and the asterisk changes this command from "remove all files beginning with note" to "remove the file note and then remove *all* other files in the directory!" So, double- and triple-check your typing when using wildcards with commands such as rm. (Better yet, use the -i option to force rm to prompt you for each deletion.) Also, quadruple-check when using the -R (recursive) option, which can result in complete destruction of your system if used improperly.

One trick you can use when working with wildcards is to use the wildcard with the ls command first. This command simply gives you a list of all the files that will be affected, without actually doing anything.

Notes on Filenames

Although Unix will technically let you get away with using just about any character in a filename (although some can't simply be typed—they have to be entered explicitly), to save yourself from migraines, you should use only letters, digits, periods, dashes (-), and underscores (_) in filenames. You should not begin a filename with a dash because Unix interprets the dash as a special character that means an option is to follow. This makes it hard to do things with the files. It is all right to include spaces in files, but you will need to quote the filenames if you are going to do that to tell the shell to interpret the string as one argument, not two separate files. A common practice, and the one I recommend, is to use underscores in filenames instead of spaces. This makes them easy to read and also eliminates the need to quote filenames. Also, avoid using filenames with special characters.

CAUTION

One serious problem with filenames that contain spaces is that they can cause you to accidentally delete files that you did not intend to delete. For example, suppose you have three files. The first is named business, the second is named letter, and a third is named business letter. Suppose you want to delete the file business letter, but you forget to quote the filename when issuing the rm command. Remember that the shell interprets a space as an argument separator unless it is quoted. Therefore, forgetting the space when issuing this command will result in the files letter and business being deleted, but the file business letter will be left untouched. This is *not* what you intended to happen. This is another good argument for not using spaces in filenames.

Dealing with Funky Filenames

Most filenames in Unix are of a simple, predictable form: alphanumeric characters, upper- and lowercase, and no spaces. However, this is just a convention; Unix fully supports filenames that contain all kinds of special characters, including spaces, quotes, parentheses, and other odd symbols that you would normally only expect to see on Windows or Macintosh files, where command-line manipulation of filenames is unnecessary. The only character that is not allowed in Unix filenames is the forward slash (/). However, although most Unix programs will only create files with well-behaved names, files that originate on Windows or Macintosh computers might end up (via FTP or other methods) on your FreeBSD machine with spaces or other funky characters in them, and you will need to know how to deal with them.

For example, here is a directory listing that contains several files with funky names:

```
*               File\1.txt      file4.txt       file6.txt
File 1          file"3".txt     file5.txt
```

These filenames are for demonstration purposes only. Don't create filenames like this in practice.

The first one is the file *. How can you remove this file? If you are new to Unix, your first reaction might be simply to type rm *, which would remove a file named *, right? Well, it will certainly remove this file, but the shell interprets the asterisk as a wildcard character. Because of this, it will remove this file and also every other file in the directory! This is obviously not what you want to happen.

The shell provides an "escape" character for cases such as this one. The escape character is the backslash (\). It tells the shell that it should interpret the next character as a normal character instead of giving it special treatment. Therefore, in this case, the command `rm -i \*` would remove the offending file while leaving the other characters untouched.

The second one is the file named `File\1.txt`. In this case, the filename itself contains the escape character. Typing **rm File\1.txt** will result in `File1.txt: No such file or directory`. The solution here is to simply escape the escape character itself, like this:

```
rm -i File\\1.txt
```

Then we come to the file named `File 1`. The shell interprets spaces as argument separators, so `rm File 1` will not remove this file. Instead, this command will attempt to remove two files: one named `File` and the other named `1`. In order to get the shell to interpret the string as a single argument, you need to quote it. In this case, `rm -i "File 1"` will do the trick.

So what about `file"3".txt`? Once again, if you simply try `rm file"3".txt`, you will see `file3.txt: No such file or directory`. This is because the shell interprets `"` as a special character. Once again, you need to escape it with the backslash. The command `rm file\"3\".txt` will do the trick.

> **TIP**
>
> Notice that the `-i` option to `rm` is used in all the previous examples. This is a good habit to get into when trying to remove files with funky names. This way, you can be sure the command you are issuing will actually have the effect you intend it to have, and it won't delete some files you don't want deleted.

Where Did I Put That File Again?

It happens to all of us. Once in awhile we create files or save files and then we simply can't remember where we put them. For situations such as this, FreeBSD provides the `find` command, which has a somewhat nonstandard syntax. Here is an example of how to use it:

```
# find . -name "lostfile*"
```

This command will find all files that begin with the name `lostfile` that are in the current directory or any directory under the current directory. Note that a search done from the root directory will check every subdirectory on the entire system—even subdirectories located on other disks or across NFS mounts. This can take quite some time on large disks. There are various options to control how far into the directory hierarchy `find` will go, and whether it will traverse filesystems or only look on the current filesystem. You can also use find to search for files based on criteria other than name, such as owner, group, and size. See the man find page for full details on this command.

A related command, called locate, does not actually search for the file but instead searches a database list of files on the system. Because of the database feature, locate is many times faster than find. The drawback is that there could be files on the system that the locate database doesn't know about and won't find. Depending on the system, the locate database is usually updated once a day or sometimes once a week (you can control the frequency of the updates; see the locate man page for more details).

That about covers what you need to know to manipulate files from the command line. Although this part of the chapter didn't cover all the available commands, you now know about the ones you are likely to use on a regular basis. For more information on each of these commands and their options, see their respective man pages.

Text-Related Commands

One of the original design goals of Unix at AT&T was for the processing of text data. Unix and FreeBSD include a large number of commands for processing text data from the command line. This chapter doesn't cover every available text command, but you'll learn how to use the most useful ones.

Counting Lines, Words, and Characters

Use the wc command to count the number of lines, words, and characters in a text file. With no options, this command gives all three. For example, the following tells me that there are 1,160 lines, 7,823 words, and 51,584 characters currently in the text file that contains this chapter of the book:

```
# wc fbu8mcu
    1160    7823    51584 fbu8mcu.html
```

wc supports the -l option to only display the number of lines, the -w option to only display the number of words, and the -c option to only display the number of characters. These options can be combined to control what information wc displays.

Viewing Text Files...More or Less

Once two separate commands, the more command is now actually a hard link to the less command. Despite its name, the less command actually is more powerful than the more command.

You can use the less (or more) command to display text files on your screen, one screen at a time. In addition, you can search the file you are currently viewing for text, and you can scroll back and forth through the file by any number of lines you specify.

Table 7.9 shows some examples of commands that can be used in `less`.

TABLE 7.9   Commands Allowed Within the `less` Program

Command	Usage
`/pattern`	If you replace `pattern` with the pattern you want to search for, `less` will find the specified pattern in the file.
Space or `f`	Scrolls forward one screen. If you type a number before pressing the spacebar, `less` will scroll forward that number of lines.
`b`	Scrolls back one screen. If you type a number before typing b, `less` will scroll back that number of lines.
Up and down arrows	Moves up and down, respectively, one line at a time in the file.
`#` **g**	If you replace # with a number and then type **g**, `less` will move to that exact line in the file.
`#` `%`	If you replace # with a number between 0 and 100, `less` will move to a new location that represents that percentage of the file.
`q`	Quits the `less` program.

These are probably the most common options you will use with `less`. Many more options are available, however. The man page for `less` is nearly 2,000 lines long. See this page for more information on the other options and commands that `less` offers.

Viewing Only the Top or Bottom of a Text File

If you want to see only the first few lines or the last few lines of a file, you can use the `head` or `tail` command, respectively.

By default, `head` and `tail` show the first 10 and last 10 lines of the file, respectively. You can change the number of lines that will be displayed by using the `-n` option followed by a number.

For the `tail` command, you can use the `-f` option to have it continually update the display with new lines as they are appended to the end of a file. This can be useful for monitoring a log file and any new messages written to it.

Searching for Patterns

A hallmark of Unix is the ability to search rapidly through a collection of files for a particular bit of text—someone's name, a command you're trying to remember, a function in a program, or the name of a service in a log file. With standard Unix command-line tools, these kinds of searches can be executed with great efficiency.

You can use the `grep` series of commands to search for patterns in text files. Three different `grep` commands are available. There is plain-old `grep`, which simply searches for patterns and basic regular expressions; there is `egrep`, which can search for extended regular expressions (which employ a large suite of special wildcards to define variable patterns); and there is `fgrep`, which searches for fixed strings (strings that must be matched literally, without wildcards). Some earlier Unix manual pages also referred to `fgrep` as "fast grep" because it was supposed to be faster than regular `grep`. In reality, though, `fgrep` is almost always slower than regular `grep`. Most man pages these days no longer refer to `fgrep` as fast grep.

Suppose you want to search the file `textfile` for the pattern `cat`. In its simplest form, `grep` looks like this:

```
# grep cat textfile
```

This command searches through every line of the file `textfile` and prints each line where the pattern `cat` is matched. Note that the command matches a pattern and not a word. This means that in addition to cat, the words *catnip*, *catbird*, *catfish*, and *concatenate* would also be matched, because they all contain the string cat. If you only want to match the actual word *cat*, enclose the string in quotes and include spaces on each side, like this:

```
# grep " cat " textfile
```

Some common options to `grep` include `-i` to perform a case-insensitive search, `-c` to suppress the display of matching lines and print the number of times the match occurred instead, `-n` to display the line number of the line in front of each line where a match occurs, and `-v` to reverse the operation and print only lines that do not match the specified pattern.

The extended regular expression matching of `egrep` is beyond the scope of this chapter, but extended regular expressions will be covered in detail in Chapter 13, "Shell Programming."

Sorting Text in a File

Sometimes, you might want to sort the text in a file into a certain order. For example, you might want to perform an alphabetical sort or a numerical sort. You can use the `sort` command for this.

By default, this command sorts based on ASCII value, and it does not ignore leading whitespace. Some of the common options are shown in Table 7.10.

TABLE 7.10   Options for Use with the `sort` Command

Option	Result
-d	Sorts using "telephone book" sorting, which ignores anything other than letters, digits, and blanks when sorting.
-b	Ignores leading whitespace in lines when sorting.
-f	Folds lowercase letters into uppercase letters when sorting. This has the effect of creating a case-insensitive sort.
-n	Sorts according to the numeric value of a field.

TABLE 7.10   Continued

Option	Result
-t	Changes the field separator that sort uses to indicate the end of a field and the beginning of the next field. By default, sort uses whitespace to separate fields.
-u	If there are identical lines in the input to be sorted, this option displays only one of the lines in the sorted output.
-r	Reverses the output of the sort.
-o	Sends the results to an output file instead of to the screen. The name of the desired file should be supplied after -o. This option has the same basic effect as redirecting the output to a file (more on input/output redirection later in this chapter).

If given more than one file on its command line, sort will concatenate the two files. If you use the -m option when supplying multiple files, sort will work faster. However, for the -m option to work properly, each input file should already be individually sorted.

Replacing Strings Using tr

You can use the tr command to search a text file for each occurrence of a certain string and replace it with a new string. The basic form of the command is as follows:

```
# tr 'a-z' 'A-Z'
```

This command would replace all lowercase letters with uppercase letters. By default, tr gets its input from standard input (which is normally the keyboard) and sends its output to standard output (which is normally the screen). This is not very useful in most cases, so normally tr is used with input and output redirection. You will learn more about input and output redirection later, but here is the basic form of tr to make it receive input from a file and also direct output to a file:

```
# tr 'a-z' 'A-Z' < file1 > file2
```

This command will read file1, replace all lowercase letters in the file with capital letters, and store the new file in file2.

You can also use the -d option with tr. In this case, tr will simply go through the file and delete each occurrence of a specified character. For example, the following will delete each occurrence of either uppercase *A* or uppercase *B* from file1 and store the results in file2:

```
# tr -d 'AB' < file1 > file2
```

The tr command is extremely flexible. When used with the proper pipes, redirections, and options, it can address a great many text-manipulation tasks that users have all too frequently written Perl scripts for, not realizing they're reinventing the wheel.

7

Showing Only Certain Parts of Lines in Text Files

Sometimes, you might be interested in only a certain part of a line in a file—just the first half of each line, for instance—or you might want to divide up each line at commas or tab characters and print out only the third field of each. You can use the `cut` command to cut only certain fields or parts thereof from a file for display. For example, suppose you have a text file named `phone.txt` that contains the following simple address book:

```
Doe, John~105 Some Street~Anytown~NY~55555~123-555-1212
Doe, Jane~105 Some Street~Anytown~NY~55555~123-555-1212
James, Joe~251 Any Street~Sometown~CA~51111~321-555-1212
```

If you only want to see five characters of each line, you can use `cut -c1-5 phone.txt`, in which the argument to `-c` (`1-5`) specifies a list of character positions, which in this case is characters 1 through 5. This results in the following:

```
# cut -c1-5 phone.txt
Doe,
Doe,
James
```

A more useful application of `cut` is to cut only certain fields from a line with regular delimiters. The following command will return the first field from a set of lines delimited by tabs:

```
# cut -f1 phone.txt
```

By default, `cut` expects fields to be separated with tab characters. However, you can change the field separator to any character you want. In this case, our address book text file doesn't use tab characters as field separators—it uses tildes (~). We can specify which delimiter character we want to use with the `-d` option:

```
# cut -f1 -d'~' phone.txt
Doe, John
Doe, Jane
James, Joe
```

Here, we have told `cut` to display only the first field, and we also told it that fields are delimited by tildes (~). Because the first tilde comes after the name, the command lists only the name of the person and leaves out the rest of the information.

Similarly, you can get a listing of all the users on your system by using `cut` on the `/etc/passwd` file:

```
# cut -f1 -d':' /etc/passwd
frank
```

```
bob
alice
joe
simba
lee
```

Formatting Text with `fmt`

The `fmt` command formats text into nice 65-character lines (by default). This is most useful for preparing a text file to be sent through e-mail, but it can be used for other simple formatting tasks as well. Here's an example:

```
Until he extends his circle of compassion to include all living things, man
➥will not himself find peace.
-- Dr. Albert Schweitzer
```

The first line contains 105 characters, which is too long to display on one line of a character-based display (and even some graphical displays if the resolution is low). The result is that either the mail-reading program will break the line in an odd place (such as in the middle of a word) or the text will go off the right end of the screen, forcing the reader to scroll right to read the rest of it. (If you've ever gotten one of those e-mail messages that looks like it is just one long line, the mail program is not breaking lines when mail is written.)

The `fmt` command will save us. Its typical use is simple, as follows:

```
# fmt quote.txt
```

```
Until he extends his circle of compassion to include all living
things, man will not himself find peace.
-- Dr. Albert Schweitzer
```

This output could then either be redirected to a mail program or to a file that could then be mailed.

Here is an example that makes it easier to see the results of the `fmt` command:

```
Until he extends
his
circle of
compassion to
include all living
things
man
```

7

```
will not himself
find peace
```

```
-- Albert Schweitzer
```

It will look like this after being run through `fmt`:

```
Until he extends his circle of compassion to include all living
things man will not himself find peace
```

```
-- Dr. Albert Schweitzer
```

This section has presented some of the most useful commands for working with text. By combining these various commands, you can perform some rather sophisticated tasks, such as analyzing Web server logs for trends. Of course, these commands have their limits. When you run into them, you might want to look into `sed` and `awk` for text processing. Both `sed` and `awk` are beyond the scope of this chapter, but you should be aware that they exist on your FreeBSD system and can be used to handle some very sophisticated text-processing tasks.

So, how can you combine the commands we've used to do more useful things? That's where pipes and input/output redirection come in to play.

Pipes and Input/Output Redirection

One of the things that makes Unix so powerful is the fact that output from one command can be used as the input to another command, and output can be redirected to other places. You can get a listing of files or the output of a program, pipe it into `grep` to filter out irrelevant lines, and then send it through `fmt` to process it for easy reading—all on the same command line. These kinds of tasks are very frequently useful in system administration tasks such as log file processing and filesystem auditing. For example, `ls` would normally display the directory list to the screen, but it can easily have that output redirected to a file, like this:

```
# ls > filelist.txt
```

This will create a text file called `filelist.txt` that contains the directory list of the current directory. This is known as *output redirection*.

If the directory list is too long to fit on the screen, you can pipe its output to the `more` program, like this:

```
# ls | more
```

You may recall that the `more` command displays text sent into it one screen at a time. This will prevent the directory list from scrolling off the screen before you get a chance to read it.

What if I want to mail the Albert Schweitzer quote to someone? Rather then type the quote into an e-mail message, you can send the file that contains the quote as the input to the `mail` command. There are actually two ways you can do this, and both have the same effect. First, you can use the `cat` command, which would normally print the file to the screen and pipe the output to the `mail` program, like this:

```
# cat quote.txt | mail useraddress
```

The following command uses input redirection to accomplish the same thing:

```
# mail useraddress < quote,txt
```

In this case, we have told the `mail` command that instead of getting the message to send from the keyboard, it should get the message from the file `quote.txt`. Although both these commands accomplish the same thing, the second one is more efficient because it doesn't have to call the `cat` program. Instead, it lets the shell handle redirection.

You can do both input and output redirection in the same command. For example, the `tr` command we used previously tells `tr` to get its input from `file1` and send its output to `file2`:

```
# tr 'a-z' 'A-Z' < file1 > file2
```

> **TIP**
>
> If you ever get confused about whether to use < or >, remember that the arrow points in the direction the data is going.

You can combine multiple pipes into a single command:

```
# cut -f1 -d' ' access.log | sort | uniq -c | more
```

This is a quick-and-dirty way of extracting useful information from an NCSA-compliant Web server log file. Specifically, this information extracts field 1, which contains the network address of each hit, pipes it to `sort`, and then pipes the sorted output to `uniq -c`. This counts the number of occurrences of identical lines and then displays each unique line, preceded by the number of times that line was repeated, and then pipes the output to `more` so that you can read it without it scrolling off the screen. Specifically, this command tells me how many hits each network address generated on my Web server.

You can also combine pipes and input/output redirection:

```
# cut -f1 -d' ' /var/log/httpd-access.log | sort | uniq -c > hits.txt
```

This is the same as the first command, except it records the information in a file instead of displaying it on the screen.

The creative use of pipes and input/output redirection is where the power of FreeBSD is really unleashed. (You can make the previous command more useful using awk, but you will have to wait until Chapter 12 to learn how.)

Command Completion and History Editing

Now that you have seen some of the basic commands available at the command line, let's examine a few of the advanced features of the more modern shells.

If you're not sure whether bash (or any program) is installed on the system, you can easily figure it out by taking advantage of the built-in command-completion features of tcsh and other feature-rich shells. Type enough of the command name for it to be unique—the first two or three letters, just to see how this works—and then press Tab. If you've entered enough of the program name for it to be uniquely determinable, the rest of the command will complete itself.

If you haven't specified enough of the program name for the shell to figure out what you want, you will get a "bell" signal (which will beep at you or give you another kind of alert, depending on your terminal program). You can then get a listing of all possible completions to the command, either by pressing Tab again (in bash) or by using Ctrl+D (in tcsh):

```
# bas[Tab]
basename   bash       bashbug
```

CAUTION

Ctrl+D is also the keystroke for deleting the character to the right of the cursor as well as for logging out of a tcsh session (if entered on a blank line). So be careful!

Tab-completion also works on filenames:

```
# ls show[Tab]
showchars.cgi*     showfavepics.cgi* showprofile.cgi*   showuploads.cgi*
showcomments.cgi* showpopular.cgi*   showrequests.cgi*
```

History editing is also a fundamental feature of the advanced shells. As you enter commands, each one is held in a buffer for the duration of your current login session, up to a limit set in your shell configuration file (100 by default in tcsh). You can scroll up and down through the commands you've entered with the up and down arrow keys; then you can either press Enter to re-execute whatever command you've selected or edit the command with the other arrow keys to correct mistakes or alter the desired result.

Each command is also entered into a history file in your home directory: .history for tcsh and .bash_history for bash. This allows your command history to span even beyond your current login session, back into previous ones; however, although the history file is readable only by its owner, you might still consider it a security risk. After all, do you really want to have a file sitting around with a record of all the commands you've entered? If that's the case, the history file can safely be deleted without any detrimental effects other than commands from previous login sessions not being available in scroll-back. You can delete your history file by entering `rm ~/.history` or `rm ~/.bash_history`, depending on the shell.

PART III

Administering FreeBSD

IN THIS PART

CHAPTER **8**

The FreeBSD Filesystem

To understand how FreeBSD operates, it is essential to have a clear idea of how the system manages files as well as the critical differences between FreeBSD's method and those of other operating systems.

FreeBSD uses the BSD Fast Filesystem (FFS). It is a common misconception that modern BSD Unixes use UFS (*Universal* or *Unix Filesystem*, depending on who you ask). In fact, many of the tools discussed in this chapter (such as mount) refer to UFS as the default filesystem type. This isn't the case. FFS is colloquially called *UFS* by many, and you can do the same—as long as you remember that the "true" UFS was used only in very early BSD-style Unixes and has been replaced by FFS in FreeBSD.

FFS is the filesystem type commonly used in FreeBSD, OpenBSD, NetBSD, and others, including Mac OS X (whose foundation, called Darwin, is based on FreeBSD and the core BSD distribution). Linux typically uses Ext2FS, Windows NT uses NTFS, and Windows 95/98/Me use VFAT. This information will be useful to know later in this chapter when we discuss mounting filesystems from other operating systems.

> **NOTE**
>
> A fuller reference and discussion of the filesystem types used in the computing world can be found at http://www.penguin.cz/~mhi/fs/.

The FreeBSD Directory Structure

If you have used any Unix or Unix-like operating system, FreeBSD's directory structure will undoubtedly look familiar to you (see Figure 8.1).

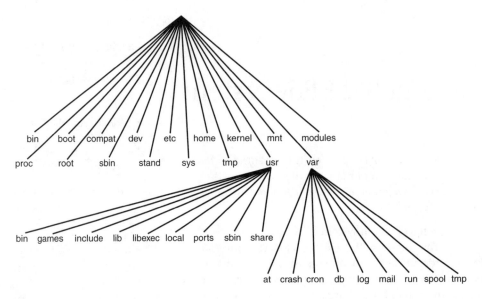

FIGURE 8.1   The FreeBSD filesystem, showing part of the hierarchical structure beginning at the root directory (/).

However, there are some key differences between the FreeBSD filesystem and the ones used by Linux, Solaris, and other Unixes. For users coming from a Windows or Macintosh background, the directory structure can be extremely cryptic. As with much in the Unix realm, the original reasons for such things as the quirky traditional naming scheme have been lost in the mists of time, but this chapter tries to shed a little light on the FreeBSD filesystem—enough, at least, to help you become familiar with its quirks so you can comfortably use the system.

Table 8.1 lists the key elements of the FreeBSD filesystem. If you issue an ls / command, you will see the top-level view of the FreeBSD filesystem, including the listed items and probably a few more which may vary depending on your specific installation. Directories are indicated with a following slash (/), symbolic links with an at (@) sign, and executables with an asterisk (*).

TABLE 8.1   Key Elements of the FreeBSD Filesystem

Directory	Purpose
bin/	Statically linked binaries are contained here. These can be used even when you're doing an emergency boot and don't have access to any dynamically linked programs or any filesystems other than /.
boot/	This directory contains the kernel, which is the master executable of the system. The kernel manages all the devices and handles networking, along with a host of other tasks. See Chapter 16, "Kernel Configuration," for more information. /boot also has configuration files and executables that are used during boot.

TABLE 8.1   Continued

Directory	Purpose
compat@	This is a symlink to directory structures which provide compatibility with other operating systems, such as Linux.
dev/	This is a special directory. Files in here are mostly devices, which are special file types that give programs an interface into any devices the kernel supports.
etc/	Long ago, this was merely a directory for random files that didn't fit elsewhere. It is now where most systemwide configuration files go, including your user (password) databases and startup scripts.
home@	This is possibly a plain directory or a symbolic link to /usr/home, depending on your installation. All regular users' home directories are contained here.
mnt/	An empty directory that's provided for your convenience as a mount point if you need to mount another disk.
modules/	Loadable kernel modules are stored here.
proc/	Contains the process filesystem (procfs) and is an interface to the process table. It's used for convenience by some programs but is not essential to the operation of the system (it can safely be unmounted).
root/	The root user's home directory. It's not in /home for security reasons so that it will be available during an emergency boot.
sbin/	Contains system binaries that are statically linked. These programs differ from the ones in /bin in that they generally alter the system's behavior, whereas the /bin programs are simply user tools.
stand/	Contains a set of hard-linked programs that provide a "mini-FreeBSD" environment during system installation and emergencies when running in standalone mode. The only program you will likely be interested in is sysinstall, which was covered in Chapter 2, "Installing FreeBSD."
sys@	A link to the kernel sources (if you installed them).
tmp/	Contains temporary files. Any user can write files into this directory.
usr/	The gateway to the rest of the system, including dynamically linked programs, user files, and programs you installed yourself. In upcoming chapters, you'll spend most of your time here.
var/	Contains variable files. These include runtime files used by programs, log files, spool directories, and other items that change with the normal operation of the system.

There are some important differences between the FreeBSD directory structure and that of similar operating systems, such as Linux. FreeBSD's structure is tightly controlled, and the clearest rule is that "anything installed by the administrator goes into /usr/local. Although other systems might allow user-installed programs the freedom to install files wherever they want, FreeBSD maintains strict structural guidelines in its ported programs and packages (see "Introduction to Packages," in Chapter 14, "Installing Additional Software"). Although a program might, by default, put its libraries in /var/lib and its configuration files into /etc, FreeBSD patches (modifies) the installation scripts so that the files would go into /usr/local/lib and /usr/local/etc, respectively. In fact, all configuration files for any software you might install will go into /usr/local/etc. If the program installs a startup script to be launched on boot, the script is placed in /usr/local/etc/rc.d. Anything in that directory is run at boot time, after the scripts in the analogous /etc/rc.d (the base system's startup scripts) are run.

The advantage of a structure this carefully controlled is that a FreeBSD system is relatively easy to maintain, and it's especially easy to re-create on a new machine (if you're upgrading to new hardware, for instance). Theoretically, you could copy the entire /usr/local directory tree from one machine to another, and everything would work the same on both machines. This is a risky proposition, however, and any such operation is likely to hit any number of unforeseen snags. Still, this kind of system portability is an ideal toward which FreeBSD strives.

An obvious disadvantage of the FFS controlled structure, though, is that if you're trying to port a program from Linux or Solaris to FreeBSD, you might experience some pain in fixing the expected paths. For instance, if you have programs written in Python on Linux, in which the Python interpreter is installed as /usr/bin/python, the programs will not run on FreeBSD because Python is not part of the base installation and are therefore installed as /usr/local/bin/python. You can easily fix this problem for one or two files, but migrating an installation with hundreds of such programs can quickly become painful. In the interest of cross-platform compatibility, it may turn out to be simplest to violate FreeBSD's structural guidelines by making the symbolic link /usr/bin/python to point to /usr/local/bin/python.

You can find a more detailed description of FreeBSD's filesystem by entering **man hier**.

Monitoring Filesystem Usage

The idea of mount points is an aspect of Unix-style operating systems that is quite foreign to Windows users. In Windows/DOS, each disk in your system is assigned a drive letter (such as C:), and each drive has its own independent filesystem. For example, a machine with two hard drives and a CD-ROM drive might have C:, D:, and E: drives that the user can switch between. In Unix, there is only one systemwide directory structure, and all disks in the system are mounted at different points in the structure. An appropriate analogy would be that a Windows system resembles an orchard, with a row of similar trees, whereas a Unix system is more like a single large tree, with smaller trees grafted onto its trunk and branches. All the grafted elements on the Unix "tree" form a single hierarchical structure (see Figure 8.2).

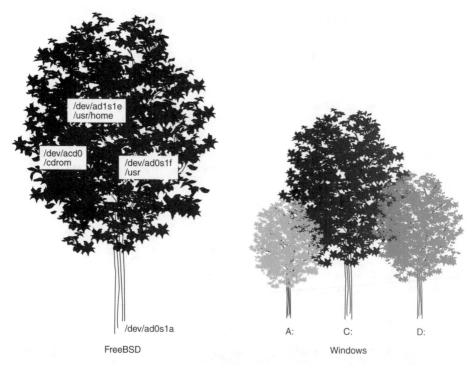

FIGURE 8.2   Diagrams of the FreeBSD (Unix) and Windows filesystem structures, using the tree analogy.

The advantage of this type of structure is that it's really easy to add more disk space to your system. To increase the pool of storage available to some part of the hierarchy, you just mount a new disk or partition there (as you'll learn later in this chapter). However, a corresponding disadvantage is that it's much harder in a filesystem like this to move the entire contents of a disk wholesale to another disk. In Windows or Mac OS, you can move your entire system to a new larger disk with a simple drag-and-drop operation, because each disk is a separate filesystem. This task is more cumbersome in FreeBSD. The hierarchical structure is better suited to a server machine with a long lifetime on the same hardware than to a desktop computer where the data often outlives the hardware.

The df (Disk Free) Command

Using the df (disk free) command is the most direct way of finding out the status of your system's disk usage. A df reading is part of every daily status check (more on this in Chapter 13, "Performance Monitoring, Process Control, and Job Automation," in the section "Using the Periodic Task Scheduler"), and it nicely encapsulates all the relevant information about your different filesystems and their respective device names.

When you enter the command `df`, you get output similar to this:

```
Filesystem  1K-blocks     Used   Avail Capacity  Mounted on
/dev/ad0s1a    128990    74314   44358    63%    /
/dev/ad0s1f    257998       44  237316     0%    /tmp
/dev/ad0s1g   8027686  1990866 5394606    27%    /usr
/dev/ad0s1e    257998    30586  227694    14%    /var
procfs              4        4       0   100%    /proc
```

Each disk slice or partition is regarded as a "filesystem" and can be mounted at any point in the directory structure. The previous output shows that this system has three slices on its main IDE disk (`/dev/ad0`) and that they are mounted at /, /tmp, /usr, and /var. This is the default setup for a FreeBSD installation. Note that the / filesystem has only about 128MB allocated to it and that /var and /tmp each have about 256MB; all the rest of the disk is allocated to /usr. This means that the system defaults expect very little to be placed into the directories other than /usr or /var, and still less to go into /var.

The numbers in the `df` output will not necessarily calculate out the way you might expect. The figures you see are subject to a number of delays and estimations due to caching and other issues. They are as accurate as possible in a system where this information must be gathered on an ongoing basis from many constantly changing sources.

> **CAUTION**
>
> Allocating a small /var slice can be dangerous because log files traditionally go into /var/log. Many administrators choose to move /var to /usr/var and create a /var symlink to point to it because log files can grow to be extremely large. We will discuss the pros and cons of different styles of partitioning in Chapter 18, "Understanding Hard Disks and Filesystems."

The du (Disk Usage) Command

Aside from the `df` command, you also need to have a more specific method for monitoring disk usage, especially if you're running a network server and you have a lot of users, any of whom might suddenly dump gigabytes of data into their home directories. For this, the tool of choice is du (disk usage). Here's an example:

```
# du -h -d 1 /home/
  23M    /home/bob
   9K    /home/fred
  31K    /home/alice
 1.5M    /home/tom
 664K    /home/pat
```

The du command tells you the size, recursively, of every directory below the one you're currently in (or the one you specify on the command line). You can specify the -d switch along with a number, which tells du to recurse only down to that depth (a necessity unless you want to be flooded with output); the -h switch (for "human readable") formats the sizes of the directories into kilobytes and megabytes. You can also use the -s option, which forces "summary" mode. In this mode, you only get a single line of output, listing the aggregate size of everything in the directory you specified. You can find more options to du, including controls for the way it handles symbolic links, in man du.

All this, of course, places the burden of watching the filesystems on you, the administrator. Wouldn't it be great if you could rely on the system to keep tabs on these things for you? Fortunately, you can—with quotas, which you'll learn about in "Setting and Enforcing User Filesystem Quotas," later in this chapter.

Mounting and Unmounting FreeBSD Filesystems

Now, we will discuss how the versatility of Unix-style filesystems can really shine. Let's say your system outgrows its single disk (/dev/ad0), and you install another disk as the primary slave so that it appears as /dev/ad1 (a SCSI disk would be available as /dev/da0, and so on). After you partition and label the disk (a procedure that is described in detail in Chapter 18), you have one or more new filesystems you can add to your system's directory structure at any point, like grafting a new branch onto the trunk of a tree.

The mount Command

Suppose, for instance, you have a system in which you have been adding new users left and right, and they keep uploading large files into their home directories. You notice (through the use of df and du) that the /usr partition is almost full, almost entirely because of /usr/home. What you want to do is add another pool of storage space and dedicate it to your users and their home directories.

You therefore buy a new 50GB disk and divide it into three partitions within the single FreeBSD slice; they are available as /dev/ad1s1e (100MB), /dev/ad1s1f (8GB), and /dev/ad1s1g (40GB). You make the third partition the largest because it's the one you want to make into the new home for your users; the other two partitions are chunks of space you want to add to other parts of the system. But for now, all you're interested in doing is turning /home into a new 40GB partition for nothing except users' home directories.

Right now, /home is most likely a symbolic link to /usr/home, so you will first want to use rm /home to get rid of the symlink. (The actual /usr/home directory that the symlink points to is not touched by this.) If /home in your system is not a symlink but is instead a plain directory, use something like mv /home /home.old to rename it for this process.

Now, create a mount point for the new filesystem. Mount points (or nodes) must be plain directories. They don't need to be empty, but after a device is mounted on a non-empty directory, whatever was originally located in that directory will no longer be accessible. To have the files and the mounted filesystems simultaneously accessible, union filesystems are needed, but this feature is not fully supported as of this writing. Therefore, to create the new mount point, issue mkdir /home.

You're now ready to mount the new filesystem. For standard FreeBSD filesystems, you do this with the mount command. Your 40GB partition is labeled /dev/ad1s1g, so give the following command:

```
# mount /dev/ad1s1g /home
```

If the command executes without any errors, you should be able to use the new filesystem immediately. Check df to see if it worked:

```
Filesystem  1K-blocks      Used    Avail Capacity  Mounted on
/dev/ad0s1a    128990     74314    44358    63%    /
/dev/ad0s1f    257998        44   237316     0%    /tmp
/dev/ad0s1g   8027686   1990866  5394606    27%    /usr
/dev/ad0s1e    257998     30586   227694    14%    /var
procfs              4         4        0   100%    /proc
/dev/ad1s1g  39245453         0 39245453     0%    /home
```

Looks like it's ready to go! You can now move the files from /usr/home (or /home.old, depending on where your home directories are in the interim) into the new /home filesystem, and your users will be free to upload to their hearts' content.

It isn't always this easy, however. Mounting filesystems is one of the areas of system administration that has the most potential pitfalls for the unwary. You may get the error message "Incorrect super block," for instance, or you may get an even less informative message, such as "Invalid argument." These messages usually stem from improperly specifying the name of the device on the mount command line; the naming conventions used by the FreeBSD labeling conventions can lead to serious confusion. A filesystem might be labeled as /dev/ad1s1e or /dev/ad1s1, depending on whether it is being addressed in "slice mode" or "dedicated mode," and certain device names with suffixes can be interchangeable with shorter names. This disk geometry esoterica is discussed thoroughly in Chapter 18.

The mount command has the -f option, which will force a mount operation. However, if a filesystem won't mount, it's usually for a good reason. It's a much better idea to find the cause for any error and fix it rather than use the -f option. Some of these causes might include an unformatted disk, a filesystem of an unrecognized type, or a "dirty" filesystem that was not shut down properly. In the latter case, the filesystem might have some inconsistencies that must be repaired using fsck (as you learn in "Checking and Repairing Filesystems with fsck," later in this chapter) before the filesystem can be mounted.

One other useful argument to note is the `options` field, in which you can specify any code words (flags) from a large list of code words, separated by commas. Most useful are the ones specifying whether the filesystem is read-only or read/write; it is read/write by default, but you can use the `-r` or `rdonly` option to make it read-only. See `man mount` for a full list of `mount` options.

The `umount` Command

There will also come the time when you have to "unmount" a filesystem; the command for this is `umount` (rather than "unmount"). To unmount the `/home` filesystem, issue the following command:

```
# umount /home
```

You can also use `umount /dev/ad1s1g` to accomplish the same result, or even `umount -a` to unmount everything except for the root filesystem.

Unmounting filesystems is a much simpler procedure than mounting them, with only one major complicating factor: For a filesystem to be unmounted, it cannot be in use. This means that to unmount filesystems such as `/usr` and `/var`, you will probably have to be in single-user mode. For the `/home` partition in the example in the previous section, any connected users will likely be in their home directories, so they will have to be kicked off the system before `/home` can be unmounted. This factor leads to the most common surprise most users find when first experimenting with `mount` and `umount`: *You can't be inside a filesystem you're trying to unmount!* If you are, you'll get a "Device busy" error message. To be safe, be in the habit of entering `cd /` before you attempt to unmount.

Like `mount`, `umount` has the `-f` option to force an unmount. But again, it's best to avoid using it unless absolutely necessary; filesystem operations have the potential to destabilize the system if done in a messy manner.

Mounting and Unmounting Filesystems from Other Operating Systems

The techniques you've just learned are all well and good for standard FreeBSD filesystems. But what if you need to mount a disk from a Linux box or from a Windows 98 or NT machine? You can do that. FreeBSD supports the filesystems listed in Table 8.2 in the `GENERIC` (default) kernel.

TABLE 8.2   Filesystems Supported in the `GENERIC` Kernel

Filesystem	Name
FFS	Berkeley Fast Filesystem
MFS	Memory Filesystem
NFS	Network Filesystem
MSDOSFS	MS-DOS Filesystem

8

TABLE 8.2   Continued

Filesystem	Name
CD9660	ISO 9660 (CD-ROM) Filesystem
PROCFS	Process Filesystem

There is also support for the filesystems shown in Table 8.3, but they need to be compiled into a custom kernel in order to work (see "Compiling and Installing the Custom Kernel," in Chapter 16).

TABLE 8.3   Additional Available Filesystems

Filesystem	Name
FDESC	File Descriptor Filesystem
KERNFS	Kernel Filesystem
NTFS	NT Filesystem
NULLFS	NULL Filesystem
NWFS	NetWare Filesystem
PORTAL	Portal Filesystem
SMBFS	SMB/CIFS Filesystem (Windows)
UMAPFS	UID Map Filesystem
UNION	Union Filesystem
CODA	CODA Filesystem
EXT2FS	Ext2 Filesystem (Linux)

Some of these latter filesystems are more stable than others. As you saw earlier, union filesystems are available as an option, but they are only partially in a working state (and can damage your system). Therefore, it is not recommended that you use them unless absolutely necessary. EXT2FS and NTFS support is also given a caveat about completeness and stability. Filesystems that are not built in to the GENERIC kernel, in general, are not included for a reason.

The ideal circumstance for a filesystem type that isn't part of the existing kernel is to be available as a kernel module in /modules, as many of the filesystems listed in the preceding tables are. If the filesystem is available as a kernel module, it will be automatically loaded when you try to mount the filesystem. At the time of this writing, these available modules include CODA, PORTAL, NWFS, NULL, NTFS, UNION, and some others that are already compiled into the GENERIC kernel and are provided in /modules for compatibility.

If you're mounting a filesystem (MSDOSFS, for example) that is supported in the default kernel, or if you decide to accept the risks and plunge ahead with mounting a filesystem that isn't initially built in, you'll find that FreeBSD does provide some handy tools for doing the actual mounting. The following tools are available in /sbin (although their names may vary according to your version of FreeBSD):

```
mount_cd9660*        mount_msdosfs*       mount_procfs*
mount_ext2fs*        mount_nfs*           mount_smbfs*
mount_fdesc*         mount_ntfs*          mount_std*
mount_kernfs*        mount_nullfs*        mount_umapfs*
mount_linprocfs*     mount_nwfs*          mount_unionfs*
mount_mfs*           mount_portalfs*
```

Each of these variations on mount corresponds to one of the supported filesystems and operates in the same way as mount. The idea is that these mount_* tools serve as an extension to the -t option to mount. The -t option recognizes only a couple internal filesystem types; if you give it an unrecognized argument, it will execute the corresponding tool from the previous list. For example, if you use mount -t nfs /mnt, the tool will actually execute mount_nfs /mnt. Knowing this, it is often easier simply to run the latter tool directly.

> **NOTE**
>
> As a further note on the stability and completeness issues regarding the not fully supported filesystem types, you should read the man mount_* pages. Each one gives a good account of what is deficient in that filesystem's support. For example, man mount_ntfs discusses the lack of full write capabilities and support for compressed files, and man mount_union warns about the feature's limited functionality and potential to damage data. Be informed!

Mounting a Windows/MS-DOS Filesystem

Let's first look at mounting a Windows 98 disk, which will be MSDOSFS for FreeBSD's purposes. The command you use for this operation is mount_msdos. This command can take some special options that we do not need to cover fully here. Examples are -W and -L, which control the locale-based character mapping for the long filenames associated with FAT32/VFAT filesystems. For this example, you can use the default settings, which assume that the ISO 8859-1 encoding will be used and that you will read and write to the filesystem as root:

```
# mount_msdosfs /dev/ad1s1 /mnt
```

For versions of FreeBSD prior to 5.0, use these settings:

```
# mount_msdos /dev/ad1s1 /mnt
```

Bear in mind that what DOS and Linux systems call *partitions* are called *slices* in FreeBSD, to avoid confusing them with traditional BSD partitions (which are subdivisions of slices). Therefore, because your Windows 98 filesystem on /dev/ad1s1 is effectively using a slice rather than a partition, you can address it simply by its slice number rather than specifying additional suffixes, as when mounting standard FreeBSD filesystems, where you use /dev/ad1s1g.

8

If you're using an extended DOS partition, you may get an "Invalid argument" error. If this happens, note that extended DOS partitions are numbered beginning with 5, so your device name will be /dev/ad1s5.

You can perform additional tricks when mounting an MS-DOS filesystem, such as mounting it as a non-root UID/GID, mounting it with a permissions mask for controlling users' access to the filesystem's contents, listing it with long filenames (instead of short filenames), and so forth. Refer to man mount_msdos for the full documentation on these options.

> **TIP**
>
> A Windows floppy disk contains filenames that can be in the standard MS-DOS "8.3" short format or in the Windows 95/98 long format, which is derived from metadata in the filesystem. If you mount a Windows floppy disk using mount_msdos, FreeBSD attempts to find any of these long filenames on the disk. If it finds any, it uses that format to list and interact with the files. However, if it finds none of these long filenames but does find short ones, it will use the short format. To force mount_msdos to use the long format, use the -1 option. The -s option forces the use of the short format.

Mounting a Linux Filesystem

Most Linux systems use EXT2FS. Because EXT2FS is not built in to the GENERIC kernel, this task involves an extra step. (EXT2FS support will eventually be available in a loadable kernel module, but not as of the time of this writing.) Chapter 16 discusses the steps involved in compiling and installing a custom kernel; the line you want to add to your custom kernel configuration file (preferably at the end of the block of options lines) is the following:

```
options    EXT2FS
```

After your system is up and running with the new kernel, you can use the following command:

```
# mount_ext2fs /dev/ad1s1 /mnt
```

Other than the kernel support, mount_ext2fs behaves almost identically to standard mount, so the surprises should be minimal.

> **Using fdisk to Gather Partition Information**
>
> You can determine what filesystem you're working with by using the fdisk command. Here's an example:
>
> ```
> # fdisk /dev/ad1
> ******* Working on device /dev/ad1 *******
> parameters extracted from in-core disklabel are:
> cylinders=1247 heads=255 sectors/track=63 (16065 blks/cyl)
> ```

```
Figures below won't work with BIOS for partitions not in cyl 1
parameters to be used for BIOS calculations are:
cylinders=1247 heads=255 sectors/track=63 (16065 blks/cyl)

Media sector size is 512
Warning: BIOS sector numbering starts with sector 1
Information from DOS bootblock is:
The data for partition 1 is:
sysid 131,(Linux filesystem)
    start 63, size 2104452 (1027 Meg), flag 0
        beg: cyl 0/ sector 1/ head 1;
        end: cyl 130/ sector 63/ head 254
The data for partition 2 is:
sysid 130,(Linux swap or Solaris x86)
    start 2104515, size 787185 (384 Meg), flag 0
        beg: cyl 131/ sector 1/ head 0;
        end: cyl 179/ sector 63/ head 254
The data for partition 3 is:
sysid 131,(Linux filesystem)
    start 2891700, size 17141355 (8369 Meg), flag 0
        beg: cyl 180/ sector 1/ head 0;
        end: cyl 1023/ sector 63/ head 254
The data for partition 4 is:
<UNUSED>
```

For each partition (or slice, as FreeBSD has it), there's a "sysid" number. 131 is an EXT2FS Linux filesystem, and 165 is FreeBSD. Everything else `fdisk` recognizes can be found in `/usr/src/sbin/i386/fdisk/fdisk.c`.

Mounting and Unmounting CD-ROM and Floppy-Based Filesystems

Now that you've had some experience mounting different foreign filesystems, it should be a snap moving on to CD-ROMs and floppy drives. CD-ROMs usually are mounted as CD9660, but floppies generally are either FFS (the FreeBSD standard) or MS-DOS.

Mounting CDs and Floppies

For CD-ROMs, the main trick is to determine the device name. IDE drives will be of the form `/dev/acd0c`, SCSI drives will be of the form `/dev/cd0c`, and miscellaneous types of nonstandard drives have other prefixes. As for the suffix, use "c" to indicate that you are addressing the entire disk in "dedicated" mode. Here's an example:

```
# mount_cd9660 /dev/acd0c /cdrom
```

TIP

See http://www.freebsd.org/doc/en_US.ISO8859-1/books/handbook/disks-naming.html for the current reference to disk names.

Mounting a floppy disk is also fairly straightforward. Use the device name /dev/fd0 (the zero specifies your first floppy drive). The kernel contains a confusing entry for fdc0, which refers to the actual ISA floppy disk controller device, but fd0 and fd1 are the device names for the drives that hang off the controller. Here's how to mount a Unix floppy disk:

```
# mount /dev/fd0 /floppy
```

An MS-DOS floppy can be mounted in a similar fashion:

```
# mount_msdosfs /dev/fd0 /floppy
```

Be careful: Floppy disks can be write protected and CD-ROMs are physically read-only, but FreeBSD does not check at mount time whether they are writable! If you mount a write-protected floppy without specifying the -r or rdonly option, you will get I/O errors whenever anything tries to write to the disk—and what happens as a result can vary with the stability of whatever program is doing the writing. Anything from a simple console error message to a complete hang of the system can happen. Therefore, if you must mount a write-protected floppy or CD-ROM from the command line, make sure you specify the -r or rdonly option to prevent programs from *trying* to write to it!

Unmounting CDs and Floppies

The other tricky thing about CD-ROMs and floppies is that because they are removable devices, there exists the potential to remove the disk while the system still thinks it is mounted. Windows (for comparison's sake) dynamically mounts and refreshes the devices whenever they are accessed for reading or writing, and Mac OS keeps track of such things by having disk mounting and physical insertion/ejection controlled entirely by software, which are therefore interdependent. FreeBSD (and other x86 Unixes) do not have the latter luxury or the former sophistication, so you must shoulder the burden of making sure the system's impression of its mounted disks is an accurate one.

Most CD-ROM drives lock when the operating system has a disk mounted, because they have soft-eject mechanisms. Such a drive will not respond when you press the eject button until you have unmounted the device. Floppies, however, can be ejected on a whim, and even CD-ROMs can be ejected through determination and the use of a paper clip. If a mounted device is ejected without being properly unmounted, and some program tries to read from or write to the device, the same kind of system destabilization can occur as described previously.

The bottom line is this: Always remember to use umount /cdrom or umount /floppy before ejecting a disk. Your system will thank you.

Other Removable Media

The field of removable media is becoming more complex every day, with USB and FireWire-based external media and rewritable CD and DVD drives coming into the market at an ever-increasing pace. Zip drives and their relatives have been around for some time. FreeBSD supports parallel port Zip drives as the vp0 device and USB Zip drives as the umass device. But dozens of new devices are in development, and each will offer its own complications in writability, removability, and mountability. Your understanding of mounting and unmounting CD-ROMS and floppies, however, can help prepare you for dealing with other removable media devices in FreeBSD.

Understanding the /etc/fstab File

You may be wondering whether there is a shortcut to all this mounting—a way to program recipes for all the mountable devices on a system—because chances are that all the flexibility offered by the mount tools will become less useful over the lifetime of a system. After you figure out the commands needed to mount your second IDE hard drive, your NFS volume from across the network, your MS-DOS floppy, and your SCSI CD-ROM, do you really have to remember those commands every time you want to mount them? No, there is indeed a better way: the /etc/fstab file.

Let's take a look at the file now, using cat /etc/fstab:

# Device	Mountpoint	FStype	Options	Dump	Pass#
/dev/ad0s1b	none	swap	sw	0	0
/dev/ad0s1a	/	ufs	rw	1	1
/dev/ad1s1f	/tmp	ufs	rw	2	2
/dev/ad0s1g	/var	ufs	rw	2	2
/dev/ad0s1e	/usr	ufs	rw	2	2
/dev/acd0c	/cdrom	cd9660	ro,noauto	0	0
/dev/fd0	/floppy	msdos	rw,noauto	0	0
proc	/proc	procfs	rw	0	0
/dev/ad1a1g	/home	ufs	rw	2	2

This file tells the system everything it needs to know about a given mount point: what device attaches to it, what filesystem type to expect, the mount options, and in what order it should perform filesystem checks when the system is booted. The fstab file is closely interrelated with the mount command. Used in conjunction, these two tools can make filesystem management a relative breeze.

> **NOTE**
>
> Don't worry about the Dump and Pass# columns; these refer to tools used in backup procedures and will be covered shortly.

The main function of the `fstab` file is to give the system a profile of mounted devices that can be activated simultaneously at boot time. With all your mount points specified in the `fstab` file, you can issue the command `mount -a` to mount them all (which is what happens during bootup). When the system goes through its filesystem checks during bootup, it runs `fsck -p` to "preen" the filesystems, making sure they are all marked "clean" (you'll learn more about the `fsck` actions in "Checking and Repairing Filesystems with `fsck`," later in this chapter). The system then runs `mount -a -t nonfs` to mount all but the NFS filesystems listed in `/etc/fstab`.

Beyond this function, though, is an even more convenient effect of this setup. After a mount point is specified in `/etc/fstab`, you no longer need to remember the `mount` command necessary to bring it online; now, the only thing you have to know is the name of the mount point:

```
# mount /home
```

This reads in all the necessary information from the `fstab` file. It knows that the device you want is `/dev/ad0s1g`, that it's a UFS (well, FFS) filesystem, and that you want it mounted read/write. Similarly, to mount a floppy disk, all you need to enter is the following:

```
# mount /floppy
```

Now, the process of mounting disks is starting to look almost user-friendly!

The `noauto` option on the `/cdrom` and `/floppy` entries tells `mount` that these filesystems should not be mounted at boot time. As with NFS resources, there is no guarantee that a CD-ROM or floppy disk will be available when the system boots, so the `noauto` option prevents `mount` from spending pointless time trying to mount a disk that isn't there. It doesn't prevent you from easily mounting it later, however. The previous command is all you need.

You can specify any of the `mount` options in the fourth column of the `fstab` file that are applicable to the filesystem in question. For instance, anything listed in `man mount` can be used, as well as anything in the filesystem's `man mount_*` page if it's a nonstandard filesystem type.

The fifth column in the `/etc/fstab` file contains the dump level numbers. These numbers are for the benefit of the `dump` command, which is a venerable Unix backup utility that operates based on levels. The dump level number tells `dump` at what level to trigger a backup for that filesystem when it is run. For example, filesystems with a dump level number of 1 are backed up only when the dump level is 1 or lower (a dump level of 0 indicates a full backup of all filesystems). Note that specifying 0 in `/etc/fstab` omits that filesystem from ever being dumped.

The sixth, or rightmost, column in /etc/fstab is the Pass# field. The pass number is a flag for `fsck`; numbers above 0 indicate the order in which the filesystems should be checked. The root filesystem has a pass number of 1, meaning that it is checked first; mounts with a pass number of 2 are checked next, in as parallel a manner as the hardware permits. A pass number of 0 means that the filesystem should not be checked; this is what you want for CD-ROMs, floppies, swap partitions, and other resources that can't become corrupted or it doesn't matter if they do become corrupted.

A fuller discussion of backup and restoration procedures can be found in Chapter 19, "FreeBSD Survival Guide," in which dump will be covered in more detail, along with other backup/mirroring methods such as CVSup.

Checking and Repairing Filesystems with `fsck`

The `fsck` (Filesystem Consistency Check) program is the equivalent of Microsoft ScanDisk and other disk utilities, at least as far as its role in the boot process and its interactive nature go. The `fsck` program runs at boot time just before mounting the filesystems out of /etc/fstab, to make sure that all the filesystems are "clean" and eligible for mounting. This is the "preen" mode that is called with the -p option. But `fsck` also exists to repair any inconsistencies that it finds and to clean filesystems that have not been marked "clean" by a proper shutdown method.

The most likely place you'll encounter `fsck` is at boot time, no matter what role it plays in your life. In the happiest circumstances, it runs invisibly just after all the devices have been identified, and all you see are a few lines like this:

```
/dev/ad0s1e:
103469 files, 858450 used, 9066025 free
(25777 frags, 1130031 blocks, 0.3% fragmentation)
```

> **NOTE**
>
> Don't worry about the "fragmentation" figure that `fsck` prints out. It looks pretty dire, but be aware that even fragmentation of 2 to 3 percent (which is the highest you'll likely see) is miniscule compared to the kind of fragmentation that occurs under Windows. It is not unusual to see a DOS/VFAT disk with 50 percent or more fragmentation; that is why defragmenting utilities sell so well in the desktop market. Unix filesystems, however, are designed with mechanisms to keep related sectors together on the fly, so fragmentation is kept to a minimum. You won't ever need to defragment a Unix hard drive. See "Blocks, Files, and Inodes," later in this chapter, for a closer look at the mechanics of data storage and fragmentation.

You may run into trouble, however, if the system has not been shut down cleanly—if power has failed or someone has hit the power switch without running shutdown first. Unix filesystems keep track of their structural information by writing that metadata to the disk in a synchronous manner, which may take multiple write cycles. If the system goes down while it's in the middle of the write sequence, the metadata becomes corrupted, and the filesystem cannot be used until it is made consistent again. This is what `fsck` is for.

If a filesystem is brought up in this "unclean" state, `fsck` drops into its investigative mode. It then walks through the filesystem block by block, examining the metadata and making sure it is consistent. This can take a very long time, depending on the size of the filesystem and the speed of the disk. When `fsck` finds an inconsistency that it cannot repair automatically while guaranteeing data integrity (see `man fsck` for details), `fsck` prompts you about whether you want to fix it. In most cases, you do. However, if you are being prompted, it's most likely that the inconsistency is so severe that you will have lost some data—usually the file or files being written at the time of the crash, which tends to mean that data loss is fairly small.

After `fsck` finishes running, you may be dropped to a # prompt. Type **boot** to continue booting or **reboot** to go through the entire boot process again. Going through a reboot might be a good idea, just to make sure it will come up cleanly without intervention. You don't want to lock the server in a cabinet and drive away, only to have it not come up the next time it crashes.

Boot time is not the only place for `fsck`, though. You also can run it from the command line at any time on mounted filesystems, although it's a bad idea to do so when the system is fully up and running! It's important that the filesystem in question not be changing while you're trying to give it a consistency check. If you have to run `fsck` on one of your system's main devices, take the precaution of dropping to single-user mode:

```
# shutdown +5
```

This command closes down multiuser mode five minutes after you issue the command. Naturally, everything from this point on has to be done at the physical console. You can't remotely administer the system in single-user mode!

> **TIP**
>
> You can also shut down the system immediately, rather than after a pause, with the `shutdown now` command.

With the system in this quiescent state, you can now use `fsck` to your heart's content. This may be necessary if during runtime you find a message in your `dmesg` output (part of the daily monitoring scripts that get sent to `root`) that says it found a bad inode or file descriptor, and you want to go directly to the root of the problem without rebooting. After you run `fsck` on one or all of your devices (use syntax such as `fsck -p /dev/ad1s1g`), you can then simply exit from the single-user shell (type **exit**) to bring up the rest of the multiuser system.

One case in which it is safe to use fsck while still in multiuser mode is when you're trying to mount a second disk with a noncritical or new filesystem that you're attempting to add. The fsck that runs at boot time will only check the filesystems that are listed in /etc/fstab. Rather than adding the new device to the fstab file and rebooting, you can simply try to mount the device. If the mount fails, telling you that you need to run fsck, do so with the syntax shown previously. Then try mounting the disk again. This mount can be done safely in multiuser mode because nobody will be writing to a device that hasn't been mounted!

> **NOTE**
>
> FreeBSD's fsck is similar in functionality to that of the fsck used on similar operating systems; however, it does lack one or two nice interface features, such as the progress bar on the Linux fsck. Be assured, though, that the core features behave almost exactly the same way.

Journaling Filesystems and Soft Updates

Many different solutions to the synchronous-write issue have been developed. You hear about journaling (or logging) filesystems, for example, which keeps a log of all metadata writes before they are executed. This log dramatically speeds up fsck because it no longer needs to comb the entire filesystem—it knows where the inconsistencies are and how to fix them.

FreeBSD does not include support for journaling filesystems; what it does have, though, is Soft Updates. Whereas journaling filesystems work by maintaining a log file of write actions, Soft Updates (which is built into the GENERIC, or default, kernel as of FreeBSD 4.5) provides a potentially superior technique. Soft Updates uses precalculated, ordered writes to eliminate the need for an external log; at the same time, Soft Updates protects the integrity of the metadata to provide filesystem consistency as good as or better than that offered by journaling. It has performance advantages over journaling as well; a filesystem can be brought up immediately at boot time, and the consistency checking is done afterward through the use of automated snapshots in a background task.

Soft Updates can be enabled on any or all of your filesystems. A toggle option in the Disk Label Editor (the utility you use to divide your disk into subpartitions and assign them to different mount points, as discussed in the section "Creating the Disk Labels," in Chapter 18) lets you set Soft Updates on whichever partitions, or filesystems, you wish. Soft Updates is particularly effective when used on filesystems that contain frequently changing data, such as /var and /usr.

In FreeBSD 5.0, a daemon called diskcheckd supports Soft Updates. Enabled by default, diskcheckd runs in the background and performs periodic filesystem integrity scans, thus dramatically reducing the reliance on fsck at boot time and the risks associated with abrupt shutdowns. The configuration file is /etc/diskcheckd.conf; see man diskcheckd

8

for instructions for and examples of using this file. Any errors that `diskcheckd` finds are logged through the `syslogd` service, described in the section "The System Logger (`syslogd`) and the `syslog.conf` File," in Chapter 10, "System Configuration and Startup Scripts." While `diskcheckd` is running, you can use `ps` to view its progress:

```
# ps -ax | grep diskcheckd
  251  ??  Ss     0:00.28 diskcheckd: ad0 13.26% (diskcheckd)
```

You can find more information on Soft Updates and comparisons between it and journaling filesystems at `http://www.mckusick.com/softdep/` and `http://www.ece.cmu.edu/~ganger/papers/CSE-TR-254-95/`.

Using `fsck` to Recover a Damaged Super Block

Chances are you'll never have to use this technique. However, according to Murphy's Law, the best way to ensure a precaution will be unnecessary is to take that precaution.

A common kind of filesystem corruption is a damaged super block—the block that contains the critical data for a device's filesystem. This corruption occurs when the system, for whatever reason, cannot read the device's super block, located on sectors 16 through 31 at the beginning of the device. The super block is such an indispensable part of a filesystem that FreeBSD keeps an alternate super block at the beginning of every cylinder group. This way, if your main super block becomes corrupted, dozens of backups throughout the device are available for you to use. The first alternate is always at block 32, and the rest are at regular intervals throughout the disk, but are much less easily predictable.

Let's say you try to mount a filesystem that you know is otherwise valid—for example, a removable hard disk that worked the last time you had it in the machine. Upon issuing the `mount` command, you get the following error:

```
/dev/ad1s1h on /mnt: Incorrect super block
```

As dire as the situation sounds, it is easily dealt with by using `fsck`:

```
#  fsck /dev/ad1s1h
** /dev/ad1s1h
BAD SUPER BLOCK: MAGIC NUMBER WRONG
LOOK FOR ALTERNATE SUPERBLOCKS? [yn] y
USING ALTERNATE SUPERBLOCK AT 32
** Last Mounted on /home2
** Phase 1 - Check Blocks and Sizes
** Phase 2 - Check Pathnames
** Phase 3 - Check Connectivity
** Phase 4 - Check Reference Counts
** Phase 5 - Check Cyl groups
148 files, 15660 used, 7038840 free (208 frags, 879829 blocks, 0.0%
```

```
fragmentation)
UPDATE STANDARD SUPERBLOCK? [yn] y
***** FILE SYSTEM WAS MODIFIED *****
```

FreeBSD makes dealing with a "damaged super block" error easy. Other platforms make you use command-line options to specify where the alternate super block is that you want to use, but the one at 32 is really the only one you know for sure is there. Using fsck in this manner, the first available alternate super block is copied over the primary one, and you should be able to mount the filesystem cleanly.

NOTE

You can determine where all the super blocks on the device are (if you're really interested) by using the newfs utility, with the -N parameter (which prints out the filesystem's stats without actually making any changes to the disk). Here's an example:

```
# newfs -N /dev/ad1s1h
Warning: 2672 sector(s) in last cylinder unallocated
/dev/ad1s1h: 14558608 sectors in 3555 cylinders of 1 tracks, 4096 sectors
 7108.7MB in 223 cyl groups (16 c/g, 32.00MB/g, 7936 i/g)
super-block backups (for fsck -b #) at:
 32, 65568, 131104, 196640, 262176, 327712, 393248, 458784, 524320, 589856,
 655392, 720928, 786464, 852000, 917536, 983072, 1048608, 1114144, 1179680,
 1245216, 1310752, 1376288, 1441824, 1507360, 1572896, 1638432, 1703968,
 1769504, 1835040, 1900576, 1966112, 2031648, 2097184, 2162720, 2228256,
 2293792, 2359328, 2424864, 2490400, 2555936, 2621472, 2687008, 2752544,
 2818080, 2883616, 2949152, 3014688, 3080224, 3145760, 3211296, 3276832,
 3342368, 3407904, 3473440, 3538976, 3604512, 3670048, 3735584, 3801120,
 3866656, 3932192, 3997728, 4063264, 4128800, 4194336, 4259872, 4325408,
 4390944, 4456480, 4522016, 4587552, 4653088, 4718624, 4784160, 4849696,
 4915232, 4980768, 5046304, 5111840, 5177376, 5242912, 5308448, 5373984,
 5439520, 5505056, 5570592, 5636128, 5701664, 5767200, 5832736, 5898272,
 5963808, 6029344, 6094880, 6160416, 6225952, 6291488, 6357024, 6422560,
 6488096, 6553632, 6619168, 6684704, 6750240, 6815776, 6881312, 6946848,
 7012384, 7077920, 7143456, 7208992, 7274528, 7340064, 7405600, 7471136,
 7536672, 7602208, 7667744, 7733280, 7798816, 7864352, 7929888, 7995424,
 8060960, 8126496, 8192032, 8257568, 8323104, 8388640, 8454176, 8519712,
 8585248, 8650784, 8716320, 8781856, 8847392, 8912928, 8978464, 9044000,
 9109536, 9175072, 9240608, 9306144, 9371680, 9437216, 9502752, 9568288,
 9633824, 9699360, 9764896, 9830432, 9895968, 9961504, 10027040, 10092576,
 10158112, 10223648, 10289184, 10354720, 10420256, 10485792, 10551328,
 10616864, 10682400, 10747936, 10813472, 10879008, 10944544, 11010080,
 11075616, 11141152, 11206688, 11272224, 11337760, 11403296, 11468832,
 11534368, 11599904, 11665440, 11730976, 11796512, 11862048, 11927584,
```

8

```
11993120, 12058656, 12124192, 12189728, 12255264, 12320800, 12386336,
12451872, 12517408, 12582944, 12648480, 12714016, 12779552, 12845088,
12910624, 12976160, 13041696, 13107232, 13172768, 13238304, 13303840,
13369376, 13434912, 13500448, 13565984, 13631520, 13697056, 13762592,
13828128, 13893664, 13959200, 14024736, 14090272, 14155808, 14221344,
14286880, 14352416, 14417952, 14483488, 14549024
```

As you can see, plenty of backups are available, but all except for the one at 32 are at odd locations. fsck does all the dirty work for you. However, it does let you specify a certain super block
if you don't want to let it pick one automatically. For example, fsck -b 2490400 /dev/ad1s1h is
the command to use the super block at sector 2490400.

Setting and Enforcing User Filesystem Quotas

Remember those users from earlier in the chapter who wouldn't stop uploading files and
forced you to buy a new disk to accommodate them? Suppose you decided that you didn't
want any single user to be able to use more than 20MB without special permission from
you. You can set this limit with quotas.

Quotas are not built into the GENERIC kernel. To enable them, you have to add the following line to your custom kernel configuration file (/usr/src/sys/i386/conf/CUSTOM, copied
from GENERIC, as discussed in Chapter 16):

```
options    QUOTA
```

See "Creating a Custom Kernel Configuration File," in Chapter 16 for information on
building a custom kernel. You also can make use of a couple switches in /etc/rc.conf to
enable support for quotas when the system is brought up. To use those switches, add these
lines:

```
enable_quotas="YES"
check_quotas="NO"
```

The first line turns on quota support globally. The second line tells the system to skip a
long, time-consuming consistency check (quotacheck -a) at boot time, which ensures that
the quota database is properly synchronized. If you want to enable this check, change the
second line to "YES" or remove the line altogether ("YES" is the default).

The last step is to turn quotas on (or off) per filesystem. This is done in /etc/fstab by
adding the userquota option and/or the groupquota option to the fourth field in each
filesystem on which you want to enforce quotas. Here's an example:

```
/dev/ad0s1f    /var    ufs    rw,userquota              2    2
/dev/ad0s1e    /usr    ufs    rw,gropquota              2    2
/dev/ad1s1g    /home   ufs    rw,userquota,groupquota   2    2
```

After making all these changes, reboot the system. Now that you're armed for battle, you're ready to start assigning quotas to users. You can assign them user by user (which is hardly practical on a high-load server) or you can set one user's quota and then use it as a prototype to apply the same settings to a range of UIDs. To set the quota for that first user, you'll need to use the built-in edquota utility, which lets you edit the attributes as a text file (much like chfn, which you learn about in Chapter 9, "Users, Groups, and Permissions"). The text editor that edquota uses is whatever is specified in your EDITOR environment variable. The default installation specifies vi, but you can choose a more user-friendly text editor, such as pico or ee, by using a command such as setenv EDITOR pico. Here's an example of setting a user's quota ("hard" and "soft" limits will be discussed later):

```
# edquota -u bob
Quotas for user test:
/usr: blocks in use: 65, limits (soft = 50, hard = 75)
      inodes in use: 7, limits (soft = 50, hard = 60)
/var: blocks in use: 0, limits (soft = 50, hard = 75)
      inodes in use: 0, limits (soft = 50, hard = 60)
```

After this user's quota has been set up, you can then clone the settings throughout your system, as follows:

```
# edquota -p bob 1001-9999
```

This will apply the same quota settings to the entire range of UIDs specified, even those that haven't been created yet!

Note the difference between blocks and inodes. Both limits will be enforced. The term *blocks* refers to the total space used (in 1KB units), and *inodes* can be understood to mean "files."

Blocks, Files, and Inodes

The different ways of looking at data on a disk can get fairly confusing, but the details are important for understanding how to read the output of tools such as df and fsck. Let's take a closer look at how storage is divided up and used.

The data block is a unit of data storage; the default size for a data block is 8,192 bytes. A data block is divided into eight fragments of 1,024 bytes each. A file that does not take up an entire data block is stored in fragments and shares that block with other files. This process is actually what fsck is referring to when it reports fragmentation.

However, if a file that is currently sharing a data block with another file grows to the point where it will no longer fit in the current data block, FreeBSD moves the entire file to a different data block. In the same circumstance, Windows simply fragments the file into an adjacent block. FreeBSD's approach ensures that for files smaller than 8,192 bytes, all the fragments for a single file are always stored in one data block. It also ensures that a file of any size is stored across as few different blocks as possible. You will never have a file that has fragments in more then one data block. This, of course, improves access time, and it prevents fragmentation from getting to the dizzy levels seen in consumer-grade operating systems.

A file really just provides a way of looking at an *inode*, which is the fundamental grouping of related data that we think of as a file. This model is necessary for a true multiuser operating system to be able to share files efficiently. Here is all the information that is contained in an inode:

- The type of file and the access modes

- The UID and GID of the owner

- The size of the file

- The time the file was last accessed and modified, and the inode changed

- The number of data blocks used by or allocated to the file

- The direct and indirect pointers to these data blocks

FreeBSD accesses data blocks with pointers located in the inodes. There are 12 direct pointers, which can access one block each. This allows direct access to a file up to 96KB. In addition, there are three levels of indirect pointers: single, double, and triple.

The *single* indirect pointer refers to a filesystem block that contains pointers to data blocks. The filesystem block contains 2,048 additional addresses of 8KB data blocks, thus allowing access to a file up to 16MB in size. The *double* indirect pointer refers to a filesystem block containing 2,048 addresses that each point to a filesystem block containing a single indirect pointer, and each one of those 2,048 single indirect pointers refers to a filesystem block containing 2,048 addresses of 8KB data blocks. This allows access to a file up to 32GB in size. Finally, the *triple* indirect pointer contains 2,048 addresses that each point to a filesystem block containing a double indirect pointer. Each of these double indirect pointers contains 2,048 addresses that each point to a single indirect pointer. And each of these single indirect pointers contains 2,048 addresses that point to a filesystem block that contains addresses for 2,048 8KB data blocks, thus allowing the triple indirect pointer to access a file that is 70TB (terabytes) in size! UFS limits the maximum file size to 1TB, though, so don't get too excited.

Soft and Hard Limits

A word or two about hard and soft limits—and the grace period—are in order here:

- A *hard limit* is strictly enforced. If a user's disk usage reaches the hard limit, the system will not permit any more space to be allocated to that user.

- A *soft limit* does not prevent the user from creating more files or using more space; instead, it triggers a timer for the *grace period*, which is seven days by default (but can be changed using `edquota -t`). After this grace period expires, the soft limit is enforced the same way as a hard limit. This allows users to use more than their allocated space (up to the hard limit) for brief periods of time. If the user's disk usage drops below the soft limit, the grace period is reset.

Once you have set these limits, you can view them as follows:

```
# quota bob
Disk quotas for user bob (uid 1015):
Filesystem  blocks   quota   limit   grace   files   quota   limit   grace
/home       1812     20000   40000           37      0       0
```

The `quota` command shows the quota information for the user specified as the final argument, or for the current user if that argument is omitted. If the user is over either of these limits, an asterisk (*) will appear after the number of blocks or files that are over the limit, and the "grace" column will report the amount of time left before the soft limit is enforced. Here's an example:

```
# quota bob
Disk quotas for user bob (uid 1015):
Filesystem  blocks   quota   limit   grace   files   quota   limit   grace
/home       28121*   20000   40000   6days   189     0       0
```

> **NOTE**
>
> To make sure that quotas are running properly, use the `mount` command with no arguments. The following is output from `mount` on a system in which the `/home` partition is using quotas:
>
> ```
> /dev/ad0s1a on / (ufs, local)
> /dev/ad0s1e on /usr (ufs, local)
> procfs on /proc (procfs, local)
> /dev/ad1s1g on /home (ufs, local, with quotas)
> ```
>
> If you don't see the `with quotas` flag, the filesystem was not properly mounted with quotas. Check `/etc/fstab`, `/etc/rc.conf`, and your kernel configuration and then try rebooting if everything looks correct.

Quotas can be turned off easily enough in one of three ways:

- Globally, by setting `enable_quotas="NO"` in `/etc/rc.conf`.
- Per filesystem, in `/etc/fstab`.

- Per user, by using `edquota` and setting the hard and soft limits to zero. Then, you could use `edquota -p` to propagate these settings throughout a range of UIDs, if you wish.

Filesystem management isn't an easy task, but once you have a firm grasp of the concepts, the versatility of Unix filesystems becomes readily apparent. Multiuser operating systems such as FreeBSD bring up all kinds of issues that don't exist on desktop systems, such as handling multiple filesystem types, monitoring usage, and enforcing quotas, but these features are what separates Unix from its less-capable contemporaries. We will continue this discussion into the area of formatting and labeling new disks in Chapter 18.

CHAPTER **9**

Users, Groups, and Permissions

U sers and file permissions are the concepts that form the central pillars of a Unix system. Administering a system that is designed for multiuser operation imposes many more restrictions than you experience when administering single-user desktop systems. These restrictions serve to prevent much of the uncontrollable complexity that occurs when every operation on a machine is, in effect, done by the "super-user" (as is the case in Windows and other such systems).

Traditional desktop operating systems, such as Windows 95/98/Me and classic Mac OS, give the impression of being multiuser operating systems; however, strictly speaking, they are not. What they use, instead, are simply profiles, or ways of presenting data according to each user's preferences. Any action the user wants to take on the local machine, such as reading files, installing programs, or shutting down the computer, is permitted because there is only one "user" with absolute control over the machine. Access to network resources is done on a "guest user" basis, without the user or the machine participating in any true authentication with a domain or its equivalent.

Windows NT and 2000, however, have taken successive steps toward becoming true multiuser operating systems like FreeBSD. Each user in the system has a separate account and a set of permissions that control access to files, printers, and other resources. Windows and FreeBSD both have the concept of a "root" user, or administrator, who has absolute power over the local machine. Both systems have groups and differ-ent layers of accessibility. In fact, Windows NT/2000 permis-sions have such complexity—inheritance upward, inheritance downward, domain users versus local users, and up to three

IN THIS CHAPTER

- Introduction to Users and Groups
- Why Use Groups?
- File Ownership
- File and Directory Permissions
- Access Control Lists (ACLs)
- Adding and Removing Users

accounts with administrative power—that even the most experienced user can get swamped. However, there is one crucial element of multiuser functionality that is native to Unix-like operating systems and foreign to desktop-bred ones: remote accessibility.

Most NT machine usage takes place at the console, with the user sitting in front of the actual computer. To do otherwise requires specialized "terminal server" software. In fact, an NT user cannot directly execute any processes on the server. Users access applications on the server through each application's client software, and the server application has to be running at all times. Windows 2000 includes "terminal server" software, which enables users to execute GUI applications on the server side, thus bringing Windows a step closer to Unix-style accessibility.

FreeBSD and similar operating systems thrive on remote accessibility. In fact, almost nothing on a Unix system takes place at the physical console but rather through terminal connections (such as Telnet or SSH), which provide a user with a command-line interface over the network. The upshot of this is that your FreeBSD machine will likely be accessed wholly from other locations and by many different users at once. On FreeBSD systems, therefore, user and group permissions play a much more important part in an administrator's life than they would on an NT system, in which the administrator can always predict which applications will be running.

> **CAUTION**
>
> SSH (Secure Shell) is an encrypted, or "scrambled," form of remote terminal connection. It provides all the functionality of Telnet (the traditional clear-text terminal application), with added security to prevent eavesdroppers from viewing terminal traffic such as your password. Today, SSH is preferred and encouraged in almost all circumstances, and Telnet should only be used when SSH is not an option. We will cover SSH in more detail in Chapter 29, "Network Security."

Introduction to Users and Groups

The users and permissions model that FreeBSD and most Unixes use is fairly simple and single layered. There are only two types of users: regular users and the super-user, or "root." Regular users are subject to user permissions that restrict what they can do; only the super-user is free of these restrictions. Other permissions models (such as that of Windows NT/2000) involve more complex layering, which is intended to facilitate certain system functions, such as authentication services and system-level processes. The simpler model of FreeBSD requires you to do a few more gymnastics when it comes to tasks such as setting up a Web server with proper permissions (covered in Chapter 25, "Configuring a Web Server"). However, the alternative—a more complex permissions system—more than likely means a less secure system, because there's so much more that can go wrong.

Everybody on a FreeBSD machine has limited permissions and a place to dwell (a home directory). To gain elevated status, you need to promote yourself to the super-user using the su command. This prompts you for the root password, which is the "key to the kingdom" and the most important piece of information you'll have to remember in maintaining your system. After you gain root access, you have as much freedom to create—or destroy—anything on the computer as you would on a single-user Windows machine.

CAUTION

Any time you are logged in as root, you should cultivate a heightened sense of security consciousness, a wariness that someone malicious could be eavesdropping to get the kind of access that you have. The root password should never be transmitted over the network in clear-text, and it should be changed every few months as a rule (see Chapter 29 for more details). You cannot be too careful with this vital piece of information.

In order to execute the su command, you need to be a member of an elite group called "wheel." Although FreeBSD has only regular users and the super-user, the wheel group effectively creates a special class of regular users—those who are allowed to *become* root (using su). You can use su and this special class to delegate administrative responsibility to others that you trust.

NOTE

FreeBSD differs slightly from most distributions of Linux and many other Unix-based operating systems in that it does not allow you to connect directly to the system (via Telnet or SSH) as root. This is a security measure. To gain root access, you must connect as a regular user—specifically, a user who is a member of the wheel group—and use the su command to promote yourself to super-user status. This means that the root password alone will not give anyone access to your system; that access also requires a user's password in the wheel group. A determined hacker will find ways to discover both of these passwords, but the added step is a significant deterrent.

If you really, *really* must turn off this feature, you can do so by editing the file /etc/ttys and adding the keyword secure in the field to the right of network in the first few entries in the Pseudo terminals section:

```
ttyp0   none              network     secure
ttyp1   none              network     secure
ttyp2   none              network     secure
```

This is, however, considered an extremely risky maneuver, and not one you should use if you can possibly stand simply logging in as yourself and using su.

Another kind of distinction among regular users is between actual login users (people who connect to the system) and automated users (such as bin, operator, daemon, nobody, and others). These user accounts exist in order to "own" certain system processes. It is important to realize that processes, just like files, are all owned by some user, and those processes are bound by that user's permissions when interacting with files and other processes.

Users never really access their files directly. Everything a user does to his or her files by giving commands is effectively done by executing processes, running with the user's assigned permissions. Those processes then operate on files and other processes, as illustrated in Figure 9.1. The processes owned by user1 can only operate on the files and processes owned by user1; permission would be denied if any of those processes tried to change any of user2's files or processes in any way. In the simplest setup, each user can change only those files and processes that he or she owns.

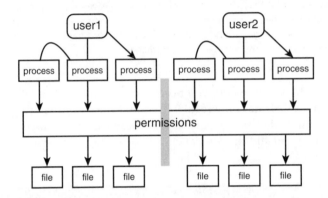

FIGURE 9.1   A user executes processes, which then operate on files and other processes.

Imagine what would happen if user1 were the super-user. That user's processes would have absolute power over any other user's files and processes. If one of user1's processes is, for instance, a program that reads a configuration file and then modifies items on the system specified in that file, imagine what would happen if an unauthorized user managed to modify the configuration file. The system would be vulnerable to complete annihilation. This is why most system processes, except those that are absolutely trusted, run under the ownership of one of the automated pseudo-users instead of running as root.

Why Use Groups?

Every user belongs to some primary group, generally a group of one that has the same name as the user. This can be changed as you see fit; for instance, you may decide to have all users belong to the "users" group as their primary group. However, having a different group for every user gives you more flexibility, as you'll see a little later. It's also a more secure model. More information on unique "personal" groups can be found in man adduser.

Each user can also belong to any other groups in the system, such as other users' "personal" groups, the wheel group, or any other group you create (by adding the user to the /etc/group file, as you'll see later). However, the super-user is the only one who can control who belongs to what groups.

We have discussed the purpose of the wheel group: to indicate a special clique of users who have the privileges to use su to gain root access. Other applications for groups are geared toward granting special privileges to certain users. In the most general case, a group exists to give one user the same permissions on a set of files or processes as another user— for example, to enable different engineers working on a software project to modify the source code files in a single central location, as illustrated in Figure 9.2. It wouldn't be very desirable if the two users had to share an account or tell each other their passwords; groups enable the two users to "own" the same group of files, with both users having the same permissions to operate on these files.

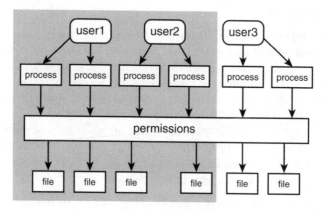

FIGURE 9.2   Two users in a group working on the same set of files. These files are still protected from other users.

File Ownership

This brings us to our file ownership model. All Unixes have the same kind of ownership structure: Every file and directory is owned by both a *user* and a *group*. However, as you will see in a moment, this does not necessarily mean that either the user or the members of the group have any particular permissions to access the file or directory.

Let's take a look at the permissions and ownership details of a set of files (see Listing 9.1). Here we use the -l option to ls to give a detailed listing, and we use the -a option to show all files, including "hidden" ones (those whose names begin with a dot).

LISTING 9.1   Set of Files Showing Ownership and Permissions

```
# ls -la /home/frank
total 3126
drwxr-xr-x   3 frank     users      512 May 12  2000 .
drwxr-xr-x  52 root      users     9216 Mar  7 13:37 ..
-rw-r--r--   1 bob       users   291090 Jan 23  2000 1.bmp
```

LISTING 9.1   Continued

```
-rw-rw-r--   1 bob      bob      2703 Dec 22  1998 contents.html
-rw-r--r--   1 frank    users    3657 Jan  9 14:11 file.txt
-rw-r--r--   1 bob      users   92195 Sep 11 21:31 1.uu
drwxr-xr-x   2 root     users     512 Jan  2 14:19 files
drwxr-xr-x  12 root     wheel    1024 Feb 18  1999 more-files
```

Seems pretty cryptic, but it really isn't. In this chapter, you learn how to decode strings such as drwxr-x, which define the *mode* of a file (the parameters that define who can access it and in what manner).

There are three modes of owner permissions on a file (or directory): *user*, *group*, and *others*. There are also three modes of access: *read*, *write*, and *execute*. These six pieces of information, referred to as *bits*, define the permissions on a file. For instance, a file's permissions configuration might tell us that the user who owns the file can read and write to it, but members of the group that owns the file can only read from it, and anybody else in the system can also only read from it. (This is the default file mode.) Similarly, a file's permission mode can tell us that anybody—user, group, or others—can read or execute the file (running it as a program) but that only the user and group owning it can write to it. Literally any combination is possible. We'll look in more detail at the permission modes and discuss how to set them a little later in this chapter.

For now, it is necessary to realize that a user can only read his or her own files if those files have their permissions set so that the user can read them. Similarly, the necessary permissions must be in place if members of the owner group are to read the files. Most of the time, this is the case; it is important to recognize, though, that ownership and permissions are not inextricably tied together.

> **NOTE**
>
> There is nothing inherent in the permissions of a file that gives its owner special power over it. The one exception—the one thing that really ties ownership and permissions together—is that a user can delete a file owned by another user, *if that file is in a directory owned by the first user*. The rm (remove) command will prompt for whether the user wants to override the file's ownership and permissions, and proceed, as shown here:
>
> ```
> # ls -l tempfile
> -rw-r--r--  1 root   users   0 Aug  7 21:44 tempfile
> # rm tempfile
> override rw-r--r--  root/users for tempfile? y
> ```

Using chown to Change File Ownership

As the super-user, you have the ability to change which users own any files on the system. Only the super-user can do this; regular users cannot "give" their files to another user or "take" them from another user. If they could, it would sort of defeat the purpose of users and file ownership!

The command to change ownership is chown (change owner):

```
# chown bob file.txt
```

This command changes the *user* owner—not the group owner—of the file file.txt to the user "bob." The file used to be owned by "frank," but now bob can read and write to the file, whereas frank can no longer write to it.

You can also use chown on a directory:

```
# chown bob /home/frank
```

This command, when used on a directory, operates on the "." entry you saw earlier in Listing 9.1. This entry is a pointer that refers to the current directory, whereas the ".." entry refers to the parent directory (this behavior is the same as in MS-DOS). Looking back at the permissions on the /home/frank directory, we can see that it is writable only by its user owner; therefore, bob is now the only one who can create and delete files in the directory. He can, however, modify any file that he owns in any directory. This interrelation between ownership and permissions will be made clearer in Table 9.1.

> **TIP**
>
> There's a useful option to chown that you as an administrator will need to know: -R. This makes chown act recursively, meaning that if you run it against a directory, the function will operate on the current directory, all files within the directory, and all files in all subdirectories below it. You'll need to use chown if you have to re-create an account, for example, and need to transfer ownership of all the user's files. Here's an example:
>
> ```
> # chown -R bob /home/frank
> ```

Using chgrp to Change File Group Ownership

Now that you know how to use chown, it's a simple matter to understand the use of chgrp, a very similar command. Its purpose is to change the group owner rather than the user owner of a file or directory, and it works exactly the same way:

```
# chgrp users contents.html
```

After this command is issued, the permissions for contents.html will look like this:

```
-rw-rw-r--   1 bob       users    2703 Dec 22  1998 contents.html
```

Because both the user and group owners have write permissions, we've just created a situation in which any member of the users group can write to the file just as bob can.

FreeBSD, by default, creates a new group for every user, so there will be a "bob" group as well as a "bob" user, and bob belongs to it as his primary group. By default, all the user's files are created with the user and group owners set to "bob." Now, if another user (for instance, frank) belongs to the bob group, he can write to those files. We now have a file-sharing mechanism in which both bob and frank have the same level of control over the files.

Using `chgrp` is really just another way of executing `chown`; if you prefer, you can use the following syntax:

```
# chown bob.users contents.html
```

This changes the ownership on `contents.html` to the "bob" user and the "users" group, whereas the following will change the group owner only:

```
# chown .users contents.html
```

Both `chown` and `chgrp` support the `-R` option, described previously, in the same way.

File and Directory Permissions

Refer to the files in Listing 9.1. It's now time to examine the permissions strings for these files and directories more carefully. The first thing you should notice is that for directories, the first bit in the string is a d. This is simply a flag and doesn't really indicate permissions that can be controlled; this flag is, however, a useful means of distinguishing between files and directories.

The rest of the bits in the string are fairly straightforward: three groups of three, showing respectively the read, write, and execute permissions for the user owner, the group owner, and others. For instance, `contents.html` is readable and writable by both the user and group owners and only readable by anyone else.

Note that a directory must have the "execute" bit set in order for its contents to be viewable; for directories, the x bit is construed as "search" rather than "execute."

The Relationship Between File and Directory Permissions

Table 9.1 shows the relationship between a user, a group to which the user belongs, and the permissions that the directory offers to the user and group, depending on its mode.

TABLE 9.1   Capabilities Granted by the Various Types of File Permissions

	Directory Writable by User	Directory Writable by Group	Directory Writable by Other
Create file	Yes	Yes	No
Delete file owned/writable by user	Yes	Yes	No
Delete file owned/writable by group	Yes	Yes	No
Delete file owned/writable by other	Yes	Yes	No
Rename file owned/writable by user	Yes	Yes	No
Rename file owned/writable by group	Yes	Yes	No
Rename file owned/writable by other	Yes	Yes	No
Modify file owned/writable by user	Yes	Yes	Yes
Modify file owned/writable by group	Yes	Yes	Yes
Modify file owned/writable by other	No	No	No

Any time you try to delete (rm) a file for which you do not have write permissions, you'll see a prompt similar to the following:

```
# rm file.txt
override rw-r--r--  bob/users for 1.uu? y
```

Note that you still might not have permission to delete the file! The override prompt appears any time you try to delete a file that isn't yours, regardless of whether you'll be successful if you type **y**. You can suppress the override prompt with rm -f.

A file that can be deleted can be renamed because you use the mv (move) command to rename a file in FreeBSD, and mv operates by copying the file and then deleting it. A file that can be read can be copied.

Beyond the standard permissions that apply to the user, group, and others, a few additional file modes have special meanings. You'll learn about these modes in the following sections, which discuss mechanisms for changing file permissions.

Using chmod to Change File and Directory Permissions

Now that you know how to read permissions on a file or directory, it's time to learn how to set them. The command for setting permissions is chmod (change mode). A file's permissions set is often referred to as its *mode*.

The chmod command can operate in two ways—numerically or symbolically—depending on your preference.

Changing Modes Numerically

The most direct way to change permissions is by setting a three-digit, octal (base-8) number that uniquely specifies the permissions for each type of ownership. Each digit refers to a certain ownership mode that controls the permissions corresponding to the user, group, and others, respectively (you'll learn about a fourth digit later in this section). A mode digit is constructed by adding together the numbers corresponding to the permission bits you want to grant. The available bits are shown in Table 9.2.

TABLE 9.2   Permissions Mode Bits and Their Meanings

Bit	Meaning
0	No permissions
1	Execute (for directories, search)
2	Write
4	Read

Therefore, you can specify a mode of "read and write" with 6, a mode of "read and execute" with 5, or a mode of "read, write, and execute" with 7.

Combine these digits into a three-digit number, and you've got a numeric way of specifying the standard permissions for a file. Table 9.3 shows a few examples.

TABLE 9.3   Some Complete Numeric Permissions Modes

Mode	Meaning
755	Read/write/execute by user; read/execute by group and others
644	Read/write by user; read-only by group and others
600	Read/write by user; no access for group and others

You can then apply the permissions to a file or directory, like so:

```
# chmod 755 testscript.sh
```

But that's only three of the four digits mentioned earlier. The fourth, "most significant" (leftmost) digit controls some "extra" features that address specific behaviors of files and directories under special circumstances. Here are the bits that make up this fourth digit and what they do:

- 0—Indicates normal permissions.

- 1—The sticky bit. This can only be set (with any effect) on directories. Within a directory with this bit set, a regular user can only delete or rename files if he owns them *and* if he has write permissions for the directory. This does not apply to executable files.

- 2—Set group ID (setgid). If this bit is set on an executable file, it will be executed with the effective group permissions of the file's group owner rather than those of the user executing it. A file can only be made setgid by the super-user.

- 4—Set user ID (setuid). If this bit is set on an executable file, it will be executed with the effective user permissions of the file's user owner rather than those of the user executing it. A file can only be made setuid by the super-user.

This fourth digit is the highest-value digit (in other words, the leftmost one), so in the earlier example where we showed what the permissions of 755 mean, we could have used the equivalent value 0755. We use the same method to construct the value for that digit as we do for the other digits, so the value 3755 would create a directory with the sticky bit and the setgid bit set, in addition to the regular 755 permissions.

Changing Modes Symbolically

As clever as the octal numeric system is, it's helpful to have a method for setting modes that's easier to remember. Fortunately, we have a symbolic method for doing just that.

Instead of giving chmod a number, you can give it between one and three flags in a single string. This string can be formatted in a number of ways, but we'll briefly cover the most common usages here.

> **NOTE**
>
> See man chmod for complete coverage of the flexible syntax of chmod and its symbolic modes.

Table 9.4 shows some examples of symbolic modes. Each is made up of a string of characters. The first character specifies the ownership mode(s), the second character indicates the modification you're making (+, -, or =), and the third is the permission bit(s).

TABLE 9.4   Symbolic Permissions Modes

Mode String	Meaning
go+w	Adds "write" permissions to the group owner and others
+x	Adds "execute" permissions for everyone
o-r	Removes "read" permissions for others
ugo=rw	Sets "read" and "write" permissions for everyone
a=rw	Same as ugo=rw
+t	Adds the sticky bit (super-user only)
+s	Adds both the setuid and setgid bits (super-user only)

To set the file file.txt so that it is "group writable," use the following command:

```
# chmod g+w file.txt
```

This symbolic method lends itself more readily to memory than the numeric method, and it will probably be a much easier way for you to perform most of your typical chmod operations.

> **TIP**
>
> The -R option works on chmod, too, the same as with chown and chgrp.

Access Control Lists (ACLs)

The Access Control List (ACL) is a new addition to FreeBSD 5.0 that gives you tighter control over who can and cannot access files and directories. Instead of just allowing or denying access based on owner, group, and everyone else, you can now grant access to individual users and individual groups. You can also set a maximum permission mask for the users and groups that are granted access through an ACL that will override the actual permissions given by the ACL.

For an ACL to work, UFS Extensions must be compiled into the kernel. The next section explains the options that must be added.

Configuring the Kernel to Support ACL

At the time of this writing, it is not known for sure whether UFS Extensions will be enabled in the default kernel for the release of version 5.0. If they are enabled, you do not need to rebuild the kernel. If they are not, you will need to add the UFS Extension options to the kernel configuration file and then rebuild the kernel.

To see whether your kernel has UFS Extensions enabled, look for the following lines in your kernel configuration file. Unless you have already built a custom kernel, your kernel configuration file will be /usr/src/sys/i386/conf/GENERIC on an Intel x86-based system and /usr/src/sys/alpha/conf/GENERIC on an Alpha-based system. The following lines should be present in order for an ACL to work:

```
options      UFS_EXTATTR
options      UFS_EXTTR_AUTOSTART
options      UFS_ACL
```

If these options are already present in your kernel configuration file, you don't need to do anything. If they are not present, you will need to add these options and then build a new kernel. See Chapter 16, "Kernel Configuration," for full details on how to configure, build, and install a new kernel.

> **TIP**
>
> Further documentation on the kernel modifications necessary for ACLs can be found in the source tree, in the README.* files in /sys/ufs/ufs.

After you have installed the new kernel and rebooted, you will need to configure the filesystems you want to use the ACL with.

Configuring Filesystems to Use ACLs

The `extattrctl` command is used to control the extended attributes on filesystems. You must use it on each filesystem you want to use an ACL with. For example, to enable an ACL on the filesystem mounted as `/usr`, follow this procedure:

> **CAUTION**
>
> The files created by the commands in the ACL-enabling process can be extremely large, possibly taking up several gigabytes of disk space on large filesystems. Make sure you have plenty of free disk space before running the commands.

1. As the root user, create the directories `/usr/.attribute` and `/usr/.attribute/system`:

   ```
   # mkdir /usr/.attribute /usr/.attribute/system
   ```

2. Change to the newly created `/usr/.attribute/system` directory (cd `/usr/.attribute/system`) and then run the `extattrctl` command to initialize the ACL attributes on the filesystem:

   ```
   # extattrctl initattr -p /usr 388 posix1e.acl_access
   ```

   On large filesystems, this command can take several minutes to complete, so be patient as the command generates the backing files needed to support the ACL.

3. When the first command has finished executing, run the `extattrctl` command one more time with a different filename as the argument:

   ```
   # extattrctl initattr -p /usr 388 posix1e.acl_default
   ```

   Once again, on a large filesystem, this command can take several minutes to complete, so be patient.

4. Reboot the system or remount the filesystems in question for the changes to take effect. After you have done so, the ACLs for the filesystem will be enabled.

Getting Information About Current ACL Settings

Use the `getfacl` command to obtain information about existing ACL settings on files or directories. For example, on a newly created file named `acltest.txt` with no ACL set and with default 644 permissions, issuing `getfacl acltest.txt` will return the following:

```
#file:acltest.txt
#owner:0
#group:0
user::rw-
group::r--
other::---
```

The first line simply shows the name of the file. The next two lines show the UID and GID, respectively, of the owner and group the file belongs to (in this case, the file is owned by root). The final three lines show the current file permissions on the file. Notice that "other" does not have any permissions on this file.

Setting the Maximum Permissions Mask

The *maximum permissions mask* controls the maximum permissions that will be given to any user or group added to the ACL list. Note that the mask applies only to users and groups that are given access to the file or directory with an ACL entry; the mask doesn't affect the owner's permissions. It also does not affect the permissions that the default group has, nor does it affect the permissions of the rest of the world. For anyone not listed in an ACL entry, the standard file access permissions apply.

The `setfacl` command is used to add, modify, or delete entries from the ACL list. The syntax is

```
# setfacl action permissions filename
```

where `action` is the action that should be performed (adding an entry, modifying an entry, deleting an entry, and so on), `permissions` is the ACL permissions that should be set, and `filename` is, of course, the name of the file or directory that the ACL should be applied to. The following example adds an ACL maximum permissions mask of read to the file `acltest.txt`:

```
setfacl -m m::r acltest.txt
getfacl acltest.txt
#file:acltest.txt
#owner:0
#group:0
user::rw-
group::r--
mask::r--
other::---
```

In the `setfacl` command, the `-m` option means that you want to add or modify the ACL entry. The `m::` specifies that you want to set a mask, and the `r` simply means "read." If you want to also set the mask to allow write permissions, you would use `m::rw`. The last entry is, of course, the name of the file you want this operation to be performed on.

After you have set the mask, `getfacl` displays the same information it displayed the first time, but this time it shows that there is a mask set.

Adding a User or Group to an ACL

To add a user or group to an ACL, you once again use the `setfacl` command. For example, to give the user "foobar" read access to the file `acltest.txt`, you can use the following command:

```
setfacl -m u:foobar:r acltest.txt
getfacl acltest.txt
#file:acltest.txt
#owner:0
#group:0
user::rw-
user:foobar:r--
group::r--
mask::r--
other::---
```

As you can see, an entry has been added to the ACL list for the user foobar. This user will now have read access to the file, even though the standard file permissions would not normally give it to him.

So, what happens if you try to give the user write permissions as well as read permissions? The following command would give foobar both read and write permissions on the file:

```
setfacl -m u:foobar:rw acltest.txt
#file:acltest.txt
#owner:0
#group:0
user::rw-
user:foobar:rw-
group::r--
mask::rw-
other::---
```

The `getfacl` output shows that foobar was indeed given write permissions to the file. Notice also that the mask has been updated automatically to give a maximum permission of read and write. If this behavior is undesirable (in other words, you do not want the mask to be updated), use the `-n` option when setting the ACL. For example, the following command sets an ACL that gives the user foobar read and write access to the file:

```
# setfacl -n -m u:foobar:rw acltest.txt
```

6

This command won't update the mask, however, even if the current mask does not allow write access.

> **TIP**
>
> The order of the options is important. The -n option must come before the action option (in this case, -m). If you reverse the order of the two options, you will get the following error:
>
> ```
> setfacl: acl_from_text() failed: Invalid argument.
> ```

> **CAUTION**
>
> Remember that if you set a new ACL without using the -n option, the maximum permissions mask will automatically be updated to allow the permissions. For example, if the mask is currently set to allow maximum permissions of read-only, and you add an ACL for a user that allows read and write, the mask is updated automatically to allow both read and write privileges. Always remember to use the -n option if you do not want this to happen.

> **TIP**
>
> When the -n option is not used and the mask is automatically updated, it will increase the permissions if a new ACL is added that has greater permissions than the mask currently allows. The mask will also automatically be lowered to the maximum permissions needed to support all the entries in the ACL. For example, if you delete an ACL entry that allows read and write access to a certain user, and after you delete this entry there are no other entries left that require write access, write access will automatically be removed from the mask. Just as you can use the –n option to prevent the automatic raising of the mask, you can use the option to prevent the automatic lowering of the mask.

After giving foobar read and write access to the file, your ACL should now look like this:

```
#file:acltest.txt
#owner:0
#group:0
user::rw-
user:foobar:rw-
group::r--
mask::rw-
other::---
```

If you want to change your mask back so that it allows maximum ACL permissions of read-only, use the following command:

```
# setfacl -m m::r acltest.txt
```

If you then run the `getfacl` command again, you get the following output:

```
#file:acltest.txt
#owner:0
#group:0
user::rw-
user:foobar:rw-          # effective: r--
group::r--
mask::r--
other::---
```

Notice that the user foobar still has read and write permissions listed. However, because of the mask, foobar's effective permissions are read-only.

You can also add several ACLs with a single command line by separating them with commas. Here's an example:

```
# setfacl -n -m u:foobar:rw,u:guest:r,g:visitors:r acltest.txt
```

This command gives read and write access to the user foobar, read access to the user guest, and read access to the group visitors. In addition, the use of the -n option prevents the mask from being updated, even if the current mask doesn't allow some of the permissions you assign in this statement.

Denying Access with ACLs

Just as an ACL can be used to allow users and groups to have access to a file or directory that they otherwise could not access, it can also be used to deny access to users and groups that otherwise would have access. For example, the following command creates an ACL entry for the user foobar that contains no permissions:

```
# setfacl -m u:foobar: acltest.txt
```

In this case, the user foobar is denied all access to the file `acltest.txt`, even if foobar is a member of the group that owns the file and that group has access to the file. The ACL overrules the standard file permissions and denies the user access, even if the standard file permissions would allow the user access.

Deleting an ACL Entry

Use the -x option with `setfacl` to delete an ACL entry. For example, the following command removes the entire entry for the user foobar:

```
# setfacl -x u:foobar: acltest.txt
```

Removing All ACL Entries

Use the -b option to remove all the ACL entries. Here's an example:

```
# setfacl -b acltest.txt
```

For more information on the capabilities of ACLs, including the capability to set default ACLs for directories, see the man pages for getfacl and setfacl.

Adding and Removing Users

Now that we have covered permissions and ownership, we need to turn our attention to expanding the system's user base to include more users and groups.

Use the adduser script to add users to the system. This program differs somewhat in workflow from the adduser and useradd scripts you might be accustomed to using on a Linux system, but it accomplishes the same thing. You must be root in order to run adduser.

The first time you run adduser, the script sets up a configuration file with a set of defaults; the next time you run it, you can use the -s (silent) option to use these defaults, and the script will only ask you for the basic details on each user. Listing 9.2 shows a sample initial run of the script.

CAUTION

Users familiar with earlier versions of FreeBSD should beware of the new first line of the adduser script, which prompts you for a regular expression that new usernames must match. The default regular expression given (which restricts usernames to alphanumeric characters or the underscore for the first letter and then the same set of characters plus the hyphen for remaining characters) is generally desirable. However, this is where the script previously prompted for the username. Don't be fooled!

If you enter a custom regular expression, be sure you know what you're doing. All future new usernames will be required to match the pattern that you enter here. If you accidentally enter an undesirable value, you can delete or modify /etc/adduser.conf to start again from scratch.

Regular expression syntax will be covered in Chapter 20, "Introduction to Perl Programming."

LISTING 9.2   A Sample adduser Session

```
# adduser
Use option ``-silent'' if you don't want to see all warnings and questions.

Check /etc/shells
Check /etc/master.passwd
Check /etc/group
Usernames must match regular expression:
```

LISTING 9.2   Continued

```
[^[a-z0-9_][a-z0-9_-]*$]:
Enter your default shell: bash csh date no sh tcsh [csh]:
Your default shell is: csh -> /bin/csh
Enter your default HOME partition: [/home]:
Copy dotfiles from: /usr/share/skel no [/usr/share/skel]:
Send message from file: /etc/adduser.message no [no]:
Use password-based authentication (y/n) [y]:
Enable account password at creation (y/n) [y]:
Use an empty password (y/n) [n]:

Ok, let's go.
Don't worry about mistakes. I will give you the chance later
to correct any input.
Enter username [^[a-z0-9_][a-z0-9_-]*$]: joe
Enter full name []: Joe User
Enter shell bash csh date no sh tcsh [csh]:
Enter home directory (full path) [/home/joe]:
Uid [1005]:
Enter login class: default []:
Login group test [joe]:
Login group is `joe''. Invite test into other groups: guest no
[no]:
Use password-based authentication (y/n) [y]:
Use an empty password (y/n) [n]:
Enter password []:
Enter password again []:
Enable account password at creation (y/n) [y]:

Name:      joe
Password: ****
Fullname: Joe User
Uid:       1005
Gid:       1005 (joe)
Class:
Groups:    joe
HOME:      /home/joe
Shell:     /bin/csh
OK? (y/n) [y]:
Added user ``joe''
Send message to ''joe'' and: no root second_mail_address [no]:

Joe User,
```

LISTING 9.2   Continued

```
your account ''joe'' was created.
Have fun!

See also chpass(1), finger(1), passwd(1)

Add anything to default message (y/n) [n]:
Send message (y/n) [y]: Copy files from /usr/share/skel to /home/joe
Add another user? (y/n) [y]: n
Goodbye!
```

Pressing Enter after every prompt accepts the default value, which is shown in brackets. Many of the prompts give you a space-separated list of choices, such as the prompt for the shell. When these choices include no, that option can be used to disable or decline whatever the prompt is offering. For instance, entering no for the shell creates the user without a valid shell, meaning that the user cannot log in to the system.

> **NOTE**
>
> As of FreeBSD 4.0 and later, the "csh" built in to the base system is actually tcsh, an extended version of csh (the C shell). You can still specify tcsh as a shell, but it's the same thing as csh.

If you like, you can put a file at /etc/adduser.message that will be e-mailed to the new user at the new local account. The user is able to read it the first time he or she logs in to the system and runs a mail program (more on reading mail can be found in Chapter 24, "Configuring E-mail Services"). To make it easier, if you have elected to send the adduser.message file, the script prompts you for a second address to send it to (for instance, an address that the person is already using), so you can be sure the user receives it.

The "dotfiles" that the script mentions are the semi-hidden shell configuration files (they are only visible if you use the -a option on ls):

.cshrc	.login_conf	.mailrc	.rhosts
.login	.mail_aliases	.profile	.shrc

These files are explained in more detail in the section titled "Shell Initialization Files," in Chapter 11, "Customizing the Shell."

Each user and group has a numeric equivalent to its name, user ID (UID), and group ID (GID). This ID is listed in the ownership information of a file or directory and is used to control processes. If you remove a user from the system, that user's files become owned by the UID number that the user left behind.

Removing a user is a fairly simple matter. The command here is rmuser, which takes the username as an argument (adduser does not), as shown in Listing 9.3.

LISTING 9.3   A Sample rmuser Session

```
# rmuser joe
Matching password entry:

joe:IRBpIrE/nkDQo:1008:1008::0:0:Joe user:/home/joe:/bin/csh

Is this the entry you wish to remove? y
Remove user's home directory (/home/joe)? y
Updating password file, updating databases, done.
Updating group file: (removing group joe -- personal group is empty) done.
Removing user's home directory (/home/joe): done.
Removing files belonging to joe from /tmp: done.
Removing files belonging to joe from /var/tmp: done.
Removing files belonging to joe from /var/tmp/vi.recover: done.
```

The line about the "matching password entry" describes the database in which all the user information is kept, which brings us to our next topic.

The /etc/passwd and /etc/master.passwd Files

All Unix-flavored operating systems have an /etc/passwd file, but the file's specific role differs from platform to platform. For some systems, /etc/passwd is the sole repository of user information (including passwords). In these cases, adding a user requires only that you add a line to the file using a text editor (vi, pico, ee, emacs, and so on). More modern operating systems, though, use a "shadow passwords" structure—a way of storing the encrypted password strings not in /etc/passwd, but in a different file that is readable only by root. This file's name varies, depending on the platform. On some platforms, it's /etc/shadow; on others, it's /etc/security/master.passwd. On FreeBSD, it's /etc/master.passwd.

Both of these passwd files are simple text databases, containing a line for each user with fields delimited with colons (:). The files contain the username, the user ID, the group ID of the primary group, the home directory, the login shell, and the full name (which also has embedded comma-delimited fields such as Office Location, Office Phone, and Home Phone).

The permissions on /etc/passwd are 0644; on /etc/master.passwd, they're 0600. This security scheme means that any user can access the information in /etc/passwd, but root is the only one who can see into /etc/master.passwd, which differs from /etc/passwd only in that it contains the users' encrypted passwords in the second field. Passwords are encrypted in FreeBSD using a hash scheme based on the MD5 algorithm. Here are examples of each:

```
/etc/passwd:
joe:*:1008:1008:Joe User:/home/joe:/bin/csh

/etc/master.passwd:
joe:$1$32iknJXS$TnJUUj9LzYGwWRZonOu/I0:1008:1008:Joe User:/home/joe:/bin/csh
```

These two files aren't the only ones that store user information, though. Flat text databases are fine for a fairly small number of users, but as the user base grows, the need for a faster, hash table–based lookup database becomes more and more obvious. On a system with 25,000 users in a linear text database, looking up a user's information can take a significant amount of time—while the user is waiting to log in!

So, FreeBSD also has /etc/pwd.db and /etc/spwd.db. These files are hash tables in db format, corresponding to the "insecure" /etc/passwd and the "secure" /etc/master.passwd, respectively. They also have the same permissions as their corresponding clear-text files. These files provide a fast lookup mechanism for large user databases, and they're generated by the pwd_mkdb program automatically every time you alter a user's information with the chfn, passwd, or adduser/rmuser command.

Speaking of which, the chfn (change full name) command is the tool you use to change a user's information. Like the edquota command we examined in the last chapter, chfn operates by invoking the editor specified in your EDITOR environment variable (vi, by default). You can then modify any of the text fields. Upon saving and exiting, the /etc/master.passwd file is rewritten, and pwd_mkdb -p is automatically run to rebuild the other three files.

It is important to understand that /etc/master.passwd is truly the "master" user database file. If you want to rebuild a user list or port one from another FreeBSD machine, you can simply place the new master.passwd file into /etc (or anywhere within the / partition) and then issue the following command:

```
# pwd_mkdb -p /etc/master.passwd.new
```

This example assumes that your new master.passwd file is in /etc as master.passwd.new. The /etc/master.passwd file is replaced with your new file, and /etc/pwd.db, /etc/spwd.db, and /etc/passwd are rebuilt. The -p option tells pwd_mkdb to generate a new /etc/passwd file; if this is omitted, /etc/passwd is left unchanged. You will probably want to use -p at all times to keep the two files synchronized.

NOTE

In FreeBSD, the /etc/passwd file itself is never consulted; it only really exists for compatibility with third-party applications. Most modern utilities look up user information from /etc/pwd.db.

The /etc/group File

Groups are handled in much the same way as users—with a text database in /etc. But because groups normally don't have passwords, there is no need for special security on the /etc/group file (the group equivalent of /etc/passwd), other than having it writable only by root.

The following is a sample line from /etc/group. Note that there are only four fields: the group name, a "dummy" field (in which passwords would go if they existed), the group ID, and then a comma-separated list of the users in the group:

```
wheel:*:10:root,bob,frank
```

There is no hash database for /etc/group because the file's information generally is referenced much less frequently than the information in /etc/passwd and because most systems have far fewer groups than users. FreeBSD's "unique groups" policy, however, makes that latter point moot. Future development may produce a hash file for groups.

Managing Groups

Without passwords, user access, and a hash file to worry about, adding a group to the system is much easier than adding a user. You can simply open the /etc/group file in any text editor and create a new line in the format listed earlier (make sure to give the new group a group ID that has not yet been used).

New groups are added automatically by the adduser script when it creates unique per-user groups. The group IDs typically match the corresponding user IDs, but that is not a requirement. You will most likely only be interested in adding systemwide groups—for example, for tasks such as running a Web server or a database back end. These groups generally ought to have group IDs in the range of 100 to 1000. The numbers above 1000 are usually used for unique per-user groups, to match the corresponding user IDs. The numbers under 100 tend to be populated by system groups that are part of the core operating system.

To add a user to a group, type the user's name into the fourth field. If there are already usernames in the fourth field, separate them with commas, as shown previously. You can remove a user just as easily—simply delete the name.

6

System Configuration and Startup Scripts

FreeBSD's startup process, like that of most Unix-like operating systems, provides you with a lot of information before it gives you a command prompt. This startup can be more complex than in operating systems such as Windows and Mac OS. However, as long as you run the right system on the correct hardware, a full startup (including the launch of all the system services, or *daemons*) can be just as quick as that of a desktop OS.

Because each Unix-like operating system does things a bit differently, FreeBSD's startup process may be unfamiliar even to Linux veterans. For example, you won't have the handy `fsck` progress meter or the neatly formatted check box columns of some distributions of Linux, and the boot manager operates quite differently from LILO (the Linux boot loader). Neither does FreeBSD have the large variety of run levels that Linux and Solaris have. Because FreeBSD's model is simpler and more direct, it can be easier to understand and deal with, but it also has pitfalls and complexities that other platforms lack.

With a little exploration, though, you'll soon have the process fully analyzed and under control.

Understanding the FreeBSD Startup Process

FreeBSD's bootstrapping (startup) process is a multistage one, with each stage typically having a very limited function and scope, and executing one crucial step before passing off control to the next stage. This chapter covers these stages in detail. Chances are you won't ever need to know the details of what happens when the system is starting up, but knowing them can't hurt!

When you first power on the machine, the first thing FreeBSD does is run the hardware checks and probes that are specified by the BIOS and the CMOS configuration. The hardware checks and probes run the memory check and the IDE or SCSI exploration that you see before the screen is cleared for the first time. This step is not OS specific; it happens the same way, no matter what you have installed on the machine.

Moving Through the Boot Process

After the BIOS prints the table showing the hardware data it has collected, it reads the Master Boot Record (MBR) of the primary disk for the first preliminary *boot block*. It is the job of this and the next two boot blocks to find and run the loader, which configures and loads the kernel. Each boot block is sequentially a little more complex than the previous one. The first two are limited to 512 bytes in size (by the size of the MBR and the size of the boot sector of a slice), so they are both very simple. Here are each of the boot blocks and their functions:

- **Boot block 0 (boot0)**—This preliminary boot block is what sits in the MBR, like LILO, and (if the FreeBSD boot manager is installed) lists the available slices (the F-key commands that follow) from which you can choose what you want to boot:

```
F1 FreeBSD
F2 Linux
F3 ??

Default: F1
```

You can press the appropriate F-key to select the slice you want or else just wait for several seconds, in which case boot block will choose the default selection and continue.

- **Boot block 1 (boot1)**—This a very simple program that runs from the boot sector of the slice you selected in boot0, and its job is to use a stripped-down version of disklabel, which divides a slice up into BSD-style partitions (this is covered thoroughly in Chapter 19, "Understanding Hard Disks and Filesystems") to find and run boot2 in the appropriate partition. There is no user interface portion to boot1.

- **Boot block 2 (boot2)**—Finally, we reach a boot block that has enough elbow room to have the necessary complexity to read files on the bootable filesystem. In earlier versions of FreeBSD, this boot block used to provide a prompt so you could tell it where to load the kernel from, if not from the default location in the bootable slice. Now it automatically runs a program called loader, which gives you this interface to the kernel command line and a lot more.

- **loader**—You can find this program in the /boot directory. It reads the /boot/defaults/loader.conf and /boot/loader.conf configuration files and loads the kernel and modules specified there. (The /boot/loader.conf file contains the overrides to /boot/defaults/loader.conf, in a similar fashion to the way /etc/rc.conf works, which we cover later in this chapter.)

The loader counts down 10 seconds while it waits for a key press from you; if it doesn't get one, it boots the kernel in its default state. If you press Enter, however, the loader puts you into its command prompt interface, in which you can control precisely your kernel boot procedure. You can boot in single-user mode (boot -s), boot an old kernel (boot kernel.old), boot from CD-ROM (boot -C), load and unload kernel modules one by one (load and unload), view the contents of files (more), or perform a number of other tasks (see man boot for details). Most of the time, you don't need all these boot options, because you boot in the default configuration. Let's say, though, that you want to load a certain kernel module (/modules/portal.ko) at boot time, rather than waiting until the system has completely booted. You also want to view the currently loaded kernel modules. You can set this up at the ok prompt, as follows:

```
ok load portal.ko
/modules/portal.ko text=0x1d18 data=0x1f4+0x4 syms=[0x4+0x8d0+0x4+0x6bf]
ok lsmod
 0x100000: kernel (elf kernel, 0x355be4)
 0x455be4: /boot/kernel.conf (userconfig script, 0x4c)
 0x456000: portal.ko (elf module, 0x3eb0)
```

Typing **?** at the ok prompt gives you a list of available commands. The two you just saw are load, which loads modules into the kernel, and lsmod, which lists the currently loaded modules. This command can be very useful during troubleshooting or if you use kernel modules that must be loaded in a specific order. For further details on the options available at the loader command line, consult man loader.

This concludes the boot block phase of the bootstrapping process. You're now well on the way to bringing the system all the way up. The final phase of the boot process is where the complete FreeBSD system starts to come into play. That's where the kernel loads itself into memory, probes its available devices, and runs the "resource configuration" scripts that construct a working environment and start up the various system services. The remaining steps are as follows:

- **Kernel**—After loader transfers control, the kernel begins to probe all the devices it can find, and the results of each probe are echoed to the screen. This is the time when you will see many boot messages. These messages are logged into the dmesg files, which you can read with the dmesg command if you need to see what the kernel had to say about a certain device.

10

> **TIP**
>
> The dmesg command is a fairly rudimentary tool, listing the contents of the system message buffer that have accumulated since the system last booted. Simply enter **dmesg** to view the list of messages or enter **dmesg | less** to view the output in an interactive pager for easier access.

- **init**—After the kernel loads, it passes control to the init process, the final stage in the startup procedure. This is signaled by the "Automatic reboot in progress" message, which involves init running the resource configuration script (/etc/rc). This script first checks all the filesystem devices in /etc/fstab for consistency, as discussed in Chapter 8, "The FreeBSD Filesystem."

  If fsck finds no problems it cannot correct on its own, it will mount all the filesystems (using mount -a -t nonfs) and continue running the rest of the startup processes. If fsck finds an unresolvable problem with the disks, it will exit to single-user mode for you to run fsck manually and repair the damage. Exit the single-user shell to continue rebooting into multiuser mode.

Finally, if all goes according to plan, you get a login prompt. This whole process usually takes no more than a minute.

Securing the Boot Process

Of concern to the security-conscious administrator is the fact that by default, if you choose to boot into single-user mode (boot -s at the loader prompt), you are not prompted for a password, and the system comes up automatically with full root access. If you're sharing the machine with anyone else, such that this person can sit down in front of the machine and physically reboot it if he or she wants to, this constitutes a grave and gaping security hole.

Fortunately, it's easy to plug this hole. In /etc/ttys, which contains terminal settings for the various access methods (the console, virtual terminals, serial terminals, and network [pseudo] terminals), you can change the setting on the console line from secure to insecure:

```
console none                         unknown off insecure
```

This tells the system to treat the console as an insecure access point and to present a challenge (login prompt) to anyone who tries to boot into single-user mode. The root password is required in order to pass this challenge point.

NOTE

The `console` terminal method is only used in single-user mode. When you're booting into full multiuser mode, multiple virtual terminals are available at the physical terminal (you can switch between them with Alt+F1, Alt+F2, and so on). These terminals always present a login prompt. The `secure` and `insecure` settings in this case control whether you can log in as root or whether you're required to log in as a regular user and then use `su` to gain root access.

If others have access to the physical terminal (even if you've secured the single-user console), you have a second security hole to plug. This security weakness results from the fact that Ctrl+Alt+Delete causes the system to reboot, whether or not you're logged in as root, or even logged in at all. The three-finger-salute works even at the login prompt. Allowing this kind of access is appropriate in some situations (a rack-mounted server in a trusted machine room, for example), but not in others. To disable it, you'll need to add an option to your kernel configuration and rebuild the kernel:

```
options         SC_DISABLE_REBOOT
```

For a detailed discussion of kernel options and configuring your kernel, see Chapter 16, "Kernel Configuration."

What Can Slow Down the Boot Process?

Your system might take longer than a few minutes to boot up. Because of the scripted, serial nature of the boot process, it's fairly simple to see where it's hanging. Two common culprits are `sendmail` and `httpd` (Apache); in both cases, the associated slowness results from a network connectivity problem or misconfiguration.

Both Sendmail and Apache have to figure out your machine's hostname. To do this, they need to perform a reverse lookup against the domain name server (DNS) configured in `/etc/resolv.conf`. (TCP/IP setup will be covered thoroughly in Chapter 22, "Configuring Basic Networking Services.") This lookup will have to time out for every configured name server before it fails and allows the startup process to proceed. Network timeouts are often fairly long, which is why networking is the most common cause of boot hangups. One solution to this problem is to make sure the name server listed first in `/etc/resolv.conf` is reachable from your FreeBSD machine. This ensures that Sendmail and Apache will be able to determine the machine's hostname and start up without delay. If this configuration is not possible, list `127.0.0.1` (`localhost`) as the first name server and disable the rest.

Incidentally, this potential slowdown is why `init` uses `mount -a -t nonfs` when doing its initial "preen" to see whether it can safely go into multiuser mode. NFS has an astonishingly long timeout period, and a process waiting for that timeout to occur can be almost impossible to kill. The `mount` command, which you learned about in Chapter 8, avoids mounting NFS resources until later, in resource configuration, so that it can come up properly in multiuser mode without user intervention.

10

However, `init` does mount all filesystems later in /etc/rc, including NFS ones. Any NFS resources that you configured for automatic mounting in /etc/fstab (for example, without the `noauto` option) have the potential to freeze the system for a long time when the /etc/rc script reaches that point. Therefore, don't auto-mount NFS resources at boot unless you're sure you'll always be able to reach them!

Resource Configuration Scripts

After `init` has been started, the remaining startup tasks in the system—the ones that start all the services and operating system processes—are handled by the resource configuration scripts. These scripts can be recognized in FreeBSD 4.x and earlier by the prefix `rc`, as in `rc.network` and `rc.firewall`. However, in FreeBSD 5.0 and later, the resource configuration scripts are managed in a different structure, inside the /etc/rc.d directory. This chapter looks at both these structures, in turn, so that you'll know what you're dealing with regardless of how recently built your FreeBSD system is.

RC Scripts Prior to FreeBSD 5.0

Anything in /etc that has a filename beginning with `rc` is a resource configuration script (a program that starts up parts of FreeBSD according to the system's configuration). Some of these scripts are called recursively from other programs, some do nothing in the out-of-the-box configuration, and some will probably never even be run. There is only one `rc` file in /etc that you should ever edit to change system startup behavior, however, and that is /etc/rc.conf, the file in which your line-item settings override the default system settings found in /etc/defaults/rc.conf. All the resource configuration scripts that FreeBSD uses are described in Table 10.1, although depending on your individual installation, some of your scripts might be different.

TABLE 10.1   Resource Configuration Scripts

Script Name	Description
/etc/rc	The main resource config script.
/etc/rc.diskless1	`init` reads these scripts if you're doing a diskless boot via BOOTP.
/etc/rc.diskless2	
/etc/defaults/rc.conf	`init` reads in this file early to fill in its laundry list of tasks to do.
/etc/rc.conf	This is the file you edit to override defaults set in /etc/defaults/rc.conf. This should be the *only* resource config file in /etc that you edit!
/etc/rc.serial	Sets up terminals and other serial devices.
/etc/rc.pccard	Runs the PC-card daemon for laptops.
/etc/rc.network	Sets up TCP/IP networking.
/etc/rc.network6	Same as `rc.network`, except for IPv6 services.
/etc/rc.atm	Called from `rc.network`; sets up ATM devices for WAN machines.
/etc/rc.isdn	Sets up the ISDN subsystem.
/etc/rc.firewall	Called from `rc.network`; configures an `ipfw` firewall.

TABLE 10.1   Continued

Script Name	Description
/etc/rc.firewall6	Called from rc.network6; configures an ip6fw firewall.
/etc/rc.i386	Architecture-specific startups for the *x86* platform, such as console options and APM.
/etc/rc.shutdown	Executed by init when it is shut down (using shutdown).
/etc/rc.suspend	Scripts used for the APM power-management daemon.
/etc/rc.resume	
/etc/rc.devfs	Configures the device filesystem. See Chapter 16 for more on this file.
/etc/rc.local	An obsolete method of adding your own startup script extensions. Use the rc.d method instead!
/etc/rc.sysctl	Sets the kernel variables specified in /etc/sysctl.conf.
/etc/rc.syscons	Sets up console settings.
/usr/local/etc/rc.d/	Directory trees containing any new startup scripts you add
/usr/local/X11R6/etc/rc.d/	(or are installed automatically by programs).

FreeBSD 5.0 and Later

The resource configuration scripts in the current system have been reorganized so that they're all inside /etc/rc.d. This organization cleans up /etc and keeps it manageable. The scripts' behavior is more or less the same as in the earlier system; some scripts are called from within others, and there is an ordering function, called rcorder, that controls the sequence in which the scripts are run. All the scripts inherit global subroutines from the /etc/rc.subr script. At the time of this writing, the new structure is referred to as rc_ng (for Resource Configuration: Next Generation).

/etc/rc.d contains a number of scripts, some of which are analogous to the /etc/rc.* scripts in the old structure. Each script is named for the service or configuration area it controls. Finally, the structure contains some scripts that control programs that may or may not be installed in the default system (for example, the Postfix mail system, which is covered in Chapter 24, "Configuring E-mail Services").

When you are working in FreeBSD 5.0 and later versions, you do have the option to use the old-style structure. In your /etc/rc.conf file, you can turn off the rc_ng option, and FreeBSD will use the /etc/rc.* files rather than the /etc/rc.d/* files to control its startup procedure. Here's how:

```
rc_ng="NO"              # Set to NO to disable new-style rc scripts.
```

This is useful for systems with pre-existing installations of FreeBSD that you are in the process of upgrading to FreeBSD 5.0. It can ease the transition if you don't want to risk destabilization from the new startup script structure. However, there is no reason to turn off the rc_ng option on a new installation.

10

The `/etc/defaults/rc.conf` File

Whether in FreeBSD 5.0 or in earlier versions, the resource configuration scripts are controlled by the same global configuration files: `/etc/defaults/rc.conf`, `/etc/rc.conf`, and the local `rc.d` directory trees. Everything else (all the other `/etc/rc.*` files or the contents of `/etc/rc.d`) should be left untouched so that future installations of FreeBSD can upgrade the files while preserving your customizations.

Take a look through the `/etc/rc` script. You'll see that it's completely automated; it works by checking whether certain variables are defined that control system configuration or whether certain files exist. If those variables or files are present, it executes a predefined, abstracted launch loop, which takes its parameters from those variables and files. Nothing in `/etc/rc` itself should be edited. In other systems, the system startup process is altered and extended by making changes to the resource configuration scripts themselves; in FreeBSD, though, the model is to automate and abstract as much as possible of the process and centralize the control files that specify the parameters.

In earlier versions of FreeBSD, there was only `/etc/rc.conf`. It contained all the variables that `/etc/rc` and related scripts would need in their default states, and any modifications to the system would be made to that file. This arrangement quickly became unmanageable, as the list of variables grew and the role of the file expanded. An administrator upgrading the system would painstakingly have to merge the old `rc.conf` with the new one—hardly an improvement over just editing `/etc/rc` in the first place.

Therefore, the solution was to create a directory called `/etc/defaults` and put a copy of `rc.conf`, with all the defaults filled in, into it. Now, `/etc/rc.conf` still exists, but the system will boot even if this directory is empty. Its purpose is to fill in overrides for the defaults in `/etc/defaults/rc.conf`. Typical overrides are for the networking configuration (IP address, hostname, gateway address, and so on) and for running daemons such as `sendmail` and `sshd`.

Let's look at a typical block in `/etc/defaults/rc.conf`, as shown in Listing 10.1.

LISTING 10.1   Excerpt from `/etc/defaults/rc.conf`

```
# named. It may be possible to run named in a sandbox, man security for
# details.
#
named_enable="NO"                   # Run named, the DNS server (or NO).
named_program="named"               # path to named, if you want a different one.
named_flags=""                      # Flags for named
#named_flags="-u bind -g bind"      # Flags for named
```

Now, you can find what `/etc/rc` will do by default. In this case, the default behavior is to not run named at all.

Typically, variables in /etc/defaults/rc.conf are grouped into these blocks, with similar prefixes keeping them related and with a single "YES"/"NO" variable serving as a "master switch" at the top. If the variable is set to "NO", generally none of the rest of the variables will matter; if it is set to "YES", all variables apply unless commented out. The second named_flags line in the listing is provided as an example in case you want to create a bind user and group for named to run as.

The /etc/rc.conf File

Let's say you do want to run named. In the simplest case, all you have to do is edit /etc/rc.conf (the "overrides" file) and add the following line anywhere in the file:

```
named_enable="YES"
```

The rest of the named_* variables in /etc/defaults/rc.conf do not need to be copied into the overrides file. Remember, every variable in the "defaults" file is loaded into memory by init, and they only matter if the "master switch" for that block has been turned to "YES". In that case, the variables will be used in the execution loop in /etc/rc to launch whatever process is controlled by the block you're working on (in this case, named).

CAUTION

As you tinker with /etc/rc.conf, it's a very good idea to keep a backup copy on hand so that you can easily back out to a known working system configuration. Create a backup file by simply copying your existing file before you begin working on it:

```
# cp /etc/rc.conf /etc/rc.conf.revert
```

To switch back to the backup version, copy or move (rename) it back to its original name:

```
# mv /etc/rc.conf.revert /etc/rc.conf
```

You can use these other variables for fine-tuning, though, and override them just as easily. Let's say your name server program is a customized version called mynamed. Let's also say that you've created a bind user and group, intending that the name server should run as this user and group so it won't be susceptible to as many security hacks. To handle that, all you need to do (assuming that mynamed has the same behavior and command-line options as named) is add these two lines to /etc/rc.conf:

```
named_program="mynamed"
named_flags="-u bind -g bind"
```

Just for curiosity's sake, you can find out what init is doing with these variables:

```
# grep "named_enable" /etc/rc*
/etc/rc.network:          case ${named_enable} in
```

Okay, so the `named` program is launched from `/etc/rc.network`. Looking in that file, you find this loop:

```
network_pass2() {
        echo -n 'Doing additional network setup:'
        case ${named_enable} in
        [Yy][Ee][Ss])
                echo -n ' named';        ${named_program:-named} ${named_flags}
                ;;
        esac
```

Here, you can see all the `named_*` variables from both `rc.conf` files being invoked. Now, when you boot the system and see named appear in the console messages after "`Doing additional network setup:`", you know that it's applying your overrides over the defaults and running the name server automatically.

> **NOTE**
>
> See Chapter 12, "Shell Programming," for a tutorial on shell scripting, which will help you in reading the resource configuration scripts.

The most typical variables that appear in `/etc/rc.conf` are the TCP/IP configuration parameters. Because these are different for every system, FreeBSD can't very well specify them in the defaults. Listing 10.2 shows a typical `/etc/rc.conf` just after a new FreeBSD installation.

LISTING 10.2   A Newly Installed `/etc/rc.conf`

```
# This file now contains just the overrides from /etc/defaults/rc.conf
# please make all changes to this file.

# Enable network daemons for user convenience.
# -- sysinstall generated deltas -- #
kern_securelevel="1"
kern_securelevel_enable="YES"
linux_enable="YES"
sendmail_enable="YES"
sshd_enable="YES"
portmap_enable="NO"
nfs_server_enable="NO"
inetd_enable="NO"
network_interfaces="fxp0 lo0"
ifconfig_fxp0="inet 10.6.7.101  netmask 255.0.0.0"
defaultrouter="10.6.1.1"
```

LISTING 10.2   Continued

```
hostname="freebsd1.testnetwork.com"
usbd_enable="YES"
```

Some of these variables are, in fact, redundant with the defaults file; still, it can be useful to have them in the overrides file, as well, because many of these features (such as the NFS server) now have a one-touch toggle control, as it were.

Many programs, when you install them, will have to install a way for themselves to start up at boot time; /etc/rc.conf is not, however, the place for these programs. This file is supposed to be touched only by you, the administrator, and by the sysinstall program when it makes changes to the core system. Another structure, the /usr/local/etc hierarchy, is in place for the startup scripts and configuration files of user-installed programs (ports and packages) and for any scripts that /etc/rc and friends do not know about.

The /usr/local/etc and /usr/local/X11R6/etc Directories

As you learned in Chapter 8, anything installed by the administrator goes into /usr/local. This is as true of startup scripts as it is of programs and shared libraries. The /usr/local/etc directory is the "local" equivalent of /etc (*local* referring to "this specific machine" as opposed to the generic components and settings found on all FreeBSD machines), and into it go all the configuration files installed by programs that you choose to install, rather than the ones controlled by the FreeBSD base system distribution.

> **NOTE**
>
> It's important to note that the difference between the /etc files and the /usr/local/etc files is *not* that the former are noneditable and the latter are editable. Just as most of the files in /etc should not be tampered with, many of the ones in /usr/local/etc also contain no user-serviceable parts or are designed not to need any modification by you in order to function (although the directory also contains customizable configuration files for installed programs). The distinction is that /etc controls the base system—for example, only those programs that are always part of a FreeBSD installation. The files in /usr/local/etc control programs that you install after the fact, from the ports collection or from packages (which you'll learn about in Chapter 14, "Installing Additional Software"). /usr/local/etc also doubles as the location for any startup scripts you write.

The main local configuration directory, /usr/local/etc, contains configuration files that administrators edit to tune their programs' behaviors. You learn more about configuring ports and packages in Chapter 14. Here, however, we're interested in the rc.d (resource configuration for daemons) subdirectory.

init turns its attention to /usr/local/etc/rc.d after it has run through all the other /etc/rc.* or /etc/rc.d scripts. Any executable files within the directory that end in .sh are executed in lexicographical order. Examples of files that are installed in here include

10

`apache.sh`, `mysql-server.sh`, and `samba.sh`. These scripts are custom built as part of the ports or packages, and each one is tuned to take a `start` or `stop` argument. When `init` runs each script, it uses the `start` argument. Note that you can just as easily run these scripts yourself during runtime—for instance, to start a newly installed service without rebooting:

```
# /usr/local/etc/rc.d/apache.sh start
```

Some ports or packages install with a secondary suffix of `.sample` (for example, `samba.sh.sample`). This suffix appears because the program has to be properly configured before it can run successfully. Apache, for instance, will run immediately after installation without any further modification to its config files (although you will no doubt be modifying them anyway). Apache, therefore, installs an `apache.sh` file, which could run the program cleanly if you rebooted it right then. However, Samba must be tuned first to run on your machine; if you ran the script right after installing it, it would fail to start the daemon. You need to rename the script to remove the `.sample` extension before it will be run on startup by `init`.

The `/usr/local/X11R6/etc` directory (which is created if you install any third-party ports or packages for X-Windows) is analogous to `/usr/local/etc`, except it is specifically tasked to X11-based programs, including GNOME panels, graphical tools, games, window managers, and so on. This directory also has an `rc.d` subdirectory, and scripts in it are executed immediately after the ones in `/usr/local/etc/rc.d`. The local startup-script directories are configurable. You can override this `rc.conf` line to add more directories if you need to:

```
local_startup="/usr/local/etc/rc.d /usr/X11R6/etc/rc.d" # startup script dirs.
```

Creating Scripts to Run Programs on System Boot

It is perhaps a bit idealistic to imagine that you will never need to have the system perform any startup tasks that are not tied to any of the carefully crafted ports/packages or the core system. You may want to run a custom daemon that you wrote yourself, for example, or clear out a common file-sharing directory every time the system boots. To do this, you can write your own shell script and put it into `/usr/local/etc/rc.d`.

Recall that `init` expects every script in the `rc.d` directory to be able to handle the `start` argument. Also, each script's name has to end in `.sh` in order to be run automatically. The following is a sample script from the man `rc` page:

```
#!/bin/sh -
#
#    initialization/shutdown script for foobar package

case "$1" in
```

```
start)
        /usr/local/sbin/foo -d && echo -n ' foo'
        ;;
*)
        echo "unknown option: $1 - should be 'start'" >&2
        ;;
esac
```

You might call this file foo.sh. Make sure it is set executable (chmod +x foo.sh)!

Technically, the program doesn't actually have to be a shell script; you can write it in Perl if you want, or even C or anything else that will run, as long as it has an .sh extension. Writing the program in anything other than a shell script is fairly bad form, though. You shouldn't have to try to fool the system! For more on shell scripting, consult Chapter 12.

The inetd Daemon and the inetd.conf Configuration File

Although there are a fair number of daemons in the base system that have .conf files in the /etc directory, the most important (and sensitive) one you will have to deal with is inetd, the "super-server." The job of inetd is to listen for connections on a specified set of network ports and fire off the appropriate server process when a request comes in.

For instance, inetd is in charge of Telnet connections; if your system allows Telnet, you can open a connection to it and receive a login prompt without any telnetd process running on the server beforehand. Every time the system receives a connection request on port 23, it creates a new telnetd process to handle the connection. Executable programs that run out of inetd (and other similar daemons) are in /usr/libexec. These programs are not generally part of your command path and are not supposed to be run from the command line; instead, they are spawned from within another process and passed certain resources (such as environment variables and network connections).

> **NOTE**
>
> The use of inetd eliminates the need for a "master" telnetd process running as root, which is a situation that could be particularly dangerous if a security vulnerability were to be uncovered in telnetd. Many daemons, including sshd, httpd (Apache), and sendmail, do run in this "stand-alone" mode rather than being called out of inetd. The master process (running as root) listens for the new connections and spawns new processes, owned by an unprivileged user, to handle each transaction. This allows for greater flexibility and speed in the program, at the expense of a centralized security risk. inetd also runs as root, so it is just as dangerous if inetd is compromised. The more daemons that run as root, the more possibilities there are for security holes to be found.

10

Examining the `/etc/inetd.conf` file reveals that nearly all entries in it are disabled in the out-of-the-box configuration, assuming you've selected the default security settings during setup. (For more information on security settings, see Chapter 29, "Network Security.") The entries in this file that are enabled are listed in Table 10.2.

TABLE 10.2   System Services Controlled by `inetd` That Are Enabled by Default

Service	Description	Port(s)/Resources Used
ftp	File Transfer Protocol	Port 21/TCP
telnet	Remote terminal	Port 23/TCP
comsat	"biff" server (notifies users of incoming mail)	Port 512/UDP
ntalk	Command-line chat server	Port 518/TCP, UDP
ftp (IPv6)	File Transfer Protocol	IPv6
telnet (IPv6)	Remote terminal	IPv6

Other services that you'll probably want to enable are listed in Table 10.3.

TABLE 10.3   Other Useful `inetd` Services

Service	Description	Port(s)/Resources Used
pop3	Post Office Protocol	Port 110/TCP
imap4	Interim Mail Access Protocol (server-side mail)	Port 143/TCP
smtp	Qmail (alternative to Sendmail SMTP server)	Port 25/TCP
netbios-ssn	Samba file sharing with Windows	Port 139/TCP
netbios-ns		Port 137/TCP
finger	Lookup user information	Port 79/TCP

To enable any one of these services, simply remove the comment (#) from the beginning of the line and then restart the `inetd` server, as follows:

```
# ps -waux | grep inetd
root    110  0.0  0.6  1032  752  ??  Ss   11:57PM  0:00.01 inetd
# kill -HUP 110
```

> **TIP**
>
> If you selected to run the system at security level 1 or higher during installation (level 1 is the "Medium" security level mentioned in the installer), `inetd` will not be running. This is indicative of the risky nature of many of the services that run out of `inetd`. If you are running at this security level and want to run `inetd`, you can run it by entering **inetd -wW**. To enable it permanently, remove or toggle this line in `/etc/rc.conf`:
>
> ```
> inetd_enable="NO"
> ```

inetd is one of the areas of FreeBSD without a lot of built-in automation or safety nets to prevent bad configurations. If you must enable services in /etc/inetd.conf, be aware that you're venturing into a nonstandard type of setup, and you should know what you're getting into. For instance, the cvs services come with a dire warning about a security hole that can be opened up with a misconfigured parameter. The Samba services (netbios-ssn and netbios-ns) expect to find the smbd and nmbd binaries in /usr/local/sbin, but they won't be there unless you have installed Samba from the ports or packages. (Running Samba from inetd instead of in standalone mode is a nonstandard, alternative configuration.)

Similarly, other services (such as pop3) try to run services installed into /usr/local/libexec. But remember, this directory is inside /usr/local, meaning that unless you explicitly installed a program there, it won't be there. Installing the popper port/package puts the necessary binary into that directory, so you can enable the service in inetd. However, if you choose instead to install the qpopper port/package (another POP3 server), the binary is qpopper instead of popper, and you have to modify the line accordingly:

```
pop3    stream  tcp     nowait  root    /usr/local/libexec/qpopper       qpopper
```

Numerous other pitfalls await the unwary. Be sure not to modify the inetd services any more extensively than you really have to. The man inetd page provides a more extensive discussion of the syntax and technique of handling inetd.

The System Logger (syslogd) and the syslog.conf File

System messages are logged to files in /var/log. The mechanism that does this is called syslogd, the system logger daemon. This daemon's behaviors are set in /etc/syslog.conf, which defines various different log files for different services. Each service or "facility" that syslogd knows about (including auth, authpriv, console, cron, daemon, ftp, kern, lpr, mail, mark, news, ntp, security, syslog, user, uucp, and local0 through local7) has a number of different "severity" levels for which you can control logging. These levels include, in decreasing order of severity, emerg, alert, crit, err, warning, notice, info and debug.

Each daemon or service that you run in FreeBSD can log through the predefined facilities of syslogd; for instance, Sendmail and other mail programs can use the system's syslog() routines to send out messages at various levels of severity, using the mail facility; the messages would be handled by syslogd as defined in syslog.conf.

By default, syslog.conf defines several logging rules, as follows:

```
*.err;kern.debug;auth.notice;mail.crit            /dev/console
*.notice;kern.debug;lpr.info;mail.crit;news.err /var/log/messages
security.*                                        /var/log/security
mail.info                                         /var/log/maillog
```

10

lpr.info	/var/log/lpd-errs
cron.*	/var/log/cron
*.err	root
*.notice;news.err	root
*.alert	root
*.emerg	*

You can interpret this to mean that all err messages from any service, debug messages from the kernel, authorization notice messages, and crit messages from mail programs will be printed out to the system console, and you will see them if you have a monitor hooked up to your FreeBSD machine. Similarly, all security-related messages go into the /var/log/security file, and all messages from mail programs at the info level go into /var/log/maillog. Almost everything else goes into /var/log/messages, the general system log file. (If you're used to Linux, this file is equivalent to what is usually called syslog.)

Certain types of messages are not merely written to log files but are sent to a variety of other types of handling mechanisms. In the default syslog.conf, messages from any service at the err, notice, or alert level are printed to any terminal where root is logged in, and emerg messages are printed to all users at all terminals. Table 10.4 shows the possible actions for syslogd messages and the syntax for each.

TABLE 10.4   Syntaxes for syslogd Actions

Syntax	Action Taken
/path/to/file	Messages are written to the specified file.
@some.hostname.com	Messages are forwarded to syslogd at some.hostname.com using the syslog network service.
user1	Messages are printed to any terminal where user1 is logged in.
root,user1,user2	All specified users receive messages on all their terminals.
*	Messages are written to all logged-in users.
| "mail root"	Messages are mailed to root.

Further details on how to configure syslogd can be found in the man syslogd and man syslog.conf pages.

> **NOTE**
>
> Each log file in /var/log is rolled over according to a different set of rules. For instance, the /var/log/maillog file is archived and restarted every day by the periodic program. Other log files, such as /var/log/cron and /var/log/messages, are refreshed through other means (often internally by the programs that write to them). Archived log files are generally compressed with gzip. To search through old log files, use gzcat in conjunction with the conventional grep:
>
> ```
> # gzcat /var/log/messages.2.gz | grep "rejected"
> ```

Notes on the /etc/rc.local File

The resource configuration script /etc/rc.local was described earlier in this chapter simply as being obsolete. Administrators who used earlier versions of FreeBSD or certain Linux distributions will recognize this file. Its purpose is much the same as the /usr/local/etc/rc.d directories—to provide you with a mechanism to extend the system's startup behavior.

The rc.d method described earlier is the preferred method of accomplishing the extending of system startup behavior because it's a more structured method. It keeps each startup task in its own script with a common interface—corralled into /usr/local and out of /etc. If you must use it, however, /etc/rc.local still works, although it doesn't exist in the default installation. You can create the file (with the proper interpreter line modeled after the other rc.* files) and put any set of shell commands into it, and it will be executed just before the rc.d scripts.

Support for rc.local is for backward compatibility only, and it may eventually be removed from FreeBSD. To make sure your system supports it, check /etc/rc for mention of the rc.local file, as shown in Listing 10.3.

LISTING 10.3   Excerpt from /etc/rc Showing Support for /etc/rc.local

```
# grep -A 5 rc.local /etc/rc
# Do traditional (but rather obsolete) rc.local file if it exists. If you
# use this file and want to make it programmatic, source /etc/defaults/rc.conf
# in /etc/rc.local and add your custom variables to /etc/rc.conf, as
# shown below. Please do not put local extensions into /etc/rc itself.
# Use /etc/rc.local
#
# ---- rc.local ----
#       if [ -r /etc/defaults/rc.conf ]; then
#               . /etc/defaults/rc.conf
#               source_rc_confs
#       elif [ -r /etc/rc.conf ]; then
#               . /etc/rc.conf
--
# ---- rc.local ----
#
if [ -r /etc/rc.local ]; then
        echo -n 'starting local daemons:'
        sh /etc/rc.local
        echo '.'
fi


# For each valid dir in $local_startup, search for init scripts matching *.sh
#
```

10

The loop that runs `sh /etc/rc.local` is what you're looking for. If it's there and not commented out, you can use `rc.local`. It is still a much better idea, however, to use the `rc.d` script method.

CHAPTER 11

Customizing the Shell

Regardless of whether you choose to operate your FreeBSD system through the X-Window GUI—particularly as an administrator—you're going to have to deal with a shell. A shell gives you all the flexibility you need to accomplish even the most complex tasks but also dictates a user experience that's arcane at best. In this chapter, we'll make ourselves at home in the shell—comfortable enough to use it as a programming environment and as a user interface.

What Is a Shell?

We've already talked about the basics of the shell and what you can do with it back in Chapter 7, "Working with the Shell." That chapter introduced the shell as a command-line interface and discussed the various shells you can use in FreeBSD and what kinds of commands are available in the shell for controlling the system. Now, we'll be looking at the shell itself in more detail and examining how it applies to the multitudes of users you might be supporting on your system and how to customize it to your taste.

You already know that a shell (in brief) is a command-line interface in which you can enter the typed commands that make the Unix computing experience so markedly different from a fully GUI-based one such as Windows or Mac OS. The shell is similar in function to the COMMAND.COM command interpreter in MS-DOS and its descendants in Windows, but it's vastly more complex and useful because it plays a much more important role than in a GUI-based operating system.

But why is it called a shell? The answer has to do with the terminology used in Unix architecture to describe the various levels of system operation in terms of a multilayered ball, with the most automated functions at the core and the user-triggered functions on the outer layer. On the inside is the *kernel*, which has been mentioned in earlier chapters and will be covered thoroughly in Chapter 17, "Kernel Configuration." On the outside of the system is the user. How does the user interact with the kernel and its surrounding support programs? Through the shell, naturally. This relationship is illustrated in Figure 11.1.

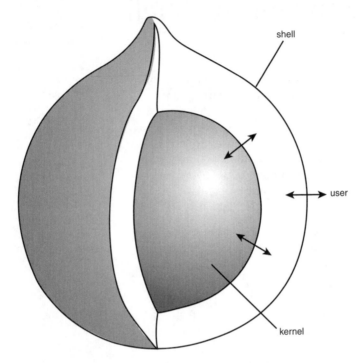

FIGURE 11.1   The kernel surrounded by the shell.

The job of the shell is to give you—the user—a safe, structured way to access the kernel. As a command interpreter, the shell takes your commands and translates them into processes that access files and devices through the kernel. It prevents you from executing unsafe code that could crash the kernel, and it helps you find and execute the programs that run the system.

In a more practical sense, the shell is simply a forking-capable utility that is executed by the system whenever you log in. The shell presents you with a command prompt, interprets your commands, and terminates when you log out. In fact, these are the only things a shell really needs to do; any program can act as a shell, which is a fact that can be used with great creativity, as you will see.

You probably will encounter the term *shell* used in a number of slightly different contexts. For instance, any program running on top of another and providing an interface to it is a type of shell; Windows 95 is technically a shell, albeit a better-disguised one than its predecessors (Windows 3.1, DESQview, and the short-lived MS-DOS Shell). Many programs will offer you the option to "shell out" to DOS or the command-line interface. This option is common in older programs that predate multitasking operating systems or terminal-based programs in which you're likely to have only one window open to the system. In these cases, "shelling out" means executing a shell program (such as the DOS or Unix command line) from within the program you're in, suspending the program while you perform operations "above" it.

In Chapter 7, we looked at the various choices of programs for FreeBSD that are specifically designed to be shells, in the sense that they are command interpreters capable of running scripts in specialized shell scripting languages. Some of these programs are sh, csh, bash, ksh, and tcsh; these shells differ subtly in their behavior and in the programming languages they support. Chapter 12, "Shell Programming," covers scripting in the Bourne shell (sh) environment, the most popular by far. However, for now we will turn our attention to a somewhat more pedestrian and everyday topic: configuring your chosen shell to fit your taste and needs.

Before we can do this, we must look at how to add shells to FreeBSD that are not included with the base system and how to change from one shell to another.

Adding Shells to the System and Making Them Available

Most users will probably be satisfied with the default FreeBSD shell, /bin/tcsh (the same as /bin/csh). It provides command-line editing, tab completion, history, and the rest of the advanced shell features missing in the more rudimentary shells. However, the fact that FreeBSD defaults to tcsh rather than bash (which is commonly used in Linux) reflects the subtle philosophical differences between the BSD tradition and the System V structure (which accounts for much of the architecture of Linux), an argument as old as Unix itself. These philosophical differences used to mean a lot more than they do today. Commercial flavors of Unix generally fall into one camp or the other and haven't changed materially in years; between Linux and FreeBSD, though, the more significant philosophical difference is between the GNU and BSD license structures. That's where we see the roots of Linux's preference for bash and FreeBSD's preference for tcsh.

Because bash is a GNU-oriented program, and because Linux tends to prefer software developed under the GNU Public License (GPL), bash is the default Linux shell. The feature sets of bash and tcsh are quite similar, but these features are accessed in different ways, and the configuration process and runtime behavior of the two shells differ subtly. If you are used to Linux, you may want to install bash in order to remain in a familiar environment. On the other hand, you might come from a system in which your shell was ksh or zsh. Installing and using these shells is no problem, as you'll learn in the next section of this chapter.

The remaining sections of the chapter examine both `tcsh` and `bash`, showing the differences in configuration and usage for each one. For additional shells, you're on your own—you'll need to install the shells and read their man pages for details.

Installing Shells from the Ports or Packages

The preferred way to install software on FreeBSD is through the ports or packages, which is described in detail in Chapter 14, "Installing Additional Software." That chapter explains how to use the ports collection and the packages for all your software-management needs. This section, however, covers the most basic commands and procedures for installing new shells.

Installing from Packages

The simplest way to install a new shell is through `sysinstall` and its interface to the package manager. Run `/stand/sysinstall`, select Configure, and then choose Packages. Select your installation medium—CD-ROM if you have the FreeBSD installation CD handy, or FTP otherwise.

After you've received the package list, go into the "shells" subsection and scroll through the list of available shells. Press the spacebar to place an × on each shell you want to install. Press Enter once you're done selecting shells to install, and you'll be returned to the main package selection screen. Use the right-arrow key to select Install and then press Enter. Then select OK at the confirmation screen showing the selected packages.

The software will now download automatically and install itself. Once it's done, exit out of `sysinstall` by returning to the Exit option at the top of the Configuration menu; then choose Exit Install from the bottom of the screen. The shell (or shells) you've selected are now installed. You can verify this installation by looking in `/usr/local/bin` and by reading the man page for the shell you've installed (for example, `man bash`).

Installing from the Ports

An alternate way to install software, also described in Chapter 14, is to use the *ports collection*. This is a rigorously structured way to compile and install the software on your own machine while guaranteeing that the installed files will be put in the proper locations (for instance, inside `/usr/local`, according to the FreeBSD hierarchy rules). If installed, the ports collection is in `/usr/ports` and contains the same hierarchical structure found in the packages as browsed through `sysinstall`.

Go into `/usr/ports/shells` and look around. This is a fairly small section of the ports collection; most of the other categories (subdirectories of `/usr/ports`) have lots more available programs for you to install. Each of the directories shown in the following directory listing contains a makefile, various checksum and patch files, and a packing list.

44bsd-csh/	esh/	nologinmsg/	pkg/	wapsh/
Makefile	fd/	osh/	rc/	zsh/
bash1/	flash/	pash/	sash/	zsh+euc_hack/
bash2/	ksh93/	pdksh/	tcsh/	zsh-devel
es/	mudsh/	perlsh/	vshnu/	

All you have to do is go into the directory and type **make**; the system will retrieve the distribution file, unpack it, patch it, configure it, and compile it. Then you need to type **make install** to install the package and **make clean** to delete all the temporary files created during the build process:

```
# cd /usr/ports/shells/bash2
# make
  ...
# make install
  ...
# make clean
  ...
```

Once this process is complete, the new shell will be installed and available for use.

> **NOTE**
>
> You may need to type **rehash** (if you're using tcsh) to force the shell program to reread your shell configuration files and the available programs in your path after installing any new programs; otherwise, you won't be able to access those programs unless you log out and then back in.

The /etc/shells File

A very important system file that you'll need to know about when working with shells is /etc/shells. This file contains the names of the installed shells on the system, listed with their full paths. The following is an example of /etc/shells on a working system with three extra shells installed:

```
# cat /etc/shells
# $FreeBSD: src/etc/shells,v 1.3 1999/08/27 23:23:45 peter Exp $
#
# List of acceptable shells for chpass(1).
# Ftpd will not allow users to connect who are not using
# one of these shells.

/bin/sh
/bin/csh
```

```
/bin/tcsh
/usr/local/bin/bash
/usr/local/bin/zsh
/usr/local/bin/ksh
```

The purpose of /etc/shells is to specify the shell programs that you, the administrator, consider "valid." The chsh program (which we'll discuss shortly) won't allow a regular user to change his default shell to any program that you have not listed in /etc/shells. This safeguard allows you to ensure that a user cannot change his default shell to a program that isn't designed to be used as one. Especially problematic are setuid programs, or programs that run with the effective UID of the user that owns them (as described in Chapter 9, "Users, Groups, and Permissions"). If a setuid program is owned by root, it can execute any action with root's privileges; it's clearly not desirable for a user to be able to attain these privileges simply by logging in.

A user's shell is specified in the /etc/master.passwd user database, in the tenth field of the user's record (or the seventh field in /etc/passwd), as you saw in Chapter 7. Here's an example:

```
/etc/master.passwd:
foo:*:$1$LXZkCuzD$7Oa8LyRgbjYOb.XrXiBad.:1001:1001::999066364:0:
➥Foo Bar:/home/foo:/usr/local/bin/ksh
/etc/passwd:
foo:*:1001:1001::Foo Bar:/home/foo:/usr/local/bin/ksh
```

If that field's value (/usr/local/bin/ksh in this example) is set to a shell that appears in /etc/shells, the user is allowed to log in using services such as FTP. If not, he is denied. Also, /etc/shells is used to generate the list of available shells that you can assign to a user during the adduser process, which we covered in Chapter 9.

An entry is added automatically to /etc/shells each time you install a shell through the ports or packages, as described earlier. Note that although only the administrator (root) can change a user's shell to a program not listed in /etc/shells, a user can log in as a shell user whether or not the assigned shell appears in /etc/shells. The shells database also controls access to the system via FTP. A common trap is for an administrator to install a shell without using the ports or packages (thus not adding an entry to /etc/shells) and then to switch another user to that new shell (because the administrator is allowed to do so). The regular user can use telnet or ssh to get to the machine without any trouble, but as soon as he tries to ftp to it, he will be inexplicably denied access. The solution to this is simply to make sure the user's shell is listed in /etc/shells. Always use the ports or packages to install shells properly.

Using Alternate Shells

Any user can change his or her assigned shell at any time. The reasons for doing this are myriad: The user might be accustomed to Linux and bash, as described earlier, or have a highly customized shell environment from another system that is only in a certain shell's configuration format (as we'll discuss shortly). Regardless of the reason, changing a user's shell is pretty easy.

Changing Your Shell While Logged In

The simplest way to use an alternate shell is simply to run it. If your default shell is tcsh, and you want to use bash (assuming that bash is available on the system), just type **bash** to open a new bash environment within your tcsh session, as shown here:

```
# bash
bash-2.04#
```

Now, when you log out, you'll have to do it twice—once to exit the bash process and again to exit the original tcsh process. When your login shell program exits, you are disconnected from the system.

Changing Your Default Shell

Running a shell other than your default one every time you log in can get tedious. Although you can do it automatically by adding the command for the second shell into your .login file (an initialization script that runs when the shell is started, as you'll learn in "tcsh/csh Files: .cshrc, .login, and .logout," later in this chapter), this still means you're running a shell within a shell, which isn't very efficient. Fortunately, any user can change his or her shell to any program listed in /etc/shells. The chsh (change shell) program is used for this task. This program differs in its behavior from platform to platform. On some platforms, such as Linux, chsh is a command-line, interactive tool that prompts for new values one by one. In FreeBSD, however, chsh is really the same program as chpass, chfn, and other user-management tools. They're all hard links to each other, and they all have the same function.

The behavior of chsh (and its identical siblings) is to open your user information in a text editor and allow you to change the values in any of the available fields. The editor used by default is vi, although this can be overridden by setting the EDITOR environment variable to the name of a different program, such as ee or pico. (We'll talk about environment variables in the upcoming section "Shell Initialization Files.")

To change your own shell, simply enter **chsh**. If you're root, you can modify another user's shell by supplying that user's login as the argument. Here's an example:

```
# chsh frank
#Changing user database information for frank.
Shell: /bin/tcsh
Full Name: Frank Allen
Office Location:
Office Phone:
Home Phone:
Other information:
~
~
```

A full discussion of how to use the vi editor is found in Chapter 6, "Working with Applications." For now, let's concentrate on the necessary commands you'll need for changing the user's shell.

Part of what makes vi so challenging is that its internal commands are so arcane and must be entered so exactly that it's easy to get to a point at which crucial data has been accidentally deleted or mangled and can't be retrieved. If you make a mistake, enter a colon (:), followed by **q!**, and then press Enter, which will force an exit without saving changes:

```
~
~
:q!
```

Let's say you want to change frank's shell permanently from /bin/tcsh to /usr/local/bin/bash. Once you're in the vi screen, obtained by typing **chsh frank**, use the arrow keys to move to the beginning of the word tcsh, immediately after the second slash (/). Type **c** (for "change") and then **w** (for "word"). A dollar sign ($) will appear at the end of the word you're changing:

```
Shell: /bin/tcs$
```

Type **bash** in place of the word tcsh and then press Esc to exit change-word mode. Now the shell is /bin/bash. The next step is to place the cursor on top of the first slash, just before bin, and type **i** (for "insert") to get a usable cursor. Enter **/usr/local** and then press Escape. The shell string should now be /usr/local/bin/bash.

Now, enter a colon (:) to go into the in-program command line and then follow it with **w** (for "write"). Press Enter to save the file. Finally, type **:q** and press Enter to quit.

The file you've now written is actually a temporary file in /etc. If your changes are valid, they will be read from that file and automatically rebuilt into /etc/master.passwd and /etc/passwd. From now on, every time the user in question logs in to the system, the login will be under /usr/local/bin/bash rather than /bin/tcsh.

If the changes you've made are not valid (for example, if the shell you specified is not listed in /etc/shells), you are given the choice to re-edit the user profile or to cancel the operation.

Non-Shell Programs as Shells

It's possible to set a user's shell to a program that isn't specifically designed to be a shell; programs such as /sbin/nologin, for example, do nothing but print out a text banner and exit. Also the user might prefer to use some programs tailored to command-line interaction with services other than the Unix filesystem (such as TinyFugue).

You can set a nonexistent program as a user's shell to prevent the user from logging in at all. You can even set a user's shell to /usr/bin/mail (the shell-based mail reader) if you want, although this will mean that the user can't do much but read mail. On the other hand, this might be the server policy you decide to set.

The chsh program will warn you if you specify a shell that doesn't exist, but it will still dutifully write it into the user database. There's nothing wrong with having a user's shell set to a nonexistent program; it simply means that the user won't be able to log in. Remember, a login shell works as follows:

- If the program can be successfully executed and attached to a pty (pseudo-terminal), the login will be successful and will not end until the shell program terminates and releases the pty.

- If the shell program can't be executed, nothing will bind to the pty, and the user won't get a command line. Instead, the user gets an error. Depending on the terminal program, the error might take the shape of a password-authentication error or a protocol failure error. In a command-line telnet session, the error might result in an explicit failure to execute the shell program after displaying the various login banners, as shown here:

```
FreeBSD/i386 (stripes.somewhere.com) (ttyp2)

login: frank
Password:
Last login: Sat May  5 18:35:52 from w044.z064002043.
Copyright (c) 1980, 1983, 1986, 1988, 1990, 1991, 1993, 1994
        The Regents of the University of California.  All rights reserved.

FreeBSD 4.6.2-RELEASE (STRIPES) #0: Wed Aug 14 20:47:38 PDT 2002
- - - - - - - - - - - - - - - - - - - - - - - - - - - - - - - - - - - - - - - - -
Welcome to the system! Today's news: nothing.
```

```
You have mail.
login: /usr/local/bin/foosh: No such file or directory
Connection closed by foreign host.
```

You can leverage this behavior of displaying the general login banners before executing a user's shell. For instance, if you have a troublesome user or group of users who have violated system policy in some way (such as by hacking), you can prevent them from logging in by setting their shells to a nonexistent program and giving an explanation of a systemwide policy enforcement change in /etc/motd. This "message of the day" file is a regular text file that the system displays as a banner to every user immediately after accepting his or her password. Edit /etc/motd in your favorite text editor to reflect anything you want all your users, including ones without valid shells, to read upon login.

An even more useful (and correct) method is to set the user's shell to a program that isn't really a shell but merely a program that prints out informative text. /sbin/nologin is a built-in program that you can set as a user's shell to disable his or her login. This shell script prints out a single line of text and then exits. The line of text is short and sweet:

```
You have mail.
This account is currently not available.
Connection to stripes.somewhere.com closed.
```

Notice that /sbin/nologin executed, attached to the pty, exited properly, and released the pty. The fact that it never presented any kind of interactive command line doesn't make it any less valid as a shell. This method of disabling an account works for any terminal program, whether using telnet or ssh, and it involves no errors or warnings. It's very elegant and extensible.

You can, in fact, assign any program as the shell, regardless of whether the program is interactive. You can make your shell /bin/ls or /usr/bin/finger, if you like. More usefully, you can create your own script or program to execute when a certain user logs in. This way, you can set up interesting services on your system, such as a customized "library" system in which guests can log in and interact with a menu, execute a certain limited set of commands, or simply get a screenful of information. The possibilities are endless!

CAUTION

A word of warning is in order: If you write a login handler for the purpose of providing custom services in C or another language in which you have to allocate your own buffer space, beware of potential buffer overflows! These are the most common types of security holes found in network services; if an attacker is able to find and exploit a buffer overflow in a program you devise yourself, and there is any way for the program to run executable code as root (for example, if it's a setuid program owned by root), your system belongs to that attacker. Be very careful in this area!

Shell Initialization Files

It's now time to discuss how to customize your shell to do what you want. You can create aliases to simplify common commands, you can automatically execute certain programs every time you log in, you can set various environment variables to your taste, and much more. These tasks are handled in the shell initialization and configuration files, which exist both at the global and per-user levels.

Because tcsh and bash have completely different sets of configuration files, we will cover them both sequentially. FreeBSD includes systemwide and default per-user config files for both shells so that you can switch from tcsh to bash on a systemwide basis if you really want to (although this is rarely necessary).

> **NOTE**
>
> When a new user is created, default shell config files are copied from /usr/share/skel (the dot prefix on each of the files is dropped) into the new user's home directory. If you like, you can copy these default files into /usr/local/share/skel, modify them to your taste, and then alter the /etc/adduser.conf file to copy its default "dotfiles" from this new location. Use this technique to make a global, pre-emptive change to all users' default shell configurations before they're even created.

tcsh/csh **Files:** .cshrc, .login, **and** .logout

The first file that tcsh looks at when it is executed is the systemwide config file, /etc/csh.cshrc, followed immediately by /etc/csh.login. Note that in FreeBSD, both these files exist, but their only contents are commented out (see Listing 11.1).

LISTING 11.1   The global /etc/csh.cshrc and /etc/csh.login Files

```
# cat /etc/csh.cshrc
# $FreeBSD: src/etc/csh.cshrc,v 1.3 1999/08/27 23:23:40 peter Exp $
#
# System-wide .cshrc file for csh(1).

# cat /etc/csh.login
# $FreeBSD: src/etc/csh.login,v 1.19.2.1 2000/07/31 20:13:26 rwatson Exp $
#
# System-wide .login file for csh(1).
# Uncomment this to give you the default 4.2 behavior, where disk
# information is shown in K-Blocks
# setenv BLOCKSIZE     K
#
# For the setting of languages and character sets please see
# login.conf(5) and in particular the charset and lang options.
```

LISTING 11.1   Continued

```
# For full locales list check /usr/share/locale/*
#
# Read system messages
# msgs -f
# Allow terminal messages
# mesg y
```

This listing shows that these config files don't really do anything, but they could if you so chose. Any change you make in either of these files, such as enabling mesg (terminal messages) globally, is applied globally. The change is overridden only if set differently by the per-user config files, which are analogous to the systemwide ones and read immediately afterward from the user's home directory (.cshrc, followed by .login).

The default .cshrc file, which comes from /usr/share/skel/dot.cshrc, does a number of generally useful things to set up the shell environment. For example, it creates several aliases to shorten commands:

```
alias h         history 25
alias j         jobs -l
alias la        ls -a
alias lf        ls -FA
alias ll        ls -lA
```

It sets the search path for programs:

```
set path = (/sbin /bin /usr/sbin /usr/bin /usr/games /usr/local/sbin
➥/usr/local/bin /usr/X11R6/bin $HOME/bin)
```

It sets various environment variables that control the behavior of many different shell tasks:

```
setenv  EDITOR  vi
setenv  PAGER   more
setenv  BLOCKSIZE      K
```

And a few other things are set as well. You can look at the .cshrc file in your own home directory to see them all.

The .login file, which is read next, is where the user can place any programs she wants to run every time she logs in. For example, the fortune program is provided in the default .login file (from /usr/share/skel/dot.login) and is encapsulated in an existence-test conditional (but it's commented out):

```
# Uncomment to display a random cookie each login:
# [ -x /usr/games/fortune ] && /usr/games/fortune -s
```

You (the administrator) or the user can also specify certain things to happen whenever the user logs out. For instance, you might write a script to clean out any temporary files owned by the user in /tmp; you could put a call to this script into /etc/csh.logout, which in its default state has no material contents:

```
# cat /etc/csh.logout
# $FreeBSD: src/etc/csh.logout,v 1.3 1999/08/27 23:23:41 peter Exp $
#
# System-wide .logout file for csh(1).
```

The logout process will also read a .logout file in the user's home directory if it exists, but there is no such per-user file installed by default.

> **NOTE**
>
> The files shown in this section are the ones run by tcsh when it is executed as a login shell. There are various other circumstances under which tcsh can be run—for example, as a non-login shell executed in order to run a shell script, invoked from the interpreter line of the script. In this case, the .login and .logout files (and their systemwide equivalents) are ignored.

bash Files: .profile, .shrc, and .bash_logout

If you've chosen to use bash rather than tcsh as your shell, it will operate in much the same way. It will first read the systemwide config and initialization files and then proceed to the per-user ones. First comes /etc/profile, which (like /etc/csh.cshrc) is materially blank but contains a few examples for options you might decide to enable, as shown in Listing 11.2.

LISTING 11.2   The Global /etc/profile File

```
# cat /etc/profile
# $FreeBSD: src/etc/profile,v 1.12.2.1 2000/07/31 20:13:26 rwatson Exp $
#
# System-wide .profile file for sh(1).
#
# Uncomment this to give you the default 4.2 behavior, where disk
# information is shown in K-Blocks
# BLOCKSIZE=K; export BLOCKSIZE
#
# For the setting of languages and character sets please see
# login.conf(5) and in particular the charset and lang options.
# For full locales list check /usr/share/locale/*
# You should also read the setlocale(3) man page for information
# on how to achieve more precise control of locale settings.
```

LISTING 11.2   Continued

```
#
# Read system messages
# msgs -f
# Allow terminal messages
# mesg y
```

Notice that /etc/profile combines the functionality of both /etc/csh.cshrc and /etc/csh.login. It's the only bash-related global file in the system; there is no systemwide logout script for bash.

The next file for bash is the user's .profile file, which primarily sets various environment variables (including PATH) and exports them in the Bourne shell style:

```
# remove /usr/games and /usr/X11R6/bin if you want
PATH=/sbin:/bin:/usr/sbin:/usr/bin:/usr/games:/usr/local/bin:
➥/usr/X11R6/bin:$HOME/bin; export PATH


BLOCKSIZE=K;     export BLOCKSIZE
EDITOR=vi;       export EDITOR
PAGER=more;      export PAGER


# set ENV to a file invoked each time sh is started for interactive use.
ENV=$HOME/.shrc; export ENV
```

The last line sets the ENV variable to the .shrc file, also in the user's home directory. This is then read in sequence with .profile. Its purpose is to define the various aliases that tcsh sets in .cshrc, as well as a few other optional things, such as customizing the prompt, that are commented out by default:

```
# some useful aliases
alias h='fc -l'
alias j=jobs
alias m=$PAGER
alias ll='ls -laFo'
alias l='ls -l'
alias g='egrep -i'


# # set prompt: ``username@hostname$ ''
# PS1="`whoami`@`hostname | sed 's/\..*//'`"
# case `id -u` in
#       0) PS1="${PS1}# ";;
#       *) PS1="${PS1}$ ";;
# esac
```

As with .logout for tcsh, bash will read and execute a .bash_logout file if it's present (but no such file is installed by default).

> **NOTE**
>
> These are the files "sourced" (that is, read as configuration files) by bash if it's executed as a login shell. If it's used as a non-login shell, though, the file it reads is .bashrc rather than .profile. This file doesn't normally exist in FreeBSD.

Customizing Your Shell Environment

You've seen a few examples already, in both tcsh and bash style, of how to customize the way your shell works through the use of the default settings in the shell config files. These can serve as perfectly valid examples of how to extend your shell's functionality. There are a few extra things you can do, though. Also, some options aren't clearly demonstrated in the default files. We'll look at how to accomplish these customizations in tcsh and in bash. In most cases, these are built-in shell commands that can be issued either from the command line directly or from within any of the shell configuration files.

> **NOTE**
>
> Full details on a large number of available built-in commands—some of which appear in csh/tcsh, some of which appear in sh/bash, and some of which appear in both—can be found in man builtin.

Customizing tcsh

The most common shell customization is to create an alias. This customization substitutes the first word of a command with whatever you choose to replace it with. Aliases can greatly simplify your work, especially if there are certain complex commands that you find yourself using on a regular basis. The simplest alias is of the type seen in .cshrc:

```
alias ll        ls -lA
```

This alias, as you would expect, replaces a command such as ll /usr/local with ls -lA /usr/local. But what if you want to perform argument substitution as well, reformatting the command's parameters according to what you enter each time? You can do that with the extremely versatile and equally convoluted command-line parsing syntax of tcsh. The man tcsh page explains this in full detail, but for our purposes, simply note that the first argument to a command in an alias assignment can be referred to as \!^ (or \!:1), and further arguments can be indicated as \!:2, \!:3, and so on. Therefore, you can create an alias like the following:

```
alias lookup    grep \!^ /etc/passwd
```

This customization allows you to enter commands such as lookup frank to extract a user's information. The unalias command allows you to remove an alias, as shown here:

```
unalias lookup
```

You can customize your prompt's appearance by setting the prompt shell variable. You can embed the output of any command (for example, by enclosing it in back ticks) as is done in Perl scripts. You can also echo the "command number" variable, which specifies an event in the editable history, with the ! character. The following example is a fairly complex one that incorporates all these tricks, plus the use of sed (a "stream editor" text processor that operates noninteractively on text fed to it at any time) to shorten the output of hostname to its first element:

```
# set prompt="{`whoami`@`hostname | sed 's/\..*//'`:!} "
{root@www:23}
```

Another use of the prompt shell variable is to reflect the directory you're currently in, which can be echoed using the pwd (present working directory) command:

```
# set prompt="{`pwd`:!} "
{/root:24}
```

Setting the command path in tcsh also involves setting a shell variable (we'll cover shell variables and environment variables in a moment). You can't add elements to the paren-thesized array "on the fly." You have to add the new path element to the string and reissue the entire set command, which is why the path is best set from within one of the config scripts rather than from the command line. The syntax specifies a list of pathnames in parentheses, separated by spaces:

```
set path = (/sbin /usr/sbin /bin /usr/bin /usr/local/bin /usr/contrib/bin
➥/usr/X11R6/bin /usr/local/sbin /usr/games . /usr/local/mystuff)
```

Another useful built-in tool is stty. This tool allows you to redefine various character mappings, a practice you might find very useful in cases where your terminal program sends unexpected characters to your programs. This is most commonly seen in confusion between "delete" and "backspace" characters or in line-delimiter characters. The first step is to see what's currently set for the characters:

```
# stty -a
speed 38400 baud; 60 rows; 80 columns;
lflags: icanon isig iexten echo echoe -echok echoke -echonl echoctl
        -echoprt -altwerase -noflsh -tostop -flusho pendin -nokerninfo
        -extproc
iflags: -istrip icrnl -inlcr -igncr ixon -ixoff ixany imaxbel -ignbrk
        brkint -inpck -ignpar -parmrk
```

```
oflags: opost onlcr -oxtabs
cflags: cread cs8 -parenb -parodd hupcl -clocal -cstopb -crtscts -dsrflow
        -dtrflow -mdmbuf
cchars: discard = ^O; dsusp = ^Y; eof = ^D; eol = <undef>;
        eol2 = <undef>; erase = ^?; intr = ^C; kill = ^U; lnext = ^V;
        min = 1; quit = ^\; reprint = ^R; start = ^Q; status = ^T;
        stop = ^S; susp = ^Z; time = 0; werase = ^W;
```

Now, if you want to set your "erase" character to ^H, specify it in just that two-character form:

```
# stty erase ^H
```

You can turn on "watch" mode, telling you who's logged in on the system and who has the various ptys, with the following sequence:

```
set watch=(1 any any)
set who="%n has %a %l from %M."
```

One thing about tcsh that you'll likely want to disable is the autologout shell variable, which is set by default to 60 minutes. This variable closes your connection if you leave the terminal idle for more than an hour. You can disable autologout easily enough with this config file line:

```
unset autologout;
```

Finally, if you set any of these built-in customization variables by editing the configuration scripts, you don't have to log out and back in to incorporate them; you can use the rehash built-in command to force a reread of all the config scripts.

Customizing bash

Aliases in bash work a bit differently from those in tcsh. The alias and substitution text are separated by an equal sign (=) rather than a space or tab. Also, there is no mechanism for performing argument substitution as there is in tcsh, so the lookup alias we created for tcsh can't be created in bash without more extensive gymnastics:

```
alias ll='ls -laFo'
```

Setting your prompt in bash can get interesting. Because bash doesn't implement shell variables in the same customized way that tcsh does, the best it can really do is to set the "primary" and "secondary" prompts as environment variables (PS1 and PS2), from which the shell reads the strings it displays to you. To get the "e-mail address" prompt you saw earlier in tcsh, use the following code (note the backslash behind the ! character, which doesn't have the same special meaning as it does in tcsh):

```
# PS1="{`whoami`@`hostname | sed 's/\..*//'`:\!} "
{root@www:17}
```

Similarly, to get a prompt that reflects the present working directory, use the following:

```
# PS1="{`pwd`:\!} "
{/root:18}
```

Setting the command path in bash involves setting the PATH environment variable. In this context, it's a colon-separated string of pathnames, together with an export statement to publish the variable into the environment:

```
PATH=/sbin:/bin:/usr/sbin:/usr/bin:/usr/games:/usr/local/bin:
➥/usr/X11R6/bin:$HOME/bin; export PATH
```

The need to export your variables is something we'll talk about in the next section.

Shell and Environment Variables

One of the biggest differences between tcsh and bash lies in the way they handle variables. You have two kinds of variables to work with: shell variables and environmental variables (you'll learn more about these variables in Chapter 12). Let's take a look at how the variable types differ and where they're used.

Environment Variables

No matter which shell you're using, you always have environment variables (variables containing values that travel with you throughout your login session and are propagated to any program spawned from within that session). Environment variables dictate the behavior of certain programs that you run. For instance, the chfn program launches the text editor specified in the EDITOR environment variable, and the TERM variable tells the shell how to format text to display properly on your screen. The BLOCKSIZE variable controls what the output numbers in commands such as du and df signify (kilobytes, half-kilobytes, or whatever the value of the variable is). A program doesn't have to be a login shell to have access to environment variables—every program has access to the same set of variables as the program that spawned it.

Whichever shell you're using, you can view all your environment variables using the printenv command, as shown in Listing 11.3.

LISTING 11.3   Sample Output of the printenv Command

```
# printenv
PATH=/sbin:/usr/sbin:/bin:/usr/bin:/usr/local/bin:/usr/contrib/bin:
➥/usr/X11R6/bin:.
MAIL=/var/mail/frank
```

LISTING 11.3   Continued

```
BLOCKSIZE=1k
FTP_PASSIVE_MODE=YES
USER=frank
LOGNAME=frank
HOME=/home/frank
SHELL=/bin/tcsh
SSH_CLIENT=192.168.173.230 50095 22
SSH_TTY=/dev/ttyp0
TERM=vt100
HOSTTYPE=FreeBSD
VENDOR=intel
OSTYPE=FreeBSD
MACHTYPE=i386
SHLVL=1
PWD=/home/frank
GROUP=users
HOST=stripes.somewhere.com
REMOTEHOST=192.168.173.230
PATHSET=true
EDITOR=vi
VISUAL=pico
```

To set an environment variable from within the shell, you would use one of two syntaxes, depending on the shell you're using. To set a variable called COLOR to gold in tcsh, enter the following:

```
# setenv COLOR gold
```

In bash, you have to first set the variable in the local session context and then export it to the shell's environment, as shown here:

```
# COLOR=gold
# export COLOR
```

Note that an environment variable must have a value; it can't simply exist in the environment with a null or undefined value.

Shell Variables

In addition to environment variables, another separate set of variables are available to your login session. These variables, called *shell* variables, apply only to the current login session and have no bearing on any other processes. They're comprehensible only to the shell process itself. In programming terms, shell variables exist in the "local" context, whereas environment variables exist in the "global" context and can be inherited by other programs.

Shell variables in `tcsh` *must* be lowercase, and shell variables in `bash` *must* be uppercase. You can view shell variables using the `set` command. Setting a shell variable in `tcsh` is also done, not surprisingly, with `set`. It's possible to set a shell variable in `tcsh` without assigning a value to it:

```
# set history=100
# set noclobber
```

In `bash`, you simply set the variable without exporting it:

```
# VISUAL=pico
```

You can also remove a variable with `unset`, as shown here:

```
# unset autologout
```

Shell and environment variables, as well as the way their inheritance properties interact and apply to shell scripting techniques, will be described more fully in Chapter 12.

CHAPTER 12

Shell Programming

In Chapter 7, "Working with the Shell," you saw how to work with the shell interactively at the command line. What you may not have known is that a powerful programming language is built in to the shell. You can use shell programming to do everything from automating a repetitive list of commands, to writing sophisticated interactive programs that process text data, to storing and retrieving information in simple databases.

Due to the modular design of the FreeBSD operating system, you can call any FreeBSD command from within a shell program. And if you can't find a FreeBSD command to do what you want, you can string commands together in "pipelines" to create new commands. As you learn in this chapter, pipelines take the output from one command and use it as the input for another command. FreeBSD has hundreds of these modular commands that each serve a small but highly specialized purpose. In this chapter, you learn how to write a simple shell program and how to use variables, arithmetic, and loops in shell programming. You also learn how to use conditional statements, file descriptors, and many of the advanced techniques of shell programming to perform a number of important tasks in FreeBSD.

Shell programs offer commands for searching text files, combining text from two files into a single file, formatting text in columns, cutting only certain fields from text files, counting characters, words, and lines in a file, performing math operations, doing file backups, compressing and uncompressing files, and much more. If you can't find a command or pipeline that does what you want, chances are you can find a free program available on the Internet that you can use in your shell program. You learn how to take full advantage of shell programs in this chapter.

Why Shell Programming Matters to You

Shell programming is sometimes shunned in favor of Perl and other languages and thought of as simply a "glorified version of DOS batch programming," but this simply is not true. In its simplest form, shell programming is like DOS batch programming in that you can use it to execute a list of commands stored in a file that could also be executed from the command line. However, you can write highly sophisticated shell programs.

Here are the top six reasons to learn FreeBSD shell programming:

- It's easy to learn. If you work with the FreeBSD command line on a regular basis, you probably are already familiar with many of the commands you can use in your shell programs.

- For many tasks, you can develop a shell program in 5 or 10 minutes that would take hours or even days to develop in C or some other programming language.

- It can save you hours of tedious work. For example, why go through 100 text files manually to make a single change, when you can write a shell program with a `for` loop that will do it automatically?

- It will teach you many new and useful ways to work with FreeBSD. You will discover useful commands you never knew existed as well as ways to do things you didn't even know could be done. You might even learn to like the FreeBSD command line. Why spend money to buy a new program to perform a certain task when you can string a few FreeBSD commands together in a pipeline to accomplish the same thing?

- Don't like the way an existing command works? You can write a new one in a few minutes with shell programming. One of the things that makes FreeBSD so powerful is the "do it your own way" philosophy. There are many ways to achieve the same end, and no one way is necessarily the best way.

- It is perhaps the ideal first programming language because it allows you to concentrate on learning programming logic and such while working with commands you may already be familiar with.

Furthermore, some of the most crucial components of FreeBSD are actually shell scripts, including (but not limited to) the resource configuration scripts in /etc and the start/stop shell scripts that control third-party daemon programs, which live in /usr/local/etc/rc.d (as you will see in Chapter 10, "System Configuration and Startup Scripts").

Having a thorough grounding in shell scripting will make it much easier for you to understand how those scripts work, and therefore to come up with clever solutions to problems that might arise with your configuration. Shell scripting is like having a jack in your trunk: Most of the time, it's just there taking up space. But when you suddenly get a flat tire, you find yourself very glad you took the time to stow it there.

It's to your advantage to take the time to understand the shell, how it interprets commands, how to send the output of one command down a pipeline to use as the input for another command, and the hundreds of specialized FreeBSD commands available for performing various tasks. You can start that learning process by working with a simple shell program, as you do in the section that follows.

NOTE

The first part of this chapter covers only commands that are available in all Bourne-type shells. The second part covers the enhanced features of the Korn and POSIX shells, such as FreeBSD uses. If you need to write shell programs that will be run on other systems and you cannot say for sure what shells will be available on those other systems, it is best to stick with the commands available in all Bourne shells. If you don't, your programs might not work on other systems that have an older Bourne shell.

NOTE

This chapter does not cover C shell scripting at all. Although it is possible to write shell scripts using the C shell, this is generally not a good idea because it lacks a lot of very useful shell-scripting features (including functions and swapping STDOUT and STDERR). C shell scripting can be a real exercise in frustration and futility. Because of this, it is recommended that you always write your scripts using the Bourne shell.

TIP

There is a lot more to shell scripting than a single chapter can cover. If you are interested in learning more about shell scripting, refer to *Teach Yourself Shell Programming in 24 Hours*, available from Sams Publishing, for more information.

A Simple Shell Program

The first rite of passage for any aspiring programmer is to write the "Hello World!" program. Here is one way to write it in the Bourne shell programming language. Enter this text in your favorite text editor and then save it as a file (the line numbers in this code are for reference only; don't include them when you enter the code):

```
1.  #!/bin/sh
2.
3.  # The legendary Hello World program
4.  # As implemented in the Bourne shell programming language.
```

```
5.
6.   echo
7.   echo "Hello World!"
8.   echo
9.exit 0
```

Next, you need to make the file executable. You can do this with the following command:

```
chmod u+x hello
```

Assuming that you named the file `hello`, this command gives the owner of the file permission to execute it.

TIP
Traditionally, shell scripts have the extension .sh so that anyone can quickly tell in a directory listing that a certain file is a shell script. The extension is not necessary, however, and in some cases you might want to leave it out to make the commands easier to type. If you're writing a shell script for end users who have no knowledge of what the .sh extension means, you can safely leave the extension off.

Next, execute the file. The following sequence shows the command you type as well as the output of the program:

```
bash$ ./hello

Hello World!

bash$
```

Understanding the Shell Script, Line by Line

Now let's look at the lines in the previous program in detail and see what each one does:

- **Line 1**—This line contains the magic character sequence #!, which tells FreeBSD that what follows is a script that should be interpreted by the program named after #!. In this case, it tells FreeBSD that it should use the Bourne shell interpreter `/bin/sh` to interpret what follows. If this were a Perl script, we would use `/usr/bin/perl`. For a Python script, we would use `/usr/local/bin/python`, and so on.

- **Lines 2 and 5**—These are simply blank lines. The shell ignores whitespace unless it is quoted (more on that later). It is a good idea to use whitespace to make your program more readable.

- **Lines 3 and 4**—These are comments. Comments in a shell program begin with # and extend to the end of the line. Comments are ignored by the interpreter. They are used for the benefit of the programmer who needs to revisit a complicated program he wrote six months ago and try to figure out what it does again.

- **Line 6**—The echo command takes whatever it receives and echoes it to STDOUT (which is normally the screen). This can be redirected, however, so that echo sends the output somewhere else, such as to a file. In this case, echo by itself simply prints a blank line on STDOUT.

- **Line 7**—The echo command here prints the string "Hello World!" to STDOUT. The quotes tell the interpreter that everything inside them should be interpreted as a single argument (that is, the shell should interpret the string as one long unit instead of many short units). Without the quotes, the shell will interpret the white-space as an argument separator. In this case, the quotes would not have been strictly necessary, but you will see later on in the chapter why quoting is important. It is a good idea to get into the habit of quoting strings such as these.

- **Line 8**—The echo command here prints a blank line again.

- **Line 9**—The exit command exits the program and returns an exit status to the invoking program. (This is normally the shell, but it could be another program, such as another shell program.) An exit status of 0 indicates that the program terminated normally. An exit status of anything other than 0 indicates that an error occurred. The exit status can be read by the calling program and used in decision-making. The calling program then determines what action it should take next, based on the success or failure of the previous program that was run.

In a program this short, setting the exit status isn't really necessary. If the exit status is not implicitly set, the exit status returned will be the exit status of the last command that was run in the script. It is best to be aware of the exit status, though, because it will become important as you start to write larger and more complex shell programs. Later in this chapter, you will see how the exit status of a command can be used in a shell script to make automatic decisions about the next action that should be performed. However, setting the exit status should not generally be necessary; if a script is written properly, it will exit with a status of 0 on its own. Otherwise, it will have inherited an error condition from one of its lines, and you as the programmer should address this rather than masking the true status with an exit statement.

Using the printf Command

The previous program could also have been written using printf instead of echo. The printf command performs a similar function, but it allows more control over how its output is formatted. The following example shows how the program could be rewritten using printf instead of echo:

```
1.   #!/bin/sh
2.
3.   # The legendary Hello World program
4.   # As implemented in the Bourne shell programming language.
5.
6.   printf "\nHello World!\n\n!"
```

If this program is run, the output it produces will look exactly the same as the previous program's.

If you have ever programmed in C before, the syntax of the printf command will look familiar to you.

The backslash is an escape character that indicates the character immediately following it has special meaning (or negates the special meaning of the character if the character would have special meaning by itself). In this case, n is a newline character. This is why we could eliminate the two echo commands to insert blank lines when we use printf, because now we can embed the newlines directly into the string we wish to print. At the end of the string, we used two newline characters because printf does not automatically insert a newline at the end. So, we want two newlines to get a blank line. Here's an example in which printf doesn't automatically insert a blank line at the end:

```
printf "Hello "
printf "World!\n\n"
```

The previous two lines in a shell script would produce the output "Hello World!", even though they are separate statements. This is because printf does *not* automatically output a newline (which in Unix implies a carriage return) at the end of a statement, the way echo does. If we had used echo in the previous two lines instead of printf, "Hello" and "World!" would appear on separate lines.

The printf command supports the formatting characters outlined in Table 12.1.

TABLE 12.1   Formatting Control Characters from printf

Formatting Characters	Description
\a	Rings the terminal's bell. In the old teletype days, this rang an actual bell on the teletype machine. These days, it usually beeps the computer's speaker.
\b	Prints a backspace character.
\f	Prints a form-feed character.
\n	Prints a newline character.
\r	Prints a carriage return. The difference between this and the newline character is that the carriage return returns the cursor to the beginning of the line but does not send it to the next line. The result is that the previous output on the line will be overwritten by whatever comes after \r.
\t	Prints a tab character.

TABLE 12.1   Continued

Formatting Characters	Description
\v	Prints a vertical tab character, which is equivalent to a linefeed without a carriage return.
\'	Prints a single-quote character.
\"	Prints a double-quote character.
\\	Prints a backslash.
\num	Prints the ASCII value of the octal 1-, 2-, or 3-bit value *num*. You will probably never use this option in a shell program.

Of course, simply being able to echo messages to the screen is not very useful. This is where variables come in.

Variables

In algebra, you learned that you can use letters to stand for unknown quantities in algebraic equations, and that these letters are called *variables*. In programming, the concept is pretty much the same, although programming variables can hold strings (strings of characters) as well as numbers.

You work with two types of variables in shell programming: shell variables and environment variables. The primary difference is that *environment variables* are available to other scripts or programs that you call from inside your shell program, whereas *shell variables* are available only to the script itself.

Variables in shell programming are loosely typed; they do not have to be declared or typeset before they can be used. All variables in shell programming are stored as strings.

Variable Assignment

In its most basic form, a variable can be set from the command line in the following manner:

```
myvar=5
```

The value 5 is now stored in the variable myvar. To access the information stored in a variable, proceed the variable name with a dollar sign ($). For example echo ${myvar} will print 5 to STDOUT, which as you recall, is normally the screen.

> **NOTE**
>
> Variable assignment is one place where whitespace *does* matter. The statement mvar=5 will assign the value 5 to the variable myvar. The statement myvar = 5 will produce an error because the shell will try to interpret myvar as a command name to execute rather than as a variable assignment.

The curly braces are optional but can help to improve code readability because they make variable names easier to spot when you are quickly scanning code. It's up to you whether you want to use the braces.

The value of a variable can also be assigned to another variable. Here's an example:

```
myvarB=$myvar
```

This line assigns whatever is in `myvar` to the variable `myvarB`. If `myvarB` already contains something (for example, the number 5), that value is overwritten by the new assignment.

In addition, it is also possible to assign the output of a command to a variable or read input from `STDIN` (which is normally the keyboard) and store it in a variable. You will see how to do this later in the chapter.

Creating an environment variable is pretty much the same as creating a shell variable. The only difference is that it must be exported. This is done with the `export` statement, as shown in this example:

```
MYVAR=5
export MYVAR
```

This creates a shell variable named `MYVAR` and then exports it so that it is an environment variable that is available to other shells started from within this shell.

Variable Names

Variable names are case sensitive and can contain letters, numbers, and underscores. The variable name cannot begin with a number, though, and it is best to avoid beginning variable names with an underscore. Use descriptive names to make program code easier to read. For example, it is much easier to guess what a variable named `avg_rainfall` probably contains than to guess what a variable named `xyz123` might contain.

CAUTION

You cannot use words that are already the names of shell commands as variable names; nor can you use any of the "reserved words" that have special meaning in shell scripting, such as `if` and `case`.

TIP

By convention, local variables use lowercase letters, and environment variables use uppercase letters. However, some people prefer to use a mixture of lowercase and uppercase letters in local variables to make them stand out from other shell commands, which are almost always in all lowercase.

Interacting with the User

Simply assigning variables inside a script and calling those variables later is not very useful. The shell provides a way for you to get input from STDIN. Normally, this input will be typed in by the user (or received from a file if STDIN has been redirected). The command that can read input from a user is read. Here is a slightly modified version of the "Hello World!" program that reads input from STDIN, which is normally the keyboard:

```
1.  #!/bin/sh
2.
3.  # Modified Hello World program that accepts input from keyboard
4.
5.  echo
6.  echo -n "Please enter your name: "
7.  read name
8.  echo
9.  echo "Hello, ${name}!"
10. echo
```

When run, this program does the following:

```
Please enter your name: Mike
Hello, Mike!
```

Notice these three important lines in the preceding program:

- **Line 6**—A new option to the echo command is introduced. The -n option suppresses the newline character that would normally be sent at the end of the echo statement. This causes the cursor to remain on the same line after Please enter your name:.

- **Line 7**—The read command accepts input from STDIN (in this case, the keyboard). The user can enter a string of text here. When Enter is pressed, read takes whatever the user entered and stores it in the variable name. The read command implies quotes; therefore the string is stored in the variable exactly as the user enters it with all whitespace preserved.

- **Line 9**—The echo command is used to insert the contents of the variable name into the string containing Hello, and the exclamation point; then, once the final string is composed, it sends the string to the screen. Once again, the curly braces are optional.

The read command can take multiple variables as arguments. When it does, whitespace is the delimiter that separates what goes into each variable. Listing 12.1 shows an example.

LISTING 12.1   Using Multiple Variables with read

```
#!/bin/sh

echo
echo -n "Enter three numbers separated by spaces or tabs: "
read var1 var2 var3
echo
echo "The value of var1 is: ${var1}"
echo "The value of var2 is: ${var2}"
echo "The value of var3 is: ${var3}"
echo
```

Here is a sample run of the previous program:

```
Enter three numbers separated by spaces or tabs: 557 2024 57240

The value of var1 is: 557
The value of var2 is: 2024
The value of var3 is: 57240
```

It doesn't matter how much whitespace you use in the input from the keyboard. When assigning multiple variables, read interprets any amount of whitespace as argument separators to determine what should go in each variable.

If read gets fewer arguments than there are variables in its list, the remaining variables after the argument list runs out will not be assigned. On the other hand, if read gets more arguments than it has variables, whatever arguments are left over will be assigned to the last variable in the list. For example, here is another run of the program that gives read more than three arguments:

```
Enter three numbers separated by spaces or tabs: 1 2 3 4 5 6 7 8 9 0
The value of var1 is: 1
The value of var2 is: 2
The value of var3 is: 3 4 5 6 7 8 9 0
```

Handling Command-Line Arguments

You can also get information from the user by reading arguments included on the command line. The shell automatically stores command-line arguments in special variables. No programming is required to actually read the arguments. Up to nine arguments can be included on the command line. These arguments are stored in the variables $1–$9. The FreeBSD POSIX shell also allows additional arguments that can be accessed with ${10}, ${11}, and so on. But this should be avoided if the program will need to run on other systems, because the traditional Bourne shell can only handle $1–$9. The variable $0 contains the name of the program itself, the variable $@ contains all the arguments, and the variable $# contains the number of arguments that were passed to the program. Here's an example:

```
#!/bin/sh
echo
echo "The name of the program is: $0"
echo "The total number of arguments received is: $#"
echo "The complete argument string is: #@"
echo "Your first name is: $1"
echo "Your last name is: $2"
echo
```

And here is a sample run:

```
bash$ ./yourname Michael Urban

The name of the program is: ./yourname
The total number of arguments received is: 2"
The complete argument string is: Michael Urban"
Your first name is: Michael
Your last name is: Urban

bash$
```

> **NOTE**
>
> The POSIX shell that FreeBSD uses also supports the getopts command, which provides a more versatile way of handing command-line arguments with a shell program. We will discuss this command when we talk about the advanced features of Korn shell programming. If you are writing Bourne shell programs (that use sh) for other Unix platforms, however, it is best to avoid the use of getopts because it is not a standard part of the traditional Bourne shell and may cause the program not to work on some systems.

Command Substitution

Among other things, *command substitution* allows you to run a command and assign the output to a variable. The command to be run should be enclosed in a backward quote (`). Be careful not to confuse this character with the single quote. The backward quote character typically shares a key with the tilde (~) character on the keyboard. Here's an example of the backward quote used to enclose a command:

```
TodayDate=`date`
```

This example runs the date command and assigns its output to the variable TodayDate. You can then access the information in this variable just as you can access the information in any other variable.

Arithmetic in Shell Programs

Although the original Bourne shell has no built-in arithmetic handlers, arithmetic can still be done using command substitution along with the expr command. Here's an example:

```
var3=`expr var1 + var2`
```

This adds the values contained in var1 and var2 together and then stores the result in var3. Note that the arguments and the operator must be separated by whitespace. expr var1+var2 will not have the intended result.

The expr command can do only very simple arithmetic—it can handle only integer arithmetic. Entering floating-point numbers will cause an error. In addition, changing the order of operations with parentheses is not supported. Division that does not return an integer value will have the decimal portion dropped. For example, 5 / 2 is 2 as far as expr is concerned. If you wish to retrieve the remainder of a division, you can use the modulus operator (%). For example, expr 5 % 2 will return 1 (5 / 2 = 4 remainder 1).

Characters that have special meaning to the shell must be escaped. For example, expr 2 * 2 will not work because the shell interprets the * as a wildcard operator. For the operation to work, the multiplication operator (*) must be escaped like this: expr 2 * 2. This protects it from the shell and prevents the shell from giving it special meaning.

expr can also evaluate true/false expressions. If the expression is true, expr returns a 1. If the expression is false, expr returns 0. Here's an example:

```
expr 2 + 2 = 4 + 1
```

This returns 0 (the equation is false).

This next example returns 1 (the equation is true):

```
expr 2 + 2 = 3 + 1
```

!= will reverse the equation. It means "is not equal to." So, for example, the equation expr 5 != 3 will return 1 (true).

expr can, of course, also evaluate less than/greater than expressions. Once again, because the < and > characters have special meaning to the shell, they must be escaped when used with expr to protect them from the shell. It is a true/false evaluation just like the "equal to" operator. If the expression is true, expr returns 1. If the expression is false, expr returns 0. For example, expr 5 \> 4 returns 1 (the expression is true). In addition, greater than or equal to (\>=) and less than or equal to (\<=) evaluations are also supported.

expr is not limited to comparing numbers. It can also compare strings. For example, expr "The quick brown fox jumped over the lazy dog" = "The quick brown fox jumped over the lazy dg" will evaluate to 0 (the expression is false unless the strings are exactly equal).

Although expr is great for simple shell scripting, as mentioned previously, its capabilities are rather limited. If you need to do floating-point math, work with complex expressions that change the order of operations, and so on, you can use a command called bc. bc is a programming language in itself for working with math. It is possible to embed expressions into your shell program and feed them to bc. The program in Listing 12.2 uses bc to compute both the circumference and the area of a circle. Note that the argument to bc is -1, the lowercase letter L. It defines the standard math library for bc.

LISTING 12.2   Using bc to Compute the Circumference and Area of a Circle

```
1.  #!/bin/sh
2.
3.  # The Following program computes both the circumference and the area
4.  # of a circle.
5.
6.  pi="3.14159265"          # Assign the value of pi to a variable.
7.
8.  # Tell the user what the program does and ask them for the radius of
9.  # the circle.
10.
11. echo
12. echo "This program computes both the circumference and the area of"
13. echo "a circle."
14. echo
15. echo -n "Please enter the radius of the circle: "
16. read radius
17.
18. # Now we will use bc to compute the answers and store them in variables.
19.
20. circumference=`echo "$radius*$pi" | bc -l`
21. area=`echo "$radius^2*$pi" | bc -l`
22.
23. # Last, we display the answers to the user and exit.
24.
25. printf "\n\nThe circumference is:\t$circumference\n"
26. printf "The area is:\t\t$area\n\n"
```

Most of the concepts used in this program have already been explained, in the sections "Variables" and "Interacting with the User." Therefore, rather than go through the program line by line, we'll just cover the concepts that are new and/or important to the operation of the program:

- **Line 6**—This line assigns a reasonably accurate value of pi to a variable called `pi`. I point this out because it shows good programming practice. We could just as easily have typed the number 3.14159265 each time we needed to use pi in the program. But assigning the number to a variable serves two primary purposes. First, it simply makes the program more readable. Second, it makes the program much easier to maintain. If we later decided that we needed more precision for the value of pi, we would only have to change one number where we assign the value to the variable `pi`. If we had used the actual number each time in the program when we needed it, we would have to find and change each occurrence of pi when we decided we need more precision.

- **Line 16**—As shown earlier, the `read` command gathers data from `STDIN`. In this case, we gather the value typed by the user and store it in the variable `radius`.

- **Line 20**—Line 20 uses command substitution and a pipe to compute the circumference of the circle and store the value in the variable `circumference`. Because bc does not accept expressions directly on the command line, we need to use the `echo` command to echo the expression we want computed and then pipe the output of `echo` to bc.

- **Line 21**—This line is similar to line 20. The caret (^) in the expression is the bc exponent operator. In this case, it raises the value stored in `$radius` by the power of 2 (you may recall from geometry that the area of a circle is obtained by squaring the radius and then multiplying by pi). We do not need to use parentheses to change the order of operation because, as you may recall from algebra, exponents have higher precedence than multiplication. Therefore, we can be assured that the exponent will be evaluated before the multiplication is done.

- **Lines 25 and 26**—These lines display the results to the user. I used `printf` here because it gives me a nicer layout than `echo`. The use of the hardware tabs with \t causes the numbers to line up in a nice column.

This is only a very simple use of bc. bc is quite powerful and can do much more than the examples you've seen here. See the man page for bc if you are interested in learning more about its capabilities, both inside shell scripts and in standalone programs.

Loops

Sometimes you might want an operation to repeat until a certain condition becomes true (or until a certain condition is no longer true). This is where looping statements come into play. The Bourne shell supports three different looping constructs for these situations. These are the `while` loop, the `until` loop, and the `for` loop. We will look at each one separately.

The while **Loop**

The while loop repeats the statements inside the loop as long as the condition that is being tested is true. Depending on your point of view, it could also be said that the while loop repeats the statements inside the loop until the condition that is being tested becomes false. If the condition is already false the first time it is evaluated, the loop will never be executed. For example, the following program uses a while loop to count to 20 and display the numbers on the screen:

```
1.  #!/bin/sh
2.  # Count from 1 to 20
3.  i=1
4.  while [ $i -le 20 ]
5.  do
6.        echo $i
7.        i=`expr $i + 1`
8.  done
```

This program introduces a few new concepts:

- **Line 3**—This line simply assigns the variable i the initial value of 1. i is a variable that is universally understood to be a loop-control counter; as with its usage in summation in mathematics, *i* typically stands for *increment*. This is one case where you can get away with not using a descriptive variable name.

- **Line 4**—The while command contains the condition to test enclosed in brackets. The bracket is actually a shorthand notation for a command called test. You will use this command a lot in shell scripting.

  Unfortunately, the test command uses a somewhat strange syntax. -le in this example means "is less than or equal to." So this means the loop will repeat as long as the variable i is less than or equal to 20. For mathematical evaluations, Table 12.2 shows all the operators that this command supports.

TABLE 12.2   Mathematical Operations for the test Command

Option	Action
-eq	True, if operand one is equal to operand two
-ne	True, if operand one is not equal to operand two
-gt	True, if operand one is greater than operand two
-ge	True, if operand one is greater than or equal to operand two
-lt	True, if operand one is less than operand two
-le	True, if operand one is less than or equal to operand two

- **Line 5**—The do statement indicates that everything after this should be done for each iteration of the loop. All statements located between the do statement and the done statement are considered part of the loop.

- **Line 6**—Prints the current value of the variable i.

- **Line 7**—Uses command substitution with the expr command to increment the value of i by 1 and then assign the new value back into i.

- **Line 8**—Indicates the end of the loop. At this point, the program jumps back up to the while statement, and the test condition is evaluated again. If i is still less than or equal to 20, the statements inside the loop are repeated again. If i is greater than 20, the loop exits and control passes to the first statement after the done statement (in this case, line 9, which simply exits the program with a 0, or successful status).

Notice that the statements inside the loop are indented. This makes it easy to pick out the statements that are part of the loop when quickly scanning the program's source code. The shell ignores the indentation, so you could have written this program without using it. I recommend you always indent loops, though, to make them easier to find when quickly scanning program source code.

> **TIP**
>
> The space between the bracket ([) and the condition to be tested is mandatory, as is the space immediately before the final bracket (]). Failing to include either one will cause an error. For example,
>
> ```
> [ $VarA -gt 5 ]
> ```
>
> will work, but
>
> ```
> [$VarA -gt 5]
> ```
>
> will cause an error.

The until Loop

The until loop is the opposite of the while loop. It performs the operations inside the loop as long as the condition being tested is not true. When the condition being tested becomes true, the loop exits. If the condition is already true the first time it is evaluated, the loop will never be executed.

The while loop and the until loop are very similar. Usually, you can use either one in a program and achieve the same results simply by modifying the condition that is tested for. For example, the counting program that used the while loop can be rewritten to use an until loop by making only two changes in line 4:

```
4.  until [$i -gt 20 ]
```

This program performs the same function performed by the earlier program that uses the while loop. The only difference is that now the loop repeats until the value of i is greater than 20, whereas before it repeated while the value of i was less than or equal to 20. The result is exactly the same, however.

Logical AND/OR Statements in while and until Loops

Both the while loop and the until loop can also work with logical AND/OR statements. A logical AND statement will be carried out if and only if both conditions are true. A logical OR statement will be carried out if either condition is true. The following code example shows a logical AND statement, which will execute the while loop only if both statements ("$VarA is equal to 1" and "$VarB is greater than 7") are true; the second statement is not true, so the loop will not execute:

```
#!/bin/sh
# Demonstrate logical AND
VarA=1
VarB=5
while [ $VarA -eq 1 ] && [ $VarB -gt 7 ]
do
        echo "VarA is equal to 1 and VarB is greater than 7"
done
```

In this example, the echo statement will not be executed. Because the while loop in this case requires both conditions to be true, the test fails and returns a 0 (false).

The following code example is identical to the previous one, except we have changed the while test to a logical OR statement. Now, only one of the conditions needs to be true. Therefore, because $VarA will always be equal to 1 in this program, the while statement will continuously execute in an endless loop (until you press Ctrl+C):

```
#!/bin/sh
# Demonstrate logical OR
VarA=1
VarB=5
while [ $VarA -eq 1 ] || [ $VarB -gt 7 ]
do
        echo "VarA is equal to 1 or VarB is greater than 7"
done
```

The for Loop

The for loop is different from the while and until loops. Instead of evaluating a true/false test condition, the for loop simply performs the statements inside the body of the loop once for each argument it receives in a list. When creating a for loop, you supply it a variable. Each iteration of the for loop changes the value of the variable to the next argument in the list. The for loop continues until the argument list has been exhausted, at which point the loop exits and the first statement after the loop is executed. The following program uses a for loop along with the bc command you learned about earlier to print the square root of all numbers from 10 through 20:

```
1.  #!/bin/sh
2.  # Print square roots of 10 - 20
3.  for num in `jot 10 10 20`
4.  do
5.     square_root=`echo "scale=5; sqrt($num)" | bc -l`
6.     echo $square_root
7.  done
```

The output from this program is as follows:

```
3.16227
3.31662
3.46410
3.60555
3.74165
4.00000
4.12310
4.24264
4.35889
4.47213
```

Note these important lines in the preceding program:

- **Line 3**—This line of the program contains the for loop. It introduces a new command called jot. The jot command can do many useful operations with numbers, including printing a string of numbers and generating random numbers. In this case, we have used jot to print a string of 10 numbers, starting with number 10 and ending with the number 20 (10 10 20). The for loop assigns each one of these values to the variable num in sequence and then performs the statements in the body of the loop for each value.

- **Line 5**—This line uses the bc command to compute the square root of the value stored in $num. The "scale=5" statement tells bc that the output should be scaled (truncated) to five significant digits after the decimal point. Notice also the semicolon after the scale statement. Semicolons can be used in place of a new line to separate multiple statements on the same line. The sqrt function of bc takes a number in parentheses and returns the square root of that number. Because the shell expands the variable to the value it contains, bc actually receives the number contained in the variable rather than the name of the variable itself. Finally, at the end of line 5, the output is piped to the bc command itself. The -1 option tells bc to preload the math function library, which contains the sqrt function.

The shift Command

The shift command is similar to the for loop. Basically, you can use a while loop along with shift to run a loop once for each command-line argument sent to a shell program.

As you'll recall from the previous discussion, command-line arguments are stored in numbered variables starting at $1 and going to $9. The shift command shifts the variables one position to the left each time it is run. This means that each time shift is encountered, the information currently stored in $1 "falls off" the end, for example, and the information currently stored in $2 is moved to $1. Here is an example:

```
1.  #!/bin/sh
2.  # This program demonstrates the use of shift.
3.  while [ $# -ne 0 ]
4.  do
5.      echo "The value of \$1 is now $1."
6.      shift
7.  done
8.  echo
```

And here's a sample run:

```
bash$ ./shift1 a b c d e
The value of $1 is now a.
The value of $1 is now b.
The value of $1 is now c.
The value of $1 is now d.
The value of $1 is now e.

bash$
```

Here are the notable lines in this program:

- **Line 3**—This line starts a while loop. You will recall from the "Handling Command-Line Arguments" section that the magic variable $# contains the number of command-line arguments. This while loop continues as long as the value of $# is not equal to zero. When the value of $# is equal to zero, all the command-line arguments have been used up, and the loop ends.

- **Line 5**—This line prints the current value of $1. Note that to actually print the literal string $1 on the screen, you have to escape the $ character with a backslash to prevent the shell from giving $ a special meaning.

- **Line 6**—When the `shift` command in line 6 is run, the variables are shifted one position to the left. $1 "falls off" the end and is no longer available, $2 becomes $1, $3 becomes $2, and so on.

One of the most common applications of `shift` (and `for` loops) is in shell programs that accept filenames as command-line arguments and then perform a group of operations on each file specified on the command line.

The `true` and `false` Statements

The sole purpose of the `true` and `false` statements in shell programming is to return a value of true (0) or false (1), respectively. You can use these statements to create infinite loops. As long as there is some condition that can break a program out of an infinite loop, it can be useful to write code that creates one. This is how programs are designed that run continuously and listen for input, such as Web servers. The following example shows a program that will loop indefinitely:

```
1.   #!/bin/sh
2.   # The following program loops indefinitely.
3.   while true
4.   do
5.        echo "This line will print forever."
6.   done
7.   echo "This line will never print since the program will"
8.   echo "never get past the loop."
9.   exit 0      # The program will never exit cleanly since it will
10.              # never get to this point.
```

Obviously, this chapter cannot show you the output of this program, because it would go on forever. Line 3 tests for a true condition. And because the argument it tests (`true`) will never return a value of false, the loop will repeat indefinitely. Lines 7, 8, 9, and 10 will never be executed because the program can never get past the loop. (To end this program, press Ctrl+C on your keyboard.)

Breaking the Loop

Sometimes, you might want to break out of a loop before the condition necessary to exit the loop has occurred. There are two statements that can be used to break a loop. The first is the `break` statement. The second is the `continue` statement.

The `break` Statement

The `break` statement will terminate a loop immediately when it is encountered, regardless of whether the condition required to exit the loop has been met. Listing 12.3 shows a slight modification to the previous "endless loop" program.

LISTING 12.3   Breaking Out of a Loop

```
1.  #!/bin/sh
2.  # The following program loops indefinitely.
3.  while true
4.  do
5.      echo "This line will print forever... But..."
6.      break
7.  done
8.  echo
9.  echo "The break statement in the loop causes the loop"
10. echo "to terminate immediately and go the first statement"
11. echo "after the loop."
```

Here's the output of this program:

```
This line will print forever... But...

The break statement in the loop causes the loop
to terminate immediately and go to the first statement
after the loop.
bash$
```

In a more complex implementation, you could have a loop that waits for some kind of input to be entered from the user's console or from the network; the loop could test continuously for the existence of a file or the value of a variable, and if that condition becomes true, a break could end the loop. Usually it is considered more elegant to write loops whose exit conditions are constructed to react properly on the right kind of input and to avoid a break when possible. In sufficiently complex programs, however, a break can be just what you need to get out of a jam.

The continue Statement

The continue statement causes the loop to immediately jump back to the top and re-evaluate the test condition. Any remaining statements in the loop are not executed. Listing 12.4 is another example that uses the "endless loop" program with a slight modification.

LISTING 12.4   Restarting a Loop Before It Has Ended

```
1.  #!/bin/sh
2.  # The following program loops indefinitely.
3.  while true
4.  do
5.      echo "This line will print forever."
6.      continue
```

LISTING 12.4   Continued

```
7.       echo "But this line will never print even though it is inside"
8.       echo "the loop because the preceding continue statement"
9.       echo "causes the loop to jump back to the top and re-evaluate"
10.      echo "the test."
11. done
12. echo "This line will never print since the program will"
13. echo "never get past the loop."
14. exit 0      # The program will never exit cleanly since it will
15.             # never get to this point.
```

This program will indefinitely output "This line will print forever." The rest of the echo statements inside the loop will never be printed because the continue statement before them causes the loop to immediately jump back to the top and re-evaluate the test condition.

Conditional Statements

Conditional statements execute if and only if a certain condition or conditions are true. They generally come in three forms: if statements, case statements, and logical AND/OR statements. These are very fundamental and useful constructs in programming; flow control depends on them (executing certain blocks of code depending on the outcome of a condition), as does the ability of a program to behave correctly upon receiving certain expected arguments (which would be handled by case statements).

if Statements

if statements test numerical expressions. If the condition is true, the statements inside the if block are executed. If the condition is false, one of two things can happen:

- Nothing. The statements inside the if block are not executed, and the program continues as if they were not even there.

- If an else statement is included inside the if block, the statements will be executed if the condition is false. In other words, this can be used to write "Do this if the condition is true, or do this if the condition is false, but do not do both" type of controls in programs.

For example, the following program uses an if statement to test the number of command-line arguments given to the program. If the command-line arguments are one or more, the program performs the operations inside the then block. If no command-line arguments were supplied, the program exits without doing anything:

```
1.  #!/bin/sh
2.  # ifprog: Demonstrate one way to use if statements.
3.  if [ $# -ge 1 ]
4.  then
5.      echo "You supplied $# command line arguments."
6.  fi
7.  echo
8.  echo "Program exiting..."
9.  echo
```

And here are two sample runs:

Run 1:

```
bash$ ./ifprog file1 file2 file3
You supplied 3 command line arguments.

Program exiting...
bash$
```

Run 2:

```
bash$ ./ifprog

Program exiting...
bash$
```

The if statement in line 3 checks to see whether the number of command-line arguments supplied is one or greater (using the magic variable $#, which stores the number of command-line arguments). If it is, the statements between then and fi are executed. ("fi" is if spelled backward. It marks the end of the if block.) If it isn't, the statements inside the if block are skipped and the program jumps to the first statement past fi, which in this case simply informs the user that the program is exiting.

Using an else Statement

We could make this program more user friendly by including an else statement that tells the user how to properly use the program rather than simply having it exit without doing anything, as it currently does. Listing 12.5 shows the revised example. Note that the operand in line 3 is a number one, not a lowercase *L*.

LISTING 12.5   A More Friendly Version of the Previous Program

```
1.  #!/bin/sh
2.  # ifprog: Demonstrate one way to use if statements.
3.  if [ $# -ge 1 ]
```

LISTING 12.5   Continued

```
4.   then
5.        echo "You supplied $# command line arguments."
6.   else
7.        echo "Usage: $0 file1 file2..."
8         echo
9         exit 1
10.  fi
11.  echo
12.  echo "Program exiting..."
13.  echo
```

Now, if the number of command-line arguments is less than one, the program will perform the else statements and give the user a usage message (remember that $0 contains the name of the command that was invoked). Notice also line 9, which tells the program to exit immediately and sets the exit status to 1 (which indicates the program terminated with errors). Statements 10–14 will never get executed if the program runs the else statements.

The then part of the if statement is required. The else part is optional. As you have seen, the then part of the if statement performs an action if the expression tested by if evaluates to true. Sometimes, however, you might want to perform an action only if the expression evaluates to false and to do nothing if the expression evaluates to true. You can do this by using a colon as a placeholder. Here's an example:

```
if [ $myvar -gt 5 ]
then
    : # Do nothing and continue after end of if block
else
    # Statements to execute if condition is false go here.
fi
```

Using an elif Statement

Sometimes you might want to test for two or more different conditions and perform a different action, depending on the results. The elif statement accomplishes this.

elif is an abbreviation for "else if." When elif statements are used, the program will go through the if statement. If it evaluates to true, its actions will be performed and then program flow will jump to the first statement after the end of the if block (where fi is located). If it evaluates to false, the first elif is checked. If it is true, the statements inside it are executed and flow jumps to the end of the if block. If it is false, the second elif statement is evaluated, and so on. Basically, evaluations are done until the program reaches an expression that evaluates to true. If none of the conditions evaluate to true, either nothing happens or the statements inside else, if present, are executed. Listing 12.6 uses much of what you have learned up to this point, including if, elif, and else to play a simple number-guessing game. Note that line 10 uses jot, a little command-line random-number-generating tool. The arguments in this case to its -r option are the number of results to return (1), the lower bound (1), and the upper bound ($up_limit).

LISTING 12.6   A Simple Number-Guessing Game

```
1.  #!/bin/sh
2.  # Number guessing game
3.  clear
4.  guess_count=1    # Initialize the guess counter to 1
5.  echo
6.  echo "Number guessing game written in bourne shell script."
7.  echo
8.  echo -n "Enter upper limit for guess: "
9.  read up_limit
10. rnd_number=`jot -r 1 1 $up_limit`    # Get a random number
11. echo
12. echo "I´ve thought of a number between 1 and $up_limit."
13. echo
14. echo -n "Please guess a number between 1 and $up_limit: "
15. read guess
16. # Check the guess against the random number.
17. while true
18. do
19.     if [ $guess -gt $rnd_number ]
20.     then
21.         echo
22.         echo "Your guess was too high. Please try again."
23.         guess_count=`expr $guess_count + 1`
24.         echo -n "Please guess a number between 1 and $up_limit: "
25.         read guess
26.     elif [ $guess -lt $rnd_number ]
27.     then
28.         echo
29.         echo "Your guess was too low. Please try again."
30.         guess_count=`expr $guess_count + 1`
31.         echo -n "Please guess a number between 1 and $up_limit: "
32.         read guess
33.     else
34.         break
35.     fi
```

LISTING 12.6   Continued

```
36. done
37. # We get to this point when the player guesses the correct number.
38. echo
39. echo "Correct!"
40. echo
41. echo "You guessed the number in $guess_count guesses."
42. echo
```

Here's a sample run:

```
Number guessing game written in bourne shell script.

Enter upper limit for guess: 10
I've thought of a number between 1 and 10.

Please guess a number between 1 and 10: 5

Your guess was too low. Please try again.
Please guess a number between 1 and 10: 8

Your guess was too high. Please try again.
Please guess a number between 1 and 10: 7

Correct!

You guessed the number in 3 guesses.
```

Most of the concepts in this program should be familiar to you by now:

- Line 3 simply clears the screen.
- Line 4 initializes a variable guess_count to store the number of guesses the player has made and sets the initial value to 1.
- Lines 23 and 30 increment the value of the variable guess_count by 1 for each incorrect guess made.
- Line 10 uses command substitution with the jot command to assign a single random number between 1 and whatever the player entered as the upper limit for the guess to the variable rand_number.
- Line 17 starts an infinite loop.

- Line 19 checks to see whether the number the player entered is greater than the random number that the program picked. If it is, the player is informed of that, the guess_count variable is incremented by 1, and the player is asked to pick another number. After the player has picked another number, it is stored in the variable guess and the while loop starts over.

  If the number the player guessed is not greater than the random number the computer picked, the elif statement is evaluated to check whether the number is lower. If it is, the player is informed of this, the guess_count variable is incremented by 1, and the player is asked to try again. After the player has entered a new number, the while loop starts over.

- Finally, if neither condition is true, the else statement is executed (we did not need to perform a test here because if the number is neither higher nor lower, it must be equal). The else statement here simply breaks out of the infinite loop, and program flow passes to the first statement after the done statement.

- The statements at the end of the program simply tell the user he guessed the correct number and then inform the user how many guesses it took him to get the correct answer by displaying the value of guess_count.

Like loop tests, if tests also support the logical AND (&&) and logical OR (||) tests to perform conditions if and only if both conditions are true, or if one of any number of conditions are true.

case **Statements**

If you need to test the same variable for multiple conditions, there is a more efficient and cleaner way of doing it than with if statements. The case statement takes a variable as an argument and then uses statement blocks to determine what to do, depending on the value of the variable. Listing 12.7 uses case statements to create a random quote generator.

LISTING 12.7   Using case to Generate Random Quotes

```
1.  #!/bin/sh
2.  # Random quote generator.
3.  quote_num=`jot -r 1 1 5`
4.  case "$quote_num" in
5.     1) echo
6.        echo "\"Until he extends his circle of compassion to include"
7.        echo "all living things, man will not himself find peace.\""
8.        echo "-- Albert Schweitzer"
9.        echo ;;
10.    2) echo
```

LISTING 12.7   Continued

```
11.        echo "\"With regard to excellence, it is not enough to know, but"
12.        echo "we must try to have and use it.\""
13.        echo "-- Aristotle"
14.        echo ;;
15.    3) echo
16.        echo "\"Imagination is more important than knowledge. Knowledge"
17.        echo "is limited. Imagination encircles the whole world.\""
18.        echo "-- Albert Einstein"
19.        echo ;;
20.    4) echo
21.        echo "\"It is not the strongest of the species that survive, nor"
22.        echo "the most intelligent, but the one most responsive to change.\""
23.        echo "-- Charles Darwin"
24.        echo ;;
25. esac
```

Once again, we use jot in line 3 to generate a random number between 1 and 4. The case block begins on line 4. The syntax is case *variable* in, where *variable* is the name of the variable that the tests should be performed on. Line 5 begins the first test. Everything to the left of the parenthesis indicates the condition that case tests for. Like the if statement, case stops at the first match it comes to, executes the statements that go with that match, and then jumps down to esac (which is "case" spelled backward). The end of the statements that go along with each condition is marked with a double semicolon. The double semicolon can be on a line by itself, or it can be placed on the same line as the last statement, as is done in the previous example.

The case statement also accepts shell wildcards. Here's an example:

```
case "$myvar" in
    a) #statements to do for a
       ;;
    b) #statements to do for b
       ;;
    *) #statements to do for anything else
       ;;
esac
```

The previous code will check to see whether $myvar is equal to *a* or *b*, and perform the appropriate statements if it is. If it is not, the last test is a wildcard that will match anything. So, if $myvar is not equal to *a* or *b*, the last group of statements will be performed.

Other wildcards supported by case include ?, which works the same way it does in the shell (as you saw in Chapter 7), and the pipe character (|), which allows case to accept a range of options. For example, Y | y) will accept either *Y* or *y* as a match for a test. You can also enclose multiple characters in brackets to match a range of characters. For example, [Yy]|[Yy][Ee][Ss]) will accept either *y* or *yes* as a match in any combination of upper- or lowercase letters.

12

CGI Programming

You've probably seen Web sites that have features such as random quotes that display on the page at each load or a random picture that changes each time the page is reloaded. The program presented previously that used case to display the quotes is one way to do this. This is called a CGI program, and it is a way for the Web server to run external programs and then send the output of those programs over the Internet to a browser. Chapter 25, "Configuring a Web Server," covers more of CGI programming.

Logical AND/OR **Conditionals**

Using logical AND/OR conditionals are basically a short-hand way of doing if statements in some cases. They use the exit status of the first command to determine whether to run the second command. Here's an example:

```
tar cvfz backup.tar.gz documents/2000/* && rm -r documents/2000
```

This command basically says, "If the first operation is successful, perform the second operation. If the first operation is not successful, do not perform the second operation." In other words, "You have to perform A and B. If A cannot be performed, do not perform B." In this case, it will attempt to archive all the files in the directory documents/2000 into a file called backup.tar.gz. If the archive operation is successful (the tar command exits with 0), the operation after && will also be performed, which removes the directory documents/2000. If the archive operation is unsuccessful (the tar command exits with some number other than 0), the operation after && will not be performed (obviously, we do not want to remove the directory if we were unable to successfully archive it).

The || is the OR operator. It basically says, "If you cannot perform A, perform B. But do not perform B if A is successful." Here is an example:

```
tar cvfz backup.tar.gz documents/2000/* || echo "Archive operation failed."
```

In this case, if the archive operation is successful (tar exits with 0), the statement after || will not be executed. If, however, the archive operation fails (tar returns an exit status other than 0), the statement after || will be executed, and an error message will be printed to the screen.

Exit Status

Most programs in FreeBSD return an exit status when they terminate. The exit status is usually 0 if successful, and some number other than 0 if something went wrong. Some programs will return a different exit status, depending on the problem. Often, this information can be found in the program's man page.

The exit status of the last program that ran is stored in the magic variable $?. Here are a couple of examples:

```
bash$ ls > /dev/null
bash$ echo $?
0
bash$
```

```
bash$ ls -2 /dev/null
ls: illegal option -- 2
usage: ls [-ABCFGHLPRTWabcdfgiklnoqrstu1] [file ...]
bash$ echo $?
1
bash$
```

The first example will set the magic variable $? to 0, as shown (the output of the ls command was redirected to /dev/null for brevity in the example). The second example, however, supplies an illegal option to ls. The command fails with an error message, and $? is set to 1.

You can use this exit status to make automatic decisions in your shell programs. The previous logical AND/OR example already introduced this to an extent. It showed how the success or failure of one command can determine whether the next one is executed. The logical AND/OR statement used in the previous section could also have been written as an if statement, like this:

```
if tar cvfz backup.tar.gz documents/2000/*
then
    rm -r documents/2000
else
    echo "Archive operation failed"
fi
```

This example combines the two examples from the previous section. The if statement reads the exit status of the tar command. If the exit status is 0, the then statements are performed, and the directory that was archived is removed. If the exit status is some number other than 0, the then statements are not performed, and the else statements are performed instead.

Another useful application of this property is with the test command. You've already seen how to use the test command with mathematical expressions. Another useful application of test is to check for the existence of AND/OR properties of a file, as in this example:

```
if [ -f program.conf ]
then
    : # do nothing
else
    touch program.conf
fi
```

This example checks for the existence of the file program.conf. If the file exists, 0 is returned and the then statement is executed. In this case, the then statement does nothing. (The colon tells it to do nothing. The rest of the line is a comment.) If the file does not exist, 1 is returned and the else statement is performed, which uses the touch command to create the file.

The test command can test for more than just the existence of a file. It can also test the attributes and type of file. Table 12.3 is a list of all the options to the test command and what they mean.

TABLE 12.3 Testing File Attributes in Shell Programs

Option	Action
-f	The file exists and is a normal file.
-d	The file exists and is a directory.
-s	The file exists, and its size is greater than zero.
-c	The file exists and is a character special file.
-b	The file exists and is a block special file.
-r	The file exists and is readable.
-w	The file exists and is writable.
-x	The file exists and is executable.
-d	The file exists and is a directory.

Setting Exit Status

Most of the scripts in this chapter have set the exit status, and by now you have a pretty good idea of what the exit status is used for. You have also seen that the exit statement is used to set the exit status. If you do not specifically set the exit status, your program will return the exit status of the last command that ran. When you do set the exit status, whatever you set will be stored in the $? variable, just like the exit status of any other program. Also, just like any other program, the exit status of your shell program can be read by other programs to make a decision about what to do next. This can be useful if you are calling a shell program from another shell program, for example.

Also, remember that you are not limited to just 0 and 1 for exit statuses. You can use many more exit statuses. Always use 0 for a successful exit and numbers other than 0 for an error exit. You can use several different exit statuses in the same program to handle different error conditions, and then the calling program can act accordingly. Here is an example of some code that uses multiple exit statuses:

```
if [ -r program.conf ]
then
    : # do nothing
else
    exit 1
fi
if [ `touch /tmp/program.lock` ]
then
    : # do nothing
else
    exit 2
fi
# main program statements here
exit 0
```

The preceding example first checks to see whether it can read the file program.conf. If it can, the program continues to the next if test. If it can't, the program exits immediately with an exit status of 1. If the program was able to read the program.conf file, it will then attempt to create the /tmp/program.lock file. If it can, the program continues. If it can't, the program exits immediately with an exit status of 2. Finally, assuming that both operations succeed, the program will continue with the main part of the program and then exit with a status of 0. This program could be called from another program and then return its exit status to that program. The calling program could then make decisions based on the exit status it received from this program.

Exit Traps

As you know, programs in FreeBSD can be terminated by sending them various "kill" signals and with various combinations of keyboard commands (Ctrl+C, for example). (See the "Terminating Misbehaving Processes" section of Chapter 13, "Performance Monitoring, Process Control, and Job Automation" for more on the kill command and its signals.) The problem with this is that if, for example, a program creates temp files, and the user interrupts the program with Ctrl+C before it has finished running, the program will not clean up after itself and will leave its temp files laying around on the disk, thus wasting space.

Fortunately, the shell provides a way to trap these types of interrupts. Here is a short sample program that demonstrates the use of trapping interrupts:

```
#!/bin/sh
# Program that demonstrates trapping interrupts
trap `echo "Interrupt received. Quitting." 1>&2` 1 2 3 15
echo -n "Enter a number: "
read num
exit 0
```

Basically, this program sets a trap for interrupts 1, 2, 3, and 15. The actions performed by the trap are located between the single quotes. If you run this program and press Ctrl+C at the prompt that asks you to enter a number, it will send signal 2 (INT) to the program, which will set off the trap and cause the message "Interrupt received" to be printed. Then, the program will exit.

You also can use the echo command in the task of shell output redirection. The 1>&2 in the echo statement redirects the output of the echo command to STDERR. This ensures that the output of the command will not accidentally be sent down a pipe to another command or redirected to another location along with the rest of the program's output. It is a good idea any time you create error messages to send the output to STDERR with 1>&2.

Normally, of course, you would use the traps to do things such as clean up temp files and such. If you need to do a lot of things in a trap, it is better to make the trap a function (functions will be covered later in the chapter).

If you want to prevent the user from being able to exit the program with Ctrl+C, you can set a trap and leave the action null, like so:

```
trap `` 2
```

This line causes signal 2 to be completely ignored.

Your program can have more than one trap, and different things can be done, depending on how the program has exited. A trap for signal 0 will be set off on all exits, normal or otherwise.

A trap for other signals will be set off only when one of those signals occurs. Table 12.4 provides a list of the most common signals you might want to trap.

TABLE 12.4   Common Interrupt Signals and Their Actions

Interrupt Signal	Action
0	Exit
1	HUP—Session hangup (or disconnect)
2	INT—Interrupt (Ctrl+C)
3	QUIT—Quit (Ctrl+\)
15	TERM—A normal kill command

NOTE

You can trap signal 15 (the default signal sent by the `kill` command). You can also trap most other signals that can be sent by the `kill` command. However, you cannot trap signal 9 (SIGKILL). SIGKILL is used as a last resort to terminate a program when all other methods have failed. Therefore, it cannot be trapped and cannot be ignored.

Functions

Functions are basically groups of statements that can be called with a single command. They can almost be thought of as "mini-programs inside other programs." Using functions in your shell programs can make your life a lot easier—for two reasons. First of all, if you need to perform the operation in multiple places in your program, you can simply type the name of the function rather than having to retype all the code each time you need to perform the operation. Second, if you later decide you need to make the operation work differently, you only have to change the function rather than go through the code and change it every place it is used. The following example demonstrates how a function is created; it shows a simple function that cleans up temp files, and so on, after a shell program exits. It then shows how to call the function:

```
#!/bin/sh
on_exit() {
    rm -rf /tmp/myprogram.*
    mv logfile logfile.old
    mail foo@bar.com < report.txt
}
trap on_exit 0 1 2 3 15
```

This function is given a name, followed by parentheses and a left bracket. Everything between the two brackets is the body of the function. The function can then be called as if it were a program, simply by using its name. As stated previously, functions can almost be thought of as "mini-programs inside other programs." Any time you type the name of this function, the statements between its brackets will be performed.

There is one important difference between calling a function and calling another program, though. The function is run in the current shell, whereas a separate program starts in a subshell. This means that a function can modify the variables and environment variables in the program that calls it. But a separate program called from inside a shell program cannot modify any of the variables or environment variables in the calling program.

File Descriptors

File descriptors are numbered IDs that are set up each time the kernel starts a process. These numbers are what the process uses to write output and read input. Three file descriptors are opened by default:

File Descriptor	Meaning
F.D. 0	STDIN. This is where standard input comes from. This is normally the keyboard, but it can be redirected to read from a file or some other source.
F.D. 1	STDOUT. This where standard output goes. It is normally the screen, but as you have seen it can be redirected.
F.D. 2	STDERR. This is where standard error messages go. Once again, this is normally the screen, but it can also be redirected.

File descriptors can be used in shell programs to make your programs both more efficient and easier to write. The exec command can be used to open a file descriptor. Here is an example of how file descriptors can make your programs both easier to write and more efficient:

```
#!/bin/sh
# open a file descriptor on F.D. 1 (STDOUT)
exec > testfile.txt
# echo some stuff to STDOUT which will now go to the file testfile.txt
echo "Line 1 of the file"
echo "Line 2 of the file"
echo "Line 3 of the file"
echo "Line 4 of the file"
echo "line 5 of the file"
exit 0
```

The exec statement in the second line of the preceding code example causes testfile.txt to be opened as STDOUT. As a result, all the echo lines are set to the file testfile.txt instead of to the screen, even though the output is not redirected in the echo statements. If you have a lot of things that need to be written to a file, this is more efficient than using shell redirection each time. It is also easier to code because you don't have to redirect the output each time.

This is also very useful when opening a file descriptor for STDIN and using read. Here is an example:

```
#!/bin/sh
# open a file descriptor on F.D. 0 (STDIN)
exec < testfile.txt
while read string
do
    echo $string
done
```

Assuming that you still have the file `testfile.txt` from the previous example, this example will output the following:

```
Line 1 of the file
Line 2 of the file
Line 3 of the file
Line 4 of the file
Line 5 of the file
```

So, what is so great about this? It demonstrates the important concept of using a file descriptor with `read`. Because the file is not closed between each call to `read`, `read` remembers the last line it read and moves the pointer to the next line in the file. This way, `read` will read each line of the file in sequence automatically.

Debugging Shell Scripts

If you write shell scripts of any complexity at all, sooner or later bugs are going to creep in. Although there is no full-fledged debugger for the shell, it does provide some primitive debugging capabilities in the form of being able to trace each action that is performed. You turn on the tracing by adding `-xv` to the end of the `#!/bin/sh` line in your script, so it looks like this:

```
#!/bin/sh -xv
```

The `-x` switch means for the shell to print every command, preceded by a plus sign (+), to `STDERR`. The `-v` switch puts the shell in verbose mode. This has the effect of causing the script to write out everything it does to the error file descriptor so that you can debug more easily.

This works best if you pipe the output to `more` or `less` so that it doesn't scroll off the screen faster than you can read it—and also if you redirect both `STDOUT` and `STDERR` to the same place so that you can see both the output of the script and the errors. Enter this simple example into a file called `xvtest` and set it executable:

```
#!/bin/sh -xv
# Demonstrate the use of tracing in shell script debugging
result=`echo "2 * 12 / (2 + 2)" | bc`
echo $result
exit 0
```

To execute this program so that you will see both `STDOUT` and `STDERR` and pipe the output to `more`, use the following command:

```
./xvtest 2>&1 | more
```

The program will produce the following output:

```
1.    ./xvtest 2>&1 | more
2.  #!/bin/sh -xv
3.  # Demonstrate the use of tracing in shell script debugging
4.  result=`echo "2 * 12 / (2 + 3)" | bc`
5.  + echo 2 * 12 / (2 + 3)
6.  + bc
7.  + result=4
8.  echo $result
9.  + echo 4
10. 4
11. exit 0
12. + exit 0
```

You can now see everything that this program did. The lines with plus signs (+) in front of them are the results of actions in the program. For example, line 3 in the preceding example assigns the results of a calculation to the variable result. Lines 4, 5, and 6 show the actions that were taken. Line 4 shows the echo command, line 5 shows the execution of bc, and line 6 shows the variable assignment, where 4 is assigned to the variable result.

This example also shows how variable expansion works. Notice lines 8, 9, and 10. In line 8, the echo statement is read. In line 9, the variable is expanded so that the echo statement becomes "echo 4". Then, in line 10, the actual output of the echo statement is produced.

Advanced Features of Korn Shell Scripting

The Korn shell contains some advanced features that can make shell programming easier and more powerful, such as built-in arithmetic and arrays. You should think carefully before using these features in a script, however, because virtually every Unix system can run a Bourne shell script, but some will not be able to run a Korn shell script. If such a script is highly specialized—requiring the advanced features of the Korn shell—and will be run only on your local system or on systems that have the Korn shell available, using this script won't present any problems. If you are writing a shell script for public consumption, however, or if this script will run on multiple systems within your organization and you cannot be sure which shells will be available on those systems, you are better off sticking to plain-old Bourne script.

That being said, this section will cover some of the advanced features of Korn shell scripting.

> **TIP**
>
> Most of the techniques given in this chapter also apply to the POSIX shell that FreeBSD ships with as /bin/sh. However, you definitely should not use these in a /bin/sh script if the script will be run on other systems that do not use a POSIX shell as /bin/sh. Because of the #!/bin/sh at the beginning of the script, the other system will try to run the script anyway. But it will bomb as soon as it hits code that it doesn't understand because that code is not part of the Bourne shell syntax.

> **TIP**
>
> Note that the bash shell can also run most scripts written for the Korn shell. However, you will, of course, need to change the first line in the script to point to the bash shell instead of the Korn shell. For example, in FreeBSD you would change #!/usr/local/bin/ksh to #!/usr/local/bin/bash. If you wanted to run the script on a Linux system, you would change the line to #!/bin/bash.

Obtaining and Installing the Korn Shell

Before you can write shell programs for the Korn shell, you need to install a copy of the Korn shell on your system. The Public Domain Korn shell is available for FreeBSD both on the CD-ROM as a package under shells (which can be installed from /stand/sysinstall or from the command line) and also in the ports tree under /usr/ports/shells/pdksh. To tell your program to run with the Korn shell, replace #!/bin/sh at the top of your shell program with #/usr/local/bin/ksh. The Korn shell is completely backward compatible with Bourne, so any script that was written for a Bourne shell will also run under the Korn shell. The reverse is not true, however. You cannot run a Korn shell script under Bourne.

When you have the Korn shell installed, take a moment to review some of the advanced features that make programming in the Korn shell easier, more powerful, and more efficient.

Built-in Arithmetic

The Korn shell has built-in arithmetic. This means you do not need to call the expr program to do arithmetic in Korn as you do in Bourne. However, like expr, Korn shell arithmetic is limited to operations on integer numbers. Because it is an internal function, however, it can perform these operations much faster than exec.

There are two ways to access the built-in arithmetic functions of the Korn shell. The first is with the let statement. Here's an example:

```
let x=7+5
```

This line assigns 12 to the variable x.

The other method is by enclosing the expression in double parentheses, as shown here:

`((x=7+5))`

This can be more readable than using `let`. It is also more readable for mathematical comparisons than using the test command in Bourne shell syntax because it allows you to use the familiar mathematical notations < and > rather than `-lt` and `-gt`. Also, unlike with `expr`, characters that would have special meaning to the shell do not have to be escaped. In Korn, you can write `((5 * 3))` rather than `expr 5 \* 3`, for example.

Korn shell arithmetic supports the common mathematical operators shown in Table 12.5.

TABLE 12.5   Korn Shell Math Operators

Operator	Description
+	Addition
-	Subtraction
*	Multiplication
/	Division
%	Modulus (returns the remainder of a division)
>	Greater than
<	Less than
>=	Greater than or equal to
<=	Less than or equal to
==	Equal to
!=	Not equal to
&&	True if both expressions are non-zero
||	True if either expression is non-zero
=	Assigns the expression on the right to the expression on the left
+=	Adds the expression on the right to the variable on the left and then stores the result in the variable
-=	Subtracts the expression on the right from the variable on the left and then stores the result in the variable
*=	Multiplies the expression on the right by the variable on the left and then assigns the result to the variable
/=	Divides the expression on the right by the variable on the left and then assigns the result to the variable
%=	Divides the expression on the right by the variable on the left and then assigns the remainder to the variable

Arrays

The Korn shell also supports arrays. An *array* is a variable that contains multiple elements, each of which contains a separate value. Arrays are useful for grouping related elements together.

You can think of an array as a box with different compartments in it. Each compartment has a number. You could access the various compartments by giving the name of the box, followed by the compartment number.

Use the `set` command to load an array. For example, suppose we want to create an array called `temperature` that contains the average temperature for each month of the year for a given area. The following command will do the trick (the –A option effectively sets the parameter, or name, of the array to `temperature`):

```
set -A temperature 57 52 58 61 63 65 71 70 68 66 64 62
```

This will create an array called `temperature` with 12 elements in it—one for each month of the year. If you are following along at your system, simply enter the previous command from a Korn shell command prompt for now (if you need to start a Korn shell, you can do so by typing **ksh** at the prompt).

To access the various elements in the array, we use a subscript appended onto the end of the array name. Elements in the array start at 0, and wildcards are accepted. Here are some examples of how this works:

```
ksh$ echo ${temperature[0]}
57
ksh$ echo ${temperature[11]}
62
ksh$ echo ${temperature[*]}
57 52 58 61 63 65 71 70 68 66 64 62
ksh$
```

Arrays can contain up to 512 elements (0–511).

If you wish to change the value of only one element in an array, you can do so by referencing the element in a variable assignment. Here's an example:

```
temperature[0]=55
```

Here are a couple of points to note regarding arrays:

- Unlike variables, the brackets are not optional when referencing the array. They are mandatory. `echo $temperature[1]` will not have the desired result. It must be written as `echo ${temperature[1]}`.

- Arrays cannot be exported as environment variables.

We could have created a separate variable for each month, of course, but the following program shows how using arrays instead can save a lot of programming time:

```
1.   #!/usr/local/bin/ksh
2.   # Demonstration of arrays and computing average temperature.
3.   set -A temperature 57 52 58 61 63 65 71 70 68 66 64 62
4.   i=0
5.   printf "\nMonth\t\tTemperature\n\n"
6.   while (( i < 12 ))
7.   do
8.           (( month = $i + 1 ))
9.           printf "$month\t\t${temperature[$i]}\n"
10          (( total_temp += ${temperature[$i]} ))
11.         (( i += 1 ))
12.  done
13.  avg_temp=$(( total_temp / 12 ))
14.  echo
15.  echo  "Average temperature for whole year: $avg_temp"
16.  echo
```

Here's the output of this program:

```
Month           Temperature

1               57
2               52
3               58
4               61
5               63
6               65
7               71
8               70
9               68
10              66
11              64
12              62

Average temperature for whole year: 63
```

This may look scary at first, but really there isn't much new here, other than the syntax, which is a little different from what you're accustomed to using in Bourne shell scripting. There is also some new logic in this program that you haven't used before, but it will make perfect sense once you look at how the program works:

- **Line 1**—Notice the difference here. This shell script starts with /usr/local/bin/ksh. If you accidentally put #!/bin/sh here instead, the program will not run, and you will get strange errors.

- **Line 3**—This line uses the set command to load an array named temperature with 12 numbers, each of the numbers being an average temperature for one month.

- **Line 4**—This simply initializes the loop counter to zero.

- **Line 6**—This line starts a loop that will continue as long as i is less than 12.

- **Line 8**—This line creates a new variable called month and sets the value to whatever is in $i + 1. This is used in the output of the program to print the number of the current month. Why do we have to add 1 to $i? Because $i is currently set to 0, and it is what we will use to get the first element out of the temperature array. Because array elements start with 0, our elements in the temperature array are numbered from 0 to 11. But this is not what we want for our month number display, so we simply add 1 to the current value of $i for each iteration of the loop.

- **Line 9**—This line prints the current value of month, followed by two tab characters and then a single element from the temperature array. Notice that we use variable substitution here. The value of $i is expanded to the number stored in $I, and this is used as the element to retrieve from the array.

- **Line 10**—This line takes whatever value is currently in the variable $total_temp, adds the number stored in the array element of temperature represented by $i to it, and then stores the new value in $total_temp, overwriting the old value. It keeps a running sum of all the temperatures added together, which will be used later to compute the average temperature.

- **Line 11**—This adds 1 to the current value of $i. So, for example, on the second iteration of the loop, $i will now be set to 1 instead of 0, and therefore the second element of the array will be printed as well as added to $total_temp. This is the last statement in the loop. If $i is still less than 12, the loop will repeat.

- **Line 13**—After the loop has completed, the average temperature is computed by taking the sum of all the temperatures stored in $total_temp and dividing by 12. The new value is assigned to avg_temp.

- **Line 15**—The average temperature for the entire year is printed.

NOTE

According to the program, the average temperature for the whole year was 63. This is a good example of how the shell's arithmetic can only handle integers. The actual average temperature for the whole year is 63.083333, but because the shell cannot handle floating-point math, it drops the decimal portion and just prints 63. If you needed more precision here, you could use the bc command to do the calculation, as you saw in Listing 12.2 to compute the circumference and area of circles with pi.

Do you see how this program saved us some work? Rather than having to go through each month manually, we were able to use a loop that increments a variable and automates the task of getting the value for each month. If we had used separate variables to store the temperatures, this task would have required a good deal more code than we used here.

> **NOTE**
>
> If you want some good practice, see if you can modify the previous temperature program to use a `for` loop instead of a `while` loop. Here is a hint: Remember that the array can accept the asterisk wildcard to show all the elements in the array.

Command Substitution

The Korn shell also supports a cleaner form of command substitution than the Bourne shell. Rather than putting commands in backquotes, you can use a syntax like the following:

```
today_date=$(date)
```

The old style is also still supported. Which one you use in Korn shell scripts is mostly a matter of personal preference.

Using `getopts`

The `getopts` command offers a better way of handling command-line arguments than the simple Bourne-style syntax used earlier in the chapter. It allows you to use the standard option syntax of `-option` that most other FreeBSD commands use. It also allows for better handling of arguments to the options.

The general syntax of the `getopts` command looks like this:

```
getopts options variable
```

Here, `options` is the list of valid options that can be supplied, and `variable` is the name of the variable in which those options should be stored. If an option letter ends with a colon, it can also take a value. That value will be stored in the special variable `$OPTARG`. Another special variable, named `$OPTIND`, stores the value of the current argument being worked on.

The `getopt` command executes once for each option it is supplied with. If used with the `while` loop, the loop will execute once for each command-line argument supplied. The following shows an example of how the `getopt` command syntax works:

```
getopts abc:d: MyVar
```

With this command, the valid options that getopts recognizes are a, b, c, and d. In addition, options c and d are followed by a value that will be stored in the variable $OPTARG. The option itself is stored in MyVar.

A simple example script using getopts follows:

```
1. #!/bin/sh
2. # Demonstrates the use of getopts.
3. for i in 1 2 3 4
4. do
5.   getopts abc:d: MyVar
6.   echo "$MyVar, $OPTARG"
7. done
```

Let's assume that you have saved this script as a program called myprog, and you invoke it as follows:

```
./test.sh -a -c foobar -b -d blah
```

Note that the order in which you specify the arguments does not matter. The output looks like this:

```
a,
c, foobar
b,
d, blah
```

If you omit any arguments, the $MyVar variable will be set to the question mark (?). The getopts command is run as many times as there are arguments. The first time it is run, $MyVar will contain a. The second time it is run, $MyVar will contain c, and the variable $OPTARG will contain the string foobar. Using these variables and the previously mentioned $OPTIND variable, the getopts command can be used for decision-making in shell programs using the same procedures used throughout this chapter (loops and conditional statements, for example).

Performance Monitoring, Process Control, and Job Automation

One of the fundamental differences between a desktop operating system such as Windows and a server operating system such as FreeBSD is process control. FreeBSD lets you control every single process on your system, whether trivial or crucial. Windows, by comparison, gives you control over only certain application processes—and very limited control at that. The only time you ever see the process table in Windows is during an emergency. In FreeBSD, it's an ever-present part of administering the system.

In Windows, for example, you can press Ctrl+Alt+Delete and get a list of desktop processes, which you can terminate if you choose. That's all you can do—and it's hard to tell what each of the listed processes does or how much of the system's resources it's taking up. But FreeBSD shows you all this information and gives you the ability to restart processes, alter their priority, give them a number of different types of termination signals, and more—all with complete visibility into which processes might be causing problems. To use a common analogy, desktop operating systems are like cars "with the hood welded shut." FreeBSD lets you pop the hood at any time.

This doesn't mean that FreeBSD is either more arcane or less stable than GUI-based desktop platforms. Savvy administrators will never end up destabilizing the FreeBSD system through poking at the processes, nor will they have to comb through an opaque table of numbers just to perform basic system functions. As you see in this chapter, the FreeBSD process table and the tools that interact with it are an embodiment of what makes a Unix system what it is: a fully accessible machine with all the moving parts exposed and all the nuts and bolts showing. This accessibility gives you the power to tune everything the system does, no matter how minute. That's the essence of Unix.

This chapter discusses several process-monitoring tools—namely ps, top, and kill. Some are more user friendly than others, and some are more versatile than others. The chapter also takes a look at the cron program, which is a scheduler for tasks that have to happen periodically—another feature that separates the servers from the desktops.

Performance Monitoring with top

The easiest to use of the process-monitoring utilities is top, so named because it was originally designed to list the top-10 processes currently running on the system, in descending order of CPU usage. The current version of FreeBSD's top by default shows you every process currently running in any state—somewhere around 30 processes on a freshly installed FreeBSD system.

The benefit that top provides is that it's interactive and works in real time. When you run it, it takes over your terminal and updates itself every second, giving you instantaneous information about the state of the system at that moment. You can also pass top commands, such as the kill and renice commands (covered later in this chapter), or give it different options for filtering the processes it shows you. This makes top an immensely useful tool for reining in an out-of-control server, fine-tuning the performance of certain tasks, or simply keeping an eye on things as you work in another window.

top Output Explained

When you run the top program, you get output similar to what's shown in Listing 13.1.

LISTING 13.1　Sample Output of top

```
last pid: 30283;  load averages:  0.51,  0.89,  0.87   up 52+15:48:43  11:19:03
126 processes: 1 running, 124 sleeping, 1 zombie
CPU states:  0.7% user,  0.0% nice,  2.8% system,  0.7% interrupt, 95.8% idle
Mem: 142M Active, 35M Inact, 59M Wired, 7496K Cache, 35M Buf, 4256K Free
Swap: 500M Total, 48M Used, 452M Free, 9% Inuse
```

PID	USERNAME	PRI	NICE	SIZE	RES	STATE	C	TIME	WCPU	CPU	COMMAND
19460	mysql	2	0	25908K	2692K	poll	0	112:20	2.20%	2.20%	mysqld
30283	bob	2	0	1360K	976K	sbwait	1	0:00	6.02%	1.56%	qpopper
30282	root	29	0	2076K	1236K	CPU1	0	0:00	3.14%	0.93%	top
245	root	2	0	868K	232K	select	1	177:39	0.00%	0.00%	healthd
18427	root	2	0	7592K	5092K	select	0	80:24	0.00%	0.00%	named
86694	frank	10	0	1700K	56K	nanslp	0	76:46	0.00%	0.00%	elm

LISTING 13.1   Continued

```
   86 root      2 -12  1296K   412K select 0  6:28  0.00%  0.00% ntpd
80717 root     10   0  2132K   472K nanslp 0  5:53  0.00%  0.00% telnetd
61945 root      2   0  1868K   360K select 0  3:29  0.00%  0.00% inetd
   80 root      2   0   916K   320K select 0  3:26  0.00%  0.00% syslogd
56054 root      2   0  2168K   584K select 0  3:12  0.00%  0.00% sshd
73772 root      2   0  8956K  2540K select 0  3:12  0.00%  0.00% httpd
40567 www       2   0  9880K  2872K sbwait 1  0:57  0.00%  0.00% httpd
40581 www       2   0 10008K  3796K sbwait 0  0:55  0.00%  0.00% httpd
```

By default, top shows all the system's processes (no matter who owns them), whether they're active, idle, or in "zombie" mode, and how much CPU time they're taking up. The first useful bit of information is in the second line—the number of processes. This number varies from system to system, but chances are that many more processes are currently running than can fit on your screen. You can press the I key to switch top into displaying only the processes that are active. Because the top program is interactive, there are a number of other commands you can issue while it is running, such as the K key followed by a process ID to kill a process. We will cover these a little later.

The next items to notice in the top output are the "load averages," which are fairly obtuse metrics you can use as a yardstick to tell at a glance how busy the system is. The exact derivation of the values is from the number of jobs executed over the last 1, 5, and 15 minutes, respectively; however, it's difficult to relate this to real-world applications. Just think of the load average as the tachometer of the system, and think "the lower the better."

Load Averages

Eventually, you will get a feel for what constitutes a high load average on your system; typically, a load should not go above 1 on a continuous basis for a server, although a desktop system with lots of graphical tools will bump it up into the 2 to 3 range (5 is considered a high load). Certain daemons stop accepting new requests at a certain load level (for example, 12 for sendmail). If the load reaches 20 or 30, chances are the system is in a feedback-loop situation (which can be thought of as a race condition), in which new processes are being created faster than the system can complete them. This only serves to slow it down more and drive the load higher, in what's not-so-affectionately termed a "death spiral."

This is one of those rare times when you might have to reboot a Unix system, because a server under this kind of load can become so tightly wedged that it will never come back—or it will take so long to complete all its processes and return to normal duty that it's faster to reboot. Either way, your remote Telnet or SSH session might be unresponsive in this condition, or you might not be running one at the time the "death spiral" occurs (in which case, the system probably won't be able to open a new connection for you to come to the rescue). This is when logging in to the physical console—or even power-cycling the machine, or shutting it down physically and rebooting, as an absolute last resort—might be the only recourse.

The header block contains more information about the RAM in the system than you'll probably ever find useful. You won't find a simple "used/free" graph of all available RAM here; instead, you see the states of all chunks of memory, including swap (virtual memory), in the fourth and fifth lines in Listing 13.1.

Don't look at the Free block and assume that it is all the memory available in the system. That block is only the memory that hasn't yet been used at all since the system was last brought online. What you should be looking at is the Active block, because that describes memory in use by active processes—programs that are currently running and not idle. The rest of the fields describe other states of use that may or may not be mutually exclusive, so adding up all the fields won't necessarily give you the amount of RAM you have. It will, in fact, probably add up to more.

The Swap fields are more straightforward. Here, data is paged in and out of the virtual memory space as needed (copied to the disk and out of RAM), and the only fields that top shows are Used and Free. The numbers here add up predictably. It's probably more useful to look at the Swap fields than at the actual RAM fields to see how well your system is doing; if there's a lot of data in Swap (50 percent or more used), it means that data has been paged in fairly recently as a result of your physical RAM being full, and you may want to consider adding more memory. A FreeBSD system rarely runs out of swap space. If it does, as with most Unix implementations, the results will usually be benign (you'll see error messages, but the system won't destabilize). The occasional unpredictable behavior or instability will surface, however. You'll want to keep your swap as little used as possible—for this reason and also because naturally everything runs faster in RAM than in swap.

Next, notice that the processes are listed in descending order in the CPU column. This column lists how much of the CPU's cycles are being used currently by each process. Don't expect the column to add up to 100 because your CPU will only be lightly used most of the time. Take a look at the headers again; the CPU states line tells you how much of the processor is being used in each of the four possible states, and you can relate these values fairly closely to the percentages in the CPU column. The WCPU field is the "weighted CPU" percentage, which we'll cover in the next section when we look at the ps command.

> **NOTE**
>
> Some programs are designed to use 100 percent of the CPU, unless actively throttled by the configuration. For example, Qmail (an SMTP daemon that we will cover in Chapter 24, "Configuring E-mail Services") or a database back end such as MySQL might run to 100 percent of the system's capacity during heavy load. This is normal behavior and should not cause concern, if the system's primary role is in running those programs.

The CPU operates in discrete cycles, many millions per second (depending on its speed). Each of these cycles is dedicated to some part of some process, and over time a process will have used enough of these cycles to add up to a number measurable in seconds. This is what the TIME column tells you. Don't let the colon separator fool you into thinking that it's an hours:minutes reading; the values in the TIME column actually represent the number of CPU seconds that the process used in system states and user states, respectively. It may take minutes or hours for a process to use enough cycles to accumulate a measurable number. If a process has a large value (such as mysqld in the sample output in Listing 13.1), it's usually because the process has been running for weeks or it has become a runaway and has been taking up some huge percentage of the CPU during its runtime. In the latter case, you can easily check by looking at the CPU column.

The next parts of top's output that you should understand are the SIZE and RES columns. SIZE is the entirety of a process's allocated size, including the text, data, and stack components. Because parts of these components are shared systemwide, this column is not accurate for seeing how much memory a process is using. Instead, RES shows the resident memory value (this column should add up to the current amount of in-use memory). Both size values are "correct," but use RES for determining the "traditional" amount of memory a process uses, the equivalent to what it would be reported as using in Windows or Mac OS.

The rest of the fields in top are less important or are self-explanatory. The C column tells you which CPU a process is using, if there is more than one. PID is the process ID, a number that is assigned to each process upon execution, and OWNER is the user who executed the process. STATE tells you which of the possible states a process is in, which isn't very informative unless it's zomb or zombie (which refers to a child process that has terminated but has not yet fully given up its process table space).

Using Interactive top Commands

You also can give top commands interactively to help sort through the information. Earlier in the chapter, you learned that you can press the I key to show only active processes. You also can press the U key to be prompted for a username; top then displays only processes owned by that username (use + as the username to show them all again). You can issue a kill command with the K key, which then prompts you for a PID to kill. The T key toggles whether the top process itself is displayed. These and other options are listed in the man top page.

With this feature set, top serves as a very good all-around summary of what's going on in the system, and it allows you to handle the majority of the process-management tasks you'll have to perform. But top isn't a total solution; it doesn't give you detailed information about the processes themselves, and its interactive nature keeps top from being a scriptable tool or something that can be used in conjunction with pipes and other programs. For these functions, you use ps.

Process Monitoring with ps

Rather than being an interactive, real-time monitoring program like top, ps works a lot more like ls (hence the name). It's an instantaneous listing of all the processes that are running at the time you execute it. It provides all the information that top does as well as extra details about many of the values.

By default, if you run ps without any arguments, you will get a listing of only the processes owned by you that are attached to terminals (that is, those that have been run from a login session). A large array of command-line options can give you more wide-reaching results, and each can be found documented in man ps. You specify these options as follows:

```
# ps -waux
```

This combination of options shows the following:

- The output in wide format (w), which allows the output to wrap to multiple lines rather than being cropped to the width of your terminal

- Usernames along with processes (u)

- All users' processes, not just your own (a)

- All processes, regardless of whether they have an associated terminal (x)

In short, this combination of options displays a list of every process on the system, with as much detail as possible.

You can filter the output in certain ways by using the built-in options. For instance, eliminate the x option to show all processes, whether they're attached to a terminal or not, and drop the a option to show only your processes (or use -U to specify another user—for example, -U frank). Many other options of this type can be found in the man page for ps. Beyond the built-in filters, though, you will need to use ps in conjunction with grep (as you saw in Chapter 8, "The FreeBSD Filesystem") to filter based on the process name. An example is shown in Listing 13.2.

LISTING 13.2   Sample ps Output, Filtered Through grep

```
# ps -ax | grep httpd
40563  ??  S      0:54.73 /usr/local/sbin/httpd
40564  ??  S      0:55.30 /usr/local/sbin/httpd
40565  ??  S      0:56.03 /usr/local/sbin/httpd
40566  ??  S      1:00.16 /usr/local/sbin/httpd
40567  ??  S      1:05.13 /usr/local/sbin/httpd
```

ps **Output Explained**

Listing 13.3 shows some sample output from ps -waux.

LISTING 13.3   Sample Output from ps

USER	PID	%CPU	%MEM	VSZ	RSS	TT	STAT	STARTED	TIME	COMMAND
root	1	0.0	0.0	528	72	??	ILs	31Jan01	1:05.94	/sbin/init --
root	2	0.0	0.0	0	0	??	DL	31Jan01	14:41.63	(pagedaemon)
root	3	0.0	0.0	0	0	??	DL	31Jan01	2:38.47	(vmdaemon)
root	4	0.0	0.0	0	0	??	DL	31Jan01	0:33.21	(bufdaemon)
root	5	0.0	0.0	0	0	??	DL	31Jan01	79:52.61	(syncer)
root	24	0.0	0.0	208	0	??	IWs	-	0:00.00	adjkerntz -i
root	80	0.0	0.1	916	320	??	Ss	31Jan01	3:27.80	syslogd -s

Processes in the output from ps are sorted by PID rather than any of the reported metrics (unless you used one of the special sorting options described in the man page). You do get most of the same information that top gives you, albeit in a more cryptic format and with a few slight variations.

> **NOTE**
>
> Output from top differs from ps output in that the %CPU column in ps is not the same as the CPU field in top; it's actually equivalent to the WCPU field. This value is a "weighted CPU" percentage that takes into account CPU cycles in which the process was in a "resident" state. Most of the time, this weighting makes no difference, but occasionally it can result in a significantly higher number reported in ps than in top or between the two columns in top. In either case, the %CPU column is calculated as an average over the preceding minute, so the values are approximate at best, and you shouldn't expect them to add up to 100 percent.

When to Use ps **Instead of** top

It's generally more useful to use top to gather metrics on your processes; ps is intended for looking up PIDs of specific processes and seeing the complete command line for each one. It's quicker than top, and scriptable. For example, you can write scripts that extract the PID for a process from the output of ps and send signals to that PID, all through the use of shell commands and pipes. This is particularly helpful when you need to rein in a runaway process or change the priority on a task. These are functions that we will now review in detail.

Terminating Misbehaving Processes

Let's say you notice the system running more slowly than you think it should; you use su to access root, fire up top, and look at the processes. Sure enough, you see something like what's shown in Listing 13.4.

LISTING 13.4   Output of top Showing a Possible Runaway Process

```
last pid: 67469;  load averages:  8.32,  5.49,  2.47   up 53+01:04:22  20:34:42
90 processes:  1 running, 88 sleeping, 1 zombie
CPU states:  93.2% user,  0.0% nice,  0.2% system,  0.8% interrupt, 5.8% idle
Mem: 153M Active, 23M Inact, 60M Wired, 7252K Cache, 35M Buf, 5112K Free
Swap: 500M Total, 44M Used, 456M Free, 8% Inuse

  PID USERNAME     PRI NICE  SIZE   RES STATE  C   TIME  WCPU    CPU COMMAND
19460 frank         2    0 25908K 2816K poll   0 131:15  0.00% 92.43% testprog
67468 root         28    0  2036K 1024K CPU0   0   0:00  0.43%  0.20% top
  245 root          2    0   868K  232K select 1 178:48  0.00%  0.00% healthd
18427 root          2    0  7592K 5124K select 0  81:01  0.00%  0.00% named
```

Aha! There's your culprit. It seems that frank is running some experimental program that's perhaps not written very well, and it's taking up almost all the CPU's available cycles. Sometimes such a "runaway" process results from an infinite loop (a piece of code that never reaches a point where it can terminate) or a memory leak (the program keeps trying to grab more memory, whether it needs it or not). Chances are, the process isn't going to exit by itself cleanly; meanwhile, it's becoming more difficult for other processes to execute and terminate. This testprog process has to go.

Using the top kill Command

To get rid of testprog or other runaway processes, press the K key. This brings up the "kill" prompt within top; this prompt is an interface to the kill command (or at least a simplified version of the command). At the prompt, enter the PID of the offending process (19460, in this case). Because you're running with root privileges, the process most likely will immediately terminate, and the system will breathe freely once more. Now, you're safe to track down what happened; you'll probably want to start by sending messages to the user and letting him know what his program did.

There are times when the top command doesn't work, though, or you may need finer control over what signals you're sending to the processes. The kill command within top is fine for simple process termination, but it's only a subset of the functionality of the command-line kill program.

The Command-line kill Program and Its Options

Its name is slightly misleading: kill does a lot more than simply terminate processes. Its full charter is to be a signaling mechanism by which processes can give each other commands of a fairly wide variety. Any user can use kill against any of his processes, but root is the only user who can kill other users' processes.

The simplest and most common usage of `kill` is for the purpose of terminating a process:

```
# kill 12553
```

This, however, sends only a certain kind of signal to the process: the TERM signal. This is a universal "quit" message that all Unix programs understand, but it isn't guaranteed to work. A number of other signals exist, too. Table 13.1 shows the more important ones.

TABLE 13.1   Commonly Used `kill` Signals

Signal	Symbolic Name	Meaning
1	HUP	Hang up, or terminate and restart
2	INT	Interrupt
3	QUIT	Quit
6	ABRT	Abort
9	KILL	Non-ignorable kill
14	ALRM	Alarm
15	TERM	Terminate cleanly

You can use any of these signals by specifying either the signal number or its symbol:

```
# kill -9 12553
# kill -HUP 12553
```

The first command sends a low-level "super-kill" signal that terminates the process, no matter what. This command makes the process quit in an unclean fashion and might leave files open or connections in an orphaned state. Use it only if plain `kill` (or `kill -TERM`) doesn't work. The second command tells the process to shut itself down cleanly and restart itself with the same arguments—rereading any input files and taking on a new PID. This is useful when you've changed something in a program's config file and need to restart the process to incorporate the changes.

> **NOTE**
>
> The `kill` program is not infallible; there are some occasions when even a `kill -9` will not terminate a process that has become completely unresponsive to signals. Some processes under certain circumstances can become "zombies," meaning that they never die and can't be killed. Most zombie processes just sit there and don't take up any significant system resources. However, if in some rare case you have a zombie process that is interfering with general system operation, a reboot may be the only way to clear it.

These signals are the only ones you're likely to use in everyday process control. The other signals are typically ignored by programs that aren't specifically written to respond to them.

Making Processes "Nice"

The kill command is one of the process-management tools that you can use both from the command line and within top. You read earlier of another tool, though, that you can use to alter a process's priority. This tool is the renice command, which alters the priority (or "nice" level) of any currently running process.

The scheduling priority is an integer value between -20 and 20, with -20 being the highest possible priority. Take a look at top; the values in the NICE column are the priorities of each process. Notice that most processes have a priority of 0. Zero priority is the default because, in most circumstances, you don't need to specify any particular priority. Still, certain services run at predefined "nice" levels to ensure they will run at a certain time or get out of the way of more important processes.

If you're not root, you can set a process to a lower priority (a higher "nice" value), but not to a higher one (a lower "nice" value).

From the command line, you can alter a process's priority to 10 using renice:

```
# renice 10 1442
```

Within top, you can type r to get the renice prompt. Enter a priority level between -20 and 20, followed by the PID of the process you want to change, and you can see the results in the NICE column. This is an easy, interactive, alternate solution to the testprog problem you saw earlier. Rather than killing the runaway process outright, you could simply set its priority to 20, which would theoretically make it back off and allow other processes to run uncontested.

The nice command provides a way to set the priority level of a process at the time you run it. You precede a command with nice and the priority level, like so:

```
# nice -10 ls
```

This starts the ls process with a priority level of 10.

> **NOTE**
>
> The priority level in the nice command is preceded by a dash, which means that positive (lower) priorities are specified as shown in the previous renice example. However, to specify a negative (higher) priority, you would have to use the following:
>
> ```
> # nice --10 top
> ```
>
> Unfortunately, though, the double-dash syntax appears not to work properly in FreeBSD as of this writing. A workaround is to start a process normally and then use renice to alter its priority while it is running, as shown previously.

Automating Processes with the cron Daemon Scheduler

Now that you've seen how to manipulate processes directly, you're ready to examine how processes can be executed automatically, without any intervention on your part. Automating tasks with the scheduler allows FreeBSD to perform daily security audits and system status updates, regularly update its runtime databases, flush log files, and perform as many other tasks as an administrator can think of. Some operating systems attach schedulers to individual applications (such as the Software Update tool in Mac OS), but the advantage of FreeBSD and other Unix-like systems is that the scheduler is an independent daemon that can run any command-line program or set of programs on any periodic schedule.

The scheduler in FreeBSD, as in most Unix-type systems, is called cron. FreeBSD's cron program was written by Paul Vixie, and it's the standard version used in most distributions of Linux and other similar systems. Like any standalone daemon, it runs all the time and looks at its input files (called crontab files) each minute to see whether they have changed or contain a task it needs to execute that minute. The cron process itself never needs to be restarted; it will automatically read in any changes when it wakes up every minute.

A global crontab file (/etc/crontab) and a directory (/var/cron/tabs) are available for individual users to create their own crontab files. It can be tempting to add your own scheduled jobs to the /etc/crontab file, but, as with /usr/local/etc/rc.d versus /etc/rc.local (refer to Chapter 10, "System Configuration and Startup Scripts"), you really should leave /etc/crontab untouched (so it can be safely overwritten by later upgrades) and create new jobs in root's personal crontab file in /var/cron/tabs. You'll see how to do this in a moment.

Anatomy of a crontab File

Let's take a look inside a user's individual crontab file. Here's /var/cron/tabs/frank:

```
# DO NOT EDIT THIS FILE - edit the master and reinstall.
# (/tmp/crontab.tqWGz91396 installed on Thu Feb  1 09:29:43 2001)
# (Cron version -- $FreeBSD: src/usr.sbin/cron/crontab/crontab.c,v 1.12.2.1 2000
/11/09 11:05:36 dwmalone Exp $)
0 3 1,15 * * cat ~frank/faq.txt | mail -s "FAQ Auto-Post" mylist@testsystem.com
```

This file has one item in it: a task to send a text file into mail to be sent out to a mailing list. The task will be executed at 03:00 on the 1st and 15th of every month. How is this schedule specified? It's done with the first five fields of the whitespace-separated data line. (The first three lines are auto-generated comments and are not processed by cron.) The fields are shown, in order, in Table 13.2.

TABLE 13.2   Date and Time Fields in a `crontab` File

Field	Allowed Values
Minute	0–59
Hour	0–23
Day of month	1–31
Month	1–12
Day of week	0–7

For instance, to create a task (we'll use the simple `ls` for these examples) that executes every night at 1:00 a.m., use the following syntax for the five fields:

```
0        1        *        *        *        ls
```

To run the same task only on Mondays, use this:

```
0        1        *        *        1        ls
```

A task that runs at the top of every hour throughout the month of March would be specified like this:

```
0        *        *        3        *        ls
```

Any field can have multiple numbers separated by commas or can contain a range (for instance, `1-10`). You can also use an asterisk (`*`) in a field to specify every occurrence of that interval. The month and weekday (fourth and fifth) fields can also use symbolic names—the three-letter abbreviations for month or weekday names. Names can also be listed as comma-separated strings, although they can't be used in ranges. In the fifth (weekday) field, `0` and `7` are Sunday.

> **NOTE**
>
> If you want to run a command every *n* minutes, or every *n* hours, you can do that by specifying a "step" value (for example, `*/n`). In the minute field, `*/5` would translate to "every fifth minute," or the equivalent of `0,5,10,15,20,25,30,35,40,45,50,55`. See `man 5 crontab` for further details on schedule formatting.

You can also use shorthand strings in place of the first five fields to specify certain often-used schedules, as shown in Table 13.3.

TABLE 13.3   Examples of Symbolic Scheduling Intervals

String	Equivalent
`@reboot`	Run once, at startup
`@yearly`	`0 0 1 1 *`
`@annually`	Same as `@yearly`

TABLE 13.3   Continued

String	Equivalent
@monthly	0 0 1 * *
@weekly	0 0 * * 0
@daily	0 0 * * *
@midnight	Same as @daily
@hourly	0 * * * *

You can use shorthand strings, for example, to specify a task to occur every night at midnight:

```
@midnight ls
0        0        *        *        *        ls
```

After the schedule fields, the formats of the `/etc/crontab` file and the individual `crontab` files diverge. The global `/etc/crontab` file has an extra field before the `command` field—a `who` field—that specifies which user should execute and own the process:

```
1        3        *        *        *        root     periodic daily
```

The `command` field can be as complex as you like; fill it in exactly as you would a command entered at the command line. You can even use a semicolon (;) to separate multiple commands that you want to run sequentially as part of the same automated job. It's important to note that for commands executed from `/etc/crontab`, `cron` will not assume the path of the user specified in the `who` field—there's a PATH statement at the top of the file that lists only a few basic system directories. This means you need to give the full path to any command you run that isn't in that path; otherwise, `cron` won't be able to find the programs to run.

If there's any output from any program executed by `cron`, that output is gathered into a mail message and sent to the owner of the `crontab` file (or the owner of the scheduled task for `/etc/crontab` items).

Creating and Editing `crontab` Files

It's easy enough for you to edit `/etc/crontab` as root and to add any schedule items you want. Because you should avoid editing `/etc/crontab` if at all possible, however, you need to understand the individual `crontab` files and how to create them.

Because each `crontab` file goes into a central directory (`/var/cron/tabs`) and is owned by its creator with permissions 0600, a security mechanism is in place to allow users to create and edit their own files there without compromising others' files. This mechanism is the `crontab` program:

```
# crontab -e
```

Here's how to edit frank's `crontab` file if you're root:

```
# crontab -e -u frank
```

Much like the `chfn` and `edquota` tools you saw earlier, `crontab` works by invoking the editor specified in the `VISUAL` environment variable (or the `EDITOR` variable, if `VISUAL` isn't set). The contents of the file (minus the first three comment lines) appear in the editor. After you make your changes, save and exit. The temporary file, which resides in `/tmp` while you're making your changes, is copied into `/var/cron/tabs`, and the header lines are added. The `crontab` file will be active the next time `cron` looks at it, at the top of the minute.

Creating Jobs to Run One Scheduled Time with the `at` Command

Okay, so `cron` is amazingly useful for regularly scheduled tasks. However, what about a task that you only want to happen once—something you want to postpone until some later time when you won't be around to execute it yourself? You could do this with `cron`, setting up a `crontab` file to have an entry that runs `crontab -u` at the end to delete itself. However, there is a better way: the `at` program.

The `at` program is actually made up of several commands: at (the job creator), atq (which displays pending jobs), and `atrm` (which lets you cancel pending jobs listed in atq). There is also a `batch` command, which is a version of at that will run only if the system load is less than some value (`1.5` is the compiled-in default).

When you use at to create a job, it reads commands, line by line, in `/bin/sh` script style. These commands can be specified either on the command line (standard input) or with a preexisting file. Either way, you simply enter the at command followed by a time-formatting string, which can take a number of fairly intuitive forms, as shown in Table 13.4 (a full discussion of the time-formatting options is available in `man at`).

TABLE 13.4   Syntax Examples of the at Command

Command String	Meaning
`at 10pm`	Executes at 10:00 p.m. on the current day or the next day if it's after 10:00 p.m.
`at 8:00am May 15`	Executes at 8:00 a.m. on May 15
`at midnight Jan 1 2000`	Executes on the first second of the year 2000
`at teatime tomorrow`	Executes at 4:00 p.m. the following day

After you type this string and press Enter, you are in standard input mode. Type your commands line by line, pressing Enter each time. When you finish entering commands, press Ctrl+D to exit and place the job into the queue. You can alternately specify an input file:

```
# at -f mycommands noon + 5 days
```

This reads a plain-text file called mycommands that contains your commands, like a batch file, and executes them using /bin/sh at noon five days from the time you entered the command.

You can view existing jobs with the atq command:

```
# atq
Date                    Owner   Queue   Job#
23:00:00 03/28/01       root    c       2
```

The following lets you cancel jobs with the atrm command:

```
# atrm 2
```

> **NOTE**
>
> The way at jobs are executed involves the atrun command. The atrun tool runs every five minutes (in the standard FreeBSD installation), reads all pending jobs for all users, and executes all jobs whose execution time has passed. You can modify how frequently atrun runs by changing its entry in /etc/crontab, although this should not be necessary.

Controlling Access to the cron and at Commands

Scheduling is so powerful that most administrators don't necessarily want their users to be able to have complete access to the cron and at commands. As an administrator, you can control access to these commands on your FreeBSD system.

Let's say, for instance, you have a troublesome user who insists on running an IRC "eggdrop" bot, and every time you kill the process, it keeps coming back—because the user has set up a crontab file to restart the process if it's not running (checking every hour, for example). The user doesn't respond to e-mail. Your options are either to disable the user's account (a fairly barbaric and messy option) or to restrict the user's access to the cron and at commands. You can restrict the user's access through the deny and allow files for both programs.

Normally, /var/cron/allow and /var/cron/deny don't exist. In this condition, anybody is allowed to create crontab files. If you create /var/cron/allow, the only users (aside from root) who can create crontab files are the ones you listed in it (in a simple text list, one user per line). Alternatively, you can put users into /var/cron/deny. This approach lets everyone create crontab files, except for the ones listed in the file. If both files exist, /var/cron/allow takes precedence.

The /var/at/at.allow and /var/at/at.deny files work the same way, but the filenames are slightly different, so take note!

Using the Periodic Task Scheduler

Now that you know how `cron` and `at` work, the function of the `periodic` command should be clear. Like `at`, `periodic` is a command that executes other commands at specified times. The difference is that `periodic` is designed to operate on a repeated basis, and its input is specified by command files in a predefined directory.

If you examine `/etc/crontab`, you will see three references to the `periodic` command:

```
# do daily/weekly/monthly maintenance
1     3     *     *     *     root     periodic daily
15    4     *     *     6     root     periodic weekly
30    5     1     *     *     root     periodic monthly
```

The `periodic` command is invoked three times, with three different arguments: `daily`, `weekly`, and `monthly`. These arguments correspond to three different subdirectories of `/etc/periodic`. Each subdirectory, named in accordance with the three arguments, contains a number of shell programs, each of which executes a specific task—in this case, a maintenance task that the system carries out either daily, weekly, or monthly, at the specified times in `/etc/crontab`. In `/etc/periodic/daily`, for example, you will find such scripts as `100.clean-disks`, `200.backup-passwd`, and `999.local`. Simply by existing in the subdirectories of `/etc/periodic`, these scripts will be run when `periodic` is executed with the name of their directory as an argument.

Scripts in the `periodic` directories are traditionally prefixed with numbers; because `periodic` executes scripts in lexicographical order, using numbers provides an easy way to define the order in which the scripts should be run. For example, `999.local` is always the last script to run in `/etc/periodic/daily`.

The output of these `periodic` runs is gathered into a mail message and sent to root (by default). This is the origin of the daily messages that your FreeBSD machine sends you each night shortly after 3:00 a.m. Reading through the source directories, you will be able to see what the system is doing to generate all the disk status, user login accounting, news, UUCP, mail, and other pieces of status it throws at you every day, week, and month.

Each script in the `periodic` directories has individual behaviors that are defined in `/etc/defaults/periodic.conf`. You can examine that file to see how each script is treated, and you can override those settings by creating an `/etc/periodic.conf` file, which operates the same way that `/etc/rc.conf` does. You can use this to send the script output to a different user or to a log file, instead of to root, for instance. You can also turn on or off the output reporting for individual scripts as well as adjust many other script-specific variables that control how the scripts themselves operate.

> **NOTE**
>
> The /etc/periodic/security directory is special; it contains scripts that specifically address security-related tasks, such as looking for new setuid programs, accounts without passwords, and kernel firewall messages. The scripts in this directory are run in a separate process and handled differently from the normal daily maintenance scripts, in order to minimize the risk of sensitive information being gleaned by an eavesdropper. This behavior can be modified by overriding the settings in /etc/defaults/periodic.conf using /etc/periodic.conf.

You can add your own scripts to the periodic directories if you wish. However, as you have seen before, it's considered safer and better form to avoid editing the global files in /etc when an alternative "local" version is available. In this case, /usr/local/etc/periodic is the location for any daily, weekly, or monthly scripts you might wish to add. The scripts are executed at the same time that /etc/crontab runs the global periodic scripts. Immediately after finishing the scripts in /etc/periodic/daily, for example, periodic will run whatever it finds in /usr/local/etc/periodic/daily, in lexicographical order as with the global location.

Adding scripts to the periodic directories is a good way to schedule specific tasks to be performed on an ongoing basis—for example, a script that cleans up a temporary directory, a database backup process, or a CVSup process that synchronizes your FreeBSD sources (you learn more about synchronizing FreeBSD sources in Chapter 17, "Keeping Up to Date with FreeBSD").

13

Installing Additional Software

Up until now, we have covered topics that are largely applicable to many different types of Unix systems. Pretty much any such system, whether commercial or open source, operates the same way regarding the filesystem structure, process automation, and general administration. What sets FreeBSD apart from its BSD brethren (Linux and commercial Unix software) is the model by which the administrator adds new software.

With Solaris, if you want to add a new piece of the software to the system, you have to find a precompiled binary for your particular platform and install it yourself (usually without the aid of installers that help you put it in the right place), because Solaris typically doesn't come with gcc (the standard GNU C/C++ compiler). Other systems, such as IRIX and HP-UX, do come with gcc, but you still have to find the source code for the program you want to install and then run its configuration script, compile it (a step that's often much easier said than done), and install it.

Different flavors of Linux take this a step further with the concept of *packages*, which are essentially all-in-one bundles that contain the proper binary for your system as well as any required libraries, plus the necessary information about where to install everything. The Red Hat Package Manager (RPM) system is a GNU-licensed packager that runs on many systems, including FreeBSD. Its popularity was a large part of what pushed Red Hat to the top of the Linux distributors, edging out the previous favorite, Slackware. RPM allows administrators to keep tabs on their installed software and to upgrade, deinstall, and add new packages with unprecedented ease.

But FreeBSD takes things to yet another level of convenience. It has its own package management system, the pkg_* tools, which this chapter covers in detail. FreeBSD also has a supplementary system called the *ports*. Ports allow you to compile software from its original sources with guaranteed, one-command simplicity.

Introduction to Packages

Jordan Hubbard, formerly one of the core developers of FreeBSD (now working at Apple as an architect of Mac OS X), is responsible for most of the initial work on the package system. FreeBSD's system has been adopted by NetBSD and other platforms and refined over the years, with the best of the independent development efforts being rolled back into FreeBSD.

By its simplest definition, a package system is a way of bundling up software (including config files, shared libraries, and documentation) and extracting it again onto another machine, in which its configuration will be valid enough that the software can run properly on the new machine. Early package managers did little more than manage the bundling and extraction processes. RPM and FreeBSD's packagers both have numerous additional features:

- They maintain a database on each machine that shows which software and which version of each package are installed.

- They can grab a remote file from an FTP site (generally, the primary distribution site).

- They keep track of dependencies or any additional packages that must be installed for the one you're installing to run.

- They can do upgrades and deinstalls as well as installations.

The difference between the two packagers is related very closely to the different development philosophies of FreeBSD and Linux. Linux has a number of different distributions, with different versions of glibc (a set of core-shared libraries not relevant to FreeBSD) and a nearly infinite variety of hardware on which the operating system can run. RPM must necessarily be quite complex in order to handle all this diversity—and indeed it is. Its command-line interface is fairly arcane and requires a lot of documentation to be used properly. FreeBSD, however, benefits from a centralized development model and a single supported hardware platform, so the package model can be much simpler, both in architecture and usage.

As we discussed in Chapter 8, "The FreeBSD Filesystem," the /usr/local hierarchy is reserved for items that you install yourself, which refers specifically to software you install from the ports and packages. Table 14.1 shows the /usr/local directory structure (although your installation may vary slightly).

TABLE 14.1   Directory Structure Within `/usr/local`

Subdirectory	Purpose
bin	Binaries (compiled programs)
etc	Configuration files
include	C include files, used for building new software
info	Various supporting types of data for building documentation
lib	Shared libraries
libexec	Supporting binaries used by other programs
man	Manual pages for installed software
sbin	System binaries (programs that alter system behavior)
share	Platform-independent materials (data files, documentation, and so on)
var	Variable files for installed software

In other words, `/usr/local` has the same hierarchy found directly within `/usr` (with the exception that man pages are found at `/usr/local/man` rather than `/usr/local/share/man`, as you might expect). FreeBSD's package system keeps anything you install in the `/usr/local` tree and out of the `/usr` tree, thus maintaining the seamless but strict separation between base and user-installed software.

Shared Libraries and Dependencies

A *shared library* is a centralized file that provides precompiled function calls. Using a shared library, a program can access certain functions without having to have those functions built in to itself. This technique, known as *dynamic linking*, reduces file size and redundancy in comparison to static linking, which compiles all necessary functions into every program. Shared libraries exist on nearly all platforms, although they have different names—for instance, Windows calls them Dynamic Link Libraries (DLLs).

FreeBSD already has a large number of shared libraries installed in the base system— enough to support all the software that's part of the base system—and provides hooks for software that you might install later. Nevertheless, you're almost certain to run across a program that needs a shared library that doesn't exist in the base FreeBSD.

In FreeBSD, basic shared libraries are stored in `/usr/lib`, and any shared libraries that you install go into `/usr/local/lib`. All programs know automatically to look first in `/usr/lib` for the shared libraries they need, and they then look in `/usr/local/lib` (as well as a couple of other places). You can control this search path in `/etc/rc.conf`, as you saw in Chapter 10, "System Configuration and Startup Scripts."

Every package has a listing of dependencies that includes both shared libraries and executables (programs). If a dependency isn't already installed, the package system automatically hunts it down and installs it before proceeding with the installation. If you later remove some program or library (via the package tools) that is a dependency for some other installed package, the tools tell you about this and refuse to proceed.

14

Obtaining Information on Installed Packages

The first step toward getting to know the packages is to explore the information about the packages you have already installed. Chances are you've installed some packages as you read earlier sections of this book, or you may have some from a custom installation. If not, don't worry—the information here will be just as useful to you later.

The tools you use to manage packages are pkg_add, pkg_delete, pkg_info, pkg_update, pkg_version, and pkg_create. Each one does pretty much what you would expect it to do; one hallmark of FreeBSD's style is to use differently named programs rather than obscure switches and parameters. Each of these tools interacts with a filesystem database at /var/db/pkg, which you can consult by simply using ls to take a quick glance at your system's package status. This repository has a directory for each installed package that includes information about the packing list (the manifest of files in the package) and the dependencies. pkg_info uses this database to print out the short descriptions of every package you currently have installed, as you can see in Listing 14.1.

LISTING 14.1   Sample Output from pkg_info

```
# pkg_info
ImageMagick-5.2.7_2 An X11 package for display and interactive manipulation of
analog-4.16         An extremely fast program for analyzing WWW logfiles
apache-1.3.19       The extremely popular Apache http server.  Very fast, very
arc-5.21e.8         Create & extract files from DOS .ARC files
aub-2.0.5           Assemble usenet binaries
autoconf-2.13       Automatically configure source code on many Un*x platforms
dict-1.4.9          Dictionary Server Protocol (RFC2229) client
elm-2.4ME+68        A once-popular mail user agent, unofficial clone
emacs-19.34b        GNU editing macros
```

You can also get lots of information on any single package with the -v switch. As with RPM, packages in FreeBSD have names with multiple parts separated by dashes—the package name, followed by the version. However, RPM files tend to be geared toward multiple platforms, so the "platform" part of the package name is not used. Instead, a FreeBSD package file takes the form *name-version*.tgz. Here's an example:

bzip-0.21.tgz

Packages are generally .tgz files (called *tarballs*), which is shorthand for .tar.gz. Using tarballs is the traditional way of archiving a directory structure under Unix—you first pack the directory into one file using tar and then compress it using gzip. To use tools such as pkg_info -v, you need to specify the full package name, including the version, as shown in Listing 14.2.

LISTING 14.2   Verbose Output of `pkg_info`

```
# pkg_info -v pgp-2.6.3ia
Information for pgp-2.6.3ia:

Comment:
PGP MIT or International version - Public-Key encryption for the masses

Depends on:
Description:
PGP (Pretty Good Privacy) is a public key encryption pack-
age to protect E-mail and data files.  It lets you  commu-
nicate  securely  with  people  you've  never met, with no
secure channels needed for prior exchange of  keys.   It's
well featured and fast, with sophisticated key management,
digital signatures, data compression, and  good  ergonomic
design.
WWW: http://www.pgpi.org/

Packing list:
        Package name: pgp-2.6.3ia
        CWD to /usr/local
File: man/man1/pgp.1.gz
        Comment: MD5:a0ab17d1fe83aaf159cb80fa1abf5462
File: bin/pgp
        Comment: MD5:625e99562f936a3d9b0ac3c5d5a94ba9
File: lib/pgp/pgp.hlp
        Comment: MD5:d5da3783ea26bc60f4b7584df4227866
File: lib/pgp/pgpdoc1.txt
        Comment: MD5:260ca85cd0263275cb7df6cd276e2b9f
File: lib/pgp/pgpdoc2.txt
        Comment: MD5:e3defe467fbf5c5c4809f8b5c13404a1
File: lib/pgp/language.txt
        Comment: MD5:bcec0f56b207846725fe7e4a612383ef
File: lib/pgp/config.txt
        Comment: MD5:b2518ad2566a9a4bce071936311d3c93
        Deinstall directory remove: lib/pgp
        UNEXEC 'if [ -f %D/info/dir ]; then if sed -e '1,/Menu:/d'
➥%D/info/dir | grep -q '^[*] '; then true; else rm %D/info/dir; fi; fi'
```

This listing tells you everything you need to know about the package—from its long
description, to its dependencies, to its packing list (with the MD5 "fingerprint" checksum
for each file, listed in its Comment field). Some files have extra information noted, such as

"deinstallation scripts," which are tasks the package manager needs to execute if you remove this package. In this listing, the directory `lib/pgp` within the designated local directory tree (for example, `/usr/local/lib/pgp`) would be deleted upon deinstallation. You can deduce from this that this package creates a whole folder for its own shared libraries within `/usr/local/lib`; it can do that because shared library directories are searched recursively. Similarly, the package manager will run the `UNEXEC` line as a shell script to remove the `/usr/local/info/dir` file, subject to some conditionals. As you can see, a well-written and well-behaved package (and just about all packages are well behaved) will erase cleanly off your system when removed, leaving nary a trace behind.

How do you know that this version is current? You can determine this easily by using the `pkg_version` tool. It works only if the ports collection has been installed—and it should be installed unless you're severely short on disk space. You learn more about the ports collection later in this chapter, but all you need to know for understanding `pkg_version` is that the ports collection (if kept up to date) has a listing of the current version of every package. The `pkg_version` tool compares the versions of every installed package to the version found in the ports collection, and it tells you whether your packages are up to date (see Listing 14.3).

LISTING 14.3   Sample Output of `pkg_version`

```
# pkg_version -v
ImageMagick-5.2.7_2      <    needs updating (port has 5.2.9_1)
apache-1.3.19            =    up-to-date with port
arc-5.21e.8              =    up-to-date with index
aub-2.0.5                =    up-to-date with index
autoconf-2.13            =    up-to-date with index
bash-2.04                *    multiple versions (index has 1.14.7,2.04)
bnc-2.8.2                =    up-to-date with index
bulk_mailer-1.12         <    needs updating (index has 1.13)
bzip2-0.9.5d             <    needs updating (index has 1.0.1)
cclient-4.8              <    needs updating (index has 2000c)
cvsup-16.1               =    up-to-date with index
demoroniser-1.0          =    up-to-date with index
```

Without the `-v` option, `pkg_version` wouldn't print the third column; you'd just get the icon in the second column. The version string would also not be appended to the package names in the first column. Either way, this provides you with a quick, at-a-glance method for telling where your maintenance efforts are needed.

Installing Packages

Now, go out and find some software to install. The first step is to find out what's available. Just about all the software available for Linux is also available for FreeBSD, because binary compatibility allows you to do anything up to and including playing back audio/video using Linux software.

Installing from `sysinstall`

If you have the ports collection installed, you can see a categorized view of all the available software by going to `/usr/ports` and just looking around at the filesystem. Your old friend `/stand/sysinstall`, however, offers an even more direct interface.

From the main menu of the `sysinstall` program, choose Configure and then select Packages. The Packages menu is shown in Figure 14.1. From there, choose CD/DVD as the installation media if you have your FreeBSD install disk handy; if not, and you're on the Net, choose FTP.

FIGURE 14.1 The Packages menu in the `sysinstall` program.

After you get the package list from whichever medium you choose, you are presented with a menu like the one shown in Figure 14.2. Scroll up and down to see the various categories, and press Enter to go into each one.

A Note on Version Branches

We won't be covering FreeBSD's version-branching system until Chapter 17, "Keeping Up to Date with FreeBSD." For now, however, you should become familiar with at least a few important bits of terminology that are crucial to the proper operation of the packages and ports.

In the Options section of the `sysinstall` program is a field to set the release name you'll be working with. Chances are you will be running a "release" version of FreeBSD (these are the versions that come on CDs). If so, the Release Name field will be set correctly for the version you're running. However, if you've upgraded your system to an interim point on either the -STABLE or the -CURRENT branch, this field may be set to #.#-STABLE, where the hash marks (#) stand for major and minor version numbers. That value won't work when you try to open the Packages menu because it's pulled in directly from the output of the `uname` command, which reports information on the kernel version. It doesn't work because the Release Name field specifies the directory on the FTP server where `sysinstall` will look for the packages, and the corresponding directory for the packages that match your system's version doesn't necessarily have the same name.

Go to `ftp://ftp.FreeBSD.org/pub/FreeBSD/releases/` (and then into your appropriate plat-form subdirectory) to see the available release directories. If your version is 4.6.2-RELEASE, the release directory you want is `i386/4.6.2-RELEASE`. If your system has been rebuilt from `-STABLE` sources, choose the most recent `-RELEASE` directory.

FIGURE 14.2   Browsing a category in the Packages menu.

At the bottom of the screen shown in Figure 14.2, you'll see the one-line "short descrip-tion" of each package. When you see the package you want, press the spacebar to mark it with an ×. Select Cancel (press the right arrow) to exit from the category. You can browse through all the available categories this way until you've selected a long list of the pack-ages you want; when you're done, select Install from the bottom of the screen to install them all in one fell swoop.

> **NOTE**
>
> Note that selecting Install is the only way to exit from the Package menus. If you don't select any packages for installation, you still need to select Install (and accept its dialog about there being nothing to install) in order to exit to the main `sysinstall` menu.

The program now goes through the list and downloads each package, one by one, unpack-ing it into `/usr/tmp` and installing it using the `pkg_add` program, the command-line element to this phase of the FreeBSD package manager (which you can also use indepen-dently of `sysinstall`). If a package has any dependencies, `sysinstall` first finds and installs them and then returns to the packages you selected.

Exit from `sysinstall` using the Exit Install option at the bottom of the screen. Your new packages are now installed—that's really all there is to it. The documentation (`man` pages) is all ready to use, config files are in `/usr/local/etc`, and the binaries are in `/usr/local/bin`. Type **rehash** to refresh the available programs that your current shell knows about (or log out and back in), and you'll be able to use the software.

As you learned in Chapter 10, some programs need to be configured before they can be used. Go into /usr/local/etc and check for a config file (usually of the style <program name>.conf or <program name>.cfg, or at least containing the program name). If the file has .sample at the end, you need to perform some additional configurations and remove the .sample part before the program can use it. Open the file with your favorite text editor and do what needs to be done, as described in comments in the file itself or in the man page for the program. After you have configured the first file, check inside the rc.d subdi-rectory for similar files and deal with them in the same way.

Using pkg_add

Few options are available for the actual installation process in FreeBSD. Because executa-bles, config files, and libraries are all kept in a standard centralized location, no dialog asks where you want to install a program or offers you any of the custom installation options you get in the desktop OS world. These installation limitations are perfect exam-ples of both the more "closed-box" approach of FreeBSD, as compared to that of Linux, and the centralized distribution model for all the open-source software available for the platform.

However, there are times when you need more control over a package than you can get within sysinstall. Examples include packages that have interactive preinstallation scripts (in which you can set options specific to that package) and situations in which the auto-mated installation in sysinstall fails. For times such as these, you need the pkg_add tool; it's used in every package installation, whether it's called directly or run by sysinstall.

The pkg_add tool is designed to operate on a .tgz file you've already downloaded (from the per-release distribution directory described earlier) or on a remote file specified by its URL. For instance, the following two procedures are roughly equivalent:

```
# fetch ftp://ftp.FreeBSD.org/pub/FreeBSD/releases/i386/4.6.2-RELEASE/
➥packages/www/roxen-2.1.231.tgz
# pkg_add roxen-2.1.231.tgz
```

and

```
# pkg_add ftp://ftp.FreeBSD.org/pub/FreeBSD/releases/i386/4.6.2-RELEASE/
➥packages/www/roxen-2.1.231.tgz
```

Of course, the latter is much more convenient, because not only does it eliminate the separate steps of downloading and installing the package, it also does all its work in /usr/tmp (or a similar temp directory) and cleans up after itself when it's done. pkg_add also keeps track of dependencies as if you were using it through sysinstall. If you use pkg_add to add a package that has dependencies, it will automatically download and install the dependencies before proceeding. This ensures that you'll have a fully functional program after it's done working.

TIP

Use pkg_add -nv to do a "dry run" install. This shows you the steps pkg_add would take during the installation, without actually doing anything.

An even more convenient way to install packages, one that does not involve your exploring through the FTP site at all, involves using the -r option to pkg_add. This is the automated "remote fetching" feature, and it eliminates the need for you to know the current version number of the package you want, or even the version of your own operating system. The package manager will figure it out for you. Simply use the name of the package you want without the version number string, along with the -r flag, and pkg_add will determine your platform type and release version and install the package in one step. Here's an example:

```
# pkg_add -r roxen.tgz
Fetching ftp://ftp.freebsd.org/pub/FreeBSD/ports/i386/packages-4-stable/
➥Latest/roxen.tgz... Done.
```

Sometimes, a package installation finishes with a screen that gives you further instructions about how to complete the configuration. This is one benefit of installing packages from the command line rather than through sysinstall. Another is that sysinstall provides no feedback about the file size of any package, so you pretty much have to just let it download with no progress feedback other than data rate. If you used a browser to find the package in its FTP directory, you'll find the package size there and at least know how far you have to go when downloading.

Notes on Package Origins

The directory structure at the FreeBSD FTP site is such that each package is actually a symlink, so the file sizes aren't actually directly available if you reach them from the preceding URL. A little digging will get you the information, but it might not be worth your while.

Note that pkg_add does work on .tgz files grabbed from any location, not just the FreeBSD site. However, beware of files from "suspect" locations; adding packages is an act of trust, allowing whoever wrote the package to specify files to be placed in user-executable locations, possibly overwriting other files. (This is why regular users are generally restricted from installing packages and ports.) Viruses and Trojan horses are fairly uncommon in the Unix world, but a conscientious administrator should have these potential threats in mind at all times, and especially when installing packages!

If you stick to sysinstall, or at least to the .tgz files found at the FreeBSD FTP site, you can be assured that all the packages are approved for use and include an MD5 checksum to verify their authenticity, which you can usually do with the md5 tool:

```
# md5 roxen-2.1.231.tgz
```

You can compare the output string from this command to the contents of the checksum file, often provided along with the package, to make sure they match.

You can also specify multiple packages, run in verbose mode, and prevent pkg_add from running preinstallation or postinstallation scripts. You can even prevent it from recording that it has installed the package. These options and more can be found in the man pkg_add page.

Updating Installed Packages

The pkg_update tool allows you to update a package using a newly downloaded .tgz of a package you already have installed. It will handle all dependencies and ensure that the new version is installed cleanly. To use it, download the .tgz package and then run pkg_update on it, like this:

```
# pkg_update newpackage.tgz
```

Removing Packages

There is no front end in /stand/sysinstall for removing packages. You really don't need one because once a package is installed, you can specify its name directly using the command-line tools.

You can use pkg_info to see which packages you have installed, as you learned earlier. You can also simply look in /var/db/pkg; the directory names are the same as the package names. After you have the name of the package you want to delete, simply use pkg_delete to remove it, like this:

```
# pkg_delete roxen-1.3.111
```

If the package has any dependencies, pkg_delete will detect them and refuse to proceed unless you've run it with the -f option to force deinstallation. It will also attempt to run any deinstallation scripts and evaluate any "require" statements; if these fail, pkg_delete will also fail (except if it's running with the -f option). As with pkg_add, you can use a number of other options, including verbose mode (-v) and "dry run" mode (-n).

Introduction to Ports

You now know about packages and the tools FreeBSD provides for interacting with them. *Ports* offer another way for you to install software in FreeBSD. You use ports to compile software directly from the source in an automated procedure that controls and safeguards the installation process as it allows you to grab the source directly from each program's distribution site.

As convenient as packages are, the traditional "Unix way" of installing new software has always been to compile it yourself. The administrator finds the distribution site (using either HTTP or FTP, or in an earlier era, a tool such as Gopher or Archie), downloads the source code bundled up in a `.tar.gz` or `.tgz` file, and unpacks it into some temporary directory. After reading the various README files for special instructions, the administrator usually runs a `configure` script that examines the system to check for a variety of function calls (these calls vary from platform to platform within the Unix world). The next step is to compile the software by running `make`—an encapsulated compiler-management tool that reads its build targets and the necessary steps from a file called `Makefile` within the main source directory. After a (hopefully) clean compile, the administrator must then find the new, freshly baked executable and manually copy it into the publicly accessible location for binaries (`/usr/local/bin`, for example). In the best-case scenario, however, there is an "install" target in the makefile, so typing **make install** copies the proper files into (possibly) the correct location.

This installation operation is (or rather, *was*) very inexact; sometimes it worked, sometimes it didn't. In the vast majority of cases it worked "sort of." Maintenance was impossible, performance was unpredictable, and the reputation of Unix for being arcane and difficult to use only grew stronger.

Enter the FreeBSD ports. Ports provide a way for you to compile software directly from the source in a regimented, structured, automated procedure that ensures the safety and integrity of the software you're installing while allowing you to grab the source directly from each program's distribution site. This means you can stay on top of the very latest developments in a piece of software without having to wait for a precompiled binary package that might not run on a heavily customized system.

Port installation also allows thousands of different pieces of software to install all their components into the proper locations in the FreeBSD filesystem without the developers even having to know about it. This is done through a widespread system of port maintainers, volunteers in the FreeBSD user community who keep track of changes in their assigned ports and maintain scripts that patch a program's build and installation procedures to operate correctly with FreeBSD. A port, then, is simply these scripts and patches in a bundle, sitting in a particular spot on your FreeBSD machine, with a customized makefile that enables you to install the software simply by typing **make install**. No downloading; no configuring; no tweaking; no copying. All that work has been done for you.

FreeBSD's port system has been so successful it has been adopted by various other systems, particularly OpenBSD and NetBSD. Its success can be attributed to two things: Its ability to keep Unix administrators who prefer to compile their own software (either through security awareness or machismo) happy, and it's ability to provide the simplicity of version tracking and maintenance that the packages boast. It's truly the best of both worlds.

The FreeBSD Ports Tree

The ports collection lives in /usr/ports. Go into that directory now and take a look around. What you see should resemble Listing 14.4. You'll notice that every category you saw in the sysinstall program is here as a directory. (The list may not be 100-percent accurate for you because categories are reorganized on a fairly regular basis.)

LISTING 14.4   Directories in /usr/ports

```
# ls -sF /usr/ports/
total 1447
    1 .cvsignore          10 devel/            1 news/
 1296 INDEX                 3 distfiles/        1 palm/
   11 LEGAL                 4 editors/          3 print/
    4 Makefile              2 emulators/        1 russian/
    1 Mk/                   1 french/           1 science/
    2 README                1 ftp/              4 security/
    4 README.html           6 games/            1 shells/
    1 Templates/            1 german/           3 sysutils/
    1 Tools/                5 graphics/         4 textproc/
    1 archivers/            1 hebrew/           1 ukrainian/
    1 astro/                1 irc/              1 vietnamese/
    4 audio/                9 japanese/         6 www/
    1 benchmarks/           1 java/             3 x11/
    1 biology/              2 korean/           1 x11-clocks/
    1 cad/                  3 lang/             1 x11-fm/
    2 chinese/              4 mail/             1 x11-fonts/
    1 comms/                3 math/             2 x11-servers/
    2 converters/           1 mbone/            3 x11-toolkits/
    2 databases/            4 misc/             2 x11-wm/
    1 deskutils/            7 net/
```

> **NOTE**
>
> The contents of /usr/ports are by their nature independent of the branched development structure of the FreeBSD operating system. A newly released copy of the system will come with a snapshot of the ports created at the time the system was released, but it immediately becomes obsolete as soon as the ports within it are revised as new versions of the ported software come out. If you synchronize your ports tree to the central repository (as we will discuss later), it's always to whatever is current at the time you synchronize. There isn't a fixed state for the ports tree attached to each release as there is with the packages. Therefore, these sample directory listings are likely to differ somewhat from what is in your system.

14

The first few directories (the ones beginning with capital letters, taking advantage of the Unix convention of alphabetizing capital and lowercase initial letters separately, in accordance with the ASCII character set) are structural elements of the ports system, adjuncts that make the system work. The rest of the directories are categories of ports. Look inside one and you'll see as many as hundreds of different port directories, as demonstrated in Listing 14.5.

LISTING 14.5   Ports Within a Category (Directory)

```
# ls -sF /usr/ports/audio/
total 230
  1 Maaate/            1 mpg123/
  5 Makefile           1 mpg123.el/
 11 README.html        1 mpg321/
  1 afsp/              1 mpmf20/
  1 amp/               1 mq3/
  1 ascd/              1 musicbox/
  1 aumix/             1 musicbrainz/
  1 aureal-kmod/       1 mutemix/
  1 autozen/           1 mxv/
  1 bladeenc/          1 napster/
```

Browsing the ports in this way is less than efficient, especially in the larger categories. That's what the README.html file is for. Remember the "short description" that each package had? That description is stored in this file, too, and there's a README.html file at both levels of directories, as well as inside (almost) every port directory. You can browse the structure in hypertext using any Web browser on the local machine: Netscape, if you're using the machine as an X-Windows workstation, or lynx if you're logged in remotely (as shown in Figure 14.3).

FIGURE 14.3   Browsing a category's README.html file in lynx.

Anatomy of a FreeBSD Port

Inside each port directory are a few files, totaling no more than a few kilobytes, that completely define all the tweaks and modifications that need to be made to a cleanly downloaded bundle of source code for it to compile and install cleanly on FreeBSD. These files are detailed in Table 14.2.

TABLE 14.2   Files in a port Directory

File	Purpose
Makefile	Contains certain variables used in the build process as well as contact information for the maintainer.
README.html	Contains the "short description" (or comment) for the port in HTML format.
distinfo	An MD5 checksum used for verifying the authenticity of the downloaded tarball.
files/	Patches that are applied to the source after it has been unpacked and support
runme.sh	files that are FreeBSD specific; these vary greatly from port to port.
patch-aa	
patch-ab	
pkg-comment	The "short description" for the port.
pkg-descr	The "long description" for the port, which usually includes the URL of the developer's distribution site.
pkg-plist	The "packing list," which lists all the files to be installed as well as keywords telling the port system what to do when the port is deinstalled (for example, when removing directories).

Makefile is the file that has the critical elements for building, configuring, installing, and maintaining a port. Listing 14.6 shows you what's typically inside Makefile.

LISTING 14.6   A Typical Port Makefile

```
# New ports collection makefile for:      amp
# Date created:          Jun 23 1997
# Whom:                  Vanilla I. Shu <vanilla@MinJe.com.TW>
#
# $FreeBSD: ports/audio/amp/Makefile,v 1.10 2000/04/08 21:23:11 mharo Exp $
#


PORTNAME=       amp
PORTVERSION=    0.7.6
CATEGORIES=     audio
#MASTER_SITES=  ftp://ftp.rasip.fer.hr/pub/mpeg/
# the author's site seems dead.
MASTER_SITES=   ftp://ftp.clara.net/pub/unix/Audio/
```

LISTING 14.6   Continued

```
MAINTAINER=      vanilla@FreeBSD.org

GNU_CONFIGURE=   yes
USE_GMAKE=       yes

MAN1=            amp.1

do-install:
        @ ${INSTALL_PROGRAM} ${WRKSRC}/amp ${PREFIX}/bin
        @ ${INSTALL_MAN} ${WRKSRC}/amp.1 ${PREFIX}/man/man1
.include <bsd.port.mk>
```

The list of variables tells you what you need to know about where the source for the port comes from, what version the makefile thinks is current, and how to reach the maintainer. The *maintainer* is a volunteer, usually unaffiliated with whoever develops the actual software, whose job is to make sure the port compiles and installs cleanly and that the most recent version of the software is reflected in the port.

Most makefiles contain targets, such as clean, install, and all. Not all the makefiles in the ports have these targets, but what they do have is an included central makefile (bsd.port.mk, which lives in the /usr/ports/Mk directory along with other included files). This file is what contains the standardized build targets. The individual makefiles in each port serve as overrides or augmentations (much in the same way /etc/rc.conf relates to /etc/defaults/rc.conf), setting the necessary variables for the build and defining additional targets that will be used in the automated compile process.

Installing and Removing Ports

Let's say that a port catches your eye and you decide you want to install it. Here's where it gets fun. All you have to do is move into the port's directory (using cd) and type **make**. This compiles the software. Then, you type **make install** to install it.

It's a simple process on the surface, but there's a lot that goes on under the hood. The make command actually executes a series of sequential make targets (described in Table 14.3). Each one depends on all the previous targets. You can specify any of these targets directly. This will build all targets up to and including the one you specify.

TABLE 14.3   The make Targets in a Port Makefile

Target	Action
fetch	Downloads the source tarball from the master site into /usr/ports/distfiles
checksum	Verifies the authenticity of the tarball using the MD5 checksum
extract	Unpacks the tarball into a work subdirectory

TABLE 14.3   Continued

Target	Action
patch	Applies the patches from the `files` directory to the source
configure	Runs the `configure` script, which prepares the source for building
build	Compiles the source

Typing **make extract**, for example, will download the source file, match its MD5 checksum, and unpack it. Although there are other targets (listed in `/usr/ports/Mk/bsd.port.mk`), you won't need to use any of them under most circumstances.

After each step in the process is complete (except for `fetch` and `checksum`), a file is created in the `work` subdirectory of the form `.extract_done`. This is how the system keeps track of which steps are completed. To see whether the `fetch` step is done, it simply checks for the existence of the file in `/usr/ports/distfiles`. The `extract` step runs the `checksum` step implicitly. After that, the steps are sequential and independent, and they check for prerequisite steps by looking for the appropriate `.*_done` files.

If you need to make any changes to the source before compiling, you can run `make patch`, thus bringing the source up to where it's ready to compile, and then make whatever changes you like. Then, you can complete the process with `make`.

Dependencies are handled automatically by the ports, just as with the packages. Any dependencies are read from the makefile during the `fetch` phase and then downloaded, built, and installed. You will get feedback in the `build` output each time it encounters a dependency, regardless of whether that dependency is installed already.

After a port is installed, an entry is made in the `/var/db/pkg` database; for all intents and purposes, it is now a package. You can use the `pkg_*` tools on it to gather information and compare its version, just as with packages installed from within `sysinstall`.

There is a `deinstall` target in the ports (`make deinstall`). This target is used when the installed port version is the same as the one in the makefile—in essence, you're deinstalling exactly the same software package you installed. If you update your ports so that the version of a port (in the makefile) is higher than the installed version, you can't use `make deinstall` to delete it. Instead you have to use `pkg_delete`, the same way as you would a package.

Upgrading a Port

If the version of a port has changed, you can simply use `make install` to install it over the old version. This can be a bad idea, however, because most of the installed files will be the same from one version to another, so if you try to delete (using `pkg_delete`) an older version of the same port or package while a newer one is installed over it, you will end up deleting most of the newer version as well. If you have `pkg_version` output like the following, you're stuck with the earlier versions in your package database, unless you're willing to deinstall all versions of the package and then reinstall the current version:

```
apache-1.3.12          <    needs updating (index has 1.3.19)
apache-1.3.14          <    needs updating (index has 1.3.19)
apache-1.3.17          <    needs updating (port has 1.3.19)
apache-1.3.19          =    up-to-date with port
```

To avoid this situation, always check for a previous version of a port before installing a new one. Use `pkg_info`, `pkg_version`, or the `/var/db/pkg` structure to see what's there already. If there's an earlier version, remove it, like so:

```
# pkg_delete apache-1.3.12
```

You shouldn't have to worry about customized config files for the port. In the apache port, for example, the `pkg-plist` file contains `@unexec` commands, which compare the configuration files with the default ones installed by the port and delete them only if they match. Even so, it's a good idea to back up important config files before removing a package or port, just in case.

It's not the end of the world to leave your old versions installed, though. This provides an audit trail so you can view your system's upgrade history, and it doesn't hurt anything to have the old versions around (except that if a port's files move around, the outdated files on your system will continue to hang around).

Updating and Maintaining Your Ports

Software changes. There are more than 4,000 ports in the collection, and each one of them is undergoing development (some at much faster rates than others). A fact of system administration is that you can't install or upgrade software fast enough to keep up with the rate of development. The best you can hope to do is keep your ports collection up to date and use the built-in tools, such as `pkg_version`, to keep track of what needs to be upgraded.

Keeping Ports Up to Date with CVSup

To keep your ports synchronized, the best tool for the job is CVSup. In Chapter 17, you learn about CVSup in detail. Because CVSup is an essential tool for working efficiently with ports, it's important that you know some of its simplest uses—and there really isn't much to it.

First, install the `cvsup-bin` package, either by using the package system or by building it from the ports. In fact, it's better to use the package version because CVSup is a tool written in Modula-3, meaning that building it from source involves building several large Modula-3 dependencies. Use the package installation to get past that for now.

Make sure you're connected to the Internet properly. Now, go into the /usr/ports/net/cvsupit port directory. This is a pseudo-port that doesn't really install anything; instead, it creates a central runtime config file for CVSup to use. Run make and then run make install. You will be taken to the cvsupit configuration (branch selection) screen, as shown in Figure 14.4.

FIGURE 14.4 The cvsupit branch selection screen.

Select the first option (".") rather than a branch name. This stands for the "head" of the source tree, and it's where the current ports are kept on the master server. Accept the defaults for the rest of the screens (where it asks whether you wish to track the ports and docs collections) and select a CVSup server from the list (the higher-numbered servers are usually less busy). When it prompts you, select No to elect not to run the CVSup update now.

> **NOTE**
>
> The function of the cvsupit port is to create /etc/cvsupfile, which you can subsequently use when running CVSup from the command line. The fact that it lets you run your first CVSup update from within the cvsupit dialog boxes is a courtesy; you're not supposed to need to do it that way more than once. After you've run cvsupit for the first time, you will be running CVSup manually from the command line or in an automated fashion with a cron job.

Open the file /etc/cvsupfile in your favorite text editor. Comment out the lines beginning with src- (tags that specify the operating sources, which you won't be updating now). Do this by placing a hash mark (#) at the beginning of each of these lines.

Now, run the CVSup update, as directed by cvsupit:

```
# /usr/local/bin/cvsup -g -L 2 /etc/cvsupfile
```

The tool 1 connects to the selected CVSup server and begins synchronizing your ports collection. You will see all changes between your installed version and the current one scroll by. CVSup operates by updating only files that have changed and then by updating only the changed pieces (by using diff patches). This allows you to update the entire ports collection while transferring only a minimum of data and using a minimal amount of bandwidth. A CVSup update can be done efficiently, even over a very small network link.

After the synchronization is complete, your ports collection is current and "up to the minute." You can now run pkg_version -v to see which ports or packages you need to update.

You will probably want to make this synchronization process a part of your system's daily routine so that your ports will never be more than 24 hours out of date. To do this, add the previous CVSup command to your daily periodic files (see "Using the Periodic Task Scheduler," in Chapter 13, "Performance Monitoring, Process Control, and Job Automation"). If it doesn't exist already, create a directory called periodic in /usr/local/etc and then another directory called daily underneath that. Create a file called something such as 100.cvsup-ports and put these lines in it:

```
#!/bin/sh

/usr/local/bin/cvsup -g -L 2 /etc/cvsupfile
```

Now, every night when the daily periodic script is executed, your ports collection will be synchronized. The output of CVSup is mailed to you in your daily system status update.

Notes on Forbidden Ports

Sometimes a port is present in the ports collection but the system doesn't allow you to build it. This is controlled by the FORBIDDEN variable in the makefile. If this variable is present, whatever text string it is set to is displayed when you try to build the port:

```
# cd /usr/ports/lang/perl5
# make
===>   perl-5.005 is forbidden: perl is in system.
```

A port can be marked "forbidden" for many reasons. In this example, it's because the program in question has been made a part of the core system, and building it from the ports would be redundant and possibly ruin the system's operation. In other cases, it's because a port might have a recently found security hole that is not yet fixed. In either case, this is a good illustration of the need to keep your ports synchronized to the CVSup server as regularly as possible.

It's seldom a good idea to override a forbidden port, but it's possible to do so by simply removing the FORBIDDEN line from the makefile. Some forbidden ports do provide a way to override the block by setting an environment variable, such as in this example of the security/ssh port:

```
# cd /usr/ports/security/ssh
# make
===>  ssh-1.2.27_3 is forbidden: OpenSSH is a superior version of SSH which has
been included in the FreeBSD base system since 4.0-RELEASE. This port is now
deprecated and will be removed at some point in the future. To override this
warning set the REALLY_WANT_SSH environment variable and rebuild..
```

As the instructions say, set the indicated environment variable and try again. Here's how if you're using csh or tcsh:

```
# setenv REALLY_WANT_SSH yes
```

And here's how if you're using bash:

```
# REALLY_WANT_SSH=yes
```

After setting the variable, run make again. The port should build cleanly.

Reclaiming Hard Disk Space Used by the Port-Building Process

After you're done building and installing a port, the work directory is still sitting there, filled with the unpacked tree of source code and compiled binary objects. This can take up a fair amount of disk space. It's always advisable to clean this directory out after installation—returning the port to its original pristine state—by running one more make command, this time with the clean target:

```
# make clean
```

This deletes the work directory and everything in it. It also cleans out the port directory for each dependency listed. However, it does not remove the tarball files from /usr/ports/distfiles; you'll have to remove these files yourself.

> **TIP**
>
> Unless you really need the disk space, you might want to leave the tarballs intact in the /usr/ports/distfiles directory. You can save a lot of time this way—if you should ever need to rebuild or reinstall a port, the system can use the file it already has, instead of having to download it again.
>
> The beauty of ports is that if a security hole or critical bug is fixed in a port that you have installed, the ports collection might solve it by placing a patch file in the files directory of the port, not by bumping the revision number of the entire distribution file (and causing you to have to download a new tarball). A simple rebuild allows you to incorporate the new patch into your old sources.

14

Periodically, you may want to issue a top-level recursive `make clean` on the entire ports collection. There's a makefile at both the `/usr/ports` level and the category level below it that enables you to do odd tasks such as building all the ports in a category at once (for example, building every "www" port by running `make` from inside `/usr/ports/www`). More usefully, it lets you clean every port at once, in one very long recursive process. You do this simply by going to `/usr/ports` and entering **`make clean`**. You can now go and get a sandwich if you want; like cleaning an oven, this process will be worthwhile but usually takes forever.

When a Port Will Not Build: Searching for Solutions and Using Upgrade Kits

As convenient as the ports collection is, it's not perfect—and with the amount of change that goes on in the tree, especially with so many ports (such as the ones related to GNOME and KDE) interrelated and constantly evolving, chances are that you'll run into some stumbling blocks now and then. The general failure behavior is for the compile process to fail with "`*** Error code 1`" or a similar message. When this happens, you can try a number of things.

First, make sure you're starting from a clean port. If there is a pre-existing work directory, it's possible that you've mixed new sources with old, resulting in an unbuildable port. Run `make clean` to start over from a clean slate.

It's also important to make sure you have the very latest ports tree available. If a port doesn't build, chances are it's a temporary condition that will have affected many other users besides yourself. A new version of the ported software might have been released since the version your ports refer to, for example, or perhaps your ports refer to a version that was newly released at the time your ports tree was installed, and some of the patches (written for a previous version) might have inadvertently become incompatible. If your ports tree is even a few days out of date, the chances are good that the port has been fixed in the meantime. Synchronize your ports tree as discussed earlier in this chapter and try building the port again (make sure you run `make clean` first).

If this doesn't work, it's time to seek outside assistance. Head to the FreeBSD Web site at `http://www.freebsd.org` and go to the Mailing Lists link, where you can search the relevant mailing lists. Make sure you check the Ports list as one of the search criteria. Then perform the search on the name of your port and some of the relevant text in the last few lines of the compiler output. If there's anything commonly failing that other people have noticed, you'll probably find something useful this way.

Still no luck? There's one more good recourse: the port maintainer. Look in the port's `Makefile` for the MAINTAINER variable, which is set to the e-mail address of the maintainer.

Send off a politely worded, undemanding e-mail containing the last (relevant) part of the compiler output, as well as information about your system (the output of uname -a, for instance). The maintainer is usually a very overworked, underappreciated individual, so be sure to express your gratitude for any help!

There may come a time when a port will fail to build, claiming that your system is "too old." It will inform you that you either need to upgrade your entire system or install an upgrade kit. This latter option is much preferable; despite its name, it doesn't upgrade your system at all, and it's very nonintrusive.

An upgrade kit is a set of updated include files that the ports collection needs in order for its customized build targets to work. Most of these include files are in /usr/ports/Mk and can therefore be brought up to date with CVSup. However, an unavoidable obstacle is that some required files are not within /usr/ports—they're elsewhere in the core system, such as /usr/share or /etc. An upgrade kit is a standard FreeBSD package that provides newer versions of these files, enabling you to continue building ports even when your ports tree is much newer than your base system. You can install an upgrade kit using pkg_add, as with any package.

Upgrade kits are distributed from http://www.freebsd.org/ports, and there is one available for updating from any supported release version to the current spot in its corresponding -STABLE branch. You can install successive upgrade kits if you need to. However, it will eventually become necessary for you to upgrade your entire system, as you'll learn in Chapter 17.

Fresh Ports

The output of the CVSup synchronization process is a useful, but hardly ideal way to keep track of which ports have changed. There's a very handy Web site (see Figure 14.5) that should be in the bookmarks or favorites of any FreeBSD administrator: Fresh Ports.

Maintained separately from the FreeBSD project proper, Fresh Ports is a database linked to the main CVS repository for the ports collection. It constantly monitors all check-ins and lists them in reverse chronological order. You can register with the Web site and set up a watch list for your favorite ports. You'll be e-mailed whenever anything on your watch list changes, and you can view exactly what the changes are to each port so that you can determine whether the change is worth upgrading for. For instance, if a port is bumped up a version or a crucial security fix has been checked in, you may well want to upgrade; however, if the only recent change is to fix a typo in an installer error message, don't bother.

FIGURE 14.5   The Fresh Ports Web site (www.freshports.org).

CHAPTER 15

Printing

Setting up a printer in FreeBSD is one of the more complex topics you will have to deal with if you administer FreeBSD. Unfortunately, FreeBSD printing is not as simple as installing a driver, selecting the printer from a Control Panel, and then printing. Printing from FreeBSD involves configuring one or more configuration files and possibly installing filters if you need to print anything more advanced than plain text. After a basic outline of the major printing processes in FreeBSD, this chapter explains how to configure the kernel, device, and communications modes, create the spool directory, install printing filters, and enable printing in FreeBSD. The chapter also covers the administration of network printing functions, and it provides troubleshooting guidance for identifying and resolving a number of common printing problems.

The first part of this chapter assumes that you have a printer connected to a parallel port. It is possible to use FreeBSD with printers that connect to the serial port. However, serial printing is very slow, and is obsolete. Only ancient printers use serial printing. In addition, this chapter assumes that you know whether your printer understands PostScript. See your printer's documentation to find out.

> **NOTE**
>
> GDI printers, sometimes also called *WinPrinters*, don't work with FreeBSD at all. These printers are usually cheaper than non-GDI printers because they move some of the printer control off of the hardware and into a software driver. These printers have disadvantages: They use more system resources because the computer's CPU has to do much of the processing, rather than letting the printer do it, and they require special drivers that are usually available only for Windows. A very long list of operating systems simply will not work with these types of printers, and FreeBSD is one of them.

The first part of this chapter assumes that you have a printer connected to a parallel port. It is possible to use FreeBSD with printers that connect to the serial port. However, serial printing is very slow, and is obsolete. Only ancient printers use serial printing. In addition, this chapter assumes that you know whether your printer understands PostScript or not. See your printer's documentation to find out.

How lpd, the Print Spooler, and the Print Queue Function in FreeBSD

lpd is the line printer daemon. This software runs in the background and waits for print requests. When it receives them, it sorts the requests through any relevant filters, converts the data to a different format if necessary, and sends the requests to the print queue.

The *print queue* is an area on the hard disk where print data is stored that is waiting to be sent to the printer. Each printer connected to the system has its own separate queue and spool area. The spool area holds the data until it can be sent to the printer. It can hold multiple jobs from the same or different users.

When a user submits a job to be printed, it is put in the queue. The *spooler* then spools the job to the printer when the printer is available. Jobs can have different priorities that determine in which order they will get printed. The spooler has several advantages over simply printing directly to the printer, as DOS used to do:

- It allows the printer to be shared by multiple users because data can be queued up to be printed, and the program that sent the data can then forget about it.

- It allows for background printing. Once again, the program that requests a print job can send the job and then forget about it. This means you don't have to wait for the program to finish printing before you can continue working in it. It also means you can shut down the program after the job has been submitted to the queue without losing the print job.

- It allows for some degree of fault tolerance. If the printer has to be reset, you will not lose the jobs that are in the queue and have to resubmit them. After the printer is back online, the remaining jobs in the queue should print normally, as if nothing happened.

Generally, the spool directories are located in /var/spool. The first printer on the system will normally spool to /var/spool/lpd or /var/spool/output/lpd. However, this can be changed by editing a configuration file, and we will look at how to do this later in the chapter.

Kernel, Device, and Communications Mode Configuration

The default kernel has support for the parallel device built in to it, so unless you have built a custom kernel and removed support for the parallel port, you shouldn't have any problems. The easiest way to check for parallel support in the kernel is by checking the kernel's dmesg output. The command dmesg | grep lpt0 will check to make sure that the first parallel device (which would be lpt1 in DOS; FreeBSD devices almost always start at 0) is supported in the kernel. If FreeBSD responds with something similar to

```
lpt0: <Printer> on ppbus0
lpt0: Interrupt-driven port
```

then the printer has support for the parallel port. If FreeBSD responds with nothing, the kernel does not have support for the parallel port. You will need to add the line device lpt to the kernel configuration file and rebuild the kernel (see Chapter 16, "Kernel Configuration," for information on how to configure and build the kernel). In addition, the line device ppbus must also exist in the kernel configuration file.

Configuring the Parallel Port Mode

You can use the lptcontrol program to configure the mode of the parallel port. Note that you will need to be root to do this. Also, there must be a printer connected to the parallel port for lptcontrol to work.

The syntax of lptcontrol is lptcontrol -x -d /dev/lpt0, where -x is one of the options detailed in Table 15.1, depending on the mode you want to set.

TABLE 15.1   The lptcontrol Mode Options

Option	Description
-i	Sets interrupt-driven mode
-p	Sets polled mode
-e	Sets extended mode (whatever extended mode the printer supports)
-s	Sets standard mode (turns off extended mode)

If your printer and your BIOS support ECP, EPP, or other forms of enhanced communication, you will want to use -e here.

Also, note that -d is optional. If you do not specify a device, lptcontrol will use the default device, which is /dev/lpt0.

For example, the following command will set the first parallel port to extended mode:

```
lptcontol -e -d /dev/lpt0
```

Maintaining Port Configuration Across Reboots

If you want these settings to be maintained across reboots, you must add the `lptcontrol` control command to one of the system startup scripts so that it is run at each system boot. You can add this control command to `/etc/rc.local` or you can create a new file in `/usr/local/etc/rc.d` that has the command in it. If you create a file in `/usr/local/etc/rc.d` that has the command in it, you will need to set the permissions on the file so that it is executable (for example, `chmod 655 filename`).

Creating the Spool Directory and Setting Its Permissions

After you have completed the preceding procedure, you are ready to set up `lpd` and configure the spooler. Begin by creating a spool directory for the printer. Print spool directories are normally located in `/var/spool/lpd`, although there is nothing that says you can't put them somewhere else.

Decide on a name for the printer you are configuring. You can name the printer just about anything you want. You can also create aliases to access the printer by other names.

After you have decided on a name for the printer, create a spool directory for it. Here's an example:

```
mkdir /var/spool/lpt/laserjet
```

After this, you will probably want to change the owner of the spool directory and also change the permissions so that users can't snoop around and look at other people's print jobs. All print spool directories should be owned by the user daemon and group daemon, and they should have read, write, and execute permissions for the user and group, with no permissions for anyone else. The following commands will correctly set the ownership and permissions on the spool directory:

```
chown daemon.daemon /var/spool/lpd/laserjet
chmod 770 /var/spool/lpd/laserjet
```

You have set up the spool directory; you will need to set up a text filter for `lpd`.

Setting Up Text and Conversion Filters

After you have set up the spool directory, you will need to set up a text filter for `lpd`. Filters are where most of the actual work is done in printing. When `lpd` sends data to a filter, it sets the filter's STDIN to the file that is to be printed and its STDOUT to the printer device. Conversion filters are similar to text filters, except they are designed to convert file formats into a format the printer can understand.

Text Filters

As its name implies, the *text filter* is the filter lpd uses when it receives plain text to print. The text filter can be as simple as a shell script that uses cat to simply pass the raw data to the printer, or it can be as complex as a program that changes the data into a completely different format. An example of a complex filter is one that uses GhostScript, which takes raw PostScript data and changes it into a format that a non-PostScript printer can understand (see the next section for more information about GhostScript).

What Is PostScript?

PostScript is a complex programming language designed to print and format graphics and text. It is device independent, meaning that any printer that understands PostScript can render a PostScript document with no special drivers. PostScript was invented by Adobe in 1985 and is supported by a wide range of printers today. It became a widely popular language for describing text and images in files because it was so portable and device independent.

Unfortunately, printers that do not understand PostScript cannot print PostScript documents. (They will print them out as just plain text, which will usually not make any sense.) However, a freely available program called GhostScript can translate PostScript into a format that non-PostScript printers can understand. This allows these non-PostScript printers to emulate PostScript with software. GhostScript will be covered later in this chapter.

A very simple text filter for lpd would look like this:

```
#!/bin/sh
/bin/cat && exit 0
exit 2
```

The generally accepted place to save a text filter is in /usr/local/libexec. (You may want to call it /usr/local/libexec/if-text, for example.) After you have saved the file, it will also need to be made executable so that lpd can run it. The command chmod 555 /usr/local/libexec/if-text will do the trick.

The first line in this filter indicates that this is a shell program that should be run with /bin/sh (the standard shell).

TIP

If any of this is unclear to you, you might want to refer to Chapter 12, "Shell Programming," before continuing with this chapter. Setting up print filters often involves a significant amount of shell programming.

The second line simply calls the cat program, which by default reads from STDIN and sends to STDOUT. The double ampersand (&&) means to do both of the statements on this line, or do neither one. In other words, if the cat command is successful, the script will exit with status 0, which indicates success. If there is an error, the part of the line after &&

is not performed, and the third line will be performed instead, which tells the program to exit with a status of 2. (If lpd receives an exit status of 2, it means the filter failed, and lpd will not try to print the file again.)

Setting Up Text Filters for Printing Plain-Text Files on PostScript Printers

The preceding simple filter will work fine for printing plain text on most non-PostScript printers. However, PostScript printers cannot handle plain-text data. If you have a PostScript printer, you will need a more complex filter that can convert the plain-text data into PostScript data.

The first thing you need to do is install a program that can convert plain text to PostScript. A program that can handle this task for you is "a2ps," which can be found in the FreeBSD ports tree. (Refer to Chapter 14, "Installing Additional Software," for more information on how to install ports.) Note that three versions of a2ps are available. They are named based on the paper size they are intended to work with.

Basically, a filter for a PostScript printer has to be able to test whether it is receiving PostScript data. If it is, nothing happens, and the data is passed straight through as it was with the earlier simple text filter. (A PostScript file is a plain-text file that has complex control codes in it that the PostScript printer can understand.) If the PostScript printer is not receiving PostScript data, the filter must convert the data to PostScript before it sends it to the printer.

All PostScript files begin with the magic character sequence "%!". We can write a shell script that checks to see whether the first line of the file begins with this sequence. If it does, we have a PostScript file, and the data can be passed straight through to the printer. If it doesn't, we have a plain-text file, and the data needs to be passed through a2ps to convert it to PostScript before it is sent to the printer.

The shell script shown in Listing 15.1 will do the trick.

LISTING 15.1 Sample Postscript Filter

```
#!/bin/sh
# Simple filter for PostScript printers

read header
ps_test=`expr "$header" : '\(..\)'`
if [ "$header" = "%!" ]
then
    # File is PostScript. Print pass through.
    Echo "$header" && cat && printf "\004" && exit 0
    exit 2
else
    # File is plain text. Convert it first.
    (echo "$header"; cat) | /usr/local/bin/a2p && printf "\004" && exit 0
    exit 2
fi
```

Save this file somewhere (`/usr/local/libexec/if-ps` might be a good choice). Make the file executable so that `lpd` can run it (`chmod 555 /usr/local/libexec/if-ps` will do the trick).

This code reads the first line of the input it is sent by `lpd` and stores it in the variable `header`. The program then uses the `expr` command to get the first two characters from the file and stores them in the variable `ps_test`. The `if` statement that comes next checks what two characters are stored in `ps_test`. If they are `%!`, this is a PostScript file and the `then` statement is performed, which passes the raw data directly to the printer. It sends the first line, "cats" the rest of the input, sends an escaped `\004` with `printf`, and finally exits with a status of 0. The double ampersand (`&&`) connects the different statements and basically says, "Either do all of these commands or don't do any of them." If for whatever reason any part of this command line fails, none of it will be performed, and the program will exit with status 2 instead—which tells `lpd` that the data could not be printed and that it should not retry.

If the first two characters are not `%!`, this file is not a PostScript file, and the `else` statements are performed instead. The `else` statements in this case first echo the first line of the program and then "cat" the rest of the input and pipe it to `/usr/local/bin/a2ps`. The a2ps program does the work of converting the file into PostScript and sending it to the printer.

Finally, when all the data has been sent, an escaped `\004` is sent with `printf`, and the program exits with a status of 0. As with the `then` statement, if any part fails, the program will exit with a status of 2 instead.

The a2ps program has many options, so if you will be printing plain-text files through a PostScript printer on a regular basis, I suggest you read the man page for a2ps. You can then modify the way this script calls a2ps to suit your needs and preference.

Printing PostScript Files on Non-PostScript Printers

If you have a non-PostScript printer, your problem is just the opposite of the one just described. You need to let plain text pass through to the printer, but you need to convert PostScript data to a format that your printer can understand.

If you never plan to print more than plain text, you do not need to worry about this. However, PostScript is the common denominator in Unix and FreeBSD when it comes to printing anything other than plain text. Virtually all word processing, graphing, drawing, and graphics programs can write a PostScript file (or send it directly to the printer). Although some applications (such as StarOffice) may have drivers for your particular printer, most Unix applications will not. Instead, they will simply output PostScript. Because of this, your printing capabilities will be severely limited if you cannot handle PostScript.

Fortunately, a company called Aladdin makes a freely available program called GhostScript that can simulate a PostScript printer. It takes PostScript input and converts it to a form that your printer can understand.

15

NOTE

GhostScript supports a wide variety of printers. A list (which may not be all-inclusive) can be obtained at `http://www.cs.wisc.edu/~ghost/doc/printer.htm`.

GhostScript is available in the FreeBSD ports collection under the "print" category. Refer to Chapter 14 for information on installing ports.

For this to work, we will need a script similar to the one in the previous section. However, the operations will be reversed. In this case, if the script detects that the data being sent is not PostScript data, that data will be passed straight through. If the data is PostScript, it will be sent through the GhostScript program to convert it to something the non-PostScript printer can understand. The script shown in Listing 15.2, taken from the *FreeBSD Handbook*, will provide PostScript functionality on an HP DeskJet 500 (a non-PostScript printer).

LISTING 15.2   A Sample GhostScript Filter for an HP DeskJet 500

```
#!/bin/sh
  #
  #  ifhp - Print Ghostscript-simulated PostScript on a DeskJet 500
  #  Installed in /usr/local/libexec/hpif

  #
  #  Treat LF as CR+LF:
  #
  printf "\033&k2G" || exit 2

  #
  #  Read first two characters of the file
  #
  read first_line
  first_two_chars=`expr "$first_line" : '\(..\)'`

  if [ "$first_two_chars" = "%!" ]; then
      #
      #  It is PostScript; use Ghostscript to scan-convert and print it.
      #
      #  Note that PostScript files are actually interpreted programs,
      #  and those programs are allowed to write to stdout, which will
      #  mess up the printed output.  So, we redirect stdout to stderr
      #  and then make descriptor 3 go to stdout, and have Ghostscript
      #  write its output there.  Exercise for the clever reader:
      #  capture the stderr output from Ghostscript and mail it back to
      #  the user originating the print job.
```

LISTING 15.2   Continued

```
     #
     exec 3>&1 1>&2
     /usr/local/bin/gs -dSAFER -dNOPAUSE -q -sDEVICE=djet500 \
          -sOutputFile=/dev/fd/3 - && exit 0

     #
     /usr/local/bin/gs -dSAFER -dNOPAUSE -q -sDEVICE=djet500 -sOutputFile=- - \
          && exit 0
else
     #
     # Plain text or HP/PCL, so just print it directly; print a form
     # at the end to eject the last page.
     #
     echo $first_line && cat && printf "\033&l0H" &&
exit 0
fi

     exit 2
```

This script looks complicated at first, but it isn't really that bad. Basically, the script reads the first line of the input, extracts the first two characters, and checks to see whether they are %!. If they are, the input is PostScript, and the then statements are executed, which send the output through GhostScript. If they are not, the file is treated as plain text and is passed straight through.

> **NOTE**
>
> GhostScript is a very powerful program that has far more options than can be covered here. For more information on GhostScript, see the documentation at http://www.cs.wisc.edu/~ghost/index.html.

> **NOTE**
>
> FreeBSD also comes with a program called lpf that can act as a print filter. It has many capabilities, including accounting (the capability to track how many pages are printed, by what users, and so on). See the man page for pac for more details on what this program can do.

Conversion Filters

As mentioned earlier, conversion filters are similar to text filters, except they are designed to convert file formats into a format the printer can understand. Conversion filters allow you to print various types of files directly from the command line with lpr and avoid having to load them into a program or convert them by hand before you print them. You specify which filter to use on the command line with an option to lpr. (lpr is the command used to print files from the command line. We will cover it in detail later in the chapter.) Table 15.2 lists the conversion options that lpr understands.

TABLE 15.2   Conversion Options to lpr

Option	Description
-d	The file is in DVI format (produced by the TeX typesetting system).
-f	Intended as a filter for printing FORTRAN source files. This is basically obsolete unless you are still writing a lot of FORTRAN code.
-c	The file contains plotting data produced by cifplot. This program is not included with FreeBSD.
-g	The file contains plotting data produced by the Unix plot routines. These routines are included with FreeBSD.
-n	The file contains data from device-independent troff (ditroff). This is not supported by any software included with FreeBSD.
-t	The file contains C/A/T phototypesetter commands for ancient versions of troff. This is probably obsolete for most people.
-v	The file contains a raster image for various image-printing devices. Most people will not use this.

By default, none of these filters is installed. Also, the option letter and the filter it calls are not hard-coded into the system. Because of this, if you have no use for a cifplot filter, for example, it is easy to have the -c option call some other filter that you might have use for.

Like text filters, these filters can be shell scripts that call standard Unix programs or stand-alone executable programs that may be provided by manufacturers of third-party software.

The following is an example of a very simple conversion filter that converts data in the GNU groff typesetting system (which cannot be understood by the printer) into PostScript (which can be understood by the printer, either directly or by sending the data through GhostScript):

```
#!/bin/sh
exec grops
```

If you read the man page for grops, you will see that it is a program that converts groff to PostScript. In this case, the file will simply be sent through grops before being sent to the printer for printing.

The filter should be saved in the directory /usr/local/libexec. (You might decide to call this filter g2ps or something similar because it converts groff to PostScript.)

If we assign the lpr option -t to this, we can now print a groff source file directly from the command line and have it come out looking correct on the printer. This would be done as follows:

```
lpe -t myfile
```

Here, *myfile* is, of course, the name of the groff source file we want to print.

You learn how to configure the print system to actually use this filter in the following section of this chapter, where we look at setting up the /etc/printcap file (the file that controls how the print system behaves).

Configuring /etc/printcap to Control Print System Functions

The /etc/printcap file is the glue that holds all of what we have covered so far together. It defines the name and aliases of a printer, what filter it uses, the conversion filters it can use, what option should be used to access the filter, where the printer spools to, and more.

An /etc/printcap file already exists on your system, but all the options are commented out. Therefore, you will need to uncomment and change options and/or add options.

The format of /etc/printcap is fairly simple. Here is a sample entry:

```
simba|lp|local line printer:\
#       :sh:\
        :lp=/dev/lpt0:sd=/var/spool/lpd/simba:lf=/var/log/lpd-errs:
    :if=/usr/libexec/if-ps:
```

The first line in this entry gives the printer name, followed by any aliases we want to define. In this case, the name of the printer is simba. It also has an alias of lp, which means it will be the default printer. Finally, the last alias is a long description of this printer.

The second line is commented out. If it is uncommented, header pages (cover pages) will be printed that give the name of the user, the name of the file, and so on. This is a good idea if you have a lot of users printing to the same printer—they can easily find which printouts are theirs when they go to pick them up.

The third line gives the information on where the printer is located. Here, :lp stands for *local printer* (as opposed to a remote printer). The printer is located on the first parallel port (/dev/lpt0, which is LPT1 in DOS). Also, :sd is the spool directory this printer uses, which is /var/spool/lpd/simba (see the section in this chapter on creating and configuring the spool directory), and :lf, which stands for *log file*, is where this printer will log any errors it encounters.

15

The fourth line specifies the input filter, or text filter, that should be used with this printer. In this case, we are using the if-ps filter (which is the text-to-PostScript filter we created earlier).

Installing Conversion Filters

If you want to install any conversion filters, /etc/printcap is also where those are handled. Install them simply by adding the appropriate option (listed in Table 15.3), followed by the name of the filter. The format is the same as the :if line for the input filter.

TABLE 15.3   Filter Options for /etc/printcap

Filter	Option
DVI	:df
FORTRAN	:rf
cifplot	:cf
plot	:gf
dittroff	:nf
troff	:rf
raster	:if

Remember that these filters are not hard-coded. Therefore, if you have no use for a FORTRAN filter, for example, you can replace it with some other filter.

Here is the line you would add under the :if line to install the groff-to-PostScript filter we created earlier:

:rf=/usr/local/libexec/g2ps:

Note that when you add this line, you will have to make a slight change to the :if line before it and add a backslash at the end. This is because lpd expects the entire line of information to be on one line. The backslash escapes the new line so that multiple lines are treated as a single line when read by the system.

Enabling lpd for Command-Line Printing

After you have configured the /etc/printcap file, you can start lpd. As root, you can simply type **lpd** from the command line to start it. If you want to have lpd start up automatically each time the system boots, add the following line to /etc/rc.conf:

lpd_enable="YES"

You should now be able to print from the command line by following the instructions in the next section. If printing doesn't work correctly, see the troubleshooting section at the end of the chapter.

Basic Command-Line Printing

The `lpr` command is used to send a file to the print spooler. At its simplest, `lpr` takes the form

`lpr filename`

where *filename* is, of course, the name of the file that should be printed. You can specify multiple filenames on the command line to cause multiple files to be printed.

You have the option of specifying a printer to which you want the data to be sent; to do so, use the `-P` option. If you omit the `-P` option, `lpr` assumes that the default printer should be used. The default printer is determined by checking these conditions in the following order listed; the first condition that is found to be true will be used as the default printer:

- If the `PRINTER` environment variable is set, `lpr` will use the name listed here as the default printer.

- If the `LPDEST` environment variable is set, `lpr` will use the name listed here as the default printer.

- The printer name `lp` is used, which should be an alias to one of the printers in the `/etc/printcap` file.

- If neither the `PRINTER` environment variable nor the `LPDEST` environment variable is set, and no printer has an `lp` alias in `/etc/printcap`, the print request will fail.

The `lpr` command also has several other options. Table 15.4 contains a list of some of the options you are likely to find the most useful.

TABLE 15.4   Options to the `lpr` Command

Option	Description
`-l`	Uses a filter that will print control codes and suppress page breaks.
`-p`	Output is formatted with `pr`, which formats pages into 66 lines per page with a header at the top containing the date and time the file was created, along with the page number and five blank lines at the bottom.
`-P`	Sends the job to a printer other than the default one.
`-h`	Suppresses the printing of the "burst" page, also known as the *banner* or *header page*. This has no effect if header pages are turned off by default.
`-m`	Sends e-mail to you, notifying you when the print job has completed printing.
`-r`	Removes the file upon completion of spooling. This option should probably not be used because it will remove the file before it has successfully printed. If it is used with the `-s` option (described next), it won't remove the file until after it has completed printing.

15

TABLE 15.4   Continued

Option	Description
-s	Uses symbolic links. Rather than copying the file to the spool directory, this option will simply create a symbolic link to the spool directory from the existing file. This allows files too large to fit in the spool area to be printed. If you use this option, be careful that you do not modify or delete the file before it has finished printing.
-#n	Here, n is the number of copies of each file that should be printed. (This feature can be disabled.)
-J job	Here, job is the name of the job that should be printed on the banner page. By default, it will be the name of the first file that is specified.
-T	Specifies the title name that pr should use on the header at the top of the page. By default, this will be the filename. This option only applies if the -p option has also been used.
-i n	Here, n represents the number of columns that the printed output will be indented by.
-w n	Here, n represents the page width in columns. This only applies if the -p option has also been used.

Printing from X-Windows

Different X-Windows applications will have different means of printing, but here is an example from Netscape if you want to print a Web page, for instance.

To print a file from Netscape, select File and then choose Print from the menu. The Print dialog box is shown in Figure 15.1.

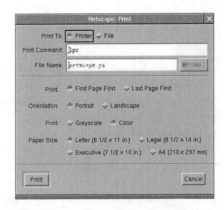

FIGURE 15.1   The Print dialog box in Netscape. Notice that if you click the File button at the top, the filename will be netscape.ps. Netscape outputs PostScript data when it prints.

In the "Print To:" section at the top, you can select whether you want to send the output to a printer or to a file. If you select Printer, the Print Command box becomes active and you can type in your command. Notice that it defaults to lpr, which is the same program you used to print from the command line. If you want, you can supply additional options to lpr here, such as having it e-mail you when it is done or print more than one copy. (See the section on lpr earlier in this chapter for details.)

Most X-Windows programs can also output to a file. When they do, they will usually create a PostScript file that can then be sent to a PostScript printer directly or run through GhostScript and sent to a non-PostScript printer.

Like many other Unix programs, Netscape has no printer drivers. It simply outputs in PostScript. This demonstrates the need for GhostScript if you are not running a printer that understands PostScript.

Printing in StarOffice

If you have StarOffice installed, you can configure its printer by double-clicking the Printer Setup icon on the desktop. You will get a dialog box like that shown in Figure 15.2.

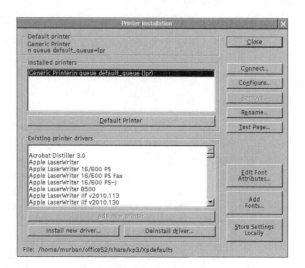

FIGURE 15.2   The Printer Configuration dialog box in StarOffice. Notice that StarOffice has printer drivers included (bottom box) for many different printer models.

Because StarOffice comes with a large selection of drivers for various printers, it eliminates the need for using GhostScript to translate PostScript. You can simply select your printer model from the list and click Add New Printer, and it will be installed as the default printer. You can then use the Configuration button and such to configure the printer.

If you do not install a printer, StarOffice uses the default "Generic Printerin queue," which sends PostScript output to lpr.

TIP

Even if you do have GhostScript installed, you will probably want to use one of the native drivers in StarOffice because it may have better support for the various features of your printer that can be accessed directly from StarOffice, without you having to modify GhostScript filter options.

Using the lpq Command to Check the Status of Print Jobs

The lpq command can be used to check the status of jobs that are waiting in the print queue. If it is called without any arguments, lpq will report the status of all jobs currently in the queue for the default printer. The default printer is checked in the following order: If the PRINTER environment variable is set, that printer is considered to be the default printer. If the PRINTER environment variable is not set, the printer that is aliased to lp in /etc/printcap will be used as the default.

lpq can also be called with a job number to show only the status of a particular job or with a username to show only the status of jobs owned by a particular user. The output of lpq will look something like this:

```
bash$ lpq -P simba
simba is ready and printing
Rank      Owner    Job    Files                      Total Size
active    mike     5      /home/murban/sample.txt    2000 bytes
2nd       mike     6      /home/murban/sample1.txt   2500 bytes
3rd       jack     7      /home/jack/myfile.txt      3200 bytes
4th       jack     8      ...                        5500 bytes
```

The -P option tells lpq to report on a printer other than the default—in this case, the printer named simba. All of the options to lpq will be explained later.

The information given by lpq is pretty self-explanatory.

The first line tells what the printer is currently doing. In this case, the printer is ready and printing. If the printer is stalled, out of paper, jammed, and so on, you may see other things listed here instead.

The example here shows four jobs in the queue; one is active, and the others are ranked as to when they will be printed. A few other things are worth pointing out. The third column, labeled Job, shows the job ID number assigned to a particular job. If you need to cancel a print job (explained later), you will need this job ID number. Also, the fourth column lists the file or files that are being printed. Notice that the fourth job in this example is listed as just three dots. This means that the pathname of the file is too long to fit in the list, so lpq simply didn't list it.

The lpq command has a few other options, as shown in Table 15.5.

TABLE 15.5   Options to lpq

Option	Description
-P *name*	Here, *name* is the name of a printer. This will cause lpq to show information on a printer other than the default one.
-1	This option will cause information about each one of the files in the queue to be displayed, even if the information causes the display to break across a line. (In the previous example, this command would cause the filename to show; it currently shows up as three dots because it is too long to fit.)
-a	Causes lpq to display the status of all local queues for all printers.

Removing Jobs from the Queue with the `lprm` Command

The lprm command can be used to remove print jobs that are currently in the queue and sometimes to remove print jobs that are currently printing. If lprm is run without any command-line arguments, it will remove whatever job is currently printing on the default printer if that job belongs to the user running lprm. If the currently running job does not belong to the user running lprm, the command will have no effect. If the root user runs lprm with no options, the command will remove the currently printing job from the default printer, no matter who the job belongs to.

Running lprm with a job number as an argument will remove the job with that ID number from the queue of the default printer, assuming that you own the job and that you are not the root user. Normal users can only remove jobs that belong to them. The root user can remove any job. Here is an example:

```
bash$ lprm 5
dfA001simba.samplenet.org dequeued
cfA001simba.samplenet.org dequeued
bash $
```

The first file that is dequeued in this example is the data file for the job. This is basically a copy of the file in the printer's spool directory. The second file that is dequeued is a control file.

Note that the system may take some time to respond when you run lprm (up to several seconds). It may seem that lprm has hung. Don't worry; it hasn't. Wait a few seconds, and you should get your prompt back.

If you try to delete a job that does not belong to you, and you are not the root user, lprm will respond with the message Permission denied.

15

The `lprm` command has a few options to modify the default behavior. These are listed in Table 15.6.

TABLE 15.6   Options to `lprm`

Option	Description
`-P` *name*	Here, *name* is the name of the printer that `lprm` should remove the job from. If the printer name is not specified, the default printer specified in the PRINTER environment variable is used. If the PRINTER environment variable is not set, the default printer aliased to `lp` is used.
.	A dash by itself will cause all jobs belonging to you to be removed from the queue. If you are the root user, all jobs in the queue will be removed.
user	Here, *user* is the username of someone on the system. This option will remove all jobs belonging to that user. This works only for the root user because normal users can only remove jobs belonging to themselves.

CAUTION

Removing a job that is currently printing will not cause the printer to stop immediately. Depending on the amount of RAM installed in your printer, there could be up to several pages of data already in the printer's buffer. This means that some of the document could be printed anyway (or if the document is small enough, almost the entire document could be printed), even if it has been removed from the queue.

NOTE

Print jobs can be removed only from the system they were sent from, even if the printer is available to more than one computer on the network.

Controlling Printers

Printers and their associated queues are controlled with the `lpc` command. This command is used by the system administrator for printer administration. Some limited functionality is available to normal users, such as displaying the status of queues and restarting the printer daemon if it has died. Among other things, `lpc` can be used to enable and disable printers, enable and disable printer queues, change the order of jobs in the queue so that files at the bottom of the queue can be printed first, and check the status of queues.

If no command-line arguments are given to `lpc`, it will start in interactive mode with a prompt. You can also supply command-line arguments when starting `lpc`. If you do this, `lpc` will start, run the arguments specified on the command line, and then exit. We will start by looking at the interactive mode of `lpc`.

Using `lpc` in Interactive Mode

If `lpc` is started with no arguments, it will run in interactive mode. The interactive mode simply gives a prompt like this:

```
lpc>
```

You can type **?** or **help** and press Enter to get a list of the available commands. Typing **help** followed by the name of one of the commands will give you a short, one-line description of what the command does.

When you type commands, they can be abbreviated to the shortest form that is not ambiguous. For example, the `status` command can be abbreviated as `stat`. However, it could not be abbreviated as `sta` because there is also a `start` command, and `lpc` would not know which one you wanted.

If you do not provide enough of the command for `lpc` to know which one you mean, it will respond with `?Ambiguous command`. If the command you specify does not exist, it will respond with `?Invalid command`.

Checking Queue Status

To check the status of a queue, use the `status` command (which, as mentioned previously, can be abbreviated `stat`). You also need to specify an argument to the `status` command. The argument can be either `all` to display the status of all daemons and queues or the name of a printer to show the status for only that printer. Here's an example:

```
lpc> status lp
lp:
        queuing is enabled
        printing is enabled
        2 entries in spool area
        waiting for lp to become ready (offline?)
lpc>
```

This gives you the status for the system default line printer. In this case, the queue is enabled, printing is enabled, and two entries are sitting in the queue waiting to be printed. However, nothing is printing because the printer is unavailable, and `lpc` suggests that it may be offline.

The `status` command can be run by both normal users and system administrators.

Disabling Printing and Stopping the Daemon

The `abort` and `stop` commands can be used by the system administrator to disable printing and also terminate the daemon that handles spooling for the printer. Both commands require an option—either `all`, which will disable printing on all the queues and terminate the daemons, or the name of a printer, which will cause the command to affect only the named printer.

The abort command terminates printing immediately and stops the daemon that handles spooling for that printer. Here's an example:

```
lpc> abort lp
lp:
        printing disabled
        daemon (pid 597) killed
lpc>
```

And here is the output of the status command after the preceding command:

```
lpc> status all
lp:
        queuing is enabled
        printing is disabled
        2 entries in spool area
        printer idle
lpc>
```

There are two important points to note about this output:

- Two entries are still listed in the spool area. The abort command simply kills the daemon and disables the printer. It does not remove any jobs from the spool area. When the daemon is restarted and the printer is enabled again, the jobs that are in the spool area will print.

- Queuing is enabled. This means you (and others) can still send jobs to the printer. They will be placed in the queue to wait until the daemon is restarted and the printer is enabled. At that point, any jobs submitted while the printer was disabled will be printed, along with any jobs that were already in the queue.

The stop command works similarly to the abort command, except it will wait until the current job has finished printing before it disables the printer and stops the spool daemon. Like abort, stop does not bring down the queue. The queue will still accept jobs that users submit and hold them for printing whenever the printer becomes available.

> **TIP**
>
> If you will be taking a printer down for an extended period of time (for maintenance, for example), consider aliasing that printer's name and its aliases to another printer in /etc/ printcap. If this is the system default printer, make sure you also alias lp to a different printer. This will redirect any print jobs sent to that printer to a different printer without requiring users to make any changes to their configuration. Preferably, of course, you will want to alias the down printer to a printer that is a similar type and is located in the building fairly close to where the down printer is located. In addition, you will probably want to send a systemwide e-mail to the affected users, letting them know where they can pick up their print jobs for the time being until the printer they normally use is available again.

The `stop` command has a similar effect. It will disable the printer and terminate the spooling daemon after the current job has finished.

Disabling Print Queuing

Neither `abort` nor `stop` disables the queue. If you are taking a printer down for maintenance, for example, and you simply issue an `abort` command to kill the daemon and disable the printer, the queue will still be available. Users will be able to continue to send jobs to this printer as if nothing is wrong, and the queue will happily accept the jobs and store them to print whenever the printer becomes available. Because of this, you will probably want to disable the queue if the printer will be down for an extended period of time. There are two ways that this can be done.

The first is with the `disable` command. It requires an argument that can either be `all` to disable all queues on the system or the name of a particular printer to disable the queue for only that printer. Here's an example:

```
lpc> disable lp
lp:
        queuing disabled
lpc> status all
lp:
        queuing is disabled
        printing is enabled
        3 entries in spool area
        waiting for lp to become ready (offline?)
lpc>
```

In this case, the queue is disabled, but printing is still enabled. This means that the printer will continue to print all jobs currently in the queue (if it can), but the queue will not accept any new jobs.

If you try to send a job to a printer with a down queue that is not accepting jobs, you will get an error similar to the following:

```
bash$ lpr myfile.txt
lpr: Printer queue is disabled
bash$
```

The other way that a queue can be disabled is by using the `down` command. Like the `disable` command, it requires at least one argument, which can either be `all` to affect all queues on the system or the name of a printer to affect only one printer.

The `down` command actually sends a `stop` command, which disables the printer and the spool daemon after the current job has finished printing, and then sends a `disable` command to bring down the queue. The `down` command can also take an optional message as an argument. The message will be written to the status file in the printer's spool directory. This will then be displayed in the output of lpq to let users know why the queue is not accepting their requests. Here's an example:

```
lpc> down lp Printer is down for maintenance.
lp:
        printer and queuing disabled
lpc>
```

If lpq is then run, it will respond with the following:

```
bash$ lpq
Warning: lp is down: Printer is down for maintenance.
Warning: lp queue is turned off
Printer is down for maintenance.
Rank   Owner     Job  Files                               Total Size
bash$
```

To enable a queue that has been disabled, simply type **enable** followed by **all** to enable all queues. Alternatively, you can type the name of a printer to enable only the queue on that printer. Here's an example:

```
lpc> enable lp
lp:
        queuing enabled
lpc> status lp
lp:
        queuing is enabled
        printing is disabled
        3 entries in spool area
        Printer is down for maintenance.
lpc>
```

Notice that although this brought the queue back up, it did not re-enable the printer. Currently, the queue will accept jobs, but they will not be printed. If you used the down command to bring down the queue, use the up command to bring it back up. This will re-enable the queue, restart the spooling daemon, and enable the printer. It will not, however, clear the status message. To clear the status message, you will need to run the restart command, as discussed in the next section.

Restarting a Spooling Daemon

If you need to restart a spooling daemon, you can use the restart command. If there is no daemon currently running, this command will start one. If there is currently a daemon running, this command will kill it and restart it (see the following caution, however). This can be used to reset a daemon that seems to have hung, for example.

The `restart` command requires an argument that can be either `all` to restart all print daemons on the system or the name of a printer to restart only the daemon for that printer. Here's an example:

```
lpc> restart lp
lp:
        daemon (pid 2102) killed
lp:
        daemon started
lpc>
```

CAUTION

Occasionally, the `restart` command kills a running daemon but doesn't restart it again, even though it claims it did. Because of this, it is a good idea to check the output of `lpq` for the printer in question. If `lpq` says in the status line `Warning: no daemon present`, it means that `lpc` stopped the daemon when the `restart` command was issued but then failed to restart it again. If this is the case, simply run the `restart` command again from `lpc`, and this will take care of the problem.

15

Cleaning the Queue Directory

The `clean` command in `lpc` causes it to clean out the queue directory. Basically, it will remove any control files and so on that cannot be printed because they are not complete print jobs. Like most commands in `lpc`, the `clean` command requires an argument of either `all` or the name of the printer spool directory that you want to clean.

Changing the Priority of Print Jobs

You can use the `topq` command to change the order of print jobs in the queue (that is, to move jobs at the bottom or middle of the queue up to the top so they print faster).

Only a system administrator can change the order of the print jobs. The basic syntax of `topq` is

```
topq printername jobnum(s), )
```

where *printername* is, of course, the name of the printer, and *jobnum(s)* is a list of job numbers you want to move to the top of the queue. You can specify multiple numbers with the command, and it will print them in the order listed. The first job listed will be moved to the top of the queue, the second will be second in the queue, and so on. For example, suppose the queue currently looks like this:

```
Rank    Owner     Job   Files                        Total Size
1st     murban    8     myfile.txt                   151625 bytes
2nd     murban    9     cardlist.txt                 38311 bytes
3rd     murban    10    lions.txt                    1113 bytes
4th     murban    12    schedule.txt                 6599 bytes
```

To reverse the order of these jobs in `lpc`, type **topq lp 12 10 9 8**. The results are shown here:

```
lpc> topq lp 12 10 9 8
lp:
        moved cfA008simba.samplenet.org
        moved cfA009simba.samplenet.org
        moved cfA010simba.samplenet.org
        moved cfA012simba.samplenet.org
lpc>
```

If we look at the queue again, here's what we see:

```
Rank    Owner       Job  Files                          Total Size
1st     murban      12   schedule.txt                   6599 bytes
2nd     murban      10   lions.txt                      1113 bytes
3rd     murban      9    cardlist.txt                   38311 bytes
4th     murban      8    myfile.txt                     151625 bytes
```

The `topq` command can also take a username instead of a list of jobs. When `topq` is used this way, it will move all the jobs from the named user to the top of the queue.

Note that `topq` does not preempt a job that is currently running. It moves the jobs listed to the top of the queue so that they are next in line, but whatever job was printing before `topq` was used will finish printing before the job moved to the top of the queue starts. If you want a particular job to print right away, you will first have to use `lprm` to remove the job that is currently printing.

Quitting `lpc`

To quit the `lpc` program, simply type either **quit** or **exit** at the `lpc>` prompt. This will put you back at the command line.

Using `lpc` in Noninteractive Mode

`lpc` can also be run in noninteractive mode. In this case, simply supply the command you want to perform, along with any parameters on the command line.

When `lpc` is run in noninteractive mode, it expects the first argument to be the command and anything that follows to be arguments to the command. Here's an example:

```
# lpc restart lp
lp:
        daemon (pid 2280) killed
lp:
        daemon started
#
```

All the same commands available in interactive mode are also available in noninteractive mode.

Controlling Who Can Use `lpc`

Sometimes you might want to give other people the ability to control printers with `lpc` but not give them full root privileges on the system. The operator group allows you to do this.

Basically, any user who is a member of the group "operator" can make full use of `lpc` without having full root access to the system. This will allow that user to change the priority of print jobs, start and stop print daemons, and bring queues up and down.

Refer to Chapter 9, "Users, Groups, and Permissions," for more information on groups and how to add users to a group.

Basic Network Printing

Basic network printing is similar to local printing. To set up a network printer in `/etc/printcap`, use a line like the following:

```
simba|lp|local line printer:\
        :lp=::rm=nova:rp=simba:sd=/var/spool/lpd/simba:lf=/var/log/lpd-errs:
```

This entry will connect to a remote printer named `simba` on the host named `nova`. Note that the local name (on line 1) does not have to be the same as the remote name of the printer. You can call the local name whatever you want. What printer the job is actually sent to is controlled by the `rp` entry in line 2. The local spool directory will hold the file only until the remote spool directory has room. Then, the file will be moved into the remote host's spool directory.

Notice that we did not have to specify an input filter here. That is because all the filtering will be handled by the remote host.

The printer on the remote host should be configured using the instructions provided earlier in the chapter for configuring a printer.

> **NOTE**
>
> CUPS (Common Unix Printing System) is an alternative to the `lpr` system presented in this chapter. CUPS is intended to be a cross-platform printing solution for all Unix environments. CUPS is not a standard part of FreeBSD, nor is it included in a standard FreeBSD installation. It is, however, available in the FreeBSD ports collection under the `print` directory. For more information on CUPS, including documentation, visit the CUPS Web site at `www.cups.org`.

15

Troubleshooting

Several things can go wrong when you use printers. This section discusses some of the most common problems and their solutions.

Printer Does Not Receive Data; Jobs Are Sitting in Queue

Check `lpq` and make sure that the spooling daemon is running. If it says `Warning: no daemon present`, you will need to use `lpc` to restart the spooling daemon. Also check `lpc` and make sure that the printer is not disabled.

Data Light on Printer Flashes, but Printer Will Not Print

This is often a symptom of sending non-PostScript data to a PostScript printer. Check your filter and make sure it is filtering text correctly and converting that text to PostScript.

Printing an Image File in GIMP or a Web Page Results in Hundreds of Pages of Garbage Being Printed

This can often be a symptom of feeding PostScript data to a printer that doesn't understand PostScript. The non-PostScript printer will try to print this file as plain text. Check out the GhostScript program and also see the section earlier in this chapter titled "Printing PostScript Files on Non-PostScript Printers."

The Printer Is Slow

Try setting the printer to polled mode (assuming this printer is on the parallel port). Use the following command:

```
lptcontrol -p
```

Remember that you will need to add this to a startup file if you want it to take effect at each system boot. See the section at the beginning of the chapter on `lptcontrol`.

Printed Output "Stair Steps"

The symptoms of the stair-step problem look something like this:

```
Line one of the file.
        Line two of the file.
                Line three of the file.
                        Line four of the file.
```

This pattern will continue until the text runs off the end of the page. This is a fairly common problem caused by differences in the way Unix and DOS/Windows interpret the linefeed (LF) character. When DOS/Windows advances to a new line, it sends both a carriage return and a linefeed. Unix, on the other hand, sends only a linefeed character and expects a carriage return to be implied. If your printer is expecting DOS-style carriage return and linefeed combinations but is only receiving a linefeed, it will advance the paper but never return the print head to the beginning of the line. There are a few ways you might be able to solve this problem.

The first is to look for an option in your printer's configuration that changes the way it interprets a linefeed character. See your printer documentation to see whether there is a way you can do this.

The second way is to create a filter that converts the LF to a combination of CR and LF.

If your printer understands HP-PCL language, the following filter is recommended by the *FreeBSD Handbook* for performing this task:

```
#!/bin/sh
#
# hpif - Simple text input filter for lpd for HP-PCL based printers
# Installed in /usr/local/libexec/hpif
#
# Simply copies stdin to stdout.  Ignores all filter arguments.
# Tells printer to treat LF as CR+LF.  Ejects the page when done.

printf "\033&k2G" && cat && printf "\033&l0H" && exit 0
exit 2
```

See the section on text filters earlier in this chapter for more information on how to install a text filter.

If your printer does not understand HP-PCL, you might be able to use the `tr` command to convert the LF into a CR/LF. A filter such as the following may do the trick:

```
#!/bin/sh
# Filter that fixes the stair stepping effect on non PCL printers.
/bin/cat | tr '\13' '\13\10' && exit 0
exit 2
```

Once again, see the section on text filters earlier in this chapter for more information on how to install a text filter.

All the Text Prints on One Line, Creating a Mess and Writing Over the Top of Existing Text

This is basically the opposite of the stair-stepping problem. This problem is rare, but it does happen occasionally. Basically, the LF is being interpreted as a CR by the printer. The print head is getting returned to the beginning of the line, but the paper is not being advanced.

To fix this problem, you will need to make changes to your printer's configuration settings so that it interprets CR and LF properly. See your printer's documentation for details on how to do this.

If you find that you cannot change the hardware settings of your printer to fix this problem, the same filter used earlier to fix the stair-stepping problem might fix this problem as well.

Kernel Configuration

This chapter covers a topic that's likely to be one of the most intimidating to a newcomer to Unix: how to configure and rebuild your kernel. This is a task that simply does not happen in the desktop PC world. However, it's a necessary part of life when dealing with an open-source system under constant development, in a world in which new devices constantly demand more functionality from a kernel. Unfortunately, kernel configuration isn't easy to do.

Configuring the kernel is at the heart of customizing FreeBSD and other operating systems like it. A well-tuned kernel will serve 100 percent of the demands that a system and its users place on it, while eliminating all the unnecessary baggage that an unoptimized kernel might have, thus making the system operate significantly faster. This chapter provides enough insight into the kernel-configuration process to eliminate the mystery and enable this kind of customizability.

The Role of the Kernel

The kernel is the master executable of the system. It's the first thing that is executed from the boot blocks when you power on the system, and it constantly runs throughout the machine's uptime. Its job is to oversee all the processes running on the system, handle TCP/IP and other networking duties, manage access to all the devices on the system, and control memory usage—to name just a few of its tasks.

Every operating system has a kernel—from MS-DOS, to Windows, to the highest-end mainframe. Some systems take greater pains to hide the kernel from the user than others do. In Windows, it's an executable in `C:\WINDOWS\SYSTEM`; in classic Mac OS, it's hidden from the filesystem entirely. In many Unix systems, the kernel's traditional place is in the root directory at the top of the filesystem. In FreeBSD, the kernel is placed in / prior to FreeBSD 5.0 and in /boot afterward. With each of these operating systems, a default (or "generic") kernel is part of every released version of the system; when a new version comes out, its changes are mostly additions to accommodate drivers for new devices that the system supports. The kernel is responsible for knowing about every kind of device that can be connected to the system. When you install drivers for a new and previously unsupported device in Windows, you generally have to reboot. That's because the drivers, libraries, and other items used by your kernel have been modified and cannot be incorporated into the system's operation "on the fly." In most cases, the system has to be restarted in order for the new resources to be used.

FreeBSD uses a *microkernel* architecture, which means that the kernel is fairly small and modular. Windows NT and Mach (the kernel upon which Mac OS X is built) are other examples of microkernels in which new devices are more frequently added through kernel modules (which can be loaded and unloaded during runtime) than by recompiling the kernel. Linux and Windows 95/98/Me are instead *monolithic* kernels, in which the kernel's code is more optimized for performance and to minimize context switching. The monolithic kernel architecture makes for kernel code that's cleaner and easier for developers to maintain, but the administrator is required to recompile the kernel every time support for a new device is added.

This isn't a terribly clear delineation—Linux operates fairly heavily on kernel modules today, and FreeBSD's kernel does have to be recompiled for a number of different reasons. The difference between a microkernel and monolithic kernel architecture is largely a philosophical one and has to do with a good deal more than simply device support. The biggest and most fundamental difference is that a microkernel has a mechanism for passing certain non-core system calls to a user-level processing level, or *ring*, instead of handling them all internally and stripping down the core of the kernel to only those functions that require the highest level of supervisor-mode execution status. Keeping only essential functions in the kernel increases runtime robustness and makes the kernel processes more understandable and manageable. This arrangement also provides a measure of inherent security in the form of reduced complexity as well as easier support for modularity when it comes to devices.

Although the ideal of total modularity is all well and good, a kernel in which every possible kind of device and option is modular and loadable during runtime is as theoretical as perpetual motion. Chances are that as you gain experience with FreeBSD, you will come to a point where you can't avoid recompiling your kernel; it's at that time that you'll undergo the rite of passage that initiates you into the circle of kernel hackers.

Why Configure a Custom Kernel?

FreeBSD comes with the GENERIC kernel installed by default. This kernel is tuned to support as wide a user base as possible so that FreeBSD will work "out of the box" on as many different machines as there are users in the world. Given the nature of *x*86-based hardware, this means that the FreeBSD kernel must hold a truly astounding number of built-in drivers. An operating system built for a tightly controlled set of hardware (such as SGI's IRIX or Apple's Mac OS X) can afford to get away with much less of this generic support, but FreeBSD is stuck with it. The GENERIC kernel also has various options for memory allocation and optimization set to lowest-common-denominator levels, and other optional elements are left out in order to keep the kernel as streamlined as possible under the circumstances. These are all aspects of the kernel that can almost certainly be configured more efficiently for your particular system.

Streamlining the Kernel

The kernel probes at boot time for every single kind of device it knows about. This is where you see that scrolling screen full of white text while the system is coming up; the kernel is looking for dozens of different kinds of devices that are enabled in the GENERIC kernel. Although it doesn't hurt anything for the kernel not to find most of them, it does take time to perform each probe. You can speed up boot time significantly by removing the unnecessary devices from the kernel. This also helps reduce the size of the kernel. Modern systems with hundreds of megabytes of RAM don't need to worry about this streamlining, but it's a worthy consideration on a machine that barely meets FreeBSD's minimum requirements.

> **NOTE**
>
> Even with the GENERIC kernel, it's possible to suppress probing for every device under the sun. That's what the boot configurator (covered in Appendix C, "Troubleshooting Installation and Boot Problems") does: It allows you to explicitly remove support for various devices that it can tell will cause IRQ or memory address conflicts (or that you know you don't have). This process does not actually change the kernel or its compiled-in elements at all, but it does prevent the kernel from wasting time looking for nonexistent devices when it's booting.

As you add devices such as USB peripherals, sound cards, SCSI controllers, and others to your system, you won't be able to use many of them unless you add support for them in the kernel. The same is true of new filesystem types (such as EXT2FS, as you saw in Chapter 8, "The FreeBSD Filesystem"). Many devices and filesystems are available today as kernel modules, but the majority still have to be compiled into the kernel, so you have little choice but to rebuild it. However, rebuilding gives you the chance to tweak other things in the system (such as the number of memory buffers, custom memory management features, and the kernel's name), so you can probably enhance your system's performance fairly significantly with one rebuild.

Symmetric Multi-Processing (SMP) support is not present in the GENERIC kernel either, by the way. If you have a system with more than one CPU, you'll need to build a custom kernel in order to take advantage of all of them.

16

Using dmesg to Get Information About the Kernel Startup

If you will be stripping unnecessary devices out of your kernel, it is imperative that you find out what devices you do have so that you don't end up accidentally removing support for your existing hardware. As mentioned earlier, the kernel probes for all its known devices at boot time, and it prints out the status of each probe, telling you which devices you must keep in the new kernel. This information isn't just printed out to the screen at boot time; it's also echoed into an internal runtime message buffer for reference at any time. The tool to use for recalling this information is dmesg.

The output of dmesg can be very long, so you'll probably want to pipe it through less, as shown in Listing 16.1.

LISTING 16.1   The Output from dmesg Piped Through less for Improved Readability

```
# dmesg | less
Copyright (c) 1992-2002 The FreeBSD Project.
Copyright (c) 1979, 1980, 1983, 1986, 1988, 1989, 1991, 1992, 1993, 1994
        The Regents of the University of California. All rights reserved.
FreeBSD 4.6.2-RELEASE #0: Wed Aug 14 20:47:38 PDT 2002
btman@stripes.somewhere.com:/usr/obj/usr/src/sys/STRIPES
Timecounter "i8254"  frequency 1193182 Hz
CPU: Pentium III/Pentium III Xeon/Celeron (598.06-MHz 686-class CPU)
  Origin = "GenuineIntel"  Id = 0x683  Stepping = 3
  Features=0x383f9ff<FPU,VME,DE,PSE,TSC,MSR,PAE,MCE,CX8,SEP,MTRR,PGE,MCA,
➥CMOV,PAT,PSE36,MMX,FXSR,SSE>
real memory  = 535736320 (523180K bytes)
config> di sn0
config> di lnc0
config> di ie0
config> di fe0
config> di ed0
config> di cs0
config> di bt0
config> di aic0
config> di aha0
config> di adv0
config> q
avail memory = 516485120 (504380K bytes)
Preloaded elf kernel "kernel" at 0xc044a000.
Preloaded userconfig_script "/boot/kernel.conf" at 0xc044a09c.
Pentium Pro MTRR support enabled
md0: Malloc disk
npx0: <math processor> on motherboard
npx0: INT 16 interface
```

LISTING 16.1   Continued

```
pcib0: <Host to PCI bridge> on motherboard
pci0: <PCI bus> on pcib0
pci0: <Intel model 1132 VGA-compatible display device> at 2.0 irq 11
pcib1: <PCI to PCI bridge (vendor=8086 device=244e)> at device 30.0 on pci0
pci1: <PCI bus> on pcib1
fxp0: <Intel Pro/100 Ethernet> port 0xde80-0xdebf mem 0xff8fe000-0xff8fefff
➥irq 11 at device 8.0 on pci1
fxp0: Disabling dynamic standby mode in EEPROM
fxp0: New EEPROM ID: 0x49b0
fxp0: EEPROM checksum @ 0x3f: 0xd3ef -> 0xd3f1
fxp0: Ethernet address 00:d0:b7:c7:74:f1
inphy0: <i82562ET 10/100 media interface> on miibus0
inphy0:  10baseT, 10baseT-FDX, 100baseTX, 100baseTX-FDX, auto
fxp1: <Intel Pro 10/100B/100+ Ethernet> port 0xdf00-0xdf3f
➥mem 0xff700000-0xff7fffff,0xff8ff000-0xff8fffff irq 11 at device 9.0 on pci1
fxp1: Disabling dynamic standby mode in EEPROM
fxp1: New EEPROM ID: 0x40a0
fxp1: EEPROM checksum @ 0x3f: 0x1829 -> 0x182b
fxp1: Ethernet address 00:d0:b7:bd:5d:13
inphy1: <i82555 10/100 media interface> on miibus1
inphy1:  10baseT, 10baseT-FDX, 100baseTX, 100baseTX-FDX, auto
isab0: <Intel 82801BA/BAM (ICH2) PCI to LPC bridge> at device 31.0 on pci0
isa0: <ISA bus> on isab0
atapci0: <Intel ICH2 ATA100 controller> port 0xffa0-0xffaf at device 31.1 on pci0
ata0: at 0x1f0 irq 14 on atapci0
ata1: at 0x170 irq 15 on atapci0
```

The output continues throughout all device checks, filesystem validations, and daemon startup blocks and then continues into runtime errors generated by various devices since you booted. You can ignore everything after you begin seeing date stamps and regular error messages. What you're interested in is the boot messages, such as the ones in the previous listing.

The first part of the boot messages, after the copyright and CPU information lines, is the kernel configuration you have set in the boot configurator. Each line beginning with config> is a command you issued in visual config mode, most likely (as with the di lines) to delete unwanted devices from the probe process. These devices won't appear later in the dmesg output. If you haven't removed these devices in the configurator, the kernel will probe for them.

Any driver accompanied in the listing by a "not found" message is a driver you can delete from the kernel. You may wish to keep two SSH terminal windows open to your FreeBSD machine: one to read the output of dmesg and another to configure the kernel. This will help ensure you don't delete anything that the system reports as "found."

The Kernel Configuration Files

At the time of this writing, FreeBSD doesn't have a visual kernel configuration utility like Red Hat Linux's linuxconf or the make config dialog-driven process in other Linux distributions. FreeBSD's kernel is configured using text files, a method that may seem quite arcane but one that does provide some flexibility the visual methods don't.

A visual configuration tool provides interactive feedback, allowing you to enable and disable devices and options on a one-by-one basis. What it doesn't do, though, is allow you to maintain multiple configurations side by side, comparing them using tools such as diff and grep, and use the base-level GENERIC configuration, previous known valid configurations, and the reference NOTES file as guidelines. Using a text file configuration also allows you to see all your device options at a glance.

An interactive visual tool can become needlessly complex and convoluted, and in asking you to decide individually whether to include every different option, it actually can detract from useful feedback. Unless you can remember the importance and consequences of every different option available in the config file, it's hard to keep track of which options you should be selecting. With the FreeBSD method, you can tune your config file until you're happy with it, incorporating changes introduced since the release of a previous version. You can even copy a "standard" configuration from another FreeBSD system and then build the kernel from it.

Assuming you installed the FreeBSD sources on your system, go into the /usr/src/sys/i386/conf directory, the location for the kernel config files. There you'll see the GENERIC file, among other items.

> **NOTE**
>
> If you're running on Alpha hardware instead of *x*86, use alpha in the previous pathname instead of i386. A number of other details in this chapter will be slightly different as well, but the process remains the same.

The GENERIC Configuration File

Open up the GENERIC file in your favorite text editor. Scroll through the various options, but don't actually make any changes just yet (you don't want to alter the GENERIC file itself). You'll see that there's a lot of built-in redundancy in the file in order to make sure your system remains compatible with all kinds of machines. The block of "required" lines will resemble the following, although it will vary depending on your specific version of FreeBSD:

```
machine        i386
cpu            I386_CPU
cpu            I486_CPU
cpu            I586_CPU
cpu            I686_CPU
ident          GENERIC
maxusers       32
```

Below this block are the "optional" lines—items that are part of the GENERIC kernel by default. Although these lines don't have to be present in order for the kernel to be valid, it just wouldn't be a very useful kernel without them. These include the block of useful kernel options shown in Listing 16.2 (a FreeBSD 5.0 kernel is shown).

LISTING 16.2   Built-in GENERIC Kernel Options

```
options        INET                        #InterNETworking
options        INET6                       #IPv6 communications protocols
options        FFS                         #Berkeley Fast Filesystem
options        SOFTUPDATES                 #Enable FFS soft updates support
options        UFS_DIRHASH                 #Improve performance on big directories
options        MD_ROOT                     #MD is a potential root device
options        NFSCLIENT                   #Network Filesystem Client
options        NFSSERVER                   #Network Filesystem Server
options        NFS_ROOT                    #NFS usable as root device, NFS required
options        MSDOSFS                     #MSDOS Filesystem
options        CD9660                      #ISO 9660 Filesystem
options        PROCFS                      #Process filesystem
options        COMPAT_43                   #Compatible with BSD 4.3 [KEEP THIS!]
options        SCSI_DELAY=15000            #Delay (in ms) before probing SCSI
options        KTRACE                      #ktrace(1) support
options        SYSVSHM                     #SYSV-style shared memory
options        SYSVMSG                     #SYSV-style message queues
options        SYSVSEM                     #SYSV-style semaphores
options        P1003_1B                    #Posix P1003_1B real-time extensions
options        _KPOSIX_PRIORITY_SCHEDULING
options        KBD_INSTALL_CDEV            # install a CDEV entry in /dev
```

The remainder of the file is taken up with "device" lines. These lines specify all the devices the GENERIC kernel has built in, and there are a lot of them. These are mostly what you will want to strip out of your custom kernel in order to optimize it. Listing 16.3 shows a sample block of device lines, of which there are several in the file.

LISTING 16.3   Some of the Device Drivers Built into the GENERIC Kernel

```
# PCI Ethernet NICs that use the common MII bus controller code.
# NOTE: Be sure to keep the 'device miibus' line in order to use these NICs!
device          miibus            # MII bus support
device          dc                # DEC/Intel 21143 and various workalikes
device          fxp               # Intel EtherExpress PRO/100B (82557, 82558)
device          pcn               # AMD Am79C79x PCI 10/100 NICs
device          rl                # RealTek 8129/8139
device          sf                # Adaptec AIC-6915 (''Starfire'')
device          sis               # Silicon Integrated Systems SiS 900/SiS 7016
device          ste               # Sundance ST201 (D-Link DFE-550TX)
device          tl                # Texas Instruments ThunderLAN
device          tx                # SMC EtherPower II (83c170 ''EPIC'')
device          vr                # VIA Rhine, Rhine II
device          wb                # Winbond W89C840F
device          xl                # 3Com 3c90x (''Boomerang'', ''Cyclone'')
```

Device Hints

FreeBSD operates using the Device Filesystem (DEVFS) and *device hints*, which provide a way of abstracting the attributes of various devices so that the system can find them without needing the attributes to be compiled statically into the kernel. These attributes used to be defined like this, in the kernel config file itself:

```
device          ata0    at isa? port IO_WD1 irq 14
device          ata1    at isa? port IO_WD2 irq 15
```

Now, however, the kernel configuration file only needs to have this line:

```
device          ata
```

This change happened because the ata device has its attributes in the /boot/device.hints file, which is consulted by the kernel at boot time. Here are the relevant lines for this example:

```
hint.ata.0.at="isa"
hint.ata.0.port="0x1F0"
hint.ata.0.irq="14"
hint.ata.1.at="isa"
hint.ata.1.port="0x170"
hint.ata.1.irq="15"
```

With these attributes kept in a central location, the kernel knows on what bus, memory address, and IRQ (interrupt request) to find the ata device. Also, you can change these attributes without having to recompile the kernel. If you prefer, though, you can still compile the attributes statically into the kernel by enabling this line:

```
#To statically compile in device wiring instead of /boot/device.hints
#hints          "GENERIC.hints"         #Default places to look for devices.
```

The /etc/rc.d/devfs script is run at boot time and controls after-the-fact symlinking and permissions tweaks that normally need to be done only once in a static, non-DEVFS system (you learn about /etc/rc.d/devfs in Chapter 10, "System Configuration and Startup Scripts"). For instance, a common task in setting up a Unix installation is to symlink /dev/mouse to /dev/cuaa0, or /dev/dvd to /dev/acd0c, because certain software expects to use the more generic device names, so you don't have to configure the system-specific devices into that software. A DVD player application will expect to find /dev/dvd, not a device label that can vary from system to system. Also, because some devices (such as DVD-R burners) must have the proper permissions so that certain users—typically those in the groups that own these devices—can write to them, the permissions on the devices must be altered with a chmod command.

Traditionally, you would issue the following commands during installation to set up /dev/dvd, after which you would never have to worry about it again:

```
# chmod 664 /dev/acd0c
# ln -sf /dev/acd0c /dev/dvd
# ln -sf /dev/acd0c /dev/rdvd
```

Now, with DEVFS, the /dev/acd0c device is set up dynamically each time you boot. To achieve the same effect as with earlier systems, you simply add these three lines to /etc/rc.d/devfs at the end of the file, and they will be applied after the dynamic devices are created.

The NOTES File and LINT

Fortunately, you aren't on your own when it comes to identifying each of these ugly-looking options and devices, or knowing which other ones are available. A file called NOTES, also in /usr/src/sys/i386/conf, describes all possible options and devices available in the current system. It's another file that you don't want to modify. Just open it in a text editor and look through its contents.

Everything in GENERIC has an entry in NOTES as well. Nothing is commented out of it except for actual comments. You can theoretically copy any configuration line (that begins with anything other than hint.) into your custom config file and then run with it. This will generally be necessary only if you add some particularly unusual device or kernel option, but NOTES is the first thing you should consult in that event.

NOTES also contains device hint lines; these are the ones beginning with hint. (as described previously). You can copy these lines either into /boot/device.hints or into the hints file for your kernel (for example, GENERIC.hints) if you want to compile them in statically.

Many items in NOTES refer to a mysterious thing called LINT. This is an old, deprecated (pre-5.0) way of looking at what is now the NOTES file. LINT was named after the lint command—a C-code debugging utility that's named for the fact that it validates the code you run it on by removing excess lint and fuzz from it. This piece of naming trivia is weird but true (and also not particularly useful or important). One of the long-running ideals (or myths) about FreeBSD is that it offers the capability to build a kernel based on the LINT file, incorporating every possible supported option and driver. This capability is almost certainly not possible, because many of the kernel options are mutually exclusive or unstable. FreeBSD does, however, provide the capability to generate an old-style LINT file by running make LINT from within the directory. This strips out all comments and hint. lines, and creates a kernel config file that you can theoretically use to build a really huge, all-encompassing kernel that probably won't have a chance of booting or even compiling.

Creating a Custom Kernel Configuration File

Here's where we actually begin the process of creating a new kernel. Remember that you don't want to modify the GENERIC file itself; it gets updated with the system sources every time you synchronize or upgrade. Therefore, to make sure your changes don't get over-written, make a copy of GENERIC to use as your custom kernel config. The name for the copy should be a single word in all caps, according to tradition. The custom kernel for this example is called CUSTOM:

```
# cp GENERIC CUSTOM
```

You can now modify the CUSTOM file all you like. The first thing you should do is go through it and change every mention of GENERIC to CUSTOM (or whatever name you chose). You also should remove redundant entries for cpu and, if necessary, modify the value of maxusers (see the following note). Here is a block from a customized kernel config on a Pentium III–class machine operating as a high-profile server:

```
machine        i386
cpu            I686_CPU
ident          CUSTOM
maxusers       64
```

> **NOTE**
>
> Don't be fooled by the maxusers setting: It doesn't actually limit the number of current logins the system will support. (That limit is controlled by the device pty <num> line.) What maxusers does is much more subtle: A number of internal table sizes are derived from it, such as the maximum number of processes allowed (16 times the maxusers setting, plus 20) and several others. Set maxusers to approximately what you expect the average number of users to be, but don't set it lower than 4 because you'll run out of processes quicker than you expect.

You can now start customizing the options and devices. Refer to NOTES to keep yourself informed about what you're modifying, and keep your other window with the dmesg output open. Don't delete anything from the config file that dmesg says the kernel found! It's in fact a good idea not to actually delete any lines. Instead, just comment them out by putting a hash mark (#) at the front of each line.

If you have any doubt about whether to disable a line that's in GENERIC, don't disable it. GENERIC definitely contains a lot of items that aren't needed on every system, but it's better to err on the side of caution when it comes to kernels, especially if you're making these changes on a production server.

Compiling and Installing the Custom Kernel

After your config file is ready to go, building the kernel is a fairly simple process. In theory, the build requires at most three commands:

```
# cd /usr/src
# make buildkernel KERNCONF=CUSTOM
# make installkernel KERNCONF=CUSTOM
```

The KERNCONF argument specifies the kernel config file to use; if you omit it, the GENERIC config file will be assumed. The first command parses the config file, sets up the build directory, builds the dependencies, and then builds the kernel itself. The second command installs it into /boot, moving the current kernel to /boot/kernel.old. (Prior to FreeBSD 5.0, these kernels are installed into /, the root.) You must then reboot to use the new kernel.

> **NOTE**
>
> The kernel has the schg (system-immutable) flag set on it, meaning that even root can't delete or overwrite it without first removing that flag. The make installkernel target attempts to remove the flag before installing the new kernel. However, if you're running with a securelevel setting of 1 or higher (a systemwide security setting that you select during installation or in /etc/rc.conf; see man securelevel for details), it won't be able to remove the flag. You'll have to reboot into single-user mode in order to complete the kernel installation; dropping to single-user mode via shutdown won't work.

If you're really sure of yourself, you can combine both the make lines into a single one, as shown here:

```
# make kernel KERNCONF=CUSTOM
```

Adding Device Nodes to the /dev Directory (If Necessary)

This section applies only to versions of FreeBSD prior to 5.0-RELEASE. If your version is 5.0-RELEASE or later, you can safely skip this section because later versions use the DEVFS filesystem interface to the system's devices and build the /dev virtual filesystem dynamically at boot time.

Many devices will be missing an entry in /dev when you add them to the kernel configuration; devices in /dev include only those that have either been part of the base system or have been added afterward explicitly. You have to create device nodes for new devices that you add to the kernel—they're not generated automatically.

Fortunately, creating the device nodes is fairly simple. All you have to do, after you reboot with the new kernel, is go into the /dev director, and run the MAKEDEV shell script:

```
# ./MAKEDEV
```

All devices supported by the running kernel will be created as device nodes or "special files" in /dev. Afterward, you have a target you can use with your command-line tools to interact with each new device. A more efficient, direct solution is to make the device node only for the new device(s) you've installed (for instance, if you've enabled the snd0 sound driver). You can enable the device by running the MAKEDEV command on it alone:

```
# ./MAKEDEV snd0
```

Recovering When Something Goes Wrong

Compiler errors are not uncommon. If you're running the same source tree that you've had since you installed the system, an error in the compile process (where the compiler fails to complete, usually citing "*** Error code 1") is probably the result of some unstable kernel option or device that you've enabled. See whether you can determine which one it is by checking the last few lines of the compiler output—the text immediately preceding "*** Error code 1" indicates errors that terminate the compilation process. Each compiler command line is echoed to the screen, so you should be able to see what component it was trying to compile when the error occurred. If it's not obvious, you can find some guidance by visiting the FreeBSD Web site (http://www.freebsd.org) and searching the mailing list archives for some of the unique words in whatever compiler errors were generated.

If you've updated your sources since installing your system, it's quite likely (especially if you're tracking -CURRENT or -STABLE) that the code is in an unstable state, and whatever errors you've encountered will probably be corrected within a few days (you'll learn more about updating sources in Chapter 17, "Keeping Up to Date with FreeBSD"). You should be subscribed to the freebsd-current or freebsd-stable mailing lists if you're such a cutting-edge FreeBSD user, and you can get help there (see the FreeBSD Web site for details on subscribing).

However, there is always the chance your kernel will build cleanly, install cleanly, reboot cleanly, and then explode without warning when it tries to boot. It might fail to mount its filesystems, it might freeze up with a kernel trap error, or it might behave according to a number of other failure modes. If this happens, don't panic—there's an easy way to get out of this predicament.

Reboot the machine and press the appropriate F-key to get past the boot loader. When you're offered the loader prompt (when it counts down from 10 seconds, giving you the option to press any key but Enter for the prompt), take it. Enter **boot /boot/kernel.old** (or **boot /kernel.old**, prior to FreeBSD 5.0) at the prompt, and your previous working kernel will be used.

Keep in mind that if you next try to rebuild the kernel and install it, /boot/kernel.old will get overwritten by the previous kernel you built that was broken. To avoid this, copy kernel.old to some filename that won't get overwritten by any automated process (for instance, /boot/kernel.frank). You can use this kernel to boot from the loader prompt the next time if it happens again.

Another possible problem is that your system boots properly and completely comes up, but system utilities such as ps, top, and w no longer work. If this happens, it's most likely because you're building your kernel from a newer source tree than your system is built from, and the libkvm library has become outdated by your newer kernel.

To get around this, you can rebuild your libkvm library, but that solution is for experts only. If you're brave, you can do this by going to the location of the libkvm code within /usr/src and attempting to make and install it by hand. You learn about that process in Chapter 17). A still better solution, though, is to always build your kernel from the same sources that your full system is built from, and only build a kernel on updated sources if you're doing a complete make world, as described in the next chapter.

16

Keeping Up to Date with FreeBSD

Every operating system has to have a way of keeping up with the times. Administrators need to get security patches, bug fixes, and support for new technologies into their installed systems without waiting for new full releases, which can take anywhere from six months to three years in the operating system world. In today's "Internet time" environment, however, hackers can compromise systems within hours of a security breach announcement, so maintaining an up-to-the-minute operating system is essential.

No operating system maker completely neglects this need. Microsoft provides large periodic "service pack" upgrades to users of Windows NT/2000. When a security breach is discovered in a Windows- or Macintosh-based consumer application, manufacturers issue the appropriate security patches for these consumer applications within a matter of days. Similar patch mechanisms are in place for Linux. You can keep FreeBSD up to date through these methods, but because the system is largely founded on its users' access to the source code (even more so than its open-source cousins), FreeBSD offers some better methods for keeping your system buttoned up against even the most current conditions.

Major versions of FreeBSD (such as 4.0 and 5.0) appear every one to two years, and interim releases (such as 3.4 and 4.6) generally appear every three to six months. But no matter how frequently a patch release becomes available, it's too infrequent to address the pressing day-to-day needs of a security-conscious administrator. In this chapter, you learn about CVSup, make world, and other real-time methods for keeping your FreeBSD system current.

Tracking the FreeBSD Sources

The easiest and most common upgrade path is simply to wait for each new official release. You get a copy of the CD or disk image file and install the new version of the operating system from it by using the methods covered in Chapter 2, "Installing FreeBSD," or as described at the FreeBSD Web site. However, upgrading to new releases isn't a real-time solution to the upgrade procedure. To really keep up with the times, you have to track the sources.

The source tree for FreeBSD is kept in a central CVS repository, mirrored across a number of redundant servers, and maintained by a fairly small core of contributors and committers. FreeBSD is structured so that the entire system is available in source form at all times for anybody to use. This structure differs from the Linux model, in which the sources for the kernel are available but each individual distribution has its own set of executables and libraries, its own filesystem structure, and its own policies for how the source for those resources should be made available. Whether you intend to modify and develop the sources and check them back in to the main tree or simply want to maintain a server with a current source distribution, you use CVS to handle the FreeBSD structure and revisions. This model gives FreeBSD developers and administrators the same level of access to the code.

The STABLE and CURRENT Source Branches Explained

Between complete releases, the FreeBSD code is in a state of constant flux. Bugs are being fixed, utilities are being patched and extended, features are being added, and the structure of the system is being reorganized. To understand this process, think of the code repository as a tree that occasionally sprouts new branches at the top as it grows. Each time a new version of the FreeBSD code (3.x, 4.x, 5.x, and so on) is initiated, it branches off from the main development codebase (or the "trunk" of the tree). As shown in Figure 17.1, the topmost branch is called CURRENT, and the next highest is STABLE. Typically, multiple branches of the code tree are undergoing maintenance at the same time, with the two newest branches in active development and earlier branches receiving sporadic maintenance.

This code development model is fairly common; it enables developers to freeze a certain feature set within a version and avoid the instability of ongoing minor tweaks and additions. Following this model, developers add new features in blocks, introducing each new feature set or restructuring with each new branch.

The thing to remember here is that CURRENT is not the branch you want to use for a production server! CURRENT refers to the very most cutting-edge branch of the code—the one where brand-new features are being tested. Consequently, it's the least stable branch of the code tree. CURRENT is intended only for developers and people who absolutely, without any possibility of alternative, must have the new features that are introduced in FreeBSD code, without waiting for them to be declared part of a STABLE version.

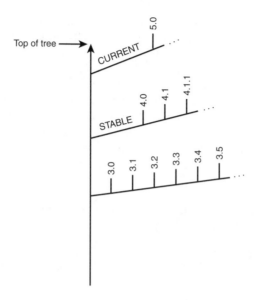

FIGURE 17.1   The FreeBSD code branches, showing the relationship of the CURRENT and STABLE branches.

At some point during development on a CURRENT branch—usually after the first release, for example 5.0-RELEASE—the CURRENT version feature set is deemed STABLE, and the CURRENT and STABLE designations each move up one branch on the tree. CURRENT becomes the tag for the newly created topmost branch, and the newly designated STABLE (formerly CURRENT) version feature set is now recommended for use on production servers. New releases are announced on both branches every few months, until the feature set in CURRENT has matured and the STABLE branch no longer meets the needs of the community. The tree then branches again, starting the cycle over.

Selecting Your Upgrade Target

You can upgrade your system at any time, no matter how far along the development in the tree is. You have two choices for making the upgrade:

- You can select any release in which the code is frozen and kept in a static repository.

- You can simply synchronize your source using CVSup (in much the same way as we discussed synchronizing your ports in Chapter 14, "Installing Additional Software") and build a new system any time you want to.

The remaining sections of this chapter discuss how to synchronize your source to either a release version target or an interim build in order to update your FreeBSD system. The only difference, in practice, between the two methods is the target tag you use in your

CVSup configuration. All tags begin with RELENG, a prefix that stands for *release engineer*. The RELENG tag signifies that a branch has been officially initiated by the release engineer on the core FreeBSD team.

Upgrading to a Release Version

To upgrade your FreeBSD system to a release version, you insert a release version tag into your CVSup configuration, which we will discuss a little later. The release version tags all have three digits, separated by underscores rather than periods, and have a suffix of RELEASE. Table 17.1 shows how release tags map to version numbers. This is an incomplete example; there are many more available release version numbers available, each with their corresponding tags.

TABLE 17.1   Mappings Between Release Tags and Version Numbers

Release Tag	Version Number
RELENG_5_0_0_RELEASE	FreeBSD 5.0
RELENG_4_6_0_RELEASE	FreeBSD 4.6
RELENG_4_1_1_RELEASE	FreeBSD 4.1.1
RELENG_3_5_0_RELEASE	FreeBSD 3.5

Upgrading to an Interim Build

Interim versions for specific releases are maintained so you can apply security patches and critical code fixes to an otherwise unchanging RELEASE codebase. If your system is built from 4.5-RELEASE sources and you want to track a code branch that incorporates all the most recent security fixes without having to worry about all the other new features and code that go into the STABLE development branch, you can synchronize your system to the RELENG_4_5 branch. This upgrade gives you RELENG_4_5_0_RELEASE, plus any critical patches that have been committed since then, but nothing that has gone exclusively into the 4.6 development tree.

To upgrade to an interim build of FreeBSD, you specify in your CVSup configuration a branch that's in development. You create your release target by leaving off the RELEASE suffix and the third digit (which signifies the patch release number). You probably won't need the second digit, because most recent releases of FreeBSD treat the second digit as the patch release number, moving toward a two-digit numbering system, as shown in Table 17.2.

> **TIP**
>
> Note that Table 17.2 is current as of Summer 2002. Due to the dynamic nature of development branches, this information will become obsolete with time. Refer to http://www.freebsd.org/doc/en_US.ISO8859-1/books/handbook/cvs-tags.html for a definitive and current table of the appropriate branch tags.

TABLE 17.2   Branch Tags and Version Designations for Interim Versions

Branch Tag	Version Designation
RELENG_5	FreeBSD 5-STABLE (the main line of 5.*x* development)
RELENG_4_6	FreeBSD 4.6-RELEASE-p# release/security branch
RELENG_4_5	FreeBSD 4.5-RELEASE-p# release/security branch
RELENG_4	FreeBSD 4-STABLE (the main line of 4.*x* development)

Upgrading with make world

In the language of FreeBSD development, the *world* refers to everything within the FreeBSD system other than the kernel. Therefore, make world refers to the process of rebuilding your FreeBSD system from the ground up. Rebuilding your entire system is certainly a more hands-on, less "prepackaged" way of upgrading than simply dropping in a CD. However, in accordance with the FreeBSD way of doing things, building your binaries from pure source is the only way to ensure your system will truly be compatible with your hardware and your setup. The make world process does involve a lot of steps and a fair amount of risk, but the regimented structure of FreeBSD helps to mitigate the risk and allows you to enjoy the advantages this method provides.

The make world process provides safeguards that would not normally be available if you were to install precompiled binaries from a CD. If any part of the source code is broken, for example, it will fail to compile in the first place, rather than waiting until the rebuilt binaries are installed on your system before revealing themselves to be unusable. The clearest philosophical difference, though, between make world and other upgrade methods is that it blurs the line between release software and interim builds.

A *release* is just a snapshot of the source where it appeared particularly stable and matched a set schedule milestone. The process of synchronizing to that snapshot is functionally the same as synchronizing to any other point in the branch—a developer-friendly approach. This blurred distinction encourages administrators to keep their code trees in sync, which provides the real advantage of ensuring that the most recent security patches and bug fixes are always at your fingertips.

All you typically have to do to update an individual part of your system is to go to that part of the source, build it, and install it (you learn about updating individual components through this method in Chapter 29, "Network Security"). You also need to plan on rebuilding the entire system—the entire world—on a periodic basis.

Making the world consists of four main steps:

1. Building the world (or everything in the core system aside from the kernel).

2. Installing the world.

17

3. Building the kernel.

4. Installing the kernel.

Before you do any of these things, though, we need to address some essential preparations and precautions.

Things to Consider Before Choosing a make world Upgrade

The risks of building your system from scratch are not insignificant. On a high-profile production server, you may deem them too great for make world to be a viable upgrade method. It's a simple matter to wait for each full release on CD, and you may prefer to go that route instead. To make an informed decision, though, you need to fully understand the risks involved in building a system from interim sources.

First, and most obviously, make world involves at least one reboot. If you're concerned about your uptime, or if your system absolutely must be online at all times (as with a high-profile network server), you would probably be best served by upgrading to each successive RELEASE version and applying the necessary patches in between releases.

Second, make world isn't a guaranteed process. The FreeBSD Group makes no claims that make world will not completely destroy your system (though the same is true for any upgrade path, really). The real issue is that frequently rebuilding the operating system gives it that many more chances to blow up. Using make world is absolutely the best way to keep on top of all the latest bug fixes, but it's also an excellent way to find yourself running a system with untested new features or code changes—or even to find that your sources won't build because, by pure bad luck, you synchronized your sources just when some unstable code was being checked in.

Remember, the STABLE and CURRENT code branches are living, breathing creatures—they're not "release" quality, nor are they intended to be. Any interim code between releases should be regarded as beta quality at best. Rebuilding the entire system between releases is really something you should do only if you're using your FreeBSD machine as a workstation or a small, noncritical server, or if there is absolutely no other way for you to get a critical bug fix or new feature.

> **NOTE**
>
> In production environments, it is a common configuration to have two identical machines: the "real" server and a clone of it used for backup and testing purposes. If you have this kind of setup, you can test the results of a make world process on the backup system before performing the same procedure on the production server.

If you do track either STABLE or CURRENT, it's absolutely essential that you subscribe to the freebsd-stable@freebsd.org or freebsd-current@freebsd.org mailing list (as appropriate). These lists serve as forums for anyone tracking the branch to discuss problems, new bug fixes or features, and possible pitfalls for anyone choosing to synchronize sources at a particular time. A committer might post to freebsd-stable@freebsd.org, for instance, warning everyone not to use make world for at least the next couple of weeks until he or she has had a chance to test a risky new feature that has just been checked in. If you're not on the mailing list and the feature turns out to be less than rock-solid, you could end up with an unstable or insecure system, which is exactly what you're trying to avoid by tracking the sources.

> **NOTE**
>
> Both mailing lists are standard majordomo lists. You can subscribe to either one by sending an e-mail to majordomo@freebsd.org, with the message body as follows:
>
> subscribe freebsd-stable
>
> Do *not* send the subscription request itself to freebsd-stable or freebsd-current! This is one of the Internet's most common mistakes! These addresses are for the actual list traffic, not for control commands.
>
> That's all there is to it. When you receive a confirmation message, return it to be added to the mailing list. To unsubscribe, do the same thing, except replace the word subscribe with unsubscribe.

It's important to note that even though you might choose not to run the make world process regularly, it's still an excellent idea, in almost all circumstances, to track the sources. Tracking sources synchronizes your sources (everything within /usr/src) to the current state of either the STABLE or CURRENT code branch; it doesn't affect the operation of your system at all. You can then choose to use make world, compiling all those sources into a completely new system. Alternatively, because the build process is as hierarchical as the filesystem in which it resides, you can simply go to any point within /usr/src and build that component individually. This is how you typically patch your system in response to a security advisory (learn more about these in the section "FreeBSD Security Advisories," in Chapter 30).

Above all, remember that upgrading a FreeBSD system is not a reversible process. You can't deinstall a newer version and have the older version still work as it used to. The best safeguard is to take as many precautions as you can.

> **Bug Tracking and Problem Reports**
>
> The FreeBSD bug-tracking database is online. You can view the status of all open bugs and feature requests at http://www.FreeBSD.org/cgi/query-pr-summary.cgi, or you can go to http://www.freebsd.org and follow the links to "Bug Reports" and the GNATS bug database.

You can also submit bug reports of your own; indeed, that's how a lot of these bugs get filed. The tool to use is called `send-pr`. When you run that command, you are placed into your preferred text editor with a template file. Simply fill out the input fields with the relevant data about the bug you're submitting. When you save and exit, the problem report is sent directly into the GNATS database and reviewed by the committers.

Of course, you'll want to make sure the bug you're reporting hasn't already been submitted. Search the preceding URL for any specific relevant text in any of the open reports. Also, don't forget to subscribe to the appropriate mailing list: `freebsd-stable` or `freebsd-current`. It's a good idea to post to the appropriate list before submitting a problem report and ask whether anyone else has seen the problem before you send it via `send-pr`. It's likely that someone has already noticed the bug and may even have a temporary workaround to suggest to you.

Pre–make world **Tasks**

So, you've chosen to rebuild your system. Whether you're going to synchronize to interim sources along one of the development branches or you want to rebuild to upgrade to the next RELEASE, there are a number of things you need to do before embarking on the rather convoluted rebuilding process. A lot of things can go wrong, so it pays to follow the game plan:

1. *Make a backup of your system.* Nothing is more heartbreaking than performing a simple, routine upgrade, only to find that your filesystem is destroyed and all your users' data irretrievably lost. Backup solutions might include tape drives, optical disks (CD-R, DVD-RAM, DVD-R, and so on), a second hard drive that you mount only when you need to mirror your first drive's contents onto it, and a second machine that you keep synchronized via NFS or CVSup (you learn about backup methods in Chapter 19, "FreeBSD Survival Guide").

> **CAUTION**
>
> Having a proper backup solution is one of the most crucial, and yet most onerous, parts of system administration. Many readers will undoubtedly ignore this warning and proceed anyway—it happens all the time—but if you can possibly manage the cost and hassle of setting up a backup solution, the benefits are absolutely worth the investment.

2. *Check the timing of your upgrade.* Pay attention to the mailing list for your chosen branch. Make sure your upgrade won't occur during a bug fix or testing phase. If the time isn't right for your upgrade and you desperately need just a certain patch or bug fix, see if there's a way to rebuild just that one component.

3. *Synchronize your sources.* Before you can really do anything further to prepare yourself for the build, you need to synchronize your sources, as explained in the section that follows. You only need to do the setup for this once; after that, it's a process that can be automated.

Synchronizing Your Source Tree with the STABLE or CURRENT Tree or a RELEASE

You have a number of ways available to you to synchronize your sources. The methods suggested by the FreeBSD developers include CTM, Anonymous CVS, and CVSup—and each one has its own particular advantages. You can read more about each of these at the FreeBSD Web site under the "Synchronizing Your Source" heading of the handbook. This chapter covers using CVSup because it's the most advanced and efficient (not to mention coolest) option available.

Using CVSup

We discussed how to set up CVSup in "Keeping Ports Up to Date with CVSup" in Chapter 14. If you haven't set up CVSup using the `cvsupit` port, as described in that chapter, refer to it now and follow the same procedure. Note these few differences, however, as you follow the procedure:

1. When `cvsupit` prompts you for the source branch to use (the first screen), select the one appropriate to your system. If you want to track the STABLE sources, select the topmost STABLE branch in the list that matches your system's major version. For instance, if you're running 4.6-RELEASE and you want the newest STABLE sources (the ones with new features and layout changes that will eventually be incorporated into 4.7-RELEASE), use `RELENG_4`. If you want to upgrade your 4.6-RELEASE system to the current snapshot of that same version but with all up-to-date critical security patches merged in, use `RELENG_4_6`. But if you're really "cutting edge" and want to run the absolute latest and least tested code of all, select the very first entry ("."), which is the head of the source tree.

2. In the next screen, simply press Enter to select all available source components. It's not really advisable or necessary to pick and choose particular components; this capability is only there for experts who need that kind of flexibility.

3. Go ahead and accept the defaults to track the ports and doc collections as well. It's a good idea to synchronize those trees at the same time. However, you can disable these secondary updates by editing `/etc/cvsupfile` and commenting them out.

When the `cvsupit` tool offers to run the update, go ahead and accept. After it finishes, you probably should add the update command to your daily `periodic` file, as described in "Keeping Ports Up to Date with CVSup," in Chapter 14. Every day afterward, you'll have sources that are no less than a day old.

Pay attention to the contents of each update output mail you get! When you're tracking STABLE or CURRENT (or a point-release/security patch branch), these messages tell you each day what has changed. This way, you'll know exactly when a crucial bug fix has been applied to a certain component you're watching.

17

Using CVSup to Synchronize to RELEASE Sources

Using CVSup is an excellent way to get the sources for a RELEASE snapshot as well as to synchronize to interim sources. To do this, you simply need to use the branch tag that specifies the release you want (as discussed earlier in the chapter). However, cvsupit doesn't let you do this automatically, because the original RELEASE codebase is usually insecure—it's missing whatever critical fixes have been merged into it. Generally, RELEASE codebases are relevant only for a few weeks after the initial release on that branch appears or until the code begins to change in response to security bulletins.

If you really want to synchronize to a RELEASE codebase, your best bet is to run cvsupit to create /etc/cvsupfile and then elect not to run the update at this time. Exit from cvsupit and open /etc/cvsupfile in your editor. It will look something like what's shown in Listing 17.1.

LISTING 17.1   A Sample /etc/cvsupfile Created by cvsupit

```
*default   host=cvsup8.FreeBSD.org
*default   base=/usr
*default   prefix=/usr
*default   release=cvs
*default   tag=RELENG_4
*default   delete use-rel-suffix

src-all
*default tag=.
ports-all
doc-all
```

Simply change the tag line to the release tag you want. For example, 4.6-RELEASE sources can be had with the following line:

```
*default   tag=RELENG_4_6_0_RELEASE
```

Now, when you run the CVSup update from this file, you have the "frozen" sources for the release you've chosen. Also, unlike with the constantly changing STABLE and CURRENT branches, if you update again a week later, nothing will have changed. You can now use make world from these sources and change the release tag in /etc/cvsupfile back to what it was before. Then, you can resume daily synchronizations so you can have all the latest source patches and updates at your disposal. This upgrade method works best if you have a critical server to keep updated.

Troubleshooting Questions

Quite a number of things can go wrong with CVSup, and because it's a type of task that has no analogue on most other operating systems, it's hard to tell when the process has gone as planned and when it has abjectly failed. Here are suggested fixes for some of the most commonly reported problems:

- **CVSup won't connect to the server I've selected (Connection refused).**

  Try picking a different CVSup server. The higher the number (for example, `cvsup8.freebsd.org`), the less traffic it is likely to be sustaining. Also, try to run CVSup at a time of day when traffic will be minimal (the middle of the night, for example).

- **CVSup connects but nothing ever happens.**

  This might occur if you're behind a firewall or a NAT router that masks your IP address. CVSup is known to work with NAT-enabled network configurations, but a misconfigured one might cause problems. Also, make sure your firewall will allow CVSup traffic. The server port is 5999.

- **CVSup deleted my entire `/usr/src` directory!**

  This occurs if you've specified an invalid branch tag. If you give CVSup a tag that the server doesn't recognize, it responds by giving you the contents of the CVS tree at the branch you've specified—which is nothing. Make sure you've got the right branch tag, and you should be all right.

The UPDATING Text File

Now that your sources are updated, you have a current UPDATING file in /usr/src. This file is a "late-breaking news" bulletin that has important information on upgrading your system, almost guaranteed to be more current than anything you read in print or online (this book is no exception). UPDATING contains a reverse chronological listing (each with a date stamp) of notable changes to the build process that you should know about. Read all of them between the top of the file and the date of your last make world.

Something to remember is that /etc is not altered automatically by the make world process. Any configuration files you have in there will not be overwritten. This ensures that your custom system setup won't be lost; it also means that whenever the default system configuration requires something new to be added to or deleted from /etc, you'll have to merge it in manually. The UPDATING file usually details cases like this. Fortunately, a neat tool called mergemaster allows for an easy merge of new files into /etc. You learn more about mergemaster in "Using mergemaster to Check for Changed Configuration Files," later in this chapter.

Merging /etc/group and /etc/passwd

Most of the /etc files don't affect your ability to build the system. However, occasionally new services are added that have to be installed with ownership matching a certain user and group. Remember that make world is not an installer application with built-in upgrade tasks; it simply recompiles and installs a new version of the operating system on top of the old. This means that make world most likely won't create the users and groups it needs if they don't already exist. You can help avoid any collisions arising from this by merging any new entries into your /etc/group file.

The new version of /etc/group is in /usr/src/etc/group. It probably won't be any longer than 20 lines or so. Open /etc/group in another terminal window. Now, check to see if there are any entries in /usr/src/etc/group that are not in /etc/group. If you find any, simply copy them over. New entries are likely to have GIDs below 100.

One easy way to compare the two files is to use diff, as shown in Listing 17.2.

LISTING 17.2   Comparing /etc/group and /usr/src/etc/group Using diff

```
# diff -c /etc/group /usr/src/etc/group | less
*** /etc/group   Wed May  2 09:57:10 2001
--- /usr/src/etc/group   Fri Aug 27 16:23:41 1999
***************
*** 8,24 ****
  bin:*:7:
  news:*:8:
  man:*:9:
- wheel:*:10:root,frank,joe
  games:*:13:
  staff:*:20:root
  sshd:*:22:
  smmsp:*:25:
  mailnull:*:26:
  guest:*:31:root
  bind:*:53:
  uucp:*:66:
  xten:*:67:xten
  dialer:*:68:
+ network:*:69:
- mysql:*:88:
- users:*:100:
  nogroup:*:65533:
  nobody:*:65534:
```

Groups in your existing /etc/group are shown with a minus sign (-), and new groups in /usr/src/etc/group have a plus sign (+). In this example, you need to copy the network group into your /etc/group file.

It's important to preserve the GIDs suggested in the new `group` file. In the unlikely event that any of the GIDs don't match, you need to fix your existing `/etc/group` to match the new file. This fix might cause some existing files in your system (that were owned by that group) to lose their permissions. You can search the system for these files with the `find` command:

```
# find / -group <GID> -print
```

You can then fix the permissions on these files with `chmod`, as you saw in Chapter 9, "Users, Groups, and Permissions."

It's even less likely that any mismatches will occur in the user database. The sources don't include a `passwd` file, just a `/usr/src/etc/master.passwd` file that's even shorter than the new group file. Quickly scan it and your `/etc/master.passwd` file for mismatches and then use `adduser` to insert any new users you find.

Merging `/etc/make.conf`

The `make.conf` files are the global configuration files that control all `make` operations, including `make world`. You don't have an `/etc/make.conf` file in a new installation of FreeBSD. However, in the same way that `/etc/rc.conf` and `/etc/defaults/rc.conf` work, there's a file named `/etc/defaults/make.conf` that specifies all the likely default settings. You can leave things as they are, but you can speed things up a bit with the judicious use of a few options.

The FreeBSD handbook suggests enabling the following lines by copying them out of `/etc/defaults/make.conf` and into `/etc/make.conf` and then uncommenting them:

```
CFLAGS= -O -pipe
NOPROFILE=      true    # Avoid compiling profiled libraries
```

These modifications help to ensure that the `make world` process will be smooth, without trying to add potentially destabilizing optimizations or unnecessary compilations into the process. You can set some other options if you want to experiment, but that's beyond the scope of both this chapter and this book.

Rebuilding Your System from Sources

You're ready to go. The rebuilding process consists of a good number of steps, so take your time with it.

The `make world` process itself consists of four main compilation steps, listed in Table 17.3. If you're feeling exceptionally confident, you can reduce the process to two steps, but for this first time, take each of the `make world` steps individually.

TABLE 17.3 Steps Involved in a Complete `make world` Process

Four-step Command	Two-step Command	Meaning
make buildworld	make world	Builds and installs everything but the kernel
make installworld		
make buildkernel	make kernel	Builds and installs the kernel
make installkernel		

The `make world` and `make kernel` commands should be used only by seasoned veterans who really know what they're doing; everyone else needs to use the four individual `make` commands. You won't be using those commands in the order shown in the table, though! You actually build the world first, build and install the kernel, and then install the rest of the world. The following sections detail the steps for this process.

Cleaning Out `/usr/obj`

This step isn't necessary if this is the first time you've done a `make world`. If it isn't, you'll probably want to clean out everything in `/usr/obj` to speed things up and prevent collisions when the system runs into files it can't overwrite.

`/usr/obj` is where the object files (compiled components) are stored after being compiled and before being installed. Deleting them, however, isn't necessarily as easy as simply doing an `rm -rf` inside that directory. Making the world creates certain files with the `schg` flag (the "system immutable" flag), which means that the files can't be deleted, even if you're root. This is a safety measure intended only to provide an extra means of protection against accidents (such as `rm -rf \.*`). To get around this and clean out the build directory properly, use the following commands:

```
# cd /usr/obj
# chflags -R noschg *
# rm -rf *
```

You won't be able to do this so easily if `securelevel` is set to 1 or higher (this is a systemwide security setting you select during installation or in `/etc/rc.conf`, as described in `man securelevel` and in "Network Security," in Chapter 29). This setting prevents you from unsetting the `schg` flags. You have to reboot into single-user mode to complete this step properly.

Starting an Output Log

Keep a log of the output from your `make world`. If anything goes wrong, you can review the log for clues and, if necessary, post the relevant parts of it to the appropriate mailing list. Chances are that because an error will cause the compile to fail immediately, you'll have the relevant lines in your scrollback buffer. It's still a good idea to have a transcript of the entire process to peruse if you need to.

Use the `script` command to create the log. This command effectively runs a shell within a shell, capturing all output into the file you choose. You remain in the script shell until you type **exit** to return to your regular shell. Here's an example showing the make buildworld command issued after a `script` log has been started:

```
# script ~/buildworld.out
Script started, output file is ~/buildworld.out
# make buildworld


...


# exit
Script done, output file is ~/buildworld.txt
```

The argument to `script` specifies the target file that will contain all the build output. It's a good idea to name this file according to the build step you're about to capture. Each time you run `script` with the same target filename it overwrites that file rather than appending to it. Therefore, you should run `script` separately—and have a separate target file—for each step in the make world process.

> **CAUTION**
>
> Don't specify a target file in /tmp! Files in /tmp are deleted on bootup, so you won't have your output files when the system comes back up.

Running and Troubleshooting make buildworld

Here's where the fun really begins. Go to /usr/src, take a final look around to make sure everything looks okay, and enter the first make step:

```
# make buildworld
```

Now, sit back and watch. The buildworld process takes an hour or two, depending on your hardware. You can speed it up by using the -j option to run multiple simultaneous processes, as in this example, which starts four of these parallel tasks:

```
# make -j4 buildworld
```

This is useful even on a single-CPU system, but if you have multiple processors, you can get still more performance from higher values (try as many as 10).

The build process takes a vaguely alphabetical, recursive path through /usr/src. You can track its progress by looking through the directories in /usr/obj. When you see it compiling things in /usr/src/usr.sbin, you know you're near the end.

As is the case with CVSup, the process of building a complete operating system is probably an unfamiliar one, and you can expect to run into some problems. Here are two of the most commonly reported problems and their solutions:

- **The compiler fails with "signal 11" errors.**

  Signal 11 refers to a segmentation fault in the compiler, which most frequently occurs due to hardware issues. Check to see whether your CPU is overclocked; this can frequently cause problems with FreeBSD when you perform processor-intensive tasks such as compiling software. If you're not overclocking, suspect your RAM or other hardware.

- **The compiler fails with a lot of "*** Error code 1 ***" lines.**

  This is the generic error when the build fails at any certain point. The buildworld process won't proceed if any part of it fails, so the last few lines of output leading up to the failure are the most useful.

To avoid the latter problem, make sure you have completely removed the contents of /usr/obj before compiling. Leaving the objects from previous builds intact can save time, but it can also cause spurious failures if the compiler fails to realize it has to rebuild some component. Clean out /usr/obj, as shown earlier, and try again.

If this doesn't help, search the mailing list archives at http://www.freebsd.org (in the mailing list that pertains to your code branch—stable/freebsd-stable or current/freebsd-current) on the relevant keywords from your output. If you find nothing useful, post a question to the relevant mailing list, citing the output of uname -a, the time of your last CVSup, and the relevant final few lines from the compiler output.

Upgrading the Kernel

Okay, your "userland" (user-accessible files, or everything but the kernel) is now built and ready to be installed. First, though, you need to get the new kernel built and installed.

Upgrading a GENERIC Kernel

If you're running a GENERIC kernel (see Chapter 16, "Kernel Configuration," for details), the process is simple:

```
# make buildkernel
# make installkernel
```

Or, even more simply:

```
# make kernel
```

Now, your new kernel is installed as /boot/kernel (/kernel prior to FreeBSD 5.0), and the old one is at /boot/kernel.old. As discussed in Chapter 10, "System Configuration and Startup Scripts," you can boot with the old one if the new one fails.

Upgrading a Custom Kernel

The upgrading process is made a bit more complex if you're running a custom kernel. The adventurous might try building a new version of the custom kernel and running with that, but you can set up a safety net by building a GENERIC kernel first and keeping it on hand to boot with if you have to. You'll also have your old kernel (the one currently running) as a fallback if all else fails.

Still within /usr/src, enter the following:

```
# make buildkernel KERNCONF=GENERIC
```

This is your first backup kernel, a GENERIC one built from the new sources. Now, if you haven't done this already, copy /boot/kernel to /boot/kernel.prev (or some other name to indicate that this is the kernel you were already running and you know works). Next, install the newly built kernel:

```
# make installkernel KERNCONF=GENERIC
```

Then, copy this kernel to kernel.GENERIC:

```
# cp /boot/kernel /boot/kernel.GENERIC
```

Now, here's how to build your first-choice kernel (the custom one built from the new sources):

```
# make buildkernel KERNCONF=CUSTOM
```

Naturally, replace CUSTOM with whatever the name of your custom kernel is. Now, install the new custom kernel as /boot/kernel:

```
# make installkernel KERNCONF=CUSTOM
```

To recap, your lineup of kernels is shown in Table 17.4.

TABLE 17.4   Newly Available Kernels

Kernel	Description
/boot/kernel	New custom kernel
/boot/kernel.GENERIC	New GENERIC kernel
/boot/kernel.prev	The old tried-and-true kernel

When you reboot, if the first kernel fails, try booting with the new GENERIC kernel. As described in "Understanding the FreeBSD Startup Process" in Chapter 10, this is accomplished by pressing a key during the countdown to get to the loader prompt, then entering **boot kernel.GENERIC**. If that fails, boot with the previously working kernel, and you'll be back to where you started.

Troubleshooting the Kernel Upgrade and Installation

Building and installing the kernel is the riskiest stage yet in the make world process, and the safeguards in the system that protect the kernel during this process add to the arcane nature of the procedure by being quite user unfriendly. Here are two few common failure modes and their solutions:

- **The compiler fails.**

  The kernel sources can fail to build for the same reasons that building the rest of the system can fail. If you can't resolve the failure yourself, try the mailing lists.

- **The system won't let me install my new kernel!**

  If you've set securelevel to 1 or higher, make installkernel won't be able to remove the schg flag on the kernel. You will have to reboot into single-user mode to complete each step of the process. Remember that when you boot into single-user mode (using boot -s from the loader prompt), none of the filesystems will mount automatically; you'll need to run mount -a before you can go into /usr/src and run the make installkernel process.

Running and Troubleshooting make installworld

After you've completed your kernels, it's time to reboot into single-user mode, which prevents multiuser processes (either run by other users or by daemons operating automatically) from altering files that you'll be upgrading. Collisions of this type can lead to serious instability. Using single-user mode is also a good idea simply because of the slight speed advantage and because it's nice to be able to bring the system back online completely upgraded and ready to go.

Reboot into single-user mode by using the reboot command. When you reach the loader (the countdown phase), press a key to get the loader prompt and then enter the **boot -s** command to bring the system up far enough for you to verify that the new kernel is working and to complete the installation.

> **NOTE**
>
> If the system fails to come up (it might crash, it may spew error messages, or there may be any number of different failure modes), first try rebooting normally to see if the behavior is different from case to case, and to try to determine what in the new kernel is causing problems. If you still have no luck, it's time to drop back to your old kernels. Reboot again, and try booting single-user with the backup kernel, as you saw a little earlier. Keep trying kernels until you reach the one you were using before you began the upgrade (which should boot without trouble—so far, the kernel is the only thing you've changed in the system). You may want to postpone your make world and try again from scratch after you've resolved the problem with your new kernel. Chances are that a kernel failure at this point is indicative of a more widespread and temporary problem that will be resolved in the source in the near future.

In single-user mode, you're root by default. The first thing to do is to mount your filesystems, so you can have access to the source tree; do this with a **mount -a** command and then verify that it worked by using **df**. Go back into /usr/src now and enter the final, most important part of the make world process. Installing the system binaries won't take as long as building them, but there is an equal chance of errors occurring—and this time, a failure will result in a partially altered system. Make sure to start your script output log before you begin this step. Here's the command for this step:

```
# make installworld
```

After this step completes, your binaries and kernel should be compatible; try running utilities such as ps and top to make sure they work properly. You'll get errors if the kernel and the binaries aren't built from the same source base, so if the utilities work, you can be pretty confident you successfully installed everything so far.

Anything that goes wrong during the make installworld step is potentially dangerous—you can end up with a partially installed system, with some of it compatible with the new kernel and some of it not. Fortunately, there are fewer things that can potentially go wrong than in the other stages. Here's the most common problem:

- **The installer fails, citing a problem with permissions or ownership.**

  This is the reason for synchronizing your /etc/group and /etc/master.passwd files before installing the world. Check again to make sure some user or group isn't missing and try again.

Using mergemaster to Check for Changed Configuration Files

There's only one step left in the make world process: merging the /etc hierarchy (and other miscellaneous areas such as /var/log and /usr/share). As you learned earlier, the make world steps don't touch /etc, in order to keep from stomping on heavily customized configurations. In earlier days, the only way to merge changes into /etc was to do it manually, a very painful and error-prone process. The mergemaster utility, a standard part of FreeBSD, makes this process a great deal simpler and safer.

A lot of safeguards are built into mergemaster; it's a very safe tool to use. Nevertheless, there always exists the risk of damaging your configuration, so as a precaution, you should make a backup copy of /etc. Fortunately, this is easy:

```
# cp -Rp /etc /etc.old
```

Running mergemaster

Typically, mergemaster doesn't really need any options; its defaults are set to sensible behaviors. This first time through, you can add the -v (verbose) option to see an explanation of what mergemaster is doing at each step. You can also use the -c option to use contextual diffs instead of unified ones. Here's the command:

```
# mergemaster -cv
```

The first thing mergemaster does is create a temporary root directory and install everything from the relevant sources into it, including the various trees of files that need to be "installed" rather than simply copied over. This "staging area," by default, is in /var/tmp/temproot. It shows you a listing of files that only exist in /etc and not in the temporary root directory (generally, these are files you have added yourself, so it won't touch them). Then, mergemaster proceeds to compare all the files in /etc and certain other locations with the new ones in /var/tmp/temproot. Whenever it encounters files that don't match, it displays the diff output in whatever pager you have specified in the PAGER environment variable (or more, by default).

When you scroll to the bottom of the diff display (or press > to jump directly to the bottom), you are given a list of choices for what to do with the new file, similar to Listing 17.3.

LISTING 17.3   Options for Merging a File in mergemaster

```
***************
*** 321,326 ****
--- 327,333 ----
  kern_securelevel="-1" # range: -1..3 ; '-1' is the most insecure
  update_motd="YES"     # update version info in /etc/motd (or NO)
  start_vinum=""                  # set to YES to start vinum
+ unaligned_print="YES" # print unaligned access warnings on the alpha (or NO).


  ############################################################
  ### Define source_rc_confs, the mechanism used by /etc/rc.* ##

  Use 'd' to delete the temporary ./etc/defaults/rc.conf
  Use 'i' to install the temporary ./etc/defaults/rc.conf
  Use 'm' to merge the old and new versions
  Use 'v' to view the differences between the old and new versions again

  Default is to leave the temporary file to deal with by hand

How should I deal with this? [Leave it for later]
```

As you can see, the default behavior is to do nothing, leaving the new file in /var/tmp/temproot for you to consider after you've finished running. This makes mergemaster a very safe utility to run.

If you select m to merge the two files, you are dropped into the sdiff environment. This shows you the old and new versions of the changed file, line by line, allowing you to choose between the left (old) and right (new) versions of each:

```
*** Type h at the sdiff prompt (%) to get usage help

pccard_beep="1"          # pccard beep | pccard_beep="2"          # pccard beep
%
```

> **TIP**
>
> Each changed line is merged individually, so the sdiff method can become tedious if you're using it to merge very long files with lots of scattered changes. You may be better off simply making a backup copy of the existing file, replacing it completely in mergemaster, and then merging in the changes later with a text editor and two parallel terminal windows.

Because each changed line is shown on different halves of the same screen, sometimes the two sides look the same because the only differences might be on the right half of the line. This isn't usually a problem (the only time it tends to crop up is on version-number lines in which a modification date appears toward the end of the line). You can get around it, though, by specifying a larger screen width with the -w option to mergemaster:

```
# mergemaster -cv -w 120
```

The sdiff command options are available by typing **h** at the prompt. Once you're done picking your way through the lines, you're brought back into mergemaster, where you are given yet another chance to review (or even remerge) your changes before moving the new file into place.

Once you're all done, mergemaster asks whether you want to delete what's left of /var/tmp/temproot. If you've left unmerged files to deal with later, select "no." You then exit from mergemaster and have the chance to go to /var/tmp/temproot to merge these remaining files by hand.

Troubleshooting mergemaster

The things that can go wrong with mergemaster, fortunately, aren't destructive to the system—especially if you have backed up your /etc directory. A few kinds of missteps are common, though, such as the following:

- **I accidentally overwrote a critical file in /etc with the generic new version!**

  Not to worry. If you kept a backup (for example, /etc.old), you can simply quit mergemaster with Ctrl+C and copy the file out of the backup directory and back into /etc.

- **mergemaster accidentally deleted the rest of the files in /var/tmp/temproot! I was going to get to those!**

  Just run mergemaster again and ignore any files you already replaced or merged. Make sure to select "no" at the last prompt, where it asks whether you want to delete the remainder of /var/tmp/temproot.

Rebooting After the Upgrade

Before you reboot, make a mental checklist:

- Have I synchronized to the latest sources?
- Have I done a buildworld?
- Did I compile a new kernel?
- Did the new kernel boot?
- Have I done an installworld?
- Do utilities such as ps and top work?
- Is /etc merged to my satisfaction?

If you can answer "yes" to all these questions, you're ready to reboot:

```
# reboot
```

When the system comes back up into multiuser mode, check ps and top again just to make sure everything's synchronized. Finally, run uname -a to see whether you agree with the kernel version:

```
# uname -a
FreeBSD stripes.somewhere.com 4.6-STABLE FreeBSD 4.6-STABLE #0: Wed Jun 26
➥21:39:53 PDT 2002 frank@somewhere.com:/usr/src/sys/compile/CUSTOM  i386
```

If it all checks out, congratulations! You've just completed a make world. You can now rest easy—at least until the next time you decide to do it.

Understanding Hard Disks and Filesystems

This chapter tries to make sense of what is surely one of the ugliest parts of dealing with a Unix system: disks. Compared to a Windows system (where a disk is automatically assigned a drive number by the BIOS) or a Macintosh (where a new disk simply appears on the desktop), Unix systems require a deeper knowledge of geometry, partitions, access modes, and other such esoterica. FreeBSD is, unfortunately, no exception.

As you learned in Chapter 8, "The FreeBSD Filesystem," the hierarchical filesystem structure of Unix does provide a more flexible way of dealing with files than is possible with traditional desktop operating systems. This flexibility comes at a price, however. To add a new disk to the FreeBSD system, it must first be installed in the proper physical position and then sliced, partitioned, labeled, and finally mounted at the selected mount point. This is a far cry from the two or three steps necessary to add a new disk in most desktop systems.

Times are changing, and the progress of hardware standards has eliminated the need for some of the really nasty underlying pencil-and-paper work that used to accompany the installation of a new disk. With the right knowledge (and the help of your good friend `sysinstall`), you can get the rest of the process under control.

IDE/ATA Access Modes

The most common type of hard disk for PC hardware is the Integrated Drive Electronics (IDE) interface. The IDE interface is so named because the controller chips that manage the disk are integrated into the drive itself, rather than on a separate host adapter card (as with SCSI). The official name for this type of interface is Advanced Technology Attachment (ATA), and ATA and IDE are often used interchangeably.

This chapter discusses both IDE/ATA and SCSI disk systems. Unless you're running a high-performance server, however, you are most likely to use IDE disks. They're inexpensive and ubiquitous, but they come with their share of annoyances and quirks. SCSI disks tend to be better made and faster, but they're also more expensive and require more expensive hardware. Regardless of whether you use IDE, however, it's worthwhile to cover these issues so you can be prepared if the need arises.

IDE provides quite adequate speed, and it's the built-in standard on all $x86$-based motherboards currently on the market. You will have to make a couple of purchasing decisions based on the highest access modes supported by the disk, the motherboard, and FreeBSD. An informed decision on this subject requires a bit of access-mode history.

PIO Modes

Programmed I/O (PIO) modes were the original standard for data transfer on PC hardware using the ATA interface. To this day, these modes exist as a fallback method, because PIO is a built-in part of the BIOS, and it requires no additional support by the operating system. Just about every modern operating system has moved on to DMA and Ultra DMA. Unless you're using very old hardware, you needn't concern yourself with PIO modes.

The five standard PIO transfer modes and their speeds are listed in Table 18.1.

TABLE 18.1   PIO Transfer Modes

PIO Mode	Maximum Transfer Rate	Defining Standard
Mode 0	3.3 MBps	ATA
Mode 1	5.2 MBps	ATA
Mode 2	8.3 MBps	ATA
Mode 3	11.1 MBps	ATA-2
Mode 4	16.7 MBps	ATA-2

NOTE

Most motherboards today use the PCI bus to talk to their hard drive chains. If, however, you've got a really old system with an ISA bus, the best it will be able to support is PIO Mode 2—anything faster is beyond the throughput limit of ISA.

DMA Modes

A fundamental problem with PIO is that it requires significant resources from the CPU to direct its data flow. This problem used to be one of the biggest reasons to use SCSI rather than IDE disks, because SCSI disks use an independent controller to take the load off the processor. DMA modes, introduced in the early 1990s and listed in Table 18.2, offer this same benefit to IDE disks by allowing the disk to bypass the CPU and communicate directly with the system RAM. DMA transfer modes require specialized electronics in the drive itself (particularly for first-party or "bus mastering" DMA disks) as well as operating system support, but this method is almost universal nowadays.

TABLE 18.2   DMA Transfer Modes

DMA Mode Standard	Maximum Transfer Rate	Defining
Single Word Mode 0	2.1 MBps	ATA
Single Word Mode 1	4.2 MBps	ATA
Single Word Mode 2	8.3 MBps	ATA
Multiword Mode 0	4.2 MBps	ATA
Multiword Mode 1	13.3 MBps	ATA-2
Multiword Mode 2	16.7 MBps	ATA-2

You may not have heard much about plain DMA during its heyday. As you can see from the table, its transfer speeds were comparable to those of the PIO modes. Although DMA disks did benefit from lower CPU overhead, this advantage was mitigated by poor support for the modes in the operating systems of the day, such as Windows 95. PIO was built in, so there was little pressure on the industry to move away from it.

Ultra DMA (UDMA) Modes

PIO truly lost prominence with the introduction of Ultra DMA. These enhanced DMA modes are now the ubiquitous industry standard, even giving SCSI a run for its money as far as performance goes, while remaining cheaper and better supported, even on low-end hardware.

Ultra DMA gave data transfer speeds a significant and immediate boost over standard DMA by clocking its transfers on twice as many points in the interface strobe, on both the "rising" and "falling" edges of the signal waveform. This technique, known as *double transition clocking*, allowed the controller to have a "free" doubling of data transfer speed, to 33 MBps, without reducing its cycle time. Subsequent incremental improvements to Ultra DMA, shown in Table 18.3, have raised the bar ever higher, aided by a new IDE cable standard that uses 80 pins rather than the 40 of the previous standard.

TABLE 18.3   Ultra DMA Transfer Modes

Ultra DMA Mode	Maximum Transfer Rate	Defining Standard
Mode 0	16.7 MBps	ATA/ATAPI-4
Mode 1	25.0 MBps	ATA/ATAPI-4
Mode 2	33.3 MBps	ATA/ATAPI-4
Mode 3	44.4 MBps	ATA/ATAPI-5
Mode 4	66.7 MBps	ATA/ATAPI-5
Mode 5	100.0 MBps	ATA/ATAPI-6

18

Any hardware made after about 1998 is designed to work in UDMA mode, and you won't have to worry about a thing if you have these four components:

- A hard disk that supports Ultra DMA mode

- An 80-pin IDE cable

- A motherboard (or IDE controller) that supports Ultra DMA mode

- Support in the operating system (or BIOS) for Ultra DMA mode

If you're missing any one of these items, your system will still run but in a reduced-speed mode, generally one of the PIO modes natively supported in the BIOS. Motherboards or controllers that don't support UDMA might prove troublesome. Issues with instability and lockups caused by controller issues can usually be solved either by upgrading the BIOS (to enable the controller to support UDMA) or by disabling UDMA in the disk itself through software utilities available from the manufacturer of the disk. These utilities typically run only under DOS or Windows and are either included with the disk or downloadable from the manufacturer's Web site.

FreeBSD fully supports Ultra DMA, making it perhaps the strongest link in this chain; you can see whether all the necessary components are present by watching the device-probing messages during boot (or using dmesg afterwards):

```
ad0: 6194MB <HITACHI_DK239A-65> [13424/15/63] at ata0-master using UDMA33
```

If the UDMA capability isn't detected and the hard disk is new but the rest of the machine's components aren't, you should find the disk manufacturer's drive management utility, boot the system from an MS-DOS floppy, and use the utility to disable the disk's UDMA capability. This will keep you running at a lower speed than the disk can go, but it's for the best. The alternative is to run the risk of crashes and lockups. Your system will thank you for not pushing it beyond its means.

SCSI Disks

If all this IDE nonsense is something you can afford to bypass, or if you will be attaching external disks to your system, your alternative is SCSI. At first glance, the litany of SCSI modes, shown in Table 18.4, looks hardly any less bizarre than that of IDE.

TABLE 18.4   SCSI Transfer Modes

Standard	Transfer Mode	Transfer Speed	Max Cable Length	Devices/IDs	Connector
SCSI-1	SCSI	5 MBps	6m	8	50-pin
SCSI-2	Fast SCSI	10 MBps	3m	8	50-pin
	Wide SCSI	10 MBps	6m	16	68-pin
	Fast Wide SCSI	20 MBps	3m	16	68-pin

TABLE 18.4   Continued

Standard	Transfer Mode	Transfer Speed	Max Cable Length	Devices/IDs	Connector
SCSI-3	Ultra SCSI	20 MBps	1.5–3m	4–8	50-pin
	Wide Ultra SCSI	40 MBps	1.5–3m	4–16	68-pin
	Ultra2 SCSI	40 MBps	12m	8	50-pin
	Wide Ultra2 SCSI	80 MBps	12m	16	68-pin
	Ultra3 SCSI	160 MBps	12m	16	68-pin
	Ultra160 SCSI	160 MBps	12m	16	68-pin
	Ultra320 SCSI	320 MBps	12m	16	68-pin

For all its "can you top this?" naming conventions, however, SCSI is relatively well behaved and predictable when it comes to its capabilities. Each successive standard is twice as fast as the previous, and although there's a truly astonishing number of different cable styles made for SCSI devices, the connector standard has remained mercifully steady over the years. This means that for the most part, any modern SCSI controller will recognize—and properly handle—any SCSI device that was built to an earlier standard.

An SCSI device chain can handle up to the number of devices specified by the standard, usually 8 or 16. That's a far cry from the strictly regimented four (primary and secondary, master and slave) of the IDE/ATA structure. What's more, the order of these devices doesn't matter; there are no such things as "masters" or "slaves" in SCSI to dictate cabling order. There's only the controller, or host adapter (which takes up one of the device IDs), and the rest of the devices.

SCSI also has clear advantages if you're using external disks. IDE/ATA provides no good way to hook an external disk to the internal bus; sometimes you can get away with using the parallel (printer) port, as with Iomega Zip drives, but this is an astoundingly slow interface and is unusable for any general purpose. SCSI is the only game in town for external disks until FireWire (IEEE 1394) becomes prevalent.

The biggest problem with SCSI is, simply, price. SCSI disks are generally pricier than similar-sized IDE disks by 50 to 100 percent. Beyond that, there's the cost of the host adapter card, which you have to buy separately from the motherboard. (Very few motherboards today are made with built-in SCSI cards, although the number is, in fact, rising.) These controllers aren't cheap.

If you're interested in going the SCSI route, you should know that there are more pitfalls to avoid that are beyond the scope of coverage here. These include terminators, the SCSI BIOS, setting device IDs (with jumpers), and what happens when you mix "narrow" and "wide" devices on the same chain. Further reference can be found in the many books dedicated to the subject or at the PC Guide Web site (http://www.pcguide.com).

18

Understanding Hard Disk Geometry

You'll see a lot of references to "hard disk geometry" in the online tutorials that explain how to prepare your disks, and you'll encounter this term every time you run fdisk (or the friendlier interfaces to fdisk that you use in this chapter). Fortunately, this is something that owners of newer hardware (that is, hardware manufactured after hard disks larger than 8GB were common) or owners of SCSI disks can skip or ignore. Disk geometry data is only there for informational purposes. The functional importance of this information is now no longer the administrator's responsibility—it's the hardware's.

One of FreeBSD's strengths, though, is that it will run—efficiently—even on older hardware that is considered obsolete for desktop use or to run Windows. Your 166MHz Pentium motherboard will support FreeBSD just fine. But there's a trap: Try to plug in a new 70GB IDE hard disk, and the system might not realize that it's any larger than 8GB. This is where the unpleasantness of disk geometry comes into play. To use the disk, you will need to use some techniques that have otherwise been made obsolete by newer BIOS technology as well as know something about the history of hard disk development.

Back in the mists of time, when registers were made only as large as cost would allow, regardless of future scalability implications, IDE hard disks reported their size as a function of their physical geometry. Four dimensions—heads, cylinders, sectors, and bytes—described the layout of the disk and subsequently its size, or the amount of data that could be stored on it (see Figure 18.1). Hard disks still have the same internal geometry as they always did; it's just no longer as important to understand it thoroughly as it was back then.

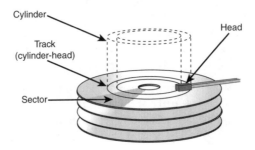

FIGURE 18.1   Hard disk geometry.

A disk is made up of a number of platters, stacked on a central spindle, with data stored on both sides of each platter and one or more magnetic *heads* reading each side. A disk with four platters and two heads per side, for example, would have 16 heads. Each platter is divided into concentric rings, or *cylinders* (not in a spiral configuration, as with optical disks such as CDs), and the combination of a cylinder and the head that reads it is called a *track* (or cylinder-head). Tracks are then divided into *sectors* (usually 64 of them, with 63 usable), and each sector stores a certain number of bytes (generally 512).

Each disk is shipped with information, usually on the label, showing how many of each of these subdivisions exist on the disk. You can calculate the total size of the disk by multiplying all of them together. The disk used for the demonstration of `fdisk` back in Chapter 9 had the following information:

```
# fdisk /dev/ad1
******* Working on device /dev/ad1 *******
parameters extracted from in-core disklabel are:
cylinders=1247 heads=255 sectors/track=63 (16065 blks/cyl)
Media sector size is 512
```

Multiplying these figures together (ignoring the blocks-per-cylinder figure) and remembering that a cylinder-head is equivalent to a track (to keep your units straight), produces the following:

```
1247 cylinders x 255 heads x 63 sectors/track x 512 bytes/sector = 10.2GB
```

But wait a minute... 255 heads? Does that make sense at all? No, first of all we'd expect the number of heads to at least be an even number. Even if we allowed for that, we're talking about what appears to be at least 64 platters, which just isn't physically possible in a half-inch-high hard disk. What we've got here is a virtual disk geometry, made possible by two successive hacks by the hard disk industry, which get around register-size limitations imposed by the original design of the disk interface in the BIOS. These two hacks are LBA and Extended INT13 modes.

LBA and the 528MB Limit

In the days of floppy disks, nobody ever thought that anyone would ever use a disk as gargantuan as 528MB; this is why that number was allowed to remain as the size limitation imposed by the number of bits the original PC BIOS (combined with the ATA/IDE standard) allocated to each of the disk geometry dimensions, shown in Table 18.5.

TABLE 18.5   Dimensional Limits on Hard Disk Geometry

Dimension	Bit Size	Maximum Value
Cylinders	10 bits	$2^{10} = 1,024$
Heads	8 bits	$2^8 = 256$
Sectors/tracks	6 bits	$2^6\text{-}1 = 63$

Therefore, a disk was allowed to have up to 256 heads, but no more than 1,024 cylinders. Because the number of bytes per sector and the number of sectors per track are relatively fixed numbers (dependent on physical limitations such as rotation speed and read reliability), and because you can't really put more than a few platters and heads into a drive you want people to be able to lift, this meant that the cylinder number rapidly emerged as the limiting factor in a disk's ultimate size. Disk manufacturers eventually converged on the ATA standard of 16 physical heads in a disk, so this meant a size limit of 528MB. The manufacturers could produce disks larger than that size by adding more cylinders—which

18

was easy because the stepper motor that moves the head's swingarm between cylinders can be controlled very precisely—but the BIOS couldn't address any of the cylinders above 1,023.

Around 1993, it became apparent that this wasn't going to fly as users' hunger for disk space continued to grow. A single video game could take up that much space! So, the BIOS manufacturers developed a scheme called Logical Block Addressing (LBA), whose purpose was to augment the BIOS disk addressing method by remapping cylinders above 1,024 to "virtual heads," thus taking advantage of all the available head numbers up to 255 that were going unused. For example, a disk with 1,852 cylinders and only 16 physical heads could actually be thought of as having 463 cylinders and 64 heads. Now the disk's calculated size was unchanged, and both the cylinder and head values were within their BIOS-imposed limits. All was well once again… for awhile.

Extended INT13 Modes and the 8.4GB Limit

The alert reader will have noticed that this scheme could only have been considered a temporary solution because eventually LBA would run out of room when both the cylinder and head numbers were completely filled—a disk size that works out to about 8.4GB. Indeed, it wasn't long—another four years or so—before disks were jostling at the 8.4GB barrier. (It should also be noted that 8.4GB was only a theoretical limit; many buggy BIOS implementations and supporting software tools used pseudo-LBA routines that introduced barriers at lower numbers.)

The solution was a newly redesigned BIOS interface, commonly called Extended INT13, which is now in general use in modern hardware and is used more and more commonly in the Windows world (where the software still must communicate with the disk through its BIOS, something FreeBSD doesn't need to do). This new interface abstracts the disk geometry addressing through a 16-byte disk-addressing packet, effectively removing any size limitation imposed by new hardware.

If your hardware is modern enough to understand the Extended INT13 modes, you're home free—disk geometry need only interest you for curiosity's sake. If you use a tool to try to extract the geometry information from a disk larger than 8.4GB, it will report 16,383 cylinders, 16 heads, and 63 sectors per track—a "code" configuration that tells the operating system not to even try to compute the disk's size from its geometry. If you see this configuration being reported anywhere, rest assured that FreeBSD is taking care of all this "geometry" nonsense itself. At least, until IDE disks reach 137GB, where they will be blocked once again by the ATA standard-imposed limit of 65,536 cylinders.

Practical Implications of Installing FreeBSD on Older Systems

If you're installing FreeBSD on older hardware, such as a motherboard from the days of LBA, you may well run into one of these limitations. You won't lose any data, but you may notice odd problems, such as your 10GB disk only reporting 8.4GB total space. If it does, you'll know what the cause is.

Many motherboard and chipset manufacturers provide BIOS upgrades, which can help you get past these problems. Check with the maker of the motherboard or chipset (consult its Web site) to see whether a firmware update is available. If not, you may have no choice but to invest in a new motherboard and CPU, or else to use lots of small disks instead of one large one.

Of course, if you've chosen instead to use SCSI or FireWire (IEEE 1394) hard drives (and if your hardware is modern, enough to support them), none of this need apply to you. These interfaces were designed with much more scalability in mind than IDE/ATA was, so their typically higher price is justified by their behavioral predictability.

Partitioning a Hard Disk

Okay, now that all the background is out of the way, it's time to get down to the action. Adding a new disk to the system involves four steps: installing it, partitioning it, labeling it, and mounting it. Depending on whether you've gone with an SCSI or IDE disk, the installation procedure varies; use the installation instructions that come with the disk.

The following examples assume you've installed a new 80GB IDE disk as the primary slave. The device name is /dev/ad1 (you can learn more about FreeBSD filesystem structure, device names, and mount points in Chapter 9). (An SCSI disk in a similar configuration would be /dev/da1; the rest of the instructions here apply just the same.) As you learned earlier, there's a lot more to a typical disk device name; the extensions beyond the initial ad1 specify additional partitioning information. This is how you refer to specific parts of a disk that you've separated for different uses—either so you can run more than one operating system from the same disk or so you can keep different parts of your system separate so they won't steal storage space from each other.

BIOS Partitions (Slices)

Every operating system allows you to partition your disk. The thing to remember about FreeBSD, though, is that it allows not one but *two* levels of partitioning. First come the BIOS partitions, addressed directly by the system BIOS in PC hardware; you can have up to four of these, which are what other operating systems think of as "partitions." If you partition your Windows or Macintosh disk, each partition is one of these BIOS partitions.

FreeBSD uses the term *slices* for these BIOS partitions, and it's important that you remember this terminology. When FreeBSD refers to *partitions*, it's talking about the second level of partitioning, which occurs within the slices. This second level contains what are properly known as the *BSD partitions*.

BSD Partitions

These BSD partitions are subpartitions that separate different parts of a FreeBSD system from each other—/var, /usr, /home, and the like. Each partition has a single letter for a name, and there are eight BSD partitions available, shown in Table 18.6. When you divide a slice into BSD partitions, the first few letters are reserved for special uses, but the remaining ones (listed as "General use") are free for you to use in the system.

TABLE 18.6   BSD Partitions and Their Purposes

Partition	Purpose
a	Root partition (/)
b	Swap
c	Addresses the entire slice, or the entire disk in "dangerously dedicated" mode
d	General use (not used by the Disk Label Editor)
e	General use
f	General use
g	General use
h	General use

Figure 18.2 shows a fully specified device name. The first part (ad1) specifies the base device name. IDE/ATA disks can be ad0 through ad3 (primary master, primary slave, secondary master, and secondary slave). Next comes the slice name, whose numbers start at 1 (s1). Finally, comes the BSD partition name (e).

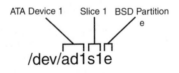

FIGURE 18.2   Understanding a disk device name.

Foreign Extended Partitions

Some other operating systems have constructs analogous to FreeBSD's partitions; for instance, Extended DOS Partitions provide a way to get subpartitions (logical partitions) into a DOS/Windows machine. Linux uses a functionally identical method. This method is in many ways more awkward than the FreeBSD solution. Interoperability between different operating systems can be fairly tricky; partitions within Extended DOS Partitions are treated by FreeBSD as additional slices on the same level as regular DOS partitions, but starting at slice 5 (after the four regular DOS partitions). To mount the second logical partition within an Extended DOS Partition on a disk installed as ad3, you would address /dev/ad3s6 rather than trying to use BSD-style partition names within a slice.

Going the other direction is even trickier. You probably won't be able to mount a FreeBSD disk in a DOS/Windows system, but you may have to do something like that on a Linux machine. Linux treats its partitions (called *slices* in FreeBSD) the same way that FreeBSD treats them, meaning that they're labeled numerically and sequentially, rather than hierarchically. To mount a FreeBSD slice under Linux, use Table 18.7 (which describes a primary slave disk with FreeBSD in its third BIOS partition/slice) as an equivalency guidance.

TABLE 18.7   Linux/FreeBSD Disk Label Equivalence

Linux Label	FreeBSD Label
/dev/hdb4	/dev/ad1s3a
/dev/hdb5	/dev/ad1s3b
/dev/hdb6	/dev/ad1s3e
/dev/hdb7	/dev/ad1s3f

This mapping scheme is reliable only if you don't have any more Linux partitions after the FreeBSD slice! Always be aware of the peril of expanding a hierarchical structure into a sequential one.

"Dangerously Dedicated" Disks

It's possible to simplify the whole hierarchical slices/partitions structure if you won't ever be using your disk under any other operating systems. Slices exist to allow a FreeBSD-formatted disk to coexist with other platforms without confusing their fdisk programs (or equivalents) with its structure. If this doesn't matter to you, you can configure your disk in "dedicated" mode.

Many sources refer to this mode as "dangerously dedicated," because unpredictable things can happen to your data if you try to mount such a disk under another operating system. Windows will ignore or nondestructively misread a "dedicated" FreeBSD disk, but OS/2 will destroy its data.

You use the sysinstall program to partition your disk. This program asks you at partitioning time (if you select the Use Entire Disk option in the Slice Editor) whether you want to use a "true partition entry" to ensure interoperability with other platforms. If you answer no, sysinstall uses "dedicated" mode, skipping the "slices" level of partitioning and dividing the entire disk into BSD partitions. Device names become greatly simplified this way; the disk described in Figure 18.2 would be simply /dev/ad1e in "dedicated" mode (the "slice" part of the name is unnecessary, so it is skipped).

The Slice Editor (fdisk) in sysinstall

To use the fdisk command in sysinstall as root, enter the /stand/sysinstall program and select Configure. Scroll down to the Fdisk option, labeled as the "Slice (PC-Style partition) Editor." Selecting this option gives you a list of all the disks the system has detected. Make sure that ad1 (the primary slave, your new disk) is listed. If it isn't, the disk hasn't been installed properly.

18

TIP

If `fdisk` doesn't detect your installed disk, check the `/var/run/dmesg.boot` file to see whether the disk was detected at all when the machine booted; if it wasn't, check your cabling and the jumpers on the disk. Remember that if you only had a single disk on the primary IDE chain before you installed the new one, its jumpers were probably set to the Single position; make sure the primary disk's jumpers are set to Master and the new disk's jumpers to Slave.

If your disk is listed, select it with the spacebar and enter the visual `fdisk` (fixed disk) editor. This utility exists in some form on every operating system, because every PC hardware–based operating system needs a way to control its BIOS partitions (slices). You can use `fdisk` directly from the command line, but its many options and potential pitfalls make interfacing with it via `sysinstall` a good idea. It's not especially wise to "work without a net" around such things as disk reformatting and repartitioning tools!

Any pre-existing partitions show up in the `fdisk` menu. A new, unformatted disk displays an essentially empty list of slices. You have a lot of flexibility in how you can handle these slices. If you really want to, you can do all your slicing here in this menu, setting up BIOS partitions for other operating systems or even for FreeBSD, in the Linux or DOS style. In most cases, however, this is unnecessary. In general, you should select the A option for Use Entire Disk to produce the results shown in Figure 18.3. Don't worry about any of the other options—they're there for flexibility and compatibility.

The utility asks whether you want to do this with a "true partition entry," as covered in the previous section. This is for you to decide. The tradeoff is device name simplicity for interoperability. The examples in this book are on a disk that is *not* dedicated, so you can see the interaction of slices and BSD partitions more clearly.

FIGURE 18.3   The Slice Editor, after choosing the Use Entire Disk option.

At this point in the process, you have three entries: a small "reserved" space for the boot manager to be installed later, a single large FreeBSD slice (`ad1s1`), and a third "leftover" chunk of negligible space that could not be made part of the main slice.

Nothing has yet been done to the disk. Select Q to quit the Slice Editor. You'll now be prompted for what kind of boot manager to install. If this is a secondary disk that you're adding to an already running system, select None. Install the FreeBSD Boot Manager (BootMgr) if you will be booting from this disk (if you're prepping this disk to be used in a new machine, for example) or to replace the existing disk in your current system. Otherwise, select Standard to do the equivalent of the DOS command fdisk /MBR, which removes operating system–specific boot managers (such as Linux's LILO and FreeBSD's BootMgr) from the Master Boot Record and makes it available to other operating systems (for example, if you're reusing the disk to make a new Windows machine).

CAUTION

The Slice Editor has a Write Changes option: the W command. This should be used before quitting the Slice Editor if, and only if, you are modifying an existing disk setup. If you're installing FreeBSD for the first time, or if you're preparing a new disk for installation, just quit the Slice Editor and move on directly to the Disk Label Editor. The W option reiterates this warning if you use it.

Creating the Disk Labels

The disk is now sliced and has been made FreeBSD friendly, but it still isn't formatted—you can't use it in your system yet. You do that next, in the Disk Label Editor.

Still in sysinstall, select Label (the Disk Label Editor). You'll again be asked to select from the list of installed disks; use the spacebar to select ad1. You're presented with the Disk Label Editor screen, a visual interface to the command-line disklabel command. This is where you assign the BSD partitions and format the disk.

CAUTION

FreeBSD's Disk Label Editor doesn't allow you to resize existing partitions. A partition can't be modified without reformatting it and losing its data, so consider carefully what your partitions will be used for before you commit your changes!

Creating a Complete FreeBSD Partition Layout

If you're just adding a new disk to the system, skip ahead to the "Adding a New Disk" section. This section of the chapter, however, demonstrates how to use the Disklabel Editor to assign BSD partitions and mount points for a complete FreeBSD system, including a root partition, /usr and /var partitions, and a swap partition. This is useful if you're going to be installing FreeBSD onto the new disk (for example if you're replacing your current disk with a larger one).

Press A to accept the "Auto Defaults for all!" settings. This automatically allocates a set of partitions that are appropriate for most systems (see Figure 18.4). You can probably go with the defaults if you plan to use your FreeBSD system as a workstation or a small server with only a few users.

NOTE

The automatic defaults specify partitions that add up to approximately 500MB, depending on your RAM size (in the case of the swap partition) and other factors. If your disk is not large enough to contain these default partition sizes, the A command will issue a warning, and you will probably want to set up your partitions manually instead.

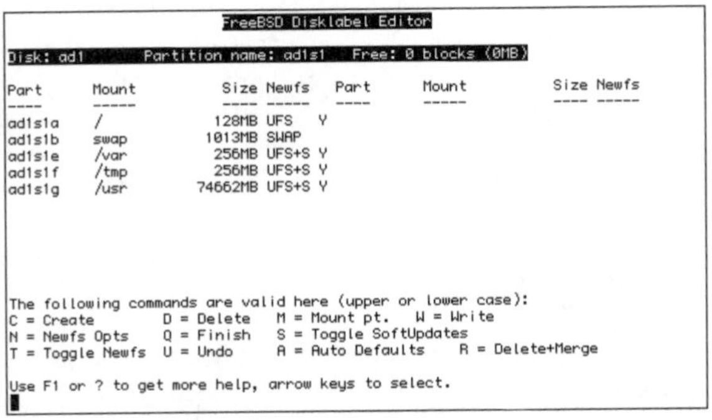

FIGURE 18.4   The Disk Label Editor, after using the "Auto Defaults for all!" option.

However, these defaults will almost certainly turn out to be woefully inadequate for a high-profile server. Mail and log files both live in the /var partition; if you have 100 users all storing their mail spools on the server, or if your Web server generates 100MB log files, the default /var size of 256MB will be exhausted almost before you can blink. You will need to allocate some more space to /var; this gives you an excellent excuse to experience some of the more flexible workings of the Disklabel Editor.

First, delete both the /var and /usr partitions. (Remember, nothing is actually done to the disk itself until you press W to write changes; right now you're just setting up the configuration for it to write.) Delete these two partitions by selecting each of them and pressing D. Now, scroll back up to the top of the screen, where the "Free:" field shows all the space you've recovered by deleting these two partitions. You can now reallocate that space as you see fit.

With the selector bar on the "Partition name: ad1s1" line, press C to create a new partition. You are given a dialog asking how much space to dedicate to the new partition. Let's give /var 2GB; that should be enough for a medium-sized server. (Give it an even higher number if you want to be really safe.) Assign this by deleting the number displayed and entering **2g** or **2048m**. Next, select FS to create a filesystem instead of a swap partition.

You're asked for the mount point; enter **/var**. The partition is created and added to the list, and the "Free:" space listed at the top is updated accordingly.

Now you can repeat the process, this time accepting the default size for the remaining partition (to use all the rest of the space on the disk) and entering **/usr** for the mount point. The resulting list will be similar to Figure 18.5.

```
                        FreeBSD Disklabel Editor
Disk: ad1       Partition name: ad1s1   Free: 0 blocks (0MB)

Part        Mount       Size Newfs  Part    Mount       Size Newfs
----        -----       ---- -----  ----    -----       ---- -----
ad1s1a      /          128MB UFS   Y
ad1s1b      swap      1013MB SWAP
ad1s1f      /tmp       256MB UFS+S Y
ad1s1e      /var      2048MB UFS+S Y
ad1s1g      /usr     72870MB UFS+S Y

The following commands are valid here (upper or lower case):
C = Create       D = Delete   M = Mount pt.   W = Write
N = Newfs Opts   Q = Finish   S = Toggle SoftUpdates
T = Toggle Newfs U = Undo     A = Auto Defaults   R = Delete+Merge

Use F1 or ? to get more help, arrow keys to select.
```

FIGURE 18.5   A customized partition layout.

Note that in the default layout, /var, /tmp, and /usr have the Soft Updates data-integrity protection system turned on (learn more about Soft Updates in "Journaling Filesystems and Soft Updates," in Chapter 8). A filesystem that has Soft Updates turned on is denoted by UFS+S; you can toggle this with the S key. Soft Updates are advisable for filesystems with lots of data that changes frequently; /var is therefore a good candidate, as is /usr.

Adding a New Disk

You can create up to eight BSD partitions on your new disk. Don't use the A option if you're simply creating more space to add to your current system; instead, with the "Partition name: ad1s1" line selected, press C to create a new partition. If you want to make one big BSD partition out of the disk (for example, if you want to add all 80GB to /home), accept the default value for the size of the partition—the entire available capacity of the slice you're in. Alternatively, you might choose to specify a size (such as "20G") for one partition and allocate the rest to another partition. It's up to you how to carve up the space.

Select FS to create a filesystem rather than swap space and then specify a mount point. FreeBSD 5.0 and later will attempt to automount the new filesystem at the mount point you specify. This means that you should specify the mount point carefully so that the proper entry in /etc/fstab can be made and the disk can be mounted cleanly after the disk-labeling process is concluded.

18

> **NOTE**
>
> Prior to FreeBSD 5.0, what you enter as a mount point isn't really important in adding new disks to the system; you can just make something up, such as /blah. The mount point only specifies what will be written into /etc/fstab for the new filesystem that will be associated with this partition, and this does not happen in earlier versions of FreeBSD unless you're doing the initial system installation.

You can continue creating partitions this way until the available space is all consumed. Delete a partition by selecting it and pressing D. Remember, the disk itself is not touched by any of these operations; no changes are written until you press W.

> **NOTE**
>
> There is an effective limit of four working BSD partitions that you can create in the Disk Label Editor. If you create more than four partitions, the "reserved" partition names will be used, beginning with a and b; c will be skipped because it has a specific reserved meaning. Beyond d, however, a "dummy" label of X will be used, and you won't be able to use the partition properly.

Writing Changes and Formatting the Disk

Formatting disks in FreeBSD is done with the newfs command, another command-line utility that is handled automatically by the front-end in sysinstall. Each filesystem in the list that has a Y in the Newfs column will be formatted when you commit changes. You can toggle this on and off with the T key.

Take a good look at the partition labels that the editor is assigning. These are listed under the Part column; you'll notice that no matter how you set up your partitions, the a through d partitions are reserved for special uses, as shown in Table 18.6. The first partition you can create yourself is e. This means that your new mountable partitions, if you're adding space to the existing system, are named ad1s1e, ad1s1f, and so on. You'll need to remember these labels for when you mount the filesystems.

When you're happy with the partition layout, press W to write the changes. The disk is partitioned, and newfs processes are fired off to format each partition you've specified. When the partitioning is completed, press Q to exit and then quit sysinstall.

Making the Filesystem Available for Use

You're almost done. All that remains now is to mount the new filesystems you've created. You may also want to set up /etc/fstab to mount the filesystems automatically on bootup (a full discussion of the mount command and how to use /etc/fstab appears in "Understanding the /etc/fstab File," in Chapter 8).

In this chapter, though, you're dealing with the simplest possible case: new, clean FreeBSD-formatted partitions. You can use the mount command in its most straight-forward way.

Create a directory to act as the mount point (for example, /mnt/newdisk). You can do this anywhere in the filesystem. Next, issue the mount command:

```
# mount /dev/ad1s1e /mnt/newdisk
```

Use the df command to verify that the disk is mounted. You can do the same for each new partition you created, placing each one at a different point in the filesystem. Unmount it with the umount command:

```
# umount /mnt/newdisk
```

Congratulations, you've tamed FreeBSD disk management!

18

CHAPTER 19

FreeBSD Survival Guide

If you were to read only one chapter in this book, this should be it. This chapter is a rough guide for new users of FreeBSD: a trail map showing how to get the system up and stable as quickly as possible. It is especially targeted at administrators coming from other operating systems who might bring certain preconceptions about how FreeBSD is going to act. This chapter can help those users to see beyond their preconceptions and avoid many common mistakes borne out of inexperience or unfamiliarity with FreeBSD.

The first few weeks with any new operating system are the riskiest—accidental misconfigurations can lead to security breaches, data loss, or general long-term disorganization. The key to surviving these first critical weeks is to get the platform-specific pitfalls out of the way and the necessary infrastructural safety nets in place so that you can tackle the more general administrative learning process at your leisure.

Newbies and veterans alike should be able to find useful information in this chapter. It summarizes the philosophical differences between FreeBSD and Windows as well as between FreeBSD and its much more similar cousin, Linux. It also offers suggestions for avoiding some of FreeBSD's general traps as well as some useful tips to help keep the system running smoothly. Finally, you'll learn about the inevitable specter of catastrophic system failure, the various weapons at your disposal for preparing for it, and—in the absence of the ability to turn back time—ways to recover from it.

Migrating to FreeBSD

At the time of this writing, and as accurately as these things can be measured (which is to say, not very), FreeBSD has approximately 15 percent of the open-source Unix Internet server market. The rest of that market is almost all Linux, with the remainder comprised of NetBSD, OpenBSD, and a few other little-known variants. In the wider server market, Windows NT/2000 claims about a 20- to 30-percent share, with Unix (both commercial and open source) estimated at about 65 percent. By any measure, this means FreeBSD is not an especially large player. However, market share alone does not dictate the quality of a piece of software (as anyone reading this book likely knows).

FreeBSD usage is growing. A steady stream of Linux-based and commercial Unix-based businesses are moving to FreeBSD for its stability and its performance, desiring an open-source solution that's free of the distribution politics of Linux (which is true because of its nature—FreeBSD is a complete operating system, whereas Linux is simply a kernel). Stories also abound of high-profile, Web-based services running on FreeBSD simply because it is the only solution that can handle the load (the services' parent companies' own operating systems notwithstanding). The end result is an increasing respect for FreeBSD in the server community, and a growing desire to move toward its tempting mixture of stability, standards compliance, openness, and power.

Migration away from Windows NT/2000 or Linux means a tradeoff of two things: software availability and established practices. These two things are the largest stumbling blocks typically faced by seasoned server veterans eyeing FreeBSD for the first time—the former applying more significantly to Windows (because more and more Linux programs are being ported to FreeBSD); the latter applying to both. The following sections look at both these migration paths in turn and address the barriers.

Migrating from Windows NT/2000

If you're switching to FreeBSD from a Windows server platform, the problems you are most likely to face involve not just what software is available but a number of fundamental differences in how the computer is used. The topological role a Windows server plays in a network is quite different from that of a FreeBSD server.

Windows NT/2000 is almost exclusively GUI based, without a mature or widely used remote administration method. This means that to use Windows NT/2000 effectively, you usually need to be physically sitting at the machine. Getting used to a command-line interface to do your work can be a daunting task, but it's crucial to Unix systems' great advantage of remote accessibility.

In this section of the chapter, you learn that setting up a FreeBSD server to provide certain common services involves much less commercial software, licensing, and client/server installation than is required to set up other servers. You learn about migrating client/server applications to the FreeBSD system, and you learn information about some of the important differences in maintaining security in FreeBSD rather than Windows 2000. An important part of keeping your system secure is keeping your system up to date; later in this section, you learn how to keep your FreeBSD system current with the latest developments. Of course, one big difference you'll notice when you migrate from Windows to FreeBSD is the change in software availability, licensing, and registration. When you move to FreeBSD, you deal with free and open-source software packages that you compile yourself, with support coming from grassroots Internet sources or third-party support services rather than from large software vendors.

> **NOTE**
>
> Built-in and third-party components of Windows NT/2000 are gradually increasing the remote accessibility of the platform. These days, you can manage services remotely that are controlled through the Services control panel, and various methods exist to acquire a DOS command line on the server machine. However, these are both subsets of the complete functionality of a system—they're limited to the functionality explicitly built in to the control mechanism you're using. Complete configurability of installed server software often relies on administrative client programs, as we'll discuss next.

Client/Server Applications

Most enterprise software for Windows servers is developed on a model in which you install the server portion physically (generally from CD). In this model, you then install an administrative portion—a *client*—on your desktop machine as well as on the machine of anyone else who will be administering the server. "Terminal server" packages are available, which allow you to directly control the server machine itself, but due to the intensely graphical Windows GUI, these tools are not simple or elegant to use. You must accept a major philosophical shift when moving to Unix.

There are virtually no specialized client/server applications for FreeBSD. Some operate through a graphical Web-based interface accessed by a common Web browser (for example, streaming audio/video servers, calendaring servers, and the like). For the most part, however, all administration takes place through a remote terminal.

SSH (or Telnet, as a recourse) is the dominant all-purpose tool for doing anything in the Unix world. Technologically, using Telnet is one of the most efficient and streamlined methods imaginable for working with the server—all you're sending and receiving is text. It's also the most versatile method, giving you much wider access to the server's operations than any graphical tool could. Naturally, though, this also means you have more power to break things. It's a tradeoff: the ease of use, safety, and directed functionality of Windows client/server software for the versatility, risk, and esoterica of terminal-based administration.

Security

Whole books have been written on the Windows NT/2000 security model, and the topic is well beyond the scope of this chapter. However, if you're used to the Windows style of users, domains, and permissions and you're moving to FreeBSD, there are a few things you'll want to know that will help you keep your security model roughly intact.

The "root" account is the equivalent of "Administrator." That is hardly a secret. However, beyond that there are a few things you can do to keep your services running with their accustomed privileges and to give your trusted administrators exactly as much power as they need—and no more. The first step is to know what some of the fundamental differences are between the Windows NT/2000 and FreeBSD security models:

- FreeBSD uses the User, Group, and Other mode bits to specify ownership and permissions, whereas Windows NT/2000 uses Access Control Lists. This scheme is discussed in Chapter 9, "Users, Groups, and Permissions."

- Windows NT/2000 has the concept of *trusted paths*, allowing for the implicit authentication of users coming from specified hosts. For instance, you can tell Windows to "trust" any user connecting from a particular computer under some or all circumstances, thus eliminating the need for user authentication where it isn't necessary. FreeBSD doesn't have this capability unless you use Kerberos, as you'll see in Chapter 29, "Network Security."

- Login names in FreeBSD must be 16 characters or fewer and contain only lowercase characters or digits. No spaces or special characters are allowed. In Windows, usernames can be as many as 20 characters long, although the same kinds of special-character restrictions apply.

- Windows NT/2000 has as many as 27 different assignable user rights for file modification and execution with various privileges. FreeBSD distinguishes between processes executed by root (the super-user), processes executed by individual users, and processes executed in setuid or "set user ID" mode, in which the process takes on the privileges of whoever owns the executed file.

- FreeBSD and Unix don't have hierarchical groups. Windows NT/2000 allows you to place a group of users inside another group, to an arbitrary depth; this is not possible in FreeBSD. All groups exist at the same "level."

- Windows "domains" don't exist in the Unix world. Instead, remote authentication services (as with the Domain Controller in Windows NT/2000) and security domains are handled by the NIS or "yellowpages" system. Details on NIS can be found in man nis.

- Peer-to-peer file sharing, done by NetBIOS under Windows, is typically done over NFS between Unix systems. You can do Windows-style NetBIOS file and printer sharing in FreeBSD by using the Samba package. NFS is covered in Chapter 32, "The Network Filesystem (NFS)," and Samba is discussed in Chapter 33, "File and Print Sharing with Microsoft Windows."

- Windows uses the Authenticode scheme for verifying code authenticity in downloaded software packages. This is a signing scheme by which downloaded software must present a "certificate" to the user for acceptance or rejection, adding a layer of security against potentially malicious software. Unix has no such standardized signing mechanism, but the FreeBSD ports/packages system provides centralized auditing and a measure of authenticity assurance suitable for nearly all applications. (This may change in the future, however, as the ports system becomes more distributed.) See Chapter 14, "Installing Additional Software," for more on the ports and packages.

Windows NT/2000 bills itself as being easier to use and make secure than Unix. The number of necessary security certifications in the Windows world suggests that this is not universally true. Windows is potentially easier to make insecure through misconfigurations that are made with the best of intentions. Although this is also possible in FreeBSD, historical data shows that it is less common. FreeBSD may suffer fewer security flaws resulting from misconfiguration because Unix is structured to encourage tighter security as a result of actions a new user might take. The large amount of concise and useful information available online for securing Unix systems certainly contributes to stronger security, as well. An excellent resource for such information is the SANS (System Administration, Networking, and Security) Institute, found at `http://www.sans.org`.

Software Equivalency

Table 19.1 lists some of the commonly used software on Windows servers and what the equivalents would be under FreeBSD.

TABLE 19.1 Windows Server Software

Service	Windows NT/2000	FreeBSD	Availability
Mail (SMTP)	Microsoft Exchange	Sendmail	Core system
Mail (POP)	Microsoft Exchange	qpopper	Ports
MAIL (IMAP)	Microsoft Exchange	IMAP-UW	Ports
News (NNTP)	Microsoft Exchange	inn	Ports
System logging	Microsoft SMS	syslogd	Core system
Web/HTTP	Microsoft IIS	Apache	Ports
FTP	Microsoft IIS	ftpd	Core system
Dynamic Web content	Cold Fusion, ASP	PHP, mod_perl, mod_python	Ports
DNS	Microsoft Active Directory	BIND	Core system
Remote access	Microsoft Terminal Server	SSH, Telnet	Core system
Directory Services	Microsoft Active Directory	OpenLDAP	Ports

It's worth pointing out that in the Windows world, unwanted interactions between different pieces of server software are often such a risk that enterprises typically will not run more than one critical service on the same machine. These systems have a dedicated mail server, a dedicated Web server, a dedicated name server—all different machines. The open-source Unix community doesn't subscribe as commonly to that philosophy for two reasons:

19

- Open-source Unix systems are often run for their low cost, so buying multiple servers often isn't within the budget of the operator or business.

- Software under Unix typically is much better behaved than under Windows, and detrimental interactions between services or daemons are much rarer and less potentially harmful.

You may or may not choose to follow the Unix method. If you do, however, you can generally feel more at ease and operate more efficiently running multiple critical services on the same machine than you could if it were a Windows server.

Keeping Up to Date

Microsoft provides system updates through *service packs*. These large collections of software revisions and binary patches appear every six months or so. Quicker responses (for instance, in response to security bulletins) come in the form of binary *hotfixes*—updates and patches that can be downloaded from Microsoft's Web site.

FreeBSD's method of keeping current can be a lot more complex than Microsoft's, but once it's understood, this method also can be easier and more effective. FreeBSD places a lot of emphasis on being available in source form for you to track if you like, keeping a local copy of the entire source tree synchronized at whatever frequency you choose. The CVSup tool makes this process both automatable and easy on bandwidth resources. If you prefer, you can also simply keep a source copy of the release version of FreeBSD that you have installed, as a substrate for source patches. Keeping a source copy is a good idea.

Any security bulletin that is sent out by the FreeBSD Security Officer contains a source patch or similar way to fix the problem. Line-by-line instructions are provided; all you really have to do is copy them verbatim to the command line, and you often don't even need to reboot after you're done.

You can, if you choose, keep your system completely cutting edge by rebuilding the entire thing from scratch, from your synchronized sources, however often you like. This process is known as make world and is covered in detail in Chapter 17, "Keeping Up to Date with FreeBSD." This is probably not something you need to do as a newcomer to the FreeBSD world. Rebuilding might prove useful later, however, as you build up experience and want to work with the very latest state of the system. For now, though, use Chapter 17 as a reference for synchronizing your -RELEASE sources so you can apply security patches and keep your system fresh.

> **CAUTION**
>
> It's always a good idea to keep a "backup" machine as a mirrored copy of your "live" machine. If you must do cutting-edge synchronization and use the newest code, do it on the backup machine first before applying the same changes to the live machine.

Migrating from Linux

FreeBSD is much more similar to Linux than to Windows NT/2000. FreeBSD and Linux are both derived from the same Unix tradition, they're both open source, and their security models are almost identical. The same software (for the most part, especially if you take into account FreeBSD's Linux binary compatibility) is available for both platforms. The same kinds of system administration problems occur on both platforms, and the same kinds of solutions tend to work as well.

Migration difficulties from Linux to FreeBSD are much more technological than philosophical, and so this section will go into more administrative detail than the section on migrating from Windows NT/2000.

Functional differences between Linux and FreeBSD can be boiled down to a few basic areas:

- Where everything in the system can be found
- Partitions and filesystem types
- Ports and packages
- Keeping in sync
- Technical esoterica

Where Everything in the System Can Be Found

The most important thing to remember about FreeBSD should be a mantra by now: Everything that you install goes into /usr/local. FreeBSD maintains this model very carefully to prevent pollution of core system areas (/usr/bin, /var/lib, and so on). Table 19.2 lists a few common locations for the resources you'll need, but bear in mind that the Linux locations might vary from distribution to distribution.

CAUTION

Some ports aren't as well behaved as others. Beware of ports that install components into areas outside /usr/local, as some such ports do exist.

TABLE 19.2 Comparison of Common Resource Locations Between Linux and FreeBSD

Resource	Linux	FreeBSD
Apache server root	/var/lib/apache	/usr/local/www
Apache configuration	/var/lib/apache/conf	/usr/local/etc/apache
Apache binaries	/var/lib/apache/sbin	/usr/local/sbin/
Sendmail executable	/usr/lib/sendmail	/usr/sbin/sendmail
MySQL database directory	/var/lib/mysql	/var/db/mysql

TABLE 19.2　Continued

Resource	Linux	FreeBSD
System startup scripts	/etc/rc.d	/etc/rc.*
User-installed startup scripts	/etc/rc.d	/usr/local/etc/rc.d
User-installed executables	/usr/bin	/usr/local/bin
User-installed libraries	/usr/lib	/usr/local/lib
User-installed shared files	/usr/share	/usr/local/share
System documentation	/usr/doc	/usr/share/doc
Documentation for user-installed software	/usr/doc	/usr/local/share/doc

Some of these resource locations differ because of the differences between the RPM method (the widely used Linux package manager) and the FreeBSD ports/packages method of software installation. Other location differences exist because of differences in the core system layout. Linux typically has more of a "System V" structure, whereas FreeBSD is, well, BSD-like. Refer to Chapter 14 for a fuller discussion of how ports and packages work under FreeBSD.

Partitions and Filesystem Types

The Ext2FS filesystem used by Linux takes a very DOS-like approach to disk partitioning: There are four primary BIOS partitions, one of which can be made into an "extended partition" with multiple "logical" partitions inside it. These partitions all appear on the same "level" to the user, even though the structure is, in fact, hierarchical. The system can be booted only from a nonextended partition, thus leading to a lot of potential confusion.

FreeBSD's hierarchical partition structure is much more overt. BIOS partitions are called *slices*, subpartitions are called *partitions* or *BSD partitions*, and the boot process handles the different levels explicitly in order to remove the mystery associated with extended and primary partitions. Setting up a disk involves first slicing and then partitioning the disk. This process is described in detail in Chapter 18, "Understanding Hard Disks and Filesystems."

FreeBSD's native filesystem is UFS/FFS. You can use your Linux disks under FreeBSD without modification, but you will need to recompile the FreeBSD kernel to support Ext2FS. See Chapter 16, "Kernel Configuration," for instructions on how to enable this option and build yourself a new kernel.

Ports and Packages

Coming from a Linux background, you may be used to installing software through the RPM utility. This is not widely used or recommended in FreeBSD. In fact, you can seriously damage your system by installing incompatible libraries into places such as /usr/lib, although it is possible to do if you really need to. The preferred method of installing and maintaining software in FreeBSD is through the package tools (pkg_*) or the ports. Chapter 14 offers a full explanation of ports and packages, but some aspects of how they work in FreeBSD are especially important to users migrating from Linux. Packages and ports provide a centralized filtering mechanism to tweak the build and installation options of software written for Linux so that it will compile properly under FreeBSD and install into the prescribed locations for user-installed materials. Ports and packages travel through the FreeBSD committers and the central download sites, rather than being available directly from the software developers themselves. This helps keep a FreeBSD system neat and tidy.

Keeping in Sync

FreeBSD is more "source centric" than Linux; because there is effectively only one "distribution" of the operating system, the entire installation is directly available in source form. The Linux world doesn't do this as effectively. Each distribution has its own structure and its own software selections. The Linux kernel itself is the only source subtree that you can be sure is the same as another Linux user's. Different distributions have different philosophies toward making the rest of their source trees available for automatic download, synchronization, and building. FreeBSD provides these tools.

This means that to keep synchronized with the latest development code, all you have to do in FreeBSD is to track the sources using CVSup, as described in Chapter 17. Security patches and hotfixes (available in Linux variously as RPMs, source patches, or binary patches) are distributed in FreeBSD both in source patch form and by checking in fixes to the central source tree. You can update your system in response to a security bulletin either by following the line-by-line patch instructions in the bulletin or by simply making sure your source tree is synchronized to a point after the fix has been made and then rebuilding that part of the system.

CAUTION

Patching system components without rebuilding the entire operating system is a method that usually works (especially for small, noncritical elements of the system), but not always. The more fundamental to the system's operation a component is, the more likely it is that you will need to do a complete `make world` in order to upgrade properly. Such fundamental areas of the system usually include the central libraries (items in `/usr/lib`) or headers (in `/usr/include`). Less-risky areas are the supporting binaries, in `/usr/bin` and `/usr/sbin`.

Working with Master Password Files

Linux and FreeBSD both use *shadow passwords*, a method of storing encrypted password strings in a file readable only by root (see "The `/etc/passwd` and `/etc/master.passwd` Files," in Chapter 9). However, whereas FreeBSD maintains an `/etc/master.passwd` file that contains all user data, with `/etc/passwd` being simply a subset (without the actual password strings), Linux does it a bit differently. Linux's `/etc/shadow` file doesn't contain any useful information other than the username and the hashed password.

19

With the combined /etc/passwd and /etc/shadow files from a Linux system, it's possible to put together a master.passwd that you can install into your FreeBSD machine and thus preserve all your users' login data. This can be done with a Perl script (available on the included CD-ROM as mkpasswd.pl), as shown in Listing 19.1.

LISTING 19.1   Sample Perl Script to Convert a Linux User Database for Use in FreeBSD

```perl
#!/usr/bin/perl
# Set this to the location of bash on your FreeBSD machine (if installed),
# or to /bin/csh to switch /bin/bash users to csh
$newshell = "/bin/csh";

open (PASSWD,"/etc/passwd");
@passwd = <PASSWD>;                     # Read in the /etc/passwd file
close (PASSWD);
open (SHADOW,"/etc/shadow");
@shadow = <SHADOW>;                     # Read in the /etc/shadow file
close (SHADOW);

foreach $user (@shadow) {
  @sdata = split(/:/,$user);
  $passhash{$sdata[0]} = $sdata[1];  # Make a lookup table based on usernames
}
foreach $user (@passwd) {
  @pdata = split(/:/,$user);
  $pdata[6] = $newshell."\n" if ($pdata[6] eq "/bin/bash\n");
  $pdata[1] = $passhash{$pdata[0]};  # Replace the "x" with the password hash
  splice (@pdata,4,0,undef,"0","0"); # Splice in extra blank fields
  foreach (@pdata) {                       # Print the combined output line
    print "$_";
    print ":" unless ($_ =~ /\n/);
  }
}
```

Make sure this script is set executable; then, log in to the Linux machine, use su to gain super-user access, and run the script sending the output into a file:

```
% ./mkpasswd.pl > new.master.passwd
```

Transfer this new.master.passwd file to your FreeBSD machine and put it into /etc (pwd_mkdb doesn't like working on input files and destinations that are on different filesystems). Open up the file in a text editor and then open FreeBSD's /etc/master.passwd in another window. You will need to modify the first block of about 15 usernames (such as daemon, bin, news, and other system pseudo-users whose UIDs are different in Linux and FreeBSD). Simply copy this block of users from FreeBSD's /etc/master.passwd into the new.master.passwd file, replacing the corresponding block in the new file.

Back up your existing /etc/master.passwd by making a copy of it. Finally, run pwd_mkdb to generate the new password files and hash databases:

```
# pwd_mkdb -p /etc/new.master.passwd
```

If this command completes without errors, don't log out yet—you need to test this while you still have super-user (root) privileges so that you can fix any problems that might exist. Also, test to determine whether you can log in as a regular user with a new terminal session. If you can't, run pwd_mkdb again on the backup file you created, and the databases will revert to their former state.

Technical Esoterica

A lot of extra little odds and ends are different between Linux and FreeBSD. Here is a list of some of the most visible:

- Device names in FreeBSD are less generic than those in Linux, but more descriptive. In other words, all Ethernet cards in Linux are eth0, eth1, and so on, so that you can easily tell that they are Ethernet cards, but you can't immediately tell one make or model from another. FreeBSD has specific drivers for each card manufacturer and model, with names that vaguely correspond to the manufacturer name (rl for RealTek, sf for Adaptec Starfire, and so on). Similarly, Linux hard drives are hda, hdb, and the like; FreeBSD's drives, depending on whether they are IDE/ATA or SCSI, are ad0 and ad1 or da0 and da1. These names tell you more about the specific kinds of devices you have; but they can be more confusing than in Linux, if you are simply trying to find which device corresponds to your Ethernet card or your hard drive.

- FreeBSD doesn't have a System.map file. Linux uses this table to look up jump vectors for commonly used kernel symbols. FreeBSD builds these symbols into the kernel, so you don't need to worry about them.

- The default shell in FreeBSD is tcsh, not bash. tcsh and csh are hard-linked to each other, so csh is the same as tcsh. If you want bash, you'll need to install it out of the ports or packages.

- The Linux binary-compatibility package (which you really should install when given the chance) creates a /compat/linux tree that contains a basic Linux binary and library structure for Linux-packaged programs that really need them. It also creates a linux.ko kernel module (you can check its status with kldstat). These structures handle Linux executables mostly transparently; some anomalies may occur, but for the most part the handling is seamless. You will certainly want to install FreeBSD-native versions of anything you can, however, from the packages or ports, if available.

19

- FreeBSD doesn't allow you to log in remotely as root unless you hack the /etc/ttys file (see the note in "Introduction to Users and Groups," in Chapter 10 for details). If you're at all concerned about security, you will want to leave /etc/ttys alone and use su to handle superuser duties.

- As of version 5.0, FreeBSD uses the DEVFS device filesystem rather than a standard /dev directory populated with "special" files. See Chapter 17 for more information on how to work with DEVFS and device hints.

- Devices on the PCI bus in FreeBSD are numbered, starting with zero for onboard devices and then increasing as they move away from the motherboard down the PCI chain. In Linux, the onboard device is typically the highest-numbered device, and the numbers decrease with distance for the motherboard. This means that on a machine with two Ethernet cards, the devices that were eth0 and eth1 under Linux might become fxp1 and fxp0 (respectively) under FreeBSD.

- Trading in your Tux t-shirts and bean bags for Daemon ones can be a little discouraging due to incomplete market penetration as of this writing.

Aside from adjusting to these minor differences, though, the transition from Linux to FreeBSD ought to be quite smooth.

Dos and Don'ts (Common Gotchas)

Every operating system has numerous pitfalls ready to snare the unwary. These pitfalls seem to be particularly dangerous when the system is newly installed. This section lists some of the most commonly made errors and some of the most valuable pointers for effective FreeBSD administration.

DO:

- Do use the ports and packages to install software. It's possible to grab the source for a particular program directly from the developer and compile it using its built-in scripts, but that just pollutes your core-system userland. If the program isn't available as a port, post to the freebsd-ports@freebsd.org mailing list and ask for it, or you can even learn the porting process and become a maintainer yourself.

- Do pay attention to the nightly, weekly, and monthly periodic output messages. Any setuid executable differences are flagged in the security report. The messages also alert you to filesystem usage, rejected mail hosts, and many other forms of visibility that are an effective "closed-circuit TV" against intruders.

- Do become familiar with CVSup. CVSup is your friend. Not only can it keep your source and ports in sync at all times, it can also serve as an effective mirroring solution, as you learn in the section "Mirrors," a little later in this chapter.

- Do install `sudo` (`/usr/ports/security/sudo`) and encourage its use. If you have to share administrative privileges with others, giving them access to `sudo` is an excellent way to limit their potential for damaging the system while enabling them to still effectively manage things. In fact, `sudo` is appropriate for *all* administrators on a system, including yourself. Never do anything as root if you can do it with `sudo` in a more restricted environment; an inadvertently trashed system teaches all good administrators to limit even their own power.

- Do use `ntpd` and `ntpdate` to synchronize your system's clock so that all the system logging and scheduled processes in FreeBSD that depend on the time being accurate can operate properly. You can do this by adding the following lines to `/etc/rc.conf`:

```
ntpdate_enable="YES"
ntpdate_flags="tick.usno.navy.mil"
xntpd_enable="YES"
```

  You can use any NTP server you like for `ntpdate`, which runs at boot time and corrects any gross time discrepancies before other services have a chance to run. You should also create an `/etc/ntp.conf` file to control `ntpd`, which runs as a daemon and keeps your clock synchronized with the NTP server (or servers) on an ongoing basis. See `man ntp.conf` for details on creating that file.

- Do be nice to the FreeBSD committers. There are only 15 or so of them, and the responsibilities of the entire operating system rest largely on their shoulders (as opposed to the collective shoulders of thousands of independent developers and distributors of Linux, or the corporate shoulders of Microsoft). That's a lot of responsibility. Be a cooperative and supportive user.

- Do decide what kind of security model you're going to have. Do you trust all your users? If so, you can get away with leaving a lot of system-level resources viewable. This way, when you have permission-collision problems (such as Web applications that must store clear-text passwords or write to a world-writable directory), you won't have to worry as much. If you don't trust all your users, though, you'll have to be much more careful. However, it's always best when running a networked server to lock down as much external security as you can. Even if you trust your local users, as long as your machine is on the Internet, it will be interesting to those who would like to break into it. See Chapter 29 for a fuller discussion of security in a networked environment.

- Do subscribe to the appropriate mailing lists for your version of FreeBSD. Unquestionably, you should be on `freebsd-security@freebsd.org` if you're running a server; `freebsd-ports@freebsd.org` and `freebsd-questions@freebsd.org` are also useful. If you're tracking the STABLE or CURRENT sources, subscribe to `freebsd-stable@freebsd.org` or `freebsd-current@freebsd.org` accordingly.

19

- Do monitor the size of your log files. Apache's `httpd-access.log` and `httpd-error.log` are notorious for eating up disk space if your Web server gets any kind of significant traffic. Use Apache's built-in `rotatelogs` utility or run a `cron` job to flush the logs occasionally. If your `/var` partition fills up, your mail, databases, and runtime files will not work.

  Also, do be sure to *read* your logs! The system isn't just writing out all that data for its health. Well, it is, actually, but it only works if you pay attention to what the system has to say.

- Do fly the Daemon banner proudly!

DON'T:

- Don't use experimental features on a production server. This isn't the place to try out new ideas such as Soft Updates and unsupported filesystem kernel modules. Try these things out on a cheaply built "hobbyist" machine or a mirrored "backup" server; then put them into practice only once you're comfortable with their use.

  Beware, however, that if your test environment is not absolutely identical to your live machine, you run the risk of software failing in the production environment even if it worked on the test bed.

- Don't port-scan your server if you're running PortSentry or another tool that blocks your route to the machine when it detects an intrusion coming from your IP address. You'll lose connectivity until you find an alternate direction from which to reach your server and delete the "blackhole" route.

  Try to be aware of any action or situation that might block remote access to your machine. If that happens, you'll require physical access to the machine in order to restore remote access.

- Don't use `shutdown` to drop to single-user mode (for high-privilege activities such as replacing the kernel) if you're running with the `securelevel` setting at 1 or higher. Using `shutdown` won't decrement the kernel security level. Instead, reboot the machine and enter **boot -s** at the loader prompt to boot into single-user mode. Simply exit the single-user shell to come back up the rest of the way. You must boot in to and exit from single-user mode at the physical console!

- Don't get hung up on uptime. If a system has 350-day uptime, this means the system has been sitting unused in a closet for a year or has not been conscientiously upgraded to keep up with security bulletins. Nonstop uptime doesn't make for such great bragging rights as one might think.

- Don't forget to add yourself to the "wheel" group at installation time! Very little is more disheartening than building a new server, driving 50 miles to the co-location facility, locking the server in a cabinet, driving home, trying to log in, and discovering you can't get root access.

- Don't make a habit of using filenames with spaces in them. This can be done with backslashes in front of the spaces, as with any other special character (for example, My\ Document.txt). There's no guarantee, however, that software will handle the filenames properly. Most of the time, it will, but there's still no guarantee.

- Don't write Perl or shell scripts on a local Windows machine and then upload them in binary mode over FTP, rather than in ASCII mode. Binary mode prevents proper translation of end-of-line characters, which occurs properly in ASCII mode. Although the body of the uploaded script might look perfectly fine, the return character at the end of the very first line (#!/usr/bin/perl) will be unrecognizable to the shell and cause the script to fail.

> **TIP**
>
> If you're having trouble with CGI programming and scripts that mysteriously fail after uploading, check the #!/usr/bin/perl script first; then make sure you're uploading in ASCII mode. Better yet, do your programming directly on the server. Excellent text-editing tools (such as vim, pico, emacs) are available for just that purpose.

Performance Tuning

In its default, "out of the box" configuration, FreeBSD is optimized to work with low-end hardware and to be extremely safe and reliable. This means that under heavy demand load, the system in its default state will perform more poorly than similarly equipped Linux or Windows servers. FreeBSD isn't an inferior platform; quite the contrary. Rather, it simply needs to be tuned for high-performance operation. The other platforms to which it's compared tend to be optimized for high performance by default, to the exclusion of low-end hardware. Very few sites that run FreeBSD servers do so without tuning the system for higher performance.

Performance tuning involves several different areas of the system, some of which require kernel reconfiguration (as you saw in Chapter 16). The following sections look at how to tune the kernel as well as components such as the disk.

Kernel Settings

You will need to tune your kernel to support high levels of traffic if your machine will be handling extreme loads. The GENERIC kernel is tuned for workstation or low-load server use so that its hardware requirements can be as low as possible. High demand for kernel resources can overload a system that hasn't been optimized to support it.

19

To optimize the kernel for handling high levels of traffic, change the MAXUSERS option setting, which is set by default to 0 (which tells the kernel to auto-tune this value). This setting is analogous to the "licenses" concept in Windows; it doesn't actually set a limit on the number of users who can access the system at once. Rather, it sets a figure from which other tuning values are derived; these values include the number of concurrent processes per user and the network memory buffers (or NMBCLUSTERS).

The maximum number of processes per user is derived from the following formula:

```
(MAXUSERS * 16) + 20
```

If you find that you're unable to run certain programs or perform certain tasks without getting "proc table full" error messages, tune the number according to this formula. Similarly, you will want to set MAXUSERS to 128 or 256 (or higher) for extremely heavily loaded systems or servers that have to maintain large numbers of processes or NMBCLUSTERS.

TIP

The NMBCLUSTERS setting, derived from the formula (MAXUSERS * 16) + 512, controls the number of available "mbufs," which you can view with netstat -m. Watch to see whether the mbufs are being used up. If they are, and raising MAXUSERS doesn't help, you can tune NMBCLUSTERS independently from its derivation from MAXUSERS. Set it in the kernel to 16384 or 32768 (or higher) for heavily loaded systems. Alternately, you can set it as a runtime kernel variable without rebuilding the kernel. Add the line kern.ipc.nmbclusters="16384" to /boot/loader.conf to set it at boot time.

Soft Updates and Asynchronous Writes

One of the features that allows FreeBSD to operate so safely on low-load systems is *synchronous writes*, meaning that the system has to wait while any write operations of filesystem metadata take place. This delay minimizes the potential harm to the filesystem due to a crash or power failure. This safeguard also makes the system run noticeably slower than comparable platforms, however, and it introduces artificial performance ceilings. You can remove these performance limitations if you so desire.

"Journaling File Systems and Soft Updates" in Chapter 8, "The FreeBSD Filesystem," discusses Soft Updates. Soft Updates is a technique by which disk write operations can be done in a software-controlled, orderly manner that speeds up disk input/output (I/O) and ensures that the filesystem remains safe should the system crash.

The Soft Updates mechanism is built in to the GENERIC kernel and is available for use at any time. The /stand/sysinstall installation utility integrates the ability to toggle Soft Updates on and off per filesystem, in the Disk Label Editor (as covered in Chapter 18). Another, more flexible, way to enable Soft Updates on a filesystem where it is not already running is to use the `tunefs` utility. FreeBSD natively uses this support program for the Fast Filesystem (FFS) natively. Run the `tunefs` program in single-user mode, in order for its changes to take effect, because filesystems on which it operates (such as /usr and /var) cannot be mounted at the time. Because `tunefs` is in /sbin, it is available in single-user mode without any additional filesystems needing to be mounted.

Reboot the system into single-user mode (enter **boot -s** at the loader prompt). At the shell prompt, enter the following commands:

```
tunefs -n enable /
tunefs -n enable /usr
tunefs -n enable /var
tunefs -n enable /tmp
```

Repeat the command for any other regular filesystems on your disk. Note that you might have to substitute /sbin/tunefs for `tunefs` in these command lines.

If Soft Updates isn't an option, an alternate way to get around the problem of synchronous writes is to force the filesystems to be mounted *asynchronously*, or in such a way that write operations do not hold up system functions. This option gives you the advantage of greatly enhanced speed, but it lacks the safety of synchronous writes. If the system should suddenly shut down while a write operation is pending, the filesystem could be damaged or even rendered irreparable.

To assume the inherent risk and mount a filesystem asynchronously, use the `async` option in the appropriate `mount` command or in /etc/fstab. A manual asynchronous mount would look like this:

```
# mount -o async /usr /dev/ad0s1f
```

To do asynchronous mounts automatically, add the `async` option to the fourth column in /etc/fstab:

```
/dev/ad0s1f            /usr            ufs      rw,async    2        2
```

Disk Geometry Concerns

If you're really interested in optimizing your system's disk access performance, you can squeeze a few extra horsepower from FreeBSD by arranging your partitions according to their placement on the disk. Because data can be transferred more quickly from the edge of a spinning disk than from the center, you can gain some speed benefits by placing your more active filesystems toward the edge.

The order in which you specify partitions in the partition table (in the Disklabel Editor in `sysinstall`) matters. The first entry in the table begins at the edge of the disk, and subsequent entries are placed further and further inward (the opposite of how data is arranged on a CD, which, incidentally, spins at different rates according to where the read head is).

The root and swap partitions are accessed the most, so place them as far outward as possible. Smaller filesystems also work better toward the edge than toward the center. With this in mind, the best layout is usually to start with a fairly small root partition, followed by a swap partition about twice the size of your physical RAM. Following this are your /var, /usr, and /home partitions, which generally tend to increase in size respectively.

> **TIP**
>
> In Unix, the algorithms that control virtual memory are optimized to work best when the swap partition is about twice the size of your onboard memory. For instance, if you have 256MB of RAM, use a 512MB swap partition. A smaller swap volume can result in speed penalties as virtual memory paging operations start to overlap each other.

A Few sysctl Tune-Ups

The sysctl program controls numerous kernel state variables, such as the kern.ipc.nmbclusters variable you saw earlier. The defaults for these variables are such that a low-end system can operate smoothly and safely, but not with great top-end performance. You can tune a number of these to higher-performance values by adding them to /etc/sysctl.conf, which is evaluated by init at boot time. The /etc/sysctl.conf file doesn't exist in the default installation; you will need to create it and add the following lines:

```
vfs.vmiodirenable=1
        # Allow the system to cache large numbers of directories
kern.ipc.somaxconn=8192
        # Maximum number of pending connections allowed
kern.ipc.maxsockets=16424
kern.maxfiles=65536
        # Maximum number of file descriptors (open files, sockets, fifos)
kern.maxfilesperproc=32768
        # Maximum number of file descriptors per process
net.inet.tcp.rfc1323=1
        # Enable timestamps and window scaling per RFC 1323
net.inet.tcp.delayed_ack=0
        # Disable TCP delayed-ACK behavior
kern.ipc.maxsockbuf=2097152
        # These seven lines increase the TCP and UDP send/receive
net.inet.tcp.sendspace=65535
        # window sizes. This can increase network throughput and speed.
```

```
net.inet.tcp.recvspace=65535
net.inet.udp.recvspace=65535
net.inet.udp.maxdgram=57344
net.local.stream.recvspace=65535
net.local.stream.sendspace=65535
```

Before you reboot with the new /etc/sysctl.conf, you can use sysctl to view the default value of those variables which are already set in the base system (some of them are not):

sysctl net.local.stream.sendspace

```
net.local.stream.sendspace: 8192
```

You can then manually set any value with the -w flag:

sysctl -w net.local.stream.sendspace=65536

```
net.local.stream.sendspace: 8192 -> 65536
```

Similarly, you may wish to set two or three variables in /boot/loader.conf, which is read by the kernel even earlier than init reads /etc/sysctl.conf. If /boot/loader does not exist, create it and add the following:

```
kern.ipc.maxsockets="5000"
➥      # Raise the max number of network sockets
kern.ipc.nmbclusters="65536"
➥      # Raise the max number of network memory buffer clusters
hw.ata.wc="1"
➥      # If you have IDE disks, this turns on IDE write caching
        # (good for data integrity, though it may negatively
        #  affect performance)
```

Helpful Manual Pages

A wealth of information is available in the man tuning page. This document is an essay describing some of the ideas we've covered here, such as disk geometry issues and how to optimize a filesystem according to the read and write demand on it.

Similarly, read man tunefs for a fuller discussion of how the tunefs command can be used to take advantage not only of Soft Updates but also of many other performance enhancements that are a part of FFS.

Finally, man sysctl offers a good description of the kernel state variable mechanism and how to use it to its full potential by tweaking the system's variables during runtime.

19

Preparing for the Worst: Backups and Mirrors

No matter how many precautions you take, no matter how much of a veteran you are, your system will be hacked, your hardware will fail, or something else will happen that will make your data unusable and recovery impossible. The only defense against this is to have the tools available for a complete rebuild from the ground up. Prepare for the worst, says one of the corollaries to Murphy's Law, and the worst will never happen. If precautions are the price we pay for safety, so be it.

Creating "Seed" Files

One way you can ensure that your custom configuration will survive a catastrophic failure is to gather together the "seed" files, which you can use to customize a new system that you build from scratch. These files can be preserved offline by burning them onto a CD or, in the absence of writable optical media, a floppy disk (remember, however, that floppies can be damaged and will deteriorate with time, so you need to make multiple copies and keep them fresh):

- `/etc/rc.conf`—The main system configuration file.

- `/etc/master.passwd`—The master user database. All other user databases can be generated from this one.

- `/etc/mail/freebsd.mc`—The Sendmail "master config" file if you have a custom Sendmail configuration. (The filename may vary according to what you have named it.)

- `/etc/fstab`—Important for re-creating your disk structure.

- `/usr/local/etc/*`—Individual config files for all the programs you've installed (the well-behaved ones, at any rate).

These are the most critical files—the ones that define your system and give it its identity. All told, they won't come to more than a few hundred kilobytes; those few hundred kilobytes can save you weeks of painful tuning and trial and error when rebuilding your system.

You may even want to package these files together into a tarball and mail it to yourself (at an account *not* on your FreeBSD machine) on a daily basis. Here's a sample command to accomplish this:

```
# tar cvfz - /etc/rc.conf /etc/master.passwd /etc/fstab /usr/local/etc |
➥uuencode seedfiles.tar.gz | mail -s "Seed Files" me@myaccount.com
```

You can put this into a shell script in `/etc/periodic/daily` or into root's `crontab` file, as you prefer.

Backups

The importance of backups can hardly be overstated. Any system administrator will tell you this. Yet, it's also no secret that doing regular backups is tedious, annoying, and expensive. Many administrators will wax lyrical about how imperative it is to have a backup scheme in place while not actually having one to wax lyrical about.

At the very least, you should become familiar with the various options for doing backups. That way, if you aren't using a backup solution, it won't be because you don't know how.

Many enterprises have a standardized backup procedure for safeguarding their data, whether it's stored on Windows, Unix, or Linux servers. This procedure can involve a central tape carousel and controller software running on a central server as well as client endpoints to that controller running on all the other machines to be backed up. The carousel controller collects data over the network from all the subscribed servers and writes tapes. The tapes can then be stored offsite so as to protect the data in the event of a fire or other catastrophic event that would render multiple onsite backups or mirrors irrelevant.

The software for these kinds of solutions is often geared toward high-end commercial platforms, and it's a rare case when a native FreeBSD client endpoint is available. Fortunately, though, many makers of such software are writing versions of their endpoints for Linux, and because FreeBSD has Linux binary compatibility, you may be able to get away with simply using the Linux software. For instance, the Legato client for Linux runs on FreeBSD, in most cases (although not without the occasional unpredictable behavior).

> **TIP**
>
> Linux software is often distributed in "RPM" format, which is used by the Red Hat Package Manager. As we've discussed before, the `rpm` utility is available for FreeBSD (in `/usr/ports/archivers/rpm`), but its use has some pitfalls. For instance, you might need to use flags. The flag `--nodeps` enables `rpm` to ignore missing dependencies that it expects to have in its own package database. The flag `--prefix=/usr/local` lets `rpm` put binaries into the standard FreeBSD location instead of `/usr`. The flag `--ignoreos` lets `rpm` ignore the fact that it's not Linux you're installing on.

In the case of Legato, native versions of the endpoint software are provided by an independent software company as part of an agreement to furnish unsupported versions of the software for platforms that Legato does not explicitly support, including FreeBSD. These packages are available in the ports at `/usr/ports/sysutils/nwclient` and `/usr/ports/sysutils/nwclient602`. These might work if the Linux version fails.

More of these specialized backup solutions are available every day, and it is becoming easier to find a commercial package that will work well with FreeBSD. However, in the event that no such option is available, you can turn to the standard Unix backup/restore tools for the backup basics.

19

Using dump

The built-in Unix utility dump is the good-old standby backup method. It operates based on dump levels specified in /etc/fstab (as you saw in "Understanding the /etc/fstab File," in Chapter 8). The dump levels enable a fine-grained "delta dump" system, in which you can do one complete dump at the beginning and then subsequently dump only new or changed files, thus saving tape space and backup time.

You'll need a drive to use as the backup device. You can use a tape drive (/dev/rsa0, the default), an external hard drive, or any device that can be mounted and written to during normal operations. SCSI has always been the interface of choice for backup devices such as tape drives, because of the speed and robustness of the interface and the general quality of the components. You'll need a SCSI controller for this, which will hike up the price a bit. Alternatively, you can wait until FireWire (IEEE 1394) devices have become fully mainstream and then use one of those. Also, IDE/ATAPI tape drives are available. However, make sure FreeBSD supports the tape drive you like before you buy it! The device need not be mounted for the dump operation to work—it will write directly to the device specified.

The following command executes a baseline backup, a complete dump of the /home filesystem:

```
# dump -0u -f /dev/nrsa0 /home
```

The 0 option (which is a zero, not the letter O) means to perform a level-0 dump (back up everything, regardless of whether it needs to be backed up or not), and the u option tells dump to update the /etc/dumpdates file, a human-readable data file that dump reads to figure out whether incremental dumps need to back up certain files.

> **NOTE**
>
> The nrsa0 device is the same as rsa0, except it specifies a "nonrewinding" device—a confusing way to do it, certainly, but this has the effect of telling the tape drive not to rewind when it's done. Tape drives, particularly SCSI ones, use this convention to tell dump how to handle the tape, as shown in Table 19.3.
>
> This is useful for when you're doing batch backups; specifying the nonrewinding tape device prevents it from rewinding after the first operation and overwriting the just-completed backup.

TABLE 19.3 Device Meta-Names as Control Options

Device Meta-Name	Effect
/dev/sa0	The actual device name
/dev/rsa0	Tells dump to rewind the tape when it's done
/dev/nrsa0	Tells dump not to rewind the tape when it's done
/dev/ersa0	Tells dump to eject the tape when it's done

After your initial level-0 dump is done, you can do incremental dumps with the same syntax, but a higher dump level number:

```
# dump -1u -f /dev/nrsa0 /home
```

The dump levels work by dumping only the files that have changed since the last dump of any lower level. Therefore, if you do a level-3 dump and then a level-4 dump later, the level-4 dump will dump only files that have changed since the level-3 dump. If you then do a level-2 dump, everything backed up with the level-3 and level-4 dumps will be backed up again. The lower the dump level, the more backups will be "forced." Level 0 is the "ultimate" backup, dumping everything regardless of previous dump states.

The typical procedure is to do a level-0 dump at the outset and then a level-1 dump at the beginning of each week, using a different tape (or set of tapes) for each week. Each subsequent day, a higher-level dump is done, often in the staggered "Tower of Hanoi" sequence suggested in the man dump page.

Recovery

When it comes time to recover, you'll be using the restore utility. This can be used either in interactive or noninteractive mode. Interactive mode is helpful for specifying a particular set of files to restore—for instance if you've accidentally deleted a file and you need it back. First, change to the directory (using cd) where you want to extract the file and then enter the interactive restore program:

```
# restore -if /dev/nrsa0
```

Within this program, you have a number of commands available to you: cd, ls, pwd, add, and delete, among others. These commands allow you to navigate among the files in the tape's backed-up directory structure, view them, and add them to a list (with the add command). You can remove files from the list (but not from the tape or disk) with the delete command. The extract command restores from the tape any files in the list at the time you issue it. Full syntax for each of the interactive restore commands can be found in the man restore page.

The following two commands add the directory called frank to the extraction list and then extract it from the tape back onto the disk:

```
restore> add frank
restore> extract
```

Alternately, you can restore everything from a tape's backup session simply with the noninteractive options:

```
# restore -rf /dev/nrsa0
```

19

A tape often will have multiple sessions of backup data on it—multiple days' worth, for example. A single tape might have a week's worth of backups, beginning with a full backup followed by six incremental backups. If you want a file from a particular day's backup, you will need to position the tape to extract from that session. The tool that does this is mt, the "magnetic tape" manipulation utility.

When you first insert a tape into the drive, it is generally rewound automatically to the beginning. To wind it forward to the third session, use the fsf (fast forward) option with mt:

```
mt -f /dev/nrsa0 fsf 2
```

Here, fsf 2 tells mt to fast-forward two sessions, putting it at the beginning of the third session. To move back to the second session, rewind the tape to the beginning (also using mt) and then fast-forward it again:

```
mt -f /dev/nrsa0 rewind
mt -f /dev/nrsa0 fsf 1
```

There are a great many more details to the dump and restore procedures that need not be fully detailed here. Using the -s option with restore in noninteractive mode to specify a certain backup session on the tape is one such procedure. Others include advanced usage of the mt utility, managing multiple tapes, remote backup devices, and so on. A good tutorial on dump and restore that covers these procedures can be found at http://www.nethamilton.net/dump.html. Also, read the man pages on dump, restore, and mt for documentation of all the capabilities of these tools.

Mirrors

Backups are certainly daunting, aren't they? It's small wonder that few people actually have the patience to do them. They do require a budgetary and time consideration appropriate to a small business at the least; a personal hobbyist system might find it difficult to justify the investment and aggravation. Fortunately, there's an alternative.

For just a little more money than it would take to set up a full-fledged tape backup system, you can instead create a mirror server—a second FreeBSD machine whose only purpose is to synchronize its files with the main server on a daily basis. You can swap those files into place should anything happen to the main server. And the tool you use to do the mirroring? You guessed it: CVSup.

Ideally, your secondary server should be in a physically different location from the main server. CVSup's incremental backup system makes it possible to do this, even if the bandwidth available between the two systems is very limited.

Setting Up a CVSup Mirroring Solution

Let's say you want to mirror four directory structures: /home, /usr/local/www, /var/mail, and /etc. (You may well want to do more than just these in your situation, but these will suffice for this example.) The first step is to set up a base directory—a configuration staging area on the main server. The base directory lets cvsupd (which is installed in /usr/local/sbin as part of the cvsup port or package, which you should already have installed) know what collections to serve to clients, such as your mirror machine.

Enter the following commands as root:

```
# cd /usr/local/etc
# mkdir -p cvsup/sup
# cd cvsup/sup
# mkdir home www mail etc
```

Now, in each of these four new subdirectories, you need to create two files: the .cvs file and the releases file. These files describe a "collection" to the cvsupd server and enable it to be served. In the home subdirectory, create a file called home.cvs with the following contents:

```
upgrade home
rsymlink *
```

Next, create a file called releases with the following contents:

```
home list=home.cvs prefix=/
```

Do this for each of the four subdirectories, changing the name of the .cvs file to match the name of the directory or collection as well as altering the contents accordingly.

Running the cvsupd Server

When you have set up the base directory, you can start up the cvsupd server. The -C option limits the number of simultaneous clients to 1, and -l (the lowercase letter L) specifies where to send logging information:

```
# cvsupd -b /usr/local/etc/cvsup -C 1 -l /dev/stdout
```

Now you're done with the main server, so you can move on to the secondary server, the one that will act as a client to the CVSup server you've just set up.

Create a file in /etc called mirror-supfile (or anything you like). The contents should be as shown in Listing 19.2, in which server1.hostname.com is the hostname of your main server, from which you will be mirroring content. You can use simple hostnames, fully qualified domain names, or IP addresses for the host parameter.

LISTING 19.2   Example CVSup Configuration File (`mirror-supfile`)

```
*default host=server1.hostname.com
*default delete use-rel-suffix
*default compress
*default preserve

*default base=/usr
*default release=home
home

*default base=/usr/local
*default release=www
www

*default base=/var
*default release=mail
mail

*default base=/usr
*default release=etc
etc
```

Notice the final entry: It's not /etc that we're mirroring the main server's /etc into but rather /usr/etc. The reasons for this is that /etc is important to each machine, where it is customized for that machine specifically; you want to mirror /etc into a safe location, rather than overwriting your secondary server's /etc with that of the main server. In any case, this is a good excuse to demonstrate the flexibility of CVSup, showing how you can "check out" a collection of files into any location on the second server.

Running the CVSup Mirroring Process

Once the `mirror-supfile` is created, you're ready to do your first mirroring operation. Start up the CVSup process:

```
# cvsup -L 2 /etc/mirror-supfile
```

You'll be flooded with output, telling you exactly what is being transferred and how. You can use Ctrl+C to break out at any time—CVSup will exit cleanly and pick up where it left off the next time through. This first transfer process will take a very long time—as long as it takes to transfer all the specified data from one server to the other via any other means. It's the subsequent processes that will be fast and efficient.

Once your /usr/etc has been transferred, you can copy the master.passwd file out of it and use pwd_mkdb, as you saw earlier in the "Migrating from Linux" section, to synchronize your users. You may choose to do this as a daily automated task if you have a lot of users or add them regularly; CVSup will skip any file that it can determine has the same checksum and the same ownership information, but the ownership information won't be the same if the users on one system don't match the ones on the other! If a file is owned by a user that doesn't exist on the secondary system, CVSup will "rsync" it every time the mirror process is run, which doesn't take anywhere near as long as transferring the entire file, but it takes much longer than simply skipping the file. Keeping the user database synchronized can speed up the CVSup process from 4 or 5 hours down to about 15 minutes.

Once the mirroring process is working smoothly each time you run it, you can add it to your /etc/periodic/daily or root's crontab, whichever you prefer. You'll get the verbose output mailed to you each night for your edification. Reduce the -L level if you want to see less output.

You can create more collections on the server side if you want; just make more directories in /usr/local/etc/cvsup/sup and add them to mirror-supfile. You don't need to restart the cvsupd process—it will pick up the new collections automatically.

NOTE

Mirroring isn't a complete alternative to incremental backups. It's a solution for an administrator who doesn't need historical auditing, revision control, or offsite backup archives. Put simply, it isn't a perfect solution for a business using FreeBSD as its server platform. Mirroring provides a quick-and-easy solution to a sudden catastrophic failure. For business use, you really can't beat tape backups, tedious as they are.

CHAPTER **20**

Introduction to Perl Programming

Perl is an interpreted programming language, particularly suited for text processing, that is widely used for such tasks as system administration and CGI scripting for active Web content. Its name stands for *Practical Extraction and Report Language* (although several less-flattering variants exist). Perl was written by Larry Wall as a replacement for awk. He is still Perl's chief architect and is currently (as of this writing) working on the newly redesigned Perl 6.

It's almost impossible to work in the Unix world or on the Internet in general today without at least some understanding of the Perl language. Despite many structural inconsistencies and quirks, Perl has managed to become the *de facto* tool for writing quick but versatile programs for just about any purpose. Perl doesn't have to be compiled like C code, and its free-form syntax-checking and its built-in data typing and memory management eliminate many of the headaches of programming in more traditional compiled languages. Therefore, Perl can be used quite effectively with very little programming expertise.

This chapter covers some of the basics of Perl so that you can take advantage of Perl's strengths without having to know enough about programming to be limited by its weaknesses. The chapter discusses Perl in just enough detail to provide a useful base for writing simple scripts and understanding the concepts in some of the more complex scripts that currently exist. This Perl foundation will help you teach yourself further Perl techniques by example, using the Perl-based utilities available in FreeBSD or any prewritten tools you might download.

> **NOTE**
>
> Many, many large books have been written on the subject of Perl. Its usefulness in today's world is so vast, its presence so ubiquitous, and its structure so complex that even those who can claim mastery of Perl are frequently surprised by hidden quirks or tricks that the language can accomplish. You'll learn more about some excellent Perl books and other resources at the end of this chapter.

Perl in FreeBSD

Some of the programs that make up FreeBSD's core installation are actually Perl scripts. The rest are generally compiled binaries, built from source code written in C, C++, or a number of other popular languages. These binaries cannot be read by a human or easily decompiled back to source form. Perl code, on the other hand, does not need to be compiled. It exists as plain text, easily readable and editable, and is run with the help of the Perl interpreter, `/usr/local/bin/perl`.

> **NOTE**
>
> Until FreeBSD 5.0, Perl was included by default in the core operating system. For a variety of reasons, it is no longer in `/usr/bin` as part of a newly installed system and must be installed from the ports (`/usr/ports/lang/perl5`).

Chapter 12, "Shell Programming," describes how to write scripts using the shell interpreter `/bin/sh` by specifying the name of the interpreter on the first line of the script. Perl scripts work the same way. The difference is that whereas shell scripts are primarily useful as "batch programs" (in MS-DOS parlance) that execute sequences of system commands as they would be entered on the command line with simple variable substitution and flow control, Perl is a fully functional programming environment that allows you to write programs as complex as Web servers or database-management systems. Because they're interpreted rather than compiled, Perl programs tend to be slower in execution (especially to start) than their C counterparts, although C programs typically take longer to develop properly. Perl's primary strengths are in string processing and text handling, however. Therefore, the ideal application for a Perl program is as a system-utility script (such as adduser) or a CGI program that performs string manipulations and operations on files. Perl can be less efficient at doing heavy-duty mathematics than a well-designed C or C++ program.

Perl is used in this capacity throughout FreeBSD. Some examples of system utilities written in Perl are adduser and sockstat. It's still more widely found in third-party applications such as majordomo, the popular mailing list manager. You will probably run into Perl programs at least as frequently in FreeBSD as you will shell scripts, so it's important to know how to work with them.

Strengths of Perl

Perl strikes a balance between the ease of use of shell scripting (a high-level approach) and the versatility of C programming (a low-level approach). The result is a language that allows you to use variables of many different data types—including data structures, importable objects, associative arrays, multidimensional arrays, and I/O handles—without having to worry about casting variables from one type to another, allocating and freeing memory, predeclaring variables, dereferencing pointers, prototyping functions, and performing a number of the other onerous tasks associated with programming in C, including compiling binaries.

Perl gives you extreme freedom to do what you like without getting bogged down in the convoluted and bug-prone details of low-level programming. The high-level tools that make Perl what it is are largely responsible for Perl's vast acceptance as the language of choice for CGI programming and server-side Web applications, a field that has grown explosively over the years due to the increase in e-commerce.

Perl's specific purpose is to provide superior string-manipulation tools: pattern matching, string replacement and translation, regular expressions, and a structure that makes it very straightforward to read and write text files using native arrays of strings. There is no need in Perl to declare a variable as being a string, an integer, a character, or any other type. Perl recognizes variable types in a cascading structure of appropriateness, assigning the necessary memory to each variable as it is modified and applying operators appropriately according to the variable's type.

Perl gives you what is arguably the best mixture of ease of use and programming power in any widely used language. Its syntax is extremely lax and flexible, letting you get away with many minor mistakes that other languages would punish severely. It's extensible (with thousands of importable library modules available throughout the Internet), it's well-documented and well-supported, and it's available everywhere—on dozens of different platforms. You can be sure that a Perl script will operate the same no matter where you run it—whether it's on Linux, Mac OS X, IRIX, Windows, or FreeBSD. This is why Perl remains the tool of choice for management utilities within FreeBSD—not just scripts that form part of the operating system itself, but in allowing the administrator to extend the system's capabilities with cron jobs, database-management tools, and CGI applications.

Weaknesses of Perl

Perl was never designed as the general-purpose language it has become. It started life as a string-processing language, and over the years more and more functionality has been heaped upon it. The result is that text-processing remains extremely fast and efficient in Perl, but it does so at the expense of structural elegance. Although Perl's strengths are very significant assets indeed, Perl is not widely regarded as a model of ideal language design.

Although Perl's laxness lets the programmer get away with many types of mistakes, this has the effect of encouraging sloppy code (much as a standards-lax Web browser will

20

encourage invalid or incompatible HTML code). Perl accepts syntax that resembles C, BASIC, Fortran, or even common language in some cases. Although this gives the language great flexibility, it also means that Perl code that's perfectly natural to one programmer might be unreadable to another. Perl's structure allows many different ways to do any given task; this results in a learning curve that grows much steeper after the initial easy introduction to the language, and it means that unless certain coding practices are enforced, Perl programs can be a severe challenge for multiple programmers to maintain. Perl is in many ways the "black sheep" of the programming language community.

Python and Post-Perl Programming

Many new projects have attempted to fill in for Perl's shortcomings since its meteoric rise to prevalence. Many, such as REBOL, Java, and Ruby, have been under development since Perl gained critical mass in the server-programming world. The frontrunner, however, is a language dating back to about the same time as Perl's beginnings: Python.

Python is an even more object-oriented language than Perl, and it has a much more regimented syntax. No C-style brackets are used; instead, tab indentations are significant, greatly simplifying the hierarchical nesting of flow-control blocks. Python also uses dotted-object hierarchies and tightly structured modules (or *dictionaries*), providing a much more direct and extensible interface to objects than Perl can.

Whereas Perl programs are compiled with each runtime, Python generates compiled bytecode (a .pyc file) at the first run of a program, which speeds up execution on subsequent occasions. This is partially necessary because, as with all object-oriented programming environments, the trade-off is speed for structure. Because of its strict object-oriented nature, in which syntactic structure and a single method of doing things are paramount to its design, Python is potentially less susceptible to bugs than is Perl. Python also is easier to maintain because it is less prone to "spaghetti code." Python lacks many text-processing capabilities, though, which is the area where Perl shines the most.

Although Python is not a part of the core FreeBSD system, it is available from the ports collection, in /usr/ports/lang/python. Its proponents continue to gain strength and credibility, and Python may eclipse Perl as the dominant interpreted programming language before too much longer.

Fundamentals of Perl Scripting

A Perl script is effectively similar to a shell script, such as those explained in Chapter 12. The first line (known as the *interpreter line*) tells the shell which interpreter to use to run the rest of the script's contents:

```
#/usr/bin/perl
```

The rest of the script, as in shell programming, is made up of variable assignments, flow-control blocks and loops, system calls, and operations on I/O handles—to name a few fundamental parts of a script's anatomy. Here's a simple example:

```
#!/usr/bin/perl

$string = "Hello world!";
$hostname = `hostname`;
if ($hostname eq "uncia") {
  print $string."\n";
  print `date`;
}
```

Notice the use of C-style curly brackets to delimit the if block, rather than the "if/fi" and "case/esac" syntax of shell scripting. Also as in C, each statement is terminated by a semicolon (;), allowing you to use multiline statements in most cases. The whitespace between the statements and operators is also optional: "$a = 1" is just as valid as "$a=1". Perl's syntax much more closely resembles that of a simplified version of C than that of the shell language. Think of Perl as a cross between shell scripting and C, incorporating the best features of both.

A Perl script doesn't need to be compiled. This makes debugging very easy: Just edit the file, make a change, run it again, see what new errors there are, and edit it again. The Perl interpreter does the "compiling" at runtime, and it doesn't write out any compiled byte-code. This makes Perl slower than full-fledged C—which is why almost all critical system functions are written in C—but it's fine for scripts that aren't especially time or performance sensitive, such as adduser or the string-processing functionality of majordomo.

To run a Perl script, you have to set it as executable. This is done with the chmod command:

```
# chmod +x myscript.pl
```

This should result in the following permissions, which we know as 0755 (see Chapter 9, "Users, Groups, and Permissions," for details on permissions):

```
-rwxr-xr-x  1 frank  frank  170 Jun 14  2000 myscript.pl*
```

> **NOTE**
>
> The script must be in a directory to which you have execute permissions, as well as itself being executable.

Now, to run the script, you would use the ./ prefix to specify the script in the current directory because you most likely won't have "." (the current directory) in your path, especially as root:

```
# ./myscript.pl
Hello world!
Sat Apr 28 15:29:17 PDT 2001
```

20

Because Perl scripts are interpreted, you don't necessarily have to make them executable in order to run them, or even have the interpreter line at the top. If you prefer, although this method is less conveniently "encapsulated" than the previous method, you can run the script as an argument to perl itself. This way you can run the program even if the script is not set executable or does not contain the interpreter line:

```
# perl myscript.pl
```

Some arguments to perl can be used in either of these contexts. The -w switch, for example, turns on warnings in which the Perl interpreter informs you of improperly written code that can execute but isn't deterministically correct. You can use the -w switch in either of the following ways if you want to ensure that the code you write is "proper":

```
# perl -w myscript.pl
```

or

```
#!/usr/bin/perl -w
```

Variables and Operators

A variable in Perl is either a scalar or an array, which are two different ways of storing pieces of data. This data can take the form of a number (expressed in any of several different ways), a string of text, or other various types of what are known in Perl as *literals*— pieces of data, such as 3 or car, whose meanings are exactly as represented. A scalar variable (the most common kind) has a name beginning with the dollar sign ($).

The nice thing about Perl is that you never have to worry about whether a number is an integer, a float, a short, a long, or whatever. You also don't need to treat a string as an array of characters, a pointer to a string in memory, or anything like that. Perl handles all that stuff internally. You don't even have to convert strings to numbers, or vice versa. Perl will recognize if a string has only numbers in it and allow you to multiply it by a number or apply any mathematical operators to it. Everything from the first nonnumerical character in a string onward is dropped, so 123blah would be treated by numerical operators as 123, and blah would be treated as zero.

Operators are available to modify these variables. There are the mathematical operators you'd expect: +, -, =, and so on. C-style incrementation operators are available (++ and --), as are space-saving composite mathematical operators (+=, -=, *=, and so on). Extra operators include exponentiation (**), modulus (%), and the comparison operators used in conditional clauses (>, <, =>, =<, ==, and !=). Strings can be concatenated with the dot operator (.) or repeated any number of times using the string repetition operator (x).

Perl makes use of more operators than you are ever likely to need to know about. Full coverage of these operators could fill an entire book, but Table 20.1 lists the purposes of some of the common operators you're likely to use when writing scripts for use in FreeBSD.

TABLE 20.1   Perl Operators

Operator	Meaning	Usage	Value of $c
+	Addition	`$c = $a + $b;`	7
-	Subtraction	`$c = $a - $b;`	1
*	Multiplication	`$c = $a * $b;`	12
/	Division	`$c = $a / $b;`	1.333...
=	Assignment	`$c = $a;`	4
+=	Implicit addition	`$c += $a;`	$c + 4
++	Incrementation	`$c++;`	$c + 1
**	Exponentiation	`$c = $a ** $b;`	64
%	Modulus	`$c = $a % $b;`	1
.	Concatenation	`$c = $a . $b;`	43
x	Repetition	`$c = $a x $b;`	444
>	Greater than		
<	Less than		
>=	Greater than or equal to		
<=	Less than or equal to		
==	Equal to		
!=	Not equal to		

Here are a few simple lines of Perl that show the use of variables, literals, and operators:

```
$a = 5;
$a++;
$b = $a ** 2;
$c = "test" . $b;
print "$c";
```

This block of code would print out the string test36. First $a is assigned to 5; then it is incremented to 6. Next, $b is assigned to $a squared, or 36. Then, $c is assigned to the string test with $b appended. Finally, $c, whose value now is test36, is printed to the screen. If that's clear to you, you understand the building blocks of Perl.

Scalars, Arrays, and Associative Arrays

Variables can be used individually or in arrays of arbitrary numbers of dimensions. You've already seen scalar variables, such as $a, $b, and $c, in the previous example; a scalar variable contains a single number or string. But each of these variables travels separately, and there will be times when you will need to work with groups of associated pieces of data. This is where arrays come in:

```
@array1 = ("blah",5,12.7,$a);
@array2 = ($a, $b, $c);
```

An array has the same kind of naming conventions as a scalar variable, except that it begins with an "at" sign (@) instead of a dollar sign. As these examples show, an array does not need to be declared with a certain size or contain only a consistent type of data. Arrays can contain numbers, strings, other arrays, or whatever you like.

You can access an element of an array using square brackets. The third element of the previous @array1 array, a scalar value, would be $array1[2]. Remember that array element numbering begins at zero!

You will also see elements of arrays addressed with the @ prefix instead of $. This prefix indicates that you can address a "slice" of an array by specifying more than one element (for example, @array1[1,2]). This example is really an array in itself with two elements. If you say @array1[2], you're talking about a slice with one element, which is effectively the same thing as a scalar variable, and it works the same way. However, for consistency's sake, you may want to keep in mind that the "preferred" method is $array1[2].

You can use the various array operators, essentially built-in functions, to set up your arrays in any way you like. Arrays are often also called *lists*. In that context, you can think of an array in "stack" terminology, which gives you the push(), pop(), shift(), and unshift() operators. These operators are listed in Table 20.2, where @array1 undergoes each of them in turn.

TABLE 20.2   List Operators

Operator	Function Result	Syntax
push()	Adds a value to the end of a list.	push(@array1,"test"); @array1 = ("blah",5,12.7,6,"test")
pop()	Removes a value from the end of a list and returns it.	$d = pop(@array1); @array1 = ("blah",5,12.7,6), $d = "test"
unshift()	Adds a value to the beginning of a list.	unshift(@array1,"test"); @array1 = ("test","blah",5,12.7,6)
shift()	Removes a value from the beginning of a list and returns it.	$d = shift(@array1); @array1 = ("blah",5,12.7,6), $d = "test"

> **TIP**
>
> You can accomplish each of these operations by setting the output of the operator to a new array, or even to the same array. Therefore, by writing @array3 = push(@array1,"test"), you can create a new array with the new lengthened contents, leaving the original array (@array1) untouched.

A further useful array function is sort(). For instance, sort(@array1) would arrange all the elements in lexicographical order, treating them as strings. You can specify an alternate sorting algorithm of your own construction to extend the functionality of the sort()

routine to do whatever you like. For instance, if you create a subroutine called `numerically()` that sorts two arguments in numerical order, you can use the following:

```
sort numerically (@array1)
```

Arrays are especially useful when you're working with relational data, either through interfaces to real databases or simply delimited text files such as /etc/passwd. Using arrays is how you would access the individual lines in a file that you've read in from standard input. We'll be looking at how that's done a bit later in the chapter.

> **TIP**
>
> You can get the size of an array by accessing it in "scalar context." The easiest way to do this is to assign the list to a scalar variable:
>
> ```
> $size = @array1;
> ```
>
> Now, $size is equal to 4.

An array can be created from a scalar string using the `split()` function. This will divide up the string based on whatever delimiter you specify, omitting the delimiter from each of the new array's elements:

```
$mystring = "Test|my name|Interesting data|123";
@mydata = split(/\|/,$mystring);
```

In the first line, $mystring is assigned to a string of four different chunks of text, separated by the pipe character (|). In the second, the `split()` function separates the string into four parts, removing the pipe characters on which the string was split, and assigns the parts to elements of the @mydata array.

Note that slashes are used to delimit the delimiter expression, and you have to escape the pipe character (|) with a backslash to make sure it's evaluated as a delimiter and not the "alternative" operator, which will make sense a little later, in the section on regular expressions. In any case, @mydata now contains the strings Test, my name, Interesting data, and 123 as its elements.

A special kind of array is an *associative* array; this is equivalent to a hash table in which the different values in the array are stored as key/value pairs. The prefix for an associative array is the percent sign (%), but each value of the array is a scalar, so you use the scalar prefix ($) to refer to the individual elements. Here's how you set up an associative array:

```
$assoc1{key1} = "value1";
$assoc1{key2} = "value2";
```

20

You can then use any of several associative array operators on the array as a whole:

```
@myvalues = values(%assoc1);
while (($mykey,$myvalue) = each(%assoc1)) {
  print "$mykey -> $myvalue\n";
}
```

Associative arrays are very useful in applications such as CGI programming, in which all the variables from HTML forms are sent to the server and read into an associative array based on the form field names.

Flow Control

What makes Perl a full-featured programming environment rather than a simple batch scripting language is its complete set of flow-control structures. These are what allow you to create complex data-flow paths and iterations in your programs.

if/elsif/else

The most common control structure is the if block:

```
if ($a == 5) {            # If $a equals 5...
  print "It's 5\n";
} elsif ($a > 5) {        # Otherwise, if $a is greater than 5...
  print "Greater than 5\n";
} else {                  # In all other cases...
  print "Must be less than 5\n";
}
```

> **NOTE**
>
> Note that the conditional clause ($a == 5) must use the *equality* operator (==) rather than the assignment operator (=). The == operator and other comparison operators (listed in Table 20.1) can always be used in conditionals. But if the items you're comparing are strings, you can use the string equivalents: eq for ==, lt for <, ne for !=, and others.

foreach

Another common flow-control player in Perl is foreach, which allows you to iterate over all the elements in an array. Here, the foreach statement divides @buffer into its component elements, assigns each one to $line for the duration of the loop it controls, and allows you to use it as many times as there are members in the array:

```
foreach $line (@buffer) {
  print $line;
}
```

If you omit the optional variable name that refers to the element the loop is looking at ($line in this example), use the default $_ variable name to refer to the current element. It's a good idea to specify a variable name here in order to prevent confusion when you're using multiple nested foreach loops.

for

Perl also has a standard for loop, which is almost identical to the for loop in C. The purpose of for is simply to iterate a specified number of times rather than over the elements of an array. The for loop is controlled by an iteration variable—generally one that isn't used anywhere else in the script—that is iterated automatically by for until it reaches your specified limit. Its arguments, as in C, are separated by semicolons. These include the name of the iteration variable, the incrementation operation, and the end condition. Here's an example:

```
for ($i; $i++; $i<100) {
  print "$i\n";
}
```

This sample for loop will print out 100 lines, numbered from 0 to 99. The first argument sets up $i as the iteration variable, and the second says that $i should be incremented upward once. The for loop will execute unless the condition specified in the third argument is false, which in this example occurs once $i has reached 100.

while/until/do

Finally, we have the while loop, which acts like a simplified version of for without the iteration variable. It has a conditional statement as its argument, which is evaluated every time the loop begins, and it keeps executing until the conditional is false. Here's an example:

```
while ($i < 100) {
  $i += 5;
  $j++;
}
print "$j\n";
```

This loop will execute 20 times, and the output of the print statement will be 20.

A variant of while is until, which has effectively the opposite meaning: It keeps executing *until* the conditional is true. The following example has the same effect as the previous while loop:

```
until($i == 100) {
  $i += 5;
  $j++;
```

20

```
}
print "$j\n";
```

Another way to use while or until is via the do...while or do...until construct. This guarantees that the loop will execute at least once, and the while or until conditional is evaluated at the end, rather than the beginning. Here's an example:

```
do {
  $i += 5;
  $j++;
} while ($i < 100);
print "$j\n";
```

Backquotes (`) enable Perl to execute any command as you would at the command line or within a shell script. Simply enclose your command in backquotes, and Perl will execute it using /bin/sh, waiting until the spawned process quits before proceeding. What's more, the output from the backquoted command is available as the return value, so you can put it into a variable for later use. Here's a commonly used example:

```
$date = `date`;
```

Note that this returned string generally has \n at the end, so you can use chomp() to snip it off, either on a separate line or by enclosing the original assignment as an expression:

```
chomp($date = `date`);
```

CAUTION

Be aware that Perl won't necessarily know your command path. Your script might work for you on your own machine, but if you put the script on another system, it might fail because the command you're trying to run can't be found. The best defense against this is to specify the full path to the command:

```
@who = `/usr/bin/who`;
```

One way to keep control over externals that must be called from your scripts is to define their paths in variables at the beginning of a script. Declaring these variables in an easy-to-find section helps other users locate and maintain them:

```
$who = "/usr/bin/who";
```

Command-Line Arguments

You can pass practically as many arguments as you want on the command line to a Perl program. These arguments, separated by whitespace (unless enclosed in quotes), are placed at runtime into the @ARGV array and are available for any kind of use:

```
# ./myscript.pl test "My String" 123
```

@ARGV[0] is now test, @ARGV[1] is My String, and @ARGV[2] is 123. This also works on CGI programs, as you will see in Chapter 25, "Configuring a Web Server." If you specify a URL with arguments separated by + characters (the usual way of doing such things), @ARGV will be populated the same way:

```
http://www.some-host.com/myscript.cgi?test+My%20String+123
```

A Simple Perl Script

The script in Listing 20.1 uses most of the techniques covered thus far in the chapter, as well as a few that haven't been covered (and that's about all it does). This script is available on the included CD-ROM as simpledemo.pl.

LISTING 20.1   Simple Demo Perl Script (simpledemo.pl)

```perl
#!/usr/bin/perl

# <STDIN> is an I/O handle referring to the standard input. In this context,
# we're using it to read in text input from a prompt. The chomp operator removes
# any trailing newline/return characters from the end of the input.
print "Please enter your name: ";
chomp ($name = <STDIN>);

srand;    # Initialize the random number generator
@namelist = ("Bob","Jane","Frank");
@colorlist = ("green","red","blue","yellow");
foreach $testname (@namelist) {
  # You can select any random element of an array by using the rand() operator
  # on it.
  $colors{$testname} = $colorlist[rand(@colorlist)];
}
while (($name,$color) = each(%colors)) {
  print "$name: $color\n";
  undef ($n);    # The undef() function undefines a variable. Works like NULL.
  do {
    $color = @colorlist[$n+1];
    $n++;
  } until ($color eq "blue");
}
```

20

Advanced Perl Techniques

Now, it's time to move on to some of the more interesting things you can do with Perl in FreeBSD. These include file access, functions, modules, and—Perl's hallmark—text-processing capabilities. The following sections take a look at each of these topics.

Text Processing

Perl's primary strength and original purpose, as mentioned earlier, is text processing. Perl evolved from simpler text-processing tools whose efficiency came from their use of regular expressions.

A *regular expression* (also often called a *regexp*) is a very highly developed way of specifying a pattern to seek in a text stream. You can use regexps to do simple searches on strings, or you can modify one to include such constraints as the beginning or end of a line, groups of certain characters, included strings of arbitrary length, or any of a number of occurrences of any pattern.

Regexps are part of many different tools in FreeBSD and other Unix-based systems, especially the pattern-matching tool grep and its variants. Perl gives you the same kind of flexibility as you have in grep but embeds it in a full-featured programming environment. This is something that almost all other languages lack. For instance, in C you have to copy strings back and forth in memory and seek through them character by character. Effectively, it's not possible without a lot of pain.

Searching with Regular Expressions

The simplest regexp pattern is a text string. To seek for a regexp in a string, use the =~ operator and enclose the regexp in slashes:

```
if ($string =~ /abc123/) { ...
```

This can be simplified even more if you're receiving a text string already, such as from the "diamond" operator (<>), which allows you to loop through a text file specified on the command line (we'll look at this in the next subsection). If this is the case, and you already have a $_ variable (the "default" variable, which you read about back in the section titled "foreach"), you can search on it implicitly:

```
if (/abc123/) { ...
```

That's all well and good. But what about searching for a more complex pattern? For example, you can modify the pattern so that abc123 will match only if it appears at the beginning of the line. This is done with the ^ anchor, as shown here:

```
/^abc123/
```

The end-of-line anchor, $, is interpreted as such only if it's at the end of the regexp. Otherwise, it's treated as a variable name prefix. Using these two anchors together, you can change your pattern to only match if abc123 is the whole line, with nothing else on it:

```
if (/^abc123$/) { ...
```

These are only the most basic of the regexp pattern controls. You can embed [abc] to specify a character "class" or any of the three letters a, b, or c. You can use quantifiers immediately after any character, class, or grouping to specify how many times it can appear in sequence. Table 20.3 shows a summary of these patterns (and not a complete one, at that).

TABLE 20.3 Regular Expression Syntax Operators

Pattern	Explanation
Text	
.	Any single character
[abc123]	Any of the characters in the group abc123
[^abc123]	None of the characters in the group abc123
[a-g]	All characters between a and g, inclusive
abc1|abc2	Alternative: abc1 or abc2
(abc123)	Grouping (for use with quantifiers or alternatives, or back references)
Quantifiers	
?	0 or 1 of the preceding text
*	0 or n of the preceding text ($n > 0$)
+	1 or n of the preceding text ($n > 1$)
*?	Forces * to the minimal match (anti-greediness quantifier)
{m}	Exactly m repetitions of the preceding text
{m,n}	n through m repetitions of the preceding text
{m,}	m or more repetitions of the preceding text
Anchors	
^	Start-of-line anchor
$	End-of-line anchor
\b	Word boundary
\B	No word boundary
Escape Codes	
\X	Escapes (treats as a literal) any character (where X is any character; for example, ".")
\r	Carriage return
\n	Line feed
\f	Form feed
\t	Tab

TABLE 20.3   Continued

Pattern	Explanation
\d	Digits (equivalent to [0-9])
\w	Word characters (equivalent to [a-zA-Z0-9_])
\s	Whitespace (equivalent to [\r\t\n\f])
\D	Not digits
\W	Not words
\S	Not whitespace
\###	ASCII character ### (in octal)
\cX	Ctrl+X character (where X is any character)

What's more, you can also add various switches to the end of the pattern, after the final slash, to change the sense of the match. An i makes it a case-insensitive search (for example, /abc/i).

> **NOTE**
>
> A word on precedence: When grouping within a regexp, parentheses have the highest precedence, followed by multipliers, then anchors, and then alternatives.

Regexps can be made as complex as the most obfuscated code you've ever seen in your life. Finishing a well-crafted regexp that does some incredibly obscure task can be one of the most satisfying parts of the Unix lifestyle.

Changing Text with Translation Operators

Of course, what's a search without the ability to replace? Perl has several built-in translation operators: the "substitution" operator (s///), the "transliteration" operator (tr///), and explicit string-manipulation functions such as substr().

To do a substitution, you will still use the =~ operator, but this time as an assignment operator rather than as a comparison. The argument to it is the s operator, then a regexp, then the replacement string, and finally any options. These are all separated by slashes, as shown here:

```
$mystring =~ s/^test[0-9]/foo/g;
```

Here's a more useful example, which translates angle brackets into HTML escape sequences to display them literally in a Web page:

```
$myhtml =~ s/</&lt;/g;
$myhtml =~ s/>/&gt;/g;
```

The g at the end means *global*, and it tells the substitution operator to do a "replace all"—that is, to changr test1, test2, and so on to foo. If this is omitted, only the first match in the string will be substituted.

What if you want to preserve that number ([0-9]) in the previous example? That's where groupings and back references come in. Anything you put in parentheses in a regexp can be repeated or recalled by number. Within the regexp, you would use \#, where # is the number of the parenthesized grouping. For example, in the regexp /abc(123)(.*)\1\2/, \1 is interpreted as 123 and \2 is interpreted as .*. Note that this doesn't start at 0, confusingly enough, but rather at 1. You can have as many of these patterns as you want.

Now, to apply this to a substitution, you can also refer to a regexp's parenthesized groupings from beyond the delimiting slash—not with \1 and \2, but with $1 and $2. These special read-only variables remain in memory after the match, too, so you can use them later on in your code. Here's how the previous example would look if you wanted to preserve the number:

```
$mystring =~ s/^test([0-9])/foo$1/g;
```

The substitution operator is all well and good, but for some functions—such as capitalizing all the letters, translating all 3s to 4s, and the like—it's cumbersome and sometimes prohibits what you want to do. That's where the transliteration operator (tr///) comes in.

The tr operator acts like a simplified and constricted version of the s operator, with a few of its functions held in check. Its operation takes one set of characters (not a regexp, just a group of characters or a range) and a second set of characters and then maps the first set onto the second set. Be careful to note that you use the = operator with tr rather than the =~ (matching) operator. Here's an example:

```
$mystring = "cat and dog";
$mystring = tr/abc/def/;
```

$mystring is now fdt dnd dog. The mappings can take on a number of interesting forms, especially if the new string is shorter than the old. If that happens, it simply wraps the shorter pattern around to make the matches fit. You can specify the d option (after the final slash) to make the matches "line up," deleting unmatched characters from the first set.

The most useful application of tr is generally for capitalization. This can be done by specifying a range on both sides:

```
$mystring = tr/A-Z/a-z/;
```

This example forces everything in $mystring to lowercase.

One of the more useful explicit text-processing functions is substr(). Its full usage is covered, along with all the other built-in functions, in any good Perl reference. As a quick summary, it takes a string, an offset, and a length and then returns just that substring. Here's an example:

```
$mystring = "cat and dog";
$newstring = substr($mystring,0,3);
```

$newstring is now cat. This is cool enough as it is, but substr() really comes into its own when used in conjunction with index(). This function will return the point in a string where a given substring appears:

```
$mystring = "cat and dog";
$newstring = substr($mystring,index($mystring,"cat"),index($mystring,"dog"));
```

This would assign "cat and " to $mystring, including the trailing space.

Using Filehandles to Work with Files

You can open a file, read it into an array, and write out a new one, or even do many at once, through the use of *filehandles*. These are I/O methods that give you a way to direct your input and output to places other than the console (for example, in to and out of files).

The simplest filehandle is the "diamond" operator, which doesn't really have a permanent filehandle at all—it's just a way to treat an incoming file (or set of files) from the command line as an input filehandle for as long as there are lines in the file to read. To use the diamond operator, use a loop like the following:

```
while (<>) {
  print $_;
}
```

Then, run your program with one or more filenames on the command line:

```
# ./myscript.pl file1.txt file2.txt ...
```

This will have the effect of printing out all the contents of the specified files, much in the way that cat would. This way of operating on a file's contents is convenient and quick. However, it's also pretty limited; the diamond operator is really a "degenerate case" of a true filehandle. Let's look at some properly specified ones to see what they can really do.

A filehandle name by convention is in all caps. It is created with the open() command, and afterward you can read from it, print to it, and close it. Here's how to read a file's contents into an array:

```
open (FH,"/path/to/file1.txt");
@contents = <FH>;
close (FH);
```

It's possible for Perl to fail to open the file, either because it doesn't exist, its permissions don't allow you to read it, or any other of a number of reasons. You can trap for failures opening the file by using the die operator; if the evaluation of an expression falls through to die, it will print its argument (if any) to standard output, and the script will quit. Here's the most common way die is used with opening files:

```
open (FH,"/path/to/file1.txt") || die ("Can't open file1.txt!");
@contents = <FH>;
close (FH);
```

Writing to files is a bit more complex because there are so many different ways you can do it. The thing to remember is that you can write to any kind of handle you can use on the command line, which includes the overwrite (>) or append (>>) redirector, or even the | (pipe) into a program. This is useful for, say, having your script write its output into an e-mail message:

```
open (FH,">/path/to/file2.txt");
print FH $_ foreach (@contents);
close (FH);
```

```
open (MAIL,"| /sbin/sendmail -oi -t");
print MAIL "From: me\@somewhere.com\n";
print MAIL "To: you\@somewhereelse.com\n";
print MAIL "Subject: Check it out!\n\n";
print MAIL $_ foreach (@contents);
close (MAIL);
```

> **CAUTION**
>
> Remember that when specifying @ characters in text strings (in e-mail addresses, for instance), you need to precede them with backslashes to prevent Perl from treating them as array identifiers. If you don't, the script will fail with an error.

The filehandle goes as an argument to print; it's important here to realize that this argument is assumed to be the built-in filehandle <STDOUT> (standard output), unless a different one is specified. There is also a <STDIN> handle. To set the default input/output filehandle, use the select() function:

```
select (FH);
```

This way, you won't have to write print FH every time. However, you'll need to switch it back to STDOUT when you're done with FH.

20

Directories have corresponding opendir() and readdir() functions; you can open a directory and read its contents into an array, like this:

```
opendir (DIR,"/path/to/dir");
@files = sort readdir (DIR);
closedir (DIR);
```

Using what you've seen so far, you can now do some pretty interesting stuff. For instance, you can open up /etc/passwd, grab all the entries that have a UID greater than 1000, and print out their usernames and full names:

```
#!/usr/bin/perl

# The following three lines open the filehandle, read the data stream
# into the @passwd array (each line becoming a member of the array), and
# then close the filehandle.
open (PASSWD,"/etc/passwd") || die ("Can't open passwd file!");
@passwd = <PASSWD>;
close (PASSWD);

foreach (@passwd) {                 # For each member of @passwd...
  @userdata = split(/:/,$_);        # Split on colons and assign to @userdata
  if ($userdata[2] > 1000) {        # If the UID is greater than 1000...
    print "$userdata[0]: @userdata[4]\n";
  }
}
```

A useful tool already! This is what makes Perl so popular. There's very little effort involved in producing programs that make your life measurably easier.

Functions

Perl has hundreds of built-in functions, many of which you've already seen. These functions cover pretty much any general-purpose necessity of programming, especially once you know how to include Perl modules that expand your available functions as much as you want. However, there will come the time in your more complex Perl programs—especially programs that span multiple Perl scripts, such as server-side CGI suites—when you will want to define functions of your own (which Perl calls *subroutines*) to accomplish your common tasks.

You can define functions anywhere in your script that you want; they don't need to have already been "declared" in order to work. For neatness' sake you might choose to put your function definitions at the end, or you might want to put them all inline, or at the top—it doesn't matter.

Let's say you want to be able to pass an arbitrary number of values to a function and have it add them together. The syntax for this would be as follows:

```
sub sum {
  $mysum += $_ foreach (@_);
  $mysum;  # This line evaluates $mysum and thus sets the function's
           # return value
}
```

The function would then be called with its name prefixed with the ampersand character:

```
$newsum = &sum(45,14,2134,89);
```

The @_ variable refers to the argument list, much in the same way that @ARGV represents the arguments passed to the program itself from the command line. For a more "traditional" style of function, the kind that most other languages have (which accept a certain number of named variables), you can do something like this:

```
sub printname {
  ($name, $number, $passwd) = @_;
  print "$name/$number" if ($passwd);
}
```

Functions bring up a common hornets' nest of issues surrounding "global" and "local" namespaces. The rule about Perl is that there are no local functions—they're all globally defined. Any variables that you define in a function are global, unless you say otherwise (for example, with the local() operator). The @_ array is already local; each time you call a function, its argument array is created as a brand-new local copy. Using local(), you can do the same with other variables, too, and have them be relevant only within the function and discarded when it's done:

```
sub sum {
  local($mysum);
  $mysum += $_ foreach (@_);
  $mysum;  # This line evaluates $mysum and thus sets the function's
           # return value
}
```

The my operator does the same thing, and it is more common nowadays. You can use my to specify a list of local variables:

```
my ($mysum, $name, $hash);
```

If you're running in "strict mode," Perl will complain unless you've properly specified your local variables within every function, and it won't let you use variables unless they're declared in a my statement. Keeping things tidy in memory isn't as big a deal in Perl because Perl programs tend to execute and quit without hanging around for a long time, but good code style does dictate practices such as these.

Perl Modules

Every good language has shared libraries of some sort, and Perl is no exception. In fact, Perl's libraries (called *modules*), which are chunks of nonexecutable Perl code with .pm extensions (for "Perl module"), have grown up as a very distributed Internet-wide grass-roots effort, much in the same way that FreeBSD's ports collection has grown. The ports and Perl modules do play an interrelated part, as a matter of fact, which we'll get to in a moment.

You can put Perl code into a .pm file in the same directory as your script (for instance, mylib.pm) and then call it using the use operator, minus the .pm extension:

```
use mylib;
```

Perl's support structure in FreeBSD is installed in /usr/lib/perl5. There aren't any Perl modules in there, though; it's up to you to install any modules you need in the course of your system's life, and those go into (surprise!) /usr/local/lib/perl5. This directory forks in two directions, with man pages in one (named for the current version of Perl) and the actual modules in the other (site_perl). Inside this (one more level down) are various directories containing module groupings for any module set you've installed. There's also an i386-freebsd directory, which contains precompiled C code that some Perl modules use for performance reasons (mathematics-heavy algorithms, for example).

Working with Modules

Modules come in groups, with a prefix and the module name separated by a double colon (::), as in C++ scoping. For example, Net::Telnet is the name of the Perl module that contains Telnet capabilities, and Net::DNS provides name-server lookup functions. These are kept in /usr/local/lib/perl5/site_perl/5.005, in the Net directory, as Telnet.pm and DNS.pm.

This directory is in Perl's search path. To bring a module into your script, use the use operator, like so:

```
use Net::Telnet;
```

Now, any function specified in that module can be used in your script as if you defined it within the script itself, simply by prepending an ampersand (&) to its name.

How do you find out which functions are in a module? By using perldoc, that's how. This utility works in a similar fashion to man, and assuming that you've installed your modules properly (for example, through the ports, as you'll see in a moment), you can look up any module's documentation the same way you'd specify it in a script. Listing 20.2 shows part of the documentation for the Image::Size module.

LISTING 20.2   Sample Documentation for a Perl Module

```
# perldoc Image::Size


Image::Size(3) User Contributed Perl Documentation Image::Size(3)


NAME
        Image::Size - read the dimensions of an image in several
        popular formats


SYNOPSIS
                use Image::Size;
                # Get the size of globe.gif
                ($globe_x, $globe_y) = imgsize("globe.gif");
                # Assume X=60 and Y=40 for remaining examples


                use Image::Size 'html_imgsize';
                # Get the size as "HEIGHT=X WIDTH=Y" for HTML generation
                $size = html_imgsize("globe.gif");
                # $size == "HEIGHT=40 WIDTH=60"


                use Image::Size 'attr_imgsize';
                # Get the size as a list passable to routines in CGI.pm
                @attrs = attr_imgsize("globe.gif");
                # @attrs == ('-HEIGHT', 40, '-WIDTH', 60)


                use Image::Size;
                # Get the size of an in-memory buffer
                ($buf_x, $buf_y) = imgsize($buf);
```

Documentation of this type will generally give you usable and accurate prototype code that you can insert into your scripts, as well as a complete listing of all available functions.

Perl Modules and the Ports Collection

The "correct" way to install Perl modules is with the ports collection. Go into /usr/ports and look through the various subdirectories. You'll see many ports beginning with p5-. These are Perl modules that have been codified into proper FreeBSD ports. (Package versions of most of them exist, too.) Many modules have compiled C components as well as multiple supporting modules and documentation, so it's definitely important to make sure everything gets installed in the proper place. The ports make sure of that.

The port for Net::Telnet is /usr/ports/net/p5-Net-Telnet, and that's the naming scheme for all of them—a dash for the double colon. Some port categories have dozens of Perl modules, all of them added to the ports out of repeated usefulness. This distributed model allows Perl to be infinitely extensible while remaining fairly unencumbered in its default installation.

To install a module from the ports, simply build it as you would any port—using cd to change to its directory and then running make and make install. Perl modules have a built-in make test target that tunes and evaluates how well the module will work on the system; this is run implicitly with the ports' make target.

You can use pkg_info and pkg_version to check which Perl modules you have installed; this is much easier than remembering to look in /usr/local/lib/perl5. The rest of the package tools work as well; you can use pkg_add to install a Perl module from its tarball, if you like, and use pkg_update to refresh it when a new version comes out.

Useful Perl Resources

Because Perl is so widespread, it's little wonder that there are so many resources for it available in as many formats as you might want. Nearly everyone involved in content provider work on the Internet needs to have some familiarity with Perl, so computer book-stores do a brisk trade in books on the subject, and the most cursory or off-topic of searches on the Web will turn up discussions between Perl hackers on how to do this or that.

The following sections list some of the more centralized and "official" sources of Perl information.

Web Sites

If you need a Perl reference, the first stop should be the Web. It's not as direct or definitive as a book, but if you don't have such a book, you're sure to find your answer on the Web in at least some form.

www.perl.org
www.perl.org is the "Perl Mongers" Web site, an independently run source of information and advocacy references. There are mailing lists you can join as well as affiliated Web sites, such as www.perldoc.com, the centralized Perl documentation database.

www.perl.com
The "official" Perl site, run by O'Reilly, is an aggregation of Perl news, tutorials, and discussions about all kinds of details of working with Perl. This is probably the most complete site for everyday Perl happenings, if not necessarily for definitive reference.

Books

Just about every Perl hacker has one of the popular O'Reilly Perl reference books on hand; for complete and easy-to-follow reference, these books are hard to beat.

The "Camel" Book

Programming Perl is the complete Perl reference book, written by Larry Wall (the father of Perl), Tom Christiansen, and Jon Orwant (O'Reilly, 2000). Nicknamed for the camel on the cover, which has become synonymous with Perl as a visual logo, this book is frequently revised to cover the most recent developments in the Perl world, and it's widely accepted as the "definitive" work on the subject. One of its best features is an alphabetized function reference, an indispensable section.

The "Llama" Book

Learning Perl, by Randal L. Schwartz and Tom Phoenix (O'Reilly, 2001) is the "camel" book's little brother; the llama is its icon. It discusses the basics of Perl (essentially the same topics covered in this chapter) in enough detail and with an engaging-enough style to cover pretty much all you'll need to get you to where Perl is no longer a foreign language to you.

Perl Developer's Dictionary

Perl Developer's Dictionary by Clinton Pierce (Sams, 2001, ISBN: 0672320673) is a comprehensive reference of all Perl functions, and one of the most complete texts on the subject available today. It's ideal for the more advanced Perl hacker who needs reference on syntax and usage more than tutorials on how Perl works.

Teach Yourself Perl in 24 Hours

This step-by-step, entry-level guide also by Clinton Pierce (Sams, 2002, ISBN: 0672320355) gives you a running start into putting Perl to practical use very quickly. Also, *Teach Yourself Perl in 21 Days* (Sams, 2002, ISBN: 0672322765) takes the tutorial to the next level of depth with lots of concrete examples.

The CPAN

The CPAN (Comprehensive Perl Archive Network) is where all the modules across the Net are pulled together and made public. This also applies to binary distributions, scripts, and other tools, as well as source code for the brave of heart. Its primary usefulness, though, is for its comprehensive module list; if there's a module you want to install that isn't in the ports collection, you'll find it here, as well as all kinds of documentation that will help you use it.

The CPAN's central site is at `http://www.perl.com/CPAN-local/`. The CPAN's purpose is to provide numerous worldwide mirrors of its resources so that everyone will have quick access to it; you can use the site's list and map to find a mirror close to you and bookmark it for later reference.

20

PART IV

FreeBSD Networking

IN THIS PART

Networking with FreeBSD

O perating systems used to be designed either for networking or for single-user desktop settings. That has all changed. In the present day, the consumer-level, single-user, non-networked PC platform is giving way to operating systems whose robustness and networkability put to shame many of the mainframe-class systems of the old days. Mac OS X (with its FreeBSD architecture and Mach kernel) and Windows 2000/XP are both examples of platforms that were built around networking as a fundamental tenet, and they are intended to replace older, formerly non-networkable systems. TCP/IP (the *de facto* transport protocol suite of the Internet) is woven tightly into the cores of these systems as it was in the mainframes, and as it is in FreeBSD.

FreeBSD is a system designed from the ground up to be a network-aware platform. Whether you're using it as a workstation or as a server, chances are you're using it for its networking strengths, and a FreeBSD machine without a network is frankly not a lot of use. It's certainly a great deal less fun.

In this chapter, you'll learn the basic principles of networking as it applies to FreeBSD and its role in the Internet.

Introduction to Networking

Networking is the ability of two or more computers to be aware of each other's existence and exchange data. In the Internet age, this basic capability can mean anything from simple awareness sensing and topology mapping to e-mail traveling from server to server, Web browsers downloading HTML pages and large movie files from HTTP servers, and peer-to-peer MP3 sharing. A networked computer has the capability to expand its usefulness beyond what the user can buy off the shelf and install from CD, instantly and without any physical media being introduced. The advent of networking and what it means for business and recreation is what has fueled the computer revolution that is very likely behind your decision to use FreeBSD.

The *de facto* standard protocol suite that runs almost all active networks these days is the Transmission Control Protocol/Internet Protocol (TCP/IP). Networking—especially FreeBSD networking—has become nearly synonymous with TCP/IP in recent years. TCP/IP, whose fundamental structure we will be examining in some detail later in this chapter, has enjoyed some thirty years of development and maturity, and its extensibility and modularity are part of what has contributed to its success. Although the first recognized computer network—the United States Department of Defense-funded ARPAnet—dates back to 1969, when its first four nodes were brought online at four universities in the western US, TCP/IP itself has its roots in a 1974 paper by Internet design pioneers Vint Cerf and Bob Kahn titled "A Protocol for Packet Network Interconnection." The Transmission Control Program, later to become split into TCP (Transmission Control Protocol) and IP (Internet Protocol), demonstrated a way that data could be sent reliably over the packet-switching networks that were then still newly discovering their usefulness. UNIX systems from Bell Labs, first released in 1977, helped to popularize the new protocol suite and some of the variants that fell into its layered structure, including UDP and ICMP. Thus, the foundations of FreeBSD's TCP/IP heritage were laid. Today, the TCP/IP suite implemented by FreeBSD is known as the *reference implementation*. Other software vendors use FreeBSD's model for determining how TCP/IP should correctly work. This is a result of FreeBSD's Unix roots and the original Bell Labs and Berkeley code that still forms the core of its networking subsystem.

The TCP/IP suite forms the backbone for the Internet and all its trappings. It's just about the only game in town for network traffic over wide area network (WAN) links, such as the telecommunications links between geographical regions. TCP/IP also is quite prevalent in local area networks (LANs). Most LANS are high-speed corporate, enterprise, or university networks connected directly through Ethernet or similar physical-link protocols.

A standardized model for the networking "stack," known as Open Systems Interconnection (OSI), establishes the general structure of TCP/IP. OSI dictates as many as seven "layers" of implementation for a computer network, each of which has its own measure of specificity and its own functional applicability to the user, the software, the operating system, and the networking hardware. The conceptual arrangement of the OSI model, as exemplified in the Internet's typical usage, is shown in Figure 21.1.

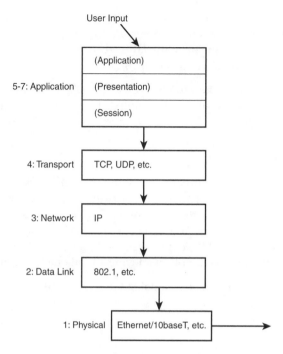

FIGURE 21.1   OSI stack layering diagram, as it is used in TCP/IP.

In an OSI stack, data travels from the highest level (the user-interface level, where it is in its most specialized form, allowing the user to interact with it using a variety of interface metaphors, such as command lines and windowing systems) progressively down to the its lowest level, where it is at its most generic and abstract form—a form that can be handled by very simple hardware and software protocols. This is achieved by each layer of the stack wrapping the data in "headers," or abstraction layers that allow the data to be decoded later by another TCP/IP stack, when the data reaches that layer on the way down. At the very bottom, the data is not "Web pages" or "e-mail." Instead, it's just ones and zeroes that the Ethernet card knows to send to another Ethernet card. All the packaging tells the remote Ethernet card what to do with the data—whether it is destined for that card's machine (in which case it should pass the data further on up the stack for decoding and delivery) or for another computer elsewhere on the network—or even on another network, in which case the data is forwarded on.

The different layers of the stack define different levels of addressing and routing specificity. The IP layer, the component that corresponds to the "network" layer of the stack, knows how to send packets of data to other computers on the Internet, as defined by their IP addresses. TCP and UDP, which you will learn about later, are protocols that exist higher up the stack, in the "transport" layer. These rely on the network layer's ability to deliver packets, but they add their own specific methods of delivery. Below IP, the "data link" layer knows nothing about IP addresses—all it knows about is the hardware addresses on other Ethernet cards on the network. However, because IP information is embedded in any packet that the data link layer receives to transmit, the receiver will know where on the Internet it's supposed to go.

Many other protocols exist at the various levels of the OSI stack, and they each play a part in routing traffic to its destination and ensuring its integrity. This chapter discusses how all these protocols fit into the TCP/IP structure and how FreeBSD deals with them.

Network Topologies

Your FreeBSD machine might be installed on a university network, in a professional co-location facility, within a corporate enterprise network, or on a home dial-up network (or dialed-up directly). These are just the most common types of settings. Different network topologies, or logical layouts of devices and data link mechanisms, are as numerous as the individual networks in the world—no two are exactly the same. However, virtually all networks share a common basic topology and a few fundamental components.

In Figure 21.2, you can see the type of topology that would be found in a typical home network. The topology shown here is also serviceable as a simplified diagram of an enterprise or university network.

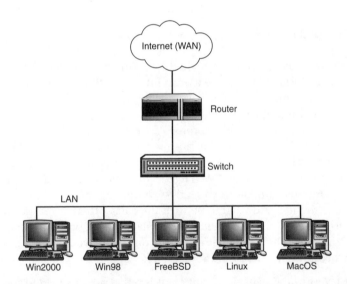

FIGURE 21.2   A basic network topology, showing a WAN and a LAN, separated by a router and comprising a number of different types of computers.

Most basic network topologies involve a WAN, a relatively low-speed serial link to the Internet, such as a T1, T3, DSL, or cable modem connection. These link types are often referred to generically as "broadband," although the mechanisms for each are widely different, and a WAN does not have to be "broadband," as the term is popularly defined. The bandwidth (or speed) of WAN links can range from the kilobits per second, in the case of 33–56Kbps modems, up through the massively infrastructural OC-3, OC-12, OC-48, and OC-192 links used between major telecommunications operators. Table 21.1 shows the equivalent speeds of most of the common WAN link types.

TABLE 21.1   Serial WAN Link Types and Corresponding Transfer Speeds

Link Type	Speed	Equivalency
Modem	Up to 56Kbps	
ISDN	56–128Kbps	
DSL	192Kbps–1.5Mbps	
Cable modem	1Mbps–5Mbps	
T1	1.5Mbps	24 DS0 lines
T3	43.2Mbps	28 T1 lines
OC-3	155Mbps	100 T1 lines
OC-12	622Mbps	4 OC-3 lines
OC-48	2.5Gbps	4 OC-12 lines
OC-192	9.6Gbps	4 OC-48 lines

These WAN link types are designed to run over very long distances. Because of their serial nature, they can carry traffic over telephone copper, fiber-optic lines, and any other infrastructure that carries standard telephone network "trunk" traffic. In fact, data traffic over these lines is indistinguishable from voice traffic; it's treated exactly the same way by phone switching equipment and travels from one geographical location to another the same way a phone call would.

NOTE

Actually, digital switching equipment is becoming more prevalent with time; whereas analog signals are opaque to any switching equipment beyond a very rudimentary level, digital signals can be differentiated easily by the right kinds of equipment. For the most part, though, WAN lines carry data and voice traffic the same way.

Another type of network topology is the Internet Service Provider (ISP) model, which involves a primary network like the one shown in Figure 21.2. This architecture also includes a secondary WAN that connects the network to a large number of home users dialing up via modems and phone lines. This is illustrated in Figure 21.3.

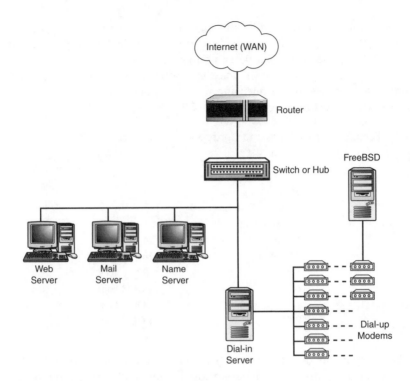

FIGURE 21.3 The ISP network architecture; home users dial up through the telephone WAN over modems to the ISP's LAN, which then connects to the Internet WAN.

After the WAN traffic reaches a DSU/CSU (which interfaces the phone company's transmission lines with your network's serial infrastructure) and router, however, it makes the transition to LAN transport mechanisms, such as Ethernet. These are physical link mechanism that, unlike serial WAN traffic, can interface directly with any computer equipped with an Ethernet card.

Figure 21.4 shows a diagram of the bandwidth capacity of the entire path from one LAN to another. This is the path that Internet traffic usually takes from a server (such as a Web site) to a client (a user's Web browser). The WAN pipe, as a rule, is narrowest right before it hits the LAN router.

Notice that although traffic in the middle of the WAN travels over lines with vastly more bandwidth than even the fastest LAN wiring, this bandwidth is divided among a great many more users than a typical LAN. Thousands, even millions of users share the thickest trunk lines during peak WAN usage periods. There are seldom more than a few hundred users competing for usage of a LAN.

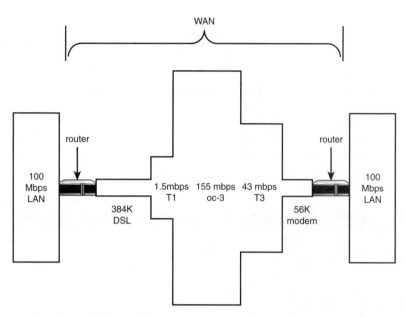

FIGURE 21.4 A schematic diagram of bandwidth availability throughout the path from one LAN (at the server end) to another LAN (at the client end), via a WAN of varying capacity.

Network Components

Any network is made up of the same types of component parts. These range in complexity from simple cables through complex computer-like devices such as routers. Each type of component exists at a different level of the OSI model; the brief view you have had of the TCP/IP stack and its layers will help to explain the conceptual difference between hubs, switches, bridges, and routers.

As with most computing equipment, the components you choose will vary in quality and in price. It's best to buy from vendors whose names you trust—Linksys, Intel, 3Com, and Netgear all make excellent infrastructural equipment, but they are by no means the only vendors you should consider. Bear in mind the features you need in your network. Will you have a pure 10base-T or 100base-TX network? Or will you need equipment that handles both? Also, pay attention to reviews to find out what models offer the best performance and quality for the price. Some components, however, offer opportunities to save on cost; you can make your own Ethernet cables, for example.

This section will examine the different components you will be working with in a typical networking topology, and later we will discuss how FreeBSD interacts with them.

Cables

The benefit of Ethernet and other LAN link types is that for very low cost, traffic can be carried between machines within a network at speeds that only the most expensive WAN links can reach. Those speeds range from 10Mbps for "standard" Ethernet, 100Mbps for Fast Ethernet, and 1Gbps for the newest standard, Gigabit Ethernet. These speeds can be achieved with cheap cables and components, making networking between computers via Ethernet a joy compared to a low-speed WAN. The downside is that Ethernet can't be used over long distances. Because the signals aren't serialized or transmitted by equipment designed to support long-distance transmission, signals degrade with cable length, particularly in coaxial (ThinNet or ThickNet) cables. Table 21.2 shows a summary of the different types of cables that can carry Ethernet traffic.

> **NOTE**
>
> It is possible to compose a WAN from pure Ethernet, although this requires equipment such as repeaters to help compensate for signal degradation.

TABLE 21.2   Types of Ethernet Cables

Type	AKA	Speed	Cable	Connector	Maximum Length
10base-2	Thin Ethernet, ThinNet	10Mbps	Thin coaxial	DB-15 DIX/AUI (to transceiver)	185m
10base-5	Thick Ethernet, ThickNet	10Mbps	Thick coaxial	BNC	500m
10base-T	Ethernet	10Mbps	UTP (CAT3–CAT5)	RJ-45	100m
100base-TX	Fast Ethernet	100Mbps	UTP (CAT5)	RJ-45	100m
1000base-T	Gigabit Ethernet	1Gbps	UTP (CAT5)	RJ-45	100m
1000base-SX			Multimode Fiber (various)	Optical	2–550m
1000base-LX			Single/Multimode Fiber	Optical	2–5km
1000base-CX			Twinax	Twinax	25m

> **NOTE**
>
> Here are a few acronym expansions:
>
> - DIX—Digital, Intel, Xerox
> - AUI—Attachment Unit Interface
> - BNC—Bayonne Neil Councelman (alternatively, British Naval Connector)
> - UTP—Unshielded twisted pair

Twisted-Pair Cables

The most commonly used cabling these days is twisted-pair cables, due to the relative simplicity and low cost of the cables and components. ThinNet and ThickNet must deal with terminators, segment-length limitations, repeaters, transceivers, BNC T-connectors (or "vampire tap" connectors for ThickNet), and unwieldy coaxial cables; DB-15 connectors had to be fitted with transceivers to connect them to coaxial or UTP Ethernet cables. Twisted-pair networks, however, connect computers' network interface cards (NICs) directly to hubs and switches via cheap cables that can be coiled tightly and connected easily to RJ-45 phone-style jacks. Ethernet cards until recently came with multiple connectors to support whatever mixture of Ethernet cables types your network might have (see Figure 21.5). Today, though, it's hard to find NICs with anything but the *de facto* standard RJ-45 connectors.

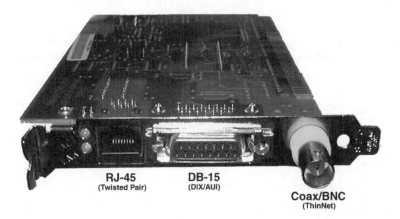

FIGURE 21.5   An Ethernet card showing the three common cable interfaces: RJ-45, DB-15, and BNC.

This standardization has resulted in an even lower cost in recent years for constructing Ethernet networks. Today, the only real use for BNC T-connectors and terminators is to make little metal sculptures, and ThickNet cable is useful only in hand-to-hand combat. The remainder of this chapter concentrates on twisted-pair cable components because of their near ubiquity in today's networks.

Twisted-pair cables are cheap and flexible, and you can make your own if you want to save even more money. RJ-45 jack crimpers can be bought at any electronics supply store, as well as RJ-45 connectors and UTP cable. Refer to the next section for information on pin-outs so that you can attach the connectors correctly.

> **NOTE**
>
> Twisted-pair cables do vary in quality, and some types are rated for higher speed than others (and have a commensurately higher cost). This quality rating can be expressed in a *supported speed*, a noise rating (citing such influencing factors as attenuation, NEXT distortion levels, and return loss), or a *category compliance* level. If your networking needs will require high-performance equipment (for instance, if you will be transmitting data at sustained speeds in excess of 100Mbps), you will want to pay the extra cost for quality cables.

Straight-Through and Crossover Cables

The two types of twisted-pair cables are straight-through and crossover. The difference lies in whether the positions of two pairs of wires in the cable are reversed from one end to the other. The type of the devices you are connecting determines which of these two cable types you must use.

Devices with RJ-45 connectors can be thought of as either "computer-type" or "hub-type" devices. Computers, routers, bandwidth managers, and other "endpoint" devices are considered computer-type devices, and they all share the same type of wiring. Hubs and switches are hub-type devices and also share the same type of wiring. Ethernet cables are wired to connect computer-type devices to hub-type devices. The rule to remember is this: Use straight-through cables between unlike devices, and use crossover cables between like devices.

You use straight-through cable to connect *unlike* devices, as in these examples:

- To connect a computer to a hub
- To connect a computer to a switch
- To connect a router to a hub

You use crossover cable to connect *like* devices, as in these examples:

- To connect a hub to a hub
- To connect a hub to a switch
- To connect a computer to a computer (for instance, to play in two-player death-match mode)

> **Uplink Ports**
>
> The exception to the Ethernet cabling rule is the "uplink" port on hubs. This special port is wired as if it's a computer-type device, so you can connect a hub's uplink port to a standard port on another hub with a straight-through cable. This became necessary in large networks, in which a very long straight-through cable would be connected to a large enterprise-wide hub or switch (in the server room, for example) and wound through walls and conduits to emerge in another room. This cable couldn't be connected directly to a standard port on a smaller hub; it had to be

fitted to an adapter and a short crossover cable before it could talk to the smaller hub. Replacing the Ethernet cable with a long crossover cable was impractical, to say the least. Hence the uplink port was born—a port that allows a hub to be connected directly to another hub for which swapping out the cable for a crossover is not a viable option. Remember, though, that connecting two hubs' uplink ports together requires a crossover cable—and that's a configuration that rather defeats the purpose, in any case.

How do you tell whether an Ethernet cable is a straight-through or a crossover cable? It's pretty easy: Hold up the two ends of the cable next to each other. If the color sequences of the wires match, it's a straight-through cable. If some of the wires appear out of place, it's a crossover cable.

The pin-out for a straight-through cable is shown in Figure 21.6.

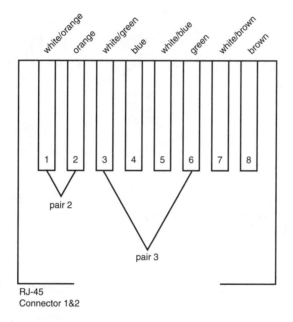

FIGURE 21.6   Straight-through cable wiring diagram.

And to make a crossover cable, reverse the positions of pair 3 (wires 1/2) and pair 2 (wires 3/6), as shown in Figure 21.7, when crimping the second end.

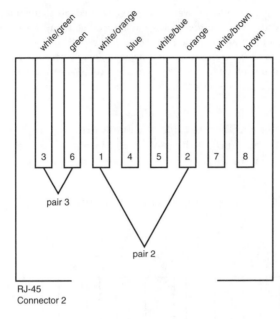

FIGURE 21.7   Crossover cable wiring diagram.

Hubs

One end of the cable connects to your computer's Ethernet card; that much is clear. However, the other end needs to connect to something, too. Far more often than not, what it connects to is a hub.

Hubs are devices with multiple RJ-45 ports, usually between 4 and 24, to which you can connect as many Ethernet cables as there are ports. These cables can connect to computers, other hubs, switches, or other network components as necessary. Hubs range in cost from about $40 to several hundred dollars, depending on quality, number of ports, and the capability to operate simultaneously with 10base-T and 100base-TX devices. Many hubs can only do one of the two speeds; an auto-sensing hub (often referred to as *N-Way*) can do either speed but costs significantly more.

Hubs range in size from small boxes no larger than your hand (or smaller) to full 19-inch rack-mountable units, and all require a power source. Some hubs are even "managed," meaning that you can telnet to them and configure each port's capabilities through a command-line interface. These hubs are naturally much more expensive than standalone hubs.

A hub is effectively a repeater, with all traffic appearing simultaneously on all ports, so a computer connected to one port on a hub will be able to see traffic to and from any other computer on the same hub. One port on a hub is usually reserved for uplink—a link to another hub, a switch, or a router higher up in the network hierarchy, as laid out earlier in Figure 21.1. This "uplink" port is usually wired so that a crossover cable is not needed between the hub and its next upstream device. This port and one of the standard ports on the hub may also be wired so that they're mutually exclusive. A five-port hub might give you the option of hooking four computers together (ignoring the uplink port) or three computers to an upstream device (ignoring the fourth standard port). This behavior might be hard-wired, it might be controllable with a pushbutton or a DIP switch, it might auto-sense the polarity, or all the ports might be simultaneously usable. These are just some of the possible variations between different hubs.

Another matter that complicates the way hubs and other devices communicate with each other is the "duplex" mode in which they operate. In half-duplex mode, a host can only be "listening" or "talking" at one time. Full-duplex mode uses twice as many wires, enabling the host to "listen" and "talk" at the same time. Therefore, a 100Mbps Fast Ethernet link in full-duplex mode can transport up to 100Mbps on each direction simultaneously, whereas the same link in half-duplex mode can only do an aggregate total of 100Mbps in both directions.

Hubs can be thought of as a cheap replacement for switches, which we will discuss next. Because the cost of switches is dropping to nearly that of hubs, we may soon see the industry move entirely to switches, with hubs vanishing into obsolescence.

Switches

A *switch* is another device that connects Ethernet devices together. A switch looks like a hub but tends to be more expensive and usually has fewer ports. It has multiple RJ-45 ports, it ranges from hand sized to rack sized, and the same companies that make hubs make switches, so it's easy to mistake one for the other on store shelves. They even operate somewhat similarly—you can plug multiple devices into a switch, and a switch used in place of a hub in a network would usually give you what appears to be the same result. The difference between switches and hubs, however, is subtle yet crucial.

On a hub, all ports share the same internal wiring. All computers connected to the hub, either directly or through another hub, exist on what's known as a *collision domain*. In a collision domain, a signal sent to one computer gets sent to all computers within the domain. It's up to each computer's Ethernet card to identify signals destined for that computer's address and to discard all others.

A switch's internal wiring is much more complex than a hub's. Each port comprises its own collision domain, and hosts connected to one port can't see any traffic destined for hosts on any of the other ports. Switches incorporate the software necessary to read each packet's Ethernet header and destination MAC address (the unique identifier for each host's Ethernet card, as we will discuss later) and determine which port has the host that should get the packet. To make that determination, a switch stores an ARP cache, which is a lookup table of which hosts are on which ports. You can often confuse a switch by moving a computer from one port to another, so it may be necessary to power-cycle the switch in this circumstance (which clears most switches' ARP caches). Managed switches, like managed hubs, have complete command-line interfaces and configurability, with the attendant high price and complexity. There are even VLAN switches, which connect multiple LANs together using many different kinds of cabling mechanisms.

Because each port on a switch has its own collision domain, switched network traffic is able to take fuller advantage of the available network bandwidth. An eight-port, 100base-TX hub with all ports in use has to divide the available 100Mbps between the eight ports. If all eight ports are simultaneously trying to do bandwidth-intensive tasks and their aggregate bandwidth demand is greater than 100Mbps, "collisions" become more common. In a collision, two ports try to transmit or receive traffic at the same time, resulting in retransmissions at the physical link level and performance well below each host's logical share of the available 100Mbps. Switches alleviate this problem. Whereas a 100Mbps hub has 100Mbps of internal wiring in total, an eight-port switch has 800Mpbs worth of wiring—the full bandwidth duplicated for every port. This is why switches tend to have fewer ports than hubs, and switches with many ports are quite expensive.

From a security standpoint, a fully switched network gives you the added benefit that machines in one collision domain can't see any traffic in any other collision domain. You can run a packet sniffer (such as `tcpdump` or EtherPeek) to put your Ethernet card into "promiscuous mode" (accepting all packets it sees regardless of whether they're destined for it) and spy on all traffic within your collision domain. Switches allow you to separate these domains so that this isn't possible. This also protects your network from being overwhelmed by a single host that floods the network with an aggressive traffic flow, whether intentional or not, that uses all available bandwidth within the collision domain. Using switches rather than hubs, along with careful network planning, can greatly increase the network's reliability, security, and performance, thus making them worth the added cost.

Switches usually have no uplink ports. Occasionally, one or both ports have a pushbutton to select whether the ports need a straight-through or crossover cable. This is the case with some two-port switches, which serve purely as a filter to keep out irrelevant traffic. As a general rule, treat ports on a switch as hub-type devices and use crossover cables to connect one switch to another or a straight-through cable to connect a switch to a hub's uplink port. Most switches can auto-negotiate the speed and duplex mode of Ethernet cards, so you generally don't need to worry.

Bridges

A *bridge* is another connecting device, in the class of hubs and switches, but it has a rather specialized purpose. It acts somewhat like a switch, but in a more complex way. A bridge is a type of switch that links different networks so that traffic from hosts on one network can travel to another network directly without having to go to a router in the interim. Think of a bridge as a type of switch that spans different networks, linking them together above the "data link" layer of the stack so that traffic from hosts on one network destined for another network can travel there directly without having to go to a router in the interim. This is useful for allowing traffic to pass from an Ethernet network to a Token Ring network, which is another style of LAN that is rapidly on the way out, so we won't bother discussing it.

Routers

A router is the most complex (and expensive) of all networking devices. Routers have full operating systems and maintain tables that keep track of where entire networks can be found. Most small networks have only one router, at the "edge" of the network (the boundary between the LAN and the WAN that connects it to the Internet), specifying which network numbers indicate the LAN and which ones should be forwarded upstream into the WAN. You can have any number of routers in your network, though, each one managing a subnetwork and subservient to the topmost router.

What's more, routers use a variety of protocols to communicate with each other and plot out what's the best way for a packet to get from one place to another. When you send out a packet, it travels upstream from router to router, until it reaches a router that knows where downstream to find your packet's destination network. That router sends your packet through the downstream route until it reaches the destination LAN and, ultimately, the destination host. Routing is the backbone of the Internet and possibly the most complex part of the way TCP/IP networking operates. You'll learn more about routing in Chapter 27, "Configuring an Internet Gateway."

TIP

You can see Internet routing in action by performing a `traceroute`; simply type **traceroute** **<hostname>** to get a listing of all the routers between you and your specified host as well as a reading of how fast that router responds. This is also useful for seeing how well the routers are performing between you and your destination host. Here's an example:

```
# traceroute freebsd.org
traceroute to freebsd.org (216.136.204.21),
➥64 hops max, 40 byte packets
 1  dot7.orrc1.pf.somewhere.com (203.152.186.253)
➥3.200 ms  0.632 ms  3.910 ms
 2  pos1-0-0.orrc5.pf.somewhere.com (192.7.4.162)
➥1.055 ms  0.634 ms  0.572 ms
 3  gr-2-0-0-1.orpa8.pf.somewhere.com (192.7.4.164)
➥1.862 ms  1.390 ms  1.426 ms
 4  so-1-0-0.orpa7.pf.somewhere.com (192.7.4.230)
➥1.366 ms  1.003 ms  3.606 ms
```

```
  5  bas1-m.pao.yahoo.com (198.32.176.135)
➡1.211 ms   1.310 ms   1.378 ms
  6  ge-0-2-0.msr1.sc5.yahoo.com (216.115.100.233)
➡2.456 ms   2.413 ms ge-1-2-0.msr2.sc5.yahoo.com (216.115.101.230)
➡4.885 ms
  7  vl44.bas2-m.sc5.yahoo.com (66.163.160.222)
➡1.925 ms   2.295 ms   2.389 ms
  8 freefall.FreeBSD.org (216.136.204.21)
➡4.577 ms 2.107 ms 3.137 ms
```

Most routers have either one or two LAN-side ports, either RJ-45 jacks or AUI ports that require transceivers—devices that translate the signal from one physical format to another—to convert the interface to twisted pair. On the other side of the router is a serial cable that connects to the DSU/CSU or other such high-speed serial converter, beyond which you have WAN traffic. Routers vary greatly in size, complexity, number and type of ports, manageability, and price. Understanding how they work is one of the most important things you can learn in the networking world.

Network Protocols

We've mentioned that most Internet traffic—HTTP, e-mail, FTP, and so on—uses TCP/IP as its transport protocol. TCP/IP itself refers to the combination of the most common "network" and "transport" protocols in use on the Internet. IP, the Internet Protocol, is the backbone of the vast majority of Internet traffic—the "network" layer of the TCP/IP stack. TCP, however, isn't the only commonly used "transport" layer protocol. There's also UDP, the User Datagram Protocol, which differs from TCP in a few key ways. IP also isn't the only means of carrying traffic at the "network" level; it has a number of contemporaries, too, but they're mostly useful on LANs. These include AppleTalk, IPX, NetBIOS, and so on. Then there's ICMP, which exists partly on the "network" layer and partly on the "transport" layer; it's the mechanism by which the ping and traceroute utilities work. We'll talk about each of these protocols in some detail next.

The Transmission Control Protocol (TCP)

TCP is a two-way transmission protocol that's designed to be *reliable*, unlike UDP. TCP has lots of built-in features to make sure the traffic it carries arrives properly at its destination. It also has features to divide large packets into appropriately sized fragments so as to transmit more efficiently.

TCP uses *retransmission* to provide reliability. Here's how a simplified version of retransmission works: When a TCP packet is sent over the network, a timeout is set by the sender, which then waits for an acknowledgment (ACK) packet to come back from the

21

other side. When it receives the ACK, the sender then proceeds to send the next packet. If the sender doesn't get the ACK within the specified timeout, it knows that either its own packet didn't make it or the acknowledgment packet got lost on the way back. The sender resends the packet and again waits for the ACK. This is a retransmission, and although it does provide reliability, it also decreases network efficiency. Each time a packet is retransmitted, it creates doubled traffic in the infrastructure, which can lead to congestion, especially considering that each packet has a certain amount of *overhead* in the size of the TCP/IP headers that must accompany it. This overhead uses up a certain amount of bandwidth, regardless of what other content makes up the packets.

A TCP connection involves an active setup procedure in which both hosts at the endpoints of the connection exchange startup tokens; disconnection at the end of a flow involves a similar exchange. This means that, unlike UDP flows, TCP flows can be accurately tracked by the system and their state can be viewed using tools such as `netstat`. TCP connections are also full-duplex, meaning that data can be sent and received at the same time, using the same packets. It's not uncommon for there to be a data payload on the ACK packets, for example. TCP has a number of other interesting features, such as a checksum that ensures the integrity of the data in the packet, automatic packet fragmenting and reconstruction, and out-of-order resequencing at the receiver level. These are all things that UDP doesn't do—or at least isn't required to do.

TCP is used in protocols in which data integrity is important and a connection can be ensured, such as Web surfing, e-mail, FTP, and the vast majority of other network applications.

The User Datagram Protocol (UDP)

UDP is a similar "transport" protocol to TCP, existing at the same layer in the OSI stack model; however, it differs from TCP in a number of key ways. The big thing to remember about UDP is that it's *unreliable*. There is no acknowledgment mechanism, no retransmission mechanism, and no true "connection" concept. UDP packets can be broadcast to anyone on the network, if so chosen, or a selected set of recipients, regardless of whether they're expecting to hear anything.

UDP packets can get lost along the way from the sender to the receiver, and neither can have any way of knowing that it missed any packets. There are no sequence numbers in UDP as there are in TCP. A sender simply spews out the traffic, and the specified recipients can receive it or not—it's up to them and the network. Any reliability in a UDP flow must be added by the application using it; an example of this is the Network Filesystem (NFS) protocol, which is described in detail in Chapter 32, "The Network Filesystem (NFS)."

NOTE

Why would a file-management and transfer protocol such as NFS, with its need for secure data integrity, use UDP? The reason is that with NFS, many hosts on the network can be using an NFS resource, and any of them can drop off the network without warning. Rather than maintaining

> all the processing overhead necessary for keeping TCP connections with these ephemeral hosts, NFS chooses UDP as its transport and provides the data integrity necessary for file transfer at the application level. Information about the complete transfer is maintained in the packets' data, so NFS can know when it's missing any pieces, or if any are corrupt.

The biggest use for UDP these days is in streaming media. Teleconferencing, streamed video, broadcast music—these protocols don't care if they miss a beat. They consist of long streams of datagrams (packets), usually very small ones, which are gathered in the order they're received by the application and then dumped to the screen or speakers. One lost packet probably won't even be missed. If network congestion occurs, the packets are simply lost at the router level (routers keep their own timeouts on their buffers), and the stream is resumed in real time when the host becomes available again—and not where it left off. There's no reason to queue up all the missed packets and dump them through at once. They're irrelevant. That's the utility of UDP.

The Internet Control Message Protocol (ICMP)

ICMP is a small "diagnostic" protocol, mostly used in tools that gauge network health. Some consider ICMP to exist on the network layer, equivalent to IP and IPX; others treat it as a transport protocol like TCP or UDP. The truth is that it has elements of both. The messages received by ICMP are handled at the "network" layer, but these messages contain IP header information, so it's difficult to say where it fits in the scheme of things.

The most common ways you'll use ICMP are with the ping and traceroute tools, both of which return information fundamental to the ICMP datagram structure. Mostly, they're built on ICMP's capability to query remote hosts for timestamps or echoes, which come back with specialized codes. ICMP can also be used to provide error messages to "transport" layer protocols, such as the "Port Unreachable" error returned by ICMP to a UDP sender that tries to talk to an unavailable port on the recipient's machine. ICMP has 16 of these error conditions it can report, as well as about as many additional functions. You generally won't need to know about them because they're really of interest only to the applications that can read them.

TCP/IP

Now that you know something about different network components and protocols, let's take a look at how they all fit together.

As mentioned earlier, the TCP/IP stack is the collection of sequential layers of protocols and their handlers, which inherit tasks and data from each other (both upward and downward). As you saw earlier in this chapter, data travels down the stack from user-level applications through the various protocols we've discussed before reaching the wire. Figure 21.8 shows a simplified version of the OSI model in which common applications and their respective "transport" components interact.

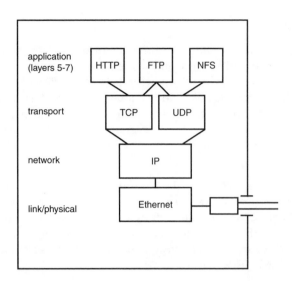

FIGURE 21.8 Simplified TCP/IP stack layering diagram, showing common applications and their path to the Ethernet link.

An application takes raw data and hands it to the transport layer (either TCP or UDP), which adds a TCP or UDP header containing information about how the remote TCP or UDP layer should decode it. The data packet now rolls down to the network layer, in which IP attaches another header containing information relevant to the remote network layer. Finally, it reaches the data link layer, in which the Ethernet driver encapsulates the whole packet in Ethernet headers and trailers and sends it out through the Ethernet card onto the network.

A receiving computer passes an incoming packet up the stack, each layer stripping off a header and following its instructions before passing the packet to the next layer, until the application receives the raw data it needs. By this time, it's generally able to ignore any details about sessions, port numbers, hardware addresses, or anything else—the TCP/IP stack at the sender's end has handled all that automatically and has packaged everything neatly in the headers, and the recipient's TCP/IP stack has read this all out and presented it to the application free of complications.

Different network devices fit at different levels of the TCP/IP stack. A bridge links multiple networks at the data link level (for instance, Ethernet and Token Ring). A switch or a router links networks at the network level (where IP addresses are meaningful).

Most operating systems in the world, including FreeBSD, handle TCP/IP the same way. A definitive reference for the structure of the protocol suite, regarded by many networking professionals as required reading, is *TCP/IP Illustrated* by W. Richard Stevens (Addison-Wesley, 1994). This multivolume text uncovers all the relevant details of how the protocols interrelate and interoperate as well as presents them in an understandable manner.

IP Addresses

The Internet Protocol enables computers on many disparate LANs to find their way to each other; this is accomplished through the hierarchical IP address system. If you've ever done anything on the Internet at all, you're probably familiar with IP addresses—at least enough to know what they look like. An IP address is typically used as a way to refer to a specific computer on the Internet, although its meaning is actually a lot more flexible than "one IP address per machine." Most generally, it's a logical designation whose purpose is to locate a machine on the Internet so that IP routers can direct traffic between it and any other machine.

An IP address is a string of 32 bits in the IP header, which specifies either what machine a packet came from or where it is destined (both addresses are present in the header). The 32 bits can be thought of also as four 8-bit bytes, each of which is expressed as a number from 0 to 255—hence, the familiar four-part dotted-decimal notation, of the form 111.112.113.114. This allows it to be treated hierarchically when dealing with Class A, B, or C subnets, as we will discuss next.

There are a few "special" IP addresses to keep in mind. First is the *network* address. This is an IP address in which one or more of its bytes are zero, such as 64.41.131.0. If the final byte is a zero, the address is a synonym for the entire 64.41.131 network and is generally used only when configuring routers. More important is if one or more of the trailing bytes are 255 (all bits set to 1). This is the *broadcast* address for the network, an address that matches all hosts on that network as defined by the mask; for example, 64.41.131.255 matches all hosts on the 64.41.131 network, and 64.41.255.255 matches all hosts on the 64.41 network. A packet sent to the broadcast address will be received and processed by all hosts on the network, which is useful for finding out which host on the network has a certain Ethernet address. We will be discussing how these matching addresses work a little later when we discuss routing and subnets.

Subnets and the Network Mask

The netmask, which travels hand in hand with IP addresses when you're configuring TCP/IP on a machine, is one of the most misunderstood parts of the whole structure, and yet potentially one of the most elegant when understood properly.

The purpose of the network mask (or *netmask*) is simply to tell a router or host whether a packet is supposed to go to the network it's on or go upstream to the next router. This is the decision that is made in a situation such as the one we just discussed in the section on ARP. When a router receives a packet (not an ARP packet, a real TCP/IP packet) and it has to decide what to do with this packet, it checks the packet's destination IP address against its own netmask.

The netmask, a 32-bit string like an IP address, usually takes the form 255.255.255.0. Let's say we have a router managing the 64.41.131 network. The router receives a packet addressed for 64.41.131.45. This is matched against the netmask in an "and" fashion, and the result matches as far as 64.41.131, the address of the network our router manages. This packet is passed on to the network. Another packet now comes in, destined for 64.41.189.45; this match against the netmask fails, and the router passes the packet upstream to the next router.

This mechanism allows you to set up subnets within your network. Let's assume you have a Class B address range to work with (64.41.xxx.xxx). Your network's main router, R1, manages this entire range, but you can put a router (R2) inside this network to manage two Class C address ranges: 64.41.131.xxx and 64.41.132.xxx. Hosts in the 64.41.131 network can be plugged into the same hub as hosts in the 64.41.132 network, as shown in Figure 21.9, but they won't speak directly to each other if their netmasks are set to 255.255.255.0, a Class C mask.

Destination IP addresses in sent packets won't match the senders' netmasks. However, if a sender host (H1) in 64.41.131 sets its netmask to a Class B mask (255.255.0.0), the addresses *will* match, and the sender would be able to send the packet directly to H2 (a host on 64.41.132). However, note that H2 won't be able to send its replies directly back to H1 because its netmask prevents this! It has to send the reply back via R2, which has multiple network addresses and subnets bound to its internal interface. You'd need to set H2's netmask to 255.255.0.0 for it to talk directly to H1 without going through the router.

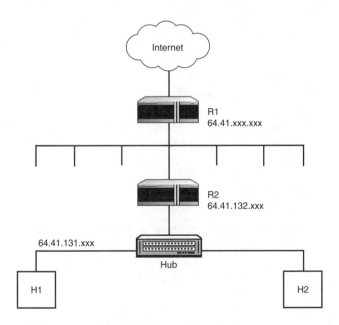

FIGURE 21.9   A network with subnets, demonstrating the packet path between two hosts whose netmasks don't permit them to communicate directly.

Netmasks don't need to be aligned on the byte boundary, either. For this reason, they're sometimes specified in pure hexadecimal format (for example, 0xffffff00 rather than 255.255.255.0). You can specify a netmask of 0xffffffc0, for instance, or 255.255.255.192. This mask will match a network of 64 hosts—the ones between 1 and 64.

Another notation used in specifying networks that incorporates the netmask is Classless Inter-Domain Routing (CIDR), which takes the form of the network address, a slash, and the number of bits that make up the mask. For example, a mask of 255.255.255.0 on our 64.41.131 network would be written as 64.41.131/24 because the mask consists of three 8-bit bytes with all bits set to 1 (or 24 bits). The 255.255.255.192 example, likewise, would correspond to a notation of 64.41.131/26. This notation is seen in routing tables and other places where succinctness is useful.

Working with IP Addresses

Typically, a single IP address is bound to a single physical port (or interface) on an Ethernet card; this is only by convention, though. The only constraint is that no two Ethernet interfaces on the same network can share the same IP address. You can bind multiple IP addresses to the same interface, though, and every interface needs to have at least one unique IP address to function. You might choose to install two Ethernet cards in your system in order to have access to two different networks at once, for example, or one address might be bound to an Ethernet card while another refers to your wireless 802.11 card. Many Ethernet cards have multiple ports, and each one can have one or more addresses assigned to it. What configuration you choose depends on how your network is set up.

You can find out the IP addresses of any Ethernet cards and other network interfaces in your system using the ifconfig utility, as shown in Listing 21.1. The -a option shows all devices, or you can specify a specific interface (such as x10) to single out. The inet line shows a configured IP address; the x10 interface in this example shows multiple IP addresses bound to a single card.

LISTING 21.1   Typical Output of ifconfig

```
# ifconfig -a
x10: flags=8843<UP,BROADCAST,RUNNING,SIMPLEX,MULTICAST> mtu 1500
        inet 64.41.131.102 netmask 0xffffff00 broadcast 64.41.131.255
        inet6 fe80::201:2ff:fe55:1256%x10 prefixlen 64 scopeid 0x1
        inet 209.154.215.246 netmask 0xffffffff broadcast 209.154.215.246
        ether 00:01:02:55:12:56
        media: autoselect (100baseTX) status: active
        supported media: autoselect 100baseTX <full-duplex> 100baseTX
10baseT/UTP <full-duplex> 10baseT/UTP 100baseTX <hw-loopback>
lp0: flags=8810<POINTOPOINT,SIMPLEX,MULTICAST> mtu 1500
```

LISTING 21.1   Continued

```
gif0: flags=8010<POINTOPOINT,MULTICAST> mtu 1280
gif1: flags=8010<POINTOPOINT,MULTICAST> mtu 1280
gif2: flags=8010<POINTOPOINT,MULTICAST> mtu 1280
gif3: flags=8010<POINTOPOINT,MULTICAST> mtu 1280
lo0: flags=8049<UP,LOOPBACK,RUNNING,MULTICAST> mtu 16384
        inet6 fe80::1%lo0 prefixlen 64 scopeid 0x7
        inet6 ::1 prefixlen 128
        inet 127.0.0.1 netmask 0xff000000
ppp0: flags=8010<POINTOPOINT,MULTICAST> mtu 1500
sl0: flags=c010<POINTOPOINT,LINK2,MULTICAST> mtu 552
faith0: flags=8000<MULTICAST> mtu 1500
```

IP Version 6 (IPv6)

Various groups, such as the KAME project (http://www.kame.net), have been working recently on incorporating support for the next generation of IP (version 6, or IPv6) into FreeBSD. IPv6 provides a 128-bit address space, with addresses effectively four times the size in IPv4 (the current version). The result is address space for 3.4×10^38 hosts—a number that we're unlikely to reach anytime soon, to say the least. Also included in IPv6 are a number of other enhancements, such as built-in encryption and authentication, connection differentiation (with flow labels), complete auto-configurability of hosts, and the abandonment of several outdated parts of IPv4 that are no longer used.

IPv6 is catching on very, very slowly. Networks are expensive to build, and retrofitting them to be IPv6 compliant generally means replacing all existing equipment with newer, more expensive, less-mature hardware. Very few companies are willing to take that plunge just yet. But in the meantime, FreeBSD has full support for IPv6 and can take advantage of the various network resources currently available for IPv6.

Networking at the Ethernet Level

The Address Resolution Protocol (ARP) and the MAC (or Ethernet) address provide the way in which Ethernet cards communicate on a LAN. ARP forms the basis for Internet routing, allowing routers to behave as destinations for LAN traffic, and then manipulate the Ethernet headers to make them compatible with the destination network.

Although IP addresses are fairly visible to us as users because we can specify them directly in our networking applications, such as Web and FTP programs, they are really just artificial constructs; they're bound to their hosts' Ethernet interfaces at the operating system level and can be changed at any time. At the bottom level of the TCP/IP stack, the data link layer, the IP address has no meaning—an Ethernet card knows nothing about what IP address the operating system has assigned to it or its hardware. Device drivers exist at a higher level than the one at which the device communicates with the network.

What the network is really interested in is what's variously called the physical address, the hardware address, the Ethernet address, or the Media Access Controller (MAC) address. Every network interface device has a MAC address programmed into it at the factory—a unique one. The MAC address is theoretically supposed to be useful as a "fingerprint" identifier for an Ethernet card (and, thereby, a computer) because no two Ethernet cards in the world ideally share one. This doesn't work out in practice, though, because MAC addresses can be forged. There is no routing mechanism for a MAC address as there is for an IP address. It operates entirely at the physical link level on a LAN and can't be forwarded by a router. The way it interoperates with IP addresses and routers is rather interesting; but first, let's take a closer look at what makes a MAC address tick.

The `ifconfig` output you saw a little earlier shows an `ether` line for the `x10` interface card. This address shows `00:01:02:55:12:56`, a typical MAC address for cards made by 3Com. The address itself is a string of six bytes (48 bits), expressed in hexadecimal and usually separated by colons. This makes for about 2,800,000,000,000,000 possible addresses—considerably more than the estimated 30 million networked computers online today. The first three bytes are used to identify the vendor (each vendor has one or more three-byte signatures assigned by the IEEE), and the other three are unique to the card. So, effectively, we really have the capacity for 16.7 million vendors, each with 16.7 million cards on the market. This does have the possibility of eventual scalability problems. It's probably for the best that the MAC address isn't used for routing!

Here's how it really works. When a newly created packet reaches the Ethernet layer of the sending TCP/IP stack, the Ethernet card must send it out onto the network and address it to the destination computer. The stack uses the MAC address instead of the IP address because, remember, the Ethernet cards on the network know nothing about IP addresses! But where does the TCP/IP stack get the MAC address of the remote computer? It has to use ARP.

ARP is what maps IP addresses to MAC addresses. If your application wants to send a packet to the IP address `10.5.6.100`, it sends the packet down the stack to the link layer. There, the stack consults the ARP cache, an OS-level table where known mappings between IP addresses and MAC addresses are stored. If the stack has never sent a packet to `10.5.6.100` before, that address won't be in the ARP table, and the TCP/IP stack must then perform an ARP query.

The ARP query is a broadcast packet, addressed to all Ethernet cards on the LAN (by setting the destination MAC address to `ff:ff:ff:ff:ff:ff`, or all bytes equal to 255, as with a broadcast IP address). The packet's payload is the IP address the stack is trying to look up: `10.5.6.100`. Every machine on the network receives this packet, but only the machine with the IP address being sought replies. After the stack receives the reply packet, its IP address and MAC address go into the host's ARP cache for future use. The packet is then sent by the sending machine's TCP/IP stack onto the network destined for the intended recipient's MAC address only.

> **NOTE**
>
> Earlier in the chapter, we talked a little bit about how switches keep their own internal ARP caches. Now that you know how ARP works, you can see how switches can keep track of which hosts are found on which ports through the use of ARP. A switch performs its own ARP queries to determine where to find a host to which it must send a packet it has received. After it adds that ARP information to its own cache, it can direct future traffic to that destination address more quickly.

Routing Between Networks Using ARP and MAC Addresses

ARP is very efficient for figuring out which packets should go where on a LAN; but what if the machine you're sending the packet to isn't on the same network as the sender? Well, that's where routers come into play. A router receives an ARP packet like any other host. When a router looks up its IP address bindings to see whether it should reply to the ARP packet, however, it finds that its internal routes are set up to send everything except traffic destined for the LAN it manages out onto the WAN toward the next upstream router. The router's TCP/IP stack sees this as a claim that the router has all nonlocal IP addresses bound to its Ethernet card on the LAN. As far as the router is concerned, it *is* the computer you're looking for, and it replies to the ARP as though it were.

The following steps are involved in a packet's journey from one host to another across the Internet:

- A host wants to send a packet to a host with an IP address that's on a remote network, so it sends an ARP request for the machine with that IP address.

- The local gateway router, which has all nonlocal IP addresses bound to its MAC address, replies that it is the destination host.

- The sending host sends the packet to the router.

- The router alters the sender MAC address in the packet's headers to match its own MAC address and then forwards the packet on over the WAN.

- The next router on the WAN receives the packet and performs a similar operation, setting the sending MAC address to its own and forwarding it on, until the packet reaches its destination network.

- The final router receives the packet, determines from the destination IP address and its own netmask that the packet is destined for a machine on its own network, and it uses ARP to find out which machine the recipient is.

- The recipient host replies to the router with its own MAC address.

- The router alters the packet's recipient MAC address to match that of the recipient host and then sends the packet directly over the LAN.

Checking ARP Cache Contents with the arp Command

ARP is handled transparently by applications and the TCP/IP stack; you'll probably never have to actually initiate ARP commands by yourself. However, there are some occasions when you'll need to tweak the ARP cache. You can check the contents of the cache by using the arp -a command:

```
# arp -a
w001.sjc-ca.dsl.cnc.net (64.41.131.1) at 0:0:c5:7c:7:f0 [ethernet]
w013.sjc-ca.dsl.cnc.net (64.41.131.13) at 0:30:65:a4:9a:5e [ethernet]
w063.sjc-ca.dsl.cnc.net (64.41.131.63) at ff:ff:ff:ff:ff:ff permanent
➥[ethernet]
```

Entries in the ARP cache do time out after a while, but there are times when you might need to clear the cache manually. Someone on the network might install a new Ethernet card in their machine and bind the old IP address to the new MAC address, which can make it unreachable if the old combination is still in your cache. You can delete cache entries by name, by IP address, or all at once (with -a):

```
# arp -d w001.sjc-ca.dsl.cnc.net
# arp -d 64.41.131.13
# arp -d –a
```

Routing

You've already learned a little bit about how IP routing works, but we'll now cover it in a little bit more detail. Configuring routes properly is one of the great skills one can develop in networking, and it pays to be able to do it correctly—or at least to have a working understanding of it so that you can perform administrative tasks that require interfacing with the routing table, such as portsentry (which we will discuss in Chapter 29, "Network Security").

A router is any device configured to act as a router, which includes actual routers or regular servers that can do the job in a pinch. Routers work by maintaining a routing table—a set of rules that says where packets that match certain IP address criteria should be sent. Because FreeBSD can be configured as a router, let's look at its routing tables as an example using the netstat -rn command (-r tells netstat to show the routing tables, and -n says not to resolve IP addresses into hostnames):

```
# netstat -rn
Routing tables

Internet:
Destination       Gateway           Flags   Refs    Use     Netif Expire
default           hsrp-gw.netnation. UGSc    126     1379327     xl0
```

```
64.41.53.101/32      localhost           UGScB       0          3      loo
net-64-40-111.netn   link#1              UC          0          0      x10 =>
ip3.somewhere.com    0:50:ba:b3:98:13    UHLW        2     357107      x10      735
ip4.somewhere.com    0:50:ba:b3:95:bb    UHLW        0       2272      x10      500
ip6.somewhere.com    0:1:2:55:12:56      UHLW        0     118941      loo =>
ip6.somewhere.com    localhost           UGScB       0          0      loo
hsrp-gw.netnation.   0:0:c:7:ac:1e       UHLW      119       8814      x10      405
64.77.63.139/32      localhost           UGScB       0          0      loo
Toronto-ppp218408.   localhost           UGScB       0          0      loo
localhost            localhost           UH         45   45210727      loo
goo.cs.und.nodak.e   localhost           UGScB       0          0      loo
```

The information in the routing table includes the following fields for each entry:

- **Destination**—This can be an IP address, a hostname, a network address (which FreeBSD displays in CIDR format, as you can see in the preceding example), or one of several special destinations, such as the "default route." This field matches the destination address of any packet the machine doing the routing sees.

- **Gateway address**—This is the "next-hop" router address where traffic to the specified destination should be sent. This can be a hostname or IP address, or for destinations on the LAN it can be a MAC address. FreeBSD also shows an entry for the link#1 gateway, which is a route matching the network of the primary network interface, from which new routes can be cloned on use (hence the C flag).

- **Flags**—This field specifies the type of route. Each letter represents a different flag, so this example shows routes with between two and five simultaneous flags. See man netstat for the meaning of each of the flags.

- **Network interface**—When a packet matches a route in the table, it is passed out through this specified interface.

IP routing grew from the distributed, adaptive defense communications network envisioned by ARPA; therefore, its nature is to dynamically update these routing tables according to network conditions. The large telecommunications hubs maintain immense routing tables with many backup links from any one place to any other place. When one route is found to be unavailable, the routing table shuffles the entries around until traffic is redirected to a working route. The result is a system in which no single router has to know anything about the route to a packet's destination other than where its own next-hop router is. Any address that isn't local (in other words, any address that isn't on the network managed by that router) is passed upstream to the next-hop router, and so on, until the packet reaches a router that has an explicit entry in its routing table—with the appropriate netmask—for the network matching the packet's destination IP address. At that point, the packet is routed out that interface and hopefully to its destination.

Routing Misconfiguration

IP routing is susceptible to misconfiguration. On the way upstream, the packet will keep moving upward until it finds an explicit match for its destination address. Someone has to explicitly add a bogus route to the table to hijack the packet on its way up the chain of routers. In its default state, the packet will reach the backbone routers without incident. However, after the packet starts downstream, every router along the way must be properly configured to route to the network that its upstream next-hop router thinks it's capable of routing to! A packet might start on its way downstream, only to find that the router that was supposed to have a further route for it to the destination actually *doesn't* have one. Naturally, without an explicit route for the packet, the router will pass the packet back to its upstream router, which will then send the packet back downstream again, beginning what is frequently referred to as a "router loop":

```
traceroute to somewhere.com (209.237.26.189), 30 hops max, 40 byte packets
 1  r2-72-core-van.nx.com (10.10.4.253)  101.878 ms  135.377 ms  85.218 ms
 2  dis2-atm1.in.nx.net (206.108.110.189)  132.023 ms  80.653 ms  81.686 ms
 3  core2-1.in.nx.net (206.108.101.45)  102.365 ms  61.537 ms  68.561 ms
 4  core2.in.nx.net (206.108.102.209)  79.989 ms  109.389 ms  115.587 ms
 5  bx3-pos5-0.in.nx.net (206.108.102.202)  86.434 ms  109.678 ms  129.128 ms
 6  sea1-nx.above.net (208.184.233.73)  91.201 ms  67.287 ms  79.369 ms
 7  core2.above.net (208.185.175.178)  74.219 ms  79.480 ms  93.121 ms
 8  sjc2.sjc2.above.net (216.200.127.117)  188.692 ms  212.627 ms  181.123 ms
 9  core1.above.net (208.184.102.25)  195.260 ms  194.973 ms  272.053 ms
10  main1.sjc1.above.net (208.185.175.246)  344.104 ms  318.313 ms
11  core1.above.net (208.184.102.25)  195.260 ms  194.973 ms  272.053 ms
12  main1.sjc1.above.net (208.185.175.246)  344.104 ms  318.313 ms
13  core1.above.net (208.184.102.25)  195.260 ms  194.973 ms  272.053 ms
14  main1.sjc1.above.net (208.185.175.246)  344.104 ms  318.313 ms
15  core1.above.net (208.184.102.25)  195.260 ms  194.973 ms  272.053 ms
16  main1.sjc1.above.net (208.185.175.246)  344.104 ms  318.313 ms
17  core1.above.net (208.184.102.25)  195.260 ms  194.973 ms  272.053 ms
18  main1.sjc1.above.net (208.185.175.246)  344.104 ms  318.313 ms
```

This "bouncing" behavior will continue, preventing proper delivery of packets until the downstream router fixes its routing tables. Fortunately, usually when this occurs it's because work is being done on the router that's at fault, and the condition is temporary, resolving itself when the backed-up routing tables are restored.

Gateways and Network Address Translation

A gateway is the router for a specific network, often used for translating addresses used by hosts on the LAN it manages to the addresses that the outside world sees. The term *gateway* is frequently used to mean *router*, and that isn't an inaccurate statement; we should clarify exactly what it means in today's parlance, though.

When you're configuring a machine's TCP/IP settings, you have to specify a gateway. This is simply the next-hop router for the machine you're configuring. Referring back to Figure 21.8, note that H1 and H2 have to have a gateway configured so that they can operate with hosts whose addresses don't match their netmasks. Generally, in this type of topology, the gateway would be R2. Depending on the type of router, H1 and H2 might not be able to reach R1 directly. It's important to consider failure modes. If R2 should be shut down, it is unlikely that it would pass LAN traffic directly through; some network devices fail into a pass-through mode, but routers seldom fall into that category.

In another type of network topology, the subnets defined by R2 might be completely unlike the R1 subnet; for instance, R1 might specify the 64.41 network, but R2 would control subnets at 192.168.10 and 192.168.11. In this case, it wouldn't do to set H1 or H2 to R1 as a gateway at all; traffic simply wouldn't reach it. The best practice is generally to set your machine's gateway to the nearest router and make sure the router is properly configured to pass traffic to the upstream router and to its managed subnets.

> **NOTE**
>
> Certain IP address ranges are "reserved" for specific private uses and cannot be assigned to hosts on public networks—data will not reach them. These ranges include 10.*.*.* and 192.168.*.*, which are commonly used in subnets and NAT topologies.

The traditional meaning of *gateway*, however, is the "edge device"—the point at which LAN traffic passes out onto the WAN. This device, generally a router, is also where network address translation (NAT) can be done. The NAT daemon on the router specifies aliases for internal routes and their translated addresses on the outside, and vice versa. NAT can be done in a one-to-one, many-to-one, or one-to-many fashion.

To use FreeBSD as a NAT router, you will want to configure and run the natd daemon; we'll discuss this in more detail in Chapter 27.

Hostnames and Domain Names

Now that you have an understanding of the way MAC addresses and IP addresses work, we can apply yet another layer of indirection to the host-finding process: hostnames and the Domain Name System (DNS). Hostnames assign human-readable names to machines that otherwise would only be identifiable by their IP addresses, and DNS is the mechanism by which those names are assigned.

Early in TCP/IP history, different networked machines were identifiable only by their IP addresses. This worked really well, until the number of online people grew so large that keeping track of all the numbers involved was tedious and error prone. Hence the introduction of the Domain Name System, a means of assigning common names to IP addresses, resulting in the much easier-to-use system we know today.

DNS records are kept in a centralized database on multiple *root servers*—the "master" name servers that hold the definitive DNS information for all the Internet—that are maintained by Network Solutions, Inc. These servers take their information from the DNS hosts they have designated as authoritative for any given domain name (for instance, `somewhere.com`). Each domain's authoritative DNS keeps the records in a database of its own, which varies from implementation to implementation. FreeBSD, like most Unixes, uses BIND, which keeps its records in `/etc/namedb`. We will discuss how to set up DNS on FreeBSD in Chapter 31, "The Domain Name Server."

Within a domain, every machine listed in the domain's DNS records has a hostname, or a simple machine name such as `tiger` or `pluto`. Combined with the domain, this results in a fully qualified domain name (FQDN), such as `tiger.somewhere.com`.

> **NOTE**
>
> It is also possible for a domain name to be fully qualified without a subdomain or hostname attached. The hostname `somewhere.com` is a fully qualified domain name, and a machine's IP address can be assigned to it.

What's important to understand for networking purposes is that the hierarchical structure of the domain name, hostname, and FQDN have no bearing on the hierarchical addressing conventions in IP addresses. The `somewhere.com` domain can have hosts with IP addresses all over the map—the DNS configuration just needs to point to them correctly. For instance, `www.somewhere.com` can be `64.41.131.45`, and `ftp.somewhere.com` can be `213.11.31.221`; it doesn't matter as far as TCP/IP is concerned. DNS is completely outside the TCP/IP stack.

Where DNS does come into play is at the application level, in which the hostname is used as an easier interface for the user than a bare IP address. A Web browser, for example, takes a DNS name and passes it to the operating system, which translates it into an IP address transparently before it even tries to connect to the requested host. To put it into the terms we've been using throughout this chapter, the abstraction that DNS provides over IP addresses is analogous to the abstraction that IP addresses provide over MAC addresses. Just as ARP associates IP and MAC addresses for use by the data link layer, a name lookup associates hostnames and IP addresses for use by the network layer.

The Dynamic Host Configuration Protocol (DHCP) and Automatic IP Addressing

The Dynamic Host Configuration Protocol assigns IP addresses to Ethernet interfaces on an as-needed basis. When an interface is to be configured by DHCP, it sends out a request at boot time to the designated DHCP server. This request, which is really a RARP query (analogous to ARP, but operating in reverse), carries the MAC address of the interface in question to the DHCP server, which responds with an IP address (and other network settings, such as the netmask) that it knows is available. The booting host then assigns this address to the interface, and the DHCP server sets up a "lease" period so that the host can boot with that same IP address on an ongoing basis.

We will be covering DHCP and how to configure FreeBSD for it in Chapter 34, "Dynamic Host Configuration Protocol (DHCP)."

CHAPTER **22**

Configuring Basic Networking Services

The last chapter offered a crash course in networking, the TCP/IP way. None of it (or very little) was FreeBSD specific or really told you how to go about setting up your system to do networking properly. The chapter did, however, lay the groundwork for the information you'll learn in this chapter. Here, you learn about the various tools you can use to configure TCP/IP.

We won't be talking about specialized network services (such as Web/HTTP, mail/SMTP, FTP, and so on) in this chapter; those topics are covered individually in later chapters of the book. Right now, we'll focus on the basics: getting the machine to be able to talk to its peers on your network.

Configuring the Network Card

As you learned in the last chapter, a computer can have multiple Ethernet cards (interfaces), and each of these cards can have multiple IP addresses and related settings. The convention is for each machine to have one Ethernet card with one IP address, but there's no reason to limit yourself in that regard. This chapter shows you how to set up as many simultaneously installed cards as you like. You also learn how to bind as many IP addresses to each card as you see fit.

The first step is to make sure you have at least one Ethernet card that FreeBSD will work with. Table 22.1 lists all the cards (more specifically, chipsets—cards from different manufacturers often use standardized chipsets that FreeBSD recognizes) that are supported in the GENERIC kernel. These cards comprise the vast majority of those used today, and your system should recognize any of these without any additional tweaking. The PCI cards are particularly well recognized by

FreeBSD. A good many other cards are supported by FreeBSD but not included in the GENERIC kernel; refer to /sys/i386/conf/NOTES (as discussed in the section "The NOTES File and LINT," in Chapter 16, "Kernel Configuration") and recompile the kernel to enable support for these cards.

NOTE

Be aware that the list of supported Ethernet cards changes fairly frequently. The devices are listed in the GENERIC kernel config file on your system, /sys/i386/conf/GENERIC. This will be the authoritative source for what cards are supported by your system.

TABLE 22.1   Ethernet Cards Supported in the Default (GENERIC) FreeBSD Kernel

Device Name	Cards Supported
PCI Cards	
de	DEC/Intel DC21x4x (Tulip)
em	Intel PRO/1000 adapter Gigabit Ethernet Card
txp	3Com 3cR990 (Typhoon)
vx	3Com 3c590, 3c595 (Vortex)
PCI/MII Cards	
fxp	Intel EtherExpress Pro/100B (82557, 82558)
tx	SMC 9432TX (83c170 "EPIC")
dc	DEC/Intel 21143 and various workalikes
pcn	AMD Am79C79x PCI 10/100 NICs
rl	RealTek 8129/8139
sf	Adaptec AIC-6915 (Starfire)
sis	Silicon Integrated Systems SiS 900/SiS 7016
ste	Sundance ST201 (D-Link DFE-550TX)
tl	Texas Instruments ThunderLAN
vr	VIA Rhine, Rhine II
wb	Winbond W89C840F
xl	3Com 3c90x (Boomerang, Cyclone)
ISA Cards	
ed	Novell NE1000/NE2000, 3Com 3c503, Western Digital/SMC 80xx
ex	Intel EtherExpress Pro/10 (82595)
ep	3Com 3c509
fe	Fujitsu MB86960A/MB86965A
lnc	Lance/PCnet cards (Isolan, Novell NE2100, NE32-VL, AMD Am7990, and Am79C960)
cs	Crystal Semiconductor CS89x0
sn	SMC 9000
xe	Xircom PC-card Ethernet

TABLE 22.1   Continued

Device Name	Cards Supported
Wireless (802.11) PCMCIA Cards	
wi	Lucent WaveLAN 802.11
an	Aironet 4500/4800 802.11
awi	BayStack 660 and others

Most Ethernet cards sold today for *x86* hardware are PCI based. This means that the PCI controller handles all the addressing automatically and you don't need to do any of the IRQ/DMA/memory address gyrations associated with ISA cards. If you're stuck with one of these older cards, though, there are a few things you need to do, such as setting the card's memory address and IRQ through a DOS utility and modifying the device hints for the card. You learn more about these accommodations later in this chapter in the sidebar "Coping with ISA Ethernet Cards."

Configuring Network Settings with sysinstall

The simplest way to configure your Ethernet card is by using sysinstall. The sysinstall method probably is familiar looking to anyone who has gone through this process on a Windows or Macintosh machine. The first time you ask sysinstall to do anything that requires a network connection (such as performing a net installation of the system, browsing packages, and various other tasks), it brings up the network-configuration window, in which you can set the TCP/IP options for your Ethernet card visually.

If you're already up and running in multiuser mode and not in the initial system installation process, you can get to this screen easily by running /stand/sysinstall, selecting Configure from the main menu, and then choosing the Media option. In this submenu, select FTP and some FTP server (it doesn't matter which; all we're doing here is triggering the network-configuration procedure, not installing any software). A dialog asks "Running multiuser, assume that the network is already configured?" Choose No to enter the network-configuration screens; the Network Interface Selection screen opens, as shown in Figure 22.1.

FIGURE 22.1   Selecting your Ethernet card in the sysinstall program.

The Network Interface selection screen presents you with a list of the interfaces that FreeBSD has found in your system. You'll probably see a number of choices that don't make a lot of sense. In the figure, you can see choices such as lp0 (the parallel port) and various PPP or SLIP options, and Ipv6 devices such as gif0 and faith0. You can ignore most of the options in the screen, because the one you want is probably at the top. The one we're using in this example is fxp1, an Intel EtherExpress Pro/100B PCI card.

When you select your Ethernet card, you're given two dialogs: a choice to let the system try to configure the card automatically using IPv6 and then another choice to let it try using DHCP. Answer No to both of these. You're then presented with the visual Network Configuration screen, as shown in Figure 22.2.

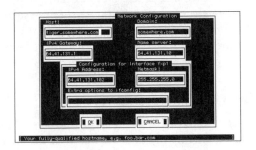

FIGURE 22.2   The visual Network Configuration screen in the sysinstall program.

Each field in this screen has a short description at the bottom of the window, but here's some further information about them:

- **Host**—This is the hostname, which is just the first part of the machine's fully qualified domain name. For instance, if your machine is www.somewhere.com, the Host: field should be set to www.

- **Domain**—This is the rest of the domain name, or somewhere.com. This can be a composite domain for networks with named subnets, such as cslab.ivyleague.edu.

- **IPv4 Gateway**—This is the IP address of your gateway router. Use the next-hop router closest to your machine, or whatever your network administrator or ISP identifies as your gateway address. If you are connected to the Internet via a DSL "modem" or similar device, its IP address (which is assigned by the ISP) should be your gateway. This router will be responsible for transmitting any traffic between your machine and any other machines in the world. As you have learned in Chapter 21, "Networking with FreeBSD," a gateway router must be on the same network as your FreeBSD machine's IP address, as defined by the netmask.

- **Name Server**—The IP address of the most reliable domain name server (DNS) in your network. You should use the DNS provided by your enterprise, ISP, or university network if at all possible; remote name servers are useful as backups, but they won't necessarily be set up to service nonlocal requests reliably. Later in this chapter you will learn how to assign multiple name servers, if necessary.

- **IPv4 Address**—This is the IP address you're assigning to your Ethernet card. It needs to be on the same subnet as your IPv4 gateway, as matched against your netmask. This was discussed in Chapter 21.

- **Netmask**—This is used to determine whether a packet's destination is on the local network. Set the field to 255.255.255.0 for a Class C network, which is the most commonly used netmask in most home configurations. Consult your network administrator to make sure what this number should be.

- **Extra options to ifconfig**—You most likely won't need to put anything in here unless you're a power user looking to tweak the performance of your interface card. Anything you put in here, such as specifying particular media types or duplex modes, will be added to the ifconfig command line that sysinstall issues in the background. You learn more about this command in "Using ifconfig to Apply Network Settings," later in this chapter.

After you've set all these options, select OK. The network settings will be applied to the card on the fly. Whatever you were doing in sysinstall continues—in this example, sysinstall connects to your selected FTP server. If the network configuration isn't successful, there's likely a problem with the network settings you entered, and you'll have to go back in and troubleshoot your settings. If you're in an enterprise network, ask your network administrator to give you the correct settings.

This process works in much the same way if you're doing a first-time installation of FreeBSD. You are presented with this configuration screen early in the install process. If you're doing a network installation, it will use the settings to pull down the system distribution.

Coping with ISA Ethernet Cards

Most PCI Ethernet cards are very trouble free. All you really need to do, especially if you have one of the commonly used cards supported in the GENERIC kernel, is plug it in, power up the machine, and watch the kernel identify the card in the boot process:

```
fxp0: <Intel PLC 10/100 Ethernet> port 0xde80-0xdebf mem
➥0xff8fe000-0xff8fefff irq 11 at device 8.0 on pci1
fxp0: Ethernet address 00:d0:b7:c7:74:f1
fxp1: <Intel Pro 10/100B/100+ Ethernet> port 0xdf00-0xdf3f mem
➥0xff700000-0xff7fffff,0xff8ff000-0xff8fffff irq 11 at
➥device 9.0 on pci1
fxp1: Ethernet address 00:d0:b7:bd:5d:13
```

However, if you're working with an old ISA card, the process can be trickier. ISA cards are set to a certain memory address and IRQ (interrupt request), and you have to pick values for both of them that aren't already used by some other device. Most Ethernet cards have a memory address of 0x300 or 0x280 and an IRQ of 9 or 10. Installing more than one of these cards means you have to configure the additional card to use an unused slot. Here's the really sticky part: This card configuration usually has to be done with a DOS utility that comes with the card.

It's fairly easy to see where the conflicts are between IRQs and memory addresses in the visual configuration menu during the initial installation of FreeBSD. Simply delete all the drivers you don't need, and if there's still a conflict between two installed devices, choose which one you want to change and what settings you want to switch to. Boot into MS-DOS with a DOS "rescue" floppy disk and then run the card's diagnostic program if you have its original disks. An Ethernet card's diagnostic program typically has a selection of common memory addresses and IRQs to set the card to use; pick one that isn't used by any other device (as reported in the visual configuration menu), set the card's firmware, and boot back into FreeBSD.

You might also need to alter the "device hints" (described in Chapter 16) for your card. These hints, kept in /boot/device.hints, control where FreeBSD expects to find the device. You can tweak them to match your card by editing that file. You should find lines such as the following:

```
hint.ed.0.at="isa"
hint.ed.0.port="0x300"
hint.ed.0.irq="10"
```

Modify the port (memory address) and IRQ lines to match the settings of your card and then reboot to activate it.

Configuring Network Settings Without sysinstall

Using sysinstall to configure your cards makes things easy in some ways; it's nice and visual, for instance, and it does everything in one place. But configuring with sysinstall is a less-than-versatile option for many of the networking tasks you may need to do. You can access the network settings more directly from the command line. Naturally, you must be root in order to run these commands in a way that alters the system's configuration.

CAUTION

Some of the functions we'll be discussing cannot be done in sysinstall, such as adding IP aliases and modifying the routing tables. In fact, if you have a customized IP setup (for example, a card with many IP aliases bound to it) and then you do an additional configuration of the card using sysinstall, you might lose your customized settings. Be aware that sysinstall is useful for the most basic and common of configuration tasks, but it should be avoided for more complex situations, for which it is not intended.

Using `ifconfig` to Apply Network Settings

The interface configurator, `ifconfig`, is the multipurpose tool for applying network settings on the fly. Its main purpose is to assign an IP address to an Ethernet card (interface), although, as with most other Unix tools, it can do a lot more. Here, we cover the most frequently used functions of `ifconfig`; check the `man ifconfig` page for further information.

First, let's use `ifconfig` to gather information on our network interfaces. In the previous chapter, you saw an example of `ifconfig -a`, which shows all interfaces and tells you which ones are available. Using `ifconfig -a` provides an easy way to find out whether your Ethernet driver is `ed0`, `fxp0`, `xl0`, or whatever. After you know, you can specify that device name as a parameter to `ifconfig` to just get that interface's settings:

```
# ifconfig fxp1
fxp1: flags=8843<UP,BROADCAST,RUNNING,SIMPLEX,MULTICAST> mtu 1500
        inet6 fe80::2d0:b7ff:febd:5d13%fxp1 prefixlen 64 scopeid 0x2
        inet 64.41.131.102 netmask 0xffffff00 broadcast 64.41.131.255
        ether 00:d0:b7:bd:5d:13
        media: autoselect (100baseTX <full-duplex>) status: active
        supported media: autoselect 100baseTX <full-duplex> 100baseTX
➥10baseT/UTP <full-duplex> 10baseT/UTP
```

> **CAUTION**
>
> We're about to go through a few configuration examples that will almost certainly cause your Ethernet interface to lose connectivity to any connected sessions. If you want to try out the functionality of `ifconfig` on your own machine, do it from the physical console rather than when you're connected via Telnet or SSH!

If you want to only change your IP address, use the following command:

```
# ifconfig fxp1 64.41.131.103
```

That's all there is to it. Note that if you don't specify a netmask, it's assumed you're setting a Class A address—and the netmask and broadcast address are set accordingly, as you can see in the updated `ifconfig fxp1` output:

```
        inet 64.41.131.103 netmask 0xff000000 broadcast 64.255.255.255
```

Let's try this again, but this time let's make it a Class C address, which means that you'll need to set your netmask, too. You do this with the `netmask` keyword in combination with the IP address. Note that `ifconfig` accepts netmasks in hex notation, in dotted-decimal notation, or by a symbolic name defined in `/etc/networks`. Therefore, the following commands are equivalent:

```
# ifconfig fxp1 64.41.131.103 netmask 255.255.255.0
# ifconfig fxp1 64.41.131.103 netmask 0xffffff00
# ifconfig fxp1 64.41.131.103 netmask your-netmask
```

You can also specify the broadcast address, although this generally isn't useful except in really exceptional networks. Note that although the broadcast address is automatically extrapolated from the IP address and netmask if you omit it (as discussed earlier), the reverse is not true: Omitting the netmask makes `ifconfig` assume a Class A mask. If you have to set the broadcast address, make sure you set both it and the netmask at the same time:

```
# ifconfig fxp1 64.41.131.103 netmask 255.255.0.0 broadcast 64.41.255.255
```

In some conditions you might need to set the Maximum Transmission Unit (MTU) of the interface. The MTU indicates the largest packet size the card can send out (in bytes); this value is usually 1500 for Ethernet cards. Sometimes, you might want to set it to a smaller value to minimize latency on low-speed WAN links. Your router usually takes care of managing transfers to minimize latency, though, so don't worry about this setting unless you have to and you know what you're doing:

```
# ifconfig fxp1 mtu 536
```

One final trick that `ifconfig` can use involves the `media` keyword, which allows you to make the card switch between the various listed media types. This capability is very handy if you have a card with multiple interfaces (such as you saw in the "Network Components" section of Chapter 21) and you want to switch from the BNC connector to the RJ-45 (UTP) connector or from the RJ-45 to the AUI connector. If you have a 10/100 Ethernet card and an auto-sensing hub that has auto-negotiated a speed of 100Mbps full-duplex with your card, you can force it into 10Mbps mode with the `media` and `mediaopt` keywords. Take a look at what `ifconfig fxp1` reports to be the supported media types (the following is a typical example):

```
        media: autoselect (100baseTX <full-duplex>) status: active
        supported media: autoselect 100baseTX <full-duplex> 100baseTX
➥10baseT/UTP <full-duplex> 10baseT/UTP
```

This example tells you that you're in auto-select mode. In that mode, the card negotiates the highest possible speed with the hub to which it's connected. Set it instead to 10BaseT mode. The `supported media:` line tells you that the keyword for this is `10baseT/UTP`, and that there's an option of `full-duplex` that you can set if you choose to (using the `mediaopt` keyword). Options are shown in angle brackets. Displayed more clearly, the media types and options for this example are as follows:

```
autoselect
100baseTX <full-duplex>
```

```
100baseTX
10baseT/UTP <full-duplex>
10baseT/UTP
```

Here's how to set this interface to each of the two available 10BaseT/UTP modes:

```
# ifconfig fxp1 media 10baseT/UTP
# ifconfig fxp1 media 10baseT/UTP mediaopt full-duplex
```

If you're doing this on a machine that's near the hub or switch where the Ethernet cable is plugged in, or if you can see the back of the computer, check the lights. You should see that the "100" light has gone out, indicating that the connection has renegotiated to 10Mpbs mode. Here's how to switch back again to the previous mode:

```
# ifconfig fxp1 media autoselect
```

Recall that full-duplex mode is where the card can both read and write at the same time, so 10BaseT in full-duplex mode means 10Mbps total in each direction. Half-duplex mode means a maximum of 10Mbps as the aggregate total of both directions. A hub can't do full-duplex mode. You need a switch if you want to take full advantage of full-duplex mode.

> **TIP**
>
> You can also find out which media types and options your Ethernet card driver supports by reading its man page (for instance, man fxp for our sample Intel driver).

Using route to Set the Gateway Router

We've now covered ifconfig in as much detail as you're likely to need. However, we haven't yet touched on how to set the gateway router or the DNS information from the command line, both of which are functions that the network configuration screen in sysinstall handles all at once. First, let's talk about gateway routers.

You don't set the gateway in ifconfig because a gateway address isn't bound to an individual Ethernet interface. Instead, FreeBSD's routing table—which allows the system to function as a full-fledged router in its own right (something you'll see how to do in Chapter 27, "Configuring an Internet Gateway")—has a single "default" route that receives all traffic not destined for any of the LANs accessible from your Ethernet cards, regardless of how many you have. This default route is what you set to specify your gateway router.

The route command is another large and complex beast, more so than ifconfig, in fact. However, because you're not actually setting up any routes right now, you need to concern yourself only with the most fundamental functions: the add and delete keywords.

> **NOTE**
>
> As long as you're on the same LAN as the FreeBSD machine, you can modify the routes—including the default route—without losing network connectivity. If you're going through these examples while connected via Telnet or SSH, you may have accidentally disconnected yourself with the `ifconfig` examples. This won't happen if you're just setting the router address, as long as there aren't any routers between you and the FreeBSD machine.

The first thing to do is to check the output of `netstat -rn`. The `netstat` tool displays the state of the routing tables and other network information; the `-r` option tells it to show the currently configured routes, and `-n` says to show the addresses numerically (rather than trying to resolve them into hostnames). This will show what default route is currently set, if any:

```
# netstat -rn
Routing tables

Internet:
Destination        Gateway            Flags     Refs      Use    Netif Expire
default            64.41.131.1        UGSc         1        1    fxp0
...
```

It seems you already have a gateway router set. This will almost certainly be the case whether the network is running properly or not; there is little error-checking in `route`, and it's pretty easy to set up a default route that would be unreachable from any of your LANs. The system might also set up a dummy default route. In any case, setting a new router address is a two-step process: You must first delete the existing default route and then you must add the new one:

```
# route delete default
delete net default
# route add default 64.2.43.1
add net default: gateway 64.2.43.1
```

> **NOTE**
>
> It's worth pointing out that the `route` command is one of those parts of Unix that gives people fits because it's implemented differently on almost every single Unix variant on the planet. The differences are subtle and syntactical; although the functionality is pretty much the same, whether you're on FreeBSD or Linux or Solaris or IRIX, the way you access that functionality is maddeningly varied. To get an idea of this lack of standardization, install `portsentry` (from `/usr/ports/security`), and look through `/usr/local/etc/portsentry.conf`. It lists no fewer than nine different ways (on nine different platforms) to use `route` to set up a "blackhole" route. It's a bit ridiculous, but that's part of the price we pay for the flexibility we demand from Unix.

Using `hostname`

Setting your machine's hostname is dead simple. All it involves is the `hostname` command, with the desired hostname (as a fully qualified domain name) as its argument:

```
# hostname tiger.somewhere.com
```

You can also print out the currently set hostname in either fully qualified or standalone format:

```
# hostname
tiger.somewhere.com
# hostname -s
tiger
```

Network Settings in `/etc/rc.conf`

Now that you have command-line tools at your disposal for setting the IP address, netmask, hostname, and gateway router, and now that you've seen how to set them manually on a one-time basis, it's time to make sure the system takes care of all that for us. That's what `/etc/rc.conf` is for, as you'll no doubt recall from Chapter 10, "System Configuration and Startup Scripts."

Recall that the system's default settings are in `/etc/defaults/rc.conf` (which shouldn't be touched), and any overrides that supersede those defaults go into `/etc/rc.conf`. If you look in the defaults file, you'll find vague, generic, disabled settings for the various TCP/IP options. You'll be enabling your Ethernet cards permanently by putting everything relevant into `/etc/rc.conf`. If you've configured the card using `sysinstall` (as we discussed earlier in the chapter), there will already be some settings in the file, such as the following (a block of "deltas" is added each time you use `sysinstall` to change the configuration):

```
# -- sysinstall generated deltas -- #
ifconfig_fxp1="inet 64.41.131.102  netmask 255.255.255.0"
network_interfaces="fxp1 fxp0 lo0"
defaultrouter="64.41.131.1"
hostname="tiger.somewhere.com"
```

> **TIP**
>
> The order in which these options are specified doesn't matter; the startup scripts read them all into variables at once.

The values written into the file by `sysinstall` include the following:

- `network_interfaces`, which sets an explicit list of the interfaces on your system

- An `ifconfig_xxx#` line for each interface, which is precisely what is passed to `ifconfig` by the configuration scripts for each card specified in `network_interfaces`

- `defaultrouter`, which sets just what you think it does

- `hostname`, which is the fully qualified domain name

All these values are read into the resource-configuration scripts when the system boots and are passed to the appropriate utilities (`ifconfig`, `route`, and `hostname`) automatically.

Perhaps you're wondering, What about DNS? We'll be getting to that shortly. DNS isn't really a part of the TCP/IP stack configuration; it's an application-level helper service, consulted independently by networking applications before any connections are really initiated, and we don't need it in place to get networking up and running.

Using `/etc/netstart`

A nice courtesy provided by FreeBSD is the `/etc/netstart` script. It's not a necessary part of the boot-time configuration process, and it can safely be removed from your system without hurting anything (although that would be silly, considering how useful it is). At one time, most network services were started explicitly within `/etc/netstart`. Back in the days when administrators had to edit scripts to add new services, it was a crucial part of the resource-configuration process. Now, though, in keeping with FreeBSD's ideal of pushing all user-level and system-level script functions apart from each other, we have `/etc/rc.network`. This system-level script runs at boot time in a cascade with the rest of the resource-configuration scripts. We also have `/etc/netstart`, a user-level script that can be run at any time.

The function of `/etc/netstart` is to read in any new configuration changes from `/etc/rc.conf` and start up the network—restarting it, effectively. If you take a quick look through the script, you'll see that there's not a lot to it. It reads in `/etc/defaults/rc.conf`, applies the overrides from `/etc/rc.conf`, and then runs `/etc/rc.pccard` and `/etc/rc.network` in sequence. Everything in `/etc/defaults/rc.conf` and `/etc/rc.conf` is available to `rc.network` when it's run at boot time, but not if you were to run it separately on your own. That's what `/etc/netstart` is for; it's a wrapper for `rc.network` that makes it behave as if the machine were just now booting.

> **NOTE**
>
> At the time of this writing, FreeBSD is in the process of transitioning to a new layout for the Resource Configuration files, which you learned about in Chapter 10. Later versions of the operating system may call scripts in `/etc/rc.d`, instead of the corresponding `/etc/rc.*` scripts that appeared in earlier versions.

The various command-line tools that we've just discussed—ifconfig, route, hostname, and the like—are all run from within /etc/rc.network, subject to various conditionals and consistency checks, and with syntax built up from the various settings to prevent input errors and potential illegal maneuvers. For everyday networking changes, /etc/netstart is the best and safest way to activate networking configuration changes, rather than running the various commands individually.

There's a caveat, however. The /etc/netstart script sets the default gateway using the route command, as you've seen; however, you can't add a new default route without deleting the old one first. The /etc/rc.network script doesn't issue a route delete default command—because it's designed to run at boot time, it shouldn't need to. So to use /etc/netstart, you have to delete the default route first. This makes using /etc/netstart a two-step process, as shown in Listing 22.1.

LISTING 22.1   Restarting the Network Using /etc/netstart

```
# route delete default
delete net default
# /etc/netstart
Doing stage one network startup:
Doing initial network setup:.
fxp0: flags=8843<UP,BROADCAST,RUNNING,SIMPLEX,MULTICAST> mtu 1500
        inet6 fe80::2d0:b7ff:fec7:74f1%fxp0 prefixlen 64 scopeid 0x1
        inet 64.41.131.101 netmask 0xffffff00 broadcast 64.41.131.255
        ether 00:d0:b7:c7:74:f1
        media: autoselect (100baseTX <full-duplex>) status: active
        supported media: autoselect 100baseTX <full-duplex> 100baseTX
➥10baseT/UTP <full-duplex> 10baseT/UTP
lo0: flags=8049<UP,LOOPBACK,RUNNING,MULTICAST> mtu 16384
        inet6 fe80::1%lo0 prefixlen 64 scopeid 0x9
        inet6 ::1 prefixlen 128
        inet 127.0.0.1 netmask 0xff000000
add net default: gateway 64.41.131.1
Additional routing options: tcp extensions=NO TCP keepalive=YES.
Routing daemons:.
```

This will work fine if you're on the same LAN as the FreeBSD machine or logged in at the console. You may have noticed, however, that this will contain a nasty trap if you're controlling the machine from elsewhere in the Internet. When you delete the default route, you effectively make the machine unable to communicate with you further, so you can't issue the /etc/netstart command (which re-enables the default route).

A trick to get around this is to put both commands on the same line, separated using a semicolon (;). This is risky because it still has the potential to result in a few dropped response packets. If everything is configured properly in /etc/rc.conf, however, your terminal connection will pick back up where it left off after just a brief hiccup:

```
# route delete default; /etc/netstart
```

Creating IP Aliases

There's nothing to stop you from assigning as many IP addresses as you want to an Ethernet card. Recalling the discussion of ARP from the previous chapter, a new TCP/IP connection looks up a LAN host by its IP address, asking for the MAC address of whatever Ethernet interface has that IP address. It doesn't do the reverse. One MAC address can answer for many different IP addresses, but one IP address can't be assigned to multiple Ethernet cards without errors and collisions resulting.

The way to assign multiple IP addresses to a single card is through IP aliasing. As with the route command, every platform does aliasing slightly differently. The syntax varies from system to system. On FreeBSD, alias is used as a keyword to ifconfig, appended after the address and all other parameters:

```
# ifconfig fxp1 64.41.131.103 netmask 255.255.255.255 alias
```

Note that the netmask is set to 255.255.255.255. This is required if the alias IP address is on the same subnet as the primary IP address for that interface. (If it's not, just use the regular netmask you would use for that subnet.) What does this mean from a TCP/IP standpoint? A netmask where all the bits are set to 1 ensures that the TCP/IP stack will only treat a packet where the destination address matches in all its bits as though it's on the local subnet; the netmask is creating a "subnet" of just that one address. All packets to and from that address thus are sent to the router and not to the LAN. If multiple aliases had the same netmask, their broadcast addresses would be the same, which would confuse the TCP/IP stack. Using an all-1s netmask is how you trick ifconfig into allowing multiple IP addresses on a single interface.

To set up IP aliases in your /etc/rc.conf, you would use the ifconfig_xxx#_alias# keyword, which works syntactically just like ifconfig_xxx#. Here's how a set of aliases in /etc/rc.conf might look:

```
ifconfig_fxp1="inet 64.41.131.131 netmask 255.255.255.0"
ifconfig_fxp1_alias0="inet 64.41.131.132 netmask 255.255.255.255"
ifconfig_fxp1_alias1="inet 64.41.131.133 netmask 255.255.255.255"
ifconfig_fxp1_alias2="inet 64.41.131.134 netmask 255.255.255.255"
ifconfig_fxp1_alias3="inet 64.41.132.161 netmask 255.255.255.0"
ifconfig_fxp1_alias4="inet 64.41.132.165 netmask 255.255.255.255"
ifconfig_fxp1_alias5="inet 64.41.132.166 netmask 255.255.255.255"
```

Mapping Names to IP Addresses with the /etc/hosts File

We need a way for hostnames to map to IP addresses. Normally, this is done with DNS, but we don't have DNS set up yet. In the meantime, we can provide mappings for hosts we know about—such as hosts on our local network—with the /etc/hosts file.

/etc/hosts allows you to build a table in which each entry lists an IP address, its most common (or "official") hostname, and any aliases (additional names that map to the same IP address). Each of these items is separated by spaces or tabs. This table is consulted before any DNS queries are made, so /etc/hosts acts both as a backup to DNS (if it's not available) and an override (if it's not serving correct information). The aliases can even be used as a shorthand for favorite hosts whose names you don't want to have to remember, as with shell aliases (which we discussed in the "Shell Initialization Files" section of Chapter 11, "Customizing the Shell").

Here are a few sample lines from /etc/hosts:

```
64.41.131.132          ns               ns.somewhere.com lion.somewhere.com
64.41.131.133          www2             www2.somewhere.com
64.41.132.165          www3             www3.somewhere.com
114.235.123.11         www.foobar.com   fred
```

With this table in place, you can connect to the listed hosts by name—either the "official" name in the second column or any of the aliases listed in the third column—even if no DNS servers can be reached.

Testing Network Connectivity with ping

After you've finished your network configurations, setting them either with sysinstall or with /etc/netstart, you can use ping to make sure the settings are correct. The ping program is a simple ICMP-based tool that checks for echoes from a specified host and reports the roundtrip time it takes each packet to get to the host and back.

The use of ping is pretty simple. You can run it against either an IP address or a hostname (or /etc/hosts alias), and it will run until you interrupt it with Ctrl+C:

```
# ping fred
PING fred (114.235.123.11): 56 data bytes
64 bytes from 114.235.123.11: icmp_seq=0 ttl=243 time=485.344 ms
64 bytes from 114.235.123.11: icmp_seq=1 ttl=243 time=351.589 ms
^C
--- fred ping statistics ---
2 packets transmitted, 2 packets received, 0% packet loss
round-trip min/avg/max/stddev = 351.589/418.466/485.344/66.877 ms
```

This is a healthy TCP/IP configuration because the specified host replied to the `ping`. However, if the host isn't reachable, the ICMP packets will time out and report the failure to connect. If this happens, something's wrong with your configuration (alternatively, the remote host might actually be down, so make sure to try multiple target hosts). The following shows a `ping` attempt that fails to reach its target:

```
# ping 64.41.131.133
PING 64.41.131.133 (64.41.131.133): 56 data bytes
ping: sendto: Host is down
ping: sendto: Host is down
ping: sendto: Host is down
ping: sendto: Host is down
^C
--- 64.41.131.133 ping statistics ---
10 packets transmitted, 0 packets received, 100% packet loss
```

Configuring DNS with the `/etc/resolv.conf` File

To use true DNS, you need access to at least one domain name server. It doesn't matter where this server is—most name servers are configured to allow queries from anywhere on the Internet, with no restrictions on who makes the queries. This practice is on the wane, however, and in most circumstances you will want to use only the name server addresses provided by your ISP or enterprise network administrator.

Name servers are specified in the `/etc/resolv.conf` file, an example of which follows:

```
search somewhere.com
nameserver 64.41.131.132
nameserver 207.78.98.20
nameserver 64.40.111.102
```

The `nameserver` keyword specifies a name server's IP address; you can have as many of these as you like, and the order in which they're listed is the order in which they're consulted. If one times out, the next server is queried. Many applications have their own internal timeouts on a DNS query that gets passed to the operating system to handle, though, so servers beyond the third or fourth probably won't provide much additional benefit.

The `search` keyword specifies the search domain—the string appended to hostnames that aren't fully qualified. For instance, if you were to do an `nslookup www`, the resolver would attach the `search` domain and perform the actual query on `www.somewhere.com`. You can list multiple search paths on the same line:

```
search somewhere.com foobar.com cslab.ivyleague.edu
```

Technically, /etc/resolv.conf is just a backup and override file, like /etc/hosts. Ideally, or at least according to design, a system should be running its own DNS daemon, which inherits its information from a master name server upstream. DNS queries, by default, are always checked against the local system's DNS if it's running. However, in the real world, you don't want to be running DNS unless you have to. It's necessary these days to have an accurate resolv.conf file containing two or three remote name servers against which to perform name lookups. If you want to run DNS on your own machine, we'll cover how to do it in Chapter 31, "The Domain Name Server."

> **TIP**
>
> Fortunately, /etc/resolv.conf can be edited and modified at any time, without any special tools to update any databases or anything. DNS lookups are only done upon request by network applications, and the resolv.conf table is consulted only at those times and opened from the file on disk, not held in memory and queried constantly, as with IP interface configuration. You can open /etc/resolv.conf in your favorite text editor, change or add nameserver entries, shuffle the order in which they're queried, and so on. The next DNS query you make through any application will query against the newly modified /etc/resolv.conf.

A Look at Other Network Configuration Files

You've already seen just about all the files containing network configuration information you're ever likely to need to work with. However, a few more files are still worth listing and briefly describing. This doesn't count config files for major network services, though; we'll cover those in Chapter 25, "Configuring a Web Server," and Chapter 31.

Most of these files have man pages; simply use man <filename>, without the path, to view them (for example, man inetd.conf). Here's a description of the files:

- /etc/networks—As you've already seen, this file contains symbolic names for subnets that you might want to use in places such as the routing table.

- /etc/hosts.allow—This is a listing of fairly complex security rules for responding to connections of various types on a per-host basis. You can use hosts.allow to reject certain hosts—whether on a particular service or on all services—or to specify an action to take when such a connection attempt is made.

- /etc/inetd.conf—The inetd "super-server" is responsible for accepting connection requests for services specified in inetd.conf and spawning a process to handle each one. Services run from within inetd include Telnet, FTP, POP3, and various miscellaneous services that you may want to disable if they're not needed. More on this in Chapter 29, "Network Security."

- /etc/services—A database of IP service types and the TCP and UDP ports each maps to. Some programs use this table to look up commonly used ports; it also provides a handy reference for what services are assigned what ports by the Internet Assigned Numbers Authority (IANA).

- `/etc/protocols`—Like `/etc/services`, this is a table providing keyword mappings for various IP subprotocol numbers. It is mostly of interest as a reference.

- `/etc/rpc`—Another table of mappings, even less likely to be of interest to the administrator. RPC lookups provide port-mapping services to requests such as NFS, NIS, and various status-reporting programs.

- `/etc/pam.d`—Pluggable Authentication Modules (PAM) provide a way to assign cascading authenticators (S/Key, Kerberos, and the like) to various services. This will be of interest when we discuss network security in Chapter 29.

- `/etc/host.conf`—If present, this file specifies the order in which name lookup sources are given priority. In the default configuration, `/etc/hosts` is consulted first, followed by the resolver in BIND (the DNS running on the local machine).

CHAPTER **23**

Connecting to the Internet with PPP

PPP stands for *Point-to-Point Protocol*. It is the protocol used for most dial-up Internet connections. If you are among the many users connecting to the Internet through a dial-up modem, you need to know how PPP works in FreeBSD and how you can make it work with as little hassle as possible.

FreeBSD comes with two forms of PPP. The first is *kernel PPP*, which involves the pppd daemon. As the name suggests, this form of PPP is implemented at a kernel level, meaning (among other things) that it must be configured and run by the root user. *User PPP*, on the other hand, runs in "userland" and is therefore accessible to normal users. Both forms have their advantages and disadvantages, as you learn later in this chapter. First, however, the chapter reviews some of the important considerations involved in choosing an ISP and setting up a dial-up connection.

Choosing an ISP

Before you can connect to the Internet, of course, you need an Internet service provider. Chances are that your city has a number of them to choose from, ranging from local independent providers to national providers such as AT&T and AOL. Try to find an ISP that allows you unlimited and unmetered access so that you do not have to worry about monitoring the hours you spend online. Here are some other questions to ask when choosing an ISP:

- *What is the subscriber-to–phone line ratio (also referred to as the "user-to-modem ratio")?* Most ISPs will be able to quote a number to prospective customers; a ratio of 6:1 is considered average. Higher ratios can become problematic; expect a lot of busy signals if your ISP has a lot of customers and not so many lines.

- *How much upstream bandwidth does the ISP have?* ISPs with lots of subscribers and not enough bandwidth can result in slow connections. Look for an ISP with at least the equivalent of several T1 lines to the Internet (a T1 line carries 1.5 Mbps).

- *Will the ISP support FreeBSD?* Many ISPs will not give you any support unless you are running Windows or a Macintosh. Avoid these types of ISPs, if possible.

- *What value-added features does the ISP offer?* Many ISPs offer value-added features such as free Web site space or multiple e-mail addresses for no extra charge. If these are features you want, ask the ISP whether they are included at no charge, or how much extra they cost (if they are available).

In addition, avoid the so-called "online services" such as AOL and MSN. They can be difficult or impossible to get working properly with FreeBSD. For best results, stick with a plain-old Internet service provider.

Gathering Needed Information

After you have signed up with an ISP, you will need to get several pieces of information:

- The communications port that your modem is on. If you know the DOS COM port, the following FreeBSD devices correspond to the DOS COM ports: COM1: `cuaa0`, COM2: `cuaa1`, COM3: `cuaa2`, and COM4: `cuaa3`.

- The IP addresses of your ISP's DNS servers. These are used to resolve domain names to numerical IP addresses.

- Your ISP's dial-up phone number.

- Your username and password.

- The type of authentication your ISP uses. This should be either a standard shell login, Password Authentication Protocol (PAP), or Challenge Handshake Protocol (CHAP). More on the different authentication protocols will be provided later in the chapter.

- Whether you have a static IP address or a dynamic IP address. If you have a static IP address, you will need to know your IP number.

All the information items except the first one can be obtained from your ISP.

User PPP Versus Kernel PPP

The two types of PPP available with FreeBSD are user PPP and kernel PPP. Both have their advantages and disadvantages. Kernel PPP must be set up by the root user, and support for it must be compiled into the kernel (which it is by default). Because it involves a daemon process that handles on-demand connections to the ISP, kernel PPP can be very efficient and seamless in operation. User PPP, however, is a scheme that exists at the user level; support for PPP need not be compiled into the kernel, so the root user does not have to be involved beyond making sure user PPP can be run in the first place. (This can be useful if you are not the administrator of the FreeBSD machine but need to use PPP anyway.) User PPP is somewhat easier to debug than kernel PPP, but because it uses a *tunnel device*—a type of "virtual network interface" that encapsulates specialized traffic inside a more generic transmission protocol—it can be somewhat less efficient than kernel PPP. The following sections discuss how to configure kernel PPP. In later sections, you learn more about user PPP.

Configuring Kernel PPP

Kernel PPP is handled by the pppd daemon. The main configuration files for the pppd daemon are located in /etc/ppp. Other than the files located there, you must edit the /etc/resolv.conf file.

> **NOTE**
>
> The /etc/ppp/ppp.conf file is used in user PPP, not kernel PPP; you can ignore it until we reach the section, "Configuring User PPP," later in this chapter.

/etc/resolv.conf

The /etc/resolv.conf file, as you learned in Chapter 22, "Configuring Basic Networking Services," determines how FreeBSD resolves hostnames to numerical IP addresses. Each line in resolv.conf contains the keyword nameserver followed by the IP address of a Domain Name Server (DNS). Nameservers are queried in the order they are listed in the file; if the first nameserver does not respond, the next listed one is checked. In addition, the keyword domain can be used in this file. If the domain keyword is present, FreeBSD assumes that any unqualified hostnames (hostnames that do not have a domain after them) are located in the domain specified after the domain keyword. Here is an example of an /etc/resolv.conf file:

```
domain samplenet.org
nameserver 111.111.11.1
nameserver 222.222.22.2
```

You can edit the /etc/resolv.conf file with any text editor. You will need to be logged in as root to do so.

/etc/ppp/options

The /etc/ppp/options file, which does not exist by default, is where most of the options for the PPP daemon go. It is read before any command-line options that you specify when invoking pppd.

The contents of this file are used to specify modem baud rates, handshaking options, routing and domain information, and connection scripts. It is possible to use kernel PPP without an /etc/ppp/options file because all the potential options have default values; however, you will most likely need to create this file and add a few basic configuration lines specific to your modem and ISP setup. The options that need to go in this file differ depending on the type of authentication your ISP uses. Here is a sample file for using simple shell login authentication and a dynamic IP address (the PAP and CHAP authentication methods are covered in detail in the next sections of this chapter):

```
/dev/cuaa0 115200
crtscts
modem
connect "/usr/sbin/chat -f /etc/ppp/chat.script"
noipdefault
silent
domain samplenet.org
defaultroute
```

Here is what each of the options listed here mean:

- /dev/cuaa0—This line sets the device that the modem is located on. In this case, this is equivalent to COM1. It also sets the port speed to 115,200 bits per second.

- crtscts—This line sets the hardware flow control of the modem to on. Hardware flow control is required for high-speed communications.

- modem—This tells pppd to use the modem control lines, wait for carrier detect before opening the serial port, and so on.

- connect—This specifies the dialer program to run along with the script that should be used. The chat program can be used to automate the modem connection with a "connect script," specified with the -f switch. This will be covered more in the next section.

- noipdefault—Use this option if you have a dynamic IP address (your ISP assigns you an IP address each time you log on). This option tells pppd to get an IP address and gateway address from the dial-up server.

- silent—This tells pppd to wait for Link Control Protocol (LCP) packets, rather than sending out its own to initiate a connection.

- domain—The domain name of your ISP should go here and may be used for authentication purposes. It appends the domain name onto the end of local hostnames.

- defaultroute—This will add a routing entry to the system routing tables while pppd is running. When pppd is terminated, the route will be removed.

If you have a static IP address, remove the line that reads `noipdefault` and replace it with a line that looks like the following:

`111.111.111.11:222.222.222.22`

Replace the first number before the colon with the IP address your ISP has assigned you. The number after the colon is the gateway address that your ISP has given you. If your ISP has not given you a gateway address, you can leave the second number off (you should include the trailing colon, however). Leaving the gateway address blank, or using the `noipdefault` option, tells FreeBSD to use the gateway address sent by the ISP during the connection setup process.

These are just a few of the many connection options you can tune in `/etc/ppp/options`. See the `man pppd` page for an exhaustive list of these options and what they can do.

> **TIP**
>
> If you installed FreeBSD on an older system (486 or older) and you have an external modem, you may find that the preceding setup produces strange results—connection resets, stalled transfers, and so on. This is because older systems did not ship with high-speed UART communication chips and may not be able to handle a port speed of 115200. If you get strange results, try reducing the port speed (specified in the `/dev/cuaa0` line in `/etc/ppp/options`) to 57600.

The Chat Script

The pppd daemon has no built-in dialing capabilities. This is where the chat program comes in. The chat program allows for an automated conversation with the modem. It uses an "expect/send" syntax; in other words, the script contains the format of the prompt to expect from the server, followed by the commands it should send in response, and so on.

Here is a sample chat script. You may need to modify this script slightly to work with your particular modem, but this one should get you started. As root, open a new file in any text editor named `chat.script` (our example uses a `chat.script` file saved in the `/etc/ppp` directory) and enter the following, all on one line:

```
ABORT BUSY ABORT 'NO CARRIER' "" AT OK ATDT5551212 CONNECT "" TIMEOUT 10
➡ogin:-\\r-ogin: foo TIMEOUT 5 sword: bar
```

The first part tells the script to abort if the modem should respond with either BUSY or NO CARRIER. Then, the script sends an AT command (which stands for ATTENTION) and waits for the modem to respond with "OK." When it does, the script uses ATDT (Attention Dial Tone) and dials the phone number given after ATDT. The script then waits for the modem to send CONNECT. When it has, it sets the timeout to 10 seconds. It then waits for the string `ogin:` (which matches either `login:` or `Login:`—whichever the server happens to send, just to be safe) from the modem; this string represents the login prompt sent by the ISP. After the script has received the login prompt, it responds with `foo`, which should be replaced with your ISP login name.

If the login prompt has not been received within 10 seconds, the script aborts. Assuming the script does receive the login prompt and sends the login name, the timer is then reset to five seconds, and the script waits for that length of time to receive `sword:` (another shortened string, designed to match the ISP's `password:` or `Password:` prompt). When the script receives the password, it sends `bar`, which should be replaced with the password you use to log in to your ISP. After the password has been sent, if your ISP's server automatically changes to PPP mode, the script is done. If, instead, you are put into a login shell, find out from your ISP what shell command needs to be issued to start PPP. Then, you can simply add this command at the end of the script.

> **TIP**
>
> If you are unsure about which prompts your ISP sends, use a terminal emulator such as `minicom` (available in the ports tree, at `/usr/ports/comms/minicom`) to dial your ISP's phone number and then perform a manual login. This will enable you to observe what prompts the ISP's server sends when requesting various items of information.

> **CAUTION**
>
> If you want to allow non-root users to start the `pppd` daemon, the `chat.script` file must be "world readable." A world-readable `chat.script` file can be a security hazard because anyone with a shell account on your system can get your Internet password from this file. It is much better to use CHAP or PAP authentication if you want normal users to be able to start `pppd`. The `chap-secrets` and `pap-secrets` files (discussed in a later section) need to be readable only by root, even if you are allowing normal users to start `pppd`. Also, if you do not want the rest of the world to be able to get your Internet password, don't forget to change the permissions on the `chat.script` file accordingly.

Starting the `pppd` Daemon

After you have completed the preceding tasks, the PPP connection should be ready to go. Simply type **pppd** at the command prompt to bring it up. If all goes well, your modem should dial and connect. If you have problems, see the troubleshooting section at the end of this chapter.

To stop the `pppd` daemon, you can either find its PID number with `ps` and then issue a `kill` command, or you can use `killall`, like this:

```
killall pppd
```

PAP and CHAP Authentication

Most ISPs these days support the Password Authentication Protocol (PAP) or the Challenge-Handshake Authentication Protocol (CHAP), and some support *only* PAP or CHAP. Both of these types of authentication start a PPP session immediately after login, instead of starting up a shell on the server side (as older PPP dial-up mechanisms used to do). This quick startup makes PAP and CHAP a little bit more efficient than a shell login.

PAP and CHAP also have one other advantage over the shell login. The chat script has to be world readable if you want any users other than root to be able to start pppd. If you use the chat script with the shell login, your password in the chat script is visible to everyone who has access to the system. With PAP and CHAP, the files that contain the passwords do not have to be world readable, so they are more secure for a multiuser system. The configuration for PAP and CHAP is a bit more complicated and requires some explanation.

Both CHAP and PAP start off in PPP mode and do not use a shell login. Also, both of them require authentication. The configuration is a little different. Let's start with the ppp options file.

At least one line will need to be added to the /etc/ppp/options file to determine what profile to use for logging in (you learn more about the profile in "Running Commands on Connect and Disconnect," later in this chapter).

At the end of the options file, add a user line. This line corresponds to a profile name (the profiles will be added later in a different file). The user line looks like this:

```
user foo
```

Replace foo with the login name you use to log on to your ISP. The following is a list of other options you might need to include:

- refuse-chap—If this statement exists in /etc/options, pppd will refuse to authenticate using CHAP, even if the remote host requests it.

- refuse-pap—Like refuse-chap, except it applies to PAP instead.

- require-chap—If this option exists in /etc/ options, pppd will require the remote host to authenticate itself using CHAP. Because your ISP's server likely does not authenticate itself to you, you will probably not use this line.

- require-pap—Like require-chap, except that it applies to PAP instead.

If you do not include either the refuse-chap or refuse-pap statement in your options file, pppd will accept whichever authentication mechanism the ISP offers first. Note also that if you reject both PAP and CHAP, the connection fails because your system does not have a way to authenticate itself to the ISP.

`pap-secrets` **and** `chap-secrets`

The `/etc/ppp/chap-secrets` and `/etc/ppp/pap-secrets` files contain the CHAP and PAP authentication information, respectively. The files follow the basic format of *username hostname password* where *username* is your ISP login name, *hostname* is the name of the host that this entry will also authenticate, and *password* is (of course) your Internet password. You can replace the hostname entry with a wildcard (*), which tells pppd that this entry can authenticate to any host. Using a wildcard is a good idea for configuring your Internet account, because if you dial in to your ISP, you are already assured that the host you are contacting is who it claims to be. A sample entry for either of these files might look like this:

```
foo * bar
```

Here, `foo` is the username, * means that this entry is good for any host, and `bar` is the password.

You can use other options in the chap-secrets and pap-secrets files, but they are generally used only if you are providing dial-in PPP service. If you are interested, further information on how to use these files can be found in the "Authentication" section of the man pppd page.

> **CAUTION**
>
> The `/etc/ppp/chap-secrets` and `/etc/ppp/pap-secrets` files should be readable only by root. Change the permissions accordingly; otherwise, anyone who has shell access to your system can get your Internet password from these files.

Dial-On-Demand and Persistent Connections

As the name suggests, *dial-on-demand* means that pppd automatically dials out whenever it detects outgoing traffic that needs to be sent. A *persistent connection*, on the other hand, is always "up" and redials the connection immediately if pppd detects a disconnect. The following subsections describe how to enable both kinds of connections in kernel PPP.

Dial-On-Demand

Dial-on-demand causes pppd to establish a dial-up connection any time it detects outgoing network traffic when the connection is not already up. The relevant statements in `/etc/ppp/` options are as follows:

- `demand`—This statement turns on dial-on-demand.

- `idle` *n*—Here, *n* is a number representing seconds. This option causes pppd to automatically disconnect after *n* seconds of being *idle*, meaning that no traffic has been sent or received over the PPP link during that time.

After you have enabled dial-on-demand, you can create a startup script to automatically start the pppd daemon each time your system boots. There are several ways to do this; but, as you have seen in Chapter 11, "System Configuration and Startup Scripts," the best way is to create a startup script in /usr/local/etc/rc.d with the single line pppd in it. This file can be called anything you want, but it's a good idea to name it ppp or something else that makes sense and tells you what it does.

23

> **TIP**
>
> If you have dial-on-demand enabled and your Internet connection seems to be starting periodically for no reason, a program is probably trying to do a DNS lookup. More often than not, Sendmail is the program causing problems. You can fix this by enabling the SMART_HOST relay definition or the nodns feature in the freebsd.mc configuration file, or by adding the IP address and hostname of your ISP's mail server to your /etc/hosts file. See Chapter 24, "Configuring E-mail Services," for information on how to configure Sendmail using the Master Config file.

> **TIP**
>
> If you have dial-on-demand enabled and you are running Fetchmail in daemon mode so that it periodically polls your mail server, this might keep the connection open all the time in addition to causing pppd to dial on a regular basis. See the "E-mail for Standalone Workstations" section in Chapter 24 for ways to stop this from happening.

Persistent Connections

You can also tell pppd to always keep the connection up. This is done by adding the persist statement to /etc/ppp/options. If this statement is present, pppd automatically tells the modem to re-establish the connection if it is lost.

> **CAUTION**
>
> Even if your ISP tells you that you have unlimited access, make sure you read the fine print. There might be a "within reason" clause or something. If you are using the persist option to keep your Internet connection open 24 hours a day, 365 days a year, your ISP may terminate your account or ask you to purchase a dedicated line. The moral of this is that unlimited access does not always truly mean "unlimited access."

Running Commands on Connect and Disconnect

When pppd establishes a connection, it checks for the existence of a file called ip-up in /etc/ppp. Likewise, when the PPP connection goes down, pppd checks for the existence of a file called ip-down in /etc/ppp. If these files exist, whatever commands are listed in them are executed.

Running commands on connect or disconnect can be helpful if, for example, you are running FreeBSD on your laptop while traveling. You could read and respond to e-mail while on a plane. Then when you get to your destination and dial in to your network, you could have pppd flush the mail queue (deliver all the mail you wrote on the plane), as well as running the Fetchmail program to download any new mail you had received. If you put the command to perform these options in /etc/ppp/ip-up, they will automatically be performed when you type **pppd** to start your dial-up connection. You could then have the ip-down script automatically kill Fetchmail if it is running in daemon mode so that it does not attempt to retrieve mail when the connection is not available.

A sample ip-up script could contain the following:

```
fetchmail mail.myisp.com
apachectl start
cd /etc/mail; make start
```

Similarly, ip-down could contain the following lines:

```
apachectl stop
cd /etc/mail; make stop
```

Configuring User PPP

Under some circumstances, kernel PPP might not be available to you. You might, for instance, not be the administrator of the FreeBSD machine in question; or the kernel might have been compiled without PPP support. If, for whatever reason, you can't or don't want to use kernel PPP, FreeBSD also provides user PPP. User PPP does not run as a daemon and does not require PPP support to be compiled into the kernel. It does, however, require a tunnel device (/dev/tun#) to be compiled into the kernel; user PPP is run through a "tunnel," meaning that the system creates a generic "virtual network interface" through which to send traffic. This interface is responsible for communicating with the PPP server, and FreeBSD does not have to do its own PPP encapsulation.

> **NOTE**
>
> Tunnels are a mechanism frequently used in cases where an application must "fool" the operating system into supporting a certain kind of specialized traffic. Other cases where tunneling is used include compressed data streams and Virtual Private Networks (VPNs), in which each packet is encrypted. Because most operating systems don't support these protocols natively in their TCP/IP stacks, a generic tunnel is used to set up a normal TCP/IP connection, and the tunnel handlers on both sides handle decrypting or uncompressing the traffic as necessary. User PPP in FreeBSD operates in much the same way.

The first thing to do when setting up user PPP is to make sure a tunnel device is available (there should be unless you have built a custom kernel and removed it). If you have built a custom kernel, check your kernel configuration file in /sys/i386/conf for the line pseudo-device tun. If this line exists, your kernel is configured to use a tunnel device.

The /etc/ppp/ppp.conf File

The /etc/ppp/ppp.conf file is the configuration file for user PPP. A sample configuration file is present in /etc/ppp that you can use to get started; it's set up to use CHAP or PAP authentication. You have to change several lines in it, however, to make it work with your ISP. Listing 23.1 shows the sample configuration file included with FreeBSD, along with explanations of the items you may have to change. You must be root to edit this file.

LISTING 23.1   Sample User PPP Configuration

```
#################################################################
# PPP   Sample Configuration File
# Originally written by Toshiharu OHNO
# Simplified 5/14/1999 by wself@cdrom.com
#
# See /usr/share/examples/ppp/ for some examples
#
# $FreeBSD: src/etc/ppp/ppp.conf,v 1.8 2001/06/21 15:42:26 brian Exp
$#################################################################

default:
 set log Phase Chat LCP IPCP CCP tun command
 ident user-ppp VERSION (built COMPILATIONDATE)

 # Ensure that "device" references the correct serial port
 # for your modem. (cuaa0 = COM1, cuaa1 = COM2)
 #
 set device /dev/cuaa1

 set speed 115200
 set dial "ABORT BUSY ABORT NO\\sCARRIER TIMEOUT 5 \
          \"\" AT OK-AT-OK ATE1Q0 OK \\dATDT\\T TIMEOUT 40 CONNECT"
 set timeout 180                    # 3 minute idle timer (the default)
 enable dns                         # request DNS info (for resolv.conf)

papchap:
 #
 # edit the next three lines and replace the items in caps with
 # the values which have been assigned by your ISP.
 #
```

LISTING 23.1   Continued

```
set phone PHONE_NUM
set authname USERNAME
set authkey PASSWORD
set ifaddr 10.0.0.1/0 10.0.0.2/0 255.255.255.0 0.0.0.0
add default HISADDR                      # Add a (sticky) default route
```

Here is what the various options mean:

- set device—This option should point to the device name that your modem is on. Here is a list of the DOS equivalents: COM1: /dev/cuaa0, COM2: /dev/cuaa1, COM3: /dev/cuaa2, COM4: /dev/cuaa3.

- set log—This option controls what types of events get logged, and it can be useful for debugging connection problems. This option will be covered more in the section on troubleshooting.

- set speed—This option sets the speed at which the serial port should run. The default setting of 115200 will work for most people. If you have problems with this on an older system, you may want to change it to 57600.

- set dial—This option is the modem control string for the dialer. It is similar to the chat script used for kernel PPP. The default script will work for most people, so don't change this setting unless you have problems or are familiar with your modem's command set.

- set ifaddr—The part of the first number (10.0.0.1/0) that precedes the slash should be replaced with the IP address assigned to you by your ISP. If you have a dynamic IP address, leave the number as-is. The second number (10.0.0.2/0) should be replaced by the gateway address your ISP gave you. If your ISP has not given you a gateway address, leave this number as-is. The third number (255.255.255.0) is the netmask. Unless your ISP has given you a netmask number that differs from this number, you should leave this number as-is. For instance, a customized ifaddr line might look like this:

  ```
  set ifaddr 64.41.131.102/0 64.41.131.1/0 255.255.255.0 0.0.0.0
  ```

- set timeout—The number here is the number of seconds of inactivity (no outgoing or incoming traffic) that will pass before the connection is terminated. It is similar to the idle option in kernel PPP.

- set default HISADDR—This line adds a default route to the routing tables for your ISP's gateway. Note that this line must appear after the set ifaddr line; otherwise, PPP will not know what the gateway address is.

- enable DNS—This option causes PPP to check with your ISP to see whether the DNS servers you have listed in /etc/resolv.conf are correct. If they aren't, PPP will update the file automatically with the servers suggested by the ISP, creating persistent entries that will last until you (or PPP) modify the file again.

- set phone—This option replaces PHONE_NUM with the phone number you use to connect to your ISP.

- set authname—This option replaces USERNAME with the login name that you use to connect to your ISP.

- set authkey—This option replaces PASSWORD with the password you use for your ISP.

If you can't use PAP or CHAP and need to use a standard Unix shell login instead, you must make some more changes to the default configuration file. First, remove the papchap section, including the set phone, set authname, and set authkey statements. Next, add the following lines after the set dial statement:

```
Provider:
    set phone "5551212"
    set login "TIMEOUT 10 \"\" \"\" gin:--gin: foo sword: bar"
```

Once again, replace foo and bar with your ISP login name and password, respectively. As with kernel PPP, include after the password any other commands you need to send to start PPP on the remote host. Like the chat script in kernel PPP, this script uses an "expect/send" syntax, in which you type what it should expect to receive from the server and then what it should respond with.

> **TIP**
>
> If you are unsure about which prompts your ISP sends, use a terminal emulator such as minicom (available in the ports tree) to dial your ISP's phone number and then perform a manual login. That way, you can observe what prompts the ISP's server sends when requesting various items of information.

Starting User PPP

If you are using PAP or CHAP authentication, you can start user PPP from the command line by typing **ppp -background papchap**. If you are using a shell login instead of CHAP or PAP, use the ppp -background provider instead. The ppp - background provider starts user PPP in the background. If all goes well, you should hear your modem dial, and after a connection has been established, the system will respond with PPP Enabled and then return you to a command prompt.

To kill user PPP, find its PID number with `ps` and then issue a `kill` command, or you can use `killall`, like this:

```
killall ppp.
```

If you want to allow normal (non-root) users to start user PPP, add a line to `/etc/ppp/ppp.conf` that reads `allow users`.

Dial-On-Demand

Like kernel PPP, user PPP also supports dial-on-demand.

To enable dial-on-demand for user PPP, you can type **ppp -auto papchap** or **ppp -auto provider** for CHAP/PAP or shell login, respectively. If you want to enable this by default at each system boot, you must add the line ppp_enable="YES" to `/etc/rc.conf`. This line sets these options, which may or may not be correct for your system configuration:

- It sets the mode to `auto` so that PPP will dial automatically whenever it detects outgoing network traffic. The link will terminate when no incoming or outgoing traffic has been detected for the period of time specified in `set timeout` in `/etc/ppp/ppp.conf`.

- It sets the profile to `papchap`. If your dial-up procedure involves a shell login, you will also need to add a line that reads ppp_profile="provider" to `/etc/rc.conf`.

- It enables Network Address Translation (NAT), which can allow other computers on the network that do not have a real IP address to access the Internet through this system. For instance, NAT allows you to assign arbitrary IP addresses—such as anything within the "reserved" 10.x.x.x address space—to machines within your home network; but on the other side of the PPP connection, each of your machines appears to share a single IP address assigned by the ISP. If this behavior is undesirable, you will need to add a line to rc.conf that reads ppp_nat="NO".

If you have made changes to rc.conf to enable dial-on-demand at system boot, you will need to reboot the system before these changes take effect.

Persistent Connections

To enable persistent connections for user PPP, you first remove the `set timeout` line from `/etc/ppp/ppp.conf`, so that that the connection doesn't terminate after inactivity. From the command line, you can then start PPP in persistent mode with the command ppp -ddial papchap or ppp -ddial provider for CHAP/PAP or shell login, respectively. If you want to enable this by default at system boot, add the line ppp-enable="YES" to the `/etc/rc.conf` file. Also add the line ppp_mode="ddial" to `/etc/rc.conf`. Adding these lines also sets a few other options that you may need to change depending on your system configuration:

- It sets the profile to papchap. If you are using a shell-based login to your ISP, you will also need to add a line that says ppp_profile="provider" to /etc/rc.conf.

- It enables NAT (network address translation), which can allow other computers on the network that do not have a real IP address to access the Internet through this system (as described earlier). If this behavior is undesirable, you will need to add a line to rc.conf that says ppp_nat="NO".

If you have made changes to rc.conf to enable persistent connections on system boot, you will need to reboot the system before these changes take effect.

Redialing

In –auto or -ddial mode, when an automatic connection attempt fails, PPP attempts to redial after 30 seconds, if another outgoing packet is detected after that period. You can change this behavior with the set redial option in ppp.conf. The syntax for this setting describes the wait period, an optional increment to add with each attempt, a maximum for the increments to reach, a wait period for trying another in a list of numbers, and a maximum number of attempts:

```
set redial secs[+inc[-max]][.next] [attempts]
```

For instance, use the following line to tell PPP to redial 20 times, pausing each time for 10 seconds more than it paused the previous time:

```
set redial 10+10 20
```

This syntax can be tweaked to achieve a huge variety of desired results. See the "Dial On Demand" section of the man ppp page for further examples.

Running Commands on Connect and Disconnect

Like kernel PPP, user PPP can run commands on connect and disconnect. It reads the files /etc/ppp/ppp.linkup and /etc/ppp/ppp.linkdown to run commands on connect and disconnect, respectively. The syntax looks like this:

```
papchap:
    commands to run here
```

Here, papchap tells PPP which profile the following commands apply to. If you are using a shell login, replace papchap with provider.

This could be used, for example, to automatically start Fetchmail and download new mail, as well as flush the mail queue and delivered queued mail automatically when PPP starts. This can be useful for a laptop user who travels (how to do this will be explained in Chapter 24).

PPP Over Ethernet (PPPoE)

Many xDSL users must set up nonpersistent PPP-based connections over an Ethernet interface; this is the case, for instance, when an ADSL modem connected to the FreeBSD machine via Ethernet does the dialing. PPPoE can be used in FreeBSD with only a few minor additions to the user PPP configuration file.

Create a new /etc/ppp/ppp.conf file as follows, replacing fxp0 with the name of your Ethernet device connected to the xDSL modem (if necessary), myisp with a keyword identifying your ISP, and yourname and yourpassword with your username and password used for logging in via PPP:

```
default:
 set device PPPoE:fxp0:myisp
 set speed sync
 set mru 1492
 set mtu 1492
 set ctsrts off
 enable lqr
 add default HISADDR
 set timeout 0
 set redial 0 0

 # Network Address Translation (NAT)
 nat enable yes
 nat log yes
 nat same_ports yes
 nat unregistered_only yes
 enable dns

myisp:
 set authname yourname
 set authkey yourpassword
```

When you want to connect to the Internet, you can then run ppp from the command line, then enter dial myisp. You should then see output indicating a successful connection, after which you should be able to access the network.

Troubleshooting PPP

If you are having trouble getting PPP to work, here are a few suggestions for trouble-shooting.

If the modem doesn't dial:

- Verify that you have selected the correct device for your modem.

- If you are using an older system, try reducing the speed to 57600. Some older systems without high-speed UARTs cannot handle 115200.

- Verify your chat script or `set dial` line. Check your modem documentation to see whether you need to be sending it some initialization string other than the default in the FreeBSD configuration files.

If the modem dials but fails to establish a connection:

- Verify that you are using the correct authentication type (CHAP, PAP, or shell login).

- Verify that you are using the correct login name and password for your ISP.

- Verify your chat script or `set dial` line. Check your modem documentation to see whether there is an initialization string you have to send.

- If you are using user PPP, you might want to try kernel PPP. (I personally had a modem/ISP combination once where kernel PPP worked fine; but user PPP, for whatever reason, simply refused to work with this particular ISP.)

If a connection is made but attempts to access remote hosts by host and/or domain name fail:

- Verify that you have the correct DNS servers listed in `/etc/resolv.conf`. Also, verify the correct setup of the `/etc/host.conf` file. It should have a line that reads `hosts` followed by a line that reads `bind`.

If the preceding suggestions do not correct the problem, try turning on logging and then attempt to connect again. This can be enabled by adding a line to `/etc/ppp/options` that reads `debug` for kernel PPP and by changing the `set log` line in `/etc/ppp/ppp.conf` to read `All` for user PPP. Messages from kernel PPP will be logged to `/var/log/messages`, and messages from user PPP will be logged to `/var/log/ppp.log`. You can monitor the messages as they are being sent by typing **tail -f /var/log/messages** or **tail -f /var/log/ppp.log**. This will show you the last 10 lines of the file and also update the display each time the file changes.

The information logged is fairly technical. You might be able to spot the problem yourself. If you can't, the contents of the log can still be useful in helping debug the problem. Your ISP might be able to use the log information to spot the problem. If they can't find it either, they might be able to call their RAS vendor and let them look at it to find the problem.

23

Finding Information for Advanced Configurations

The inforsmation presented in this chapter should be enough to get most people up and running with their ISP. However, both kernel PPP and user PPP are extremely complex, and this chapter cannot cover all the options available. If you need to do more advanced configuration, both kernel PPP and user PPP have detailed man pages that describe all the options available. The kernel PPP man page can be accessed with man pppd, and the user PPP man page can be accessed with man ppp. In addition, sample configuration files are located in /usr/share/examples/ppp.

Configuring E-mail Services

W hat's the Internet without e-mail? Probably not even the Web, with its flashy graphics and its commercial opportunities, has quite the usefulness and cachet of the Internet's oldest application, electronic mail. Every Unix server in the world has e-mail capabilities built in to it—not just the capability for users to send and receive mail, but for the system itself to act as a full-fledged mail server. FreeBSD is no exception.

The catch is that configuring Sendmail, the venerable SMTP server application that forms the e-mail backbone of Unix and the Internet, is perhaps the most daunting system administration task you'll face. After all, Sendmail is perhaps unique among server software in that it has a config file *for its config file*. But don't worry, this chapter outlines and gives you a solid grounding in the use of Sendmail. You learn how to configure and manage the program for secure and reliable performance, but you're spared the exhaustive coverage of details that could make Sendmail seem overwhelming or needlessly complex.

This chapter also covers another side of e-mail: POP and IMAP. These are the protocols remote clients use to receive e-mail. Fortunately, their use is nowhere near as complicated as Sendmail.

Introduction to SMTP

The Simple Mail Transfer Protocol (SMTP) is one of the oldest protocols on the Internet—nearly as old as e-mail itself. SMTP's purpose is to transfer plain-text messages from one host to another. This transfer often occurs in sequence, as when a dial-up client running Windows sends an e-mail message to the ISP's mail server, which then transfers it to the recipient's mail server. SMTP sequences rarely get much longer than this example, though. It isn't like the Internet itself, with its router-to-router hopping of individual packets. The sender's SMTP server communicates directly with the recipient's SMTP server.

SMTP itself is, as its name suggests, simple. An SMTP client—such as a desktop e-mail program or a relaying SMTP server—initiates a connection to TCP port 25 on the remote SMTP server, followed by an automated greeting code, some optional authentication commands, and a couple more commands to establish what type of transaction the sender is attempting. Then, the recipient asks for the message, and the sender sends it. Finally, a termination command is sent, and the connection is closed. That's about all SMTP is ever really used for, and there really aren't many other capabilities designed into the protocol.

No specialized software is necessary for using SMTP; in fact, you can execute a completely valid SMTP transaction right from the FreeBSD command line. Listing 24.1 is an example of such a transaction. Note that the bold type indicates your input during the session.

LISTING 24.1   Executing a Valid SMTP Transaction

```
# telnet destination.com 25
Trying 64.41.134.166...
Connected to destination.com.
Escape character is '^]'.
220 destination.com ESMTP Sendmail 8.11.1/8.11.1; Wed, 16
➥May 2001 22:55:37 -0700 (PDT)
HELLO stripes.sender.com
250 destination.com Hello w012.z064002043.sjc-ca.dsl.cnc.net [64.2.43.12],
➥pleased to meet you
MAIL From: frank@sender.com
250 2.1.0 frank@sender.com... Sender ok
RCPT To: bob@destination.com
250 2.1.5 bob@destination.com... Recipient ok
DATA
354 Enter mail, end with "." on a line by itself
From: frank@sender.com
To: bob@destination.com
Subject: Testing, 123...

This is a test message.
.
250 2.0.0 f4H5uCu53501 Message accepted for delivery
QUIT
221 2.0.0 destination.com closing connection
Connection closed by foreign host.
```

As you can see, communication between the two servers is done with four-letter command codes, by convention in caps, and with arguments that are incorporated into the message headers. The message that `bob@destination.com` receives will come up in his e-mail program with the following headers:

```
From: frank@sender.com
To: bob@destination.com
Subject: Testing, 123...
```

The headers are separated from the body of the message by a single blank line. A single dot on a line by itself marks the end of the message body; when the receiving SMTP program sees this, it delivers the message by appending it to the recipient's mailbox file (`/var/mail/bob` if it's a FreeBSD machine). And that's all there is to it.

A full-featured SMTP program such as Sendmail transmits its messages using a few extra commands to enhance performance and efficiency, but functionally it uses exactly the same method as the example you've just seen during the actual connection. Sendmail's complexity lies mostly in areas outside the actual SMTP transaction.

The reason the client has to communicate first with its own ISP's SMTP server, rather than connecting directly to the recipient's, is to take advantage of *queuing*. With queuing, an SMTP server can keep each message it receives from a client (on either a local or remote machine) in a "holding area" directory (commonly referred to as a *queue*), where it waits for a connection to the final recipient's SMTP server. This connection might be immediately available, in which case the message spends almost no time in the queue. If the connection isn't available, however, the message sits in the queue until a connection opens up, at which time the SMTP program sends it.

> **NOTE**
>
> Queuing is an application-level behavior of SMTP servers. The benefits of queuing for SMTP are much like those of DNS, which enhances the functionality of Internet applications while not actually being a part of the TCP/IP stack.

The benefit of queuing is that it converts e-mail delivery from a "synchronous" to an "asynchronous" process, where both clients need not be involved at all phases of the transaction. Queuing removes from the dial-up client the burden of looking up the destination host's SMTP server, queuing the message, and retrying the connection at regular intervals. When the client dials up, it can make a single connection, upload all its pending e-mail messages into the outgoing SMTP queue, and then disconnect. The client is thus freed of the mail-sending task.

24

Mail Transfer Agents (MTAs) and Mail User Agents (MUAs)

The schematic diagram for an e-mail message's path from one person to another is shown in Figure 24.1. Whether the user is on a dial-up connection from a remote site or sitting at the console on the mail server itself, the path the message takes is the same: From the user's input into the Mail User Agent (commonly known as an *e-mail client program*), the message moves into the sending SMTP server's message queue, where the Mail Transfer Agent (MTA; for example, Sendmail) pulls it out as soon as a connection to the receiving SMTP server becomes available and transmits it. (Because this process transmits a message that doesn't originate or terminate on the SMTP server machine itself, this step is known as *relaying*.) On the remote system, the MTA places the received message into the recipient's mailbox, where it can be read online with a server-side Mail User Agent (MUA) or downloaded to a client-side MUA through POP3.

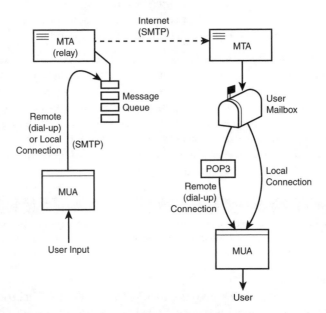

FIGURE 24.1   Diagram of an e-mail message's path from one user to another, showing the roles of MUAs and MTAs.

As a FreeBSD administrator, you'll be interested in the way Sendmail operates as an MTA, both in sender (relay) and receiver roles. This section also discusses MUA programs—both the local kind that users run on the FreeBSD machine and the remote kind that operate by uploading and downloading messages. You learn how these programs interact with the "holding areas" of the MTAs: the message queue and the user mailboxes.

Common MTAs

Here are a few of the Mail Transfer Agent programs routinely used on the Internet:

- **Sendmail**—By far the most widely used MTA, Sendmail was developed by Eric Allman in 1983, and has developed into a cross-platform *de facto* standard with both a commercially supported and a freeware component. Sendmail, Inc. (http://www.sendmail.com) is a fully functional corporation that exists to support Sendmail for commercial Unix and Linux resellers; the Sendmail Project (http://www.sendmail.org) is the free, volunteer-supported component, with grass-roots resources positioned in the traditional open-source way for users of systems such as FreeBSD in which Sendmail is bundled.

- **Microsoft Exchange**—The Windows equivalent of Sendmail, as well as of a multitude of other types of message transfer (such as POP3, NNTP, LDAP, and calendaring), Exchange is commercially developed and "closed source," in the Microsoft tradition.

- **Postfix**—Written by Wietse Venema as an alternative to Sendmail, Postfix is designed to be faster, more secure, and easier to operate than Sendmail. We'll talk more about Postfix at the end of this chapter.

- **Qmail**—Another response to Sendmail, Qmail was written by Dan Bernstein and is gaining rapidly in popularity due to its reputation for security and speed (although Postfix is reputedly faster). Also, unlike Postfix (which attempts to mimic Sendmail in its interactions with the system, for instance, where it keeps its spool and config files), Qmail uses its own structure and doesn't try to ease the transition for Sendmail users. Qmail is a good choice for administrators running the EZMLM mailing list manager, also by Bernstein, with which Qmail is tightly integrated.

A great many more MTAs are in general use throughout the Internet; the ones ported to FreeBSD can be found in /usr/ports/mail.

Common MUAs

Mail User Agents are even more numerous than MTAs. Because Windows and Macintosh e-mail clients (such as Microsoft Outlook/Outlook Express, Eudora, Apple Mail, Netscape Mail, and so on) are so widely understood, the following list contains only the more popular MUAs available for FreeBSD:

- **Pine**—Ostensibly an acronym for "Program for Internet News and E-mail," rumors persist that the name of this open-source product of the University of Washington is actually an acronym for "Pine Is Not Elm." In either case, Pine is quite widely used, providing an intuitive user interface, many modern message-handling features, and a message composer that incorporates the stalwart pico editor, which comes packaged with Pine.

- **Elm**—The genesis of Pine (at least, if you believe the name), Elm evolved from the ancient `mail` and `mailx` programs that performed e-mail duties for the university and government networks that predated the modern commercial Internet. Primitive by today's standards, Elm still claims many loyal users.

- **Mutt**—Conceived as a "mongrel" MUA and incorporating features from Elm, Pine, and a number of other programs, Mutt claims to be the most advanced of them all—and it just may be. It has features the others don't, including many that require a graphical client-side MUA in other contexts as well as a great deal of customization.

- `mail`—The ancestor of all the modern user-friendly e-mail clients, the command-line utility `mail` is available on all Unix platforms (including FreeBSD) and gives a user rudimentary access to e-mail even when nothing else is available. It can also be scripted and incorporated into programs quite usefully.

Note that the e-mail agents listed here are all shell oriented, meaning that they run in a Telnet or SSH session, monopolizing that session's window. This means they're (almost) exclusively text oriented, and such things as inline images and HTML formatting won't work (although they can be configured to open attachments in helper applications, if you're running them on a graphical FreeBSD workstation). However, it also means that you can check your mail using these programs no matter where you're computing from—just open up a Telnet or SSH session from wherever you are. You'll also be virtually guaranteed to be safe from the Windows/Outlook-oriented viruses that plague the Internet.

For more information on the Mail User Agents available for FreeBSD, see the "E-mail Applications" subsection of Chapter 6, "Working with Applications."

Configuring Basic E-mail Services with Sendmail

FreeBSD comes with Sendmail installed and already configured to serve basic e-mail needs right out of the box. All you have to do to enable Sendmail (so that it starts at boot time) is add the following line to /etc/rc.conf:

```
Sendmail_enable="YES"
```

Once the system is up and running, you can send a message to anyone on the Internet, and they can send one to you—provided you have a few things set up properly. For the most part, these aren't configuration items for Sendmail itself but rather for the system in general—Sendmail relies on the system to have a few guarantees in place before it will operate without a hitch.

You can decide to replace Sendmail with another MTA, such as Postfix or Qmail; you learn how to do that at the end of the chapter. Meanwhile, because Sendmail's default configuration works well for the vast majority of servers, we'll talk about how to manage Sendmail effectively.

Sendmail File Layout

There are three places in the system that concern Sendmail:

- /etc/mail—Configuration files for Sendmail

- /var/mail—User mailboxes

- /var/spool/mqueue—Message queue files

Sendmail itself is located at /usr/sbin/sendmail, and its log files are written to /var/log/maillog (which is rotated on a daily basis by the periodic job, which we discussed in Chapter 13, "Performance Monitoring, Process Control, and Job Automation").

> **NOTE**
>
> Some systems historically put the Sendmail binary in /usr/lib/sendmail. Some programs expect to find Sendmail there, including certain old Web tools that were developed without FreeBSD or Linux in mind. If you run these programs, you might want to violate the FreeBSD directory structure so far as to create a symbolic link from this historical location to the current one:
>
> ```
> # ln -s /usr/sbin/sendmail /usr/lib/sendmail
> ```

The mailbox files (mail spools) in /var/mail are plain-text files, each named for the user who owns it and with permissions set to 600 (readable and writable only by the owner). New messages are appended to the end of the recipient's mail spool file. There are also temporary POP lock files that have zero length and a name of the form .username.pop. They receive the contents of the corresponding mail spool file while a POP3 connection is open, and any untransferred remnants are then copied back into the mailbox. We'll be talking more about how the POP3 server works later in this chapter.

Configuration Files

Here are some of the files in /etc/mail that you'll find important when running Sendmail.

/etc/mail/sendmail.cf

This is the main Sendmail config file. However, unlike just about every other config file for every other program, you're not intended to edit this file to alter Sendmail's behavior. Rather, you should make changes at a higher "macro" level in the master config (.mc) file and then compile a sendmail.cf file from that.

The sendmail.cf file contains options, rule sets, and features—all in a format that can be very daunting and nearly not human readable. It's best to leave sendmail.cf alone unless absolutely necessary.

`/etc/mail/freebsd.mc`

The `/etc/mail/freebsd.mc` file is Sendmail's "master config" file. It contains a list of features and options that override the defaults in the standard config file, much in the same fashion as `/etc/rc.conf` overrides `/etc/defaults/rc.conf`. With `freebsd.mc`, though, the format of the settings is much more bizarre. Commands are given in the `m4` macro language (which is barely used outside of Sendmail configurations). The `.mc` file is then compiled together with the default `cf.m4` file from the Sendmail source in `/usr/share/sendmail` or `/usr/src/contrib/sendmail` to create a `.cf` output file. You can then install this file as the new `sendmail.cf` file.

Sound confusing and backward? It is, yes. However, the process has come a long way in recent versions of FreeBSD. It used to be the case that to regenerate your `sendmail.cf` file, you had to go into the source directory on your own, figure out which `.mc` file was the one that most closely matched your system, make changes according to the online documentation as best you could, and then dig out the cryptic `m4` compilation command that produced the output file—which you then had to install by hand. The state of things today is greatly improved over that, although it's still not what anyone would call user friendly.

Each line in the `m4` language contains the string `dnl` at some point; this stands for "delete through newline," and it marks the end of the readable line (each line must have one). To comment out a line, place the `dnl` at the beginning. Otherwise, put it at the end.

There's a makefile in `/etc/mail` that allows you to create a new `.cf` file from the `freebsd.mc` file simply by typing **make cf**. Then you install this output file (`freebsd.cf`) into `sendmail.cf` using `make install`:

```
# make cf
/usr/bin/m4 -D_CF_DIR_=/usr/share/sendmail/cf/ /usr/share/sendmail/cf/m4/cf.m4
➥freebsd.mc > freebsd.cf
# make install
install -c -m 444 freebsd.cf /etc/mail/sendmail.cf
```

The file `/etc/mail/Makefile` has a number of other uses, as you'll see in a moment.

> **NOTE**
>
> A *makefile* (conventionally named `Makefile`) is a special file that sits in the top level of any tree of source code; it contains "build targets," which allow you to compile the code in a certain predefined way. We covered the makefiles used by the ports in Chapter 14, "Installing Additional Software." In that chapter's example, you could compile the programs in a port with the `make` command, but the target `install` would specify to the `make` command that you wanted to run whatever installation procedures were prescribed in that port's makefile.
>
> In `/etc/mail`, the makefile that FreeBSD provides allows you to compile the various databases that comprise a Sendmail configuration, and even control Sendmail itself. It's not a config file itself, per se. Rather, it's a part of the system. Therefore, you should *not* modify it unless you know what you're doing.

`/etc/mail/aliases`

There's a mailbox in `/var/mail` for every user on the system; however, someone having an e-mail address on your machine doesn't require that they have an account. You can always set up aliases to map incoming e-mail addresses to any other address, whether it's another account on your machine, an address somewhere else on the Internet, or even a pipe to a file or program. The default `/etc/mail/aliases` contains examples of all these. An alias line contains the alias name, a colon, a space or tab, and the target address or pipe:

```
tiger: bob@stripes.com
fsmith: frank
pager: "¦/usr/local/bin/pageme"
dump: ">>/home/frank/dump2me"
mylist:include:/home/frank/list.txt
```

This last example is an "include" alias, which reads in a list of addresses from a plain-text file at the specified location. This is an easy way to manage a mailing list. Just make changes to the included file, and the alias will always be up to date.

Traditionally, and as a matter of "netiquette," a system has a number of administration aliases for various purposes that are all aliases for root. Some of these "pseudo-accounts" include abuse (the address for reporting junk mail or malicious activity originating at your server), postmaster (the person who runs the mail server), and webmaster (the person in charge of the Web server). Some of these are already aliased to root in the default configuration, and others you may have to enable by uncommenting them.

After you make any change to `/etc/mail/aliases`, you have to rebuild the `aliases.db` file, which is a hash table version of the aliases file that provides fast lookups (as with `/etc/master.passwd`, which we discussed in Chapter 9, "Users, Groups, and Permissions"). You can use the traditional newaliases command to do this, or for consistency's sake with the rest of the maintenance tasks, use make aliases:

```
# make aliases
/usr/sbin/sendmail -bi
/etc/mail/aliases: 25 aliases, longest 10 bytes, 254 bytes total
chmod 0640 /etc/mail/aliases.db
```

The command shown here will not return any output if the aliases database is up to date.

> **NOTE**
>
> Using global aliases isn't the only way to redirect mail from one local address to another, or to an external address. For instance, if a user wants all his incoming mail to be forwarded automatically to some external address, you could use `/etc/mail/aliases` to do the trick, but this involves root access. There's a better way, if the user has a full account on the system.

24

All a user has to do to forward mail to another address is to create a `.forward` file in his home directory, containing the forwarding e-mail address. This can be done with any text editor, or even simply with `echo`:

```
# echo "frank@somewhereelse.com" > .forward
```

Removing this file will cause mail forwarding to stop.

/etc/mail/access

The access database provides a way to apply certain rules to single hosts, subnets, or whole groups of addresses—an excellent anti-spam provision. Applicable rules include OK, REJECT, RELAY, DISCARD, and 550 <message>. The contents of the default /etc/mail/access file show examples of how the address/hostname field can be formatted:

```
cyberspammer.com              550 We don't accept mail from spammers
FREE.STEALTH.MAILER@          550 We don't accept mail from spammers
another.source.of.spam        REJECT
okay.cyberspammer.com         OK
128.32                        RELAY
```

The addresses on the left side can be complete hostnames or IP addresses, or else they might be only partial ones; cyberspammer.com will match any hostname in the cyberspammer.com domain, and 128.32 covers the entire 128.32.xxx.xxx Class B network. The right side contains the rules, which can be any of the following:

- OK accepts messages from the specified host, regardless of whether that host might fail other checks in the system (such as the anti-relaying provisions that we will discuss shortly).

- REJECT refuses connections initiated by the specified host.

- DISCARD silently drops messages after accepting them, making the sender think the message has been successfully delivered.

- RELAY enables relaying for the specified host, overriding other checks (as with OK).

- 550 <message> specifies a "rejection" message that is displayed to a sender matching the host specification. This message will appear during the SMTP session and will be included in an error e-mail message that is sent back to the sender.

After you've made changes to /etc/mail/access, the access.db file must be regenerated. You can do this with the make maps target, which regenerates any of the feature map files that have been changed since the last time make maps has been run. Follow this command with make restart to restart the Sendmail master process with the new access.db file:

```
# make maps
# make restart
Restarting: sendmail sendmail-clientmqueue.
```

`/etc/mail/local-host-names`

Formerly `sendmail.cw`, this file specifies all the hostnames that your server claims to be. This information becomes especially important if you're hosting multiple domains and doing mail service for all of them (virtual hosting). In that situation, if you don't add each relevant domain name to the `local-host-names` file, an incoming message destined for a domain you host will bounce back to the sender with the dreaded message `MX list for <domain> loops back to myself; local configuration error`.

 # cat /etc/local-host-names
```
somewhere.com
www.somewhere.com
bobsmachine.com
```

The `local-host-names` file has a simple format: a list of hostnames, one per line. The file doesn't exist in the default installation, but you'll need to create it if you add more domain or hostname aliases to your machine via DNS. After adding names to the list, run `make restart` to restart the server:

 # make restart
```
Restarting: sendmail sendmail-clientmqueue.
```

`/etc/mail/virtusertable`

Also on the subject of virtual hosting, `/etc/mail/virtusertable` provides a way to map addresses on one domain that you host to local accounts, other addresses, or error messages. This is somewhat like a hybrid of the access database and the `aliases` file.

Let's say you're hosting a secondary domain called `mycave.org`. You want `webmaster@mycave.org` to go to the local user bill, `info@mycave.org` to go to a remote address `anne@elsewhere.com`, and all other addresses (`@mycave.org`) to be rejected. This could be done with the following tab-separated rules:

```
webmaster@mycave.org    bill
info@mycave.org         anne@elsewhere.com
@mycave.org             error:nouser User unknown
```

Note that the order in which these rules are specified doesn't matter; when you build the `virtusertable.db` hash table, each rule has its own lookup value, and the ordering in the `virtusertable` file is irrelevant. As with the access database, you need to rebuild `virtusertable.db` and then restart the server. This is easiest to do with `make maps`, though bear in mind that this rebuilds *all* the map databases in `/etc/mail` that have been modified:

 # make maps
```
/usr/sbin/makemap hash virtusertable.db < virtusertable
chmod 0640 virtusertable.db
```

```
/usr/sbin/makemap hash access.db < access
chmod 0640 access.db
# make restart
Restarting: sendmail sendmail-clientmqueue.
```

An excellent and complete discussion of virtual hosting and the use of the `virtusertable` file can be found at the Sendmail Consortium information site (`http://www.sendmail.org/virtual-hosting.html`).

NOTE

By the way, `/etc/mail/Makefile` and all these convenient targets for rebuilding the various configuration databases are additions to FreeBSD and are not part of Sendmail as released by its developers. Other operating systems don't provide these conveniences. If you're going to be maintaining a Sendmail installation on a Linux system or some other platform, you'll want to know the underlying commands beneath each of the build targets in the makefile so that you can accomplish the same tasks. The documentation at `http://www.sendmail.org` is very helpful in this regard.

DNS Resolution Issues

Running a successful Sendmail server really requires that you have accurate DNS information set up for your machine. If you simply install FreeBSD, assign an available IP address to it, and attempt to send mail, it might bounce back to you complaining that the remote server "could not resolve your hostname." Many SMTP servers, including Sendmail in its default configuration, do not accept mail from senders without fully qualified domains in their addresses or resolvable DNS names.

Before you try to put Sendmail to full use on your machine, you'll need to make sure you have reverse DNS lookups correctly set up. You can check this with the `nslookup` command, giving it your machine's IP address as an argument:

```
# nslookup stripes.somewhere.com
Server:   lion.somewhere.com
Address:  64.41.131.132

Name:     stripes.somewhere.com
Address:  64.41.131.102
```

This output shows a correctly resolving reverse DNS setup, one in which Sendmail will work just fine. However, you may get something like the following:

```
# nslookup stripes.somewhere.com
Server:  lion.somewhere.com
Address:  64.41.131.132

*** lion.somewhere.com can't find stripes.somewhere.com:
➥Non-existent host/domain
```

This means you'll have problems sending and receiving mail until DNS is set up properly. You learn more about DNS in Chapter 31, "The Domain Name Server."

> **NOTE**
>
> You should check against a remote DNS to be absolutely sure of the DNS configuration for your machine; sometimes, a local name server plays tricks on you by reporting information only it knows about—information that hasn't propagated to the rest of the Internet.

Controlling Sendmail

Sendmail operates by keeping a single "master" process running and listening on port 25 for incoming connections, with additional processes for handling queue runs, sending messages to remote recipients, and other tasks. The master process is started at boot time from /etc/rc. Starting and stopping the Sendmail master process is made easy by the makefile and the integrated nature of the resource configuration files in /etc. To start the process, simply go into /etc/mail and enter **make start**:

```
# make start
Starting: sendmail sendmail-clientmqueue.
```

This command pulls in relevant configuration details from the systemwide resource configuration files, in which flags such as -q30m (do a queue run every 30 minutes) and -bd (run as a background daemon) are centrally specified. It will even refuse to start the process if the sendmail_enable variable in the rc.conf files is set to NO.

Restarting or stopping the master process is equally simple:

```
# make restart
Restarting: sendmail sendmail-clientmqueue.
# make stop
Stopping: sendmail sendmail-clientmqueue.
```

You can see what state each Sendmail process is in by using ps in wide mode in conjunction with grep; each process reports its position in the queue as an argument against its name in the process table. The following example shows the master process (51248) and a process in the middle of a queue run (54150):

```
51248  ??  Ss     0:00.17 sendmail: accepting connections (sendmail)
54150  ??  I      0:00.02 sendmail: ./f4GKwVW16827 mail.backstreetboys.com.:
➡user open (sendmail)
```

The Message Queue

Sendmail's operation is split into two parts: incoming messages and outgoing messages. Incoming messages waiting to be delivered to local users by Sendmail sit in /var/spool/mqueue. A similar directory, /var/spool/clientmqueue, holds messages that local command-line MUA users have submitted for Sendmail to deliver. In Sendmail's default configuration, a new sendmail -q process is started every 30 minutes, stepping through each queued message in both queue directories and attempting to deliver it to its destination. This continues for five days, at the end of which an "undeliverable" message is returned to the sender with the relevant error headers attached.

> **NOTE**
>
> The /var/spool/clientmqueue directory is actually fed by a single standalone Sendmail process that is bound only to the localhost interface; this is a security measure that eliminates the need for Sendmail to be setuid root in order for outgoing mail users to write their messages to the queue directory.
>
> Messages in the incoming queue, /var/spool/mqueue, should never build up, technically, because once a message has reached the server there should be no reason why delivery to a local user would fail temporarily.
>
> The outgoing "submit" Sendmail daemon is enabled by default, but you can disable it (returning to the model where a single Sendmail master process controls both incoming and outgoing mail in the same location, /var/spool/mqueue) by setting the following option in /etc/rc.conf:
>
> sendmail_submit_enable=NO
>
> Refer to /etc/mail/README for further details on other advanced configuration options concerning the split Sendmail model.

If you have some messages in your queues (which you almost certainly will if you've been using the system for any length of time), you can browse through them at will. Unlike opaque systems such as Microsoft Exchange, in which queue files are kept in a database without an easy way to tweak or even see the files waiting to be sent, Sendmail provides full access to queued messages.

> **CAUTION**
>
> Queued messages are just plain-text files, able to be read and edited by regular text editors. This gives the administrator great control over how the mail system operates; however, it also provides an opportunity for the administrator to abuse his or her power by looking through the content of pending messages. If you run a system in which you trust your users, be sure they can trust you too!

The first tool that comes with Sendmail is called `mailq`. It provides a way to list the current state of all messages waiting in the queue. Note that when called with no arguments, `mailq` reports on the contents of the incoming queue, `/var/spool/mqueue`. The `-Ac` option instead tells it to look at the outgoing queue, which is likely to be much more useful:

```
# mailq -Ac
                /var/spool/clientmqueue (2 requests)
----Q-ID---- --Size-- -----Q-Time----- -----------Sender/Recipient-----------
f4H1Ahu36976    6246 Wed May 16 18:10 MAILER-DAEMON
                (Deferred: Operation timed out with mlists.acmecity.com.)
                              <fred@acmecity.com>
f4GKwVW16827     706 Wed May 16 13:58 www
                (host map: lookup (hotamil.com): deferred)
                              bob@hotamil.com
```

Using `mailq`, you can keep an eye on what kind of mail transfer errors frequently occur on your system. If people often forget to specify complete e-mail addresses or misspell common mail server hostnames, you can address that problem through education and tutorials. If you're getting a lot of hostname lookup errors, this might point to a configuration problem on your end. `mailq` is an excellent diagnostic tool.

The queue also gives you the ability to fix mistakes in messages on the way out. Let's say, for instance, you have an entry like the second one in the `mailq` output shown earlier. The erroneous recipient domain is the result of a simple typo; you can either wait five days for Sendmail to give up trying to find `hotamil.com` and send the message back to you as an error, or you can fix this problem right in the queue.

To do this, go into `/var/spool/clientmqueue` and look for the files matching the ID of the entry in the `mailq` output. These would be the files `dff4GKwVW16827` and `qff4GKwVW16827`. The first contains the message body, and the second contains the message headers in an interim format. Simply open up the file with the headers (`qff4GKwVW16827`) in a text editor, replace all occurrences of `hotamil.com` with `hotmail.com`, save the file, and wait for the next queue run. The message will go through cleanly this time.

If you can't wait that long, force a queue run by running `sendmail -q -v -Ac`. (The `-q` switch tells Sendmail to do a queue run, `-v` tells it to echo the results of the entire session verbosely, and `–Ac` tells it to use the outgoing queue, `/var/spool/clientmqueue`.) This gives you the added bonus of a look into exactly how Sendmail does its SMTP transactions with all the remote systems. With each message Sendmail processes, it will echo to the session all the output from the transaction, just as in the example at the beginning of the chapter. You'll get to see all the interesting greeting messages that various administrators program into their MTAs, visible only to other MTAs, and therefore often quite creative. You can use Ctrl+C to exit at any time—messages are removed from the queue only after they've been successfully transferred.

24

Understanding Relaying

One of the most recent additions to Sendmail is protection against spam (unsolicited e-mail) through anti-relaying rules. These rules have been available for a long time, but only recently—as of Sendmail version 8.9—has the default configuration been to disallow relaying of messages from one server to another.

For a legitimate dial-up or remote user to use your SMTP server to send a message to another remote recipient, your server has to act as a relay, forwarding the message on to the recipient even if the message didn't originate from and wasn't addressed to anyone on its machine. Functionally, as illustrated in Figure 24.2, this is exactly how a spammer would send an unsolicited message to the same recipient through the same SMTP server: The spammer must relay.

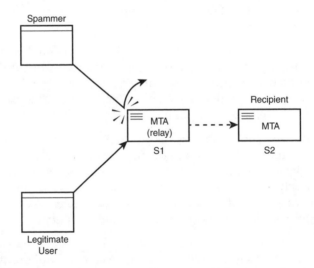

FIGURE 24.2 Relaying. Spammers and legitimate users, if they're not local to S1, must use S1 as a relay to forward their messages to S2.

How Relaying Works

Relaying is usually allowed by what's known as the "MX record," a line in the SMTP server's network DNS database (either served from the same machine as the SMTP server or another server in the same network), which tells all the machines within that network that your SMTP server (S1) is a legitimate mail exchanger for them.

Sendmail, in its default configuration on FreeBSD, will accept mail from senders whose MX record points to S1, defining it as the MTA for the network. This prevents people from outside the network from using S1 as a relay; if they try, they'll get their messages bounced back with a `Relaying denied` error.

> **NOTE**
>
> You can find out what the registered MX host is for a domain by using the `host` command:
>
> # **host somecompany.com**
> somecompany.com has address 164.199.3.78
> somecompany.com mail is handled (pri=30) by mail-1.somecompany.com
>
> You can then connect directly to this host to perform raw SMTP transactions (for testing purposes, for example).

Configuring S1 to Allow Users to Relay

This configuration is great for ISPs or enterprise networks that have a fully defined network, DNS entries for all the hosts in that network, and a proper MX record pointing to the relaying SMTP server. But what about standalone Internet hosts, which might have users all over the world trying to use their Sendmail servers to transmit mail? Each of these users, when trying to send a message through S1, from wherever they happen to be, will get a `Relaying denied` error back.

To avoid this problem, you can specifically configure S1 to allow these users to relay. There are a number of ways to do this, many of which are extremely inadvisable in some situations:

- Add "trusted" sender domains to the file /etc/mail/relay-domains, which doesn't exist in the default installation. Any host within a listed domain will be permitted to relay through your server. You have to restart Sendmail after modifying this file. This is easy and effective, but as soon as you add a large, popular domain to this file that might contain spammers as well as legitimate senders, its benefit is lost.

  Add domains to this file one per line, as with /etc/mail/local-host-names (which you saw earlier in this chapter):

  # **cat /etc/mail/relay-domains**
  good.host.com
  23.144.12.115

Note that local mail senders will be rejected unless the domains specified in their addresses are in /etc/mail/local-host-names.

- Use the access database (/etc/mail/access). This feature allows you to set up an OK or RELAY rule for each known host or domain from which your users will be connecting. This works well for small impromptu networks or for a few remote hosts at easily identifiable addresses, but it doesn't scale well for lots of users on dynamic addresses. For instance, if you're running a standalone server on the Internet that hundreds of different people connect to in order to send mail, it's going to be impossible to add all their IP addresses to /etc/mail/access, because most dial-up users have dynamic addresses these days. Administrators running servers in this kind of situation should probably advise users to send their mail through their own ISPs' SMTP servers instead of through yours.

- Enable any of the five or six relaying exception features available in Sendmail by adding them to /etc/mail/freebsd.mc and regenerating the sendmail.cf file (as shown earlier). There's a feature that lets you allow relaying based on whether the From: header is set to an address at your domain (relay_local_from), although this is easily forged by spammers and therefore using it isn't usually advisable. There's also an optional feature to perform a check against one of the Real-time Blackhole Lists, which are centrally maintained databases of known spammers (most that exist today require paid subscription). This feature is in the default freebsd.mc but is commented out; to enable it, move the dnl to the end of the line and rebuild the config file. This may be an advisable solution for ISPs.

- As an absolute last resort, turn off relay checking altogether by enabling the promiscuous_relay feature. This will allow any valid user to send mail through your Sendmail server; however, it will also allow any spammer to do the same. Some independently run databases on the Internet keep records of all "open" mail servers, and some service providers use these databases as "blackhole" lists of their own. You don't want your server to end up in these databases! If it does, some legitimate mail from your users or their correspondents may be blocked due to their ISPs blocking mail to or from your server. It's an incredibly bad idea to run an open mail server.

As a general rule, the best solution to the relaying problem is simply to instruct all your users to use the SMTP servers provided by their own dial-up Internet Service Providers. These services will always have their own SMTP servers that are open to their own customers. Because the headers in a mail message (such as the From: address) are all derived from the message body and therefore completely under the control of the e-mail client program, there's no reason for a remote user to want to use your SMTP server if he already has one of his own.

The Sendmail Consortium has an excellent page on relaying rules and your various available configuration options at http://www.sendmail.org/tips/relaying.html.

Introduction to POP3

You now have a sound understanding of SMTP and Sendmail, and you have the tools you need to configure your server according to the needs of almost any typical Internet server. But SMTP is only half of the equation. For e-mail to get completely from one user to another, there's another process that needs to take place: downloading the mail through the Post Office Protocol, known as POP.

The Post Office Protocol enables users to access their mailboxes from remote client machines and download their messages. POP became necessary once it was clear that there would ultimately be a great many more Internet users who used graphical client-side e-mail programs on their own dial-up computers, rather than server-side shell clients such as Pine and Mutt. Shell-based clients read mail directly out of the user's mailbox file. To use an MUA such as Microsoft Outlook or Qualcomm's Eudora, however, the client has to connect to the mail server in which the user's mailbox file is stored (refer to Figure 24.1), determine whether there are any new messages since the last time it checked, and if so, download them. The client program then displays these new messages and optionally deletes them from the mailbox file on the server.

Unlike SMTP, POP3 (the current and standard version of POP) requires authentication. This is sensible because although security really isn't an issue for sending mail, it's absolutely essential to receiving mail. After all, anybody can drop a letter in the outgoing post office mailbox, but only the legitimate receiver can open his or her mailbox and retrieve it. Authentication makes it a little less easy to simulate a POP transaction than an SMTP one. Simulating a POP transaction is also a lot less necessary, however, largely because POP3 requires very little in the way of configuration. There's not a lot that can go wrong. However, the POP3 server, Qpopper, is not included in the core FreeBSD installation. To enable POP3 service you must install Qpopper out of the ports (`/usr/ports/mail/qpopper`). This program is derived from the original Berkeley POP server program but is currently developed semicommercially (but in a free and open-source fashion) by Qualcomm, the makers of Eudora.

The POP3 server runs from out of `inetd`, the "super-server." `inetd` listens for TCP and UDP connections, and upon receiving one on TCP port 110, it looks up the service name in `/etc/services`, determines how to handle requests for that service type, and fires off a Qpopper process from `/usr/local/libexec/qpopper`. (This location—in the `libexec` directory—tells you that Qpopper is not a program intended to be run from the command line. Rather, it's only supposed to be invoked by other programs.) This process handles the transaction, authenticates the user, locks the user's mailbox, figures out which messages need to be downloaded, and serves them. This works just fine for most systems. Although Qpopper does in fact provide a rather large number of configuration options, most of them are useful only for tweaking extra performance out of the server—a valuable thing to know how to do if your server is a high-profile one. For most purposes, all you have to do is install the port and enable the service.

> **NOTE**
>
> You may have your system configured so that `inetd` is not running (for example, for security reasons, as outlined in Chapter 29, "Network Security"). If this is the case, `qpopper` can be run in standalone mode, like Sendmail. We will discuss how this is done in a moment.

It's important to note that, by default, POP3 transactions are done in clear text. This means that POP3 is a source of potential password leaks and a security risk.

In version 4.0, Qpopper enables encrypted connections through the Secure Sockets Layer (SSL) libraries, which are part of FreeBSD and also used in such protocols as SSH (Secure Shell) and secure HTTP. The following section describes how to configure Qpopper to take advantage of this security measure.

Configuring a POP3 Server with Qpopper

You can take your POP3 server configuration to several different levels. You can simply install the server and let everyone use it; you can run it in standalone mode, which avoids having to run `inetd` if you don't want to; you can enable "server mode," which enhances performance, depending on your circumstances; and you can enable encrypted sessions through TLS/SSL. These latter options are not mutually exclusive. We'll be looking at each of them in turn.

Basic Qpopper Installation and Configuration

Getting the POP3 service up and running without concerning yourself too much about performance or security is a simple matter. Go to the `qpopper` directory in the ports collection (`/usr/ports/qpopper`) and then build and install it from there, as described in Chapter 15. Alternatively, you can install the `qpopper` package using `sysinstall` or the package tools.

Next, you need to enable the POP3 service in the `inetd` super-server. You do that by adding a line to `/etc/inetd.conf`. Open up the `inetd.conf` file and find the lines regarding POP3, as shown. Add or uncomment the pop3 service using the following syntax:

```
# example entry for the optional pop3 server
#
#pop3   stream  tcp   nowait  root   /usr/local/libexec/popper    popper
pop3    stream  tcp   nowait  root   /usr/local/libexec/qpopper   qpopper -s
```

> **NOTE**
>
> For legacy purposes, there's a port that's simply called `popper`. It is actually Qpopper in an earlier form, and it's generally deprecated by this point. The one you want to use is `qpopper`.

Now, restart inetd by using `killall`:

```
# killall -HUP inetd
```

You can check to see whether the POP3 service is available now by connecting to port 110 on your machine via Telnet (type **QUIT** to exit the session):

```
# telnet localhost 110
Trying 127.0.0.1...
Connected to localhost.
Escape character is '^]'.
+OK Qpopper (version 4.0.2) at stripes.somewhere.com starting.
➥<4763.990313780@stripes.somewhere.com>
QUIT
+OK Pop server at stripes.somewhere.com signing off.
Connection closed by foreign host.
```

If you get this response from the server, congratulations—you have a working POP3 server.

Enabling Standalone Mode

Certain security settings turn off the inetd super-server; for instance, if you chose a Medium or High security setting during your system installation, the following line would have been added to your /etc/rc.conf, thus preventing inetd from being run at all:

```
inetd_enable="NO"
```

On a security-conscious system, you don't want to have to reenable inetd just so you can run POP3 services. This is what standalone mode is for. It isn't an option available by default, but a quick tweak to the makefile makes it pretty easy.

In /usr/ports/mail/qpopper, edit the makefile and alter CONFIGURE_ARGS to add the --enable-standalone option:

```
CONFIGURE_ARGS= --enable-apop=${PREFIX}/etc/qpopper/pop.auth \
                --enable-nonauth-file=/etc/ftpusers \
                --with-apopuid=pop --without-gdbm \
                --enable-keep-temp-drop \
                --enable-standalone
```

Now, run make and make install to build a version of Qpopper that runs in standalone mode. It will still be installed in /usr/local/libexec, though. Don't move it from this location, because this will make deinstallation more difficult later.

You'll need to start up the standalone Qpopper process from a script during system boot; this can be done by creating a startup script in /usr/local/etc/rc.d called, for example, qpopper.sh, as you saw in Chapter 10, "System Configuration and Startup Scripts." Make sure that Qpopper isn't enabled in inetd if you do this!

Enabling Server Mode

If your system has *only* users who access their mailboxes through POP3—where none of the users have shell access or run shell-based, server-side mail programs—you might choose to enable server mode for Qpopper.

Server mode allows Qpopper to run in a streamlined fashion. Instead of copying the mail spool file to a temporary copy, locking it, making changes, keeping track of mail that arrives during the session, and merging the locked session spool back to its original location, the server can work directly from the mailbox file itself. Be aware, however, that server mode can be dangerous, particularly if you have users who access their mail spool files through other methods. For that reason, you should use server mode only if your system serves mail exclusively through POP3, and if it's under enough load for you to consider this performance-boosting measure to be necessary.

You can enable server mode in a number of ways. The easiest is to use the -S switch on the command invocation line, whether in inetd.conf or on the command line if you're using standalone mode:

```
pop3    stream tcp    nowait root    /usr/local/libexec/qpopper    qpopper -s -S
```

This will put Qpopper into server mode for all users at all times. You can do it per user, though, or per group, if you prefer. Group control is best done through a configuration file. To make Qpopper use a config file, create one in /usr/local/etc/qpopper (for example, qpopper.conf) and then indicate it on the command line in inetd.conf with the -f option:

```
pop3    stream tcp    nowait root    /usr/local/libexec/qpopper
➥qpopper -s -S -f /usr/local/etc/qpopper/qpopper.conf
```

Now, in the qpopper.conf file, specify the name of a group to include or exclude from server mode using the group-server-mode or group-no-server-mode keywords. The following example turns server mode on for members of group1 and group2, and off for members of group3:

```
set group-server-mode=group1
set group-server-mode=group2
set group-no-server-mode=group3
```

You can also do this on a per-user basis. You may choose to configure Qpopper this way if different users on your system want to interact with Qpopper differently—if some want to use it in server mode and others don't. To do so, you need to add the -u switch to the command invocation line (to enable per-user configuration files). Then, each user to

whom the mode should apply needs to have a file in his or her directory called
.qpopper.options, which contains the line set server-mode. Alternately, if you don't
want each user to be able to modify his or her .qpopper.options file, use the -U switch
instead of -u, and place a corresponding per-user file in /var/mail called
.<user>.qpopper.options (where <user> is the username in question). This allows you to
turn on server mode on an individual basis. Don't use the -S global server mode switch if
you do it this way! This will only confuse the program as to whether you mean it to set
server mode globally or per user.

Enabling SSL Encryption

The Secure Sockets Layer (SSL) is a set of libraries included in FreeBSD that encrypt traffic
on a given service so that even if the packets carrying that service's traffic are captured by
an eavesdropper, they can't be descrambled without the proper encryption keys. SSL is
most frequently used on Web traffic, as you'll see in Chapter 29; however, it's use is not
limited to HTTP and can be very beneficial on services such as POP3.

By default, Qpopper will build with implicit TLS/SSL support. However, to take advantage
of it, you need to create and install security certificates. First, create a directory for your
certificates:

```
# mkdir -p -m665 /etc/mail/certs
# chown root:mail /etc/mail/certs
# chmod 660 /etc/mail/certs
```

Next, use openssl to generate a certificate request. This will require you to enter several
accurate pieces of information about your organization. In the example shown here, "..."
represents the long interactive session that results in a certificate request file. Afterward,
make sure the permissions on the private key file (cert.pem) only allow root to view it:

```
# openssl req -new -nodes -out req.pem -keyout /etc/mail/certs/cert.pem
...
# chmod 600 /etc/mail/certs/cert.pem
# chown root:0 /etc/mail/certs/cert.pem
```

Once this is done, you'll need to register the certificate with a Certifying Authority (CA),
such as VeriSign, and submit the certificate request in req.pem to the CA. Then you'll get
back a signed certificate. Concatenate this onto the end of cert.pem:

```
# cat signed_req.pem >> /etc/mail/certs/cert.pem
```

Now, add TLS/SSL support to the config file at /usr/local/etc/qpopper/qpopper.conf,
restart the server (if it's running in standalone mode), and SSL encryption is yours. Any
client that supports SSL will now be able to negotiate a secure connection if configured to
do so.

24

The following lines are what should be added to the `qpopper.conf` file:

```
set tls-support = stls
set tls-server-cert-file = /etc/mail/certs/cert.pem
```

If you want, you can emulate a Certifying Authority yourself to create a self-signed certificate that you can use to make sure the system works. However, SSL-enabled clients won't trust this certificate and will require the user to manually approve it before continuing.

First, create the test CA's private key (making sure to remember the passphrase you enter) and then create the CA certificate:

```
# openssl genrsa -des3 -out ca.key 1024
...
# openssl req -new -x509 -days 365 -key ca.key -out ca.crt
```

Now, you can self-sign the certificate request you created earlier (`req.pem`):

```
# openssl x509 -req -CA ca.crt -CAkey ca.key -days 365 -in req.pem
➥-out signed-req.pem -Cacreateserial
```

This should allow you to run an SSL-enabled Qpopper server and test its functionality. Make sure to get the real CA-signed certificate at some point!

For More Information

The official Web site for Qpopper is `http://www.eudora.com/qpopper`. It has a lot of useful information, including a PDF document (in the Documentation section) that definitively describes all the possible configuration options of Qpopper. It's written from a Linux viewpoint, so many of the pathnames quoted in the documentation are slightly different from your installation.

Even more information, particularly on the use of configuration files, can be found in the `man qpopper` page.

Configuring an IMAP Server with IMAP-UW

The Internet Message Access Protocol (IMAP) is an alternative to POP that some users prefer. You will probably want to support it on your mail server, along with POP and SMTP services, to make the package complete. The fundamental difference between IMAP and POP is that whereas POP downloads each message from the server and stores it in the mail program, IMAP mail is accessed and manipulated wholly on the server.

An IMAP client, like a server-side shell-based mail client, can have multiple mail folders and transfer messages between them as if they are local. Messages are transferred to the client only when requested, and they are not deleted unless the user explicitly deletes them. This provides the mobile flexibility of shell-based MUAs such as Mutt and Pine with the user convenience of graphical client-side mail programs such as Outlook and Eudora. Most, if not all, mail clients that support POP also support IMAP.

The most popular Unix IMAP server is IMAP-UW, by the University of Washington (the same group that produces Pine, a popular MUA that you'll learn about shortly). It's available in the ports, at /usr/ports/mail/imap-uw, or in the packages collection (refer to Chapter 14 for details on installing software from the ports or packages). Add USE_SSL=YES to both the make and make install command lines to build with SSL support.

> **NOTE**
>
> The IMAP-UW port warns of a security issue where known buffer overflows in the server daemon allow IMAP users to gain shell access with their own user privileges. This may or may not be an issue for you. If you allow shell access to your users anyway, it won't be a problem. If you don't allow shell access, though, this represents a security hole. Your choices are to wait for an update that fixes the problem, to look for alternative IMAP servers, or to disable IMAP altogether and rely on POP for your clients' mail services.

The IMAP-UW package consists of a mailbox test program (mboxtest) and four daemon executables that go into /usr/local/libexec. Two of these, ipop2d and ipop3d, are POP servers (for POP2 and POP3, respectively), which you don't need to install if you're already running qpopper. However, these POP daemons do have the capability to pipe POP commands to the IMAP server, so they can provide an upgrade path for existing POP clients to move to IMAP if you want to migrate to an exclusively IMAP environment.

Installation of IMAP-UW is fairly simple. There are no configuration files to edit for the program itself; all that is necessary is a modification to /etc/inetd.conf (because the IMAP server operates out of inetd, like qpopper) and optionally to /etc/pam.d/imap.

The commented-out line in /etc/inetd.conf will work just fine for IMAP-UW. Just uncomment it:

```
# example entry for the optional imap4 server
#
imap4   stream  tcp     nowait  root    /usr/local/libexec/imapd        imapd
```

Then, restart inetd:

```
# killall -HUP inetd
```

The IMAP daemon listens on TCP port 143. You can test whether it's set up properly by connecting to port 143 via Telnet. End the session by pressing Ctrl+] and typing **quit**:

```
# telnet localhost 143
Trying 127.0.0.1...
```

```
Connected to localhost.somewhere.com.
Escape character is '^]'.
* OK [CAPABILITY IMAP4 IMAP4REV1 LOGIN-REFERRALS AUTH=LOGIN] localhost.somewhere.com
➡IMAP4rev1 2001.303 at Sun, 10 Jun 2001 11:21:26 -0700 (PDT)
^]
telnet> quit
Connection closed.
```

The installation script suggests changing the entries in /etc/pam.d/imap (which controls cascading authentication layers) to be a little more strict. Do this by uncommenting the commented-out lines:

```
auth    required      pam_nologin.so      no_warn
auth    sufficient    pam_opie.so         no_warn      no_fake_prompts
auth    requisite     pam_opieaccess.so   no_warn
auth    required      pam_ssh.so          no_warn      try_first_pass
auth    required      pam_unix.so         no_warn      try_first_pass
```

You can do the same for the pop3 PAM script (/etc/pam.d/pop3) to provide the same enhanced strictness.

> **NOTE**
>
> You may notice warnings in your /var/log/messages file or your IMAP client software indicating that the mailbox is "vulnerable" and urging that /var/mail have "1777 protection." This is a security check done by the IMAP-UW server (Pine does it, too).
>
> FreeBSD's mail directory permissions are 775, meaning that all programs that access or create files in /var/mail must be set (using setgid) to the mail group. However, IMAP-UW does not run setgid. Therefore, when creating lock files (preventing mailboxes from delivering mail while receiving new messages), it can't do so in /var/mail. The suggested workaround is to change the permissions on /var/mail to 1777, allowing non-privileged users to add and delete files. However, only the proper users can modify their own files. This isn't an ideal solution, but it will suffice in most cases.

You can use SSL/TLS encryption with IMAP, just as with POP3. When building it from the ports, use make USE_SSL=YES and make install USE_SSL=YES instead of simply using make and make install. You can then generate a certificate using make cert, or you can simply copy the certificate file you may have created for qpopper into /usr/local/certs (where IMAP-UW expects to find it). For consistency's sake, you might want to alter your qpopper configuration to point to the same certificate in /usr/local/certs if you will be using it for both secured services.

An alternate way to provide security for both POP3 and IMAP is to use stunnel, which you learn about in "Securing E-mail Services (POP3 and IMAP)," in Chapter 29.

E-mail for Standalone Workstations

Knowing how to run a full-fledged e-mail server is an excellent system administration skill. But this skill won't help you much if your FreeBSD machine isn't intended to be an Internet server providing mail services for dozens of users. What if you're just running a workstation, in the same way that someone might run a Windows desktop machine, with a Gnome or KDE desktop and graphical productivity applications instead of server tools?

Fortunately, a standalone workstation's e-mail setup is much less complex than that of a full-scale server. Still, it's important that you know how to control the standalone workstation environment, and there are some interesting tricks that make standalone computing with FreeBSD quite convenient.

Using Fetchmail to Retrieve E-mail from POP3 and IMAP Servers

Most consumer operating systems have e-mail client programs (such as Outlook, Eudora, Netscape Messenger, and so on) that have their own internal, built-in mechanisms for checking POP3 or IMAP servers. Each one gets your mail in its own way and then stores it in its own fashion internally. Some MUA programs of this type exist for FreeBSD, and they work just fine.

However, you might choose instead to run an MUA such as Mutt, Elm, or Pine on your workstation, just as you would on a server. These programs operate directly on the system's central /var/mail directory and your mail spool file inside it, rather than keeping their own internal cache of downloaded messages. This allows you to share the mailbox between programs, search through it using command-line tools, and participate in any number of other testaments to the versatility of Unix.

But to get the messages from the POP3 or IMAP server where your e-mail address stores them (for instance, all mail to a frank@earthlink.net address would collect on the earthlink.net servers) to your local FreeBSD workstation, something needs to make the POP3 or IMAP connection and deliver the new messages from the remote mailbox to your local one. That something is Fetchmail, a small but versatile utility written by Eric Raymond.

Fetchmail can be installed out of the ports (/usr/ports/mail/fetchmail) or packages. It operates on the basis of a .fetchmailrc file in your home directory. This file specifies remote POP3 or IMAP servers to poll for new mail, the intervals at which to check, and numerous other options. Fetchmail then retrieves new mail as specified and relays it to port 25 on your workstation, where Sendmail is listening (in the default configuration). It then will deliver the mail to your local mailbox according to all the rules that would normally apply, such as .forward files and mail aliases.

Once Fetchmail has been installed (it is available in the FreeBSD ports collection in the mail directory), you will need to configure the .fetchmailrc file in your home directory before you can use it. This can be done in one of two ways.

The first method involves using the `fetchmailconf` program. This is a graphical configuration program for Fetchmail that is written in Python and uses the TK toolkit (a toolkit for building graphical user interfaces in X-Windows. Although `fetchmailconf` comes with the Fetchmail program, it requires Python and TCL/TK to be installed in order to work. (Python and TCL/TK are both popular languages available for many different platforms.)

The second method of configuring Fetchmail involves creating the `.fetchmailrc` file manually. The format of the configuration file is straightforward, and the Fetchmail man page is extremely good, covering in detail every option that can go in the `.fetchmailrc` file. This is the method we will cover in this chapter.

Configuring the `.fetchmailrc` File

In your home directory, open a new file called `.fetchmailrc` in your favorite text editor. The `.fetchmailrc` file you create here will contain three sections: global options, server options, and user options.

> **CAUTION**
>
> It's very important that the `.fetchmailrc` file sections appear in exactly the order shown here. Also note that no options that belong to a previous section can be used after a new section has been started. One of the most common causes of errors in `.fetchmailrc` files is having options in the wrong order or in the wrong place.

This chapter doesn't cover all the options available to `.fetchmailrc` because there are far too many. However, we will create a sample setup for retrieving mail from a POP3 server. As mentioned before, the man page for Fetchmail is extremely detailed and informative. Use the information presented in this section as a starting point for getting Fetchmail up and running. Then, refer to the man page for Fetchmail for any advanced configuration you wish to do.

The first section of the `.fetchmailrc` file contains the global options. These options will apply to all the mail servers and user accounts that will be listed later on in the configuration file. It is possible to override some of the global options with server- or user-specific options, but as a general rule, these will apply to all the servers and accounts that Fetchmail checks. Here is an example of a simple global configuration section and the options it might contain:

```
set daemon 600
set postmaster foobar
set logfile ./.fetchmail.log
```

These are the most common options used in the global section. Here's an explanation of each line:

- The first line causes Fetchmail to run in daemon mode and check for new mail every 600 seconds (10 minutes). When Fetchmail is started, it will check for new mail and move itself into the background as a daemon. After that, it will check for new mail every 600 seconds. If this line is not present, when you invoke Fetchmail, it will check for new mail and then terminate immediately and not check again.

- The second line is the fallback address. Basically, any mail that Fetchmail receives that is not addressed to a local user will be sent to this account on the local system. You should probably set this to the same user you will be running Fetchmail as.

- Finally, the third option sets a log file in which Fetchmail will log its activity. Alternatively, you can use the line `set syslog` instead, which will cause Fetchmail to use `syslogd` for logging. `syslogd` is the system-logging daemon that handles the logging of other system events.

The next section of the `.fetchmailrc` file is the server section, which contains information on each mail server that should be checked for mail. Here is a sample server section that is configured to check one e-mail server:

```
poll mail.samplenet.org
proto pop3
no dns
```

Several other server options are available. See the Fetchmail man page for full details. Here are the options shown in this example:

- The first line causes the server `mail.samplenet.org` to be checked for new mail at the interval configured by the `set daemon` option in the global section, as well as each time Fetchmail is invoked manually. The alternative would be `skip mail.samplenet.org`. In this case, this server would be skipped and not checked for new mail at the regular intervals or when Fetchmail is invoked manually. If the skip option is used, the server will only be checked for new mail when it is specified on the command line when invoking Fetchmail.

- The second line tells Fetchmail the protocol to use with this server. In this case, it is POP3. Other legal options are POP3, IMAP, APOP, and KPOP.

- The third option tells Fetchmail not to perform DNS lookups on multidrop. If you are running over a dial-up Internet connection, you will probably want to include this line.

The third and final section of the `.fetchmailrc` file is the user section, which contains information about the account itself. Here is a sample user section of `.fetchmailrc`:

```
user foobar
pass secretword
```

```
fetchall
flush
```

Here are some points to note in this example:

- The first and second lines contain the username and password, respectively, that you use to access the mail on your ISP's mail server.

- The third line tells Fetchmail that it should retrieve all messages from the server, including those that have already been read.

- Finally, the fourth line tells Fetchmail that it should flush the server (delete the messages it downloads off the server). This line is not strictly necessary because this is the default.

Several more user options are available, including options that cause Fetchmail not to delete mail off the server that it downloads, and so on. See the Fetchmail man page for full details.

The complete Fetchmail configuration file looks like this:

```
set daemon 600
set postmaster foobar
set logfile ./.fetchmail.log

poll mail.samplenet.org
proto pop3
no dns

user foobar
pass secretword
fetchall
flush
```

From top to bottom, this file basically says the following: "Check for new mail every 600 seconds. Send any unaddressed mail to the user foobar. Log the actions to .fetchmail.log. Check the server mail.samplenet.org for new mail every 10 minutes using the POP3 protocol, and do not attempt to do DNS lookups. Use the username foobar and the password secretword to log in to the server, fetch all the messages, and delete the messages off the server after they are downloaded."

> **CAUTION**
>
> Because the .fetchmailrc file contains your username and password for the mail server, its permissions should be set so that only you, the user running Fetchmail, can read this file. The permissions should be no higher than 600. You can set the permissions to the correct value by

typing **chmod 600 .fetchmailrc**. This will allow only the owner of the file to read or write to it. Fetchmail will complain and refuse to run if you attempt to start it with a `.fetchmailrc` file that has permissions greater than this.

This brief introduction to Fetchmail should get you up and running with a basic configuration. For more advanced options, see the man page for Fetchmail. It is very detailed and fully explains all the options available for the `.fetchmailrc` file.

Sendmail Configuration for Standalone Workstations

For Fetchmail to work, Sendmail (or some equivalent) has to be running on port 25 to accept incoming messages. However, Sendmail is configured by default to handle outgoing mail, and for good reason; it's not generally a good idea to run your workstation with no MTA at all. For example, Mutt and other shell-based mail clients send messages by passing them directly to Sendmail, rather than by connecting remotely to some external SMTP host. This prevents relaying-related issues, as discussed earlier.

Still, you can do a few things to tweak Sendmail's performance and configuration so that it's optimized for use in a system that isn't connected to the Internet at all times. The first such configuration is the "smart" mail host, and the second is an automated mail spool run.

Find the following lines in `/etc/mail/freebsd.mc`:

```
dnl Dialup users should uncomment and define this appropriately
dnl define(`SMART_HOST', `your.isp.mail.server')
```

Uncomment the `define` line by removing the dnl, and change `your.isp.mail.server` to the appropriate mail server name. Rebuild the config file by running `make cf` and `make install` from inside `/etc/mail`.

This change allows your workstation to operate like any desktop operating system in which each mail client makes its own SMTP connection to the SMTP server provided by the dial-up ISP, which then relays the mail on to its final destination. Because you might be using shell-based MUAs such as Mutt and Pine, which send mail by passing it directly to Sendmail rather than trying to make their own in-program SMTP connections to a defined SMTP relay, you need a centralized way to make these mail clients behave like their commercial Windows counterparts. Defining `SMART_HOST` forces Sendmail to direct all outgoing mail to your dial-up SMTP server.

The reason for all this is because most SMTP servers will reject mail that comes from an unresolvable IP address, and many ISP networks don't provide DNS lookup information for their dial-up clients. If you don't define `SMART HOST`, this limitation will prevent your FreeBSD workstation from being able to send mail reliably to a good percentage of the mail hosts on the Internet. However, because you have an available SMTP server at your

ISP, and because this server will relay mail from all its dial-up customers (because that's how Windows MUAs work), you can rest assured that defining SMART_HOST will get all your messages to their destinations.

Another configuration item you can tweak is the outgoing message queue. By default, Sendmail does a queue run every 30 minutes (using the `-q30m` command-line option, set in `/etc/defaults/rc.conf`). If you're a dial-up user who connects for only brief periods, this interval might be too long. You can add a line to `/etc/rc.conf` overriding the default interval:

```
sendmail_flags="-bd -q10m"
```

However, an even more efficient way to handle this is to leave the default `-q30m` untouched and to simply do a queue run as soon as you connect to the Internet. As you'll recall, you can initiate a queue run with the `sendmail -q` command, optionally adding `-v` for entertainment or debugging purposes.

Doing this by hand is sure to become tedious, though, so you can add `sendmail -q` to your `ppp-up` script, which we discussed in Chapter 23, "Connecting to the Internet with PPP."

A Look at Some Sendmail Replacements

Although Sendmail is still widely recognized as the industry-leading MTA by a wide margin, it's not without its faults. It is widely criticized for its barely comprehensible configuration files, the "master config" file in its otherwise almost-unknown m4 format, the proliferation of different runtime files (such as the access database and `virtusertable` file), and its comparative bulk and sluggishness. If you're comfortable with the way Sendmail works in its default configuration (which usually doesn't take much extra effort), you may have no need to complain. However, if you find you need more speed and less resource consumption, you can choose a replacement program. Replacements for Sendmail abound, each with its advantages, disadvantages, and die-hard supporters.

> **NOTE**
>
> A file called `/etc/mail/mailer.conf` controls an abstraction layer that allows you to drop in a replacement for Sendmail and have the system still operate as before. Its content is a set of aliases or pointers that define commands such as `sendmail` and `mailq` (which are really just aliases to specific Sendmail options; for instance, `sendmail -bp` for `mailq`) to refer to a specific binary, which by default is `/usr/libexec/sendmail/sendmail`—the actual Sendmail Consortium MTA program.
>
> `/usr/sbin/sendmail` is really a symbolic link to `/usr/sbin/mailwrapper`, which uses the `mailer.conf` file to tell it how to redirect calls for those Sendmail-related commands. If you install a replacement program such as Postfix, its installation script will modify `mailer.conf` for you so that you can continue to type **sendmail** or **mailq**, and `mailwrapper` will redirect those commands off to the new Postfix binary instead of the default Sendmail.

Postfix

Perhaps the largest and most compelling Sendmail alternative right now is Postfix, developed by Wietse Venema with primary goals of speed and security. Also, its structure tends to be very "Sendmail-like," which makes it a good choice for an administrator of a large and entrenched Sendmail system that needs to be given a performance boost.

The speed of Postfix is reported to be extremely good, easily faster than Qmail, for example, although this is difficult to measure empirically. The downside to Postfix is that it's still quite new and therefore doesn't have the maturity or the advanced features that Sendmail or Qmail has.

The Postfix home page is at `http://www.postfix.org`.

Qmail

Dan Bernstein wrote Qmail specifically to provide an alternative to Sendmail that was fast and secure. On those fronts it succeeds quite well and is gaining popularity in a lot of high-profile Internet services, such as Hotmail, Network Solutions, and Yahoo! mail. The internal structure of Qmail is built up from scratch, not adapted from the Sendmail structure; this means that the configuration and the file structure for a Qmail installation don't much resemble their counterparts in Sendmail. Qmail is a good choice for an administrator who wants speed and security but doesn't know enough about Sendmail to be attached to it. It's also integrated tightly with the EZMLM mailing list manager, also by Bernstein, so Qmail would serve you well if you use EZMLM.

The Qmail home page is at `http://www.qmail.org`.

Exim

Developed at Cambridge University, Exim offers a Sendmail alternative whose chief advantage is a helpful complement of documentation, developer support, and mailing lists. It's also reputed to be very easy to configure, largely due to these sources of help, and more mature than some of the other alternatives.

However, Exim has had historical problems with security, and it's one of the poorer choices of Sendmail alternatives when it comes to modularity or advanced features. It's still a high-performance server, though, and can speed up SMTP services by a significant amount over Sendmail.

The Exim home page is at `http://www.exim.org`.

Smail

An older MTA, Smail claims easy configurability and tight security as its hallmarks; its configuration structure is nowhere near as complex as Sendmail's (its nearest relative is Exim), but its command-line syntax has some similarities with that of Sendmail. However, Smail appears to be on its way out as a viable Sendmail alternative because development efforts seem to be petering out.

CHAPTER **25**

Configuring a Web Server

Whether e-mail or the Web is the true "killer app" of the modern Internet is really a toss-up these days. Although e-mail, the venerable workhorse of online applications, has quietly changed the way we communicate forever, there isn't anything quite like the flash of the Web and its potential as a full-fledged entertainment and commerce medium. In any case, it's probably pretty safe to assume that if you're setting up a FreeBSD server, you want it to be a Web server as well as providing e-mail and shell access. This isn't universally the case, though, so whereas FreeBSD ships with Sendmail installed to do e-mail services with almost no additional configuration, there is no equivalent Web server application installed by default. You have to get your own from the ports or packages.

For 90 percent of Web server functions, Apache is the server of choice. There are a number of other servers you can use instead, such as Roxen and AOLserver, but Apache has slowly built up so much of the market share in polled Internet servers over the years that it's the leading choice by a wide margin.

The Apache Project, located at www.apache.org on the Web, is one of the best examples of the open-source philosophy at work, producing software that gets the job done better and in more compliance with published standards than just about all the alternatives. It's also suitable for all kinds of environments—from small, low-traffic informational Web sites to full-scale e-commerce sites with hundreds of concurrent connections—with the addition of plug-in modules allowing you to take advantage of such server-side technologies as database connectivity and built-in Perl scripting.

This chapter will discuss how to configure Apache for each of these types of installations. First, however, we will look at the structure of the HTTP protocol and see how a thorough understanding of it will enable you to operate an efficient Internet server.

Introduction to the HTTP Protocol

The Hypertext Transfer Protocol (HTTP) is the backbone of the World Wide Web. Developed in 1993 to support information exchange at CERN in Switzerland, HTTP is a very simple protocol, involving no authentication and only a few possible client commands. It's optimized for the lightweight serving of small (several kilobytes at most) text files, in keeping with the original intent of HTTP as a means of disseminating inter-linked informational pages in the newly developed markup language understood by HTTP browsers, known as the *Hypertext Markup Language* (HTML).

Although originally not intended for this purpose, HTTP is now used for the transfer of large binary files, often including many inline images requested at once from an HTML page as it renders. This kind of data transfer was seldom done in the early days of the Web (GIF and JPEG image support in 1994 was sporadic across various platforms). In response to this change, certain augmentations have been made to the HTTP specification. The most important of these is the HTTP/1.1 standard, which provides features such as *pipelining* (combining the responses to many simultaneous requests into a single response stream), although the standard is still only partially supported in most browsers.

Unlike SMTP, FTP, and many other such popular protocols, HTTP is *stateless*, meaning that there isn't a concept of a "session" where a client connects to a server, performs several transactions, and then ends the connection. HTTP permits only a single request per connection, and therefore it's really not possible to determine how many users are connected to a Web server at any given time (except for downloads that are currently in progress). This also means there aren't any of the topological issues associated with protocols such as SMTP: Relaying, MX records, queues, and so on aren't relevant to HTTP. Instead, the problems that an HTTP server administrator faces have mostly to do with bandwidth, CPU, and memory resources, and with their most efficient use as concurrent activity grows with the popularity of the Web site.

HTTP Request Structure

The structure of an HTTP/1.0 request is about as simple as it can get. You can simulate an HTTP transaction by connecting to port 80 of an HTTP server and issuing a GET request, (which can contain multiple lines) in the following form:

```
# telnet www.somewhere.com 80
Connected to www.somewhere.com.
Escape character is '^]'.
GET / HTTP/1.0

HTTP/1.1 200 OK
```

```
Date: Sun, 20 May 2001 22:45:55 GMT
Server: Apache/1.3.20 (Unix)
Content-Location: index.html
Vary: negotiate,accept-language,accept-charset
TCN: choice
Last-Modified: Fri, 31 Mar 2000 01:45:46 GMT
ETag: "6531f-54e-38e4034a;3a977613"
Accept-Ranges: bytes
Content-Length: 1358
Connection: close
Content-Type: text/html
Content-Language: en
Expires: Sun, 20 May 2001 22:45:55 GMT

<HTML>
<TITLE>test page</TITLE>
<BODY>
test
</BODY>
</HTML>
```

You could instead issue a HEAD request of the same form, to retrieve the headers only, not the message body. You enter a blank line to indicate the end of the multiline request (press Enter twice).

The first block of response lines is the headers, so you can easily tell what kind of HTTP server is at the other end. Each HTTP server has its own unique signature on the Server: line. This signature tells you the name of the server software and the platform that it was built for; bear in mind, though, that even though it says "Unix", this doesn't actually tell you anything about the operating system that the server is running, which could be anything from Linux to HP-UX. The rest of the lines, especially the Content-*: lines, contain information that help the Web browser lay out the page. For instance, Content-Length:, when present, allows the browser to report how much data there is left in the download, and Content-Type: tells the browser how to render the requested file (as HTML, plain text, GIF or JPEG image data, and so on).

An HTTP/1.0 request allows a number of extra lines to be included in the request, including lines specifying cookies, accepted encodings, preferred languages, and so on. Aside from the request line, which must appear first, the order of the rest of the lines doesn't matter. However, these are optional; only one line (the request line itself) is required. An HTTP/1.1 request is almost the same as HTTP/1.0, except that a second line is also required—the Host: line. This is an addition to the protocol intended to support virtual hosting, where a single Web server can answer for many different hostnames. This means that the client has to specify the hostname whose Web content it wants to see. Because a

25

Web browser looks up the server's IP address from the hostname the user specifies and then makes the HTTP connection based on the IP address (which is how TCP/IP applications operate, as you saw in Chapter 21, "Networking with FreeBSD"), the server knows nothing about what hostname the user is trying to reach unless the client supplies the `Host:` header, as shown here:

```
# telnet www.somewhere.com 80
Connected to www.somewhere.com.
Escape character is '^]'.
GET / HTTP/1.1
Host: www.somewhere.com
```

All major browsers today, including text-only browsers such as Lynx, support HTTP/1.1-style `Host:` headers. (However, whether they formulate their requests to claim HTTP/1.1 support is inconsistent. Netscape Navigator, for instance, supports many HTTP/1.1 features, but it issues its requests as HTTP/1.0 anyway.) This means that virtual hosting based on the `Host:` header (rather than by IP address and network-level IP aliases) is now almost exclusively the method of choice, greatly simplifying matters. We'll talk more about virtual hosting later in this chapter.

Response Codes and Redirects

Although there are only a few request methods (`GET`, `HEAD`, and `POST`, plus several more for HTTP/1.1), the server can return a wide variety of responses. These responses are three-digit numeric codes, and they're grouped on meaning by the first digit. Table 25.1 shows the complete set of HTTP response codes and what they mean, particularly in the context of Apache and its features.

TABLE 25.1   HTTP Response Codes

Numeric Code	Name	Meaning
2XX—Success		
200	OK	Standard success code.
201	Created	
202	Accepted	
203	Partial Information	
204	No Content	
3XX—Redirection		
300	Multiple Choices	`MultiViews` or `CheckSpelling` found multiple matches.
301	Moved Permanently	Trailing slash was omitted.
302	Moved Temporarily	Redirect found.
304	Not Modified	Cached copy is okay to use.

TABLE 25.1   Continued

Numeric Code	Name	Meaning
4XX—Client Error		
400	Bad Request	
401	Unauthorized	Must authenticate to continue.
403	Forbidden	Server permissions or configuration do not permit access.
404	Not Found	File does not exist.
5XX—Server Error		
500	Internal Server Error	Server-side (CGI) program failed (generic error).
501	Not Implemented	
502	Bad Gateway	
503	Service Unavailable	Resources to process the request are not available.

You're probably quite familiar with 404 and 403 errors, and 500 errors will be familiar to you if you've ever done any CGI programming. However, one little-understood code is 304. This code is never seen by a user because it's intended purely for a browser's use; nonetheless, it's one of the most commonly used codes by a production server, as you would see if you were to look through the access log (/var/log/httpd-access.log).

When a client has to make a request for a file that it already has in its cache (such as an inline GIF image in an HTML page), it performs a GET request with the If-Modified-Since field set to the date and time the image was last downloaded. This causes the server to evaluate whether the file has been changed on the server since that time. If it has, it sends the file (with a 200 success code); if it hasn't, it returns a 304 (Not Modified) code, telling the browser that it's okay to display the copy that it has in its cache, thereby saving the trouble of serving the file all over again.

Another code frequently seen by browsers but not people is 301 (Moved Permanently). This code most often occurs when someone requests a URL of the type http://some.host.com/Subdirectory, where Subdirectory is the name of a directory on the server. The correct form of the URL that accesses the index of that directory is http://some.host.com/Subdirectory/, with a trailing slash. Notice, however, that if you enter the URL without the trailing slash, you'll still get the page—but the browser attaches the slash for you. This is because it received a 301 code for the first request, redirecting it to the same URL with the slash appended. The URL in your browser was updated, the browser made a second request, and the correct page was served. For this to work seamlessly, the server needs to know exactly what its hostname is; this is the purpose of the ServerName directive in Apache, which we will discuss a little later in this chapter.

25

More information about HTTP, its structure, response codes, and much more can be found at the W3 Consortium Web site, www.w3.org/Protocols. The original HTTP/1.0 specification is laid out in RFC 1945, and HTTP/1.1 in RFC 2068.

Obtaining and Installing Apache

Apache's name is derived from its original nickname "A Patchy Server," since it grew out of a series of patches applied against the industry-standard, but limited, NCSA httpd server in early 1995. Apache is one of the most widely ported pieces of software in the world today. It runs on dozens of different operating system platforms, from AIX to Windows to BeOS to Mac OS X, as well as, of course, FreeBSD. Probably the most complete HTTP implementation available anywhere, Apache is also seen by many as the epitome of the open-source ideal; its success demonstrates how a free, grassroots development effort can compete with large, commercially developed packages from market-leading software companies to become the *de facto* standard solution. Apache claims at least a 60-percent market share at the time of this writing—a figure that continues to grow.

Obtaining Apache is a matter of installing it from the ports (/usr/ports/www/apache13 or /usr/ports/www/apache2) or packages. At the time of this writing, Apache 1.3 is the mature code branch, with most of its bugs and security issues solved long ago; it's the codebase that has built Apache's popularity and reputation, and it will probably do everything you need it to do. However, it has a few structural quirks (such as a forking model, where it spawns a new Apache process to handle every single request). Apache 2.0 is a complete rewrite that incorporates kernel threading and greater modular architecture for major performance benefits. This chapter primarily covers Apache 1.3 because of its more widespread deployment and its long history of stability; however, the chapter also includes discussions of those areas where Apache 2.0 diverges in usage or behavior from Apache 1.3.

> **NOTE**
>
> The installed support files for the 1.3 and 2.0 versions of Apache are kept separate in order to allow administrators to maintain parallel installations and transition gradually to the new version. If you install Apache 2.0, the configuration files will be in /usr/local/etc/apache2, and the documentation and library paths will similarly end in /apache2 instead of /apache. In this chapter, the examples will discuss file locations that end in /apache; make the necessary adjustment if you are working with Apache 2.0.
>
> Nearly all of the operational directives are identical between Apache 1.3 and 2.0, but some filenames and paths may differ.

One interesting advantage that Apache has for FreeBSD users is that many parts of it were developed explicitly in a FreeBSD environment. These components include the URL Rewrite module (mod_rewrite) by Ralf Engelschall and a number of performance-tuning options. Its development environment also means that Apache fits well into the FreeBSD directory structure, as we'll discuss in a moment.

The Apache source distribution is available from a number of worldwide mirror sites, if your ports collection is unable to get it from the main, central site. These mirrors, as well as the definitive collection of Apache documentation, can be found at http://httpd.apache.org.

Apache File Layout

After installing Apache, you'll notice that a new directory has been created in /usr/local for the server's root directory. This new directory, /usr/local/www, contains several subdirectories for various purposes, some of which are symbolic links. The map of Apache's file layout is shown in Figure 25.1. As you would expect, everything installed as part of Apache is underneath /usr/local, except for log files (which go into /var/log with all the rest of the system's log files).

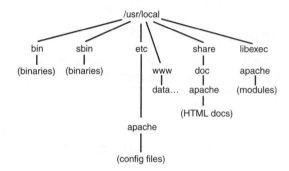

FIGURE 25.1   Map of the Apache file layout, showing the relationship of config files, the server document root, and support binaries.

Actually, a few of these directories are in a temporary, installation-only file structure that prevents the install script from "clobbering" existing files on a live server. For instance, /usr/local/www/data is the location where the default configuration expects to find the document root; however, this location is a symlink to /usr/local/www/data-dist, and it contains only generic HTML files in a variety of language variants that, if left unchanged, will tell a visitor to your site merely that Apache has been installed correctly. Your first step after installing Apache from the ports or packages should be to remove the symbolic link (rm /usr/local/www/data) and replace it with a regular directory (mkdir/usr/local/www/data) into which you will later put your Web content. Similarly, /usr/local/www/cgi-bin is a symlink to /usr/local/www/cgi-bin-dist, itself a regular directory. If you put files into cgi-bin, they will actually go into the cgi-bin-dist directory, unless you change cgi-bin to be its own regular directory.

Files in /usr/local/etc/apache, which we will discuss in a moment, also have -dist or -std variants—there are no symbolic links here, but the -dist files are the only ones that are touched when you reinstall or upgrade. This gives you a "safety net" and reference file in case you change something in your live configuration files that you can't fix without hints.

As with Sendmail, Apache's file layout in FreeBSD is considerably different from the layout in an Apache installation on other platforms. Each one differs slightly, so knowing the FreeBSD layout well won't necessarily help you if you have to maintain Apache on Linux, Solaris, or Windows.

Here's one tip that may help: There's usually a "server root" directory, such as /usr/local/www on FreeBSD, in which everything Apache-related lives. On Linux, this is often in /var/lib/apache; however, in this style of installation, very nearly everything associated with Apache—including config files, binaries, logs, sources, and build configuration scripts—lives in or under that one directory. Although this doesn't have the benefit of FreeBSD's rigid and consistent structure, at least you'll be able to find just about everything in one place in such an installation.

Configuring Apache

Just as in /etc/mail (which you saw in Chapter 24, "Configuring E-mail Services"), /usr/local/etc/apache (the Apache configuration directory) contains a number of files, some of which are of interest to us and some of which are not. Let's take a look at each of them in turn:

- `httpd.conf`—This is the main Apache configuration file. These days, everything is consolidated into this one file, rather than being grouped into as many as three more specific files.

- `mime.types`—This file provides a lookup table between filename extensions and MIME types (`Content-Type` headers) in files that Apache sends. This is how browsers know how to handle files they download.

- `magic`—An alternative method to MIME types is `magic`, which tries to determine a file type by looking for certain patterns within the file, making filename extensions unnecessary. This is the same method that's used by the `file` command.

- `ssl.conf`—A configuration file that enables Secure Sockets Layer encryption (the SSL module, mod_ssl, is included by default in Apache 2.0). See "Securing Apache" in Chapter 29, "Network Security," for details on using mod_ssl to run a secure Web server.

- `highperformance.conf`—This configuration file is only a "stub" to demonstrate what kinds of modifications you might want to make to `httpd.conf` in order to tune your Apache server for optimum performance. It contains many useful examples of such configuration options but should not be used as a drop-in replacement for `httpd.conf` itself.

- **access.conf and srm.conf**—These files used to contain certain parts of what is now incorporated into httpd.conf (these files don't exist in Apache 2.0). They will still be read if you put configuration items into them, which is why they're still here (to maintain compatibility with legacy installations). However, these files have become unnecessary and can be ignored.

Again, note that .default versions of all these files exist. Immediately after a clean installation, these are copies of the regular versions of each file. After you've made changes to the regular versions over the course of regular usage, though, if you install a newer version of Apache, only the .default files will be touched by the installation scripts. This allows you to upgrade your system and merge in new configuration options at your leisure, using diff or some other method.

Using httpd.conf

The httpd.conf file is long and detailed, but (unlike /etc/mail/sendmail.cf) it's entirely human-readable and very well commented. Every one of the configuration directives is set to a sensible default value; you can modify any of them that you want, and the inline documentation explains quite clearly what each one does. If you misconfigure something, Apache will tell you exactly what's wrong when you try to start it up.

25

> **CAUTION**
>
> Before you make any changes to httpd.conf, be sure to make a backup copy (for instance, httpd.conf.bak) so that you can easily revert to your previous working configuration.

Immediately after installation, Apache can be started up and will serve requests properly. However, just to be safe, you should first set a couple of configuration directives. Find each of these in the httpd.conf file and alter it accordingly:

```
#
# ServerAdmin: Your address, where problems with the server should be
# e-mailed.  This address appears on some server-generated pages, such
# as error documents.
#
ServerAdmin you@your.address

#
# ServerName allows you to set a host name which is sent back to clients for
# your server if it's different than the one the program would get (i.e., use
# "www" instead of the host's real name).
#
#ServerName new.host.name
```

The second directive, ServerName, is used in 301 redirections (discussed earlier in the chapter). If the trailing slash is left off of a request for a directory index or listing, Apache responds with a 301 code (Moved Permanently) and the URL to which the browser should go. Apache has to construct this redirection URL from the information it has from the client's request, which (as you've seen) contains only the portion of the URL beginning with the slash after the hostname—for example, if the requested URL is http://some.host.com/images/foo, the request is /images/foo. If it's an HTTP/1.1 request, it contains a Host: header, which Apache can use to rebuild the full URL, but otherwise it's on its own unless you've specified the server's hostname with the ServerName directive.

HTTP/1.1 does cause a few other repercussions regarding the ServerName directive. If you're doing name-based virtual hosting, which we'll get to shortly, Apache uses ServerName to match a virtual host with a request based on its Host: header. Each virtual host must have a ServerName specified, but even if you're not doing virtual hosting, it's a good idea to define ServerName to help Apache construct its redirection URLs and match requests with the single main host configuration, effectively treating the default configuration as a virtual host that must match a Host: header.

We could go through all the available configuration directives here, but too many of them are equally important relative to each other and unimportant relative to the default configuration. Authoritative documentation can be found at the Apache Group's Web site at http://httpd.apache.org/docs/.

Using .htaccess **Files and Overrides**

Although httpd.conf provides global configuration options, many of them can be overridden on a per-directory basis without the server having to be restarted. You do this by placing a file called .htaccess, containing any directives you want to override, into the directory to which you want it to apply. On every request that comes in, the global configuration that was loaded into memory from httpd.conf is consulted, followed by every per-directory configuration file (.htaccess) sequentially down the path to where the requested file is. Each successive .htaccess file can override previously seen directives, but otherwise an .htaccess applies to its own directory and all subdirectories.

Whether .htaccess files can be used depends on the AllowOverride directive. As you can see by reading through httpd.conf, AllowOverride is set to None at the operating system root level and again on the /usr/local/www/data directory; therefore, .htaccess files are ignored by default. However, you can turn them on by replacing AllowOverride None (in the /usr/local/www/data block) with any of the directives in Table 25.2, or any combination thereof (for example, AllowOverride AuthConfig Limit).

TABLE 25.2   AllowOverride Configuration Options

Directive	Allows .htaccess Files to Override
AllowOverride Options	The Options directive
AllowOverride FileInfo	File-typing directives, such as AddType and ErrorDocument
AllowOverride AuthConfig	Authorization directives, such as Require and Auth*
AllowOverride Limit	Host access directives, such as Allow, Deny, and Order
AllowOverride All	All of the above

NOTE

The Options directive is one of the largest and most versatile configuration items in Apache; it controls the availability of many of Apache's most significant features, such as ExecCGI (the ability to execute CGI scripts), Includes (server-side includes), and MultiViews (versatile content negotiation). These features can be added to or subtracted from the current configuration at any level in the hierarchical directory structure. Refer to http://httpd.apache.org/docs/mod/core.html#options for full coverage of the Options directive and how to use it.

After changing httpd.conf accordingly, restart the server (as we will discuss in a moment). You can now put an .htaccess file into any Web-accessible directory and place into it any configuration directives that Apache allows in .htaccess files (for details on these, see http://httpd.apache.org/docs/).

The httpd.conf file contains a commented-out block for controlling user directories (in /home); if you plan to run a server where your users can have sites of their own, but you want to make sure browsers that support various data-changing HTTP/1.1 methods (such as DELETE, COPY, and MOVE) can't exercise them, you might want to uncomment this block:

```
#
# Control access to UserDir directories.  The following is an example
# for a site where these directories are restricted to read-only.
#
#<Directory /home/*/public_html>
#    AllowOverride FileInfo AuthConfig Limit
#    Options MultiViews Indexes SymLinksIfOwnerMatch IncludesNoExec
#    <Limit GET POST OPTIONS PROPFIND>
#        Order allow,deny
#        Allow from all
#    </Limit>
#    <LimitExcept GET POST OPTIONS PROPFIND>
#        Order deny,allow
#        Deny from all
#    </LimitExcept>
#</Directory>
```

25

Note that the `AllowOverride` here allows `.htaccess` files to override `FileInfo`, `AuthConfig`, and `Limit` directives, but the `Options` directives are set at the global level.

NOTE

In accordance with historical convention, per-user document directories are called `public_html`; therefore, a request for `http://some.host.com/~user/` would show the documents in `/home/user/public_html`. Also traditionally, if there's an `index.html` file present, Apache will serve that file instead of the directory listing. (Microsoft servers generally use `Default.htm` for this function.) You can specify as many of these index filenames as you like using the `DirectoryIndex` directive. Apache will try each filename you specify, in the order in which you enter them.

Starting and Stopping the HTTP Daemon

The Apache installation process in the ports collection will start the server automatically. You can verify this by looking for `httpd` processes using `ps` and `grep`:

```
# ps -waux | grep httpd
root      220   0.0   2.0   4436 2456   ??   Ss  Sat02PM   0:02.79 /usr/local/sbin/httpd
nobody    303   0.0   2.0   4496 2548   ??   I   Sat02PM   0:00.01 /usr/local/sbin/httpd
nobody    304   0.0   2.0   4460 2452   ??   I   Sat02PM   0:00.00 /usr/local/sbin/httpd
nobody    305   0.0   2.0   4460 2452   ??   I   Sat02PM   0:00.00 /usr/local/sbin/httpd
nobody    306   0.0   2.0   4460 2452   ??   I   Sat02PM   0:00.00 /usr/local/sbin/httpd
nobody    307   0.0   2.0   4460 2452   ??   I   Sat02PM   0:00.00 /usr/local/sbin/httpd
nobody  13963   0.0   2.0   4468 2468   ??   I   Sat10PM   0:00.00 /usr/local/sbin/httpd
```

Note that Apache uses a forking model, where one "master" process (the one owned by root in the output shown here) listens on port 80 for incoming requests and then forks off a copy of itself (owned by the unprivileged pseudo-user `nobody`) as a child process to handle each request. The master process never actually serves any requests on its own.

NOTE

It's very dangerous to have a Web server that can serve requests as root, because that means it can execute programs as root—a situation that's one small CGI script away from an exploit that can wipe your entire hard disk clean.

Under the forking model, where dozens of `httpd` processes might be running simultaneously, killing and restarting every one of these processes is impractical, to say the least. There's a better way to stop and restart the server, though. All you have to do if you want to stop the server is to kill the master process. To restart the server, send the master process an `HUP` signal, upon which it will kill all its child processes, restart itself, and respawn its children.

Even this process is still fairly messy, though, and it involves using tools such as ps, grep, and kill in a fairly arcane manner. Fortunately, Apache provides us with a handy tool for this purpose: apachectl, which is installed into /usr/local/sbin and is therefore part of your default program path.

> **NOTE**
>
> In Apache 2.0, the apachectl support program is merged with the httpd program itself; if you call apachectl with any of the arguments we discuss here, it is actually passing those arguments to httpd, which now handles such commands internally. Therefore, the command httpd -l (which we will discuss later in this chapter) is equivalent to apachectl -l, and httpd start will have the same effect as apachectl start.
>
> Apache 2.0 is threaded instead of fork based, meaning that it involves many fewer httpd processes than does Apache 1.3.

Starting and stopping Apache using apachectl is quite easy:

```
# apachectl start
/usr/local/sbin/apachectl start: httpd started
# apachectl stop
/usr/local/sbin/apachectl stop: httpd stopped
```

After you've made any changes to any of the files in /usr/local/etc/apache, you must restart Apache. This is also made easy by apachectl:

```
# apachectl restart
/usr/local/sbin/apachectl restart: httpd restarted
```

The apachectl restart command does the equivalent of sending a kill -HUP to the master httpd process: All child processes will be killed, even if they're in the middle of serving files to clients—and those clients will have their connection abruptly dropped. If you want to restart Apache in a less-intrusive way—for example, if you have a high-load server whose data integrity is critical—you might choose instead to perform a "graceful restart," which uses a SIGUSR1 signal instead of a SIGHUP signal. This less-urgent signal allows the master process to restart itself without killing its child processes, meaning that in-progress transfers will not be dropped:

```
# apachectl graceful
/usr/local/sbin/apachectl graceful: httpd gracefully restarted
```

One other common use for apachectl is the configtest command. This will cause Apache (whether it's running or not) to read in the config files from /usr/local/etc/apache and report any configuration errors, just as the start command would—except that it does not actually start the server if it finds no errors. This is an excellent diagnostic tool and an implicit part of both the restart and graceful commands. apachectl uses configtest to determine whether the configuration is valid before trying to restart the server; if the configuration isn't valid, it leaves the running processes alone. This prevents a `restart` or `graceful` command from inadvertently killing your server:

```
# apachectl graceful
/usr/local/sbin/apachectl graceful: configuration broken, ignoring restart
/usr/local/sbin/apachectl graceful: (run 'apachectl configtest' for details)
```

> **TIP**
>
> If Apache isn't running, apachectl `restart` or apachectl `graceful` will start it.

> **TIP**
>
> Another useful apachectl command is apachectl `configtest`, which allows you to see whether your httpd.conf file is valid. If there are illegal directives or syntax errors, apachectl will tell you about them without affecting the running Web server. This is an excellent way to experiment safely with new configuration options.

Basic Access Control with Apache

Certain parts of your Web site will almost certainly need to be protected from being viewed by the general public; access control allows you to restrict these sections to authorized users either by hostname/IP address or by password authentication. We'll take a look at both of these methods.

Access Control by Address

Let's say you want to restrict a certain file, directory, or set of files and directories to a short list of fixed IP addresses or hostnames. You can do this at the global (httpd.conf) level, if you have a permanent area of your site (such as a set of administration scripts) that you want to keep secure; or more efficiently for regular users or for temporary private resources, you can use an .htaccess file in any directory at or above the level of the items you want to protect.

Begin by making sure that .htaccess overrides are enabled in the part of the site that you want to protect. As you saw earlier, you can use `AllowOverride Limit`, at the /usr/local/www/data level or further down in the directory structure with another <Directory> container, to enable the use of the access-control directives `Allow`, `Deny`, and `Order`. Because Apache directives are all read in at the same time, you need to specify the order in which to read the `Allow` and `Deny` directives; otherwise, they'll override each other in ways you don't intend.

To close off a directory to everyone but certain specified addresses or hostnames, put an .htaccess file in that directory with the following contents:

```
Order deny,allow
Deny from all
Allow from 64.41.131.102
Allow from stripes.somewhere.com
Allow from nowhere.com
Allow from 10.5.100
Allow from 10.67.22.211/255.255.255.0
```

As you can see, a number of different address formats are allowed; these are just matching rules, where if the connecting host matches any of these hostname or network patterns, it will be allowed access. Similarly, you can have the directory open to everybody *except* certain hosts:

```
Order allow,deny
Allow from all
Deny from l33t.hacker.com
Deny from 192.168
```

You must place these commands inside a <Directory> or <Location> block if you're doing this in httpd.conf; you can also use <Files> or <FilesMatch> to list certain files, wherever in the system they might be, which should be subject to the access control:

```
<Files "*.jpg">
  Order deny,allow
  Deny from all
  Allow from 64.41.131.102
</Files>
```

FilesMatch can be used to specify filenames matching regular expressions, as in this example, which would match all .gif, .jpg, .jpeg, and .png files:

```
<FilesMatch "\.(gif|jpe?g|png)$">
  Order deny,allow
  Deny from all
  Allow from 64.41.131.102
</FilesMatch>
```

Note, however, that <Directory> and <Location> are not available in .htaccess files.

The <Limit> block, despite its name, is not required for the previous access controls to work. Rather, its purpose is to list certain access methods to which the access controls should apply. For instance, you might choose to limit only GET and POST but leave all other methods unrestricted. Likewise, you could use <LimitExcept> to specify the only methods to which the access controls should *not* apply. You saw an example of this earlier, in the commented-out block controlling user directories within /home.

Access Control by Password

Sometimes, it's not practical or desirable to limit access by address. A privileged portion of your site might be made available to registered users who have paid a fee, for example, and these users might not come from a predictable IP address. This is where it's much more sensible to use password authentication for access control.

Apache stores its own username and password databases, distinct from the systemwide one in /etc/master.passwd and its relatives. This is for security purposes, and it's an extremely bad idea to try to merge the two authentication schemes together, so don't even think about it. The FreeBSD password database is for authenticating shell users who actually have an account on the system, whereas the Apache authentication databases control access to certain parts of your Web site for Web surfers. You might have a situation in which these two areas of functionality overlap (such as an intranet server for a company), but don't be tempted to try to serve both from the same database. If you succeed, it will be a study in insecurity and irresponsible system administration techniques. This practice is explicitly discouraged by the Apache Group and will earn you a great deal more scorn than respect from your peers. It's not worth it.

To password-protect a portion of your Web site, you'll need to use an .htaccess file (or equivalent configuration in httpd.conf)—including the appropriate use of <Directory>, <Location>, and <Files> blocks—just as with per-address access control. The contents of this file or configuration block are considerably different, though, involving an entirely different module in Apache to do the access control. A simple example of such a block follows:

```
AuthType Basic
AuthName "Restricted Area"
AuthUserFile /usr/local/www/.htpasswd
Require valid-user
```

This example includes the minimum number of directives needed to make password-protection work; each of these directives, or their alternatives, is required. These directives are a little confusing, so let's look at them individually:

- **AuthType**—This can be either Basic or Digest; Basic is the only one that really concerns us.

- **AuthName**—This is just a name for the "realm" or the area you're protecting. This name pops up in the authentication window in the user's browser (for example, "Enter username for 'Restricted Area' at www.somewhere.com"), helping to tell the user which area he or she is entering and which username and password are needed. This can be anything you want, except it must be enclosed in quotes if there are spaces in the name.

- **AuthUserFile, AuthDBUserFile, and AuthDBMUserFile**—One of these directives must be used to specify the location of the file that contains the user/password database for the realm. (Each realm can have a different user database file if you like.) If it's a pure text file, use AuthUserFile; if it's in db or dbm format for lookup speed purposes (a good idea if there are a lot of users in it), use AuthDBUserFile or AuthDBMUserFile accordingly. We'll cover how to create plain-text or db/dbm user databases in a moment.

- **AuthGroupFile, AuthDBGroupFile, and AuthDBMGroupFile**—These directives work in the same way as the AuthUserFile ones, except that they specify groups of users from the file indicated with AuthUserFile, allowing you to restrict access to a group rather than just to certain users. This directive isn't required, but if you do use it, an AuthUserFile directive (and associated user database file) needs to be present for its users to be recognized as part of the listed groups.

- **Require**—This tells Apache how to authenticate the user. The argument can be valid-user (any user present in the AuthUserFile file who enters the correct password), user <username> <username>... (a list of users), or group <groupname> <groupname>... (a list of groups).

Adding Users

Once you have the access control block set up and apachectl configtest reports that the configuration is okay, it's time to add users. First, let's see how to make a plain-text user database, the kind for which you'd use an AuthUserFile directive. The command to use is htpasswd, which in FreeBSD is in /usr/local/bin and therefore part of your path:

```
# htpasswd -c /usr/local/www/.htpasswd frank
```

The -c flag is only necessary the first time; this tells htpasswd to create the file because it doesn't exist yet. You will then be prompted for the user's password, which you must enter twice (as usual). To do this in a script, you can use the -b option and specify the password as another argument:

```
# htpasswd -b /usr/local/www/.htpasswd joe Pr1d3L4ndz
```

Another useful option is -m, which causes htpasswd to use an MD5-based encryption algorithm rather than the system's crypt() routine; this may provide you with better security. Other options can be found in the man apachectl page.

> **CAUTION**
>
> The user database file can be anywhere in the system that the Web server user (nobody) can read, and it can be named anything you want, although having the name begin with .htpasswd is traditional and protected from view by the default server configuration. However, it's a very bad idea to put the file anywhere where it can be accessed by a user with a Web browser! To wit, don't put it anywhere inside /usr/local/www/data or in any user's public_html directory; instead, use Web-inaccessible locations such as /usr/local/www or directly inside a user's home directory. You don't want people downloading your user database and cracking it!

Plain-text user databases work great for small lists of users; however, once you start working with dozens or hundreds of users, the time it takes to look up a user's password makes the authentication process cumbersome or even nonfunctional. The solution to this is to use a true database file, either in db or dbm form, and to use the appropriate AuthDBUserFile or AuthDBMUserFile directive. The support program that allows you to work with the database files is /usr/local/bin/dbmmanage:

```
# dbmmanage /usr/local/www/.htpwddb adduser frank
New password:
Re-type new password:
User frank added with password encrypted to NtMDxy6jwyW7A using crypt
```

This example will create a db-style database file called /usr/local/www/.htpwddb, which you can then access with the AuthDBUserFile directive. The dbm equivalent can also be used if necessary, but you shouldn't have to. See man dbmmanage for further details on the user management commands you can use.

Adding Groups

Listing groups in a plain-text file (AuthGroupFile) is quite easy. Each line contains the group name, a colon, and then the list of users in the group:

```
mygroup: frank joe alice
```

The group file should probably be kept in the same place as the user file, and with a similar name; however, because the group file doesn't contain any passwords, security considerations aren't quite as critical.

Group files can be managed with dbmmanage as well, but this practice is usually unnecessary because (as with /etc/group) there are seldom anywhere near as many groups as there are users. You can use AuthGroupFile in conjunction with AuthDBUserFile if you wish to mix formats; this is probably the simplest way to maintain a large user list along with a small group list.

Access Control by Address and Password

It's possible to require that a user satisfy both address restrictions *and* password authentication before access control allows access to a restricted area. This is done with the `Satisfy` directive:

```
Allow from 64.41.131.102
Require valid-user
Satisfy all
```

`Satisfy all` is the default setting if both `Allow` and `Require` directives are present; this behavior means that the incoming user must meet the `Allow` requirements *and* supply a valid username and password before access will be granted. You can also use `Satisfy any` to tell the server that the user must supply a valid password *or* be coming from an allowed address; this is useful if you want users at certain locations to have unconditional access to an area, but require authentication from all other users (for instance, if you're providing a service that you must administer as a regular user, but you don't want to be forever entering passwords for access).

Virtual Hosting

Virtual hosting is the practice of keeping the Web site contents for multiple different domains or hostnames on the same server; a single installation of Apache serves requests for all of them. For instance, `www.mystore.com` and `www.frankspage.com` might both be configured in DNS to point to the same IP address on your FreeBSD machine, and Apache is responsible for serving both of them, as well as its own hostname (as specified in the `ServerName` directive).

As you've seen, HTTP/1.0 provided no indication of what hostname the HTTP client was trying to reach (as specified by the user), so in earlier days, virtual hosting had to be done by pointing each hostname to a separate IP address and then binding each IP address as an IP alias to the same Ethernet card. Each virtual host was then specified by IP address, so a request coming in from a Web browser would always be sure to get the correct Web site in response. The downside was that binding these large blocks of IP addresses to the same card became unwieldy, and it caused unnecessary consumption of IP address space (which, as you saw in Chapter 21, is not infinite).

The need for this cumbersome process has been much alleviated, however, by HTTP/1.1. The mandatory `Host:` header specifies what hostname the client is trying to reach. Therefore, "name-based" virtual hosts are the norm on the modern Web. Clients that don't support the `Host:` header are almost unheard of these days, so we will be discussing only name-based virtual hosts; if you're interested in address-based virtual hosts, you can find information on them at the Apache Web site.

The bulk of the `httpd.conf` file specifies the "default" server—a global set of definitions that apply to all requests that Apache receives. In the default server, the `ServerName` directive is used primarily for constructing 301 redirection URLs, as discussed earlier. However, you can then set up small sets of overrides to these global settings, which are used if the Host: header matches a certain specified hostname. These groupings of over-rides make up what are known as *virtual hosts*.

Let's say your server is called stripes.somewhere.com, and that's what your main ServerName directive specifies. To configure name-based virtual hosts, you need a NameVirtualHost directive with an argument of * (the wildcard specifies "all hostnames"), followed by as many different <VirtualHost *> blocks as you like:

```
NameVirtualHost *

<VirtualHost *>
  ServerName www.somewhere.com
  DocumentRoot /usr/local/www/data
  ServerAdmin webmaster@somewhere.com
  ErrorLog logs/www.somewhere.com-error_log
  CustomLog logs/www.somewhere.com-access_log common
</VirtualHost>

<VirtualHost *>
  ServerName www.frankspage.com
  ServerAlias frankspage.com
  DocumentRoot /home/frank/public_html
  ServerAdmin frank@frankspage.com
  ErrorLog logs/www.frankspage.com-error_log
  CustomLog logs/www.frankspage.com-access_log common
</VirtualHost>
```

Inside a <VirtualHost> container, the ServerName directive determines the hostname to match against the client's Host: header, and a match will result in the corresponding set of overrides (the appropriate <VirtualHost> being applied to the configuration). DocumentRoot specifies where in the filesystem the incoming request should be mapped, and the ErrorLog and CustomLog directives specify alternate log files for each virtual host. ServerAlias provides a way of listing multiple alternate matching hostnames for a virtual host. You can also include any other directives you like, as long as they're allowed inside a <VirtualHost> block—apachectl configtest will tell you if they're not allowed.

It's important to note, though, that in the setup shown earlier, a request for the default server (stripes.somewhere.com), or for any other hostname that maps to the server's IP address but doesn't match any of the <VirtualHost> blocks, will not be answered by the default server; the default server never answers requests for any address that is specified for name-based virtual hosts (in the NameVirtualHost directive). It exists only to specify the default configuration set. Because we've used the * wildcard to specify name-based virtual hosts on all IP addresses, the default server will never itself service a request. In the absence of a <VirtualHost> matching the requested hostname, the server that responds will be the first <VirtualHost> that appears in the config file (www.somewhere.com in this case).

A more correct configuration than the previous one, then, would be this:

```
NameVirtualHost *

<VirtualHost *>
  ServerName stripes.somewhere.com
</VirtualHost>

<VirtualHost *>
  ServerName www.somewhere.com
  ServerAlias *.somewhere.com
  DocumentRoot /usr/local/www/data
  ServerAdmin webmaster@somewhere.com
  ErrorLog logs/www.somewhere.com-error_log
  CustomLog logs/www.somewhere.com-access_log common
</VirtualHost>

<VirtualHost *>
  ServerName www.frankspage.com
  ServerAlias frankspage.com
  DocumentRoot /home/frank/public_html
  ServerAdmin frank@frankspage.com
  ErrorLog logs/www.frankspage.com-error_log
  CustomLog logs/www.frankspage.com-access_log common
</VirtualHost>
```

Virtual hosts can be done in a myriad of other ways, allowing you to specify different IP addresses and ports to match certain groups of <VirtualHost> blocks. Examples of the syntax for these methods can be found at http://httpd.apache.org/docs/vhosts/.

Introduction to Apache Modules

One of Apache's greatest strengths is its modular structure. All configuration directives are part of one module or another, and while in earlier versions of Apache these modules were all painstakingly turned on or off at compile time, nowadays almost all modules are available as dynamic shared objects (DSOs) and can simply be loaded at runtime.

25

Built-in Modules

To see which modules are compiled statically into Apache, use `httpd -l`:

```
# httpd -l
Compiled-in modules:
  http_core.c
  mod_so.c
suexec: disabled; invalid wrapper /usr/local/sbin/suexec
```

This means that the directives in the Core module and the mod_so module are the only ones guaranteed to be available. The Core module provides access to the most fundamental directives without which Apache could not run at all; mod_so enables DSO support, which makes it possible to load all the approximately 32 further modules that ship with Apache, as well as any additional modules that you might choose to install.

> **NOTE**
>
> Ignore the note about suexec; this is a utility that allows Apache to run in a setuid wrapper, executing requests as a specified user (usually different for every virtual host). The suexec wrapper isn't installed by default; you can read more about it at http://httpd.apache.org/docs/suexec.html. Also, in Chapter 29, "Network Security," we cover CGIwrap, a more versatile alternative to suexec.
>
> Note that Apache 2.0 may not display the line about suexec.

Dynamically Loaded Modules

Dynamic modules are functional libraries that can be added to or removed from the Apache server at the time you run it, instead of having to be compiled into the httpd binary. These modules (also known as DSOs, or *Dynamic Sharable Objects*) allow you to trim down the size of your running httpd processes by eliminating modules you don't need. This can easily be done at runtime by commenting out the unnecessary modules from httpd.conf. If you decide later that you need the functionality in a certain module, just re-enable it and restart Apache. A complete listing of all the Apache modules and which directives are part of each module can be found at http://httpd.apache.org/docs/mod/.

To enable a module, you need both the LoadModule directive (which dynamically links the module into the httpd process) and the AddModule directive (which enables the module's directives in the correct order for further use in the configuration file). If you look in httpd.conf, you'll find LoadModule and AddModule directives for all the bundled Apache modules, which are installed into /usr/local/libexec/apache. Something to note about LoadModule is that each LoadModule directive is processed inline before proceeding, so the order in which the modules are specified matters. If a module depends on another module already being linked in, the dependency must be invoked first. The default configuration has all this correctly handled for you.

Third-Party Modules

The real strength of Apache's modular structure comes with third-party modules. These modules are linked in at runtime with the rest of the available Apache modules, providing additional functionality and configuration directives—usually to give Apache the ability to process certain kinds of server-side content more efficiently. One popular module is mod_perl, which embeds a Perl interpreter into Apache, greatly speeding up Perl CGI scripts by obviating the need for Apache to start up a subshell process and execute the CGI program within it (you learn more about mod perl in an upcoming subsection of this chapter). Another is mod_php4, a module that gives Apache the ability to parse and serve dynamic PHP pages (the Unix analog of Microsoft's ASP technology). Over 50 third-party Apache modules are available in the ports collection in /usr/ports/www; they're the ones beginning with mod_.

Building Modules with apxs

Early in the development of the first third-party modules, when DSO support was experimental at best, compiling a third-party module meant having the Apache source available, tweaking the build configuration files in both the Apache source and the module's source, and cross-compiling them into a single, hybrid binary. Although this was technically a "modular" approach (which is to say that it was better than having to patch the code manually into the Apache source itself), it still wasn't what anyone would call easy to handle. It still involved building a new executable each time a new version of either Apache or the module became available, and it still involved a fair amount of code hackery to get it to work.

Enter apxs, the Apache Extension tool. This support program, residing in /usr/local/sbin, is built along with Apache to take advantage of the already compiled binary's DSO support (the statically compiled mod_so module) to provide a self-contained build framework that's fully aware of all the capabilities of your httpd binary. You no longer have to have the Apache source code around in order to build third-party modules; apxs compiles and converts modules in raw source form or already compiled objects into .so objects that can be loaded into Apache with the LoadModule directive, along with the rest.

You will most likely never need to use apxs directly; it's a compile-time tool used transparently by the build tools in the ports collection. All you have to do to build a third-party module, just as with any other port, is to go into the module's directory in /usr/ports/www and type **make**. apxs does the rest. If a new version of Apache is released, it can be built and installed on its own, and third-party modules will continue to work. Likewise, if a module is updated, you can simply rebuild and reinstall it. This is true modularity at its best.

More information on apxs, if you're interested, can be found in the man apxs page.

25

mod_perl

One of the most popular third-party modules is mod_perl. Although Perl is still the most popular choice for CGI programming (which we'll discuss shortly), executing Perl scripts means a fair amount of overhead for Apache. When an HTTP request is made for a Perl CGI program, Apache must start a shell process and run the script within it, feeding the results back to the client.

With mod_perl, a Perl interpreter is built directly into Apache. Specialized directives define certain file types as executable Perl scripts that Apache can execute itself; further, each Perl script that Apache executes is held in compiled form in memory for later use. This eliminates the startup overhead usually associated with CGI execution, making the response of server-side programs a great deal faster.

More information on mod_perl is available at http://perl.apache.org.

mod_python

In keeping with the rise of Python as the likeliest inheritor of Perl's crown as the server-side programming language of choice in the future, mod_python provides the same kind of benefit to Apache for Python that mod_perl does for Perl. The Python interpreter is made directly available to the Apache executable, allowing Apache to run Python programs without any of the execution overhead of doing it through CGI.

The mod_python home page is at www.modpython.org.

mod_php

PHP, the wildly popular dynamic page-generation tool for Unix, is made a part of Apache through the mod_php3 and mod_php4 modules. The directives enabled by this module family let Apache serve .php files completely natively, executing their embedded scripting functionality to generate the final form of a page before sending it to the client. When you build and install mod_php4, your httpd.conf file is automatically updated to provide support for the .php and .phps file types.

More information on PHP and mod_php4 can be found at www.php.net.

A great many more modules are available, providing Apache with enough expanded functionality to keep you busy for a long time. Apache's modularity has only fairly recently become completely entrenched, and the widespread availability of standardized third-party modules, coupled with the FreeBSD ports collection, makes for an unprecedented new era in extensible HTTP server administration.

Server-Side Includes

One popular feature of Apache is the ability to process *server-side includes*, or calls to internal Apache functions that are embedded into plain HTML files and processed by Apache before being sent to the browser. Server-side includes let you perform feats from simply echoing environment variables into a page to importing modular HTML fragments or executing server-side programs each time the page is requested.

Server-side includes are embedded into what's known as *parsed HTML*, which is effectively just regular HTML that Apache parses when the page is requested. Apache searches through parsed HTML for server-side includes and processes each one in turn before sending them on to the client. Each include is of the following form:

```
<!--#command attribute=value attribute=value ... -->
```

CAUTION

The syntax of a server-side include statement is critical; it must be of exactly the form shown here. The opening string `<!--#command` must not contain any spaces; otherwise, Apache will treat the directive as an HTML comment and ignore it.

You can use your browser's "View Source" function to see whether any malformed server-side include statements have been ignored by Apache and passed through verbatim to the browser.

In this generic example, `command` can be `include`, `exec`, `config`, `echo`, or a few other possibilities. The `attribute=value` pairs are ways of setting or reading variables, which you can set yourself using includes or read in from the available environment variables.

First, to turn on server-side includes in Apache, uncomment the following two lines in `httpd.conf` (or add them to the appropriate `.htaccess` file):

```
AddType text/html .shtml
AddHandler server-parsed .shtml
```

Note that these lines might be found in different sections of the `httpd.conf` file. Make sure they both appear in the same "container" (`<Directory>` or `<Location>`). This can be difficult to determine, because some containers have a lot of comment blocks and extra text that can make the structure confusing.

NOTE

In Apache 2.0, the `AddHandler` directive is separated into a number of more specifically tasked directives; the second line in this example becomes an `AddOutputFilter` directive:

```
AddOutputFilter INCLUDES .shtml
```

TIP

The `.shtml` extension is the widely accepted Unix standard for server-parsed HTML files; however, other variants exist, such as `.shtm` and `.stm`. To enable these as well as `.shtml`, make duplicates of the directive lines shown here and alter the duplicates accordingly:

```
AddType text/html .shtml
AddHandler server-parsed .shtml
AddType text/html .shtm
AddHandler server-parsed .shtm
```

Next, add the `Includes` option to the `<Directory>` or `<Location>` block (or `.htaccess` file) that controls the area of the Web site that concerns you:

```
Options +Includes
```

The `AddType` directive maps a class of files (by their filename extensions) to a MIME type, extending the basic set that is stored in `/usr/local/etc/apache/mime.types`. The `AddHandler` directive assigns a handler (an internal way for Apache to process a file that is requested by the user) to a certain extension—in this case, `.shtml` (the traditional extension for HTML files that you want Apache to parse before serving). With these two directives in place, any `.shtml` file will be parsed for server-side includes on its way to the client.

NOTE

Aside from containing server-side includes, the only difference between `.html` and `.shtml` files is the filename extension. They're both regular HTML files. If you put a server-side include into an `.html` file, simply rename it to have an `.shtml` extension if you want it to be parsed before being sent to the browser. A server-side include in an `.html` or `.htm` file will show up unparsed in the client's HTML source for the page.

CAUTION

Be aware that parsing any file causes more resource drain on the CPU and memory than simply passing the file unparsed to the browser. It's best to avoid unnecessarily parsing plain HTML files; otherwise, Apache will suffer a performance hit, which might be a critical consideration for you.

A few examples of useful server-side includes follow:

- `<!--#echo var="HTTP_USER_AGENT"-->`

  Prints the user's browser identifier string into the page. A fuller discussion of the available environment variables will appear later in this chapter when we cover CGI programming.

- `<!--#set var="e-mail" value="me@somewhere.com"-->`

  Sets the variable called `e-mail` to the string `me@somewhere.com` for the remainder of the page (unless overridden later with a similar directive).

- `<!--#include virtual="/toolbar.html"-->`

  Embeds the contents of `/toolbar.html` into the page. SSIs are parsed recursively, so a file included this way can have its own includes.

- `<!--#config timefmt="%A %B %d, %Y"-->`

  Sets the time format for any server-side includes that output a date and time. The format string is the same as for the `date` command; see `man date` for more details.

- `<!--#flastmod file="index.shtml"-->`

  Displays the date and time that `index.shtml` was last modified, in the time format specified in the `config timefmt` example.

- `<!--#exec cgi="/cgi-bin/counter"-->`

  Executes a CGI script called `counter` and displays its output.

If you put directives like these into an `.shtml` file and they don't seem to be working, view the page's source. The directives should not appear in their server-side include form in the HTML code. If you see any, it means they haven't been parsed out, which means the Apache configuration hasn't been set up properly to support server-side includes. Make sure that your `AddType` and `AddHandler` (or `AddOutputFilter`) directives are correctly specified and that they apply to the part of the site you're using.

> **TIP**
>
> The default page displayed in a directory when no filename is specified is `index.html`, but using the `DirectoryIndex` directive, you can change this or even specify a list of filenames to try:
>
> ```
> DirectoryIndex index.php index.php3 index.html index.shtml
> ```
>
> Apache looks for each of these files in turn in a bare directory request, and only if none are found (and `Options Indexes` is enabled) will it display a file listing for that directory.
>
> If you prefer, you can simply use the following instead:
>
> ```
> Options +MultiViews
> DirectoryIndex index INDEX
> ```
>
> `MultiViews` tells Apache to look for any file matching the requested base filename (without the extension), and `DirectoryIndex index` says that any file in the directory called `index.*` (with any extension) should be served, generally in alphabetical preference. This way, you can account for `index.htm`, `index.HTM`, and `INDEX.HTML` files, however your users happen to name their files.
>
> `MultiViews` can cause a performance hit, however, so you should consider your server's current CPU load before enabling `MultiViews` on a commonly accessed directory.

A full tutorial on server-side includes, showing everything from conditional flow-control to external CGI execution, can be found at `http://httpd.apache.org/docs/howto/ssi.html`.

Introduction to CGI

Conventional Web sites made up of static HTML pages are fine in their way. Server-side includes let you embed a lot of useful functionality into regular HTML pages. However, for true Web applications (such as e-commerce sites, message boards, databases, and anything where the system tailors its content to the actions of the user), you need a server-side programming environment to handle the user's input and control the requested output. The standard way to do this is CGI, the *Common Gateway Interface.*

CGI exists as a "mediator" protocol, a layer of the Web server that allows you to use HTML forms to take in users' data, which the server (through CGI) feeds in a common format to any program on the server, regardless of what language it's written in. A CGI program can be a Perl script, a compiled C binary, a shell script, or anything else that can be executed by the Apache user (nobody). The output of the program is routed back through Apache directly to the Web browser. This means that, for example, you can write a CGI program that reads in variables from an HTML form, processes them, opens a pipe to Sendmail to mail the contents of the variables to you, and prints out an HTML response to the user. You'll see how to do this in a simple Perl script in just a moment.

Enabling CGI in Apache

There are two ways to use CGI programs in Apache. The first, cleanest way is with the ScriptAlias directive, which defines a certain directory as containing only CGI programs and maps it to a virtual path (as seen by the Web browser):

```
ScriptAlias /cgi-bin/ "/usr/local/www/cgi-bin/"
```

This line, which is enabled in httpd.conf by default, tells Apache that the /cgi-bin/ URL (http://stripes.somewhere.com/cgi-bin/) is a designated CGI directory and that everything in it should be treated as a CGI program. If you put anything in this directory that isn't a CGI program, it will return a 500 Server Error code, a failure to execute it as a CGI. You can add as many additional ScriptAlias lines as you like. The filesystem path to the CGI directory (for example, /usr/local/www/cgi-bin/) need not even be in the normally Web-accessible path; you can point the alias to anywhere in the system that's readable by the nobody user. This prevents people from being able to look at the contents of the directory or navigate to it from other directory listings. You generally don't want people to be able to access your CGI programs directly, anyway—they're typically called from links or as form actions, which we will discuss shortly.

> **NOTE**
>
> Note that the trailing slash on /cgi-bin/ is specified. This is another security measure, designed to prevent unauthorized access to the directory listing. A CGI program as Apache sees it through ScriptAlias is the name of the program (for example, script.cgi) that is appended to the ScriptAlias virtual path (for example, /cgi-bin/), so the slash is required in order for the server to construct the proper path (for example, /cgi-bin/script.cgi). If the trailing slash were

omitted, the bare directory itself would also be aliased, meaning that a client could issue a request for the /cgi-bin directory and get a listing; you probably don't want that. 301 redirects don't apply here.

NOTE

Because all files in a directory specified by ScriptAlias are treated as CGI scripts, you don't need to have filename extensions on each of these programs. You can have a program called /cgi-bin/test as well as one called /cgi-bin/hello.cgi; but outside the /cgi-bin/ directory, CGI scripts must have the .cgi extension or whatever extension you have configured using AddHandler, as you will see next.

The other way to enable CGI programs is to use the Options directive to add the ExecCGI option to an area of the server specified by a <Directory> or <Location> block. This is useful for enabling CGI programs in your users' public_html directories, allowing the server to execute programs as CGI based on their filename extensions (for example, .cgi) and whether they're set executable. The following example will turn on CGI execution of all users' executable .cgi files, no matter where they are:

```
<Directory /home/*/public_html>
  Options +ExecCGI
  AddHandler cgi-script .cgi
</Directory>
```

If a CGI file (whether in a ScriptAlias directory or mapped to a handler by extension) can't be executed for any reason, the user will get a 500 Server Error message; this is a generic error condition, one that can be generated by numerous different server-side causes and can't really be used for debugging, other than to know that something *is* wrong. You can look at Apache's error log to get a more detailed diagnostic message. Here's an example of an error log from an unsuccessful request for a Perl script called blah in /usr/local/www/cgi-bin:

```
# tail /var/log/httpd-error.log
syntax error at /usr/local/www/cgi-bin/blah line 3, at EOF
Execution of /usr/local/www/cgi-bin/blah aborted due to compilation errors.
[Tue May 22 22:06:26 2001] [error] [client 64.2.43.44] Premature end of
➥script headers: /usr/local/www/cgi-bin/blah
```

The first two lines of output are directly from Perl, exactly the same as if the script had been run on the command line. The third line is Apache telling us that it tried to execute the script, but it quit before printing out any HTTP headers, such as Content-type: (which is required for a valid CGI script). Our task, then, is to make sure the program is written correctly for CGI execution.

Writing CGI Programs

The format in which CGI variables are passed to a server-side program is as a URL-encoded text string, with each variable separated from its value by an equals sign (=) and from other variables by ampersands (&). The script sees it as being fed in via standard input (STDIN).

Perl is the most common language for CGI programming and therefore the two terms are (incorrectly) often used synonymously. Don't confuse the two: Perl is useful for a great many things besides Web programming, and CGI encompasses all conceivable languages, even ones that don't exist yet. Still, the prevalence of Perl in the CGI programming world makes it the object of our attention right now.

Perl's strengths, as you saw in Chapter 20, "Introduction to Perl Programming," are in text processing and ease of development; this makes it an ideal candidate for situations when you need to read in variables from an HTML form (such as a user's name, e-mail address, mailing address, and comments) and process them into a form you or the system can use. A typical Perl CGI program is invoked as the action of the HTML form:

```
<FORM NAME="myform" METHOD="POST" ACTION="/cgi-bin/post2me">
```

When the user submits this form, all its variables are submitted through the CGI interface to post2me, the Perl program whose job it is to handle them. The first thing this script must do is read in the variables from standard input and format them into an associative array for easy access:

```
read(STDIN, $buffer, $ENV{'CONTENT_LENGTH'});
@pairs = split(/&/, $buffer);
foreach $pair (@pairs)
{
    ($name, $value) = split(/=/, $pair);
    $value =~ tr/+/ /;
    $value =~ s/%([a-fA-F0-9][a-fA-F0-9])/pack("C", hex($1))/eg;
    $value =~ s/~!/ ~!/g;
    $FORM{$name} = $value;
}
```

This code does some security parsing to prevent malicious form input from being sent to the program. Specifically, if you write a CGI program that prints a user's form input out into an HTML file, a user can embed some malicious HTML code into his input that calls a server-side include that runs some program on the server. Because any program executed through HTTP requests is run by the unprivileged nobody user, this usually amounts only to an annoyance. Still, it's a security hole that must be addressed, and this code block disables any potentially malicious HTML tags by inserting spaces and dashes where appropriate.

After your script has read in the form input, each form variable is available as a key in the %FORM array; the contents of the HTML input field called e-mail, for instance, are in $FORM{'e-mail'} and can be used however you like.

Next, your script must print out a valid HTML header. You have two choices here: You can print HTML code to standard output, effectively writing a new HTML page from within the script, or you can redirect the user to a different URL while the script does its work. The former is done with a Content-type: header, which can be any valid MIME type (it's up to the browser to know how to handle it), followed by a double newline, the standard signal for the end of the header block:

```
print "Content-type: text/html\n\n";
```

Anything printed out by your script after this header is part of the response body, rendered as HTML by the browser. You can use a type of text/plain to force the browser to display it as plain text, or any other type, according to your needs.

The latter method, a redirect, is done with a Location: header and a redirection URL:

```
print "Location: http://www.somewhereelse.com/path/to/file.html\n\n";
```

Anything printed after this header vanishes because the browser will have already moved on to this new URL.

Environment variables are also available to CGI programs, and an HTTP connection comes with a great many pieces of interesting information. Some of these include HTTP_REFERER (the referring URL), HTTP_USER_AGENT (the browser the user has), REMOTE_HOST (the user's hostname), and many more. You can see them all by accessing the printenv script, which is included as part of the default Apache installation in the /usr/local/www/cgi-bin directory. You can access it at the URL http://www.somewhere.com/cgi-bin/printenv, substituting your FreeBSD machine's hostname or IP address, as appropriate. Within Perl, your environment variables are accessible as keys in the %ENV array, so you can access the REMOTE_HOST variable as $ENV{'REMOTE_HOST'}.

Let's look at a simple Perl CGI program, which reads in three variables—name, e-mail, and comments—from an HTML form, mails them to you, and prints a formatted thank-you note to the user. This script, which is shown in Listing 25.1, is available on the included CD-ROM as sendcomments.cgi.

LISTING 25.1   A Sample Perl CGI Program

```
#!/usr/bin/perl

read(STDIN, $buffer, $ENV{'CONTENT_LENGTH'});
@pairs = split(/&/, $buffer);
foreach $pair (@pairs)
{
```

25

LISTING 25.1   Continued

```
    ($name, $value) = split(/=/, $pair);
    $value =~ tr/+/ /;
    $value =~ s/%([a-fA-F0-9][a-fA-F0-9])/pack("C", hex($1))/eg;
    $value =~ s/~!/ ~!/g;
    $FORM{$name} = $value;
}

print "Content-type: text/html\n\n";

open (MAIL,"| /usr/sbin/sendmail -oi -t");
print MAIL "From: $FORM{'name'} <$FORM{'e-mail'}>\n";
print MAIL "To: you\@your.hostname.com\n";
print MAIL "Subject: Form output\n\n";
print MAIL "$FORM{'name'}, from $ENV{'REMOTE_HOST'} ($ENV{'REMOTE_ADDR'}),
➥has sent you the following comment:\n\n";
print MAIL "$FORM{'comment'}\n";
close (MAIL);

print qq^<HTML>\n<HEAD>\n<TITLE>Thank you!</TITLE></HEAD>\n^;
print qq^<BODY><H3>Thank you!</H3>\nThanks for your comments!</H3>\n
➥</BODY>\n</HTML>^;
```

You'll want to tune this script to your own needs—replace the dummy To: header with one that mails to your real e-mail address, making sure to keep the backslash in front of the @ symbol. This sample script doesn't do very much in and of itself, but after some experimentation you'll find that the basic principles we've covered here form the heart of server-side programs, from the smallest feedback forms to the largest online databases and e-commerce systems.

A CGI program does not have to be called from an HTML form or with the POST method. You can use a direct URL to call a CGI script that doesn't need to have any variables posted directly into an associative array such as %FORM. Such a URL would look like this:

http://www.somewhere.com/cgi-bin/sysinfo?frank+3

This URL calls the sysinfo program in the /cgi-bin/ directory. Everything after the question mark is known as the *query string,* and its contents are available to the script as elements of the @ARGV array. Arguments are separated by plus signs (+). The sysinfo program would have the string frank available as $ARGV[0] and the number 3 as $ARGV[1].

TIP

You can also access the entire query string as the environment variable QUERY_STRING, or $ENV{'QUERY_STRING'} in Perl.

CHAPTER **26**

Configuring an FTP Server

Once the foremost method of transferring files from one point in the Internet to another, the File Transfer Protocol (FTP) is now becoming eclipsed by the more glamorous and versatile HTTP. However, although FTP is a very rudimentary protocol, it is designed more specifically for large file transfers than HTTP is and therefore is able to do a number of things that HTTP cannot—including operating with more speed and efficiency. FTP's prevalence is fading, but it will always have a place in the Internet, as long as such services as authenticated downloads and two-way transfers are needed.

FreeBSD comes with an FTP server built in, and you can replace it with a different server if you desire. The built-in FTP server is quite complete and secure; it allows you to transfer files to and from your FreeBSD machine without any additional setup. This chapter discusses some of the details of the File Transfer Protocol and how it works. The default configuration of the FTP server is quite basic, but the information you learn in this chapter will help you take advantage of the more advanced features available to you.

Introduction to the File Transfer Protocol

To the uninitiated, FTP and HTTP seem to be quite similar. Both allow file transfers, both support a form of user authentication, and the two protocols often appear to be used interchangeably on the Web—a binary package or large multimedia file might be linked from a Web site via either the `http://` or the `ftp://` protocols, which seem to do the same thing with regard to downloading the file to your computer.

However, a little further investigation shows us that the two protocols are designed for considerably different purposes and therefore support widely different feature sets. Table 26.1 shows a contrast of these crucial areas of difference.

TABLE 26.1 Comparison of FTP and HTTP Functionalities

Feature	FTP	HTTP
Session based	Yes	No
User authentication built in	Yes	No
Primarily intended for transferring	Large binary files	Small text files
Connection model	Dual connection	Single connection
Primarily geared toward download/upload	Both	Download
Supports ASCII and binary transfer modes	Yes	No
Supports content typing (MIME headers)	No	Yes
Supports file system operations (mkdir, rm, rename, and so on)	Yes	No

The biggest difference between FTP and HTTP is that FTP is *session based*, meaning that a complete connection is initiated between the client and server, multiple commands are sent back and forth, and finally the client terminates the connection by choice. (HTTP, as you will recall, is a stateless protocol—a single request, followed by a single or pipelined response, comprises the whole HTTP "session.") FTP goes even beyond a single connection, as a matter of fact. A complete FTP session contains two connections: one for passing commands and status messages back and forth (control connection), and another to handle the actual file transfers (data connection). Figure 26.1 shows a diagram of a complete FTP connection.

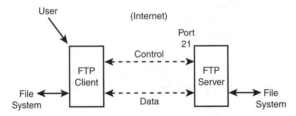

FIGURE 26.1 An FTP session, with both the control and data connections established.

An FTP client, such as the ftp command built in to FreeBSD, opens the control connection to TCP port 21 on the FTP server. This connection remains open throughout the session. When the user enters a command, such as ls or get picture1.gif, the client and server negotiate a pair of TCP ports between which they will open the data connection, which exists for as long as the response listing or file is being transferred, after which it is closed. A separate data connection is opened for each such a transfer. A complete, typical FTP session is shown in Listing 26.1.

LISTING 26.1   A Command-Line FTP Session

```
# ftp spots.somewhere.com
Connected to spots.somewhere.com.
220 spots.somewhere.com FTP server (Version 6.00LS) ready.
Name (spots.somewhere.com:frank):
331 Password required for frank.
Password:
230 User frank logged in.
Remote system type is UNIX.
Using binary mode to transfer files.
ftp> cd mydir
250 CWD command successful.
ftp> ls
150 Opening ASCII mode data connection for '/bin/ls'.
total 484
-rw-r--r--  1 frank  frank   43175 Apr  8 01:14 addresses.txt
-rw-r--r--  1 frank  frank  100523 Apr  8 01:14 contents.html
-rw-r--r--  1 frank  frank   37864 Apr  8 01:14 directions
-rw-r--r--  1 frank  frank   37308 Apr  8 01:14 lk_logo.gif
-rw-r--r--  1 frank  frank   52427 Apr  8 01:12 picture1.gif
-rw-r--r--  1 frank  frank   18648 Apr 24 13:04 picture2.jpg
-rw-r--r--  1 frank  frank  175325 Apr  8 01:14 resume.html
226 Transfer complete.
ftp> get picture1.gif
local: picture1.gif remote: picture1.gif
150 Opening BINARY mode data connection for 'picture1.gif' (52427 bytes).
100% |***************************************************| 52427       00:00 ETA
226 Transfer complete.
52427 bytes received in 4.99 seconds (10.25 KB/s)
ftp> quit
221 Goodbye.
```

26

The first part of the connection is the username and password authentication stage, just as you would get in a Telnet connection. Similar to Telnet, FTP user authentication operates directly on a user's account information on the machine running the FTP server. This authentication process differs from HTTP user authentication, which is actually a function of Apache and not of HTTP itself and requires Apache's own user databases to be separately maintained.

In order to log in via FTP, the user must either have a valid user account on the server machine or must log in via "anonymous FTP," if the server allows it (a common practice that we will cover later in this chapter).

A number of user commands are available in FTP, behaving in much the same way as their familiar shell counterparts: `ls`, `cd`, `mkdir`, `pwd`, and so on. These commands help you navigate through the directory structure and modify remote files as if they were on the local (client) machine. There is also an `lcd` command that allows you to change directories on the client machine, in case you want to download a file to a different location from the one where you started the FTP program. Additionally, there are the `put` (upload), `get` (download), `mput` (multiple upload), and `mget` (multiple download) commands, which control the file transfers themselves. These user commands are translated into client commands (such as `RETR`, `STOR`, `CWD`, and `LIST`) that the FTP server understands. The server responds with three-digit response codes, much as in HTTP. The meanings of the response codes aren't especially important to know, so we won't cover them here. See `man ftpd` if you're interested in seeing the complete list of FTP client commands (this manual for the server outlines the client-commands the server recognizes).

> **NOTE**
>
> FTP file transfers can be done in one of two modes: ASCII or Binary. ASCII mode is used for transfers of plain text, in which all data is transferred as alphanumeric characters and end-of-line symbols are translated to or from whatever the client's platform uses, such as CR/LF for DOS/Windows, CR for Macintosh, and LF for Unix. Binary mode is useful for transferring a stream of untranslated data. Some FTP clients, such as the one built in to FreeBSD, automatically detect which type is appropriate and then switch to that mode when the transfer begins. Other clients require that you select either ASCII or Binary mode before transferring files. Use the `bin` and `asc` commands to switch modes.
>
> It's very important, especially when transferring files from one platform to another, to use ASCII mode to transfer plain-text files such as HTML pages and Perl scripts. This ensures that end-of-line characters are translated properly. Binary mode can cause Perl scripts to fail to run if uploaded from a non-Unix client. Binary mode, however, is necessary for images, executables, and any other kind of binary data; binary files transferred in ASCII mode will be corrupted on the destination machine.

The default FTP server that ships with FreeBSD, which you learn about in this chapter, is the standard BSD `ftpd` daemon. It runs from within the `inetd` super-server, like `telnetd` and Qpopper, rather than as a standalone daemon. It lacks a few features supported by some of its alternatives (such as WU-FTPD and ProFTPD), but it also lacks a number of security holes that are inevitable with more complex software. You learn more about these alternative daemons at the end of this chapter; meanwhile, the following sections discuss how to make the most of the FreeBSD FTP server.

Overview of the FTP Directory Structure

Unless you've enabled anonymous FTP logins, the file layout of the FTP server is very simple. The FTP server file layout is integrated with the system in the same way that most other core services are. There are several configuration files in /etc, some of which do double-duty as systemwide resource files used by other services. Individual users' home directories are considered part of the FTP server layout, because each authenticated user connects directly into his or her home directory.

If you've enabled anonymous FTP, there's a server root area just as in Apache; this is created at the time when you elect to enable anonymous FTP, as you'll see in the later section of this chapter, "Allowing Anonymous FTP Access." The default location for the FTP server root is /var/ftp, and several subdirectories exist to help the server manage FTP users who don't actually have user accounts on the system.

Authenticated and Anonymous FTP

When a user who has an account on the server logs in via FTP with his or her username and password, the server provides access to the user's home directory and all its files. The user can enter an ls command to verify that this is the area to which he has access, by examining the files present there. Each regular user thus connects into a different point on the FTP server when logging in as a user—his or her home directory.

Anonymous FTP provides a way for a user without an account to connect. An anonymous user opens the connection, enters **anonymous** or **ftp** as his or her username, and any text string (conventionally the user's e-mail address, although this isn't enforced or authenticated in any way) for the password. The user is then given access to a "public" FTP area: /var/ftp, the home directory of the ftp user (which is also created when anonymous FTP is enabled).

There's a fundamental difference between regular account users and anonymous FTP users, though. Anonymous FTP is in a chroot "jail" by default, meaning that to the user, /var/ftp appears to be the server root (/). Nothing outside /var/ftp is accessible or even visible. A regular account user can enter a command such as cd /usr/local to move to any part of the system and access files with the same readability permissions as in a terminal session, but an anonymous FTP user can't get out of /var/ftp at all. An anonymous user who enters cd /pub will be taken to /var/ftp/pub.

You can specify additional users who must be "chrooted" in the same way as anonymous FTP logins by adding them to the /etc/ftpchroot file. That's just one example of the configuration files that control the FTP server.

> **CAUTION**
>
> Authenticated users have FTP access to your FreeBSD machine by default, but you have to specifically enable anonymous FTP—if you want it. Allowing anonymous FTP effectively opens up your system to a form of unauthorized, untraceable access. You should only enable anonymous FTP if you have a good reason!

26

Configuring the FTP Server

The FTP service involves a fairly large number of configuration files; some of them exist in /etc, and some are in /var/ftp/etc. The reason for this is that some of the files have to be accessible by anonymous FTP users, and, as you've seen, such users can't see any files outside of /var/ftp. Here are a few of the files in /etc that apply globally to the FTP server as a whole (not all of them exist in the default installation—some must be created manually):

- /etc/ftpusers—A "blacklist" of users who are disallowed FTP access. Add usernames to this file to prevent them from logging in via FTP.

- /etc/ftpchroot—Any users listed in this file will be placed in a chroot "jail," similar to that of anonymous FTP, limiting the user's access solely to his or her home directory.

- /etc/ftphosts—Allows you to configure virtual hosts, much like with Apache (as you saw in Chapter 25, "Configuring a Web Server"). You'll learn more about virtual hosting later in this chapter.

- /etc/ftpwelcome—A welcome notice. The contents of this file are displayed to everyone who connects, immediately after the connection is opened, before the login prompt.

- /etc/ftpmotd—A second welcome notice (message of the day); this one appears after a regular account user has logged in.

- /etc/shells—You encountered this file in Chapter 11, "Customizing the Shell." Its purpose is to ensure that anybody logging in to the system has a valid shell, thus preventing people from logging in to accounts such as bin, tty, and nobody, which don't have shells listed in this file.

Beyond the config files in /etc, a number of additional files control anonymous FTP. These aren't just config files, either. If /var/ftp is mapped to / for anonymous users, that means the tools in the system binary directories (such as /bin) are as inaccessible as the files in /etc. The FTP server relies on a few system tools—notably /bin/ls and /bin/date—to generate file listings to send to the client. These tools have to be available to anonymous users, too; that's what the /var/ftp/bin directory is for.

The /var/ftp tree contains the following files and directories. Any anonymous user can see these files, but none of them are inherently "dangerous" for users to see (the /var/ftp/etc files don't contain any passwords, for example):

- /var/ftp/bin—This directory contains ls and date executables. These are provided because they're necessary for the FTP server to be able to generate directory listings, and the system /bin/ls and /bin/date programs are not available if you've configured the server to chroot or have limited the anonymous FTP user's access to within /var/ftp. (This is the default behavior.)

- `/var/ftp/etc/passwd` and `/var/ftp/etc/group`—As with the tools in `/var/ftp/bin`, these are copies of the default `/etc/passwd` and `/etc/group` files, whose purpose is to provide file ownership mappings during directory listings. Because anonymous FTP access is limited to what's in `/var/ftp`, these files must exist in order to show who owns the various files in `/var/ftp`. Typically, any files in the public FTP area will be owned by root or another system account because they will be put there by you, as the administrator. Other usernames, because they don't exist in `/var/ftp/etc/passwd`, will not be mapped and will appear to FTP users as raw UIDs for files owned by them.

- `/var/ftp/etc/ftpmotd`—Operates the same way as `/etc/ftpmotd`, except that this one is displayed to anonymous FTP users instead of regular login users. From their perspective (with the `chroot` making `/var/ftp` appear to be `/` to them), this *is* `/etc/ftpmotd`.

- `/var/ftp/pub`—Visible to anonymous FTP users as `/pub`, this is where all download-able files should go. The hierarchy under `/pub` is up to you to determine, but convention says at least that `/pub` should contain everything that's meant to be of interest to the public.

- `/var/ftp/incoming`—This optional directory has world-writable permissions with the "sticky bit" set (1777). This means that any anonymous user can upload files into this directory. This can be dangerous; having an open upload directory is an invitation for people to use it as a trading point for MP3 files and pirated software. Use this option only if you really need to!

One final configuration file that concerns the FTP server is `/etc/inetd.conf`. As mentioned earlier, `ftpd` runs as a subsidiary to the `inetd` super-server, and as such it won't work if `inetd` isn't running. First, use `ps` to check to see whether the daemon is serving requests, using the `-w` (wide format), `-a` (all users' processes), `-u` (user-oriented fields shown), and `-x` (processes that aren't necessarily attached to terminals) options:

```
# ps -waux | grep inetd
root    1640  0.0  0.6  1048  780  ??  Ss   Thu08PM  0:00.15 inetd -Ww
```

If you don't see the `inetd` process running, you may have turned it off in `/etc/rc.conf`; check there for the `inetd_enable="NO"` line and remove or disable it if it's present. Second, open up `/etc/inetd.conf` and make sure the `ftpd` service is enabled:

```
ftp    stream  tcp    nowait  root    /usr/libexec/ftpd       ftpd -l
```

If this line is commented out, uncomment it, and restart `inetd` (using the `killall -HUP inetd` command). Check your configuration by trying to connect to the server (`ftp localhost`). If you are presented with a login prompt, you're in business. If not, look over the preceding steps again; kill `inetd` completely and restart it if necessary.

26

Controlling FTP Access

FTP access is not something you should enable lightly; although it's crucial for your users to have access to FTP for uploading files (such as Web pages) to your server, it's also a potential source of security issues—it's a clear-text mechanism, meaning that all data (including passwords) is transmitted unencrypted and available to anybody eavesdropping with packet-sniffing software. As you'll learn in Chapter 29, "Network Security," most major clear-text services can be superseded by a secure equivalent: Telnet with SSH, HTTP with Secure HTTP, and POP3 and IMAP with their own built-in encryption layers. FTP, however, is inherently insecure, and although several secure solutions have been put forth (such as Brian Wellington's sftp and corresponding sftpd), unencrypted FTP holds out as the last widely used insecure data-transfer protocol, difficult to replace and a virtual requirement for a fully functional server. You learn more about how to secure FTP in Chapter 29; meanwhile, be aware that special care must be taken when enabling FTP access to your users to ensure your system's security.

With this in mind, you need a way to lock out certain users from being able to connect to the system via FTP. This can be done in a number of ways. The two most convenient involve the /etc/ftpusers and /etc/shells files. A third, /var/run/nologin, controls whether the server accepts connections at all.

The /etc/ftpusers File

The simplest way to forbid a certain individual user (or a group of users) from connecting to the FTP server is to add that user's login name to the /etc/ftpusers file, which exists in the default FreeBSD installation and contains the names of the various system pseudo-users (such as operator, bin, tty, and so on). These users have null passwords, and ftpd will not allow anyone with a null password to connect; keeping the usernames in /etc/ftpusers provides an extra layer of security.

You can add any username to the file, and because ftpd reads all relevant configuration files with each new connection, there's no need to restart any processes. Try connecting to the FTP server as a disallowed user, and you should get a response similar to the following:

```
# ftp localhost
Connected to localhost.somewhere.com.
220 stripes.somewhere.com FTP server (Version 6.00LS) ready.
Name (localhost:frank):
530 User frank access denied.
ftp: Login failed.
ftp>
```

> **NOTE**
>
> Note that the `access denied` message appears immediately after the server receives the user-name—it doesn't prompt for a password. This prevents passwords from being sent over the wire, providing an extra security precaution in the case where you've disabled a user out of concern regarding an eavesdropper sniffing for passwords.

You can also add any group name to /etc/ftpusers; simply precede the name with an "at" (@) symbol (for example, @users). Any user who is part of any group listed in the file will be disallowed access.

The /etc/shells File

After seeing whether the user is listed in /etc/ftpusers, ftpd checks the shell associated with the user and sees whether it's listed in /etc/shells. If it isn't, the user will get the same kind of access denied message as with /etc/ftpusers. You can leverage this functionality to prevent a user from logging in with a terminal program or with FTP, by changing the user's shell to /sbin/nologin (which you saw in Chapter 11—it simply prints out an account not available message and exits, and it's not listed in /etc/shells) or something similarly constructed.

The /var/run/nologin File

To turn off FTP logins completely, without modifying /etc/inetd.conf or any other such config files, you can simply place a file called nologin in /var/run. If ftpd sees this file, it will respond to all connections as follows:

```
# ftp localhost
Connected to localhost.somewhere.com.
530 System not available.
ftp>
```

You can use touch /var/run/nologin to create the file (with zero length) and disable FTP logins. Remove the file (rm /var/run/nologin) to re-enable the FTP server.

Allowing Anonymous FTP Access

By default, anonymous FTP is not enabled; the easiest way to enable it, if you choose to do so, is through sysinstall. Run /stand/sysinstall; then enter the Configure and Networking sections. Scroll to the Anon FTP option and press the spacebar to enter the Anonymous FTP Configuration screen, shown in Figure 26.2.

The default options are generally appropriate for a typical FreeBSD system. The UID, Group, and Comment fields control how the new ftp user will be created. This user's home directory is set to /var/ftp, which is how anonymous FTP works—the ftp login is treated as a regular user that behaves as if it's listed in /etc/ftpchroot, so anybody logging in as ftp (or its alias, anonymous) will be put into a chroot jail at /var/ftp.

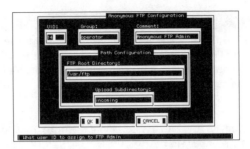

FIGURE 26.2   Anonymous FTP configuration options.

You can change any of the fields to suit your system (for instance, if you already have a user with a UID of 14, or if you want a name for the upload directory that's different from incoming). When you select OK at the bottom of the screen, the ftp user will be created, as will the /var/ftp tree with its necessary subdirectories.

Note that /stand/sysinstall doesn't provide the capability to disable anonymous FTP after it has been enabled, but you can do this a number of ways. The following methods are ranked in descending order of preferability:

- Add the ftp user to /etc/ftpusers (probably the easiest and cleanest method).
- Change the permissions on the /var/ftp tree so that its contents can't be read by regular users—0700 will work.
- Remove the /var/ftp tree.
- Remove the ftp user.

Similarly, you can disable the upload (incoming) directory by simply removing it, or else by changing its permissions to 755 (the default directory permissions, in which only the owner—root—can write into it). Re-enable it (or any other directory to which you want anonymous users to be able to upload files) by changing its permissions to 1777—for instance, chmod 1777 /var/ftp/incoming.

Virtual Hosting

If you have multiple IP addresses bound to your machine, you can map different FTP server behaviors to each one. This virtual hosting mechanism is controlled with the /etc/ftphosts file, which does not exist in the default FreeBSD system (you need to create it).

Each virtual host is defined on its own line, with fields specifying alternate config files for each host separated by whitespace. Table 26.2 describes the various fields, their meanings, and the default values (the ones that the server uses without an /etc/ftphosts file present).

TABLE 26.2   Virtual Hosting Table Fields in `/etc/ftphosts`

Field	Description	Default
Hostname	The hostname or IP address of the virtual host. Note that FTP has no equivalent of the `Host:` header of HTTP/1.1, so FTP virtual hosts are defined purely on the IP address of your machine where the client is connected. If you use a hostname in this field, `ftpd` uses the IP address to which it resolves. Bear this in mind when adding virtual hosts.	N/A
User	The user whose home directory is used for anonymous FTP access in this virtual host. Anonymous users are jailed (via `chroot`) into this directory, so equivalents of `/var/ftp/etc` and `/var/ftp/bin` should be present.	`ftp`
Statfile	The log file that tracks all FTP transfers for the virtual host.	`/var/log/ftpd`
Welcome	The welcome message displayed upon initial connection to the FTP server.	`/etc/ftpwelcome`
MOTD	The second welcome message, presented after a successful user login.	`/etc/ftpmotd`

A few sample virtual hosts in `/etc/ftphosts` follow. If a field is left blank or has a hyphen (-), the default value is used:

```
64.41.131.106   frank   /var/log/ftpd-frank   /home/frank/hi   /home/frank/hi2
ftp2.me.com     ftp2    -                     /etc/ftpd2welcome    -
64.41.131.107   ftp3    /var/log/ftpd-3       -                    -
```

Using Alternate FTP Servers

Many alternate FTP server packages exist; the two most popular are Washington University's WU-FTPD and the highly configurable ProFTPD. Both of these packages provide features that are not available in the default FTP server, including extremely flexible configurability and extra security measures.

WU-FTPD

Originally developed at Washington University to host the WUarchive (once one of the most popular file-sharing and distribution locations on the Internet), WU-FTPD has gained in popularity to become the most frequently used FTP server in the world. It's the default FTP daemon in Linux and many commercial Unix brands. WU-FTPD's configuration differs from FreeBSD's default `ftpd` in a few subtle ways, and it has a few features that the default `ftpd` does not, such as a configuration-checking tool, on-the-fly compression and archiving, and limitations on access and transfers by time and date. You might choose to install WU-FTPD to maintain compatibility with an existing non-FreeBSD system.

WU-FTPD is available as a package or in the ports (/usr/ports/ftp/wu-ftpd). After installing it, you can switch to it from the FreeBSD ftpd by commenting out the ftp line in /etc/inetd.conf and replacing it with one that points to the new ftpd:

```
ftp      stream  tcp     nowait  root    /usr/local/libexec/ftpd ftpd -l
#ftp     stream  tcp     nowait  root    /usr/libexec/ftpd       ftpd -l
```

> **TIP**
>
> WU-FTPD is installed as /usr/local/libexec/ftpd, and its man page can't be accessed directly with man ftpd—you'll get the page for the default system ftpd. To see the correct page, use the -M option to use an alternate man path, like so:
>
> man -M /usr/local/man ftpd

More information on WU-FTPD is available at http://www.wu-ftpd.org.

ProFTPD

ProFTPD was developed with the intention of creating an FTP server that could be managed with configuration files that resembled those of Apache. The server's config file has hierarchical configuration blocks like those in httpd.conf (as you saw in Chapter 25) and directives that are similar in style to those of Apache. The result is a server that has very Apache-like, access-limiting features as well as a high level of configurability, especially for administrators familiar at all with Apache. It's available as a package or from the ports (/usr/ports/ftp/proftpd).

One difference between ProFTPD and its relatives is that it can be run in standalone mode, like Apache, rather than from inetd. If you do run it from inetd, replace the default ftp line with one pointing to /usr/local/libexec/proftpd:

```
ftp      stream  tcp     nowait  root    /usr/local/libexec/proftpd      proftpd
#ftp     stream  tcp     nowait  root    /usr/libexec/ftpd       ftpd -l
```

The ProFTPD home page, www.proftpd.org, has much more information on ProFTPD's capabilities and configuration directives.

Configuring an Internet Gateway

Routing and gateways were covered briefly in Chapter 21, "Networking with FreeBSD," as was the concept of NAT (Network Address Translation). Chapter 22, "Configuring Basic Networking Services," also covered routing a little bit, but mostly in the context of configuring a host to use a router. This chapter explains how to configure FreeBSD to serve as a router or a gateway as well as how to set up Network Address Translation. The chapter begins with a few short definitions of each of the items we will be discussing.

The Basics of Routers and Network Address Translation (NAT) in FreeBSD

Like its name suggests, a *router* is a network device that determines how datagrams sent over the network get to their final destination. This is a very simple definition. A more accurate definition is that a router connects two networks together and determines how datagrams get from one network to another.

> **NOTE**
>
> A *datagram* is a packet of digital information. It contains addressing information as well as the data to be transmitted. Not all datagrams necessarily take the same route to get to their destinations, even if they all have the same origin.

To better understand what a router does, look at the following two figures. Figure 27.1 shows two sample networks for a fictional global company that has offices in New York and Denmark.

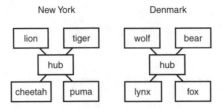

FIGURE 27.1   A sample global network for a fictional company, with several hosts in its New York office and several hosts in its Denmark office.

In the network in Figure 27.1, the hosts named `lion`, `cheetah`, `tiger`, and `puma` all know about the existence of each other and can communicate with each other at the New York office. Also, the hosts named `wolf`, `bear`, `fox`, and `lynx` all know about each other and can communicate with each other at the Denmark office. The problem here is that the networks are isolated. None of the hosts in the New York office know anything at all about any of the hosts in the Denmark office, and vice versa. There is no way for network information to travel between the two offices. In order for data to be able to flow between these two offices, we need to install a couple of routers. Figure 27.2 shows the same network, but this time we have installed a router at each office.

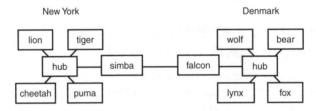

FIGURE 27.2   The same network as shown in Figure 27.1, except that a router is installed on each end of the network.

After the router is installed, one change needs to be made to the hosts on the network: They simply need to be told about the existence of the router in the office. (See Chapter 22 for information on how to tell the hosts about the existence of the router.)

The hosts in the New York office still know nothing at all about the hosts in the Denmark office, and the reverse is also true. So what has changed about this setup? Well, the hosts in the network now know about the existence of the router in their office. If each host is configured to use this router as the default router, it will send to the router any outgoing traffic for an unknown host. The router then worries about routing the network traffic to the correct destination.

For example, suppose that the user of `cheetah` wants to establish a network connection with `lynx`. As mentioned before, `cheetah` knows nothing about the existence of `lynx`. So, when `cheetah` generates traffic to `lynx`, it will simply pass that traffic off to `simba`, which is the router in the New York office. The router `simba` does know about the existence of `lynx`, and it also knows that it can get network traffic to `lynx` by passing it to the router in Denmark (`falcon`). The router in Denmark then sends the traffic to `lynx`.

This is a very simple example. In a real scenario (especially when sending transoceanic network traffic), several routers will usually be involved, each passing the traffic to another until it gets to the proper destination. If you want an analogy, you can think of routers as being like air traffic controllers, and network traffic as being like aircraft. An aircraft en route from New York to Denmark will be handed off between several different air traffic controllers until it finally reaches its destination.

Okay. So why do we need a router? Why not just tell the hosts in New York about the hosts in Denmark, and vice versa, so that they can communicate with each other directly? There are two primary reasons why it is not done this way:

- **Ease of maintenance**—This might not seem like a big deal with only eight systems. But now think of a network the size of the Internet. Without routers, every single system connected to the network would have to know how to contact every other system on the network. Obviously, when you are dealing with millions of systems, this would quickly become a maintenance nightmare.

- **Reduced traffic congestion**—If the two offices were just connected by one big network, then all network traffic would have to be sent to all computers. If, for example, `lion` sends network traffic to `cheetah` (both in the New York Office), this traffic would also get sent through the pipe, across the Atlantic Ocean, and into the Denmark office. This would occur even though the hosts in Denmark couldn't care less about this traffic because it is not for them. Imagine the network congestion if any time any host on the Internet sent network traffic to another host, that traffic had to also go to every single other host on the Internet. And besides that, transoceanic leased lines are expensive—you are usually charged by the amount of bandwidth you use. That means you don't want to use the line when you don't have to. The router acts as a "door" that keeps traffic intended for one of the local hosts inside the local network. Only traffic not intended for one of the local hosts will be sent outside of the local network. (This also increases security because you don't have internal network traffic being broadcast over the Internet and such.)

What Is a Gateway?

In general network terminology, a *gateway* is a router that allows the rest of the clients on the internal LAN to access the outside world, hence the name "gateway." Because of this, the terms *default router* and *gateway* are virtually interchangeable in most networking circles these days. In our example in the previous section, the routers `simba` and `falcon` could be called gateways.

If you want to get really technical, the preceding definition of a gateway is incorrect. According to the technical definition, a gateway is a router that can route between two different types of networks. However, virtually no one goes by this definition anymore, so we are not going to, either. Instead, we will use the commonly accepted definition throughout this chapter, and the terms *default router* and *gateway* will be used interchangeably.

One of the most common uses of a gateway is to allow multiple hosts to share a single Internet connection.

What Is NAT?

NAT, which stands for *Network Address Translation*, is a way for multiple hosts to connect to the Internet using a single IP address. The magic involved in how this works is beyond the scope of this book, but basically NAT works by having a NAT gateway attached to the network in question. When the internal hosts want to send or receive Internet content, their request goes through the NAT gateway. The NAT gateway "hides" the internal IP address and sends all requests from the hosts connected to it out on the Internet with a single IP address (which is the IP address owned by the NAT gateway). Responses that are sent back are sent to that single IP address (which is owned by the NAT gateway). The NAT gateway then routes the data to the proper internal host, which does not need to have a registered IP address. There are two primary advantages of this method:

- It conserves IP addresses. The IP address pool is a limited resource, and there is no reason to waste IP addresses where they are not needed. NAT prevents you from having to register an IP address for each one of your systems. The only system that needs a public and registered IP address is the NAT system. The rest of them can all have private, internal IP addresses.

- If you are a home or small office user, it allows you to share a single Internet connection with multiple computers, and you won't have to purchase additional accounts from your ISP. You can also share a single modem and a single phone line, preventing you from having to install additional phone lines if more than one computer will use the Internet at the same time.

To illustrate some of the ways you can configure various types of routing services on FreeBSD, this chapter presents a few sample scenarios. We begin by looking at sharing a single modem and Internet connection at home or in a small office.

Configuring a NAT Gateway in FreeBSD

In this scenario, you will generally have a single Internet connection, which may or may not be over a modem. You have several systems that need to access the Internet. Figure 27.3 shows an example.

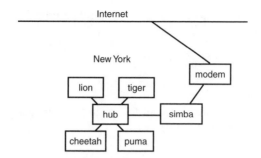

FIGURE 27.3   A simple gateway setup. The router simba has a connection to the Internet via a modem. The idea is to allow lion, cheetah, and lynx to share this modem and access the Internet through simba.

> **NOTE**
>
> A variation of this system might be that you have a classroom and want to provide laptops with wireless Internet access. This will also be discussed later on in this section because it is just a variation of a NAT gateway.

In this type of setup, your system will have two network interfaces in it. For example, ppp0 will be the modem interface—the interface to the Internet. The other interface will usually be an Ethernet interface (for example, ed0). This interface will be the interface to the internal network. The job of the gateway is to act as a "door" between these two interfaces by passing packets back and forth between them. It connects the Internet with your internal network. When traffic comes in from the Internet over interface ppp0, it will be passed to interface ed0 to be sent to the proper host on the network. When outgoing traffic for a host on the Internet arrives from a host on the local network through ed0, it will be passed to the ppp0 interface so that it can be sent out over the Internet to the remote destination. Before this can occur, however, you need to enable packet forwarding so that network traffic can flow between the two interfaces.

Enabling Packet Forwarding

In order for your system to act as a gateway, it must be able to forward packets between network interfaces. Your system will be handling incoming and outgoing Internet traffic for other computers on your network, so when the system receives a packet that is not addressed to it, it needs to forward that packet to the correct destination. By default (and to conform with Internet standards), packet forwarding is turned off, so FreeBSD will drop any packet it receives that is not addressed to the system it is running on.

You can enable packet forwarding in one of two ways. The first goes through the Sysinstall program. However, it is easier to do this manually because only one line needs to be added to a single file to enable packet forwarding. The manual method is the one we will cover here.

Open the file /etc/rc.conf in your favorite text editor and add the following line:

```
gateway_enable="YES"
```

Once you have restarted the system, packet forwarding will be enabled, and the system can now forward packets between interfaces.

Enabling NAT for Systems Without Static IP Addresses

If all the systems on your network have real static IP addresses, the preceding is all you need to do. You can now configure the other systems on the network to use the host simba as their gateway. These hosts, in turn, will send any traffic that they do not know how to deliver to the system that is configured as the default gateway. The default gateway system will then worry about handling this traffic.

> **NOTE**
>
> This section and the ones that follow assume that you already have a working Internet connection on the system that you wish to configure as the gateway to the Internet. If this is not the case, see Chapter 22 for setting up network access on a LAN (this chapter also applies to you if you are accessing the Internet through ADSL or a cable modem). If you need to configure an Internet connection over a modem, see Chapter 23, "Connecting to the Internet with PPP," for more information on setting up a modem Internet connection.

Most of the time, however, if you are configuring an Internet gateway, the other systems on the network will not have a real IP address that is registered. Instead, they will just be using internal IP addresses. In this case, you still have a little more work to do. You will have to enable NAT for these other systems to be able to access the Internet.

If you are using PPP over a dial-up Internet connection, the method used to enable NAT will depend on whether you are using User PPP or Kernel PPP. If you have not set up an Internet connection yet, I recommend you use User PPP if you want to use NAT, because it is the easier of the two to configure to work with NAT.

If you are using Kernel PPP or you need to set up NAT for an Internet connection that is not PPP, the procedure is a bit more complex.

The NAT setup procedure has been divided into the following two sections. You only need to read the section appropriate to your situation.

Using User PPP

The User PPP program in FreeBSD has NAT capability built in to it, so it is very easy to enable. You can simply use the -nat option to ppp to enable NAT. Simply add it to whatever other options you are currently using to start PPP (see Chapter 23 for more details).

The only other thing you should need to do is configure your Windows, Macintosh, or other client to use the new gateway server. This will be covered later on in this chapter in the "Configuring Clients to Use the New Gateway" section.

Using Kernel PPP or a Dedicated Ethernet Connection to the Internet

If you are using Kernel PPP or you have a dedicated Internet connection (ADSL, cable, T1, OC3, and so on), the configuration is a little more complicated. In this case, you will need to use the NAT daemon (natd), which requires a firewall in order to work. To enable the firewall, you will need to build a new kernel. This is not difficult to do, however. You can simply add the following two lines to your kernel configuration file:

```
options IPFIREWALL
options IPDIVERT
```

You can add to the kernel configuration file various other options that have to do with the firewall, such as logging. A detailed discussion of firewalls is beyond the scope of this chapter, but you may want to read the "Configuring a Firewall" section of Chapter 29, "Network Security," before you build a new kernel with firewall support. This way, you won't have to build yet another kernel if you later decide you want another option for the firewall that you didn't include in the kernel the first time around.

Also, if you are unclear about how to build a new kernel, see Chapter 16, "Kernel Configuration," for more details.

Once you have finished building a new kernel, you will need to enable natd.

Configuring and Enabling natd

The NAT daemon natd can be enabled either by configuring network settings in Sysinstall or by manually editing the /etc/rc.conf file. Once again, if you already have basic networking set up, it is easier to simply make the necessary changes manually rather than go through Sysinstall, so this is the method we are going to cover here.

Open the file /etc/rc.conf in your favorite text editor and add the following lines:

```
natd_enable="YES"
natd_interface="ppp0"
```

The natd_interface line in the previous example assumes that you have a modem connection to the Internet and that it is on the interface ppp0. If you have a dedicated connection over an Ethernet device (such as ADSL, cable, T1, or OC3), you should replace ppp0 with whatever network interface your connection to the outside world runs on.

A few other options to natd are available that control things such as logging. If you are interested in the other options, see the man page for natd.

27

Don't exit and save the modified `rc.conf` file yet because there is at least one more option you have to add. This has to do with the firewall.

Enabling and Configuring the Firewall

At a minimum, you will need to add the following line to `/etc/rc.conf` to enable the firewall:

```
firewall_enable="YES"
```

There are various ways to configure the firewall rules, and you should see Chapter 29 for full details. But here is a quick description of my preferred method.

In addition to the previous line, add the following line to `/etc/rc.conf`:

```
firewall_type="/usr/local/etc/firewall.conf"
```

Save the changes you made to `/etc/rc.conf` and exit your editor. You can then create the file `/usr/local/etc/firewall.conf`, in which you simply put the firewall rules (except for the default rule, which by default will deny anything that is not specifically allowed—see Chapter 29 for more details).

If you do not want to deny any types of network traffic and simply want to pass everything through, the following rules will work in `/usr/local/etc/firewall.conf`:

```
add divert natd all from any to any via ed0
add allow all from any to any
```

Using this rule basically has the same effect as not having a firewall at all, because it simply passes all traffic and doesn't deny anything.

Allowing people to see the firewall rules that your system is using can be a security hazard, so you should set the permissions on the file so that only root can read it. The command `chmod 600 /usr/local/etc/firewall.conf` will do the trick.

> **CAUTION**
>
> The firewall rules described previously are very insecure because they allow all types of network traffic from any source and will happily pass that content to any one of the systems that is using this gateway. This compromises the security of your network. Because of this, allowing all traffic is not recommended. Again, see the section "Configuring a Firewall" in Chapter 29 for information on how to configure the firewall to block potentially dangerous types of traffic.

Once you have completed all the previous steps, reboot the system for the kernel changes to take effect and for the firewall and `natd` to load. Your gateway should now be configured. The only thing left to do is inform the clients of the existence of the gateway. The configuration of various clients will be covered next. For the client types that are not covered, see your system documentation.

> **CAUTION**
>
> Make sure you configure the firewall for the first time from the actual system on which you are setting up the firewall. If you accidentally misconfigure the firewall and reboot remotely, you will lock yourself out of your own system. By default, the firewall denies all traffic, so this is relatively easy to do by accident.

Configuring Clients to Use the New Gateway

The procedures for configuring a client to use the gateway vary, depending on the type of operating system you are running. We will cover configuring Windows, Macintosh, FreeBSD, and Linux clients in this section.

Note that all the following configuration instructions assume that you already have basic networking configured and that they simply show you how to set up the system to use the gateway. If you do not have basic networking configured on the system yet, see the documentation for your system for instructions on how to do this.

Configuring Windows 95/98 Clients

To configure a Windows 95 or 98 client to use the gateway, double-click the My Computer icon, double-click Control Panel, and then double-click Network. This will bring up the configuration dialog box shown in Figure 27.4.

FIGURE 27.4 The Network dialog box in Windows 98. Windows 95 and Windows Me may look slightly different.

From this dialog box, click TCP/IP and then click the Properties button. This will take you to the TCP/IP Configuration dialog box. Click the Gateway tab, and you will be given the dialog box shown in Figure 27.5.

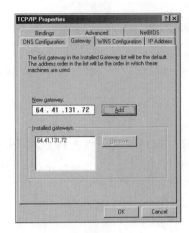

FIGURE 27.5   The Gateway tab and its dialog box in Windows 98.

Simply enter the IP address of the gateway in the New Gateway box, as shown (assuming, in this case, that the IP address of the gateway system is 64.41.131.72). Then, click the Add button, and the new gateway will show up in the list of installed gateways. Click OK to save the changes and then click OK again to leave the Network dialog box. In Windows 95 or 98, you will have to restart your computer for the changes to take effect, and you will be informed of this fact. Windows Me will probably not require a reboot.

After the reboot is complete, you should now be able to access the Internet from the Windows system.

Configuring Mac OS and Mac OS X Clients

Macintosh clients are potentially easier to set up to use your FreeBSD gateway than Windows because all TCP/IP configuration options are in the same window, and no reboot is necessary.

In the classic Mac OS (version 9 or earlier), open the TCP/IP control panel, as shown in Figure 27.6, and select Manually from the Configure drop-down menu if it is not already selected. Put your gateway's IP address into the Router Address field. When you close the window, it will prompt you to save the changes. When you do so, the new settings will be immediately applied.

In Mac OS X, open the System Preferences and then select the Network panel, shown in Figure 27.7. As in Mac OS 9, select Manually from the Configure menu and fill in the gateway IP address in the Router field. Click Save to commit the changes. The new network settings are immediately in effect.

In both these situations, you have the option to configure the built-in Ethernet card, the AirPort wireless card, or other network devices. Make sure you repeat this process for all relevant devices.

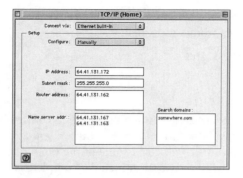

FIGURE 27.6   Configuring the TCP/IP settings under Mac OS 9.

FIGURE 27.7   Configuring the TCP/IP settings under Mac OS X.

Configuring FreeBSD 5.0

To configure FreeBSD for a default gateway, add the following line to the /etc/rc.conf file:

```
defaultrouter="64.41.131.162"
```

Of course, you will need to replace the IP address in the preceding example with the IP address of the gateway interface on the FreeBSD system that is serving as a gateway.

The change will not take effect until you have rebooted the system.

27

If you don't want to restart the system, you can add the default route manually with the following command issued from a root shell:

```
route add default 64.41.131.162
```

Configuring Linux Clients

Because of the lack of standardization in Linux, how you configure your Linux system to use the FreeBSD gateway will depend on the distribution you are using. We will not cover all the distributions here, but we will cover some of the more popular ones. (The documentation accompanying your distribution includes complete configuration instructions for that distribution.)

CAUTION

Because there is a lack of standardization between Linux distributions, the examples in this section may not work for your distribution. See the documentation for your particular Linux distribution if you need help configuring your system to use a gateway.

Red Hat Linux

Red Hat Linux network configuration is controlled by the file /etc/sysconfig/network. To use the new FreeBSD gateway, the following line should exist in the file:

```
GATEWAY=64.41.131.162
```

Replace the IP address in the preceding example with the IP address of the gateway interface on the FreeBSD system that is serving as a gateway.

Make sure you check to see whether the line already exists before adding this line because having two GATEWAY lines could cause a conflict.

You will need to restart the Red Hat Linux system before the changes take effect.

If you don't want to restart the system, you can add the default route manually with the following command issued from a root shell:

```
route add default gw 64.41.131.162
```

Slackware Linux

In Slackware Linux, the initial part of the network setup is controlled by the file /etc/rc.inet1. This file handles basic network setup, including routing. To use the new FreeBSD gateway, the following line should exist in the file:

```
GATEWAY="64.41.131.162"
```

Replace the IP address in the preceding example with the IP address of the gateway interface on the FreeBSD system that is serving as a gateway.

Make sure you check to see whether the line already exists before adding this line because having two GATEWAY lines could cause a conflict.

You will need to restart the Slackware Linux system before the changes take effect.

If you don't want to restart the system, you can add the default route manually with the following command issued from a root shell:

```
route add default gw 64.41.131.162
```

Configuring Wireless Internet Access

Wireless network access has recently become very popular because it does not require wires to be strung around, and it also does not require network connection jacks, which eliminates the common problem of not having enough network connection jacks. Any PC that has a wireless networking card can communicate with the network. Indeed, many notebook computers are shipping with wireless networking capabilities built in to them.

One of the most common applications of this technology is Internet sharing for school classrooms. Each student can have a notebook computer on his or her desk and have access to the Internet through a central server.

Configuring FreeBSD to work as a wireless gateway for this type of setup is almost identical to configuring a normal gateway, as already discussed. The only real difference is that you will need to have a wireless networking card installed in the FreeBSD system.

Table 27.1 lists some of the wireless network interfaces that FreeBSD currently supports, along with the corresponding devices that need to be present in the kernel configuration file. Note that support for new devices is being added on a regular basis, so check the hardware compatibility list on the FreeBSD Web site for the latest information.

TABLE 27.1   Wireless Network Interfaces That FreeBSD Currently Supports

Wireless Interface	Kernel Device
Aironet 4500/4800 802.11	device an
AMD Am79C930-based cards	device awi
Xircom CNU/NetWare Airsurfer	device cnw
Lucent WaveLan 802.11	device wi
Lucent WaveLan (ISA only)	device wl

With the exception of the cnw and wl devices, support for these adapters is included in the default GENERIC kernel. So, unless you have a wireless network card that requires the cnw device or the wl device, you should be okay unless you built a custom kernel and removed support for these devices.

If you do need to build a new kernel to support your wireless network card, see Chapter 16 for details on how to do this.

Once you have your wireless network card working, simply follow the same procedures mentioned earlier in this chapter to configure the gateway and the clients.

Routing Between Three or More Networks

In all the situations up to this point, the router configuration has only needed one route. For example, our `simba` gateway only has one connection to the Internet, and it only serves one network. Figure 27.8 shows how this works.

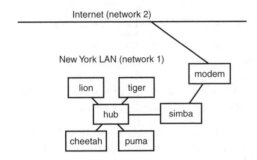

FIGURE 27.8   The gateway `simba` here only needs to route packets between two networks, which are the local LAN and the Internet.

In this simple example, the hosts `lion`, `cheetah`, `lynx`, and `puma` use `simba` as their default gateway to communicate with systems on the Internet. Likewise, `simba` also has a default router, and it is set to the router at the ISP. For a dial-up PPP connection, this is transparent to you because the default route will be added automatically when the PPP connection is established, and it will be deleted automatically when the PPP connection terminates. You do not need to worry about this, but you should be aware that your gateway has a default router it uses, just as your clients that use the gateway use it as a default router.

However, sometimes you might have a more complex configuration, such as that shown in Figure 27.9. In this situation, `simba` acts as the default router for its own network as well as serving as the default router for `falcon`, which is itself a default router for another network.

In this example, in addition to serving the clients on its own network, `simba` is actually serving as an Internet service provider to the network served by the router `falcon`. This means that `simba` now needs to route between three networks. For this to work, we need to add another route to `simba` so that it knows what packets should be routed to the network served by `falcon` as well as how to get them there.

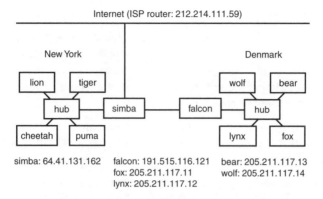

FIGURE 27.9   A more complex gateway setup. In this case, simba acts as a default router for its own network as well as serving as the default router for falcon, which is itself a default router for another network.

The network served by `falcon` owns a Class C address block. Notice that all the addresses on the network begin with the base address of `205.211.117.xx`. Also, notice that `falcon` has an IP address of `169.151.116.121`. To get `simba` to route packets to the network served by `falcon`, we can add the following lines to `/etc/rc.conf`:

```
defaultroute="212.214.111.59"
static_routes="falcon"
falcon="-net 205.211.117.0 169.151.116.121"
```

In this case, the IP address `212.214.111.59` is the default router for `simba`. In other words, any packets that `simba` receives that are for hosts it doesn't know about will be sent to this router. `212.214.111.59` is the router at the Internet backbone provider that serves `simba`.

We have also added what is called a *static route*. This is an entry in the routing table that is static—it does not change. In this case, we have told `simba` that any packets it receives that have a destination with a base address of `205.211.117.0` should be routed to the address `169.151.116.121`. This is the IP address of `falcon`, which itself serves as a router for another network. As you can see, all the hosts on the network served by `falcon` begin with an IP address of `205.211.117.xx`. Therefore, any packets that `simba` receives that are intended for any of these hosts will be routed to `falcon` rather than to the default route of `212.214.111.59`. In addition, any packets received by `simba` that are intended for clients on its own network will be routed directly to those clients rather than sent to the default route.

In order for the static routes to take effect, you will need to reboot the system. It is recommended that you reboot the system, but if you do not want to, you can add the static routes manually so they will take effect immediately. In the previous example, this can be done with the following command from a root shell:

```
route add -net 205.211.117.0 169.151.116.121
```

27

Dynamic Routing

All our examples so far have used static routes, which are routes that never change. This is because in our examples up to this point, the routers have only had one connection to the Internet. For example, in the previous section, simba accessed the Internet through the router at its ISP, and falcon accessed the Internet through simba. In both cases, these were the only access points that the router had to the Internet.

Sometimes, however, you may have multiple Internet connections or multiple routes to the same network. In this case, static routing does not work well. This is where dynamic routing comes in.

Dynamic routing uses a routing daemon, along with a routing protocol to discover new routes, and dynamically adds them to the routing table. In addition, dynamic routing automatically deletes routing entries from the routing table when they are no longer valid.

Several router daemons are available for FreeBSD. The one that is included with the FreeBSD base system is called routed. It is a fairly old program, and it uses a fairly old routing protocol known as RIP (Routing Information Protocol). RIP has some security problems, so there are better choices available for routing than routed. Other routing daemons available in the FreeBSD ports collection include gated and zebra, both in the "net" directory of the ports tree. For more information on installing software using the FreeBSD ports collection, see Chapter 14, "Installing Additional Software."

A discussion of how to configure the routing daemons is beyond the scope of this book. See the man pages and documentation for the routing daemon that you decide to use for more information.

The good news is that you probably won't need to run a routing daemon, anyway. As mentioned before, the only time you will need a routing daemon is if you have multiple routes to get to the same network (for example, multiple Internet connections). If you don't have multiple routes to the same network, then using static routing entries, as discussed previously, will work fine.

Enterprise Routing and DMZ

A variation of the previous concept of routing between multiple networks is the *DMZ* concept, which is fairly common in enterprise environments.

The problem here is that you may need some systems behind the gateway to have real IP addresses (such as Web servers), but you want the rest of the systems to use NAT. This is usually done by having a gateway that has three network interfaces in it. One interface is the outside link to the Internet, the second is for the systems that should use NAT, and the third is for the systems that should not use NAT. The interface that serves the systems with the real IP addresses is known as the *demilitarized zone* (DMZ). More information on DMZ setups can be found in the section "Using a Firewall" in Chapter 29.

Configuring a Database Server

Sooner or later, all large and popular Web sites are faced with the decision of whether to provide visitors with customized, dynamic content served from a database. For commercial sites, it's almost a requirement to supplement the static Web content with a database back end, populated with customer profiles, product catalogs, user preferences, and all sorts of other information that allows the administrator to present a customized interface to the user. Even noncommercial sites can benefit from using databases, though. This chapter covers the fundamentals of database back-end usage as it applies to any site administrator, whether commercial or not. Using the freely available MySQL and PostgreSQL packages, you can develop a data store to attach to your Web server. This chapter will teach you what you need to know in order to efficiently administer the server, to construct the database your Web site needs, to optimize its performance, and to protect its security.

Databases aren't just for the Web, either. Long before the Web existed, databases were an integral part of commerce and engineering. But a database cannot be of any use without a good interface to the data inside it, and the Web is only the most recent such interface mechanism to achieve widespread use. Because databases can be used for a great many things other than providing dynamic Web content, this chapter explains how you can use databases both in a general, stand-alone context and in the context of Web connectivity.

Introduction to Database Design and Administration

Connecting a Web site to a database can be a daunting prospect. On Windows, the process is made easier by such standardized interfaces as Open Database Connectivity (ODBC), but that's not really available on FreeBSD. Nor does FreeBSD have access to native versions of the most popular high-end database packages, such as Oracle, MS-SQL, and IBM DB2, or to what have become the standard Windows-based dynamic-content page-layout languages, ASP and ColdFusion. Creating dynamic Web content in FreeBSD is accomplished largely through the use of open-source alternatives to those packages. MySQL, PostgreSQL, and other similar databases fulfill the role of the back end itself, and PHP, Perl, and Python provide tools that furnish us with the connectivity into those back-end data stores.

Figure 28.1 illustrates the schematic layout of a Web site with dynamic content that interacts with a database back end. The user (the visitor to the site) opens the front-end content page in a browser. This content is rarely written in pure HTML. Instead, most Web page content is written in a language such as PHP, ASP, ColdFusion, Perl, or a similar framework. These languages include both the HTML that lays out the page and the calls into the database that return the information the page's code uses to fill out the interesting parts of the page. For instance, a database might contain all of a bank customer's transactions in the past month. When the user accesses the page with the proper parameters to extract those transactions, the content page prints out standard HTML headers, images, and layout elements common to the site. Then, the page accesses the database and performs a *query*. The database returns the results of that query to the code in the content page, which then formats the customer's data appropriately (wrapping it in HTML, in most cases) and prints it into the page. The page then finishes the job by printing out more common HTML, such as footers and disclaimers.

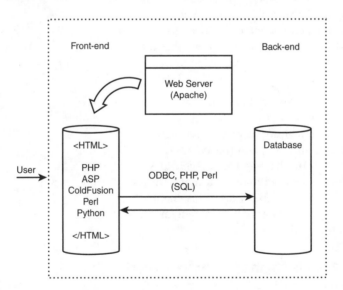

FIGURE 28.1   A diagram of a Web site that uses dynamic database-driven content. The Web page content and server (the front end) send queries to the database (the back end) using Structured Query Language (SQL) via a conduit layer such as ODBC, PHP, or Perl; the database returns the results of those queries through the same conduit to the front end, where it is formatted for display on the page.

The two large conceptual divisions of the Web site database system are in the back end (the database itself) and in the front end (the content engine and HTML output). We will turn our attention first to the back end so that you can become familiar with how database queries work, because that is the foundation not only of the Web applicability of databases but also of all other possible uses of databases.

SQL: Structured Query Language

Early work on the theory of relational databases (that is, databases in which data is stored in multiple *tables* of varying sizes that can contain not just data but relations between data elements) by E.F. Codd resulted in IBM, in the late 1970s, creating a language called SEQUEL (Structured English Query Language), later shortened to SQL. This language attempted to standardize into an English-like syntax the methods by which data could be extracted from or inserted into a database. Using terms such as SELECT <data> FROM <table> and WHERE <field> IS NOT NULL, the syntax of SQL is easy to learn—although the concepts behind what that syntax describes can be rather more challenging.

A database is organized as shown in the simple example in Figure 28.2. This diagram shows a database named PictureArchive that contains a number of tables (two are shown). These tables each represent a grouping of similar *rows* of data—each row, or *entry*, has a number of fields (columns) that contain data comprising a row. For instance, in the Users table shown, a single row would contain a user's ID, full name, e-mail address, and age. Each of these columns is specified as a certain data type—integer, character/string, floating-point number, Boolean, and so on. A row can have blank entries in its fields, which are usually represented by the NULL value.

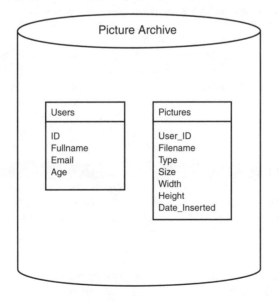

FIGURE 28.2   Diagram of a simple database.

The Pictures table works the same way: It's a grouping of a different set of data, with different fields, that is nonetheless useful as part of the PictureArchive database. This table contains fields such as the filename of a picture that has been added into the system, its type, size, and so on. But what makes relational databases so useful is the ability to associate tables together via *relations* between their elements. The Pictures table contains a field with the ID of the user who owns it; this will allow us to access the data in all kinds of creative ways, as you will see.

> **NOTE**
>
> The conceptual structure of a database, its tables, and their columns is typically referred to as a *schema.*

Basic SQL Syntax

Beginning with the PictureArchive sample database, let's assume that its tables already contain some data—that the tables are populated and in general use. The most common thing to do with a database is to extract data from it. You do this with the SQL command SELECT.

> **TIP**
>
> SQL query commands are case insensitive; SELECT, Select, and select will all work the same. Case sensitivity does apply in some cases to the data in the fields, as you learn later in this chapter. Also, the names of databases, tables, and columns are case sensitive. However, for the purposes of these examples, we will use all caps to denote SQL keywords and mixed case (as in PictureArchive) to denote named objects such as tables and columns.

A SELECT command, like most SQL commands, is structured to flow like common English. First, after the verb SELECT, comes a noun—the name of the field (or fields) that you want to extract. Next comes FROM, followed by the name of the table from which you want to extract the data. Finally, at the end of the query comes a semicolon (;). Here's an example:

```
SELECT * FROM Users;
```

> **TIP**
>
> Don't forget the semicolon at the end of the SQL query! This is probably the most common mistake among SQL novices. If you leave off the semicolon before pressing Enter, the interface will allow you to keep entering text as part of the same SQL query. Queries can span multiple lines.

This command, entered either by hand into a MySQL or PostgreSQL database command line or passed invisibly to the program by a PHP or Perl interface, tells the database to return all the data in the Users table—without any sorting or limitations. This data will either be returned programmatically to the interface that called it or printed in tabular form to the command line.

If the response contains a lot of data but you're only interested in users who match certain criteria, you can further narrow your query in a number of ways. The first is to specify only certain fields to extract, instead of entering the asterisk (*), which is a shorthand for "All fields." Here's an example:

```
SELECT Fullname,Age FROM Users;
```

Fields requested in this way can be specified in any order; they can even be repeated within the same query. The response in this example will return only the full name of each user and the user's age.

Next, you can limit your search still further by using the WHERE keyword. This allows you to apply any number of criteria to your queries; WHERE can specify that a field must be equal to, less than, greater than, not equal to, or have any of a number of other relationships to a certain value. This value can be supplied explicitly in the query, or it can be the name of another field, as you'll learn in a moment. For now, limit the query to those users over the age of 18 by using the "greater than or equal to" operator. Note that when field contents are specified, they should be surrounded with quotes:

```
SELECT Fullname,Age FROM Users WHERE Age>="18";
```

Similarly, you can use the LIKE keyword and the percent (%) wildcard to specify that you want to list all users over age 18 and who have e-mail addresses at AOL:

```
SELECT Fullname,Age FROM Users WHERE Age>="18" AND Email LIKE "%aol.com";
```

You've now addressed a fairly narrow range of users from the Users table. But maybe the output is still too long for your purposes; maybe you only want the top 20 such users, sorted in descending order of age. You can do this by adding LIMIT and ORDER BY clauses:

```
SELECT Fullname,Age FROM Users WHERE Age>="18" AND Email LIKE "%aol.com"
➥ORDER BY Age DESC LIMIT 20;
```

If your query cannot fit on a single line, don't worry—SQL queries can contain multiple lines, and they terminate only with a semicolon. This sample query could also be entered as follows:

```
SELECT Fullname,Age FROM Users
WHERE Age>="18"
AND Email LIKE "%aol.com"
ORDER BY Age DESC
LIMIT 20;
```

28

The additional clarity that this gives you will be invaluable when you find yourself writing really long, complex queries once you've become a SQL expert.

That's about it for a basic extraction of data from a single table. You use a similar process to insert data into a table, though it's a little bit more mathematical in its look and feel. You begin with the INSERT INTO statement, followed by the table in question; then, in parentheses, you enter the names of the columns into which you're adding data (you can insert into only a few fields if you want to, leaving the rest in that row as NULL). You then enter the VALUES statement, followed (in parentheses) by the values you want to insert, listed in the same order as the fields were specified:

```
INSERT INTO Users (Fullname,Email,Age) VALUES ("Sam
➥Jones","sjones@somewhere.com","25");
```

Updating data in a row (or group of rows) uses syntax that borrows from both the SELECT and INSERT commands, as in these examples:

```
UPDATE Users SET Age="26" WHERE Fullname="Sam Jones";
UPDATE Users SET Fullname="Somebody Under 18" WHERE Age<"18";
UPDATE Users SET Age=Age+1;
```

Finally, to delete a row from a table, you use a syntax similar to what you've seen already:

```
DELETE FROM Users WHERE Age<"13";
DELETE FROM Users;
```

The second line in this example will delete all entries from the Users table. Use this command with the same caution with which you would use rm -rf *! If you ever find yourself entering a DELETE or UPDATE query that has no WHERE statements in it, double- and triple-check that you're doing what you want to be doing. You'll thank yourself for your caution.

Joins

You can use the four query commands you just learned to do a number of useful things when operating on single tables. But the true strength of relational databases occurs when the contents of multiple tables are "joined" together, using relations specified in the query. Queries can be made arbitrarily long and complex through these methods, limited only by your imagination and the processing capability of your computer.

You already know how you would go about selecting all the information from the Pictures table for pictures owned by a particular user (for instance, the user with the ID number of 5):

```
SELECT Filename,Type,Size FROM Pictures WHERE User_ID="5";
```

But all this gives you is the data that's in the Pictures table. A more interesting feat would be to get the user's full name as well as the picture data for all his pictures. This is done with a join. The simplest kind of join, referred to as an *inner join*, is constructed by specifying multiple tables, separated by commas, and a WHERE clause, which cements the two tables together with a relation between their fields:

```
SELECT Fullname,Filename,Type,Size FROM Users,Pictures
WHERE USER_ID="5"
AND Users.ID=Pictures.User_ID;
```

As you can see, tables and their columns are referenced in SQL in the dotted "object" fashion, with periods separating the table names from their members. If the column names are all unique, as they are in this example, you can omit the table name, like so:

```
SELECT Fullname,Filename,Type,Size FROM Users,Pictures
WHERE USER_ID="5"
AND ID=User_ID;
```

However, if both tables had an ID field, the dotted notation specifying the respective tables would be required so as to avoid ambiguity.

> **NOTE**
>
> For style points as well as rigorous safety, keep in mind that "best practice" in SQL is to always use the fully qualified versions of object names when you're working with multiple tables—that is, use the hierarchical dotted form that includes the table name. It involves more typing and longer queries, but it's much less likely to cause problems and is much easier to debug when it does.

Inner joins aren't the only kind of joins. *Outer joins* are also quite useful and can take the form of *left* or *right*. These distinctions have to do with how the tables are aligned with each other and which table is considered more "important" than the other, as specified by its side of the comma or JOIN statement in the query.

28

An inner join will return all rows in which the fields specified in the WHERE clause that joins the tables can be matched. For instance, in the PictureArchive example, the join you just saw would return all pictures whose User_ID corresponds to an ID that exists in the Users table. However, it's possible for a picture to have a User_ID that does not exist in the Users table, and it's possible for a user to have no pictures in the Pictures table that are associated with him. An inner join will not show these users or pictures; instead, it shows only those that can be matched together.

Let's say you want to get a listing of all users and their associated pictures, even if some users don't have any pictures. You use LEFT JOIN to produce this listing:

```
SELECT Fullname,Filename FROM Users
LEFT JOIN Pictures ON Pictures.User_ID=Users.ID;
```

In the output that follows from this query, the Filename field will be NULL for some users; but for users with multiple pictures, a row will appear for each picture.

You can use RIGHT JOIN if you want to specify the table on the right of the JOIN statement as being "more important." For example, if you wanted to get a listing of all the pictures in the system, whether or not the user they're associated with exists, you could do it like this:

```
SELECT Fullname,Filename FROM Users
RIGHT JOIN Pictures ON Pictures.User_ID=Users.ID;
```

However, not all database systems fully support RIGHT JOIN; for compatibility's sake, it is usually better to stick to LEFT JOIN and merely reverse the positions of Users and Pictures in the query.

Advanced Querying Techniques

The query statements and join techniques you have just learned are by no means the only ways in which to access data in a database. A number of little tricks can help make queries easier and more flexible. Most of these are additional keywords available in the SELECT clause.

Grouping is a handy tool that has some hidden complexities. Let's say you want to repeat the LEFT JOIN example from before, only you want to collapse each user down to a single line and output the number of pictures each user has, using the COUNT() operator. Like many such operators that take column names as arguments (such as MAX(), MIN(), AVG(), and SUM(), all of which take either a column name or another function as input), this operator requires the use of a GROUP BY statement at the end of the query:

```
SELECT Fullname,COUNT(Filename) FROM Users
LEFT JOIN Pictures ON Pictures.User_ID=Users.ID
GROUP BY Users.ID ORDER BY Fullname;
```

If a user has multiple pictures in the database with the same filename, you can use DISTINCT to ignore the duplicates and NULL values:

```
SELECT Fullname,COUNT(DISTINCT Filename) FROM Users
LEFT JOIN Pictures ON Pictures.User_ID=Users.ID
GROUP BY Users.ID ORDER BY Fullname;
```

CAUTION

Note that when you group results by a certain field, you technically can't guarantee the results of any fields beside the grouping field and the output of the grouping function. For instance, suppose you issued the following query:

```
SELECT Fullname,Email,Filename,COUNT(Filename) FROM Users
LEFT JOIN Pictures ON Pictures.User_ID=Users.ID
GROUP BY Users.ID ORDER BY Fullname;
```

In this case, the Email and Filename fields might conceivably come from anywhere in the grouping, susceptible to the vagaries of the inner workings of the database program. Even if the field's contents cannot possibly vary in the current query (as with Email in this example, because all of a user's grouped rows will be the same), always try to avoid selecting fields other than the two nonvariable ones in a GROUP BY query.

Another popular advanced tool is the AS statement. This statement lets you effectively "rename" a column or the result of a mathematical operation, creating an *alias* for use later in the query. For instance, you can use the AS statement to give the output of a grouping operator a different name that you can then use in ORDER BY or GROUP BY clauses. If, for example, you want to get each user's count of pictures, sorted in descending order of the count and accessible under the new column name of pic_count, you could do the following:

```
SELECT Fullname,COUNT(Filename) AS pic_count FROM Users
LEFT JOIN Pictures ON Pictures.User_ID=Users.ID
GROUP BY Users.ID ORDER BY pic_count DESC;
```

The LIMIT clause has more flexibility than you have seen in previous examples. You can specify an offset, which can be very useful in creating multiple pages of output data. This offset is the number of rows to be subtracted from the top of the output before the LIMIT is applied. Let's say you want to return all of a user's pictures in groups of 20; to specify the third group of 20 (in other words, pictures 41 through 60), you would use the following query:

```
SELECT Filename,Type,Size FROM Pictures
WHERE User_ID="5"
ORDER BY Filename LIMIT 40,20;
```

28

SQL is a language with vast versatility and commensurate complexity. Techniques such as subselects, stored procedures, priority execution, and the remaining grouping and mathematical functions are beyond the scope of this book, but they can be found in the SQL reference guides available at the MySQL and PostgreSQL Web sites.

Using the MySQL and PostgreSQL Open-Source Databases

Now that you have a grounding in how SQL is used in all databases that support it (which is to say, almost all of them), you can turn your attention to the common open-source databases typically used under FreeBSD. These are MySQL and PostgreSQL.

In recent years, the field of open-source database software packages has narrowed to include fewer, but more useful, solutions. It used to be the case that the administrator had to choose between dozens of different solutions, all of which had some basic functionality but seemed to be missing something crucial—and each one was deficient in something different. But recently the development efforts on MySQL and PostgreSQL have turned them both into packages that are every bit as full featured as the commercial solutions they propose to replace. Even the limitations that separate these two packages from each other have grown fewer and fewer.

Today, whether you choose MySQL or PostgreSQL is largely a matter of personal taste and philosophy. MySQL is by far the more widely used and better supported open-source database system, and it's also considerably faster. That's why the examples shown in this book concentrate on MySQL syntax and usage. PostgreSQL, however, supports more advanced features than does MySQL, and it may be a better choice for high-end servers for which transactional data integrity and feature set are of critical importance. But either one will provide excellent support for all of a typical administrator's needs.

How Do MySQL and PostgreSQL Differ?

MySQL is developed by employees of MySQL AB, a commercial software company, whereas PostgreSQL is a more traditional open-source project. PostgreSQL has contributors from all over the globe, with varying areas of expertise. The two packages differ in many architectural details because of this. The most fundamental differences between the two packages are those of developmental philosophy; most other discrepancies can be traced to this root cause.

The primary goal of MySQL is to focus on performance and reliability, instead of implementing all the newest features, which MySQL AB considers to be the source of an unacceptable risk of instability. PostgreSQL's priorities tend to be directed more toward a complete feature set. PostgreSQL development seeks to implement as much flexibility and functionality as possible, with the goal of creating a complete replacement for any top-end commercial product. MySQL tends to be developed more slowly than PostgreSQL for this reason. MySQL's roadmap for future development includes some features currently supported by PostgreSQL, but MySQL developers consider these secondary in priority to code stability and performance.

An example of this difference in philosophy is that PostgreSQL requires a periodic VACUUM operation in order to clean up the space that has been relinquished through DELETE and UPDATE commands. Because the VACUUM command tends to use a great deal of overhead, a PostgreSQL database may not be the best choice for a system that must have 24/7 availability. MySQL lacks some features found in PostgreSQL that may be of use to administrators with particular goals; but because MySQL's core feature set is more robustly designed, it does not have such a need for cleanup procedures and therefore is potentially more suited to mission-critical 24/7 service.

The features PostgreSQL supports but that MySQL does not support include subselects, foreign keys, views, stored procedures, and triggers, among others. Some of these features are really very cool and provide an excellent level of functionality to the administrator. If you are interested in creating a site with which you can experiment and learn what SQL can do, PostgreSQL may be a good choice for you. If, however, you are interested in running a high-performance server where availability and speed are of critical importance, MySQL may be a better choice.

> **NOTE**
>
> Both the PostgreSQL and MySQL database projects are striving toward compliance with the ANSI SQL standard, but neither supports it fully.

Finally, an operational difference between the two packages is that MySQL provides a complete command-line environment for interacting with the system directly through a terminal. The MySQL environment includes a number of commands that are not part of SQL but have special meaning within that environment, such as SHOW PROCESSLIST and SET PASSWORD. The PostgreSQL command-line interface is more austere; shell commands are given with terse backslash codes, and all other commands issued at the command line are interpreted as SQL queries.

> **NOTE**
>
> PostgreSQL is free under all circumstances, although commercial support is available for a fee. MySQL, however, has a licensing policy whereby if you run it in a commercial context in which you prefer not to be restricted by the terms of the GPL under which MySQL is licensed, MySQL AB requests that you pay a license fee. See the MySQL Web site, www.mysql.com, for details.

Installing MySQL

MySQL can be easily installed from the packages or ports, as discussed in Chapter 14, "Installing Additional Software." The port directory you will want, if you choose to build

MySQL from the ports, is /usr/ports/databases/mysql323-server. (This directory name may change as the version number of MySQL increments.) Go into the directory and type **make** and then **make install**.

CAUTION

Before installing MySQL, make sure your /var partition is sufficiently large to support the size database you anticipate running. The /var partition must be large enough for all your data as well as for the runtime internal table structures the database may create. A partition of at least 100MB is recommended for a medium-sized database with moderate complexity. Refer to Chapter 18, "Understanding Hard Disks and Filesystems," for details on partitioning your disks.

After the package has been compiled and installed and you have started the MySQL server (/usr/local/etc/rc.d/mysql-server start), you will need to set up the initial security on the root user. By default, root has full privileges in MySQL's access control system as well as a blank password. Needless to say, it's a bad idea to leave this unchanged! The first thing to do after installation completes is to issue the following commands:

```
# mysqladmin -u root password <new_password>
```

Replace <new_password> with the new root password for super-user access to your MySQL database.

CAUTION

When upgrading from an earlier version of MySQL, it is not usually necessary to back up and restore your database files—but, as the installation script tells you, it's still a wise precaution. To begin this process, dump your databases (as explained later in the "Performing Database System Backups" section of this chapter) and shut down your MySQL server (/usr/local/etc/rc.d/ mysql-server.sh stop). Next, perform a make install operation and then restart the server. If there are any problems, you can restore your databases from the dump files.

Installing PostgreSQL

PostgreSQL can be easily installed from the packages or ports, as discussed in Chapter 14. If you choose to build PostgreSQL from the ports, use the port directory /usr/ports/ databases/postgresql7. Go into the directory and type **make**, make the choices you want in the full-screen option menus (or choose the defaults), and then perform a make install operation.

CAUTION

Unlike with MySQL, an upgrade from an earlier version of PostgreSQL requires that you dump your databases and restore them after the upgrade. Refer to "Performing Database System Backups," later in this chapter, for details on how this is done.

After the initial installation, a new user (pgsql) will have been created, as will a new startup script (/usr/local/etc/rc.d/010.pgsql.sh). Don't run this script to start the server yet, though; you first need to set up a few things manually. First, run the initdb command; this sets up the *database cluster*, which is the base directory for all the database files that will be created. The port installation procedure suggests using the default location of /usr/local/pgsql/data for this, and so here is the procedure to follow:

```
# su -l pgsql
$ mkdir data
$ initdb
The files belonging to this database system will be owned by user "pgsql".
This user must also own the server process.

creating directory /usr/local/pgsql/data... ok
creating directory /usr/local/pgsql/data/base... ok
creating directory /usr/local/pgsql/data/global... ok
creating directory /usr/local/pgsql/data/pg_xlog... ok
creating directory /usr/local/pgsql/data/pg_clog... ok
creating template1 database in /usr/local/pgsql/data/base/1... ok
creating configuration files... ok
initializing pg_shadow... ok
enabling unlimited row size for system tables... ok
creating system views... ok
loading pg_description... ok
vacuuming database template1... ok
copying template1 to template0... ok

Success. You can now start the database server using:

    /usr/local/bin/postmaster -D /usr/local/pgsql/data
or
    /usr/local/bin/pg_ctl -D /usr/local/pgsql/data -l logfile start
```

> **TIP**
>
> You may wish to change PostgreSQL's database cluster directory to something like /var/db/pgsql, to correspond to MySQL's use of /var/db/mysql; after all, database content is variable and should properly be kept in /var. Another compelling reason you might choose to do this is if you have separate disks for the /usr and /var partitions. Having your database files and your nonvariable Web content on separate drive spindles can provide a very substantial performance benefit, especially if they're also on different IDE channels.
>
> The PostgreSQL startup script calls for su -l, which changes to the pgsql user and executes the process that starts up the PostgreSQL server. The -l option reads in the .cshrc or .profile shell

---

environment file for the pgsql user, and each of these files sets the PGDATA environment variable to /usr/local/pgsql/data. In order to change the database cluster location to /var/db/pgsql, you will not only have to create that directory and run initdb -D /var/db/pgsql instead of the initdb command in the example shown here, you will also have to edit ~pgsql/.cshrc and ~pgsql/.profile and change the PGDATA lines (which currently specify $HOME/data or ${HOME}/data) to /var/db/pgsql.

You can now try to start the server by ignoring the lines at the end of the initdb process and instead running /usr/local/etc/rc.d/010.pgsql.sh start. If it starts successfully, congratulate yourself. However, if you get a message such as IpcSemaphoreCreate: semget(key=5432003, num=17, 03600) failed: No space left on device, along with an explanation that you need to raise your kernel's limits on semaphore sets, you will unfortunately need to recompile your kernel (see Chapter 16, "Kernel Configuration"). Here are the kernel options you will need to add or update:

```
options         SYSVSHM
options         SHMMAXPGS=4096
options         SHMSEG=256

options         SYSVSEM
options         SEMMNI=256
options         SEMMNS=512
options         SEMMNU=256
options         SEMMAP=256
```

Constructing a Database System

Now that your database system is installed, it's time to get started creating a working database. This is a process that involves careful planning and design; you can't just indiscriminately create tables and columns without an eye toward maximum efficiency. Likewise, you can't simply assume that you'll be able to go back and redesign the system later as you learn how it should be done. Although database schemas can be changed, it's not terribly easy to do so, and in some cases it can't be done without loss of data or without destabilizing your own Web application code built on top of the existing schema.

Before you do anything else, you may as well create your database. This amounts to little more than creating an empty directory (via the MySQL or PostgreSQL interface) that will hold your tables and indexes. Log in to the database using the mysql command-line interface and issue the CREATE DATABASE command as follows:

```
# mysql -p
Enter password:
Welcome to the MySQL monitor.  Commands end with ; or \g.
Your MySQL connection id is 8 to server version: 3.23.51

Type 'help;' or '\h' for help. Type '\c' to clear the buffer

mysql> create database PictureArchive;
Query OK, 1 row affected (0.02 sec)
```

In PostgreSQL, you can use the command-line tool createdb (which you must run as the pgsql user) to open up the new database, as shown here:

```
# su -l pgsql
$ createdb PictureArchive
CREATE DATABASE
```

Designing Tables

Before you begin creating the tables for your database, it's best to come up with a conceptual diagram for how your data will be organized and how the relations will be mapped. This is typically done with an Entity-Relationship (E-R) diagram. A sample E-R diagram is shown in Figure 28.3.

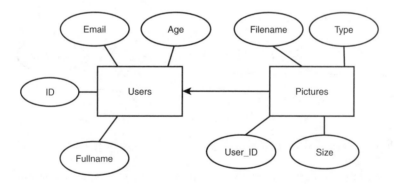

FIGURE 28.3   Sample E-R diagram showing a simple relation between two tables, Users and Pictures.

In this diagram, two sample tables (Users and Pictures) are denoted by rectangles, and their component attributes (columns) are shown as ellipses. Relations between tables are shown with arrows, their shape and direction chosen by convention to indicate the type of relationship. Because the User_ID column in Pictures refers explicitly to the ID field in Users, we can use an arrow directly from the Pictures table to the Users table, showing that it's a "many-to-one" relationship. Arrows in E-R diagrams point toward the "one" side of such a relationship; in a "one-to-many" relationship, the arrow would point from Users to Pictures. In a "one-to-one" relationship, such as one where a second table has one entry per user, a double-headed arrow would be used.

In more complex data sets, you will want to use tables that represent relations between other tables, possibly with the addition of further data fields. Let's say you want to add a table to PictureArchive that describes a set of layout profiles for the Web site (so that each user can select the way the site appears for himself). This new table, called Prefs, would have fields such as Background_color, Text_color, a Boolean value describing whether or not to display the user's e-mail address, and an integer ID. This table must be related to each user somehow, but the Prefs table doesn't have a field that refers to a specific user (like Pictures does), because each entry in Prefs should be assignable to any number of different users. You don't want to add another field to Users to specify the Prefs ID for each user. Therefore, the solution is to create a new table, called User_Prefs, that contains the "many-to-one" relationship between Users and Prefs. The E-R diagram for this is shown in Figure 28.4.

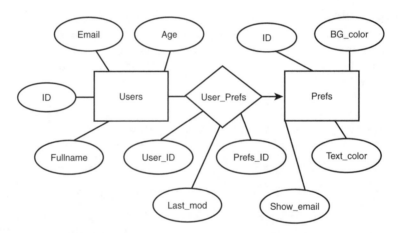

FIGURE 28.4   Sample E-R diagram showing data entities and relationship sets.

The User_Prefs table is represented with a diamond, because it is just a relationship set, rather than a table of data in its own right. It contains just three columns: User_ID, Prefs_ID, and a third column called Last_mod, which stores the date (in Unix time, an integer) when the user last updated his preferences.

This way, each time a user updates his preferences (through some mechanism in the Web site that you create, as you'll learn later), the update process simply creates a new entry in the User_Prefs table rather than an existing entry having to be updated. The insertion of the new entry could be accomplished with a query like the following, executed (for instance) by a CGI script:

```
INSERT INTO User_Prefs (User_ID,Prefs_ID,Last_mod)
VALUES ("5","3","1030745048");
```

Then, when the user views his page, your code can query the database for the most recent entry in User_Prefs for this user, find the Prefs_ID, and query for the attributes of that Prefs entry in order to generate the page according to those attributes. Here is an example of those queries:

```
SELECT Prefs_ID FROM User_Prefs
WHERE User_ID="5"
ORDER BY Last_mod DESC LIMIT 1;

... [ Extract the value of Prefs_ID into $prefs_id, as we will see later ]

SELECT Background_color,Text_color,Show_email FROM Prefs
WHERE ID="$prefs_id";
```

Alternatively, if you're even more adventurous, you can combine these into a single query with a join:

```
SELECT Background_color,Text_color,Show_email FROM User_Prefs,Prefs
WHERE User_Prefs.User_ID="5"
AND User_Prefs.Prefs_ID=Prefs.ID
ORDER BY Last_mod DESC LIMIT 1;
```

You can even do a three-way join to get all of a user's information out of the Users table as well as his latest entry in Prefs, as shown here:

```
SELECT Fullname,Email,Age,Background_color,Text_color,Show_email
FROM User_Prefs,Users,Prefs
WHERE Users.ID="5"
AND User_Prefs.User_ID=Users.ID
AND User_Prefs.Prefs_ID=Prefs.ID
ORDER BY Last_mod DESC LIMIT 1;
```

Planning out the structure of your tables in this way, before you even begin creating them, will save you a lot of heartache later on when you might otherwise have had to redesign everything from inside a running system.

Creating Tables

Now that you have a working design in mind for your database, you can begin creating tables. This is done with the CREATE TABLE query command. The syntax for this command is fairly simple, but it does require the knowledge of what kinds of data types are available. The most common of these are shown in Table 28.1, although more types are available as well and are fully documented at the MySQL and PostgreSQL Web sites.

28

TABLE 28.1   Commonly Used Column Data Types

Type Name	Description
INT, INTEGER	A "signed" integer from –2147483648 to 2147483647. This type can have the UNSIGNED attribute.
FLOAT	A floating-point number.
CHAR(*n*)	A string of *n* reserved bytes, up to *n*=255.
VARCHAR(*n*)	Like CHAR, except only as much space as is required to store the string is consumed. This type is preferable to CHAR. You can specify BINARY to make string comparisons case sensitive.
BLOB	A binary large object, holding text or binary data (such as images), with variable storage (like VARCHAR). The maximum size is 65KB. There are also TINYBLOB (256 bytes), MEDIUMBLOB (16.7MB), and LONGBLOB (4.3GB).
TEXT	Same as BLOB, except that string comparisons are case insensitive. There are also TINYTEXT, MEDIUMTEXT, and LONGTEXT.
ENUM	A set of permissible strings (for example, "Red","Green","Yellow").
BOOLEAN	"True" or "False". Not supported by MySQL.

Let's create the tables discussed already in the PictureArchive example. The Users table needs to have an integer ID field, text strings for the Fullname and Email fields, and another integer for Age. The following code creates that table:

```
CREATE TABLE Users (ID INT, Fullname VARCHAR(64), Email VARCHAR(32), Age INT);
```

The Prefs table will have an integer ID, six-character text fields for the two color fields (which you will populate with hex values), and an ENUM for Show_email (because MySQL doesn't have BOOLEAN). This code creates that table:

```
CREATE TABLE Prefs
(ID INT, Background_color VARCHAR(6),
Text_color VARCHAR(6), Show_email ENUM("Y","N"));
```

After entering the CREATE TABLE commands, issue a DESCRIBE Users command to view your handiwork, as shown here:

```
mysql> DESCRIBE Users;
+----------+-------------+------+-----+---------+-------+
| Field    | Type        | Null | Key | Default | Extra |
+----------+-------------+------+-----+---------+-------+
| ID       | int(11)     | YES  |     | NULL    |       |
| Fullname | varchar(64) | YES  |     | NULL    |       |
| Email    | varchar(32) | YES  |     | NULL    |       |
| Age      | int(11)     | YES  |     | NULL    |       |
+----------+-------------+------+-----+---------+-------+
4 rows in set (0.00 sec)
```

After some data has been entered into a table, the output from any queries you make at the command line will be returned in a tabular format, along with the time it took to process the query. If the columns are too wide for your screen, they will wrap rather than truncate; this can lead to a confused-looking display. Being selective in which fields you query for will help keep the output readable.

The following example shows a couple multiline INSERT queries that populate the Users table, followed by the tabular output from a judiciously restricted SELECT query:

```
mysql> INSERT INTO Users (ID,Fullname,Email,Age)
    -> VALUES (1,"Joe Smith","jsmith@somewhere.com",22);
mysql> INSERT INTO Users (ID,Fullname,Email,Age)
    -> VALUES (2,"Alice Walker","awalker@elsewhere.com",31);
mysql> SELECT ID,Fullname,Email,Age FROM Users;
+----+--------------+-----------------------+------+
| ID | Fullname     | Email                 | Age  |
+----+--------------+-----------------------+------+
|  1 | Joe Smith    | jsmith@somewhere.com  |  22  |
|  2 | Alice Walker | awalker@elsewhere.com |  31  |
+----+--------------+-----------------------+------+
2 rows in set (0.00 sec)
```

Indexes and Keys

You now have working tables that can be used in active queries. Setting up a complete database is not quite that simple, however. One other thing to consider when designing your tables is how they will be *indexed*. Indexing determines the ordering of data within a database and is what allows databases to be as fast as they are. Think about looking up a word in the dictionary; if you were looking for the word *sleep*, but you didn't know what "alphabetical order" was, you could literally spend weeks searching linearly through the dictionary until you found it. But because you know where the letter *S* is in the alphabet, you know how to zero in directly on the word and find it very rapidly.

Computers are the same way. If they have no indexing scheme by which to look up a piece of data, they can only search linearly through the data store for it—although they can do it faster than we can, it's still an unacceptably slow solution in most high-performance database contexts. Therefore, we have to create appropriate indexes (which for computers are similar to our concept of alphabetical order) and keys (such as the first letter of *sleep*) to help the database find its way through the data.

All tables of entity data (those that would be depicted with rectangles in an E-R diagram) should have a *primary key*. This is a column specifically designated to be the value upon which the data in the table should be automatically indexed. Values in this column should be specified as NOT NULL (in other words, they can't have a NULL value—a blank input value will become 0 for numeric data types and an empty string for text types). All values in the primary key column must also be unique.

This sounds like a role tailor-made for the integer ID columns in our tables. Indeed, the best practices in creating tables often call for the first column in every table to be a numeric ID that's the primary key and that also has the AUTO_INCREMENT attribute specified. This makes the column behave in a special way: If you insert rows into a table with an AUTO_INCREMENT column (which must also be a primary key), you can simply leave the value for that column blank or NULL, and the database will automatically fill in the next unused integer (the highest number in the column plus one) for each new row. This is perfect for the purposes of this chapter; you'll get a new unique ID number for each entry you put into your tables, and you don't even have to calculate it yourself.

Normally, you would specify these attributes at table-creation time:

```
CREATE TABLE Users (ID INT NOT NULL PRIMARY KEY AUTO_INCREMENT,
Fullname VARCHAR(64), Email VARCHAR(32), Age INT);
```

However, because in this case your tables are already created, you can use the ALTER TABLE command to change the ID column to your taste:

```
ALTER TABLE Users CHANGE ID ID INT NOT NULL PRIMARY KEY AUTO_INCREMENT;
```

> **NOTE**
>
> PostgreSQL does not have AUTO_INCREMENT; instead, it has a special data type called SERIAL. The SERIAL data type is not subject to the same keying restrictions as AUTO_INCREMENT, but it acts much the same. Use SERIAL instead of INT to create an autoincrementing ID field.
>
> Note that in PostgreSQL, if you specify NULL (instead of 0) for the ID field in an INSERT operation, NULL will be entered instead of the next available integer, which you would get if you simply didn't provide a value for that field. NULL trumps the SERIAL property in PostgreSQL. MySQL's AUTO_INCREMENT, by contrast, is invoked on any NULL or 0 entry into such a field.

You can specify other keys on other columns in the table by using the KEY attribute after the variable name at table-creation time or by using the ALTER TABLE command. Issuing this command creates an index on each key you specify. You can also create indexes based on multiple columns. This approach is useful when the unique combination of two columns taken together is what's usefully unique in a table. You can create indexes based on multiple columns like so:

```
ALTER TABLE Users ADD INDEX (Email,Fullname);
```

This code will result in a MUL tag (for "multiple," meaning that the table has multiple indexes) appearing in the Key column of the output of describe Users.

It's very important to try to anticipate which tables will be accessed a lot and which will have a large amount of data. Indexing these tables properly, with the keys being the columns on which those tables will most frequently be searched, can cause unbelievably dramatic improvements in performance.

Maintaining Security

Accessing your databases as root isn't really an especially good idea. You will likely want to enable other users—regular users—to access certain databases on your system; this is especially true when you connect the database to the Web. Each database has access privileges that can be given to individual users at different hosts, and a properly set up database system has those privileges doled out completely but carefully.

Let's say your PictureArchive database needs to be accessible by the user frank on the local system. frank needs to have the ability to create tables, add data to them, select and delete data from them, update them, and drop them. (The ability to create and drop tables is necessary in order for him to handle temporary tables.) You can grant frank these privileges with the GRANT command in MySQL:

```
GRANT CREATE,SELECT,INSERT,UPDATE,DELETE,DROP ON PictureArchive.*
TO frank@localhost IDENTIFIED BY '<password>' WITH GRANT OPTION;
```

If you want to be more lenient, you can use GRANT ALL PRIVILEGES instead of explicitly listing the privileges to grant. You can also grant privileges on specific tables within PictureArchive (by entering the name of those tables instead of the asterisk, which means "all tables"), or you can grant them on all tables on all databases by entering *.* in place of **PictureArchive.***. Replace <password> with the password frank wishes to use; putting it in single quotes as an argument to IDENTIFIED BY will hash the password and put it into the system in an encrypted format. Finally, the optional WITH GRANT OPTION gives frank the ability to grant privileges to other users himself.

The analogous functionality in PostgreSQL is the createuser tool, which provides the same options in an interactive fashion at the regular system command line, as shown here:

```
# su -l pgsql
$ createuser -P
Enter name of user to add: frank
Enter password for user "frank":
Enter it again:
Shall the new user be allowed to create databases? (y/n) y
Shall the new user be allowed to create more new users? (y/n) y
CREATE USER
```

To provide user-level security on the databases, you may wish to edit /usr/local/pgsql/pg_hba.conf and uncomment the following sample lines (and comment out the current active configuration lines):

```
# TYPE      DATABASE    IP_ADDRESS    MASK          AUTH_TYPE  AUTH_ARGUMENT
local       sameuser                                md5
local       all                                     md5  admins
```

28

If you wish, you can create a file called `admins` in `/usr/local/pgsql/data`, with one database username per line; only those users will be allowed to work with the databases. You can do the same with each new database you create—simply add a different file for each database, with the name of the user who owns it, and the name of the file in place of `admins` in this example.

Alternatively, you can enforce a policy whereby local users can connect, without passwords, only to their own databases (those that have names that match the usernames). For instance, the user `frank` would have a database called "frank." This can be done with the following configuration line:

```
local     all                                             ident    sameuser
```

Writing Administration Scripts

You've reached the next level in our breakneck tour through the world of databases; now that the tables in the sample databases are set up, you can now move on past the use of the interactive command line and learn how to automate some of the longer, more painful queries. The MySQL or PostgreSQL command line will always be useful for design and tinkering purposes. However, some tasks that must be done on a regular basis and require long, involved queries demand that you find a less frustrating way to accomplish them.

Perl and Python both provide toolkits with which you can write scripts to interface with the database. These toolkits enable you to issue queries, extract data, process it, and feed data back into the system, all within loops and conditionals and all the other programmatic benefits that those languages offer.

Database Connectivity with Perl

As a courtesy, the necessary Perl modules for connectivity to MySQL are installed along with the MySQL port. These also are located in `/usr/ports/databases/p5-Mysql`; the documentation can be read with `perldoc Mysql`.

The crucial part of these modules is the setup part of any script that intends to connect to a MySQL database. This setup block includes the following lines, which should go right at the top of the script:

```
use Mysql;
$dbh = Mysql->connect(undef, "PicureArchive", "frank", "<frank's password>");
```

After you add these lines to the script, you have a database handle to work with: `$dbh`. A whole suite of operations can be performed on this handle; this chapter doesn't discuss all of them—just the most important operations. You will find the rest in the `perldoc Mysql` documentation.

Issue a query of any type to the database by using the $dbh->query method and setting it to a variable that acts as a handle to the results:

```
$queryh = $dbh->query("SELECT Filename,Type FROM Pictures WHERE User_ID='5'");
```

You can now use the fetchrow method to get the first row of the output. The way this works, you can keep calling fetchrow over and over (in a loop) until there is no more output; this is how you can apply the same Perl code to each line of output from the database, in whatever order your SQL query specifies:

```
while (@picdata = $queryh->fetchrow) {
  print "$picdata[0], $picdata[1]\n";
}
```

Here is a list of other operators that may be useful:

- **$dbh->quote**—Surround a variable with this operator to quote its contents properly in a query; for example, to ensure that a full name such as "Bob O'Shea" will be properly inserted without the apostrophe causing confusion in the query string, use $dbh->query("INSERT INTO Users (Fullname) VALUES (".$dbh->quote ($fullname).")");.

- **$queryh->numrows**—This will return the number of rows that the query in $queryh will return.

- **$queryh->insertid**—If your query was an INSERT and the table had an AUTO_ INCREMENT column that generated a new ID, this function will return that ID so you can use it for future queries.

To connect to PostgreSQL in Perl, you will need to install the /usr/ports/databases/ p5-Pg port. This module provides much the same functionality as the p5-Mysql module does; you can set up a database connection with the following commands:

```
use Pg;

$conn = Pg::setdbLogin(undef,undef,undef,undef,"PictureArchive",
➥"frank","<frank's password>")
```

Next, submit a query with the $conn->exec method:

```
$result = $conn->exec("SELECT Filename,Type FROM Pictures WHERE User_ID='5'");
```

Then use $result->fetchrow as in the MySQL example you saw previously in this chapter. All the possibilities for the $result handle can be found in the perldoc Pg documentation, in the section titled "2. Result."

28

> **NOTE**
>
> For both these connectivity packages, the examples describe queries being executed in *autocommit mode*, meaning that each query is sent to the database as soon as it is formulated (using `$dbh->query` or `$conn->exec`), and results are immediately available to `fetchrow` commands. Each package contains analogous commands that can be used to operate in a mode where queries are not automatically committed. This approach is often very useful for operations that must be *atomic* (that is, treated as a single instruction that cannot be interrupted by other processes that can potentially change the state of the database between the start and end of the operation). Atomic operations are considered much safer than nonatomic ones, and it's good database coding practice to use them wherever possible. Refer to the `perldoc` documentation for each package for details.

Database Connectivity with Python

Python's connectivity is built upon the Python Database API Specification 2.0. Apart from the details of the setup lines and how the connection itself is set up, the command syntax for accessing MySQL and PostgreSQL databases is exactly the same. First, build and install either the `py-MySQLdb` or the `py-pyPgSQL` ports, both in `/usr/ports/databases`, depending on which database you are using.

To set up a connection to a MySQL database, use the following initialization lines:

```
import MySQLdb
db = MySQLdb.connect(database="PictureArchive");
```

If you're using PostgreSQL, the setup lines will look like this:

```
from pyPgSQL import PgSQL
db = PgSQL.connect(database="PictureArchive");
```

The preceding lines set up the connection to the database. Next, you can create a *cursor*, or statement handle, with the `db.cursor()` operator:

```
cur = db.cursor ()
```

Now you can begin issuing queries. Python's database API defaults to non-autocommit mode, so you can issue as many queries as you like before committing them, as shown here:

```
cur.execute ("INSERT INTO Users (Fullname,Age) VALUES ('Joe Smith','22')")
cur.execute ("INSERT INTO Users (Fullname,Age) VALUES ('Alice Walker','31')")
db.commit()
```

Perhaps the easiest way to handle multirow responses from queries is to use the `fetchall` command, which will retrieve all result rows into a multidimensional array. The following lines show how to use this command:

```
cur.execute ("SELECT * FROM Users")
r = cur.fetchall()
r
[[Joe Smith, 22], [Alice Walker, 31]]
```

As with the Perl modules for database connectivity, a great many more operations can be done through these interfaces. Refer to the Python Database API Specification 2.0 site (`http://www.python.org/topics/database/DatabaseAPI-2.0.html`) for full documentation of these features.

A Perl Script to Populate a Database

In this section, we will look at a simple script written in Perl. This script interfaces with a MySQL database. Its purpose is to read in a set of text files in a directory, each of which contains the information for a particular user in a system. The script will parse each file, which is of the following form:

```
User's full name
User's e-mail address
User's age
```

It will then insert each user into the Users table in the database, using the `AUTO_INCREMENT` column to create unique ID numbers for each user, and finally will return the number of rows that are in the table after all the operations have completed. The script is shown in Listing 28.1 and is included on the CD as `populateUsers.pl`.

LISTING 28.1   `populateUsers.pl`—A Perl Script for Populating the Users Table of a Database

```perl
#!/usr/bin/perl

use Mysql;

$filepath = "/usr/local/www/data/users";
$dbh = Mysql->connect(undef, "PictureArchive","fred","<fred's password>");

opendir (DIR, "$filepath");
@userfiles = sort readdir (DIR);
closedir (DIR);

foreach $file (@userfiles) {
  open (USER,"$filepath/$file");
```

28

LISTING 28.1   Continued

```
  @userdata = <USER>;
  chomp ($_) foreach (@userdata);
  close (USER);
  $inserth = $dbh->query("INSERT INTO Users (Fullname,Email,Age) VALUES
➡('$userdata[0]','$userdata[1]','$userdata[2]')");
  $num++;
}
$counth = $dbh->query("SELECT ID FROM Users");
$count = $counth->numrows;
print "There are $count users in the table, $num of which are newly added.\n\n";
```

Connecting a Database to the Web

Nothing we have discussed so far in this chapter is exclusively related to the Web. The databases you have set up can be used by local users of the system, administered by automated scripts, and even accessed remotely by database clients on other machines if configured to do so. But most databases these days are being set up so that their content can be accessed by Web browsers. Fortunately, because you have now learned all the fundamental concepts necessary for understanding Web database connectivity, making that next step should be a breeze.

Using Perl and CGI to Access Database Content

As we discussed in Chapter 20, "Introduction to Perl Programming," and Chapter 25, "Configuring a Web Server," the Common Gateway Interface (CGI) is a standardized API by which data (stored in variables) is passed from Web forms into back-end programs that process it and return it to the Web server. Any Perl script can be made into a working CGI program simply by making sure of the following:

- Its permissions are set correctly.

- It's in a location accessible by the Web server.

- It prints out the appropriate HTTP headers before it outputs content.

The same goes for programs written in Python, C, or any other language. For the purposes of the following discussion, we'll use Perl.

You have already seen how to create a Perl script that interfaces with a MySQL or PostgreSQL back end. And, you've seen (in Chapter 25) how to create a Perl script that can handle data submitted through a Web form. Creating a script that does both of these things is a simple matter of merging the functionality of the two kinds of scripts. The sections that follow explain how to accomplish this merger.

Inserting Data into the Database

Let's say you have a Web form that takes a user's information (the same fields that you saw earlier in the Users table) and passes this information to a CGI program that then inserts the information fields into the database. To accomplish this, you simply have to make sure the script is set up to handle form input as well as database connections. Here's how to do that:

```perl
#!/usr/bin/perl

use Mysql;

$dbh = Mysql->connect(undef, "PictureArchive","fred","<fred's password>");

read(STDIN, $buffer, $ENV{'CONTENT_LENGTH'});
@pairs = split(/&/, $buffer);
foreach $pair (@pairs)
{
    ($name, $value) = split(/=/, $pair);
    $value =~ tr/+/ /;
    $value =~ s/%([a-fA-F0-9][a-fA-F0-9])/pack("C", hex($1))/eg;
    $value =~ s/~!/ ~!/g;
    $FORM{$name} = $value;
}

print "Content-type: text/html\n\n";
```

Now, when someone accesses the Web form page (which refers to this script in the ACTION field of the <FORM> tag, as you saw in Chapter 25), the variables from that form's fields are available to you in the %FORM array.

The code in this block performs several operations on the form input to prevent the user from inserting malicious HTML code instead of legitimate names and ages. However, when dealing with databases, there is an additional caveat: You must ensure that the data submitted by the user is compatible with the functions that insert it into the database as well as with the database itself. This is where the $dbh->quote function comes into play.

In a loop similar to the one in Listing 28.1, you can quote the input strings in the following way:

```perl
$inserth = $dbh->query("INSERT INTO Users (Fullname,Email,Age) VALUES
➡(".$dbh->quote($FORM{'fullname'})."," .$dbh->quote($FORM{'e-mail'})."," 
➡".$dbh->quote($FORM{'age'}).")");
```

The $dbh->quote function will properly escape all quotation marks, apostrophes, and other special characters to ensure they don't interfere with the text, as entered by the user,

28

being inserted into the database without being truncated or translated—or even causing the script to fail (which would have happened if someone had entered a string with double quotes in it!).

Similar failures may occur if a user attempts to input data that's incompatible with the type of column it's supposed to go into. For instance, if Age is defined as an INT column, and a user enters "I'm not telling!" for his age, a value of zero will be entered; similarly, if a VARCHAR field is only 10 characters long, and the user enters a string longer than that, the string will be truncated upon insertion into the database. Still other conditions can cause the query operation to fail completely, returning an error, and the entire script will crash.

For this reason, it's important to implement your own consistency-checking code in your script before the data gets to the database. For instance, you can ensure that data going into an INT column is a nonzero integer by putting it into a conditional loop, as shown here:

```
if (int($FORM{'age'}) {
  $updh = $dbh->query("UPDATE Users SET Age='$FORM{age}' where id='$userid'");
} else {
  print "Error!";
}
```

> **CAUTION**
>
> Be aware that using single quotes around field names in associative array elements, such as $FORM{'age'}, won't work in this kind of query (where the entire query string is double quoted and the field contents are single quoted). Perl lets you get away with leaving out the single quotes within the variable, as shown here, but this can be an invitation to trouble. It may be safer for you to reassign the contents of $FORM{'age'} to another variable (for instance, $age) before using it in the query.

Another safeguard is to use the MAXLENGTH attribute in your HTML form input fields. For instance, if the length of a VARCHAR column is 64 bytes, you can use the following HTML code for the corresponding form input field:

```
<INPUT NAME="fullname" MAXLENGTH="64">
```

This will prevent the user from entering any more than 64 characters, and you won't have to worry about the input data getting truncated when it's inserted.

Good coding practices dictate that error-trapping should be done as close as possible to the user. With Web-to-database programming, you're dealing with three different layers of code separating the user from the data store: the front end (HTML and JavaScript), the CGI layer (Perl, Python, or C), and the back end (the database APIs and the built-in table-consistency safeguards). The best-designed Web applications have as much error-checking implemented in HTML and JavaScript as possible; then the CGI programming layer is used to catch more esoteric cases. Ideally, the database itself should never be exposed to input errors that fall through from those upper layers.

Creating a Search Form

Now that you know how to insert data into the database from a Web form, you're ready to implement something a little more generally useful: a search form. A single HTML input field ($FORM{'keywords'}) can take an arbitrary set of words, separated by spaces. Then the Perl code underlying it will divide that string into its component words and search the database for matches against each one. If more than one word matches a certain entry, you want to get a better "score" for that entry and sort the results according to that score. Even better, you want to add weight to an entry that matches *all* the keywords in order. Here are the basic steps for creating the back-end code to handle this type of search form:

1. Check to make sure there is something in the input field. Then, create a *temporary table*, which is a table that exists only for the duration of this program and is dropped at the end of the $dbh session. (This table, called Queries, will hold all the queries—wildcards and all—you plan to execute.)

2. Split the contents of the input field into the @querywords array.

3. Create $comboquery, which is going to be a string of all the keywords separated by the % wildcard; this will be the query term that should match entries with all the keywords, in order. If you search for this term as well as for all the keywords individually, its score should reflect all the matches of the individual words, plus that of its combined match. Therefore, it should be your topmost result. Add a final % to it and then push it onto the @querywords array.

4. Go through each keyword and create a variable with that word surrounded by % wildcards and quote it to protect your database. Then, insert it into the temporary Queries database.

You now have a table full of queries ready to perform.

The following examples show how these steps are executed in Perl. We begin with the form-handling preamble discussed earlier; after that, the steps you have just seen are pointed out in comments in the code.

```perl
#!/usr/bin/perl

use Mysql;

$dbh = Mysql->connect(undef, "PictureArchive","fred","<fred's password>");
```

28

```
read(STDIN, $buffer, $ENV{'CONTENT_LENGTH'});
@pairs = split(/&/, $buffer);
foreach $pair (@pairs)
{
    ($name, $value) = split(/=/, $pair);
    $value =~ tr/+/ /;
    $value =~ s/%([a-fA-F0-9][a-fA-F0-9])/pack("C", hex($1))/eg;
    $value =~ s/~!/ ~!/g;
    $FORM{$name} = $value;
}

print "Content-type: text/html\n\n";

# Here begins the handling of the form input.
if ($FORM{'keywords'}) {                              # Step 1

  $sth = $dbh->query("CREATE TEMPORARY TABLE Queries (Query VARCHAR(255))");
  @querywords = split(/\s/,$FORM{'keywords'});        # Step 2
  $comboquery = $FORM{'keywords'};                    # Step 3
  $comboquery =~ s/\s+/%/g;
  push (@querywords,$comboquery);
  foreach (@querywords) {                             # Step 4
    $_ = $dbh->quote('%'.$_.'%');
    $sth = $dbh->query("insert into Queries (Query) VALUES ($_)");
  }
```

Now, you can execute the query. Here, you're searching filenames in Pictures, and a unique picture is defined by both User_ID and Filename, so we'll group by both of those. The COUNT() of the results you'll call Score, and you'll sort by that column in descending order:

```
  $searchh = $dbh->query("SELECT Filename,User_ID,COUNT(Filename) AS Score
➥FROM Pictures WHERE Filename LIKE Query GROUP BY Filename,User_ID
➥ORDER BY Score DESC");
```

Finally, you can assign the contents of each result row to an array and print out some appropriate HTML code, which you can season to your taste:

```
  while (@searchdata = $searchh->fetchrow) {
    print "$searchdata[0] (Score: $searchdata[2])<BR>\n"
  }
}
```

Needless to say, a more sophisticated searching algorithm can certainly be constructed, and it can be even easier to design a more efficient one. MySQL has a concept called *full-text indexes*, and you can define a TEXT field to have a FULLTEXT index, and then you can perform specialized searches on that column with great speed and efficiency. Refer to the MySQL documentation (http://www.mysql.com/doc/en/Fulltext_Search.html) for details on how this is done.

> **NOTE**
>
> Note that FULLTEXT searches will not work on keywords smaller than four letters; because the indexing code is tuned to work best on very large data sets, searches on small data sets will produce very weird results.

Session Locking and Data Integrity

If your Web application has a lot of users accessing it at the same time, it's important to code your application's database operations to be as atomic as possible. As we discussed earlier, an atomic operation is one in which all commands and responses are executed in a single instruction so that no competing processes can interfere and potentially cause a change in the state of the database while your operation is executing.

MySQL and PostgreSQL both support the concept of *transactions*, where instead of issuing queries in autocommit mode (where commands are sent to the database engine as soon as they're entered, and the response data is immediately returned), you can create an atomic operation by using the BEGIN and COMMIT commands as well as any number of query operations in between. The use of these commands in a transaction is shown here:

```
BEGIN;
SELECT * FROM Users;
UPDATE User_Prefs SET Last_mod='$now' WHERE Last_mod > '$now';
COMMIT;
```

The queries are not executed until the COMMIT command is given, and while the queries are operating, the tables in use are locked. When locked, the tables cannot be accessed by any other processes, which have to wait until this process is completed.

In order to use such transactions in MySQL, you must begin the session with the following command:

```
SET AUTOCOMMIT=0;
```

PostgreSQL will automatically drop out of autocommit mode at the first BEGIN statement. Also, if you use the Perl or Python modules to connect to PostgreSQL, it will be in non-autocommit mode automatically. In fact, you can choose to use the BEGIN and COMMIT methods in the query context or through the dedicated database API commands, which do the same thing. In MySQL, transactions are a much newer addition to the engine and are most easily executed directly as SQL query commands.

The ROLLBACK command can be used instead of a COMMIT to cancel any queries that have been issued since the BEGIN command. If, for instance, you're working at the database command line and you mistakenly issue a DELETE FROM User command, as long as you started with a BEGIN statement you can enter **ROLLBACK** and the deletion will be reversed. Needless to say, using the BEGIN command is a desirable (if somewhat onerous) habit to develop!

CAUTION

If you're using transactions, don't forget to use COMMIT after you've made your (intentional) changes! It's an easy step to leave out of your code, but if you do, it won't necessarily be obvious in debugging.

Security Concerns

CGI programs that connect to database back ends (particularly MySQL, which is entirely password based) have one big security weakness: The password for connecting to the database must be hard-coded into the script or read in from another file. However you choose to implement this, if the Web server is running as the nobody user, it will execute the CGI program under the ownership of nobody; any file that contains the password must be readable by the nobody user.

If you put the password in a file that's readable only by root, the CGI program won't be able to get access to it. However, if you leave it hard-coded into a file that the nobody user can read, anyone on your system can write his own CGI program that can read that same file and print it out for all to see—or use it to connect to your database and issue a few DROP DATABASE commands. This is an inherent flaw in database security as it currently exists in the Unix world, and there's no elegant solution to it.

The easiest workaround is to disallow regular users from running CGI scripts. You may also be able to come up with creative solutions using CGIwrap (which is covered in Chapter 29, "Network Security"). But what it ultimately comes down to is a question of what kind of security level you want to enforce. *Do you trust your local users?* If so, you can probably get away with living dangerously. But if you don't trust the users with accounts on your system not to try to hack the database access password out of your scripts, you probably shouldn't be running a database with sensitive or critical data on that same server.

However, if you're running PostgreSQL, you can implement security that does not depend on passwords. The configuration we discussed earlier using ident and sameuser will only allow a user to access his own database; it doesn't allow the user to access any other databases. This type of configuration helps to prevent local users from breaking into databases where they don't belong—and you don't have to worry about your password being exposed by a malicious CGI program.

Using PHP to Provide Database-Driven Content to Web Pages

You may be wondering whether writing your own Web applications from scratch is the only way to include database-driven content in your dynamic pages, or if there's a better and cleaner way, such as using Microsoft's ASP or Macromedia's ColdFusion. The answer is yes, there is. It's called PHP, which originally stood for "Personal Home Page" but now is itself the official name of an open-source HTML preprocessing framework that has become very widely used throughout the Unix Web-hosting world. PHP's official Web site is www.php.net.

PHP consists of commands that can be embedded into HTML, and they are parsed out in much the same way that server-side includes are parsed in .shtml files, as you saw in Chapter 25. A PHP file has the extension .php, .php3, or .php4, and Apache is reconfig-ured at installation time to recognize those files and pass them through the PHP module before serving their content to the user.

This chapter's discussion of PHP will be brief, but it should be enough to get you started. If you've already become familiar with the more difficult concepts presented by database design, SQL, and Perl/Python connectivity, then PHP in this series of conceptual phases should be like dessert after a long meal.

Installing PHP

The PHP project is maintained and driven forward by the Apache Software Foundation, which means PHP and Apache are very closely intertwined in their operation. PHP is installed as an Apache module, mod_php4, which links to libraries that harness the Zend processing engine upon which PHP is based.

PHP can be installed from the ports or packages. The name of the package is mod_php4, and if you choose to install it from the ports, it's located in /usr/ports/www. When you type **make**, you are presented with a list of options to compile into PHP. Select support for either MySQL, PostgreSQL, or both, depending on which database you're using. You can also choose to enable support for the GD imaging library, mcrypt encryption, OpenSSL, XML, and other add-ons. Unless you already know you have need for these, you can ignore these additional options.

> **NOTE**
>
> If you're running Apache 2.0, you will want to define the WITH_APACHE2 environment variable before typing **make**. See Chapter 11, "Customizing the Shell," for details on setting environment variables.

At the end of the installation process, the automated installer script will modify your httpd.conf file to enable recognition of .php and .php4 files and assign them to the PHP handler. You may wish to examine the `httpd.conf` file after this and make sure nothing has been accidentally broken in the process.

Flow Control and Programming Techniques

The tag format for PHP commands is `<?php ... ?>`. A number of internal PHP commands can go between these two bookend tags; you can use `echo()` to print text, you can perform string operations on variables (including the HTTP connection variables, such as `HTTP_USER_AGENT`), and you can do flow control. For instance, the following `if` statement can be used to print different blocks of HTML code depending on the state of a variable:

```
<?php
if ($a > $b) {
?>
<B>A is greater than B.</B>
<?php
} else {
?>
<B>B is greater than or equal to A.</B>
<?php
}
?>
```

The syntax for naming and assigning variables is very like Perl. PHP includes such Perl-like control structures as `foreach`, `while`, and `do...while`, although the equivalent to Perl's `elsif` is `elseif`. There is also an array context, although the prefix for an array is `$`, as for a scalar. Also, as with Perl, PHP's variable types do not have to be declared by the programmer but are handled internally and derived from context. Lines of PHP code end with a semicolon (`;`).

Within a `<?php ... ?>` block, you can define variables and functions on as many lines as you want; you can almost pretend that it's a Perl program. Anything in a `<?php ... ?>` block will be parsed out of the HTML file it's embedded in and then replaced with the output from any functions you call. You can put PHP code blocks wherever you like throughout the file.

Interfacing with the Database

For the purposes of this chapter, what interests us is how to make PHP interact with MySQL and PostgreSQL. Fortunately, the methods for doing this are very similar to the Perl-based techniques we have already covered.

The initial MySQL database connection is set up using the `mysql_connect` and `mysql_select_db` functions, as follows:

```
$conn = mysql_connect("localhost", "frank", "<frank's password>");
mysql_select_db("PictureArchive");
```

For PostgreSQL, the database setup commands are as follows:

```
$conn = pg_connect("dbname=PictureArchive user=frank
➥password=<frank's password>");
```

A large number of connection options can be specified in the `mysql_connect` or `pg_connect` argument string, whether in the `parameter=value` format shown in the PostgreSQL example or the ordered list of values for the MySQL example (either format will work for either database). Because PostgreSQL depends to a certain extent on environment variables, you can set the defaults for many of these options by defining them in the environment for the Web server. Use Apache's `SetEnv` directive to set these in `httpd.conf` or a `.htaccess` file, as shown here:

```
PGHOST=localhost
PGPORT=7890
PGDATABASE=PictureArchive
PGUSER=frank
PGPASSWORD=<frank's password>
```

For MySQL, PHP has a number of functions, such as `mysql.default_user`, `mysql.default_password`, and `mysql.connect_timeout`, that can be set within the global PHP configuration file, `/usr/local/etc/php.ini`. Note that this file must be copied or renamed from `php.ini-dist` before it will be read.

Once your database connection is set up, you can then issue a query in much the same way as you have seen in earlier examples, using `mysql_query` or `pg_query` as follows (note that the two functions take the database connection identifier and the query in reverse order from each other):

```
<?php
$result = mysql_query("SELECT * FROM Users",$conn)
    or die("Invalid query");
?>
```

```
<?php
$result = pg_query($conn,"SELECT * FROM Users")
    or die("Invalid query");
?>
```

PHP operates in autocommit mode for both databases. As soon as you issue a `mysql_query` or `pg_query` command, the query is submitted, and you can then begin to work with the results in `$result`:

```
while($rowdata = mysql_fetch_row($result)) {
  print "$rowdata[0]: $rowdata[1]<BR>\n";
}
```

28

This syntax is very Perl like. If you look through the PHP documentation at
`http://www.php.net/manual/`, under the headings "MySQL Functions" and "PostgreSQL
Functions," you will find a large number of well-documented functions that operate very
similarly to the Perl database interfaces with which you are already familiar.

The biggest advantages of PHP over homegrown Perl or Python scripts are that because the
server-processed code is all embedded into plain HTML files, you can maintain the layout
of your pages with much more ease. You can edit the HTML in these same files without
the danger of breaking permissions or disabling the executable code. And because the files
are parsed internally by Apache, you will see a significant decrease in processing overhead,
because starting up individual CGI processes for each page view is a very expensive way
for a server to run.

Security Concerns

PHP potentially opens your system up to a large number of security weaknesses. PHP is
susceptible to many of the same exploits that threaten CGI programs, and it has a few
new areas of susceptibility of which you should be aware.

The files that include database connection passwords, whether the HTML/PHP files themselves or include files, are subject to access by local users writing CGI programs to access
the files' contents. To address this problem, you will need to take the same precautions
you would take with a Perl or Python connectivity setup (as explained earlier in this
chapter). Similarly, issues exist with virtual hosting and PHP files that are executed outside
the main server root in the users' `public_html` directories (if you choose to allow it; a
tightly secured server will run all PHP scripts from within the restricted `/cgi-bin` directory
and not allow regular users to run them). Because all PHP files are parsed and executed
with the same permissions and ownership, one user's actions can potentially affect other
users' database code or files. Again, you will want to review your security policy: How
much do you trust your local users?

Perfect security is a myth, and security and convenience are mutually exclusive. The more
lenient you are in allowing users access onto your system, the less safe you are from malicious activity by your own users. Fortunately, for the purposes of database connectivity,
the only sector from which to fear an attack is your local users, because most Web-enabled
database systems don't have their database back ends open to nonlocal connections.
However, those local users can cause a great deal of trouble if you've allowed them onto
the system.

Refer to the online PHP security documentation at `http://www.php.net/manual/en/`
`security.php` for a thorough discussion of the ways in which a PHP server can be attacked
and compromised.

Optimizing Database Performance

No matter how well you have designed your database schema, as your site becomes more and more popular and heavily used, it is likely that certain parts of its functionality will bog down. Perhaps you've forgotten an index in a certain crucial table. Perhaps you're doing a complex join where a series of temporary tables would be computationally cheaper. Or perhaps your dynamic pages are simply far too complex, and you need to create a cache of static information that's updated on a regular basis in order to speed up on-demand queries at the expense of instantaneous accuracy.

At the top-level view, it might seem impossible to figure out what's slowing things down; all you see might be a perpetually high load average in top. Fortunately, there are some ways to find out just what the database is doing in those queries. The following sections discuss these techniques.

Monitoring Database Usage

MySQL has a command called SHOW PROCESSLIST. Entered at the MySQL command line, this command will show you all the queries currently in progress:

```
mysql> SHOW PROCESSLIST;
+--------+-------+-----------+---------+---------+------+--------------------+-----------------------------------------------------------------------------+
| Id     | User  | Host      | db              | Command | Time | State
| Info
|
+--------+-------+-----------+---------+---------+------+--------------------+-----------------------------------------------------------------------------+
| 625441 | root  | localhost | PictureArchive | Query   | 0    | NULL
| show processlist
|
| 625443 | frank | localhost | PictureArchive | Query   | 0    | Copying to tmp
table | select name,dirname,id,count(*) from artists,pictures where
id=pictures.artistid and display='Y' gro |
| 625444 | frank | localhost | PictureArchive | Sleep   | 1    |
| NULL
|
+--------+-------+-----------+---------+---------+------+--------------------+-----------------------------------------------------------------------------+
3 rows in set (0.01 sec)
```

If you see dozens of processes listed in this output table, with a `Time` value in the hundreds (of seconds), then you know you have a problem—particularly if all the queries seem to be doing the same thing. If you can determine from the structure of the query where in your code it's being called from, you can look at the tables involved and make sure that the query is doing its joins on indexed columns and that the joins are sensibly constructed. You may also be able to redesign the code so that the query in question is called at a different time, when the CPU is not quite so busy with other queries.

The `EXPLAIN` command offers a more direct, if somewhat cryptic, way to drill down into your queries to see what's costing CPU cycles. This command, when placed in front of a `SELECT` statement, will display a table showing the tables involved in the query, the possible keys it will search on, the size of each table, and other information about how the query is being performed. You can check the table definitions to see whether all the possible keys are being indexed properly. If they aren't, you can index them using `ALTER TABLE` (as explained earlier in "Indexes and Keys").

The following examples use a more complex version of the same database you've seen in this chapter, including some tables that haven't been used before:

```
mysql> EXPLAIN SELECT NAME,DIRNAME,ID,COUNT(*) FROM Artists,Pictures WHERE ID=Pic-
tures.Artist_ID AND
Display='Y' GROUP BY Artist_ID ORDER BY Created DESC LIMIT 5;
+----------+-------+-------------------+-----------+---------+------------+------
+------------------------------------------+
| table    | type  | possible_keys     | key       | key_len | ref        | rows |
Extra
|
+----------+-------+-------------------+-----------+---------+---------+-
----------+------+----------------------
-----------------------+
| Artists  | range | PRIMARY,Display   | Display   |       2 |
NULL      | 1615 | where used; Using temporary; Using filesort |
| Pictures | ref   | PRIMARY,Artist_ID | Artist_ID |       4 | Artists.ID |   38 |
Using index
|
+----------+-------+-------------------+-----------+---------+------------+------
+------------------------------------------+
2 rows in set (0.18 sec)
```

`EXPLAIN` in PostgreSQL can be tuned toward helping you root out the expensive processes that cause slowdowns in your queries through explicit "cost" analysis. The following example shows the use of `EXPLAIN` in PostgreSQL:

```
PictureArchive=# EXPLAIN SELECT Artists.Name, Pictures.name FROM Artists
➥LEFT JOIN Pictures ON Artists.ID=Pictures.Artist_ID;
NOTICE:  QUERY PLAN:


Merge Join  (cost=823.39..1012.89 rows=10000 width=32)
  -> Index Scan using Artists_pkey on Artists  (cost=0.00..52.00 rows=1000
width=16)
    -> Sort  (cost=823.39..823.39 rows=10000 width=16)
        -> Seq Scan on Pictures  (cost=0.00..159.00 rows=10000 width=16)


EXPLAIN
```

Here, you see a join being performed between the Artists and Pictures tables, but there is no key in Pictures to help the database engine search for the elements upon which to perform the join. Costs of each operation are summed upward; as you work your way up the tree, you can see the overall cost of the query increasing. The sequential scan and sort operation at the bottom of the tree is causing a significant hit on system performance. If you had an index on the Artist_ID key in Pictures, the database wouldn't have to do a sequential scan and could instead do an index scan, which is much faster, as shown in this example:

```
PictureArchive=# CREATE INDEX Pictures_Artist_ID_key ON Pictures ( Artist_ID );
CREATE
PictureArchive=# EXPLAIN SELECT Artists.Name, Pictures.Name FROM Artists
➥LEFT JOIN Pictures ON Artists.ID=Pictures.Artist_ID;
NOTICE:  QUERY PLAN:


Merge Join  (cost=0.00..628.56 rows=10000 width=32)
  -> Index Scan using Artists_pkey on Artists  (cost=0.00..52.00 rows=1000
width=16)
  -> Index Scan using Pictures_Artist_ID_key on Pictures  (cost=0.00..439.06
rows=10000 width=16)


EXPLAIN
```

Here, the overall cost range is reduced from 823.39 through 1012.89 down to 0.00 through 628.56. (These units aren't very meaningful outside of the database context but can be compared internally very effectively.) It seems this maneuver has gained some very positive results.

Creating Temporary Tables

This may not seem obvious at first blush, but sometimes it's more efficient to create a temporary table than to do a complex join. Programmatically, it may appear that the most elegant solution to a problem is to accomplish the task in as few lines of code as possible—and in fact in traditional programming languages this is mostly true. But databases don't quite work that way.

If you find yourself joining three or four tables together in a single query, and you notice that the query takes an extremely long time to execute, consider for a moment what the database is being asked to do. It must align four separate (possibly very large) disparate groupings of data together, associating keys from each table with keys from another table. This process takes place in a conceptual matrix whose complexity rises by another degree with each table that's added to the mix. The multidimensional data structure that the database must hold in memory is enormous during this join, and searching through it becomes a monstrous task.

To avoid this problem, experiment with temporary tables. You can create a temporary table by simply preceding a SELECT statement with CREATE TEMPORARY TABLE <t_name>, where <t_name> is the name of the table; you can then select from this table (using the SELECT command) later in your session. Be sure to apply the appropriate indexes after the table is created. If you do this, a direct SELECT from the new table—even including the temporary table creation and indexing queries—might be orders of magnitude faster than a complex join that nonetheless you've managed to condense into a single query.

> **NOTE**
>
> Temporary tables only last until the end of the current database session; in the command-line context, temporary tables that you create will be there until you log out. In a Web scripting context, the tables are dropped when the database handle is destroyed—when you issue a disconnect command through the programmatic toolkits or when the script completes.
>
> Temporary table names exist in private namespaces, so multiple temporary tables with the same name can exist as long as they've been created by different database sessions.

Using Cache Tables

If your queries are large and complex but they just can't be made any faster or more efficient by indexing, you may have no other option than to go to a cache table. This is a table whose contents are nothing more than values that are refreshed on occasion from the results of much more complex queries. What you're doing, in effect, is creating a layer of indirection—a table from which users can get their information very quickly, with a direct and uncomplicated query, but whose contents might not be accurate until refreshed by a periodic process that performs the complex queries and inserts their results into the cache table.

This is one area where Perl scripts that are not CGI programs will come in handy. You can run a cron job that executes a Perl script every 10 minutes, for instance, that connects to the database and refreshes the cache by running the complex queries. The script can operate in an atomic fashion, by issuing a BEGIN statement, followed by the series of queries, and finally a COMMIT; this way, queries that will potentially change the data involved in the complex queries are deferred until the refresh is complete.

The system will be a little slower to respond while the refresh process is running, but in between—for 10 minutes at a stretch, or an hour, or however frequently you run your cron job—everything will be almost immeasurably faster.

Performing Database System Backups

Finally, we must address the issue of backups. It's a fact of life that hardware suffers failures, usually when least convenient or welcome. It's also a fact that running software written with the best of intentions can result in unintended consequences. Even the most seasoned veterans have war stories of times when they froze, stared dumbfounded at the screen, and then sank their heads into their hands, sobbing at the sight of an irretrievably dropped database.

MySQL and PostgreSQL don't have the "live" backup mechanisms that high-end commercial databases such as Oracle and DB2 do. (Many third-party backup software makers have applications that interact with the database, lock it piece by piece, and save backups to tape or across the network.) What they do have, however, is the ability to be locked and "dumped," like any properly designed database. The sections that follow look at a few of the tools that are necessary for creating usable backups.

Dumping the Database

MySQL has two methods for dumping its databases to disk: mysqldump and mysqlhotcopy. mysqldump is a command-line tool that locks the database, preventing any new connections, and then copies the structures of all tables, followed by the contents of all tables, into STDOUT or an output data file. This file, whose name typically ends in .sql, is a long list of SQL commands that, if run in sequence, will re-create the database structure and then repopulate all the data. The mysqldump program must be run as a user who has access to the database; it is usually safe to do this as root, but it's a good idea to specify the user who owns each database with the -u <user> or --user=<user> option. You can also specify the user's password with the -p <password> or --password=<password> option. Generally, you will want to do this as a cron job, with the mysqldump command inside the owner readable–only crontab file; but if you're concerned about local security, you can create a special "backup" user who has SELECT and LOCK TABLES access to all databases, but no other privileges. That way, if the user's password is intercepted, an attacker won't be able to do anything destructive.

The mysqldump command is executed like this:

```
mysqldump --user="frank" --password="<frank's password>" PictureArchive
➥> /usr/local/www/db/PictureArchive.sql
```

If you're running this as a cron job, you might want to precede this command with something such as mv /usr/local/www/db/PictureArchive.sql /usr/local/www/db/ PictureArchive.sql-old and then a semicolon. This will move the old dump file out of the way so the new dump file can be created. Then it will run the dump, all in one command.

If you want to quickly make a snapshot of the entire database directory without creating a dump file, you can use mysqlhotcopy. This is a Perl script that locks the tables and copies all their associated files into a new specified location; if your database becomes corrupted or lost, you can simply shut down MySQL, move the files into their appropriate locations under /var/db/mysql, and restart the server. To run mysqlhotcopy, do the following:

```
mysqlhotcopy --user="frank" --password="<frank's password>" PictureArchive
➥/usr/local/www/db/PictureArchive
```

As for PostgreSQL, the pgdump command is the equivalent of mysqlhotcopy. It is easiest to run pgdump as the pgsql user who owns the database; create pgsql's crontab file with crontab -u pgsql:

```
pgsql PictureArchive > /usr/local/www/db/PictureArchive.sql
```

Restoring the Database

Restoring from a .sql file output from mysqldump or pgdump is conceptually very simple. It's just a "replay" of SQL commands, which theoretically will re-create the entire database in every detail—first by rebuilding the tables and all their indexes and then by reinserting all the data.

To restore a MySQL database from a .sql file, you must first create the database (if it has been deleted or dropped) and then use the following command:

```
mysql -p PictureArchive < /usr/local/www/db/PictureArchive.sql
```

You will be prompted for your password. (Alternatively, you can specify the frank user with -u or --user=, and Frank's password with -p or --password=, as you saw earlier in this chapter.) After this is accepted, the .sql file will be read into the database, and through the use of SHOW TABLES and a few DESCRIBE <table> and SELECT queries, you should be able to verify that everything has been properly restored.

The process is almost exactly the same in PostgreSQL. First, use su to change to the pgsql user; then create the database (using createdb, as you saw earlier) if it doesn't already exist. Then start psql, reading in the .sql file:

```
psql < /usr/local/www/db/PictureArchive.sql
```

If all goes well, you should be back up and running.

Designing for Restorability

The backup/restore process isn't perfect, however. Because the tables and content are being re-created from a series of commands, and because those commands are automatically generated by the dump programs, it's conceivable that a configuration that you were able to set up manually cannot be re-created properly by the automated tools.

One potentially complicating factor, particularly in MySQL, is AUTO_INCREMENT. This special kind of INT column must be a primary key, UNIQUE, and NOT NULL by definition. Ideally you should never have to specify the values in an AUTO_INCREMENT column manually; you should end up with a different positive integer for every row in the table. However, you *can* go into the database and manually specify that an entry in the table should have a value of 0.

When MySQL attempts to re-create this table, it will insert this row while explicitly specifying a value of 0 for the AUTO_INCREMENT column. However, the value of 0, as you will recall, is treated as a special case and reassigned to the maximum value of the column plus one. Therefore, if you have code in your Web application that is hard-wired to treat this row a certain way because it has a unique ID of 0 (for example, if you have a table of preference settings containing a row of "defaults" that is identified by its special ID number of 0), it will not find that row there after the restore. As a result, your scripts will break; you'll have to examine the tables and reassign the value manually.

Of course, a better solution is to avoid messing with the values in an AUTO_INCREMENT column in the first place.

Most problems of this nature are such that you won't be able to see them coming, but the proper precautions you should have taken will seem blindingly obvious in hindsight. The best advice one can give on a subject like this is to encourage you to learn from your experience as rapidly as possible—nothing will rack up the Unix guru points faster than an embarrassing failure.

28

29

Network Security

System security is arguably the most important part of any administrator's job, whether it applies to a Windows server, a commercial Unix system, or FreeBSD. More books have probably been written about security issues than about any other topic—and with good reason. It's an immensely complex subject, but one that's crucially important to the success of a networked system. Although this chapter can't cover every facet of system security, it offers a good, general overview of the topic and includes information on all critical aspects of the topic.

This chapter helps you develop a security policy for your FreeBSD system based on the risk factors it faces in its role as a server or workstation. This chapter will give you the tools you need to monitor your system's perimeter, keep on top of alerts that are raised in the field, patch your system in response to those alerts, and make sure the services you provide to your users are not opening your system up to attack. It also gives you some idea of what you can do to recover when—not if—your machine is hacked.

Choosing a Security Model Based on Your Security Risks

The Internet today is not an especially friendly place for servers, and as an administrator you must always fear and prepare for the worst. The proliferation of "rootkit" tools—prepackaged weapons that attackers can use to gain super-user access to your system—and published attack scripts provides unfortunate fodder for countless individuals with nothing better to do than pursue destructive hobbies. You must assume that your system is being probed for security weaknesses at all times and expect the situation to grow more dangerous with each new published exploit. Your only defense is to keep your system as up to date as possible, act on new security advisories as soon as they're released, and be educated about the real dangers that threaten your system and where the greatest risks lie.

Security Models

You can adopt one of several models of security for your system, based on your system's setup and use patterns and your philosophy toward the security needs the system presents. The security model you choose will dictate how careful you must be about certain administrative duties, such as password policies, open services, encrypted traffic, and so on. Here's a short list of some security models, each defined by a general statement that sums up the administrator's assessment of security risks:

- **I trust everybody on the Internet.** Most certainly an inadvisable model under any circumstances, this is nonetheless the philosophy that guides the lack of security safeguards surrounding many amateur servers, and the administrators of those systems—who seldom maintain them properly—ultimately pay the price for it. Often found on university systems, especially those that have been around since before the Internet became so rich in hacker activity, systems administered with this philosophy have many open services, don't require encrypted logins, have loose account and password policies, and are easy targets for hack attacks.

- **I trust anybody on my system's network.** This philosophy is common in small enterprise networks where the server is protected from the general Internet by a firewall, and the internal network is made up of employees of a single company or department at a university. In this model, malicious users on the internal network are rare, especially if the organization is small, so the system can afford to provide unencrypted services, give accounts to anybody who asks for them, and even have disabled login security and passwords.

  Unfortunately, in large organizations, it has become the case that attacks on servers maintained under this model—attacks from *within* the network, by people who are supposed to be trustworthy—are more frequent than attacks from outside. If your organization is large, you must assume that you *cannot* trust everybody on your system's network, and instead choose a different security model.

- **I trust my local users.** Administrators that maintain this philosophy tend to be more paranoid than administrators of the systems described previously in this list's first two models. This security model is characterized by a tight network security policy: screening of users before new accounts are granted, encrypted network services (either required or encouraged), unnecessary services turned off, and crack-resistant passwords. However, local users are allowed to access internal services and see sensitive information (such as encrypted password strings). The idea is that once users are approved and given accounts, they can have the run of the system, and betrayal of that trust is grounds for removal from the system. This model is appropriate for hobbyist systems that serve a "low-risk" audience (for example, a fan Web site or community e-mail service), or for high-profile commercial Internet servers where only a few trusted people actually have user accounts.

- **I trust only myself and other administrators.** The model favored by the most paranoid system administrators, this model not only has tight network security as the preceding model, but tight local security as well. Regular users are denied access to system configuration files and server-side program code through carefully crafted permissions. The administrator must watch each user carefully to make sure nothing unauthorized is being done, and special measures (such as custom shells, chroot jails, and the disabling of certain commands) are often taken to restrict each user's access to the system's resources. This model is useful for high-profile servers that provide e-mail or Web hosting services to hundreds or thousands of users from indeterminate or anonymous backgrounds.

Once you've decided what model is appropriate for you and your system for network and user-level security, you need to decide where the risk areas are for that model and what you can do to combat the exploitability of those areas.

The Security Risks You Face

"Perfect security" is a myth; only superhuman effort can keep a system so completely buttoned up that no attack can ever get through. The next best thing, however, is to know which areas of your system are at greatest risk and how those risks can be combated.

Security risks for a network server can be grouped into three major categories:

- **Root compromise**—An attacker takes advantage of unencrypted transmissions or known programming weaknesses in server software (most commonly *buffer overflows*, or weaknesses in input boundary checking in server software) to gain super-user access to the system. He then installs tools of his own to conceal his presence from your system-monitoring tools (such as last and ps) and can steal any of your critical data or use your system as a base point for further hacking activities.

- **Privacy compromise**—If network traffic to and from your system is not encrypted (scrambled), an attacker can view any of it, including passwords (potentially leading to root compromise) or any user's critical or private communications.

- **Denial of service**—An attacker uses brute-force methods such as flooding your server with large amounts of legitimately constructed traffic, thus swamping its ability to serve traffic to normal clients and potentially crashing the system.

Within each of these categories of security risks, the most common threats result from these specific security weaknesses:

29

- **Insecure (weak) passwords**—Passwords that can be guessed by software using common words and sequences.

- **Clear-text services**—Services in which passwords and other sensitive information can be obtained just by "sniffing."

- **Unnecessary and exploit-prone services**—If you don't need to provide a service, don't. It can only cost you in the end.

- **Open SMTP relaying**—Allowing spammers to use your SMTP server as an open relay for broadcasting junk mail.

- **Unfiltered network access**—Run a firewall to prevent unauthorized or undesirable traffic from getting to your machine.

- **Outdated and vulnerable software**—The older a piece of software is, the greater the chances someone has found a way to break in through it.

Each of these weaknesses is a potential problem on FreeBSD in its default configuration. The sections that follow show you how to close these security gaps and find the necessary tools to maintain a system that will stand up to the inevitable hacker (or, more properly, "cracker") attacks that will be leveled against it.

Password Policies

If your users have insecure passwords, all the other security measures you might take may well be moot. Probably the most responsible thing you can do as the administrator of a FreeBSD system is to institute a password policy, requiring (or at least encouraging) your users to use passwords that cannot be easily guessed or decoded.

Users frequently find passwords inconvenient, and strict password policies doubly so. If allowed, a user will try to use his or her username, telephone number, hostname, a word such as "password," or strings of convenient-to-type characters, such as repeated letters or numbers. If you choose to expire users' passwords after some period, the first thing a user will try, when prompted to choose a new password, is to reuse the password from the previous period. However, an axiom of security is that "convenience and security are mutually exclusive," meaning that to increase one, you must sacrifice the other. Increased convenience brings about decreased security. There's no easy way around that truth.

When a user chooses a password using the system's passwd program or a script that calls the same routines that passwd uses, a few loose checks are performed. By default, passwords must be at least six characters in length, but that's about the only built-in measure that prevents people from choosing weak passwords. You can use the following techniques to take your password policy to the next level.

> **TIP**
>
> An ideal password is at least eight characters long (the longer the better, actually, and contains a mixture of capital and lowercase letters, numbers, and punctuation marks or meta-characters. To keep your system security strong, you must ensure that users follow these guidelines when picking a password with the `passwd` program in FreeBSD.
>
> Although the only password security measure currently enforced by the default `passwd` program in FreeBSD is that passwords must be at least six characters long, the FreeBSD development community is working to incorporate further weak-password checks into the `passwd` program. You learn how to use the `login.conf` program to set a minimum password length and to require periodic password updates in "Forcing Password Expiration," later in this chapter.

Enforcing Secure Passwords with `Crack`

The first priority in maintaining secure user password practices is to prevent users from choosing insecure passwords in the first place. As of this writing, the best way to make sure your users aren't using easily guessable passwords is to periodically try to guess them yourself. A tool called `Crack`, available in the ports collection at `/usr/ports/security/crack`, helps you do just that. Although it may appear to be a "hacker" tool, `Crack` is primarily intended as a security-auditing tool for system administrators, allowing you to perform "dictionary" attacks (trying a plethora of English words as potential passwords) as well as a number of other commonly used "convenience" passwords: repeated strings, the user's login name, groups of numbers, and so on. `Crack` helps you determine which of your users are using insecure passwords. You can then contact these users directly and ask them to adhere to the password rules you set.

You can build and install the `Crack` port using the instructions in Chapter 14, "Installing Additional Software." The new `/usr/local/crack` directory's permissions enable only root to list its contents or run any of its programs. To check your system's user database for weak passwords, go into `/usr/local/crack` and run the `Crack` program like this (note the capitalization):

```
# ./Crack -fmt bsd /etc/master.passwd
```

The `Crack` program builds some utilities, compiles some dictionaries, and then launches its arsenal against `/etc/master.passwd`. `Crack` sends its output into runtime files that you can analyze with the `Reporter` program, as shown here:

```
# ./Reporter -quiet
---- passwords cracked as of Sun Jan 14 12:17:41 EST 2001 ----

979693112:Guessed frank [frank] Frank Jones [/etc/master.passwd /bin/tcsh]
979693187:Guessed joe [password] Joe User [/etc/master.passwd
➥/usr/local/bin/bash]

---- done ----
```

`Crack` reports only the users whose passwords were successfully guessed. In the sample output, the cracked passwords are shown in the first set of brackets; Frank's password is `frank`, and Joe's password is `password`—both very weak passwords that can be guessed by an attacker with little effort. You can then contact these users and remind them of the password policy, requiring them to change to stronger passwords.

Once you're done running `Crack`, clean up the runtime tools and output files with the following two commands:

```
# make tidy
# rm run/F-merged
```

> **NOTE**
>
> As FreeBSD continues to develop, it's highly likely that there will be support in the `passwd` program for automatic password-strength checking such as that done manually by `Crack`; in fact, the libraries that `Crack` uses are available at `/usr/ports/security/cracklib`. On systems such as Linux, `cracklib` has been developed into a Pluggable Authentication Module (PAM), a mechanism that FreeBSD supports as well (see `man pam`), but FreeBSD doesn't have `cracklib` support fully integrated into PAM as of this writing. For now, though, if you're an adventurous sort willing to work with source code and experimental software, and you're interested in incorporating the `cracklib` routines into the `passwd` program, you can learn how at `http://www.kearneys.ca/ ~brent/FreeBSD/passwd42.html`.

Forcing Password Expiration

By default, passwords in FreeBSD do not expire. However, one common part of a secure password policy is to require users to change their passwords every so often, with the expiration interval chosen by you.

To do this in FreeBSD, you need to modify the `/etc/login.conf` file. This file controls system capabilities and behaviors, such as the number of allowed processes, the maximum allowed process size, the allowed number of simultaneous open files, and certain shell behaviors (learn more about this file in `man login.conf`). Each of these controls can be assigned to a "class" of users; you can assign users to classes with the `chfn` command (as you have seen in the "The `/etc/passwd` and `/etc/master.passwd` Files" section of Chapter 9, "Users, Groups, and Permissions"). By default, users aren't associated with any particular class, so the values in the `default` class apply to everybody:

```
default:\
        :passwd_format=md5:\
        :copyright=/etc/COPYRIGHT:\
        :welcome=/etc/motd:\
        :setenv=MAIL=/var/mail/$,BLOCKSIZE=K,FTP_PASSIVE_MODE=YES:\
        :path=/sbin /bin /usr/sbin /usr/bin /usr/games /usr/local/sbin
➡/usr/local/bin /usr/X11R6/bin ~/bin:\
```

```
        :nologin=/var/run/nologin:\
        :cputime=unlimited:\
        :datasize=unlimited:\
        :stacksize=unlimited:\
        :memorylocked=unlimited:\
        :memoryuse=unlimited:\
        :filesize=unlimited:\
        :coredumpsize=unlimited:\
        :openfiles=unlimited:\
        :maxproc=unlimited:\
        :sbsize=unlimited:\
        :priority=0:\
        :ignoretime@:\
        :umask=022:
```

The backslash (\) characters "escape" the line breaks, allowing you to specify all these properties on different lines, thus keeping the file readable.

To set a password expiration date, you put an extra line into the default class, specifying the passwordtime property. The line can go into the block at any point, but the easiest place to add it is right at the top, between the class name and the first existing property line:

```
default:\
        :passwordime=90d:\
        :passwd_format=md5:\
        :copyright=/etc/COPYRIGHT:\
        :welcome=/etc/motd:\
```

This example sets passwords to expire after 90 days. You can also use time values such as 2y (2 years), 6w (6 weeks), and 24h (24 hours). Now, because /etc/login.conf is a database that must be compiled into a hash table (as with the tables in /etc/mail, which you learned about in "Configuring Basic E-mail Services with Sendmail," in Chapter 24, "Configuring E-mail Services"), you must run the cap_mkdb program to generate the hash table and enable your changes:

```
# cap_mkdb /etc/login.conf
```

From now on, the login procedures will require users to choose a new password every 90 days. Note that when the passwordtime property is set, passwd writes the time of the last password change into the sixth field of /etc/master.passwd:

```
frank:$1$LXZkCuzD$7Oa8LyRf5jYOb.XrXiB3d.:1060:100::999066364:0::
➥/home/frank:/bin/tcsh
```

> **TIP**
>
> You can also use `login.conf` to alter the default minimum password length. This is done with the `minpasswordlen` value:
>
> `:minpasswordlen=8:\`
>
> This sets the minimum acceptable password length to eight characters.

Assigning Initial Passwords

When you're setting up a new user's account, it can be tempting to set a simple initial password, such as `Temp123` or `ChangeThis`. This seemingly innocuous practice, however, can seriously compromise your system's security—especially if you use the same temporary password for every new user you add.

You can mitigate this risk by coming up with a random password for each user; you can use any scheme you want to generate passwords (such as the first initials of song titles), but doing it yourself can become tiresome quickly. One good way to generate a unique and unguessable password is to use the `md5` tool and a few random keystrokes:

```
# md5 -s "asdsad"
MD5 ("asdsad") = b5b037a78522671b89a2c1b21d9b80c6
```

You can then assign the first seven or eight characters of this string (for example, b5b037a7) as the new user's password, with instructions telling the user how to use `passwd` to change this password to something more memorable. You might choose to incorporate this scheme into a small Perl script that does an MD5 hash on the output of `rand()` to generate a new password. A tutorial on programming Perl can be found in Chapter 20, "Introduction to Perl Programming."

Onetime Passwords with S/Key

If you're really serious about password security, you can do what they do at government offices and super-secure businesses: You can assign onetime passwords to your users, shifting part of the security burden from your own shoulders onto those of your users. The idea is that each user gets a set of passwords (or a means to generate one on-demand), each of which are only good for a single login attempt. Onetime passwords are generated by the `key` program, which has variants on all major platforms, and there's even a platform-agnostic Java key calculator at `http://www.cs.umd.edu/~harry/jotp/src.html`. (FreeBSD uses MD4 for its calculations.)

When the user attempts to log in, the server presents him with a "challenge" phrase and a number. The user then uses the `key` program to generate a password for that one login attempt and enters that password. This password is then never used again; at the next login attempt, he must generate a new password using the new number presented in the server's challenge.

Onetime passwords are good candidates for use on systems in which you don't obligate your users to use SSH instead of Telnet (as we will discuss shortly). Because a new password has to be generated by the user with the key program on a local system, with the user feeding into it the server's challenge phrase and the user's own secret password, which is never transmitted over the wire (except during initial key setup), an eavesdropper can never get any useful data by sniffing the connection. Once the password is used once, it can't be used again. The user can transmit his onetime password in clear text without fear.

> **NOTE**
>
> S/Key is as much a tool for a security-conscious user as it is a way for the administrator to enforce good security practices. Many parts of S/Key setup (for example, the keyinit program) are the user's responsibility to maintain. If a user feels strongly about keeping his passwords private, he might choose to use onetime passwords, even if he has the option to do otherwise.

Let's say you want to make it so that the user Frank cannot log in with his usual Unix password from a remote host but instead must use S/Key onetime passwords. While logged in to the server (preferably securely, as with SSH), he must use the keyinit program to set up S/Key authentication:

```
# keyinit
Adding frank:
Reminder - Only use this method if you are directly connected.
If you are using telnet or rlogin exit with no password and use keyinit -s.
Enter secret password:
Again secret password:

ID frank s/key is 99 st28077
COL APT HELM TAB DRY TRIM
```

> **NOTE**
>
> If Frank is not securely connected to the server (as with a clear-text Telnet connection), he ought to use keyinit -s. Without the -s, keyinit incorporates the key program into its own operation. Frank enters his secret key-generating password (which is used only for calculating S/Key onetime passwords and shouldn't be the same as his Unix password) and transmits it over the network to the server. If the connection isn't secure, the secret password is susceptible to interception, making any further attempts at security moot. The -s option requires Frank to use the key program locally—on his own Windows, Macintosh, or Unix machine—to generate a password that he must then enter into keyinit at the s/key access password: prompt (which only appears if the -s option is used).

29

After Frank has used `keyinit` to set up his S/Key mechanism and has added an entry for his login to `/etc/skeykeys`, you must create the file `/etc/skey.access` (if it doesn't already exist) and add the following line:

```
deny user frank
```

The `/etc/skey.access` file tells FreeBSD under what conditions a remote user is permitted to use his regular Unix password, and under what conditions he must use an S/Key onetime password. A line in `skey.access` specifies a rule beginning with `permit` (allowing either an S/Key or Unix password) or `deny` (requiring an S/Key password), followed by as many conditions as you like. These conditions can specify certain users, groups, remote hostnames or networks, or login terminals (you can read a full description of the conditions in `man skey.access`). The sample line you just saw requires that when Frank tries to log in, only an S/Key password is permitted—not his Unix password.

The next time Frank uses Telnet to connect to your system, his login prompt will look like this:

```
# telnet stripes.somewhere.com
Trying 64.41.131.102...
Connected to stripes.somewhere.com.
Escape character is '^]'.

FreeBSD/i386 (stripes.somewhere.com) (ttyp2)

login: frank
s/key 99 st28077
Password:
```

> **NOTE**
>
> As mentioned earlier, S/Key provides a way to make even clear-text Telnet logins secure.
> However, if you have a tight security policy, you should require your users to use SSH and disable
> Telnet logins altogether. If Frank were to use SSH to connect, the S/Key behavior would be the
> same as in the example, although the output lines would look somewhat different.

Frank must now use the `key` program (or its equivalent) on his own machine to figure out what password to enter. He has to feed into it the challenge information presented by the server: the iteration count (99 in this case, meaning that there are 99 logins left before Frank must run `keyinit` again), followed by the "seed" string (`st28077` here, the same as you saw in the `keyinit` example). These numbers, combined with Frank's secret password, generate an S/Key password made up of six short, uppercase English words:

```
# key 99 st28077
Reminder - Do not use this program while logged in via telnet or rlogin.
```

```
Enter secret password:
COL APT HELM TAB DRY TRIM
```

Frank now enters this string of words as his password and is granted access. An attacker, if he intercepted the words, would be out of luck—they only went across the wire once (on the way to the login prompt). The next time the system asks for Frank's S/Key password, the iteration number will be 98, and the password will be different. The iteration keeps counting down until it hits zero, at which time Frank must run `keyinit` again to set the counter back to 99; otherwise, he will be denied access and you'll have to get involved (by changing his rule in `/etc/skey.access` from `deny` to `permit` until he's reinitialized S/Key).

> **TIP**
>
> If he wants, Frank can generate multiple keys at once by using `key` with the `-n` option. He can then print out these keys and take them with him if that's more convenient or secure for him:
>
> ```
> # key -n 5 50 st28077
> Reminder - Do not use this program while logged in via telnet or rlogin.
> Enter secret password:
> 41: SHOT YOU BIEN GIN JUDD AS
> 42: CHOW AVIS DOES EMIT FLAM WORK
> 43: DOCK ATE ANN WAS JOCK OAT
> 44: WALE AWL ELK LETS AWK WALE
> 45: GIFT BERT ROD GRIN YANG EAST
> ```

The S/Key password challenge is also issued as part of the `su` command, helping to prevent the actual root password from being transmitted over the network at any time.

To turn off S/Key for a user, remove that user's entry from `/etc/skeykeys` and any mention of him from `/etc/skey.access`.

Kerberos

One last authentication method that deserves mention is Kerberos. Developed as a centralized login-management system at the Athena cluster at MIT, Kerberos provides a way for users to authenticate with a central server on a network and be issued "tickets" for performing tasks such as Telnet, FTP, POP3, and NFS, without having to log in each time. As long as the hosts on your network between which you're running traffic support Kerberos and subscribe to the master server, the Kerberos subsystem takes care of all the authentication chores for you. FreeBSD allows you to set up a Kerberos master server to which other hosts in the network subscribe, or to simply support Kerberos in a network where it's already running.

Until fairly recently, Kerberos has been a scheme that was really useful only in legacy situations or at MIT. Its usefulness is in streamlining often-used tasks in large LANs, such as those found at universities or hierarchical enterprise networks, and there aren't many situations left where Kerberos is especially important in today's networking atmosphere. It's less a security measure than a way of eliminating unnecessary work in pure Unix environments. However, because many enterprise networks use Kerberos to provide centralized, encrypted login services, and because Windows 2000's security model is largely tied together with Kerberos (albeit a somewhat modified version), it's once again becoming increasingly important and ubiquitous. You may need to set up your FreeBSD machine to integrate with it.

If you want to enable Kerberos in FreeBSD, you can do so. `kerberos_server_enable="YES"` in `/etc/rc.conf` will start up the services that manage a master Kerberos server; if you're working with an existing master server, you can uncomment the appropriate lines in `/etc/pam.conf` to enable centralized authentication for the services that support it. Here's an example:

```
login   auth    sufficient      pam_kerberosIV.so           try_first_pass
```

You can read more about Kerberos in the `man kerberos` page and in the online FreeBSD handbook (`http://www.freebsd.org/handbook`).

Avoiding Problems with Clear-Text Services

Transmissions between your client machine and the server (in applications such as Telnet, e-mail, and HTTP) might seem secure to you; after all, your passwords are hidden, and everything travels in tiny packets of data that flow out onto the network along with many millions of other tiny packets. Who could have the patience to apply the networking equivalent of a wiretap and piece together the fragments of an interesting transaction? They'd have to be on the same network segment as your LAN or the LAN at the opposite end—or at some trunk service provider along the way—and they'd have to possess stealth and equipment befitting James Bond. And even if they did, they'd have to eavesdrop on many different such sessions in order to unearth anything they could use. Who could have that kind of spare time?

Anybody, that's who. Security in clear-text services (applications that don't encrypt, or scramble, their transactions) is a myth. Even more importantly, *security through obscurity*—the notion that your communications or services are secure because you think nobody pays attention to them—doesn't work, as this myth has been proven wrong repeatedly over the years. Don't fall prey to the false notion that hackers aren't interested in cracking your system. You should always assume that your traffic is constantly being watched by a hacker with malicious intent.

Using `tcpdump` to Monitor Traffic

You can illustrate the risks inherent in your network's clear-text services by using a *packet sniffer*, a software tool that watches all packets on your network segment and displays the ones that interest you. A sniffer operates by putting your Ethernet card into "promiscuous mode," where it accepts all packets that it sees on the network, rather than discarding packets not addressed to it (for information on packets, see Chapter 21, "Networking with FreeBSD"). The sniffer then applies all kinds of highly configurable filters to the traffic it sees. This is how an eavesdropper can extract the relevant packets from the storm of traffic to capture a transaction with ominous ease.

FreeBSD's built-in packet sniffer is `tcpdump`, available in `/usr/sbin`. Its use is barred to regular users, who get a `Permission denied` error on the `/dev/bpf0` (Berkeley Packet Filter) device; only the administrator (root) can use the program. The purpose of `tcpdump` is not to log the actual data of the TCP/IP packets it sees (you might want to look into `tcpflow`, available in the ports at `/usr/ports/net/tcpflow` or into WildPackets' EtherPeek for that functionality). Instead, `tcpdump` is much like `Crack` in that it's intended as an administrative security-auditing tool that allows you to see how much unencrypted traffic is being sent to and from your system, and to watch for suspicious network activity that might indicate illicit pursuits on the part of your users.

> **NOTE**
>
> It's possible to use `tcpdump` to spy on the activities of your users, regardless of whether they're doing anything wrong. A warning in the GENERIC kernel configuration file reminds you to consider the ethical issues involved with using a packet sniffer. It all depends on what kind of system you're running, naturally, but packet sniffers are the equivalent of telephone wiretaps or hidden security cameras, and you should use `tcpdump` only under circumstances in which you would be comfortable using wiretaps and hidden cameras to gather information.

The configuration of `tcpdump` is quite complex, and it allows you to do a lot of very useful and versatile things. All we're interested in right now, though, is demonstrating the dangers of clear-text TCP/IP traffic. Let's set up a simple monitoring filter on the Telnet port (TCP port 23):

```
# tcpdump -x port 23
tcpdump: listening on fxp0
20:14:19.076941 w044.z064002043.sjc-ca.dsl.cnc.net.54109 >
➥w012.z064002043.sjc-ca.dsl.cnc.net.telnet: S 1972342903:1972342903(0)
➥win 32768 <mss 1460,nop,wscale 0,nop,nop,timestamp 465710 0> (DF) [tos 0x10]
                    4510 003c e44b 4000 4006 8024 4002 2b2c
                    4002 2b0c d35d 0017 758f 9077 0000 0000
                    a002 8000 001b 0000 0204 05b4 0103 0300
                    0101 080a 0007 1b2e 0000 0000
```

29

```
20:14:19.077050 w012.z064002043.sjc-ca.dsl.cnc.net.telnet >
➥w044.z064002043.sjc-ca.dsl.cnc.net.54109: S 1734674412:1734674412(0)
➥ack 1972342904 win 17520 <mss 1460> (DF)
                          4500 002c c9c2 4000 4006 9acd 4002 2b0c
                          4002 2b2c 0017 d35d 6765 07ec 758f 9078
                          6012 4470 349c 0000 0204 05b4
...
20:14:19.677472 w044.z064002043.sjc-ca.dsl.cnc.net.54109 >
➥w012.z064002043.sjc-ca.dsl.cnc.net.telnet: . ack 195 win 33580 (DF)
➥[tos 0x10]
                          4510 0028 e458 4000 4006 802b 4002 2b2c
                          4002 2b0c d35d 0017 758f 910a 6765 08af
                          5010 832c 0c49 0000 5555 5555 5555
^C
134 packets received by filter
0 packets dropped by kernel
```

The `-x` option tells `tcpdump` to output the first part of each packet's payload in hexadecimal; if this option is omitted, `tcpdump` only outputs the link-level headers. You may want to use `-w <filename>` to send `tcpdump` output into a file so that you can peruse it more easily.

Because `tcpdump` is not designed as "spyware," it does not decode the hexadecimal output for you. You can, if you wish, convert it to plain human-readable text with a hex editor such as `/usr/ports/editors/hexedit`. However, if you're interested in the contents of the packets, you will want to use a different program (such as `tcpflow`).

Adding Extra Security with Encrypted Protocols

The `tcpdump` data isn't encrypted at all. It only takes a little bit of effort to be able to see the complete contents of every packet sent via Telnet. It's even easier with tools that do the packet decoding for you, such as `tcpflow`, `tcpshow`, and EtherPeek. If these packets contain a user's login session, an attacker using any of these programs would know the user's login password and could use it to log in to your system. This security gap endangers POP3, IMAP, FTP, and HTTP traffic, too, as well as just about every small and nonessential service, such as Finger and Syslog. Safeguarding against the use of these sniffer programs is especially important in systems where passwords or any other sensitive data is transferred. Protecting communications is as much a privacy issue as it is a security concern.

Fortunately, there's a way to combat the problems of sniffer programs. You can use an encrypted alternative to any of the major data-transfer protocols, many of which are part of the default FreeBSD installation. For instance, SSH is a secure alternative to Telnet, and SSL is a method for encrypting Web traffic and other services. Sealing the security holes inherent in clear-text services is only a matter of knowing the encrypted versions exist, implementing them, and convincing your users to adopt them.

Securing Terminal Traffic (SSH)

Terminal traffic, which is typically from the Telnet or `rlogin` application, is a result of remote users interacting with Unix systems; you are probably accustomed to connecting to your FreeBSD machine remotely both to use it and to perform your administration duties. However, terminal use is probably the riskiest type of clear-text traffic—and it's the easiest to fix. FreeBSD comes with a complete SSH (Secure Shell) package designed to supplant Telnet and `rlogin`. The SSH package is called OpenSSH, and it was developed originally for OpenBSD. OpenSSH allows users to establish a completely encrypted tunnel to your server, protecting their login passwords and any command-line activity from snooping intruders.

The SSH server, `sshd`, runs on port 22 as a standalone daemon that, like Apache, spawns off new `sshd` processes when new connections come in. To enable the SSH server, add the following line to `/etc/rc.conf` (if it's not already there) and then reboot (or simply type **sshd**):

```
sshd_enable="YES"
```

The SSH client is a replacement for Telnet. To use it instead of the command-line `telnet` program, issue the `ssh` command instead of the `telnet` command:

```
# ssh stripes.somewhere.com
```

Instead of letting the server issue its own `Login:` and `Password:` prompts, the SSH client itself prompts for your password, assuming the remote username is the same as the local one. You can specify an alternate username with either of a couple of different methods:

```
# ssh stripes.somewhere.com -l frank
# ssh frank@stripes.somewhere.com
```

The `ssh` program establishes the encrypted connection and passes the login data to the server in a secure fashion. From that point on, it acts just like a regular Telnet connection—there's no difference as far as the user is concerned. A user on a FreeBSD, Linux, Unix, or Mac OS X system can use this process to connect to your machine.

Users on desktop client systems such as Windows or classic Mac OS have a little bit more work to do. These platforms have no command-line SSH client programs, but there are some excellent graphical terminal programs that incorporate both Telnet and SSH functionality: Windows users have SecureCRT (from Van Dyke, `http://www.vandyke.com`) or SSH (from SSH Communications Security, `http://www.ssh.com`), and Mac OS 9 users can use NiftyTelnet/SSH or MacSSH. The Windows programs tend to be commercial products, whereas most of the Mac programs are shareware.

29

Your task lies in convincing your users to switch to SSH rather than using Telnet. Let them all know via your published server policy that they are advised to use SSH to protect themselves at their option; however, this doesn't guarantee they will use it, and you as the administrator are still faced with the threat of an attacker who sniffs the connection of someone who has chosen not to use SSH. A more heavy-handed but complete approach is to disable Telnet entirely and require your users to use SSH instead. To disable Telnet, comment out the `telnetd` line from `/etc/inetd.conf`:

```
#telnet  stream  tcp    nowait  root    /usr/libexec/telnetd    telnetd
```

Then, restart the `inetd` process:

```
# killall -HUP inetd
```

> **NOTE**
>
> SSH has two popular protocol flavors: SSH1 and SSH2. FreeBSD supports both, but SSH1 is less well designed and potentially more likely to exhibit security vulnerabilities than SSH2. You can disable SSH1 by adding the following line to `/etc/ssh/ssh_config`:
>
> ```
> Protocol 2
> ```
>
> However, note that not all consumer SSH clients have full support for SSH2. Don't worry about disabling SSH1 unless you have to.

Securing E-mail Services (POP3 and IMAP)

POP3 and IMAP are arguably even more vulnerable to clear-text security risks than Telnet. If your users have set their e-mail clients to connect to the server every five minutes or so to check for new messages, a plainly visible login and password transaction occurs with each one of these connections, resulting in an even higher likelihood of password compromises—especially because these services send their sensitive data at predictable, regular intervals. If you're enforcing SSH rather than Telnet on your server, it's in your interest to do the same for your e-mail services.

You learned in Chapter 25 how to secure the Qpopper program to use the built-in Secure Sockets Layer (SSL) tools in FreeBSD to encrypt POP3 connections. You can use the same method to secure IMAP, employing the IMAP-UW software package. You can enable SSL support in IMAP-UW by generating a certificate with a Certifying Authority (as you learned in "Enabling SSL Encryption," in Chapter 24). If you have a certificate generated for a different service (Qpopper, for example) on your site, you can use the same certificate for IMAP-UW. Refer to the IMAP-UW documentation at `http://www.washington.edu/imap/` for more details.

The stunnel program provides an alternative way to encrypt both POP3 and IMAP. stunnel manages your SSL certificates centrally and doesn't use each service's built-in SSL support. Also available in the ports (/usr/ports/security/stunnel), stunnel allows you to set up a universal SSL tunnel for any service on the system that you choose. If you install stunnel from the ports, its default startup script (/usr/local/etc/rc.d/stunnel.sh.sample) starts a listener process on port 993 (for IMAP) and 995 (for POP3), which are the generally accepted ports for the secure versions of these protocols, as you can see in /etc/services.

NOTE

Remember to rename stunnel.sh.sample to stunnel.sh, as you learned in the section titled "Resource Configuration Scripts," in Chapter 10, "System Configuration and Startup Scripts." The .sample suffix is there to make sure you look at the script's contents to ensure the paths to the .pem certificate files are correct.

If you choose to use stunnel, you'll still have to generate a certificate, just as you do with Qpopper and IMAP-UW. The stunnel certificate should be placed at /usr/local/etc/stunnel.pem. Once it's in place, your POP3 and IMAP clients should be able to connect to the appropriate ports to establish a secure connection (993 instead of 143 for IMAP, and 995 instead of 110 for POP3).

CAUTION

Many of the popular e-mail client programs, such as Microsoft Outlook, support SSL encryption for POP3 and IMAP, but others have support for only one of the two, or neither. In other e-mail client programs, such support is incomplete or optional. Requiring users to use SSL might mean requiring them to switch e-mail programs, something not many people like to do.

Also, note that stunnel is not a replacement for POP3 or IMAP. Rather, it's an augmentation—the generalized addition of SSL capability to any specified service. This means that the regular POP3 and IMAP services must still be enabled; you can't remove these services from /etc/inetd.conf. You'll need to use IPFW (as you will see later in this chapter) to disallow connections to these ports from any host other than localhost if you want to enforce a "secure connections only" policy.

Securing FTP

FTP, as you learned in Chapter 26, "Configuring an FTP Server," is another clear-text service that has inherent password authentication and therefore has the potential to be compromised by an attacker watching the wires. FTP is used frequently by users to do things such as uploading Web pages, but it isn't used at predictable, regular intervals like POP3 or IMAP. This makes FTP a bit less risky to your system than Telnet, but still worth securing.

Fortunately, secure FTP is just as easy to implement as SSH. If you've enabled SSH (as you learned to do in "Securing Terminal Traffic," earlier in this chapter), secure FTP is available to your system. Encrypted FTP sessions actually operate over the SSH channel, with the SSH client establishing a terminal connection, starting the `/usr/libexec/sftp-server` program on the server end, and opening the necessary connections back to the client over encrypted channels. The secure FTP client then operates transparently to the user, just like a regular FTP program.

On FreeBSD, the built-in `sftp` program that's a part of OpenSSH serves the purpose of handling the client end of a secure FTP session. On Windows, the SSH Communications Security package provides a secure FTP client that works with FreeBSD. The previously mentioned Mac OS clients (NiftyTelnet and MacSSH) also have secure FTP capabilities, and Mac OS X has the command-line `sftp`.

An alternative way to perform file transfer over a secure channel is to use `scp`. This enables you to copy files to and from a remote server using login authentication, much in the same way that `rcp` works (see man `rcp` and man `scp` for details), except that `scp` operates via the encrypted SSH tunnel. Some SSH clients, such as NiftyTelnet/SSH for the Mac, support file transfer via this method.

To use `scp` to transfer a file from your local machine to a remote SSH server, use a command like the following:

```
# scp file.txt stripes:
frank@stripes's password:
file.txt                100% |*****************************|   511       00:00
```

The remote hostname is specified with a trailing colon (`:`) and can be either the source or destination argument. Either of these arguments can also contain full pathnames to the file's location. Using `scp` is a quick way to transfer files securely if you don't need all the features of full-fledged FTP.

Securing Apache

HTTP, the protocol over which the Web travels, is probably the most visible service on the Internet today, and more and more sensitive information is being sent over the Web with each passing day. Secure HTTP is vitally important to e-commerce, because it protects clients' credit card numbers and billing information—arguably just as critical as protecting login names and passwords. Secure HTTP is especially important if your business depends on your clients' confidence in the privacy with which you handle their information. FreeBSD's flagship HTTP server, Apache, must be secured if you intend to use it for any kind of commercial or privacy-sensitive purpose.

Securing HTTP was one of the earliest widespread uses for SSL. Until recently, integrating Apache with SSL was a matter for commercial software vendors who developed products based on Apache, and there were comparable but competing versions of SSL-enabled Apache available for free. However, since the release of Apache 2.0, SSL is integrated into the software in the default installation, and enabling it is a much simpler matter. However, for the benefit of users who might still be using Apache 1.3 or earlier, we will cover the SSL implementations designed for that version.

> **NOTE**
>
> Secure and clear-text HTTP are intended to operate side by side. It's not a good idea to serve all HTTP requests through SSL, and rarely is it done. High-traffic Web sites would suffer a speed impact from the processing overhead of encrypting every page and image (regardless of whether it contains sensitive information), and convenience and convention discourage the practice. Most public Web data has no need for encryption—after all, it's public. But switching to secure mode when a customer enters an online purchasing page or information-gathering form helps to provide your Web users with assurance that they're now in a more heavily protected area. Remember, you're serving the user's expectations and confidence as much as the user's data.

Apache-SSL

Apache-SSL is the "official" secure implementation of Apache prior to version 2.0. Apache-SSL has a more limited feature set than mod_ssl, being primarily concerned with stability and performance rather than with advanced features. Development on Apache-SSL is not very active these days, largely because of the tightly controlled feature set and the lack of known bugs.

The Apache-SSL binary is called httpsd rather than httpd; the idea is that you would run a regular httpd to serve regular HTTP requests on port 80, and httpsd to handle encrypted requests on port 443. Of course, this means you would have to have a version of Apache without SSL installed as well to accomplish this.

You can install Apache-SSL from the ports at /usr/ports/www/apache13-ssl, and the official Web site is http://www.apache-ssl.org.

Apache with mod_ssl

mod_ssl is a more complete and active implementation of SSL on HTTP than Apache-SSL. mod_ssl is a standard Apache module that links OpenSSL into Apache, taking advantage of the modern modular architecture of the software. It's more streamlined than Apache-SSL, and it incorporates many more features and a more versatile configuration model. The apache13-modssl port installs a single httpd executable, for example, just like the regular apache13 port, except that the configuration files have special tuning to enable SSL connections when requested:

```
<IfDefine SSL>
Listen 80
```

29

```
Listen 443
</IfDefine>
```

You can add further modules to Apache with `mod_ssl`; these include `mod_perl`, `mod_php`, and all the rest in `/usr/ports/www`. The focus of `mod_ssl` is a rich and complete feature set and easy configurability; it's not necessarily as fast or robust as Apache-SSL, but statistics on this are scarce.

In Apache 2.0, `mod_ssl` is compiled into the `httpd` binary by default, and the configuration options for it are given in the basic configuration file `/usr/local/etc/apache2/ssl.conf`, which you can incorporate into your `httpd.conf` as necessary.

Apache with `mod_ssl` can be installed from `/usr/ports/www/apache13-modssl`; the official Web site is `http://www.modssl.org`.

Running a Secure Web Server

Installing either Apache-SSL or Apache with `mod_ssl` makes maintaining your Web server a little more complex. As mentioned earlier, Apache-SSL operates under the assumption that you will run a regular `httpd` to handle regular clear-text HTTP connections, and `httpsd` for encrypted requests on port 443. This means that a separate `httpsdctl` program controls Apache-SSL, operating the same way as `apachectl` with the regular Apache. Furthermore, an `httpsd.conf` program is added to `/usr/local/etc/apache` in parallel with `httpd.conf`. These separate programs aren't present if you install Apache with `mod_ssl`—the functionality is rolled into a single set of files (you saw these files in Chapter 25, "Configuring a Web Server").

The ports (both `apache13-ssl` and `apache13-modssl`) install complete Apache directory trees—including icons, sample HTML pages, dynamic modules, and configuration files. For this reason, you must take care when updating the parallel installations of Apache-SSL and regular Apache. The `mod_ssl` version only has a single installation, replacing the standard Apache installation, so the maintenance is potentially much simpler.

Managing Your OpenSSL Certificates

Create your OpenSSL certificates, again using the method you learned in "Enabling SSL Encryption" in Chapter 24. Note that `mod_ssl` expects to find its certificate in `/usr/local/etc/apache2/ssl.crt/server.crt` and its private key in `/usr/local/etc/apache2/ssl.key/server.key`. You can adjust the directives in your Apache configuration file, which specify those files to point to the location of your existing systemwide security certificates. Alternatively, be sure to place copies of those cert files into the locations that Apache expects.

Your OpenSSL certificates are read much more interactively by a Web browser than by other secure services, so you must take special care to be sure that the certificates match reality. If the hostname in the certificate doesn't match the server's hostname or if the certificate isn't signed by a recognized Certifying Authority (in other words, it's self-signed), the user gets a dialog showing all the information about your certificate and asking for confirmation on whether the browser should accept it. This dialog can bewilder your users and undermine their confidence in your site's security.

Even if your certificate matches your site's information properly, the user can view the certificate's contents through a Web browser's Security Information feature, so all the fields you specify when generating the certificate request will be visible to any interested party. Bear this in mind—it's fairly difficult to change the information on a certificate once it has been signed.

Poorly Written CGI Scripts

Clear-text traffic isn't the only potential security hole in an Apache installation. If your security model is one where you don't necessarily trust your local users, you should be equally concerned with the possibility of users' CGI scripts running amok on the system (whether intentionally or accidentally) and destroying files. Many files in Apache's document root are owned by the nobody user (especially files created dynamically by your own server-side programs); the same nobody user executes every user's CGI programs as well. Given those facts, it's a simple matter for a user CGI program to be able to delete or modify anything else on the server owned by nobody.

It's easier than you might think for this to happen. All it takes is for a user to design a CGI program to remove his or her own unneeded files, but to mistakenly code the program to prepend the wrong path to the filenames. The same might happen in a program that prints data out into a file, potentially corrupting other users' data. Even the most seasoned CGI veterans have fallen prey to this trap. The danger is naturally much higher if you have a malicious user on your system who decides intentionally to write a destructive script to be executed by Apache as nobody.

The solution to this problem is to run Apache within a "wrapper" program that intercepts user CGI programs, performs security checks on them (making sure the permissions are appropriate), and executes them as the users who own them rather than as nobody. This has traditionally been done with the suexec wrapper that comes with Apache, but an easier-to-use and more flexible solution is CGIWrap, by Nathan Neulinger.

Making CGI Scripts Safer with CGIwrap

CGIWrap, available in the ports at /usr/ports/www/cgiwrap, provides two security advantages: It protects users and the server root from attack by poorly written CGI scripts, and it also enables users' CGI programs to write files that the users themselves can modify or delete in the shell.

In an ideal world, where programs are always written perfectly and nobody tries to sabotage others' files, a user CGI program would be executed by the user who owns it, rather than by the unprivileged nobody user. However, it's not an ideal world—people write

29

buggy CGI scripts, and hackers abound. It's a fairly simple matter for a user to create a CGI program owned by root, put it in his directory, and wait for it to be executed as the owner (the super-user), unleashing its destructive payload against any files in your system.

CGIWrap protects your system against such problems. It's not a complete or ideal solution, but it reduces the security risks associated with user CGI scripts so that you can put your administrative efforts elsewhere. By running security checks against all user CGI programs before executing them, and by running each program as its owner, CGIWrap shifts the risks inherent in a badly written CGI from you onto the script's owner.

When you install CGIWrap from its port directory, the `cgiwrap` program (a precompiled binary) goes into your top-level `cgi-bin` directory, `/usr/local/www/cgi-bin`. Rather than operating as a wrapper around Apache itself as `suexec` does, CGIWrap has to be called explicitly by your users, with a URL of the following form:

```
http://www.somewhere.com/cgi-bin/cgiwrap/frank/myscript.cgi
```

Or as a server-side include:

```
<!--#include virtual="/cgi-bin/cgiwrap/frank/myscript.cgi"-->
```

This executes the `myscript.cgi` program in `/home/frank/public_html/cgi-bin`. All of a user's CGI programs must go inside his or her `public_html/cgi-bin` directory, which the user needs to create if it doesn't exist already.

> **TIP**
>
> CGI programs outside the `public_html/cgi-bin` directory will not be run through CGIWrap, so it's important that you disable CGI execution outside the server `DocumentRoot`. To do so, make sure you don't have an `Options +ExecCGI` directive in a block that defines your users' directories.

The official CGIWrap home page is at `http://cgiwrap.unixtools.org/`, for further reference.

> **Preventing SMTP Relaying**
>
> It can be construed as a security weakness for your Sendmail server to be open for anybody to send mail through it. These days, an open mail relay is almost synonymous with a mail server that's being used by spammers to broadcast junk mail, and that constitutes a theft of your services. Furthermore, you're subject to a form of denial of service if other mail service providers add your host to a "blackhole" list—a list of banned remote addresses with which they refuse to exchange any mail—as a result of your server being an open and unprotected mail relay.
>
> It is critical to configure Sendmail so that your own legitimate users and their correspondents can continue to use your SMTP server, but unauthorized spammers—who want to send mail that neither originates on nor is destined for your server—cannot. You can find a full description of how this can be achieved in the "Notes on Relaying" section of Chapter 24.

System Security Profiles and Kernel Security (`securelevel`)

The FreeBSD kernel runs with five different levels of security, controlled by the `kern_securelevel` option in `/etc/rc.conf`—levels -1 through 3. Each of these settings corresponds to a profile that controls such things as whether the kernel can be replaced on the disk, whether kernel modules can be loaded or unloaded, whether certain file permissions and flags can be set or altered, and whether filesystems can be mounted on demand. The profile also controls whether utilities such as the IPFW built-in firewall can be disabled or modified (you learn more about IPFW later in this chapter). As you learned in Chapter 16, "Kernel Configuration," you can raise the `securelevel` setting only during runtime—you can never lower it, except by rebooting. More information on kernel security can be found in `man securelevel`.

During installation, you saw a second multilevel network security profile set in FreeBSD. You can see it again in `/stand/sysinstall`, under Configure, followed by Security. This menu allows you to choose one of two different systemwide security profiles: Medium or Extreme. These profiles control whether services such as Sendmail, `sshd`, and `inetd` should be run, and they also have a very rough correspondence to the kernel security levels. Table 29.1 shows a breakdown of each of these security profiles and what options each sets in `/etc/rc.conf`. The table also includes the Low and High security profiles, which existed until FreeBSD 4.6; if your system was originally installed with an earlier version, you will probably see all four profiles. (The `/stand` directory is not updated if you upgrade FreeBSD.)

TABLE 29.1 Systemwide Security Profiles

Profile Name	`/etc/rc.conf` **Settings**
Low	`sendmail_enable="YES"`
	`sshd_enable="YES"`
	`portmap_enable="YES"`
	`inetd_enable="YES"`
Medium	`sendmail_enable="YES"`
	`sshd_enable="YES"`
	`inetd_enable="YES"`
High	`kern_securelevel="1"`
	`kern_securelevel_enable="YES"`
	`sendmail_enable="YES"`
	`sshd_enable="YES"`
	`portmap_enable="NO"`
	`nfs_server_enable="NO"`
	`inetd_enable="NO"`

29

TABLE 29.1   Continued

Profile Name	`/etc/rc.conf` **Settings**
Extreme	`kern_securelevel="2"`
	`kern_securelevel_enable="YES"`
	`sendmail_enable="NO"`
	`sshd_enable="NO"`
	`portmap_enable="NO"`
	`nfs_server_enable="NO"`
	`inetd_enable="NO"`

As you might expect, the Extreme profile is restrictive—almost to the point of making the system unusable. The kernel `securelevel` is set to 2, meaning that the kernel can't be modified (with kernel modules) or replaced without rebooting into single-user mode; the only way to mount or unmount filesystems is explicitly with the `mount` and `umount` commands (implicit, on-demand mounting, as with `amd`, is not allowed). Additionally, `inetd`, Sendmail, `sshd`, the NFS server, and other services are not enabled.

The High profile is a little less restrictive, with a `securelevel` of 1, meaning that filesystems are more easily mountable but the kernel still cannot be modified. Sendmail and `sshd` are enabled, but the rest of the services from the Extreme profile are not.

Of course, because the security profiles work purely by setting options in `/etc/rc.conf`, you can mix the settings from Table 29.1 to your taste, creating a security profile that fits the model by which you're running your system.

CAUTION

Generally, you should never enable a service that you don't think you'll need. If it doesn't serve a useful purpose for you, it is at best useless; at worst, it offers a security vulnerability that opens your system up to security breaches. Therefore, you should play it safe wherever possible.

Using a Firewall

It's undeniable that firewalls (machines that operate as routers with filters) are almost indispensable to Internet server maintenance. Bored "script kiddies" with nothing better to do than to try to hack systems with easily accessible hacking tools make it imperative that you protect your system. Most administrators need protection that goes beyond simply electing not to run certain services and keeping on top of security bulletins. You need a generalized shield at the kernel level that prevents your system from being accessed at all on certain ports, from certain hosts, or over certain protocols. Firewalls, particularly the IPFW firewall that comes with FreeBSD, provide an answer to this need.

A firewall can prevent the vast majority of casual attacks by only allowing traffic that you designate as valid to enter your system. Even the most expensive and robust firewall, however, can be made useless through a simple misconfiguration. Most ineffective firewalls are made that way through misconfigurations rather than poor quality or design.

> **CAUTION**
>
> There is no substitute for a properly designed and well-maintained security policy used in conjunction with a competent firewall; don't be fooled into thinking that if you just buy a more expensive firewall, your network security problems are solved. That's the type of thinking that leads to a great many security breaches on the Internet today.

A firewall enables you to configure your system to filter packets based on the criteria you specify, discarding unwanted traffic at the kernel level (before it reaches any critical system services). Firewalls also help you with administrative accounting, keeping statistics on the usage of your system and seeing how much traffic comes from where.

IPFW does both of these things; you can run it directly on your FreeBSD machine, or you can use it on a system acting as a gateway router protecting multiple hosts on the inside LAN. Figure 29.1 shows this latter case, with a FreeBSD machine with three Ethernet cards acting as a gateway router (as you saw in Chapter 27, "Configuring an Internet Gateway"), passing packets between the inside (LAN), "demilitarized zone" (DMZ), and outside (WAN) networks (you learned about gateway routers in Chapter 27).

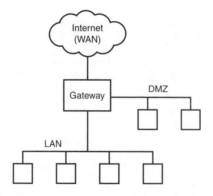

FIGURE 29.1   A diagram of a gateway router providing firewall services, showing the LAN, DMZ, and WAN interfaces.

> **NOTE**
>
> The demilitarized zone, or DMZ, is a network that is exposed to the WAN traffic directly, rather than being on the LAN. A DMZ is particularly useful in cases where the IP addresses on the LAN are translated (as you learned in "IP Addresses," in Chapter 21). A DMZ provides an enterprise or

ISP with a network on which to place untranslated "edge" machines such as Web servers, mail gateways, and other hosts that need to be accessible from the general Internet.

A DMZ may or may not be configured to be protected by the firewall rules in the gateway router. Usually this is desirable, but some specialized cases require that the DMZ be exempt from the LAN's firewall rules. Your network situation will dictate your needs.

Enabling the Firewall

IPFW is not supported in the GENERIC kernel. As you learned in Chapter 16, you can compile certain options into a custom kernel to enable IPFW, including IPFIREWALL, IPFIREWALL_VERBOSE, and IPFIREWALL_VERBOSE_LIMIT=10. You don't need to build a new kernel, however, in order to use IPFW; it's available as a kernel module, which is loaded automatically by the /etc/rc.network script. To enable the firewall without rebuilding the kernel, add the following lines to /etc/rc.conf:

```
firewall_enable="YES"
firewall_type="open"
```

If you don't specify that the firewall type should be open, the only rule that IPFW will start with is the default one, with an index of 65535 (the maximum), specifying deny ip from any to any. In other words, if you reboot with IPFW in its default configuration, your machine will be completely blocked off from the network, and you'll have to have physical console access to it in order to get it back.

> **CAUTION**
>
> It's dangerous to experiment with IPFW if you don't have console access, because it's very easy to put your machine into an unreachable state. Until you are comfortable enough with IPFW to know exactly what you're doing, always make sure you can access the machine via the console in case something goes wrong.
>
> If you do end up blocking your machine from the network through experimentation with IPFW, the only way to recover is to go to where the machine is physically located and log in from the console. From there, you can disable IPFW by removing the lines in /etc/rc.conf, or you can configure it properly and reboot.

The open setting changes the default rules so that IP traffic is passed (allowed) by default, rather than blocked. Blocking traffic by default creates a truly secure system, but it can be excessively restrictive for systems that exist within a secure environment. At the same time, allowing traffic by default (blocking only specified IP traffic) eliminates the possibility of having complete system security. Use the open setting if your system is in a network that's already behind a firewall; you probably don't need to apply the same kind of protection twice.

Once your /etc/rc.conf is set up properly, reboot. Alternatively, you can run the /etc/netstart script from the physical console (not from a remote terminal, which is *very* dangerous because it can cause your machine to lose network connectivity and become inaccessible). You will know the firewall has been enabled properly if you see the following lines:

```
Kernel firewall module loaded
Flushed all rules.
00100 allow ip from any to any via lo0
00200 deny ip from any to 127.0.0.0/8
00300 deny ip from 127.0.0.0/8 to any
65000 allow ip from any to any
Firewall rules loaded, starting divert daemons:.
```

You can also use kldstat to check whether the IPFW module has been loaded automatically:

```
# kldstat
Id Refs Address    Size      Name
 1    3 0xc0100000 355be4    kernel
 2    1 0xc0eee000 6000      ipfw.ko
 3    1 0xc0f19000 12000     linux.ko
```

You now have full access to the ipfw command, which lets you set rules on what kinds of traffic to allow and view the accounting information accumulated by IPFW.

Configuring IPFW

The ipfw command is used to either add or delete rules from the kernel filter and accounting system. The rules are constructed in a syntax that flows somewhat like natural English; it's made up of an action (such as deny), a protocol to which the action applies (such as tcp), and an address specification involving a from clause and a to clause. A rule such as deny tcp from badhost.com to any, for example, blocks TCP traffic from a host called badhost.com. You would add this rule to the kernel firewall like this:

```
# ipfw add deny tcp from badhost.com to any
```

A number of variations on this theme are possible. You can specify an address based on a network mask either with a mask pattern (for example, 255.255.255.0) or with a CIDR bit-mask (for example, /24). You can also block individual ports rather than an entire system; this technique prevents hosts within a large ISP with unpredictable IP addresses from targeting a single service on your machine. Such a rule might look like this:

```
# ipfw add deny all from evil.isp.com/16 to www.somewhere.com 80
```

29

Similarly, you can exempt hosts from earlier rules by adding `allow` rules as exceptions, like so:

```
# ipfw add allow all from goodhost.evil.isp.com to www.somewhere.com 80
```

Note that IPFW rules are entered in a "chain," in which each rule is evaluated in the order it was specified. Each rule has an index number, normally spaced by 100 from its neighbors, which you can control by specifying the index number after the `add` or `deny` keyword in an `ipfw` command; this is how you can indicate the execution order of your rules. View the existing rule set with `ipfw -a list`:

```
# ipfw -a list
00100   0     0 allow ip from any to any via lo0
00200   0     0 deny ip from any to 127.0.0.0/8
00300   0     0 deny ip from 127.0.0.0/8 to any
00400   0     0 deny tcp from badhost.com to any
00500   0     0 ipfw add deny all from evil.isp.com/16 to www.somewhere.com 80
00600   0     0 ipfw add allow all from goodhost.evil.isp.com to
➥www.somewhere.com 80
65000 1214 79688 allow ip from any to any
65535   1    40 deny ip from any to any
```

The index number is shown in the first column; the number 65535 rule, as you saw earlier, is the default deny rule that rejects anything that falls through from above. The open setting puts an `allow` bucket above the `deny` rule; however, the `allow` rule has a high index number to help ensure that it comes after any other rules that you might add through regular usage.

The second and third columns show usage statistics, displaying the total number of packets and bytes that have matched each rule, respectively. This is how you can tell whether your rules are being effective.

Troubleshooting IPFW

You might find that what you think is a very straightforward configuration results in completely unpredictable results. For instance, you might have added a deny rule for all hosts and an allow rule for your own remote machine's IP address, but you find you still can't access the FreeBSD machine.

Always remember that IPFW rules are specified and applied in subsequent order. A rule that comes later in the list supercedes a rule specified earlier in the list; a packet is compared against each rule in the order specified by the index number. In most cases (although it depends to a certain extent on the action taken and the system settings), the packet continues to be checked against further rules that might match in a more specific manner; this is how "exception" rules work. However, the "default" rule, with index 65536, only matches packets that match no other rules.

Make sure your index numbers apply the rules in increasing order of specificity. To make configuration easier, consider using a firewall configuration file, as we'll discuss shortly.

You can specify a number of different firewall types in /etc/rc.conf. Each keyword has a different meaning, as shown in Table 29.2. The exact definitions of these profiles can be deciphered from the shell script code in /etc/rc.firewall.

TABLE 29.2   Available Firewall Types

Keyword	Meaning
open	Allows access to all, from all
closed	Disables all IPs except on the loopback (lo0) interface
client	Sets up rules designed to protect just this machine
simple	Sets up rules designed to protect the whole network
unknown	Loads no rules except for the default deny rule at index 65535
<filename>	Loads rules from <filename>

For your purpose, if your setup is uncomplicated, a "canned" IPFW profile such as client or simple might be appropriate. However, you're likely to need a specialized configuration as your system continues to evolve.

Using a Firewall Configuration File

Because firewall rules are not persistent (they are flushed with each reboot), you will want to maintain your firewall with a configuration file if you have customized firewall settings. This also has the benefit of being easier to maintain and faster to troubleshoot than working with IPFW from the command line.

Put your specialized rule set into a file of your choice; for this example, call it /etc/firewall.conf. List your desired rules in that file, omitting the ipfw command itself:

```
add deny tcp from badhost.com to any
add deny all from evil.isp.com/16 to www.somewhere.com 80
add allow all from goodhost.evil.isp.com to www.somewhere.com 80
add 65000 allow all from any to any
```

Now, change the firewall_type in your /etc/rc.conf file:

```
firewall_type="/etc/firewall.conf"
```

The next time you reboot or run /etc/netstart, the rules from /etc/firewall.conf will be loaded with indexes of 100, 200, 300, and so on. An allow all rule at index 65000 provides a default behavior of passing traffic rather than denying it, which is desirable in most cases (unless you only want specified hosts to be able to access your machine).

For further reading on IPFW, see the man ipfw page and the online *FreeBSD Handbook* at http://www.freebsd.org/handbook.

Preventing Intrusions and Compromises

Firewalls, password policies, and encryption go a long way toward protecting your system from malicious access. They still aren't enough, though, to defend against a really determined hacker who has a "rootkit" or other tool designed to take advantage of some known weakness in one of your system's services.

You can use a variety of tools in Red Hat Linux that go beyond the functionality of a simple firewall to dynamically block suspicious hosts, monitor for intrusions, and control access to individual services on a host-by-host basis. The following sections describe a few of these tools.

Using PortSentry

PortSentry, from Psionic Software, is a daemon that monitors all incoming network traffic to detect port scans—preliminary attacks in which a hacker probes your system for open services that can be exploited. PortSentry listens in on a list of ports you specify. When PortSentry detects traffic that might indicate a port scan, it blocks that host from accessing your system by wrapping it in a blackhole route (a route that silently discards packets from a given IP address or range) or IPFW rule. All future connection attempts from the offending host are discarded.

PortSentry monitors both TCP and UDP traffic, dynamically building a "killfile" table of sorts—a list of banned addresses—that acts like an antibody against a virus. PortSentry reacts to suspicious activity by blocking it before it has a chance to cause any damage.

PortSentry is an open-source tool and can be installed out of the ports (`/usr/ports/ security/portsentry`). The `portsentry` binary is installed into `/usr/local/bin`, and the configuration file is `/usr/local/etc/portsentry.conf`. Open this file in your favorite text editor; it needs to be edited in order for PortSentry to work properly.

You must decide which set of ports you want PortSentry to monitor. There are three available sets, in pairs beginning with `TCP_PORTS` and `UDP_PORTS`:

```
# Un-comment these if you are really anal:
#TCP_PORTS="1,7,9,11,15,70,79,80,109,110,111,119,138,139,143,512,513,514...
#UDP_PORTS="1,7,9,66,67,68,69,111,137,138,161,162,474,513,517,518,635,640...
#
# Use these if you just want to be aware:
TCP_PORTS="1,11,15,111,119,540,635,1524,2000,5742,12345,12346,20034,31337...
UDP_PORTS="1,7,9,69,161,162,513,635,640,641,700,32770,32771,32772,32773...
#
# Use these for just bare-bones
#TCP_PORTS="1,11,15,110,111,143,540,635,1080,524,2000,12345,12346,20034...
#UDP_PORTS="1,7,9,69,161,162,513,640,700,32770,32771,32772,32773,32774...
```

The first set is quite large; it is intended for a very strict security policy in which any remotely suspicious port will trigger a blocking rule. The second set is more moderate, and the third is minimal, watching only the ports that a remote user can't possibly be contacting unless he's performing a port scan or trying to run an exploit.

The middle set, the "if you want to be aware" grouping, is enabled by default. To switch to one of the other two, comment out the middle set and uncomment the one you want. If you like, you can create your own set. Make sure that none of the ports used by your core services are included in this list! For example, port 143 is listed in all three sample sets, but 143 is the IMAP port. If you're running IMAP services, make sure to remove port 143 from the list. If you're not, however, leave it in—it will trap attackers who try to exploit IMAP-related security flaws.

After choosing the ports to be monitored, you must choose a method by which to block suspicious hosts. You can do this through IPFW (if you're running it, as discussed earlier in the chapter) or through blackhole routes (if you're not running IPFW). Choosing a method involves uncommenting a single line beginning with KILL_ROUTE, which specifies the system command that PortSentry should use to block an offending host.

For a system running IPFW, uncomment the line in portsentry.conf containing /sbin/ipfw, like so:

```
# For those of you running FreeBSD (and compatible) you can
# use their built in firewalling as well.
#
KILL_ROUTE="/sbin/ipfw add 1 deny all from $TARGET$:255.255.255.255 to any"
```

If you're not using IPFW, use the blackhole route method, which, despite the comments, works just as well as IPFW:

```
# FreeBSD (Not well tested.)
KILL_ROUTE="route add -net $TARGET$ -netmask 255.255.255.255
➥127.0.0.1 -blackhole"
```

Once you've enabled a blocking method, PortSentry is ready to run. However, as of this writing, the PortSentry port doesn't come with an automated startup script. You can use the script shown in Listing 29.1 (available on the companion CD as portsentry.sh); set it to be executable, and copy it into your /usr/local/etc/rc.d directory to start up PortSentry each time your system boots.

LISTING 29.1   Sample PortSentry Startup Script

```
#!/bin/sh

PORTSENTRY="/usr/local/bin/portsentry"
```

LISTING 29.1   Continued

```
case "$1" in
    start)
        ${PORTSENTRY} -tcp && echo " Starting PortSentry TCP mode..."
        ${PORTSENTRY} -udp && echo " Starting PortSentry UDP mode..."
        ;;

    stop)
        killall `basename ${PORTSENTRY}`
        ;;
    *)
        echo ""
        echo "Usage: `basename $0` { start | stop }"
        echo ""
        ;;
esac
```

> **TIP**
>
> While PortSentry is running, you can see which ports it's listening on by using the `sockstat` command:
>
> ```
> # sockstat
> USER     COMMAND    PID    FD PROTO  LOCAL ADDRESS      FOREIGN ADDRESS
> root     portsent   2432   0  udp4   *:1                *:*
> root     portsent   2432   1  udp4   *:7                *:*
> root     portsent   2432   2  udp4   *:9                *:*
> root     portsent   2432   3  udp4   *:69               *:*
> root     portsent   2432   4  udp4   *:161              *:*
> root     portsent   2432   5  udp4   *:162              *:*
> ...
> ```

Each time PortSentry detects an attack attempt, it lists the host and ports that triggered the detection in `/usr/local/etc/portsentry.blocked.tcp` for TCP attacks and `/usr/local/etc/portsentry.blocked.udp` for UDP attacks. PortSentry uses these lists to keep track of which hosts it has already blocked so that it doesn't try to block them again later. You can also use these files to see what hosts have been caught by your attack-detection system. These files are cleared out automatically each time PortSentry starts up. When you reboot, both IPFW and the routing table are cleared of any entries that were added during runtime, so a host that was blocked once will have access to you again if you reboot—at least until it tries to probe your ports again.

If you're using the IPFW KILL_ROUTE method, view the current blocking rules with `ipfw -a list`:

```
# ipfw -a list
00001    1      44 deny ip from 209.237.26.165 to any
```

If you're using blackhole routes, use `netstat -rn`:

```
# netstat -rn
Routing tables

Internet:
Destination        Gateway        Flags     Refs     Use     Netif Expire
...
209.237.26.165/32  127.0.0.1      UGScB      0        0       lo0
```

The B flag indicates a "blackhole" route, in which packets are simply discarded.

Each time an attack is detected, `/var/log/messages` receives lines indicating what PortSentry is doing about it:

```
Jun  2 23:50:56 stripes portsentry[2430]: attackalert: Connect
➥from host: 209.237.26.165/209.237.26.165 to TCP port: 1
Jun  2 23:50:56 stripes portsentry[2430]: attackalert:
➥Host 209.237.26.165 has been blocked via wrappers with
➥string: "ALL: 209.237.26.165"
Jun  2 23:50:56 stripes portsentry[2430]: attackalert:
➥Host 209.237.26.165 has been blocked via dropped
➥route using command: "/sbin/ipfw add 1 deny all
➥from 209.237.26.165:255.255.255.255 to any"
```

Another tool from the makers of PortSentry is Logcheck (available in `/usr/ports/security/logcheck`); it analyzes this and other log files and sends you a daily report on any unusual activity or detected attacks.

29

As with IPFW, be careful when testing PortSentry. It's very easy to trigger an attack detection; if you do, the system from which you're administering your FreeBSD machine becomes blocked. That can happen, for instance, if you telnet to port 1 "just to see what happens." What will happen is that your host will be blocked, and further connection attempts will simply time out.

> You will have to connect from a different host or the physical console to remove the mistakenly applied rule, either through an `ipfw delete 1` or `route delete <IP address>/32` command.
>
> If you want to protect certain hosts (such as your own machines) from ever being blocked by PortSentry, add their IP addresses to the `/usr/local/etc/portsentry.ignore` file.

Using `/etc/hosts.allow`

The `/etc/hosts.allow` file lets you block certain hosts from accessing certain services on your system. This file is like a manual version of PortSentry. You can specify a block of rules for a given service and apply each rule to a certain IP address or set of addresses; each rule either allows or denies matching hosts access to the service. Here's a sample block of rules from the default `/etc/hosts.allow` file, with a few extra lines added to show sample syntaxes:

```
sendmail : localhost : allow
sendmail : .nice.guy.example.com : allow
sendmail : .evil.cracker.example.com : deny
sendmail : 231.21.15.0/255.255.255.0 : deny
sendmail : 12.124.231. : deny
sendmail : ALL : allow
```

Because you've seen how IPFW works, the format of these rules is pretty easy to figure out. A rule has at least three fields:

- The service (specified by process name)

- The matching hostnames or IP addresses

- The action to take (or multiple actions, if there are four or more fields)

The first two columns can be lists (multiple entries separated by spaces), and the host column can match a variety of different ways: a leading dot to specify an entire DNS subnet or a trailing dot to do the same for an IP address. Separate an IP address and a netmask with a slash to specify a network. The block should end with a "default" rule, specifying whether to allow or deny access to the service by default. Generally, if you're running the service, there's a good reason for it; you'll probably want your default rule to be "allow" so that clients other than ones you've explicitly allowed can access that service.

You can use `/etc/hosts.allow` to specify actions other than simply "allow" and "deny." You can use it to make unauthorized access to a service, trigger an e-mail to you, or execute a program that does some kind of reverse probing against the remote host (although this is probably not a good idea—it can be fun to "fight fire with fire," but it's bad form, and dangerous, to stoop to the level of the hacker who attacked you). This file can execute any shell command in response to a match for a given rule. The default rule for the fingerd service shows an example of this type of configuration:

```
fingerd : ALL \
        : spawn (echo Finger. | \
        /usr/bin/mail -s "tcpd\: %u@%h[%a] fingered me!" root) & \
        : deny
```

The %u, %h, and %a codes and additional configuration options are described in man 5 hosts_access and man hosts_options.

Using Tripwire

You can use intrusion detection to provide security that goes beyond outright blocking of suspicious hosts. A sufficiently wily hacker will be able to get past your security checks, no matter how carefully you set them up. If that happens, you need to be able to see whether he got into the system and caused any damage. If your system has been "owned," you want to know about it as soon as it happens, and the exact extent of the damage.

Tripwire, available at /usr/ports/security/tripwire, is a widely used intrusion-detection tool. Tripwire keeps an authenticity record of every program on the system. It compiles an "authoritative" record on your programs when you first run it during installation, and it adds records of new programs when you install them. On a daily basis, Tripwire compares a new record of every program on the system to the authoritative record. If Tripwire detects any differences in the programs (for example, if the sshd executable has suddenly changed size or had its contents or meta-data altered in any way), it notifies you via e-mail. That e-mail gives you an immediate notification that your system has been compromised.

When you first install Tripwire, it builds its initial database of program "fingerprints" during the make install phase, and it writes this out into a file in the /var/db/tripwire directory. This file is signed with local and site passphrases that you specify at installation time; therefore, you don't have to worry about the database file being tampered with. If it's modified without your knowledge, Tripwire will warn you that a security breach has occurred at the next time you use it.

You must first create a configuration file for Tripwire. This is done with the twadmin utility; in this case, we'll use the -m F mode (Create Configuration File), specifying the site keyfile with -S and the input configuration file at the end:

```
# twadmin -m F -S /usr/local/etc/tripwire/site.key
➥/usr/local/etc/tripwire/twcfg.txt
Please enter your passphrase:
Wrote configuration file: /usr/local/etc/tripwire/tw.cfg
```

29

From now on, you can have the system run tripwire every night in the periodic tasks (you learned about these tasks in Chapter 13, "Performance Monitoring, Process Control, and Job Automation"). When tripwire is run with the --check argument, it operates in integrity-check mode, scanning all the files specified in /usr/local/etc/tripwire/ twpol.txt for mismatches against the database of file fingerprints. If any inconsistencies are found, it reports them, as with this example, in which the file modification time of /usr/sbin/sshd has been changed:

```
# tripwire --check
...
===============================================================================
Rule Summary:
===============================================================================


-------------------------------------------------------------------------------
  Section: Unix File System
-------------------------------------------------------------------------------


  Rule Name                       Severity Level   Added   Removed  Modified
  ---------                       --------------   -----   -------  --------
  Invariant Directories           66               0       0        0
  Sources                         100              0       0        0
  Temporary directories           33               0       0        0
  Tripwire Data Files             100              0       0        0
  Local files                     100              0       8        0
  Tripwire Binaries               100              0       0        0
  Libraries, include files, and other system files
                                  100              0       0        0
* System Administration Programs  66               0       0        1
  User Utilities                  100              0       0        0
  X11R6                           100              0       0        0
  NIS                             100              0       0        0
  (/var/yp)
  /etc                            100              0       0        0
  Security Control                100              0       0        0
  Root's home                     100              0       0        0
  FreeBSD Kernel                  100              0       0        0
  FreeBSD Modules                 100              0       0        0
  /dev                            100              0       0        0
  Linux Compatibility             100              0       0        0
  (/compat)

Total objects scanned:  466299
Total violations found:  1
```

It may well be that you expect this file to be different from what Tripwire expects; you may have installed an updated version of sshd, for example. Whenever you update files that Tripwire is monitoring, you should update the Tripwire database to reflect the new information. You can update it with the --update option:

```
# tripwire --update
```

This command reruns the entire Tripwire database-generation process, which scans the entire filesystem and writes out an updated database file signed with your site and local passphrases (for which you are prompted when you run the program).

If you *really* want to make sure your Tripwire database is secure, and you don't even trust the built-in signing mechanism that protects it, you can create a Tripwire floppy disk— placing the database in a separate location from the computer is the most secure method of all to ensure data integrity.

Unfortunately, a Tripwire database is too big to fit on a floppy; however, you can remove items from the Tripwire "policy" to make the database file smaller. Do this by editing /usr/local/etc/tripwire/twpol.txt, removing or commenting-out the lines specifying file locations you don't want, and then creating the actual (non-human-readable) policy file by issuing the twadmin command with the -m P (or --create-polfile) argument:

```
# twadmin -m P -S /usr/local/etc/tripwire/site.key
➥/usr/local/etc/tripwire/twpol.txt
```

Then, when the database file that results from another tripwire --update run is less than 1.44MB in size, you can go to /usr/ports/security/tripwire and use the make floppy command to automatically create a floppy disk with the Tripwire database file and the associated tools copied to it. You should note, however, that going to the length of creating a Tripwire floppy disk is considered completely unnecessary today, now that the local database files are themselves protected.

Air Gaps

When you keep your Tripwire database on a floppy disk or other removable media, you're using an *air gap*—a security condition where no automated process can possibly get data from one side of the "gap" to the other. Any system in which data can move via software from point A to point B is potentially susceptible to penetration by a sufficiently ingenious hacker. Given enough time and effort, someone intent on infiltrating your data will be able to access your archives— even if you go to such lengths as having a second "hidden" hard drive that mounts itself automatically during the night to perform a backup operation. That's still an automated procedure and therefore vulnerable to anyone willing to try to break its security.

Properly designed hospital and government networks maintain critical databases on machines that have no connection to any machines on the network; they're separated by an air gap and are therefore secure…at least as far as the administrators physically in charge of the systems can be trusted. An air gap is a "last-resort" security measure, the ultimate in decreased convenience

29

for the sake of guaranteed security. If you keep your data in a physically separate location from any machine connected to the network, no hacker can break into it.

When you keep your crucial data on a floppy disk, CD-R, or other removable media, you are employing an air gap that protects your data from being compromised, even if the entire networked system is infiltrated. That is, of course, unless you leave that removable disk in the drive.

If You Think You've Been Hacked...

As you learned earlier, you should assume that your system—no matter how secure—will be hacked at some point. Although Tripwire and PortSentry can take a great deal of the drudgery of intrusion prevention and detection off your shoulders, you should still be on the alert for subtle and subjective changes in how the system behaves. Here are some simple ways you can monitor your system's security:

- Keep an eye on top, as described in Chapter 13; monitor what your system's load is over long periods, and see whether it gradually gets higher; if it does, investigate to see what might be causing this.

- Don't ignore mysterious behavior changes such as login prompts that seem to be formatted wrong or command-line output that doesn't look right.

- Look through /tmp and /var/tmp periodically, watching for anything executable or setuid or very large. Also, clear out those directories regularly.

- Watch your system's log files in /var/log; be on the lookout for messages that seem suspicious, such as anything with long strings of garbage characters. These are almost certainly hack attempts probing for buffer overflows.

In short, be constantly on the lookout for anything out of the ordinary. Such ad hoc watchfulness is sometimes the only way to notice that your system isn't behaving the way it should.

> **NOTE**
>
> A favorite place to find evidence of hacker activity is in /dev. That's where packet-sniffing tools are often placed by intruders running prepackaged "rootkits" or scripts. However, because FreeBSD now uses a dynamically generated DEVFS device filesystem, this is less of a worry—but it still doesn't hurt to keep an eye out.

If you do suspect that you've been hacked (and especially if you find any evidence of it), you must assume that the damage is greater than it appears. The most common mistake for an administrator to make who has discovered evidence of a security breach is to simply disable a few services and assume that the attacker has gone away. Often, this may be the case; however, treating all such incidents in this manner is an invitation to disaster. All it takes is for the attacker to have installed a "backdoor" of some kind that lets him return and cause much more destructive damage than before.

If you suspect you have been hacked, or "owned," here are some steps you must take:

1. Disconnect the system from the Net immediately. No matter what backdoors the attacker has installed in your system, he can't do anything if the system isn't on the network (in other words, it's behind an air gap). This prevents a hacker who realizes that he has been discovered from covering his tracks by wiping your hard disk clean.

2. Check /var/cron/tabs and /etc/crontab for new entries; also check atq for jobs the attacker has left to be run in his absence. The system may be off the network, but cron jobs will still run, and the hacker can still trash your system in this way unless you clear out any suspicious pending jobs.

3. Don't try to contact the attacker or let him know that you're on to him. Even after you've removed your system from harm's way, the attacker will vanish if he realizes you're trying to track him down, and law enforcement will have a much harder job finding him. Let him think you've simply taken the machine offline to recover from the damage.

4. Gather together your log files from /var/log, and wherever else your programs might have them, and comb them for entries that might indicate where the attacker came from and how he gained access. If you are running any services for which security bulletins have been recently posted, and you haven't updated those services to remedy their vulnerabilities, it's almost a certainty that that's how the attacker gained access.

5. Take as much useful information as you can find to the National Infrastructure Protection Center (NIPC) Web site, http://www.nipc.gov (or the equivalent for your country's cybercrime investigation agency, if you're not in the United States), and fill out an incident report. This arm of the FBI is in charge of investigating cybercrime and hacker activity, and provided they have enough concrete information from your affected data, they can swiftly track down the perpetrator. Most hacker activity is committed by "script kiddies"—casual vandals who use tools prepackaged by others to exploit certain known vulnerabilities. These types of hackers usually can be found and prosecuted quite successfully.

6. Back up your important data—Web documents, configuration files, home directories, and everything in /usr/local—and reinstall the operating system. To be really thorough, wipe the hard disk clean, reinstall FreeBSD from scratch, and restore the local data. Use the daily output of Tripwire to tell you to what extent you need to "nuke and pave" the machine; beware of backdoors that may have been installed among your own installed programs in /usr/local, or even among your Web documents or configuration files.

29

7. Update all your services to the most recent versions, referring to all relevant security bulletins, before putting the system back online. Be especially vigilant for the first few days after bringing the system back up; the hacker may continue to try to break in. Pay especially close attention to your log files during this period; the more evidence you can gather, the easier it will be for the NIPC and FBI to do their job.

Denial of Service (DOS) Attacks

Although it isn't technically a security issue, another type of malicious network activity has nonetheless become quite important to system administrators recently. This is the Denial of Service (DOS) attack.

DOS attacks don't involve any compromise of a system's security or privacy. Rather, they are simply brute-force floods, sending so much traffic over a network that legitimate traffic is lost in the shuffle. The goal is often to crash the server through sheer overwhelming volume of data and number of requests. These kinds of attacks are much harder to defend against than directed hack attacks, which can be foiled through the use of IPFW, PortSentry, and the other tools we have already discussed. The impact of a DOS attack cannot be eliminated; it can only be mitigated because DOS attacks are made up completely of legitimate traffic, indistinguishable from your actual mission-critical data flow. The problem is just that there's too much of it.

Sometimes, a DOS attack can be identified as coming from a certain source, and you can block it by adding a firewall rule to deny traffic from or to that source. However, many recent attacks hide the actual source—ping (ICMP) broadcast attacks look as if they're coming from a certain source address, which is actually the victim address that receives the brunt of the attack. Distributed DOS, or DDOS, attacks work even more insidiously, with hundreds or even thousands of compromised desktop machines unwittingly taking part in the attack, so tracking down the actual culprit is pretty much impossible.

Certain configuration options in various servers and in the kernel can help to prevent your system from completely submerging during a DOS attack. The following sections look at a few of these measures; however, bear in mind that they can only serve to increase your system's chances of surviving a DOS attack—they can't neutralize the attack itself, nor can they guarantee that the attacker won't simply try harder until your system does succumb.

Limiting Server Forks

Many DOS attacks are targeted against services such as Apache, Sendmail, or others that operate by *forking* a new process to handle each incoming request. If an attacker sends an overwhelming number of requests to the service, it will fork off so many processes that the CPU and memory will eventually become exhausted, possibly destabilizing your system.

You can mitigate the risk of a server fork attack by making sure that all your forking services have built-in limits to the number of simultaneous child processes they can have. These limitations can impact the services' ability to fulfill legitimate requests during normal operation, but that tradeoff may be what saves you during a DOS attack.

Apache has a `MaxClients` directive (by default set to 150) that keeps more than that number of requests from being serviced at once. A wily attacker, however, can repeatedly request a processor-intensive CGI script until Apache is creating executable processes faster than they can complete. Requests for executable processes are much more likely to trigger a runaway server than are requests for static HTML pages. If you can get the system to accept a Telnet or SSH login, shut down Apache (`apachectl stop`) until the attack is over. That may be the only way to recover from such an attack.

Fortunately, most HTTP DOS attacks are traceable to a single client IP address, which you can block with IPFW rules or with a `deny from` directive in Apache itself. If this doesn't work, though, you can always decrease `MaxClients` to the point where even if the server is maxed out, the clients can't swamp it.

There's a similar feature in Sendmail: `MaxDaemonChildren`, disabled by default, which you can enable by uncommenting it in `/etc/mail/sendmail.cf` directly and restarting the server (`make restart`). Apart from this, Sendmail has a built-in brake that prevents it from starting new processes if the system load is over 12; however, this mechanism has too much lag during a fast-moving attack for the server to respond well, so it may be necessary to explicitly limit the number of children Sendmail can have at a time.

> **TIP**
>
> Other directives in Sendmail that you can use to help foil attackers (or anybody using your server too aggressively) are `QueueLA`, `RefuseLA`, `DelayLA`, and `ConnectionRateThrottle`. These directives are documented with comment lines in `sendmail.cf` itself and should be fairly self-explanatory. For instance, `QueueLA` (which in its default state is set to 8, but disabled) can be uncommented to make Sendmail queue messages automatically rather than attempting to deliver them, if the load average is higher than 8.

A potential general solution to fork attacks, even defending against those that might originate from your own system (a renegade or clumsy user, for example), is to modify `/etc/login.conf` to put limits on the CPU, RAM, and open file usage that a user can have. Create a class for the user that runs the service in question—nobody in the case of Apache, or an individual local user whose resources you want to limit—and use `chfn` to put the user into the class. An example `login.conf` class might look like this:

```
baduser:\
        :cputime=30m:\
        :openfiles=24:\
        :maxproc=32:\
```

```
:memoryuse=16m:\
:tc=default:
```

Then, use `cap_mkdb /etc/login.conf` to enable this new class and enforce these limits on any user in it.

Defending Against Springboard Attacks

A *springboard attack* leverages the resources of your own network to achieve its ends. Whereas brute-force and forking attacks require a high-powered attacker doing a lot of work, an attacker can launch a springboard attack simply by injecting a carefully constructed set of requests into the network. Those requests make the network's own infrastructure its own worst enemy.

An attacker can launch a broadcast ping (or *Smurf*) attack, for example, by sending normal ping requests to your network's broadcast address (which multiplexes the requests out to all hosts on the network). The hacker spoofs the requests' source address so it appears to be a different host. Typically, that host is a hapless victim who suffers a lot more than you do in this type of attack, because every host in your network turns around and floods the victim with ping responses. The multiplication effect of this kind of attack can be disastrous for the victim, and the source is very difficult (if not impossible) to trace.

> **NOTE**
>
> Another kind of springboard attack injects a UDP packet between two servers' `echo` service ports. This packet causes the servers to enter into an "echo war" that can be stopped only by shutting off the `echo` port (FreeBSD shuts off the `echo` port by default).

Springboard attacks are best prevented at the network's edge router; Smurf attacks can be prevented by configuring your router not to respond to broadcast ping requests. If your router is a FreeBSD machine (see Chapter 27 for information on using FreeBSD as a router), the `icmp_bmcastecho="NO"` setting in `/etc/defaults/rc.conf` prevents it from responding to these kinds of requests, which are almost never used for any good purpose.

ICMP error messages are another common source of springboard attacks. The `ICMP_BANDLIM` tool (compiled into the `GENERIC` kernel by default) limits the rate at which responses to ICMP error messages are sent, limiting such an attack's effectiveness. In FreeBSD 5.0 and later, `ICMP_BANDLIM` is no longer even an option—it can't be disabled. You can, however, tune the number of ICMP responses your machine will handle per second with the `sysctl` command:

```
# sysctl net.inet.icmp.icmplim=100
net.inet.icmp.icmplim: 200 -> 100
```

Use `sysctl -a` to determine what the currently set value for the variable is, as shown here:

```
# sysctl -a net.inet.icmp.icmplim
net.inet.icmp.icmplim: 100
```

Physical Security

The most secure system in the world can always be compromised if there's a possibility that an unauthorized person can gain physical access to the server machine itself, because no amount of software security can defend against someone with a screwdriver.

Secure co-location facilities are vital for a commercial or otherwise high-profile Internet server. Such a facility provides locked server cabinets in locked machine rooms, and only employees of the facility are generally allowed to open the cabinets and physically access the machines. Your system might itself be in a rack-mounted case with a locked front panel and BIOS security measures that warn you if the panel has been removed.

Anybody with physical access to the machine can reboot it into single-user mode, which doesn't prompt for the root password in the default configuration. You can change this so that it does prompt for a password by telling `/etc/ttys` that the console is "insecure," meaning that you can't guarantee that anybody accessing it is authorized:

```
console none                            unknown off insecure
```

However, this doesn't stop an intruder from being able to boot from a floppy disk or CD to compromise your system. Other devices attached to the machine can also be used to gain unauthorized access: modems, for example, or wireless networks, which should not be a part of any machine from which you're trying to restrict physical access. The bottom line is that you cannot secure your system unless you control all physical access to it.

Other Security Resources

This chapter has covered a few general security topics as they apply specifically to FreeBSD. However, the subject of network security is vast, and it grows each day as more and more malicious users try to find ways to bring down the Internet's core services.

A number of excellent resources are available on security, both FreeBSD specific and general, that you would do well to check out.

The `man security` Page

Compiled by Matthew Dillon, the `man security` page contains a long discussion of general security topics and good administrative habits. It also provides miscellaneous tips for preventing break-ins and DOS attacks. This page is the basis for a number of online resources, including part of the *FreeBSD Handbook*.

Mailing Lists

Join the `freebsd-security@freebsd.org` mailing list. Do this by sending a message to `majordomo@freebsd.org`, with `subscribe freebsd-security` in the message body. This list is where the most up-to-date discussion of security issues takes place. As an administrator, you will need to keep abreast of the most recent developments so you can defend against each new vulnerability as it becomes known.

Another useful security list, geared toward Unix security issues in general, is Bugtraq. This list receives advisories of all major issues that arise in Internet security, sometimes before their full impact on FreeBSD is known. Bugtraq is hosted at `http://www.securityfocus.com`, where you can subscribe to the list or search its archives.

FreeBSD Security Advisories

Security advisories are sent out by the FreeBSD Security Officer onto the `freebsd-announce@freebsd.org` and `freebsd-security@freebsd.org` lists to warn of newly discovered vulnerabilities. Each advisory is also archived at `http://www.freebsd.org/security/`.

An advisory contains a complete discussion of the nature and impact of a vulnerability, whether it exists in part of the core FreeBSD system or in a program in the ports collection, whether it's FreeBSD specific or not, and how to work around or solve the problem. Because it would be inviting hackers to a free lunch to disclose the exact nature of a vulnerability before a fix is available, advisories are released only after a solution has been found. This is one good reason to be subscribed to `freebsd-security@freebsd.org`, because there will be discussion of a vulnerability there even before the advisory is released.

Fixes to vulnerabilities in ports or packages usually mean simply synchronizing your ports tree and rebuilding the port in question (see Chapter 14). A fix to the core FreeBSD system, though, is usually checked into the appropriate -STABLE or -CURRENT source tree; to take advantage of it, you will need to rebuild that part of your system after synchronizing your sources. If the fix is in a sufficiently fundamental part of the system code, you may need to do a complete `make world` to make your system secure. Instructions on how to do this are in Chapter 17, "Keeping Up to Date with FreeBSD."

Web Resources

The FreeBSD Security Information page, `http://www.freebsd.org/security/`, contains resources and links geared toward the FreeBSD administrator or developer. Security advisories are archived here, as are various tips and tricks for reducing your risk factors.

The FreeBSD Security How-To (`http://people.freebsd.org/~jkb/howto.html`) is a lengthy discussion of various methods by which you can secure your FreeBSD system. It covers many topics discussed in this chapter, and many more that are not.

CERT (http://www.cert.org), the Internet's foremost security advisory site, maintains resources on security vulnerabilities in all different operating systems and is widely regarded as the authoritative source of alerts and recovery information. CERT also handles incident reports; you can report a break-in there, and they will work with the proper authorities to catch the perpetrator.

SecurityFocus, the site that hosts Bugtraq, is a security news site covering topics from intrusion-detection systems to virus protection. It also has numerous articles on good security practices and how to run a system responsibly. It doesn't have much in the way of FreeBSD-specific material, but much of its information can be applied to any platform. The URL is http://www.securityfocus.com.

Books

Two books suggested in /etc/rc.firewall are *Firewalls & Internet Security*, by William R. Cheswick and Steven M. Bellowin, for general network security topics, and *Building Internet Firewalls, 2nd Edition*, by Brent Chapman and Elizabeth Zwicky, for fuller coverage of firewall theory and practice.

Further books and papers on security are listed and scored for usefulness at the SecurityFocus site, under the "Library" link.

29

CHAPTER **30**

Virtual Private Networks (VPNs)

If you have reached this stage in this book and have paid careful attention to the previous chapters on security and server management, it's clear you have an active interest in being a security-conscious network citizen. Even if you're not a network administrator, you have learned the importance of keeping the transactions associated with your everyday computing as secure as possible. You use SSH for your remote terminal operations, you encrypt your POP3 and IMAP e-mail traffic, and you implement a secure password policy. Your online life is about as secure as it can be.

However, that all changes as soon as you start talking about networking protocols beyond basic e-mail and terminal traffic. Network security can become particularly complex when it incorporates aspects such as Network Address Translation (NAT), firewalls, and corporate LANs that are not accessible from anywhere on the public Internet. How are you supposed to do Windows file sharing with your company's corporate LAN servers if you're at home or on the road? How can you be sure your communications with the office are encrypted no matter what protocol you're using?

This is the role of the Virtual Private Network (VPN) model. This chapter introduces the underlying concepts of VPNs, describes some of the various types of VPN implementations and topologies, and guides you through configuring your FreeBSD machine to support a VPN, whether as a client (dialing in to a remote private network) or as a server (allowing other clients to access the network your FreeBSD machine is protecting).

What Is a VPN?

Corporate networks are protected from prying public eyes through various methods, many of which you have already seen in this book. Arguably the most common situation is for a company's network to be situated behind a firewall device that performs Network Address Translation (NAT) of IP addresses within the company to a single "masked" address visible from the outside. The idea behind this configuration is that machines within the network can access resources out on the Internet, but machines on the Internet cannot contact the "masked" corporate machines directly.

> **TIP**
>
> Network Address Translation is an Internet connection technique that enables multiple hosts to connect to the Internet using a single IP address. NAT is fully described in Chapter 27, "Configuring an Internet Gateway," in the "What Is NAT?" section. It is possible to perform NAT operation as well as VPN services on the same FreeBSD machine, as you will see in this chapter.

Protected in this way, servers within the corporate network are free to implement lax security policies (allowing employees to share resources among corporate servers without encryption or even authentication) and LAN-level network services (such as Windows file sharing and videoconferencing). The employees don't need to worry about security for these services, because nobody outside the corporate LAN is capable of accessing anything inside it. This is an ideal configuration...as long as all the company's employees are within the corporate network at all times.

But what happens when employees want to work from home? What if members of the sales team want to check their e-mail and access marketing documents from internal corporate servers while they're in a hotel halfway around the world? Because of the firewall and NAT, they have no way of contacting the internal servers directly; if they try to look up the servers' hostnames, their external DNS servers will be unable to map the names to meaningful IP addresses. If they try to connect directly to the servers' internal IP addresses, the Internet routers will be unable to find a way to the network containing the translated IP numbers (usually reserved ranges such as 10.x.x.x and 192.168.x.x). The employees have no way to get into the network; they're locked out by virtue of being topologically located outside the company's private LAN.

This is where a Virtual Private Network comes in. Conceptually, a VPN allows a client machine on the *outside* of the private network to join itself to the translated IP address pool used *inside* the network. The packets that carry data from the machine to the corporate servers travel over public Internet routers, but they're encrypted so as to protect them from the watchful eyes that drove the company behind a NAT firewall in the first place. Such encryption creates a *tunnel*, which is the term for the extra layer of encoding and packet headers that allows normal IP packets to be routed between machines whose configurations would not otherwise allow them to communicate. The conceptual layout of a VPN is shown in Figures 30.1 and 30.2.

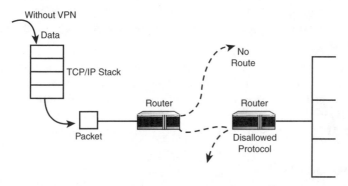

FIGURE 30.1   Without a VPN, a packet either has no route to the translated corporate IP network or is rejected by the firewall as coming from an illegal source.

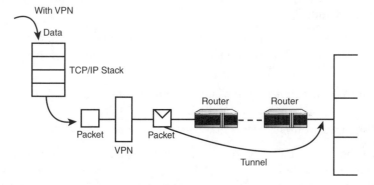

FIGURE 30.2   When a VPN is added to the client's packet path, each packet is encrypted and given a new IP destination, which sends it through the tunnel to a VPN server at the corporate network that decodes it.

A VPN is created through an authentication sequence in which the client machine exchanges keys with the VPN server in order to establish that it is a legitimate member of the corporate network. (Typically, a VPN would be used by an employee, and his username and password for the corporate network would be suitable to gain VPN access. This method is secure because the VPN authentication scheme is itself encrypted.)

30

Subsequently, the client machine is given a new virtual interface with an IP address that is compatible with the addresses of machines within the private network. With a VPN in place, DNS lookups of corporate servers work; LAN-level services such as Windows file sharing also function normally (even though the packets are encrypted and actually travel across the Internet instead of just the LAN). Best of all, the whole process is encrypted so that sensitive corporate data is not exposed to anybody who might want to sniff the public network for such treasures.

Each operating system handles VPN functionality in its own way. FreeBSD's implementation involves more work than some but is considerably more automatic in many ways than some other platforms. This automation is largely due to the optional support for IPSec (Secure IP) in the kernel, rather than a reliance on third-party tools (you learn more about IPSec in "VPN Services in FreeBSD: IPSec," later in this chapter).

VPN Topologies

All VPNs have a few basic components in common:

- **A private network**—The network is often a Class C subnet managed by a router, or it's a block of IP addresses translated by a NAT firewall into as large an internal virtual network as is necessary.

- **A VPN server**—The server sits just inside the router or is incorporated as part of the router itself, as in the case of many modern routers from Cisco and other manufacturers.

- **A client**—The client is somewhere out on the Internet.

The details of these configurations, however, can vary quite a lot.

Figure 30.3 shows the kind of topology likely to be used by employees on the road. A single machine uses a standard dial-up ISP (such as found in a hotel or an airport) to connect to the Internet. This machine then contacts the corporate VPN server, which has an IP address that's not translated and is therefore accessible directly from the Internet. This VPN server performs the necessary authentication and serves up the client's tunnel IP address, allowing it to communicate with the machines inside the NAT network.

A more ambitious layout is shown in Figure 30.4. Here, the VPN client is actually a FreeBSD machine serving as a NAT gateway and firewall for a home (local) network, the kind likely to be used by an employee who frequently works from home. The FreeBSD machine creates a permanent tunnel to the private network over the Internet but is itself operating as a router managing a network of machines of various types. Each of these machines has the VPN client machine set as its gateway router; if one of the machines tries to open up a connection to the private network, the FreeBSD machine will have a permanent route (the VPN tunnel) into which to send the connection. Normal requests to the Internet will be passed upstream to the regular ISP's router, unaltered. The machines on the local network do not need to undergo any special configuration in order to inter-operate seamlessly with the machines at the corporate site. This topology enables large companies to maintain multiple branch offices in widely separate locations around the country or the world, while at the same time allowing employees at any location to access the resources at any other location as though they are all plugged into the same switch at the central office.

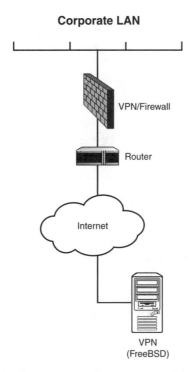

Corporate LAN

VPN/Firewall

Router

Internet

VPN
(FreeBSD)

FIGURE 30.3   A single machine connects to the Internet and communicates directly with the corporate VPN server to set up a tunnel.

The same principles underlie both the simple and the more complex topology just described. Next in this chapter, you learn the techniques for putting these principles into action. First, we look at how to configure FreeBSD as a VPN client to connect to a remote VPN server, regardless of whether your topology involves a local network. Afterward, you learn how to create a VPN server so other machines can tunnel into your own private network.

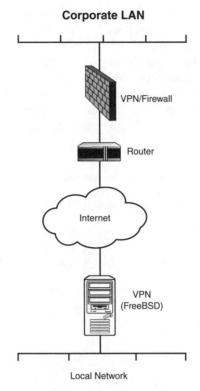

FIGURE 30.4   Two networks are connected by a permanent VPN tunnel; the machines on either network can now all freely communicate with each other, with no additional configuration on the individual machines.

VPN Services in FreeBSD: IPSec

VPN services in FreeBSD are conducted using IPSec, or *Secure IP*. The IPSec protocol is routed like IP, but it contains a payload that's encrypted and authenticated. This payload needs to be descrambled by the machine at the other end using the key exchanged during the tunnel-setup procedure. IPSec is an industry-standard protocol that has been supported in FreeBSD for some time as the result of the work of the KAME project (www.kame.net). It is not built in to the default FreeBSD kernel; however, you can enable it easily by building a new kernel.

Preparing Your System

To add IPSec support to your FreeBSD kernel, add the following three options lines to your kernel configuration file (consult Chapter 16, "Kernel Configuration," for details on modifying your kernel if you're unfamiliar with the process):

```
options  IPSEC          #IP security
options  IPSEC_ESP      #IP security (crypto; define w/ IPSEC)
options  IPSEC_DEBUG    #debug for IP security
```

For FreeBSD systems earlier than 5.0, add this line as well to the configuration:

```
pseudo-device    gif 4
```

Recompile your kernel and restart your system.

With these kernel options added, your machine will have two internal databases you will have to know about when configuring IPSec:

- **The Security Policy Database (SPD)**—Used for determining your tunnel's *policy*, or which packets it should be encrypting

- **The Security Association Database (SAD)**—Maintains the encryption keys used to decipher the encrypted packets received via the tunnel

These two databases can be manipulated using the `setkey` command, which is part of the FreeBSD system.

You will next need to install `racoon` (note the spelling), which is a tool developed by KAME to facilitate the exchange of keys during the creation of an IPSec tunnel. The `racoon` program can be installed from the ports at `/usr/ports/security/racoon`. (Refer to Chapter 14, "Installing Additional Software," for more information on using the FreeBSD ports collection.) The purpose of `racoon`, as far as basic VPN setup is concerned, is to automatically manipulate the SAD and create a VPN tunnel upon startup of the computer.

In order to set up your tunnel, you will need the following few pieces of information:

- Your own machine's IP address

- The VPN server's IP address

- The remote private network address and netmask

- The "shared key," which is a passphrase that will need to be stored in a privileged-access file on both sides of the tunnel

The most important piece to remember is the shared key; this will have to be agreed upon in advance by you and the administrator of the remote VPN server. The shared key is stored in the file `/usr/local/etc/racoon/psk.txt`, which does not exist in the default `racoon` installation. This file contains line-by-line pairs of peer IP addresses and their respective shared keys; a file located at `/usr/local/etc/racoon/psk.txt.dist` contains sample lines to show you the required format. Create your own `psk.txt` file in that directory and add to it the following line, where `<IP address>` is the address of the remote

30

VPN server and `<shared key>` is the shared key agreed upon by you and the administrator of the server:

```
<IP address>        <shared key>
```

In other words, if the server's IP address is 221.222.223.224 and the shared key is "somesecurestring," you would add the following line:

```
221.222.223.224    somesecurestring
```

> **NOTE**
>
> The two fields in the shared key line you add to your `psk.txt` file can be separated by either tabs or spaces, as is the case with most configuration files.

Next, make the `psk.txt` file secure by giving it a permissions mode of 600 (readable only by the owner) and ensuring that it's owned by root; otherwise, `racoon` will refuse to read the file:

```
# chmod 600 /usr/local/etc/racoon/psk.txt
# chown root /usr/local/etc/racoon/psk.txt
```

Finally, enable `racoon`'s configuration file by renaming /usr/local/etc/racoon/racoon.conf.dist to racoon.conf; then make a couple modifications to ensure smooth operation over the Internet WAN. Change the `lifetime time` and `lifetime byte` fields, specified in the `sainfo anonymous` block, to `36000 secs` and `50000` KB, respectively. (Add the lines if they are not present in the default configuration.)

> **CAUTION**
>
> As should be your standard practice by now, make a backup copy of your `racoon.conf.dist` file before you edit it. Instead of renaming it to `racoon.conf`, you might instead want to copy it (`cp racoon.conf.dist racoon.conf`) and keep the distribution file in an untouched form.

When you are done, the block should look like this:

```
sainfo anonymous
{
        pfs_group 1;
        lifetime time 36000 sec;
        lifetime byte 50000 KB;
        encryption_algorithm 3des ;
        authentication_algorithm hmac_sha1;
        compression_algorithm deflate ;
}
```

Also, add the `lifetime 50000` KB line to the corresponding point in the `remote` anonymous block:

```
remote anonymous
{
        ...
        nonce_size 16;
        lifetime time 1 min;     # sec,min,hour
        lifetime byte 50000 KB;      # B,KB,GB
        initial_contact on;
        support_mip6 on;
        ...
}
```

Connecting to a FreeBSD VPN Server

It may be that you are fortunate enough to have another FreeBSD machine as the server for your VPN connection. If this is the case, you can set up both machines in the same way, with their `racoon` configurations mirroring each other.

However, `racoon` only works if you have set up the SPD and SAD using the `/etc/ipsec.conf` file, which does not exist by default. First, enable the reading of that file at startup time by adding an override line to `/etc/rc.conf`:

```
ipsec_enable="YES"
```

Also, you will need to add the `gif0` virtual interface to your available network interfaces and configure it according to the local and remote IP addresses so that the kernel can route tunneled traffic to the proper destination. Assuming you already have one Ethernet interface called `fxp0`, the `network_interfaces` line in `/etc/rc.conf` should look like this:

```
network_interfaces="fxp0 gif0 lo0"
```

IPSec in FreeBSD works as shown in Figure 30.5. Both VPN peer machines have two network interfaces. On the server side, one of the interfaces is "private" and on the same LAN as the address-translated private network to which you want to connect, and the other is the "public" IP address in the untranslated address space. On your local machine, which only has one physical Ethernet card, your private IP address is really just an internal "dummy" address, because your machine isn't routing any traffic except to itself. However, the `gif0` device needs the private address in order to route properly. You will need to bind both your public and private addresses to your single Ethernet card.

30

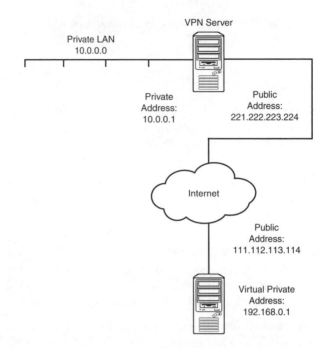

FIGURE 30.5   Each of the peer machines in the VPN connection has a "public" and a "private" IP address. The private address on the local machine is a dummy address bound to the same card as the public address.

Suppose that your machine's IP address in the public space is 111.112.113.114 and that this address is already bound to your fxp0 card. You can create a virtual address of 192.168.0.1 for use with the IPSec tunnel. Add the following line to /etc/rc.conf immediately after the line that configures the card:

```
ifconfig_fxp0_alias0="inet 192.168.0.1 netmask 255.255.0.0"
```

Furthermore, suppose that the remote VPN server's public IP address is 221.222.223.224 and that this server manages the internal, private Class A network 10.0.0.0, on which its own private IP address is 10.0.0.1. You now can configure the local machine's gif0 device by adding the following lines to /etc/rc.conf (here, explanations follow each line but would not appear in the actual code string):

```
gif_interfaces="gif0"
```

This line establishes that gif0 is the name of your virtual private interface.

```
ifconfig_gif0="inet 192.168.0.1 10.0.0.1 netmask 255.0.0.0"
```

This line tells FreeBSD to assign the virtual private address 192.168.0.1 to the gif0 interface and connect it to the remote private address 10.0.0.1 at the other end.

```
gifconfig_gif0="111.112.113.114 221.222.223.224"
```

This line creates the "public" side of the connection, directing traffic from your public address 111.112.113.144 to the public address of the VPN server, 221.222.223.224.

Finally, create /etc/ipsec.conf and add the following lines to it:

```
flush;
spdflush;
spdadd 192.168.0.1/32 10.0.0.0/8 any -P out ipsec
  esp/tunnel/111.112.113.114-221.222.223.224/require;
spdadd 10.0.0.0/8 192.168.0.1/32 any -P in ipsec
  esp/tunnel/221.222.223.224-111.112.113.114/require;
```

The spdadd lines are what control the SPD and assign the rules for what traffic FreeBSD should encrypt. Note that there are two such rule lines, and they're mirror images of each other; this is because you're creating a virtual routing mechanism, and routers must be bidirectional.

The first spdadd line applies to all traffic originating from your machine's private network (192.168.0.1, with a CIDR mask of /32, making the network synonymous with your single IP address) and destined for the remote private LAN (10.0.0.0, a Class A network). It specifies that all traffic matching that pattern should be routed across the tunnel between the two public addresses, 111.112.113.114 and 221.222.223.224.

> **TIP**
>
> Classless Inter-Domain Routing (CIDR) is a network mask notation introduced in Chapter 21, "Networking with FreeBSD." A CIDR mask of /32 describes a network that matches all 32 bits of the given IP address (a netmask of 255.255.255.255), or in other words, that given machine only. A CIDR mask of /8 means the mask is only 8 bits long, or 255.0.0.0, which describes a Class A network.

Replace these numbers with the addresses that are correct for your configuration; make sure to set up the second line as a mirror image, as shown here.

Restart the machine to ensure that all the configuration items are read properly and cleanly.

> **NOTE**
>
> A remote FreeBSD VPN server will likely be configured similarly to your own machine, using
> `/etc/ipsec.conf` and `racoon`. However, it is critical that it have its own configuration rules that
> mirror those on your own machine. The remote FreeBSD VPN server must be configured to send
> encrypted traffic to your machine through its own `gif0` interface. Add (or have the remote
> machine's administrator add) the appropriate `spdadd` lines, which would be the same as the ones
> shown here. The lines are symmetrical, so if you reverse the numbers, they turn out to be the
> same set of lines as on your local machine, except for the `in` and `out` tags:
>
> ```
> spdadd 10.0.0.0/8 192.168.0.1/32 any -P out ipsec
>     esp/tunnel/221.222.223.224-111.112.113.114/require;
> spdadd 192.168.0.1/32 10.0.0.0/8 any -P in ipsec
>     esp/tunnel/111.112.113.114-221.222.223.224/require;
> ```

Now that the kernel is set up to use the `gif0` virtual interface, there's only one thing left
to do: You must run `racoon`, which monitors outgoing flows and sets up the appropriate
key exchange. This process happens transparently and may cause a slight delay in the first
few packets you send.

When you installed `racoon`, it created a startup script in `/usr/local/etc/rc.d`. This script
automatically starts `racoon` at boot time. However, if you need to start `racoon` while the
machine is already running, you can do so by invoking the script with the `start` parameter:

```
# /usr/local/etc/rc.d/racoon.sh start
```

Try sending a ping to a machine on the remote private network (for example, `ping`
`10.1.1.10`). If you get a reply, your VPN tunnel is up and running!

Connecting to a Windows 2000 VPN Server

Most of the time the remote VPN server will not be a FreeBSD machine. It's far more likely
these days to be a Windows 2000 server. However, this should not present a problem; with
a few tweaks to `racoon.conf` on your end, you should be able to connect to a corporate
Windows server seamlessly.

The first thing to note is that a Windows 2000 server assigns identifier addresses dynamically; therefore, in the `remote anonymous` block, comment out the whole set of lines
beginning with `my_identifier`:

```
#my_identifier address;
#my_identifier user_fqdn "sakane@kame.net";
#peers_identifier user_fqdn "sakane@kame.net";
#certificate_type x509 "mycert" "mypriv";
```

Next, change the `proposal` sub-block to list the encryption and checksum methods preferred by Windows 2000:

```
proposal {
        encryption_algorithm 3des;
        hash_algorithm md5;
        authentication_method pre_shared_key ;
        dh_group 2 ;
}
```

Finally, go down into the `sainfo` anonymous block and alter it to match the following:

```
sainfo anonymous
{
        pfs_group 1;
        lifetime time 36000 sec;
        lifetime byte 50000 KB;
        encryption_algorithm 3des,des,cast128,blowfish ;
        authentication_algorithm hmac_sha1,hmac_md5;
        compression_algorithm deflate ;
}
```

Now, you must do some configuration on the Windows end. Run the `mmc` program from within a Command Prompt window. Go to the Add/Remove Snap-In option in the Console menu. Add the IP Security Policy Management snap-in by clicking the Add button, then selecting the snap-in from the pop-up window. Select to install it for the local computer (the default option). Close the Add/Remove Snap-in window to finish the process. Next, click IP Security Policies in the tree listing and then select Create IP Security Policy from the Action menu. This starts a wizard. Don't activate the default response rule (uncheck the check box it offers you); instead, edit the properties when given the option to do so. In the Properties dialog, click the Add button to add a new rule. Make sure the rule has the following properties:

- The rule does not specify a tunnel.

- The rule applies to the LAN.

- To protect the key exchange, use a string—the same "shared key" string as you put into `psk.txt` (somesecurestring) in the earlier example.

In the next screen, create a new IP filter so that only traffic from a source address of your Windows machine's subnet (or any IP address) to a destination of your FreeBSD machine's specific IP address is subject to the security policy. Select this new filter. Select the filter action Require Security and press Edit to modify the rule so that the topmost line has the following properties (use the Move Up and Move Down buttons):

30

- AH is disabled.

- ESP Confidentiality is 3DES.

- ESP integrity is MD5.

Finish the wizard and examine your list of rules. It should look like Figure 30.6.

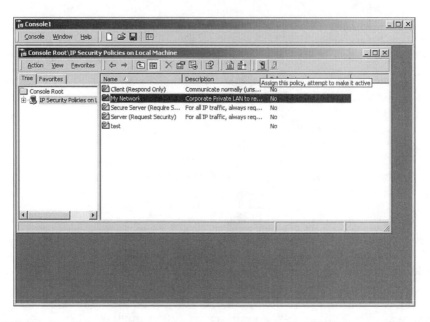

FIGURE 30.6 The IP Security Rules dialog showing the new filter you have created; click the check box preceding the filter's listing to toggle on the filter.

Using the Component Services management program (one of the Administrative Tools in the Control Panel), restart the IPSec Policy Agent, as shown in Figure 30.7. You should restart the agent after each change you make during debugging because this ensures the changes you make are always currently in use.

Activate the new policy by clicking the check box that precedes the filter listing in the My Network Properties dialog shown in Figure 30.6 (clicking the check box toggles on the filter). Now, in another Command Prompt window, run the `ipsecmon` program to monitor the tunnel rules in action. In a third window, try to ping your FreeBSD machine. The first ping will emit a "Negotiating IP Security" message, but subsequent pings should go through successfully. If this occurs, your IPSec tunnel is functional.

FIGURE 30.7   Enabling the new security policy using the toggle switch in the mmc program.

FreeBSD as a VPN Server

It won't always be the case that you only have one FreeBSD machine to connect to a remote Virtual Private Network. You might have to set up a routed, translated subnetwork of your own, for example, and create a permanent VPN tunnel to the remote network for the use of multiple machines on your own subnet. Fortunately, because you have set up the gif0 interface to use a virtual private IP address on your own local machine, making the jump to a fully routed VPN link should be child's play.

All that's required is a second Ethernet card on your machine that's plugged into the local private network. Follow the same instructions listed in the previous section, except for the part where you alias the private address (192.168.0.1) to the public Ethernet card. Instead, assign that address to the second Ethernet card. Then, set up the spdadd lines to reflect the network address of the whole network you're managing instead of just your own single machine. For instance, the following lines in /etc/ipsec.conf would allow you to tunnel the entire private 192.168.0.0 network (Class B) to the remote VPN server, enabling the machines on your network to communicate with the machines in the remote 10.0.0.0 network, and vice versa:

```
spdadd 192.168.0.0/16 10.0.0.0/8 any -P out ipsec
  esp/tunnel/111.112.113.114-221.222.223.224/require;
spdadd 10.0.0.0/8 192.168.0.0/16 any -P in ipsec
  esp/tunnel/221.222.223.224-111.112.113.114/require;
```

Routing and Firewalling

One final point to note is that to run a proper subnetwork, your FreeBSD machine will have to be doing all the routing and NAT/firewall work for that network; otherwise, you

30

will have to have dedicated equipment on your end to handle those tasks, the same as on the remote end.

Figure 30.8 shows a topological layout of the network, including several potential, correct locations for the VPN device or functionality (indicated by "VPN" in a dashed box). VPN can be handled by a dedicated machine, or it might be consolidated into the same machine as the firewall or router. If your FreeBSD machine is doing all these tasks itself, you probably won't have to worry; if it's not, however, you must ensure that each piece of functionality is positioned properly in the network so that the right addresses are visible to the devices that need them. Particularly bear in mind that if you have VPN functionality in the network at any point, your firewall will almost certainly have to be set up to allow its traffic through with specialized rules. Moreover, your router will have to be able to route the tunnel traffic to and from the VPN device. Most VPN misconfigurations stem from incorrect firewall or router rules that don't take into account the specialized addressing needs of the VPN tunnel.

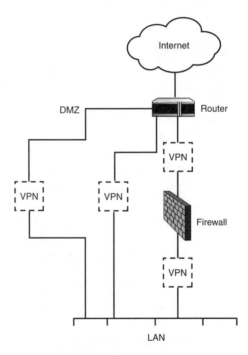

FIGURE 30.8   A topological diagram of a subnetwork, including the LAN, firewall, NAT, router, and WAN as well as five potential locations for the VPN device.

> **NOTE**
>
> Refer to Chapter 27, "Configuring an Internet Gateway," for details on routing a subnetwork using FreeBSD as well as NAT configuration. See Chapter 29, "Network Security," for more on firewalls.

The Domain Name Server

In Chapter 21, "Networking with FreeBSD," and Chapter 22, "Configuring Basic Networking Services," you learned how DNS (the Domain Name System) provides a common naming scheme for finding hosts on the Internet, eliminating the need for users to memorize IP addresses. You also learned about the process of setting up a FreeBSD machine to gather domain name information from a designated server. However, you now come to the topic of configuring the FreeBSD machine to act, itself, as a domain name server, providing lookup information to itself and to any client machines that wish to use it.

Domain name service is one of the most complex single subjects in network administration. Although it's fairly easy to set up a Web server on each of as many different servers as you might install in a network, the installation of a name server is something that typically is done just once. In many cases, the installation is handled by a "guru" whose efforts quickly become folklore to the rest of the network staff, resulting in a DNS setup that is hard to maintain or even understand. Administrators who know DNS inside and out are far less numerous than those who don't. This chapter cannot attempt to describe DNS exhaustively. For that purpose, there are lengthy books devoted to that subject. This chapter's purpose is to enable you to set up FreeBSD as a name server in any of several common configurations.

Introduction to DNS Structure, Functions, and Software

DNS is a hierarchical protocol, operating across the Internet in a fashion similar to how routing works. A number of "root servers" are maintained by Network Solutions, Inc., as well as other bodies, distributed geographically around the Internet for redundancy reasons. Each domain name (for example, `somewhere.com`) is defined in backward order from the root zone, with the domain suffix—`com`, `org`, `net`, and so on—being the topmost layer of the hierarchy directly under the . (a single dot), which refers to the root zone. Below each of the suffixes (commonly known as *top-level domains*, or *TLDs*) are the regular domain names, each typically defined not by the root servers but by individual DNS hosts on the Internet. The `somewhere.com` domain, for example, would have its DNS administered by a server on its own network, such as `ns1.somewhere.com`. This server is the "authoritative" DNS host for that domain. A central registry—also maintained by Network Solutions—keeps records of these individual domains so that the root servers can provide authoritative lookup information on them. You define these "host records" when setting up a new name server by submitting a form to Network Solutions or any of its peer registrars.

When a client makes a DNS request, it queries the name server configured in its TCP/IP settings—usually a server on its own network, as shown in Figure 31.1. If that server cannot answer the request, it passes the request on to its upstream DNS forwarder if one is available. If not, the request goes directly to the root servers.

The root servers don't maintain any authoritative DNS data of their own. All they have are host records, which you will come to know as *NS records*, which point to the authoritative name servers for each domain. The root servers send back a DNS response that refers the requester to the authoritative name server for the domain the client wants to find out about. This server sends back the requested DNS data to the local DNS machine, which passes it back through to the client.

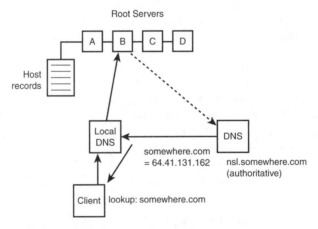

FIGURE 31.1   A Diagram of a DNS lookup, showing the path from a client to the local DNS, the root servers, and the authoritative name server.

The local DNS might keep lookup information around in its cache for a period of time specified by the authoritative name server. This speeds up the query process, allowing local clients to get immediate responses to their DNS queries from the local server without the queries having to travel out over the Internet. However, this means that changes to DNS records at the authoritative DNS will not be available to the client until the expiration period has passed. Until that time, the DNS information the client sees is "stale" and potentially inaccurate. The time period between DNS cache updates can be controlled for each domain using the Time-To-Live (TTL) value, which you will learn more about later in this chapter.

DNS Software: BIND

DNS software is ubiquitous. For Unix systems, which account for the vast majority of name servers on the Internet, the software of choice is BIND, by the Internet Software Consortium (ISC). BIND, short for *Berkeley Internet Name Domain*, consists of one major daemon program (named), a set of resolver libraries that provides the ability to perform name lookups, and various administrative tools. BIND is built in to FreeBSD, although it is not enabled by default.

Zones

BIND allows you to define *zones*, which are logical groupings of IP addresses and hostnames that exist at a certain level in the DNS naming hierarchy. For example, com. is a zone under the root (.) zone, and somewhere.com. is a zone that exists underneath the com. zone. Note that zone names always end in a dot, referring to the root zone—this will be important when you create your zone files! *Subdomains* are zones managed by the individual domain name servers; cluster.somewhere.com. is a zone that can have multiple machines inside it—indeed, it can have as many further subdivisions within it as you are willing to configure. These zones provide *forward DNS lookups*, or mappings from names to IP addresses.

Similarly, *reverse DNS lookups*—or mappings from IP addresses to hostnames—are managed in zones. Because DNS and IP addresses have their roots in the ARPAnet (see Chapter 21 for details) and have not changed fundamentally in structure since that time, a reverse DNS zone name is of the form CCC.BBB.AAA.in-addr.arpa. This is a name constructed of the IP address space in reverse order, with .in-addr.arpa appended to it. For example, the 64.41.131.* network would be defined by the zone 131.41.64.in-addr.arpa.

Each zone that your name server will manage must be defined in a *zone file*—a formatted set of definitions that maps hostnames to IP addresses (or vice versa) within the zone. A zone file also contains parameters for the behavior of the zone, such as the caching expiration period. The zone files are the most critical part of proper DNS configuration; we will be discussing them in detail later in this chapter.

BIND Files and Programs

Because BIND is a built-in part of FreeBSD, you don't need to worry about installing it or making sure the proper files are in the proper places. It is worthwhile, though, to know what programs are involved in name server operations and where you will be making your configuration changes:

- **/usr/sbin/named**—The name server daemon itself. It listens on port 53 for DNS lookup requests.

- **/usr/sbin/ndc**—The name daemon controller program. This is the tool you will use to start, stop, reload, and monitor the named server.

- **/etc/namedb**—All your BIND configuration and runtime status files, including zone definition files, are in this directory (or any subdirectories of it that you create).

- **/etc/namedb/named.conf**—The master BIND configuration file. This file tells BIND which domains you are to manage as well as how to handle each one.

Enabling the Name Server Daemon

Enabling BIND in FreeBSD is the simplest part of configuring it. All you have to do, just as with other built-in FreeBSD services we have discussed, is add the following line to /etc/rc.conf:

```
named_enable="YES"
```

With this option set, named will run automatically at boot time. To start it without rebooting, use the ndc tool:

```
# ndc start
new pid is 12717
```

The server should now be running. However, this is only scratching the surface of a complete BIND configuration.

> **NOTE**
>
> For maximum efficiency, put a nameserver line into your /etc/resolv.conf file, referring to the loopback address (127.0.0.1) as your primary name server. This way, you will be able to perform DNS lookups the quickest way of all: from your own machine. Make sure this line appears before any additional servers:
>
> ```
> search somewhere.com
> nameserver 127.0.0.1
> nameserver 64.41.131.167
> ```

Running BIND in a Sandbox

As you saw in Chapter 26, "Configuring an FTP Server," it's sometimes advisable (for security purposes) to run certain services within what's known as a *sandbox*, or a directory structure that's been pruned off so as to appear that it's all that exists in the filesystem. In FTP, this is known as a `chroot` jail; the effective "root" of the filesystem is changed so that the server and the processes it creates cannot see outside their own directory structure above a certain point. BIND provides the same kind of capability, although most of the documentation refers to it as a "sandbox" rather than as a "`chroot` jail." The concept is the same, however.

A common sandbox configuration is to have a directory called `sandbox` within `/etc/namedb`, with `named` pruning itself off into that directory as soon as it is started. This ensures that if `named` is compromised (which is possible because vulnerabilities continue to be found in versions of BIND to this day), the damage is restricted to that directory. Create the `/etc/named/sandbox` directory and then change its ownership and permissions to the unprivileged `bind` user and group:

```
# chown -R bind:bind /etc/namedb/sandbox
# chmod -R 750 /etc/namedb/sandbox
```

Next, create `/etc` and `/var/run` subdirectories inside the sandbox. Copy `/etc/localtime` into `/etc/namedb/sandbox/etc`. The server will write runtime files into `/var/run`, and it needs the `localtime` file to process the serial numbers found in zone files and to log dates properly:

```
# mkdir /etc/namedb/sandbox/etc
# cp /etc/localtime /etc/namedb/sandbox/etc
# mkdir -p /etc/namedb/sandbox/var/run
```

Finally, add the following line to `/etc/rc.conf`:

```
named_flags="-u bind -g bind -t /etc/namedb/sandbox"
```

Note that when using the `ndc` program to control `named` (as you will see in this chapter), you must use the `-c` option if you're running `named` in a sandbox. The syntax would take the following form:

```
# ndc -c /etc/namedb/sandbox/var/run/ndc start
```

Also note that if you configure `named` to log to a file, the file must be inside the sandbox for `named` to be able to write to it.

Working with the BIND Configuration File (named.conf)

In order to make your name server do anything useful, you need to make sure that it is topologically in the right place with respect to its clients and the rest of the network and that it is configured to interoperate properly with other name servers. A misconfigured name server can result in deluges of DNS traffic between your server and the root servers as it tries futilely to synchronize its data. Your `/etc/namedb/named.conf` file must be constructed properly, so it needs to be understood properly.

> **CAUTION**
>
> As should be a habit by now, be sure to make a backup copy of your `named.conf` file (such as `named.conf.bak`) before you make any changes to it. Always leave yourself the option to revert to your previous working configuration!

Fortunately, BIND 8 (the version included in FreeBSD at the time of this writing, probably soon to be replaced with BIND 9, which can be installed from the ports) greatly simplifies many of the esoteric details of name server configuration that were the norm in BIND version 4 and earlier. BIND 8, which immediately replaced BIND 4, introduced a lot more configurability and at the same time eliminated many elements that were obsolete or poorly designed. Listing 31.1 shows a sample `named.conf` file, giving you an idea of its syntax and structure.

LISTING 31.1   Sample `/etc/namedb/named.conf` File

```
/*
 * A simple BIND 8 configuration
 */

logging {
    category lame-servers { null; };
    category cname { null; };
};

options {
    directory "/etc/namedb";
};

zone "somewhere.com" {
    type master;
    file "somewhere.com";
};

zone "131.41.64.in-addr.arpa" {
    type master;
    file "131.41.64.in-addr.arpa";
};

zone "elsewhere.com" {
    type slave;
    file "slave/elsewhere.com";
    masters { 113.125.2.145; };
};
```

LISTING 31.1   Continued

```
zone "." {
    type hint;
    file "named.boot";
};

zone "0.0.127.in-addr.arpa" {
    type master;
    file "localhost.rev";
};

zone "0.0.0.0.0.0.0.0.0.0.0.0.0.0.0.0.0.0.0.0.0.0.0.0.0.0.0.0.0.0.0.0.IP6.INT" {
        type master;
        file "localhost.rev";
};
```

As shown in the listing, a configuration file consists of a number of blocks (or *statements*) in C-style syntax, with substatements allowed within curly brackets ({}). All possible statements are listed and described in the man `named.conf` page. Some of the most useful ones are options, controls, logging, and zone.

Comments in `named.conf` are also C style; single-line comments are done with double slashes (//), and block comments are done with the /* *comment* */ syntax. Shell-style comments (#) are also supported.

The `named.conf` file that exists in the default installation of FreeBSD has a few of the statements shown in Listing 31.1 and a few that are not. It also has a lot of inline documentation that describes how to use each of them.

Whenever you make a change to `named.conf` or to any of the zone files (which we will discuss later in this chapter), restart `named` using the `ndc` program:

```
# ndc reload
Reload initiated.
```

Using a Forwarder

Recalling the topology shown in Figure 31.1, a *forwarder* is a name server at an "upstream" network—a larger network "closer" to the root servers—that allows you to request DNS information from it. (Note that access to a name server can be restricted, as you will see.) A good candidate for a forwarder is your uplink ISP's name server, if your FreeBSD machine is acting as a name server for a home network. Normally, if your machine can't answer a DNS request on its own, it must query the root servers (found in /etc/namedb/named.root) for the authoritative reply. These extra steps take time and add to the packet traffic on the network.

It really isn't necessary for everyone to get authoritative answers all the time. It's perfectly acceptable in most cases to work from nonauthoritative DNS information, such as that from a caching name server:

```
# nslookup www.freebsd.org ns.somewhere.com
Server:  ns.somewhere.com
Address:  64.41.131.172

Non-authoritative answer:
Name:    freefall.freebsd.org
Address:  216.136.204.21
Aliases:  www.freebsd.org
```

Configuring your FreeBSD system to query one or more forwarders allows it to benefit from the cache of the upstream name server, rather than to fetch authoritative data on every query. The downside (as we discussed earlier) is that the cached data can become "stale" by as much time as the authoritative server's zone file specifies it should (a period frequently measured in days—though most forwarders do use reasonably short TTL values, which mitigates this drawback). Figure 31.2 shows a DNS query path in which a forwarder is involved. The forwarder does most of the work, building up its cache through queries of its own and in service to its own clients. The downstream DNS that points to it needs only to query the forwarder, thus preventing unnecessary lag and query traffic.

TIP

The deluges of DNS traffic mentioned earlier are often caused by name servers that are improperly configured, never to take advantage of caching name servers. These forwarders are what prevent too much unnecessary traffic from swamping low-bandwidth links—for instance, in cases where a DNS host serving as the authoritative name server for a domain is on a small DSL or dial-up link. Without caching name servers, every host on the Internet would have to send DNS queries to that overloaded name server directly. With forwarders, the load on the target host's link is greatly reduced. Using a forwarder is a way to act as a good network citizen and make your own queries faster and more efficient.

To enable a forwarder, replace `127.0.0.1` in the `forwarders` block of the `options` statement with the upstream name server's IP address (`127.0.0.1`, the localhost address, will not work here) and uncomment the block by removing the `/*` and `*/` comment tags:

```
/*
        forwarders {
                127.0.0.1;
                66.114.72.112;
        };
*/
```

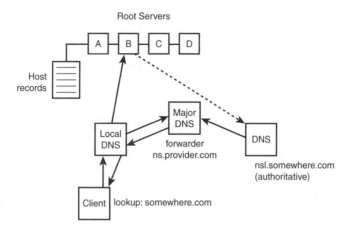

FIGURE 31.2   A Diagram of a DNS lookup involving a forwarder providing cached DNS information in a nonauthoritative capacity to the local DNS and the client.

You can specify as many forwarders as you like, and named will consult each one before giving up and querying the root servers. You can additionally uncomment the forward only; statement in the options block to force named to consult only the forwarders on all queries. Normally, your machine will consult the forwarders for DNS data unless it appears that the forwarders are unreachable or broken, in which case it makes full queries to the root servers. Setting the forward only; option prevents it from making root server queries on any occasion.

Master and Slave Configurations

Each zone block defines a domain or subdomain that your FreeBSD machine will administer. Most commonly, a zone block defines a domain of the form somewhere.com:

```
zone "somewhere.com" {
    type master;
    file "somewhere.com";
};
```

All that's absolutely necessary in this block is the name of the domain or subdomain (without the trailing dot that will usually be associated with a zone name), the type statement that defines whether it's a master or slave configuration for that domain, and the name of the file that contains the zone information. Let's examine what it means for a name server to act as a master or a slave for a particular zone.

The type substatement can be master, slave, stub, forward, or hint. The most commonly used of these are master and slave; the rest are used in special circumstances only, which we will look at shortly.

A `master` zone indicates that the server is authoritative for the zone; it means the server has a master copy of the zone file, defining name-to-address mappings that are to propagate throughout the Internet, and any changes to it must be made manually—but those changes override the information in every other name server's DNS cache when the existing information expires.

A `slave` zone is a replica of the master, with a zone file derived from the one that the master has. Slave servers can provide authoritative answers to DNS queries. A `slave` zone block looks like this:

```
zone "elsewhere.com" {
    type slave;
    file "slave/elsewhere.com";
    masters { 113.125.2.145; };
};
```

The `masters` substatement contains a semicolon-delimited list of master servers from which to transfer zone information. These masters can be actual authoritative master zone servers or they can be other slaves. The `file` statement in a `slave` zone refers to the name of the autogenerated zone file that `named` will create when it transfers it from the master. In this example, the `elsewhere.com` file is created within the `/etc/namedb/slave` subdirectory; you can use a directory structure like this to separate out your authoritative (`master`) zone files from the autogenerated (`slave`) files.

> **TIP**
>
> When you set up a `slave` zone on your server, run `ndc reload` to cause BIND to perform a zone transfer and create the new zone file at the location you specify in the `file` statement. Sometimes, the file will not be updated immediately if you make a change to the `master` zone file, even if you do an `ndc reload`. If this is the case, simply delete the `slave` zone file and reissue the `ndc reload` command to transfer the zone data again and re-create the file.
>
> Make sure that the `/etc/namedb/slave` directory exists before you issue the `ndc reload` command; otherwise, the command will fail.

Other Zone Types

As described in `man named.conf`, you can have three other types of zone blocks. These types are as follows:

- **stub**—A `stub` zone works in the same way as a `slave` zone, except that it transfers only the NS records—the records specifying where clients can find valid DNS information for the specified domain.

- **forward**—You can use a `forward` zone type to forward all requests for the zone to another server or set of servers. A `forwarders` block can be specified in this type of zone statement, operating like the global one in the `options` block; this enables you to override the global `forwarders` list.

31

- **hint**—A hint zone is only really used in connection with the initial list of potential root servers, found in /etc/namedb/named.root. This initial list is not actually the authoritative list of root servers; it's a list of "hints" for BIND, specifying servers that will have the current true list of root servers. The contents of the true list has a habit of changing as network conditions vary.

Restricting DNS Access

BIND has the capability to restrict access based on Access Control Lists (ACLs). ACLs are not a requirement, but they can make configuring your server much simpler, allowing you to use shorthand names for lists of addresses that you tend to reuse. An ACL is specified in an acl statement, which defines a name for the list and contains the criteria for which hosts are included in the list. These criteria can take a number of forms, and they can be recursive; in other words, an ACL can contain other ACLs. The following ACLs are predefined for you:

- **any**—Allows all hosts

- **none**—Denies all hosts

- **localhost**—Allows the IP addresses of all interfaces on the system

- **localnets**—Allows any host on a network for which the system has an interface

Other types of list elements that are allowed can be IP addresses (for instance, 111.112.113.114), networks in CIDR format (for instance, 111.112.113/24), a "negated" version of either of these (!111.112.113.114, which means "any host but 111.112.113.114"), or a key statement (used in secure DNS transactions, which are beyond the scope of this chapter). When you're compiling a list of ACL elements, it's best to put the more specific elements before the broader ones because the list is evaluated in the order in which it's specified. If a host matches any element, it will be allowed, regardless of whether a later "negation" element would have matched it. Put all such exceptions toward the beginning of the list.

Because named.conf is read sequentially, an ACL must be specified in the file before it can be referred to later in other statements. For best results, put all acl statements toward the top of your named.conf file, above the options block. A sample ACL would be the following:

```
acl "my_list" {
  localhost;
  localnets;
  another_list;
  !132.112.14.124;
  132.112.14/24;
};
```

This list first contains the built-in `localhost` and `localnets` ACLs and then includes another ACL called `another list`, which would be defined elsewhere in the file. Then a negated "exception" host appears (132.112.14.124), with the "!" prefix exempting it from the 132.112.14/24 subnet that comes next. Thus, this ACL contains everything in that subnet except for the single host 132.112.14.124.

Once you have a list specified, you can use it along with other address list elements later in a zone statement (to control access to requests for just that zone) or in the global `options` statement. Here's a list of the available access-control statements:

- `allow-query { address_list_elements; ... };`

  Specifies which hosts are allowed to perform ordinary DNS queries. `allow-query` may also be specified in a zone statement, in which case it overrides the `options` `allow-query` statement. If not specified, the default is to allow queries from all hosts.

- `allow-transfer { address_list_elements; ... };`

  Specifies which slave servers are allowed to receive zone transfers from this server. `allow-transfer` may also be specified in the zone statement, in which case it overrides the `options` `allow-transfer` statement. If not specified, the default is to allow transfers from all hosts.

- `allow-recursion { address_list_elements; ... };`

  Specifies which hosts are allowed to make recursive queries through this server. If not specified, the default is to allow recursive queries from all hosts.

- `blackhole { address_list_elements; ... };`

  Specifies a list of addresses that the server will not accept queries from or use to resolve a query. Queries from these addresses will not be answered.

For example, you could restrict queries globally to members of the `my_list` ACL that we specified earlier. You also could restrict queries for the `somewhere.com` domain to the members of `my_list`, as well as to an additional network, and restrict zone transfers only to two specified slave servers with the following partial configuration:

```
options {
    directory "/etc/namedb";
        allow-query { my_list; };
};

zone "somewhere.com" {
    type master;
    file "somewhere.com";
        allow-query { my_list; 64.2.43/24; };
        allow-transfer { 64.2.43.167; 123.15.221.3; };
};
```

Creating a Zone File

The zone file is where the mappings for hostnames to IP addresses within a domain or zone are defined; it's also where the most mistakes are commonly made in a BIND configuration, so we will cover it in detail.

The format of a zone file (often referred to as a *master zone file* or simply *master file*) is quite complex and regimented, although there are certain things you can get away with. A "living" zone file in an existing BIND setup can be all but incomprehensible. It helps to understand what kinds of primitives (directives) are allowed and how each one is specified, as well as the shortcuts that are allowed and commonly used.

First, consider the sample zone file, and its components, shown in Listing 31.2. Note that semicolons (;) are the comment characters in zone files.

LISTING 31.2   A Sample Zone File for the somewhere.com Domain

```
$TTL 3600

        somewhere.com. IN SOA stripes.somewhere.com. root.somewhere.com. (
                            20010610        ; Serial
                            10800           ; Refresh
                            3600            ; Retry
                            604800          ; Expire
                            86400 )         ; Minimum TTL

        ; DNS Servers
        @       IN NS           stripes.somewhere.com.
        @       IN NS           spots.somewhere.com.

        ; Machine Names
        localhost       IN A    127.0.0.1
        ns1             IN A    64.41.131.162
        ns2             IN A    64.41.131.163
        mail            IN A    64.41.131.167
        @               IN A    64.41.131.162

        ; Aliases
        www             IN CNAME        @
        ftp             IN CNAME        www.somewhere.com.

        ; MX Record
        @               IN MX   10      mail.somewhere.com.
```

Although it may look as though this is an unformatted mess, there is in fact a distinct structure to it. Listing 31.2 consists of six basic elements:

- A $TTL directive

- The SOA (Start of Authority) record

- A block of NS (Name Server) records

- A block of A (Address) records

- A block of CNAME (Canonical Name) records, which define aliases

- An MX (Mail Exchanger) record

Aside from the directives, each element of the file is a *resource record* (RR), defining the properties of a name within the zone relative to a certain "origin." The following sections look at each of these elements in turn.

Directives

The zone file format allows for a number of different basic directives. These are global settings for the entire file, and each one is specified in capital letters beginning with a dollar sign ($). Directives can appear anywhere in the zone file, and each subsequent directive of the same type overrides any previous ones.

Of all the available directives, only $ORIGIN is generally very useful in practice:

- **$ORIGIN**—Syntax: $ORIGIN <domain-name> [<comment>]

    $ORIGIN is what will be appended to any unqualified name in a record. An unqualified name is, for instance, www; if www is listed in a record in a zone file with the $ORIGIN directive set to somewhere.com., the record will be defined as www. somewhere.com. (with the trailing dot).

    If $ORIGIN is not set within the zone file, it is assumed to be the same as the name of the zone specified in the zone statement that refers to it. If an $ORIGIN directive doesn't have a trailing dot, it is not "absolute," meaning that it will be appended to any previous $ORIGIN strings. For example, the directive

    ```
    $ORIGIN com.
    $ORIGIN somewhere
    www                     IN   CNAME stripes
    ```

    is equivalent to

    ```
    www.somewhere.com. IN   CNAME stripes.somewhere.com.
    ```

    Be careful when handling these trailing dots! If your domains are not resolving properly, check the dots first and make sure your $ORIGIN statements combine to the proper string.

31

- **$INCLUDE**—Syntax: $INCLUDE <filename> [<origin>] [<comment>]

  The $INCLUDE directive imports the file specified by <filename> and processes it as if it were a part of the zone file at the point where $INCLUDE appears. For the duration of the included file, $ORIGIN is set to <origin> if specified.

- **$TTL**—Syntax: $TTL <default-ttl> [<comment>]

  $TTL sets the default time-to-live (in seconds) for any records where the TTL value is not set. Generally, this is useful only for such things as *negative caching*, where BIND caches the fact that a record *does not* exist for a certain period (in other words, the TTL). In a resource record (RR), the TTL is the field that appears before the class column—blank in the records shown in Listing 31.2 (the IN field is the class). These records inherit the value of $TTL shown at the top of the listing, which is 3600 seconds in the example.

- **$GENERATE**—Syntax: $GENERATE <range> <lhs> <type> <rhs> [<comment>]

  $GENERATE is used to create a range of records that differ by an *iterator*, or a step value. In other words, you can automatically specify a large list of name records whose names and mapped IP addresses fit a certain formula:

  - **<range>**—This can be one of two forms: start-stop or start-stop/step. If the first form is used, step is set to 1.

  - **<lhs>**—This describes what will vary between the newly created records on the left-hand side of the record. Any single $ symbol within the left-hand side is replaced by the iterator value. If <lhs> is not an absolute name, the current $ORIGIN is appended to it. Use a 0 as a placeholder if nothing on the left-hand side should be iterated.

  - **<type>**—Can be any one of PTR, CNAME, or NS.

  - **<rhs>**—Does the same as <lhs>, except for the right-hand side of the record.

The $GENERATE directives

```
$ORIGIN 0.0.192.in-addr.arpa.
$GENERATE 1-2   0 NS    ns$.somewhere.com.
$GENERATE 1-127 $ CNAME $.0
```

are expanded by BIND into the following:

```
0.0.0.192.in-addr.arpa. NS    ns1.somewhere.com.
0.0.0.192.in-addr.arpa. NS    ns2.somewhere.com.
1.0.0.192.in-addr.arpa. CNAME 1.0.0.0.192.in-addr.arpa.
2.0.0.192.in-addr.arpa. CNAME 2.0.0.0.192.in-addr.arpa.
...
127.0.0.192.in-addr.arpa. CNAME 127.0.0.0.192.in-addr.arpa.
```

Start of Authority (SOA) Records

Next we come to the first resource record in a zone file: the Start of Authority (SOA) record. This is the most important part of a zone file, and the most commonly botched. Many mistakes are the result of the counterintuitive style of the SOA record's format. To understand this record, you need to look at it piece by piece.

Here's the sample SOA record from Listing 31.2:

```
somewhere.com. IN SOA stripes.somewhere.com. root.somewhere.com. (
                      2001061000        ; Serial
                      10800             ; Refresh
                      3600              ; Retry
                      604800            ; Expire
                      86400 )           ; Minimum TTL
```

The SOA, like all records, has the following basic form:

```
<name> [<ttl>] [<class>] <type> <value>
```

If <name> is not absolute, the current $ORIGIN is appended. In this case, the name is absolute (it ends with a dot).

The <ttl> field is omitted because the sample file has a global $TTL directive specifying it. IN (for "Internet") is the class; BIND supports other kinds of classes, but we're not interested in them here. If in was specified in the zone statement in named.conf, this field is redundant and can be omitted.

The <value> field for most records is quite simple: an IP address, a hostname, or some symbolic name. For the SOA record, though, it's much more complex. It begins, first of all, with the name of the authoritative name server for the zone (stripes.somewhere.com). The next piece of information is the e-mail address of the administrator of the domain, with the @ sign replaced by a dot. It also has a trailing dot at the end. In our example, the administrator (root@somewhere.com) is specified as root.somewhere.com., which will be used by BIND to mail status notifications to the responsible party.

> **NOTE**
>
> The reason for the @ sign in the administrator e-mail address being replaced with a dot is that the @ symbol, in a zone file, has a special meaning. It's shorthand for the current value of $ORIGIN and will be expanded by BIND into a fully qualified domain name.
>
> Note that the @ symbol must be the complete key if you use it; it can't be expanded implicitly, as in www.@ or some similar construct.

Following the administrator address is a parenthesized block of settings; the parentheses specify a block in which line breaks are ignored, so you can format the values for better clarity. These are the numbers that define how the zone data will behave on the Internet:

- **Serial Number**—The serial number is the way BIND keeps track of how recent a zone file is. Each time you update the zone file, you must increment the number so that BIND knows to refresh its information from the file. Standard practice is to use the format YYYYMMDDNN for this number; the final two digits are for revisions within a day. Update the number to reflect the current day when you make a change.

> **NOTE**
>
> When you use ndc reload to refresh a master zone file's information, BIND will automatically determine that the data needs to be refreshed, regardless of the serial number. However, keeping the serial number accurate is a good habit to be in; it will ensure proper operation in cases such as manually refreshing slave zone data.

- **Refresh**—This number, in seconds, specifies how frequently slave servers should check the master for updated zone data. If the master's serial number has changed since the last zone transfer, a new zone transfer will be performed.

- **Retry**—If the master server cannot be contacted, the slaves will retry at intervals specified by this number (in seconds).

- **Expire**—If the master server cannot be contacted within this time (in seconds), the slave servers discard all their data for the zone.

- **Minimum TTL**—This number (in seconds) specifies how long "negative cache" responses (which indicate the absence of a piece of data) should be kept.

Name Server (NS) Records

Listing 31.2 showed the following sample Name Server (NS) records:

```
; DNS Servers
@        IN NS          stripes.somewhere.com.
@        IN NS          spots.somewhere.com.
```

These records specify the DNS servers that are allowed to give authoritative answers to queries about the zone. Note that the @ symbol refers to the current $ORIGIN (which, in this case, is somewhere.com.) and that both server names have trailing dots (indicating that they are absolute).

You can create NS records for subdomains, or zones within the current zone. For instance, suppose you have a cluster of machines within a zone called cluster.somewhere.com., with their DNS information handled by their own name server (ns.cluster.somewhere.com). A valid NS record for that server, allowing external hosts to query it for the cluster's IP addresses, would be

```
cluster IN NS          ns.cluster.somewhere.com.
```

Recall that by leaving the trailing dot off of `cluster`, the current `$ORIGIN` (`somewhere.com.`) is appended to it by BIND.

Address (A) Records

The Address (A) record is what you use to associate a hostname with an IP address. Our example had the following records:

```
; Machine Names
localhost       IN A    127.0.0.1
stripes         IN A    64.41.131.162
spots           IN A    64.41.131.163
mail            IN A    64.41.131.167
@               IN A    64.41.131.162
```

The meaning of these records is fairly straightforward. The unqualified names on the left-hand side are expanded with the current `$ORIGIN`. Therefore, `mail.somewhere.com` would resolve to `64.41.131.167`. Similarly, the `@` symbol expands so that a query for `somewhere.com` would return `64.41.131.162`.

Names that are defined in A records are known as *canonical names*, as opposed to *aliases* (which are defined by CNAME records).

Canonical Name (CNAME) Records

Canonical Name (CNAME) records are used to create aliases. The terminology is such that in our example from Listing 31.2, the alias name `www` (which expands with `$ORIGIN` to `www.somewhere.com.`) points to the canonical name `@`, or `somewhere.com.` (whose IP address is defined in the A block):

```
; Aliases
www             IN CNAME        @
ftp             IN CNAME        www.somewhere.com.
```

CNAME records are often useful in that they are not immediately bound to an IP address. You can use CNAME records to point to names in another zone, for example, which can then be controlled by the owner of that zone. Also, CNAME records are helpful in reducing the number of changes that must be made in a zone file if an IP address changes.

Mail Exchanger (MX) Records

Mail Exchanger (MX) records define which hosts are to be used for mail delivery to addresses in the zone. Sendmail (and other MTAs) look up the most preferred MX record within a zone and open a connection to it; you can find out the MX hosts for a domain with the `host` command:

```
# host somecompany.com
somecompany.com has address 207.114.98.18
somecompany.com mail is handled (pri=100) by mail.uu.net
somecompany.com mail is handled (pri=5) by mx-1.somecompany.com
```

Each MX record has a "priority" number associated with it, and mail servers for a domain are tried from lowest to highest numerical value until a successful SMTP connection can be made. The priority is specified as part of the value field in the record, as in our example:

```
; MX Record
@                   IN MX   10 mail.somewhere.com.
```

> **CAUTION**
>
> An MX record cannot point to an IP address. Also, many MTAs and mail clients will complain if they detect an MX record that points to a CNAME. Make sure your MX records point to defined names specified elsewhere with A records!

Pointer (PTR) Records

Pointer (PTR) records are the reverse of A or CNAME records and are used in reverse DNS zone files (for example, `131.41.64.in-addr.arpa`) to map IP addresses to domain names. An example of a reverse DNS zone file is shown in Listing 31.3.

Because a reverse DNS lookup only returns a single name, multiple PTR records for the same IP address are useless and only confuse matters. For this reason, reverse files are often shorter than their forward counterparts.

Reverse DNS Zone Files

A reverse DNS zone file, defining a zone of the form `131.41.64.in-addr.arpa`, is used to map IP addresses to names. Files of this sort are referenced in `named.conf` and propagated to slave servers just like forward DNS zone files. Listing 31.3 shows a sample reverse DNS zone file.

LISTING 31.3   A Sample Reverse DNS Zone File for the 131.41.64.in-addr.arpa Zone

```
$TTL 3600

131.41.64.in-addr.arpa. IN SOA stripes.somewhere.com. root.somewhere.com. (
                    2001061000      ; Serial
                    10800           ; Refresh
                    3600            ; Retry
```

LISTING 31.3   Continued

```
                          604800          ; Expire
                          86400 )         ; Minimum TTL


   @        IN NS    stripes.somewhere.com.
   @        IN NS    spots.somewhere.com.


   162      IN PTR   stripes.somewhere.com.
   163      IN PTR   spots.somewhere.com.
   167      IN PTR   mail.somewhere.com.
```

Note the use of PTR records instead of A or CNAME records. The name that each PTR points to is the true canonical name for that IP address. There is also no need for an MX record in a reverse file because MX records cannot be associated with IP addresses in the first place.

Making a `localhost` Zone File

A special zone file must exist for the `localhost` zone (`0.0.127.in-addr.arpa`) to work properly. There's a shell script in `/etc/namedb` to help you create one. The script is called `make-localhost`, and it reads in a template (`PROTO.localhost.rev`) and fills in information that it derives from your input. Because it isn't set executable, you must run it with the `sh` command:

```
# sh make-localhost
Enter your domain name: somewhere.com
```

The resulting file, `/etc/namedb/localhost.rev`, should look something like Listing 31.4.

LISTING 31.4   Autogenerated `localhost.rev` Zone File

```
;        From: @(#)localhost.rev 5.1 (Berkeley) 6/30/90
; $FreeBSD: src/etc/namedb/PROTO.localhost.rev,v 1.6 2000/01/10
➡15:31:40 peter Exp $
;
; This file is automatically edited by the `make-localhost' script in
; the /etc/namedb directory.
;


$TTL    3600


@       IN      SOA     stripes.somewhere.com. root.stripes.somewhere.com. (
                        20010612        ; Serial
                        3600    ; Refresh
                        900     ; Retry
```

LISTING 31.4 Continued

```
                          3600000 ; Expire
                          3600 )  ; Minimum
        IN      NS      stripes.somewhere.com.
1       IN      PTR     localhost.somewhere.com.
```

Make sure to create this file before fully deploying your DNS service!

Configuring a Caching Name Server

It's entirely possible to run a name server that is not authoritative for any zones. This is what's known as a *caching name server,* and its job consists solely of making DNS queries when prompted by clients and storing the results for later use. This is the opposite effect of the forward only; option we discussed earlier in this chapter. Whereas a forward only; name server would pass off all requests to its forwarder to handle, a caching name server performs all requests that are asked of it by itself and caches the results. Other name servers can use this server as a forwarder, leveraging the work that it has already done.

To configure a caching name server, simply omit any zone statements from your named.conf file other than the ones necessary for its own operation. Listing 31.5 shows such a configuration.

LISTING 31.5 A Sample /etc/namedb/named.conf File

```
/*
 * A simple BIND 8 configuration
 */

logging {
    category lame-servers { null; };
    category cname { null; };
};

options {
    directory "/etc/namedb";
};

zone "." {
    type hint;
    file "named.boot";
};

zone "0.0.127.in-addr.arpa" in {
    type master;
```

LISTING 31.5   Continued

```
    file "localhost.rev";
};

zone "0.0.0.0.0.0.0.0.0.0.0.0.0.0.0.0.0.0.0.0.0.0.0.0.0.0.0.0.0.0.0.0.IP6.INT" {
        type master;
        file "localhost.rev";
};
```

Because a caching name server is simply a "degenerate case" of a fully configured name server, you can easily expand your server's functionality by adding additional zones as time goes on. There is no real fundamental difference between the two "modes."

Your DNS configuration will change with time as your network evolves. Each time a new host is added to your network or changes its name, and each time you take on or remove the name service authority for a zone, you will need to make changes to the configuration. It's a good idea to keep in practice with DNS administration so that these tasks become more natural with time.

The Network Filesystem (NFS)

N FS, the *Network Filesystem*, is the Unix way of performing file sharing. Windows and Mac OS both have their own file-sharing mechanisms, enabling networked computers to access files on remote machines on a LAN as if they were local. NFS provides the same benefits, with a few extra features that other sharing protocols don't have.

This chapter will describe how to configure your FreeBSD machine to operate as an NFS client and/or server, sharing files with other Unix machines on your LAN or across the Internet.

Introduction to NFS

Windows uses NetBIOS/SMB for its file sharing, and Macintoshes use AppleTalk. These are both peer-to-peer protocols, with each system broadcasting its presence onto the LAN, and all machines being able to mount each other's shared folders dynamically. NFS is a bit different in that it's a client/server protocol, with designated servers sharing items that can be mounted remotely by specified NFS clients. This model is designed for the centralization of file sharing, as is common in enterprise or university networks, rather than for peer-to-peer file transfers. However, with the proper configuration, NFS can do almost everything that the other protocols can do, and more, with the exception of server discovery.

Under both Windows and Mac OS, the built-in file-sharing protocol on a computer broadcasts information about its own shared folders (or *shares*) and asks for responses about other available shares on the network. These "discovery" queries and responses are sent out by each machine on the network and trigger frequent responses from all other machines— resulting in a very "chatty" network environment. NFS doesn't have a corresponding discovery mechanism. As you will see, each NFS client has to know where to find each server and mount it manually. However, this does mean that the network is much quieter due to a lack of discovery traffic.

This less-convenient structure of NFS does have its benefits. The centralized model provides better security; a server can control exactly which clients are able to connect to it—for example, by hostname or IP address, or by centralized login, as with NIS or Kerberos. Another feature of NFS is that because it does not depend on LAN broadcasts for server discovery, it can be used across the Internet just as easily as across the LAN. A client in Boston can mount a share from a server in San Francisco, if necessary. By contrast, NetBIOS/SMB and AppleTalk only can operate within "domains" or "zones" on the local network (although AppleTalk/IP can cross the Internet freely).

As far as FreeBSD is concerned, NFS is a filesystem just like any other. You can mount an NFS share over the network just as if you were mounting a floppy disk or a new hard drive partition, as you saw in Chapter 8, "The FreeBSD Filesystem." Shares will even be mounted automatically if their resources are requested and the client machine is properly set up to do it. We will go over the procedure of mounting an NFS share later in this chapter.

The client/server structure of NFS is designed so that you can centralize the resources in your network. For example, an enterprise might give all its employees home directories on a central Unix machine, and every other system in the network that supports NFS will be able to mount those home directories and access them remotely, rather than requiring each machine to have its own copy of every home directory. Figure 32.1 shows this kind of network topology in action. The same can be done for build directories (in a software development environment) or shared applications that are centrally installed (as in a university workstation cluster). NFS mounts can be used in conjunction with NIS (centralized login management) to provide the entire network with user authentication; then, file ownership and permissions on every file in a mounted share will work just as on the NFS server machine itself. You can even install FreeBSD over NFS if you mount the installation CD-ROM on the NFS server and point Sysinstall toward it.

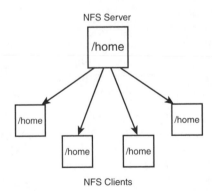

FIGURE 32.1   An enterprise network with central NFS-mounted home directories.

An interesting aspect of NFS is that it's primarily based on UDP, rather than TCP. As we discussed in Chapter 21, "Networking with FreeBSD," UDP has none of the reliability or connection-centric structure of TCP and is inherently unreliable. Although it seems odd that a data-conscious network protocol would use UDP as its transport mechanism, spewing datagrams from server to client without any guarantee of their integrity, NFS is actually one of the best examples of UDP used properly. Full TCP connections aren't really needed, especially on a LAN. NFS clients come and go as machines on a network come up and shut down, and TCP connections would just get in the way of data streams sending files and directory information back and forth between the endpoints on request. An NFS mount can stay dormant for days and then suddenly be called into use again. UDP allows the shared resources to be immediately available without connection startup overhead or lag time, and if a host drops off the network, it's no big deal to the server.

Data integrity is maintained by the NFS software itself, keeping checksum and sequencing information in the packets' payload and doing all the work that TCP would otherwise have done. However, NFS clients that operate over TCP do exist, and the NFS server supports them, too. NFS over TCP is primarily intended for mounts that take place over a WAN, in which dropped packets are much more likely, and the benefits of full TCP connections mitigate the benefits that UDP offers on LAN connections.

> **NOTE**
>
> One downside to using UDP, though, is that if a client tries to contact an NFS server that isn't there, it can take forever to time out. The lack of a full TCP connection means that more primitive methods are necessary to determine whether a server is not responding. We will talk about some of the ways to avoid running into the lengthy NFS timeout later in this chapter.

> **CAUTION**
>
> NFS doesn't have any built-in security or encryption, so it should be used over the Internet only if you're working with files that can safely be exposed to the public. Mission-critical or sensitive data should never be sent over wide-area NFS, except inside a LAN protected by a firewall or through an encrypted VPN tunnel.

A FreeBSD machine can be configured to be an NFS server, an NFS client, or both. Depending on how you configure it, the system will run a few different processes that manage the end of the NFS connections it will handle. We'll talk first about setting up a FreeBSD machine as an NFS server and then about configuring it as a client.

Configuring an NFS Server

Setting up your FreeBSD machine to be an NFS server involves a one-line addition to /etc/rc.conf:

```
nfs_server_enable="YES"
```

Also, make sure that `rpcbind_enable` (`portmap_enable` prior to FreeBSD 5.0) is set to `"YES"`, because it is disabled by default unless you override it. The `rpcbind` (or `portmap`) daemon needs to be running in order for NFS to work because the NFS server needs a mechanism by which to tell its clients which port to connect to. UDP services operate with only one "connection" per port, so while initial connections to the NFS server take place on the server port 2049, these connections are mapped by remote procedure call (RPC) services, provided by `rpcbind`, to a new and unused server port. Note that `rpcbind` services are fairly insecure and subject to a number of recurring security issues; for this reason, it's not a good idea to have an NFS server exposed to the Internet without a firewall protecting it. See Chapter 29, "Network Security," for more on firewalls.

When you set the `nfs_server_enable` option and reboot, FreeBSD starts two kinds of daemon processes—three if you count `rpcbind`—after reading the contents of the `/etc/exports` file to determine what to share via NFS. The following sections look at each of these components to explain what they do and how to control them.

NFS Daemon (`nfsd`)

The NFS server daemon, the equivalent of `sshd` or `httpd`, is `nfsd`. A certain number of `nfsd` processes are started when the network is initialized (the default is four); these processes are assigned to service NFS clients when they connect, one process per client. In the default configuration, a maximum of four clients can connect to your NFS server at the same time. You can tune this with the `nfs_server_flags` setting in `/etc/rc.conf`:

```
nfs_server_flags="-u -t -n 4"
```

The `-n` flag can be set to any number you like; set it to the highest number of concurrent NFS clients you expect to be connected to your server at any one time. The `-t` and `-u` flags tell the `nfsd` processes to serve both TCP and UDP clients. Other flags are available for you to tweak, if you like. For instance, specify `-h 64.41.131.102` among the other flags to bind the NFS servers to the interface with the address `64.41.131.102`. (You can also use a hostname instead of an IP address.) This can be necessary if your server has multiple network interfaces; the UDP mechanism is such that if you don't tell `nfsd` for which specific IP addresses it should serve requests, its responses are not guaranteed to come from the address that the client contacted. You can list as many addresses as you need with multiple `-h` flags. For example, let's say you have a server acting as a gateway with two network cards—one on the "inside" and one on the "outside" of the network. Your "inside" card has two IP addresses bound to it, and you want to serve NFS shares only to clients on the inside. You can set up NFS like this:

```
nfs_server_flags="-u -t -n 4 -h 64.41.131.102 -h 64.41.131.116"
```

Then, you can block access to the NFS service on the outside interface with an IPFW rule, like so:

```
ipfw add deny udp from any to 64.41.131.10 nfsd
```

Refer to "Using a Firewall," in Chapter 29, for more information on how to configure firewall rules using IPFW.

NFS Mount Daemon (mountd)

Whereas nfsd is the program that provides the connection end of each individual NFS mount, a second program is in charge of listening for new NFS client requests (on TCP port 2049). This program is mountd, the mount daemon. It is executed automatically along with the nfsd processes during the network setup procedure at boot time if nfs_server_enable is set to "YES".

mountd takes incoming NFS connections and passes them to nfsd processes. It's also in charge of keeping track of the NFS shares you have specified in /etc/exports. To restart NFS services after making changes to /etc/exports, you need to send an HUP signal to mountd, as you will see shortly.

There aren't too many useful options for mountd. The default settings in /etc/defaults/rc.conf, which you can override in /etc/rc.conf, are as follows:

```
mountd_flags="-r"
```

The -r flag allows mountd to serve regular files rather than only directories, to maintain compatibility with certain diskless workstations that boot via NFS. The -l flag allows you to log all NFS mount requests, and the -n flag allows NFS shares to be mounted to remote systems such as Windows PCs that don't share the same ownership and permissions model as Unix.

Determining What to Share with the /etc/exports File

The /etc/exports file lists what directory trees should be shared via NFS as well as who should be allowed to share them. If /etc/exports does not exist or is not readable at the time the network is started, the nfsd and mountd processes are not started.

The full format of /etc/exports is defined in man exports. A basic export line specifies one or more directories that should be exported (shared), any of several options, and then an optional list of hosts (by IP address, network, netgroup, or hostname) allowed to share the specified directories. For example, the following line shares the /home directory and all its subdirectories to anybody who connects:

```
/home -alldirs
```

Note that the -alldirs option can only be specified if the share is the mount point of a filesystem (for example, /usr or /home). If it isn't, the share will not be made available.

A share that can be accessed only by three specified hosts and is read-only would look like this:

```
/usr2 -ro -alldirs stripes.somewhere.com spots.somewhere.com 64.41.131.165
```

TIP

You can create groups of hosts by specifying them in the file /etc/netgroup, which does not exist in the default installation. A group can be specified in the following form:

```
groupname (host, user, domain) (host, user, domain) ...
```

For instance, to create a group called desktops that contains three particular hosts (named sol, luna, and terra), the line would look like this:

```
desktops (sol,,) (luna,,) (terra,,)
```

A netgroup defined on usernames would look like this:

```
developers (,frank,) (,bob,) (,alice,)
```

You can then use any of these netgroup names instead of hostnames in /etc/exports to confine an NFS share to members of that group.

File ownership in an NFS share is mapped based on the UIDs of each file and directory. If the usernames and UIDs on the server and client machines are the same (for instance, if the machines' logins are synchronized via NIS or Kerberos), the permissions will match. However, if UID 1045 maps on the server to the username bill, but UID 1045 on the client is john, John will own the files in the share that the server thinks Bill owns. When exporting a share containing files owned by many different users, make sure the infrastructure is in place to provide consistent mappings between UIDs and usernames on all the machines on your network.

You can use the -maproot=<username> or -maproot=<UID> option to map ownership so that the username matching <username> or the user ID matching <UID> on the client machine will have full root permissions in the share. For example, here's how to share the entire filesystem of the NFS server with anybody in the 64.41.131 network, with the client user frank having full read/write access to all the files:

```
/ -maproot=frank -network 64.41.131 -mask 255.255.255.0
```

After making any changes to /etc/exports, you need to restart the mountd process (assuming it's already running). Do this by accessing the runtime PID file:

```
# kill -HUP `cat /var/run/mountd.pid`
```

NOTE

You can't have multiple export lines for mount points within the same partition or filesystem. This is to prevent problems in cases where the export permissions for different shares in the same filesystem would conflict. An NFS client cannot access one filesystem from within another that it has mounted, and the same access permissions must apply for all shares within a filesystem. The following setup is illegal:

```
/home/frank 64.41.131.102
/home/joe 64.41.131.102
```

However, this one is correct:

```
/home/frank /home/joe 64.41.131.102
```

You can use the showmount program (with the -e, "show exports list" option) to display the valid shares and their permissions. This is how you can tell whether your /etc/exports setup is valid:

```
# showmount -e
Exports list on localhost:
/usr                        Everyone
/home/frank                 64.41.131.102
/home/joe                   64.41.131.102
/                           64.41.131.0
```

Starting NFS Services Without Rebooting

The cleanest way to start NFS services is to reboot the system. However, if you need to start the services and you don't want to reboot, simply issue the following commands as root (omitting the rpcbind command if it's already running):

```
# rpcbind
# nfsd -u -t -n 4
# mountd -r
```

Then, you can use showmount -e to make sure the NFS shares are being exported properly.

Configuring an NFS Client

If your FreeBSD machine will be mounting NFS shares from other servers, you will need to configure it as a client. Technically this isn't really necessary—you can mount an NFS share in a rudimentary fashion right out of the box. However, configuring the system as an NFS client gives you a few features that ensure speedy and reliable performance, such as the nfsiod dispatcher.

To set up an NFS client machine, simply enable the following line in /etc/rc.conf:

```
nfs_client_enable="YES"
```

This setting enables the NFS Input/Output Daemon, nfsiod, which helps to streamline NFS client requests and tunes a few kernel settings to improve access time. This is all handled automatically in the /etc/rc.network script at boot time, along with the NFS server settings (which you saw earlier).

NFS Input/Output Daemon (nfsiod)

The nfsiod daemon isn't required for proper NFS client operation, but it helps to speed things up. The nfsiod daemon operates by allowing NFS read and write operations to be done in an asynchronous manner, with "read-ahead" and "write-behind" operations occurring in the background, rather than having to wait for each sequential step in the process to complete. Just as with nfsd, there should be as many nfsiod processes running as there are mounted NFS shares on the client machine. You can tune the number of processes with the nfs_client_flags setting in /etc/rc.conf, which uses the -n option to create four processes by default:

```
nfs_client_flags="-n 4"
```

There aren't any other settable options for nfsiod. To start it without rebooting the machine, simply run it from the command line:

```
# nfsiod -n 4
```

Mounting Remote Filesystems

Mounting an NFS share is done with the mount_nfs command, which is a shorthand command for mount -t nfs (as you learned in Chapter 8). In its most common form, you would pass to it two arguments: the host and share names in a combined string, and the local mount point:

```
# mount_nfs spots:/home /home2
```

A successful mount will result in no output. You can check whether the mount was successful with the df command:

```
# df
Filesystem        1K-blocks      Used    Avail Capacity  Mounted on
/dev/ad0s1a          992239     54353   858507      6%   /
/dev/ad0s1f        26704179   4872963 19694882     20%   /home
/dev/ad0s1e         9924475   1642343  7488174     18%   /usr
procfs                    4         4        0    100%   /proc
spots:/home         9924475   1642343  7488174     18%   /home2
```

If you go into the /home2 directory, you'll see all the directories within /home on the NFS server, with each file's ownership mapped based on UID, as discussed earlier. The filesystem will remain mounted until you explicitly unmount it with the umount command:

```
# umount /home2
```

> **CAUTION**
>
> Remember to leave any NFS-mounted directory before you try to unmount it with umount! You will get a "device busy" error if you try to unmount a filesystem while you're still inside it.

NFS shares can be mounted in a great variety of ways, and the options are laid out in the man mount_nfs page. Some of the more useful are the -T option, which forces TCP transport rather than UDP (useful for mounts done over WAN links), and the -s and -x <seconds> flags, which allow the mount to time out and disappear after a specified period and then fail (a "soft" mount). Here's an example:

```
# mount_nfs -s -x 60 spots:/home /home2
```

> **TIP**
>
> Another useful option is -i, which enables interruptibility. Normally, if you have mounted an NFS share and the server becomes unresponsive or unreachable, any filesystem calls you make (commands that deal with the shared files, such as ls) can hang in such a way that even pressing Ctrl+C (the termination signal) won't stop them. The -i option makes it so that Ctrl+C will force the command to fail, returning control to you.

As with other filesystem types, you can add NFS mounts to /etc/fstab to set up predefined mount points, thus simplifying the mount process. Place any options you would otherwise pass to mount_nfs in the Options column, separated by commas, as shown here:

```
# Device          Mountpoint     FStype   Options         Dump    Pass#
spots:/home       /home2         nfs      rw,-T,-i,noauto 0       0
```

With a table entry like this, you can mount an NFS filesystem with the mount command:

```
# mount /home2
```

Mounting Remote Filesystems Automatically at System Boot

All filesystems in /etc/fstab are automatically mounted at boot time, unless the noauto option is present. You can specify that remote NFS shares should be mounted at startup by simply adding them to /etc/fstab, as you just saw. However, there are a few things to watch out for.

Most notably, NFS has an extremely long default timeout period, and the phase during startup when filesystems are mounted is a synchronous, blocking process. If your NFS server or servers cannot be found—for instance, if the server machine isn't running, or if your own machine's network connection is not configured properly—the boot process can hang for an intolerably long period before NFS gives up and allows the system to finish the boot procedure.

You can solve this problem by placing the noauto option in /etc/fstab, as you saw in the earlier example. However, this means that you have to mount each NFS share manually after the system is fully booted. There's a better way to handle this—the -b option. Here's an example:

```
# Device                Mountpoint      FStype  Options      Dump    Pass#
spots:/home             /home2          nfs     rw,-b         0       0
```

The -b option tells mount to make a quick attempt to contact the server, and if it can't, to fork off a child process to continue trying to connect while the boot process continues on. Similarly, if you mount a share from the command line using -b, the process forks into the background and returns you to the command prompt. The following is the output you would get when trying to mount the share specified in the preceding sample /etc/fstab line, after trying for 60 seconds:

```
# mount /home2
spots:/home: nfsd: RPCPROG_NFS: RPC: Port mapper failure - RPC: Timed out
nfs: Cannot immediately mount spots:/home, backgrounding
```

The background mount_nfs process will keep trying to mount the share until it's successful. This method is particularly useful in computing clusters or labs in which NFS-mounted resources are nice to have but not required for correct operation—for example, a cluster in which an NFS mount contains popular user programs or games, but all critical system functions are available on disks on the local system.

Auto-Mount Daemon (amd)

The auto-mount daemon, amd, makes NFS mounts even more convenient. This daemon allows you to mount NFS shares (and other filesystem types, as a matter of fact) dynamically, simply by working in the directory in which the share would be mounted, without ever having to bother with mount commands.

FreeBSD provides a basic way to set up amd. Simply add the following line to /etc/rc.conf:

```
amd_enable="YES"
```

When the system is booted with this option, amd runs with the options specified in the amd_flags setting, which are such that anything in the /host or /net directories—both of which are created automatically by amd—will auto-mount by name. You can also start it in the same way as it would be at boot time by issuing the following command:

```
# amd -a /.amd_mnt -l syslog /host /etc/amd.map /net /etc/amd.map
```

With amd running, use the cd command to move into the /host directory. Look around, and you'll notice the directory is empty:

```
# cd /host
# ls
#
```

However, try listing by name as if there were a directory there with the same name as a known NFS server on the network:

```
# ls stripes
home
```

So, it seems that there's indeed a directory called stripes in the /host directory, and inside it is a home directory—which contains everything that the stripes:/home share has. You've just auto-mounted that share into the /host directory, simply by listing it as a directory name. /host/stripes/home is functionally the same thing as the /home2 mount point we manually created in our earlier example. The df command will verify it:

```
# df
Filesystem     1K-blocks     Used    Avail Capacity  Mounted on
stripes:/home   9924475   1642345  7488172    18%    /.amd_mnt/stripes/host/home
```

> **NOTE**
>
> Notice that NFS shares mounted in this manner actually appear to be mounted inside a directory called .amd_mnt in the root directory. This directory doesn't actually exist; it's just a type of short-hand used by the amd daemon for bookkeeping purposes.

To specify a permanent location for a mountable NFS resource, simply make a symbolic link to the appropriate path within /host or /net:

```
# ln -s /home2 /host/stripes/home
```

From now on, whenever you go into the /home2 directory, the stripes:/home share will automatically mount and give you access to its files. When the share is no longer in use, it will automatically unmount.

> **TIP**
>
> You can specify much more complex amd mount maps, which are more direct methods of mounting filesystems at particular points, with the /etc/amd.conf file. This file doesn't exist in the default FreeBSD installation; see man amd.conf for details on its format and capabilities.

CHAPTER 33

File and Print Sharing with Microsoft Windows

NFS is an excellent solution for file sharing between Unix machines, where Unix permissions and file metadata (such as modification times) must be preserved from machine to machine. However, NFS isn't widely supported on many consumer operating systems. Windows and classic Mac OS support it only through third-party applications, and—more importantly in an enterprise environment—there isn't any "discovery" mechanism built in to NFS to allow clients to browse lists of available servers.

When you put a FreeBSD machine into an existing network, chances are that most of the computers already there will be running Windows. True interoperation with these clients and with existing Windows file servers requires that FreeBSD share files the same way Windows does. This method involves SMB, the *Server Message Block* protocol, and the *Common Internet File System* (CIFS), which is gradually replacing it.

File sharing over SMB/CIFS is not a built-in part of FreeBSD. However, an add-on package called *Samba* gives a FreeBSD machine the ability to act as a Windows file server and participate in all the same file-sharing activities as true Windows clients.

Samba is an open-source, volunteer project originally begun by Andrew Tridgell and now developed collaboratively by the general Unix community. It provides a Unix machine (such as FreeBSD) with the capability to do everything that Windows file sharing can do, including appearing in network browsing lists, securing connections based on NT domain and username logons, and providing network print services. Samba also includes tools that provide many of the administrative functions of a Windows NT/2000 server. With the addition of the smbfs kernel module to allow FreeBSD to operate as a Windows file-sharing client (you learn more about smbfs later in this chapter), you can use a FreeBSD machine in a Windows network environment with just as much functionality as a native Windows machine would have.

This chapter will guide you through configuring Samba. Here, you'll learn how to add Windows-like file-sharing and printer-management capabilities to your FreeBSD system, including integration into Windows workgroups and domains so that your system is indistinguishable on the network from native Windows PCs.

NOTE

The official Web site for Samba is www.samba.org, from which you can select any of a number of different geographical mirror sites.

SMB/CIFS and Samba

SMB, dating back to documents published in 1985 by IBM and later further expanded by Microsoft and Intel, is a generalized system for sharing all kinds of system resources over a local network. Such resources include files, printers, serial ports, and software abstractions such as named pipes. It's a protocol that operates in a client/server fashion, even if Windows file sharing on the surface appears to be a peer-to-peer structure. SMB is a fundamental part of many operating systems, including MS-DOS, Windows, OS/2, and Linux—although the primary uses for SMB today are in Windows and promulgated by Microsoft.

SMB and CIFS commands are sent over network protocols such as IPX, NetBEUI, Banyan VINES, and DECnet. These protocols operate at the "network" level of the stack, the same level as IP (as you saw in Chapter 21, "Networking with FreeBSD"), and are therefore not limited to TCP/IP transport. However, the most commonly used transport for SMB is NetBIOS (Network Basic Input/Output System, described in RFCs 1001 and 1002) traveling over IP, operating with both TCP and UDP components. This is the protocol used in Windows file sharing.

Browsing

An advantage that SMB has over protocols such as NFS is that it supports automatic server discovery, or *browsing*. In Windows, if you open the Network Neighborhood or My Network Places window, it will display the names of all the available SMB servers on the local network. This list is built up dynamically, with each machine sending out periodic broadcast packets looking for the "master browser" of the network (a computer with a definitive list of local and remote SMB hosts) and announcing its own presence. Every other machine on the network builds its "browse list" from those broadcasts.

The name of each machine, as it appears in the network browser window (as shown in Figure 33.1), is its *NetBIOS name*, a designation that Windows allows to be up to 15 characters long. Although Windows makes you input a NetBIOS name in uppercase, it shows up in the network browser window with only the first letter capitalized. Under other operating systems (such as FreeBSD), the NetBIOS name is the same as the machine's hostname, truncated to 15 characters if necessary.

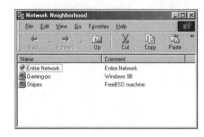

FIGURE 33.1   The Windows network browser window, showing a FreeBSD machine running Samba.

NetBIOS names are handled by a form of name service, somewhat like DNS names, but mapping the displayed NetBIOS machine names to particular machines based on other criteria as well as the IP address (because NetBIOS isn't restricted to IP). Samba's name server component is separate from the actual SMB data server.

One drawback to NetBIOS is that it operates only on a LAN; NetBIOS packets are broadcast based and therefore aren't forwarded by routers. The Windows Internet Name Service (WINS) protocol exists to link Windows sharing zones on different networks, thus mitigating this issue somewhat.

Security, Workgroups, and Domains

Access to SMB shares is controlled at various levels. The topmost level restricts access based on host IP address or by password authentication from viewing any of the file server's contents. Beneath that, each individual share (a directory, printer, or other resource) has its own access permissions and optional host/password restrictions as well. Finally, within a share, individual files are subject to access permissions based on the authenticated user or host that has gained access to the share.

User authentication with passwords can be handled in a distributed way (by each individual sharing host) or in a centralized way (by a central network logon server). This is the difference between "workgroups" and "domains" in Windows. A *workgroup* is a collection of machines that agree to appear in one another's network browser windows, and each individually handles its own authentication and security. A *domain* is a group of machines whose security duties are handled by a central server to which all member machines must be subscribed.

Samba provides the ability to restrict access on all these levels, as well as to act itself as a "master browser" (in workgroup context) or as a domain controller (the central logon authority in a domain environment). You will see how this is done shortly.

File and Print Sharing with Macintosh Clients Using AppleTalk

Samba won't provide SMB/CIFS capabilities for communicating with Macintosh clients. For that task, consider AppleTalk. This LAN-level protocol suite operates over its own transport layer or over IP, and it's used by many enterprise and university networks.

The software package that provides AppleTalk functionality to Unix platforms, called *netatalk*, is available in the ports collection. To install AppleTalk support, build netatalk from the ports at `/usr/ports/net/netatalk`. (Ignore the `netatalk-asun` port and install only the basic netatalk port; if you install both ports at once, AppleTalk won't work.)

Enable the `NETATALK` option in your kernel configuration. See Chapter 16, "Kernel Configuration," for information on building a custom kernel. The netatalk port installs a number of configuration files—one for each necessary daemon—along with `.dist` (or distribution) reference copies. The daemons run in the default installed configuration; you can change some of the config files to tweak their behavior. Every Macintosh on the network will see the machine in its AppleShare zone in the Chooser (or in the Connect to Server window in Mac OS X).

See the official netatalk Web site at `http://netatalk.sourceforge.net/` for fuller descriptions of the various tools in the netatalk package and links to other documentation.

Installing and Configuring Samba

Samba is available in the ports at `/usr/ports/net/samba` or in the packages. Refer to Chapter 14, "Installing Additional Software," for details on how to install a package or port.

Once you have installed the Samba package, a variety of new items will be installed, including daemon executables (in `/usr/local/sbin`), administrative tools (in `/usr/local/bin`), documentation and examples (in `/usr/local/share`), and configuration files that go into `/usr/local/etc`. Some of the possible config files don't exist in the default installation; you have to create them from scratch if you want to take advantage of their functionality. There are also code pages (in `/usr/local/etc/codepages`) that map Windows character sets to Unix ones.

The only configuration file that exists in the package is `smb.conf.default`, which you must rename to `smb.conf` for it to work. Similarly, the `/usr/local/etc/rc.d/samba.sh.sample` startup script must be renamed to `samba.sh`. In the very easiest way to get Samba running, you only need to edit `smb.conf` and modify the `workgroup` line to reflect the workgroup or domain of which your machine is a part:

```
# workgroup = NT-Domain-Name or Workgroup-Name, eg: REDHAT4
    workgroup = MYGROUP
```

Samba will now start automatically when the system boots. To start it manually, run the `samba.sh` script with the `start` parameter:

```
# /usr/local/etc/rc.d/samba.sh start
  Samba#
```

> **NOTE**
>
> There is no line break in the script output after the service name `Samba`. This cosmetic flaw exists because during startup, each service in `/usr/local/etc/rc.d` is started sequentially, and the echoed output of each startup script goes onto the same line. Being able to start services from the `rc.d` startup scripts is a convenience feature, not the primary intended functionality.

The smbd and nmbd Daemons

If the `samba.sh` script runs successfully, you will notice two new processes running—`smbd` and `nmbd`—as shown here:

```
# ps -waux | grep mbd
root  3855  0.0  1.5  2368 1816  ??  Is  2:43PM  0:00.00 /usr/local/sbin/smbd -D
root  3857  0.0  1.2  1940 1496  ??  Ss  2:43PM  0:00.02 /usr/local/sbin/nmbd -D
```

The `smbd` daemon is the actual data server, the process that handles SMB/CIFS requests from connected Windows clients—file transfers, print jobs, listings, and so on. Unlike NFS, SMB doesn't require a separate process to be running for each simultaneous connection; the master `smbd` process forks off a new copy of itself for each new client session and handles all that client's requests for the duration of the session. The `-D` option specifies that `smbd` should operate as a standalone daemon, listening for requests on TCP port 139.

Operating in parallel with `smbd` is `nmbd`, the NetBIOS name server. It's the process that allows Windows clients to see the FreeBSD machine in the network browser view, as you saw in Figure 33.1. It also has the job of responding to client requests for a particular NetBIOS host if it's specified by name; if a Windows client uses the `\\<name>` syntax to connect to a particular server by name, the client sends out a broadcast name request asking for the IP address of the server with that NetBIOS name. It's the job of `nmbd` to send back a response with the requested host's IP address so that the client can open an SMB request directly to the server. It's somewhat like DNS (in that it maps a common name to a direct address), and it also has a lot in common with ARP (in that it operates on a LAN through broadcast name requests, rather than to a designated central name server).

smb.conf and SWAT

The main configuration file for Samba is `/usr/local/etc/smb.conf`, in which you can set any of dozens of different options and create shares with customized settings. In this file, lines beginning with # or ; characters are comments; the usage in `smb.conf.default` (the sample config file) is to use the # characters as comments and the ; characters to enable and disable configuration lines.

Each option is pretty well documented in comments in `smb.conf.default`. However, it can become very daunting to try to keep track of everything in that file because there are so many possible options (listed in `man smb.conf`) that you can set, with so many subtle differences between them. There's an alternative method to administering `smb.conf`, however, if your network circumstances permit it. This method involves SWAT, the *Samba Web Administration Tool*, which is shown in Figure 33.2.

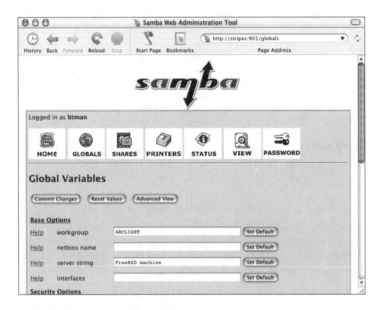

FIGURE 33.2   SWAT, the Samba Web Administration Tool.

SWAT comes with the Samba port and allows you to configure Samba graphically through a Web browser interface. This graphical configuration capability simplifies the process of managing the `smb.conf` file and reduces the risk of errors. As a Web application, however, the security risks associated with SWAT are significant. SWAT authenticates users against the system user database in `/etc/master.passwd`; authentication passwords are sent in clear text over the network from your client machine to the Samba server you want to configure. Unless you're configuring Samba from the local machine (`localhost`, using X-Windows), this presents a security risk. The risk can be managed a number of ways, but it's still not foolproof. You must take one of the following routes when deciding to run SWAT:

- Access SWAT only from `localhost`. This prevents any traffic from being sent over the wire at all.

- Operate entirely behind a firewall that allows no traffic from the outside. The `smb.conf` file is owned by root, by default, so your browser must log in to SWAT using the root password, sent over the network in clear text, with each HTTP request you make to the SWAT program. This should never be done on a network in which the password could be exposed to a malicious eavesdropper.

- Create a "dummy" user (for example, smbowner), and change smb.conf to be owned by that user (using chown). When running SWAT, log in as that user, not as root. Don't use the dummy username for any other tasks on the server; also, don't give the user any privileges, a shell, or a home directory. Be aware that if the password for this user is sniffed, an intruder can easily alter your Samba configuration. However, he won't be able to do anything else.

If the security risks are acceptable to you, and you can adhere to one of these methods of accessing SWAT, you can enable it by adding the following line to /etc/services in the appropriate spot (901 is a suggested port—any unused TCP port will do):

```
swat       901/tcp
```

Next, add the following line to /etc/inetd.conf:

```
swat    stream  tcp     nowait  root    /usr/local/sbin/swat    swat
```

Finally, restart inetd:

```
# killall -HUP inetd
```

You can now access SWAT by the URL http://stripes.somewhere.com:901, substituting your Samba server's hostname or localhost, as appropriate. You will be prompted for a username and password. Use the system username you have decided to use for SWAT access: root, if your security situation allows it, or the dummy user otherwise.

SWAT allows you to access and modify your shares and printers as well as global settings; you can also view the current status of the server and do Samba user management. If SWAT recognizes that the username under which you are logged in has full access to the smb.conf file, you will see all seven action buttons shown in Figure 33.2. Otherwise, you will see only four, allowing you to view Samba information and status, but not make any configuration changes.

Because SWAT operates as a front end to smb.conf, and because SWAT is not necessarily a viable administrative option, the rest of this chapter will concentrate on configuring Samba through smb.conf directly—not on SWAT's equivalent actions.

Sharing Directories

Many examples for how to configure a shared directory can be found in smb.conf.default. To enable any of them, make the appropriate change in smb.conf; then stop and restart Samba:

```
# /usr/local/etc/rc.d/samba.sh stop
# /usr/local/etc/rc.d/samba.sh start
```

Share examples are displayed below the `===== Share Definitions =====` line in `smb.conf`. Each share's name is listed in brackets, and the configuration lines following it apply until the next bracketed block. The `smb.conf` file begins with a `[global]` block, allowing you to set global parameters; the rest of the blocks each define a share whose settings override the previously defined global settings, much in the same way `httpd.conf` works for Apache (as you saw in Chapter 25, "Configuring a Web Server").

TIP

The `man smb.conf` page lists all available configuration parameters and describes in detail what each does. However, you may find it easier to view the page in HTML format, in which headings and examples are set apart with text formatting and made easier to read, as well as being contextually hyperlinked. Refer to the online documentation at `http://samba.org/samba/docs/man/smb.conf.5.html` for the formatted version.

To share a regular public directory, define a share block like this:

```
[my-public]
    comment = Public Stuff
    path = /usr/local/share/samba-stuff
    public = yes
    writeable = yes
    printable = no
    write list = @staff
```

With this share enabled, a client will see a share called `my-public` at the top level of the server's share listing. However, unless the user is authenticated and is a member of the Unix group `staff`, the files in the share will be read-only. Remove the `write list` line to make the share writable by all users. Note that `writeable = yes` is equivalent to saying `read only = no`.

By default, a `[homes]` share is defined and enabled. This special share is built in, allowing access to each user's home directory on the Samba server if the Windows client connects to it with the proper credentials (you learn about user-level and share-level security a little later):

```
[homes]
    comment = Home Directories
    browseable = no
    writeable = yes
```

Because this share is set as not browsable, home directories that are not owned by the client user are not displayed; if a client connects as a valid user with a home directory on the Samba server, his or her home directory (labeled with his or her username because that's the name of the directory in Unix) appears as one of the available shares. No other users' home directories appear.

Sharing Printers

Like [homes], [printers] is a special share that behaves a little differently from regular shares. Under FreeBSD, all attached printers that are defined in /etc/printcap are available to Samba users. Chapter 15, "Printing," explains how to set up your FreeBSD machine to support local printers in /etc/printcap.

By default, the [printers] share is set up like this:

```
[printers]
   comment = All Printers
   path = /var/spool/samba
   browseable = no
# Set public = yes to allow user 'guest account' to print
   guest ok = no
   writeable = no
   printable = yes
```

As stated in the embedded comment, you can make your printers public so that anyone on the network can use them. This involves the use of a *guest user*, which you learn about in an upcoming section of this chapter. Note that public is a synonym for guest ok, so you would change the guest ok line to yes instead of adding a public = yes line to allow the guest user to print.

In Samba 2.2.0 and later, Windows 2000/NT printing RPCs are supported, meaning that you can push the appropriate printer drivers to a client that lacks them. For documentation on this feature, see the Samba Web site.

Access Control

Samba access control involves a number of abstract concepts that can be very difficult to reconcile. Windows user authentication schemes include LAN Manager (LANMAN), Windows NT/2000, Windows 95/98/Me, and Windows for Workgroups—all subtly different in how they handle encryption, login names, and challenge/response.

In Samba, there are two widely used ways to perform access control: user level and share level. The default setting is user level, defined by the security option:

```
# Security mode. Most people will want user level security. See
# security_level.txt for details.
   security = user
```

User-Level Access Control

In *user-level* security, the client presents a username/password pair to the server upon the initial setup of the connection. The server determines whether to accept the client based on the username/password pair and the identity of the client machine itself. If it accepts the client, all shares are accessible.

It can be tricky to set up user-level security properly. The Windows username, which is defined either when logging in to a local profile or to a domain controller in a Windows session, must exist on the Samba server as a regular Unix user (or mapped to a Unix user). For instance, if the Windows user Harris logs on to his Windows machine, opens up the Network Neighborhood window, and tries to connect to our Samba server, he will be denied access (and given a password prompt for a share called \\STRIPES\IPC$) unless the user `harris` exists on the Unix machine.

> **TIP**
>
> Instead of authenticating users directly on your FreeBSD machine, you can specify `security = server`, instead of `security = user`, and then use the `password server = <NT-Server-Name>` line to specify the machine name of the server you want to do the authenticating. That server must be running in user-level mode, whether it's a real Windows server or another Samba machine. Samba will pass off the task to this second server and authenticate the user based on what the other machine says.

> **NOTE**
>
> In Windows NT/2000, the password prompt allows you to enter a username as well as a password. However, in Windows 95/98/Me, all you get is a password prompt, and the username is derived from the login name.

Samba users must exist in a password database at /usr/local/private/smbpasswd, similar to /etc/master.passwd in that encrypted passwords are stored in it for each local Unix user. When Samba is installed, users from /etc/master.passwd are converted into Samba format and placed into /usr/local/private/smbpasswd, with both the LANMAN password and the Windows NT password (both are present for compatibility) set to strings of 16 X characters—indicating that the user cannot log in.

To enable a user, you must set the password to something valid; you can do so with the `smbpasswd` program. It works similarly to `passwd`, prompting you for your old Samba password and then requiring you to enter a new one twice, unless you're root—in which case, you need not supply the old password, and you can change any user's password as well as your own:

```
# smbpasswd harris
New SMB password:
Retype new SMB password:
Password changed for user harris.
```

By default, early versions of Windows 95 and NT did not use encrypted passwords. They sent passwords in clear text over the wire, as with Unix. With an update to Windows 95 and with Windows NT Service Pack 3, encrypted passwords became the default behavior, alterable only by changing Registry keys. To integrate properly with recent versions of Windows NT/2000, and with Windows 98 and later, you must enable password encryption in Samba. You do this by enabling the encrypt passwords parameter after reading the document at /usr/local/share/doc/samba/textdocs/ENCRYPTION.txt, which describes the mechanism of encrypted passwords in detail. Refer also to Win95.txt and WinNT.txt in the same directory, as the comments near the encrypt passwords directive admonish:

```
# You may wish to use password encryption. Please read
# ENCRYPTION.txt, Win95.txt and WinNT.txt in the Samba documentation.
# Do not enable this option unless you have read those documents
  encrypt passwords = yes
```

CAUTION

Encrypted passwords—although they seem like a sensible security measure—actually decrease security on the server end. The encrypted Samba passwords that are stored in the /usr/local/private/smbpasswd file are the same as the passwords that are sent over the wire. Encrypted Samba passwords, therefore, are equivalent in security to passwords stored in clear text. An intruder who gains access to the smbpasswd file could immediately log in as any user (including root) through Samba, whereas the encrypted passwords in /etc/master.passwd must be cracked through some brute-force method. (By contrast, a Unix password is transmitted in clear text and *then* encrypted on the server and compared to what's in the password file; this arrangement renders a compromise of the server's password file itself harmless.) Guard the smbpasswd file just as carefully as you would master.passwd, if not more so!

TIP

You can map Windows users on a many-to-one basis to Unix users, allowing you to give groups of Windows users the same privileges as a single Unix user. To do this, create a file containing mappings—for example, /usr/local/etc/smbusers.map. The format of this file is with one mapping per line, as follows:

```
<unix-user> = <win-user-1> [<win-user-2> ...]
```

Next, enable it by adding the following anywhere in the [global] section of smb.conf:

```
username map = /usr/local/etc/smbusers.map
```

Each aliased Windows user must log in with the correct password for the Unix user to which he or she maps.

Share-Level Access Control

In *share-level* access control, a client can connect to the Samba server without any username/password authentication and receive the list of shares; the client will be refused access only if denied by IP address in the smb.conf file (the hosts allow line). However, each share has its own user authentication, using the same password scheme as you already saw in the discussion on user-level access control. A public share, in which access is open to all, can be entered without any barriers. A share that is restricted to a particular user (such as a home directory from the [homes] block), however, presents the same username/password challenge as user-level security presented at the initial connection.

More details on the workings of user-level and share-level security can be found in the documentation file at /usr/local/share/doc/samba/textdocs/security_level.txt.

Guest User

For some Samba services, notably printing, you will want any user on the network to be able to have access regardless of authentication. You accomplish this with a guest account. A guest account is an unprivileged user account that has access as a Unix user only to the service you want to provide. Note that guest users are primarily intended for Samba servers running in share-level security mode, because guest user access is allowed or disallowed on a share-by-share basis.

To enable a guest user, uncomment the guest account line in smb.conf:

```
# Uncomment this if you want a guest account, you must add this to /etc/passwd
# otherwise the user "nobody" is used
  guest account = pcguest
```

You must then add the pcguest account (or any other name you choose) to the system using adduser. Use chfn to tune the user's capabilities; the ftp user (created by sysinstall if your system allows anonymous FTP—see Chapter 26, "Configuring an FTP Server," for details on FTP server setup) is a good model for the Samba guest account.

With this account enabled, any Windows user connecting to the Samba server will have full access to any share where the guest ok or public parameter is set to yes. No authentication challenge will be presented for that share.

The guest only = yes parameter can be specified to indicate that only guest connections are permitted for a service.

Samba Log Files

In /var/log, there are various log files for Samba, one for each type of service and for each client that has connected. These files' names are of the form log.<service>:

```
# ls -l /var/log/log.*
-rw-r--r--  1 root  wheel   468 Jun  9 12:42 /var/log/log.gaming-pc
-rw-r--r--  1 root  wheel  2343 Jun  9 14:49 /var/log/log.nmb
-rw-r--r--  1 root  wheel  1606 Jun  9 14:44 /var/log/log.smb
```

The `log.nmb` and `log.smb` files report status and error conditions for the `nmbd` and `smbd` servers, respectively. Additionally, whenever any errors are reported for any connecting client host (such as authentication failures), these messages are printed into a `log.<name>` file for that client. Note that this can result in a lot of files cluttering up your `/var/log` directory. You can switch to a combined log format by commenting out the `log file` line in `smb.conf`:

```
# this tells Samba to use a separate log file for each machine
# that connects
;   log file = /var/log/log.%m
```

SMB errors for individual hosts will go into `log.smb` with this line commented out.

Another useful line to modify is the `max log size` line, which is set to 50KB by default. This control allows you to set the "rollover" size for any of the log files. When any Samba log file reaches the size you've designated, the file's renamed by appending `.old` to the filename, and new log entries are added to a new file. The `.old` file is overwritten at the next rollover.

```
# Put a capping on the size of the log files (in Kb).
   max log size = 50
```

Samba Variables

Configuration parameters in `smb.conf` don't have to be hard-wired. You have a number of variable substitutions at your disposal, so you can set certain options to be dynamically determined, depending on the conditions of the connection. For example, you can set an option to reflect the client's username with the `%u` variable, allowing you to set a parameter such as `path = /usr/local/share/user-files/%u`. The user `harris` would thus receive the path `/usr/local/share/user-files/harris`.

Here are a few of the most useful variables:

- `%u`—The client's username.
- `%g`—The primary group name of `%u`.
- `%S`—The name of the current service, if any.
- `%H`—The home directory of the user given by `%u`.
- `%h`—The Internet hostname of the Samba server.
- `%M`—The Internet hostname of the client machine.
- `%L`—The NetBIOS name of the Samba server. This allows you to change your config based on what the client calls you; your server can have a "dual personality."
- `%m`—The NetBIOS name of the client machine.
- `%I`—The IP address of the client machine.

- **%T**—The current date and time.

- **%$(envvar)**—The value of the environment variable envvar.

The complete list of variable substitutions is available in man smb.conf.

Other Samba Components

The Samba package includes a number of additional tools:

- **smbclient**—A simple FTP-like client that allows you to connect to remote SMB shares and print to remote Windows printers.

- **testparm**—A configuration file syntax checker that tests your smb.conf for correctness; similar to apachectl configtest for Apache.

- **testprns**—Tests whether the printers specified in /etc/printcap will work properly with Samba.

- **smbstatus**—Displays current connections to the Samba server. SWAT, as you saw earlier, has a page that shows the formatted output of this command in a Web browser.

- **nmblookup**—Allows you to make NetBIOS name queries like those made by Windows hosts connecting directly to SMB shares by name.

- **make_smbcodepage**—A tool that allows you to create new SMB code page definitions for Samba.

These tools also are described in man samba; each one has its own man page for further details. Finally, these tools are in addition to the smbd, nmbd, and smbpasswd utilities discussed previously in this chapter. Each of those has its own man page as well.

Future Samba Development

At the time of this writing, the most recent version of Samba in the ports is 2.2.6. This version incorporates many recent enhancements to Windows networking, enabling features that are new in Windows 2000 and XP and increasing the level of interoperability between Windows and Unix file servers. Some of the new features are as follows:

- Automatic downloading of Windows NT/2000 printer drivers from the Samba server, if they are not present on the client machine

- Unification of Windows NT/2000 and Unix Access Control Lists (ACLs) and remote manageability of such lists from Windows machines

- Built-in Windows NT/2000 login authentication

- Microsoft Distributed File System (DFS) support and the capability to act as a DFS server for Windows clients

See the documentation at http://www.samba.org for further details on these and other new features.

Accessing Shared Files on a Windows System (the smbfs Filesystem)

SMB file sharing can work both ways. Samba allows you to set up your FreeBSD machine as an SMB server only, but there is a way to set it up as a client and mount a remote SMB share like any other filesystem. This involves smbfs, available as a standard kernel module as of FreeBSD 4.4, and in the ports (/usr/ports/net/smbfs) in earlier versions.

The smbfs implementation in FreeBSD includes an smbfs.ko kernel module in /modules and a mount_smbfs tool in /sbin that works like all the other mount_* tools you saw in Chapter 8, "The FreeBSD Filesystem." The best documentation for smbfs is found in the man mount_smbfs page.

To mount an SMB filesystem using smbfs, use mount_smbfs with a few basic options. The -I flag specifies the hostname or IP address, and the two remaining arguments are the remote share name (of the form //<user>@<NetBIOS name>/<share name>) and the local mount point. To mount the share called public from a Windows machine called gaming-pc onto the local /smb/public directory, use the following syntax:

```
# mount_smbfs -I 64.41.131.139 //guest@gaming-pc/public /smb/public
```

You will be prompted for a password. Use a blank password if the share is set to allow full access; use the appropriate password if the share is set to read-only or password-protected mode.

> **NOTE**
>
> The smbfs.ko kernel module is loaded automatically when needed by mount_smbfs. If you want to, you can load it at boot time by adding the following line to /boot/loader.conf:
>
> smbfs_load="YES"
>
> However, this is probably not necessary.

To add an SMB share to /etc/fstab, use the following syntax:

```
//guest@gaming-pc/public    /smb/public      smbfs   rw,noauto 0    0
```

The mount -a process that occurs during startup will mount this share automatically when the FreeBSD system boots.

33

Dynamic Host Configuration Protocol (DHCP)

DHCP, which stands for *Dynamic Host Configuration Protocol*, is a network protocol that allows a client to obtain its IP address, name server information, gateway server information, and several other network-configuration options from a server that is running a DHCP server.

This chapter will show you how to configure a DHCP client on your FreeBSD system (so that it can obtain an IP address from a DHCP server). It will also show you how to configure a DHCP server.

How DHCP Works

A detailed discussion of how DHCP works is beyond the scope of this book, but here is a basic rundown of what happens.

In FreeBSD, a client program called dhclient allows FreeBSD to act as a DHCP client. When a system configured to use DHCP boots and dhclient starts, it will send out broadcast requests on port 68. These requests are sent in UDP format.

If there is a DHCP server on the network, it will be listening to port 68 for these requests. When it receives a request for configuration information, it will check its database for a free IP address that can be assigned to the client. It will then send back all the configuration information that the client requests on port 67, once again using UDP. The IP address that is assigned to the client will be removed from the pool of available addresses so that it is not assigned to another client that requests DHCP configuration information.

The client that is running DHCP will be listening on port 67 for this configuration information from the server. When the client receives this information, it will configure itself to use the information that the server has sent.

IP Address Leases

When the DHCP server assigns an IP address to a client, the client does not own the address. Instead, the address is leased. The lease term is configured on the DHCP server. The information about how long the lease is good for is sent to the client along with the configuration information.

The leasing of IP addresses serves two purposes:

- If the DHCP server cannot be contacted, the client will check its database to look for a lease that is still valid. Assuming it has a valid lease, the client can continue to function normally, even if the DHCP server is currently down.

- It automatically places IP addresses that are not in use back in the pool after the lease expires. This helps conserve IP addresses. For example, when a guest from a branch office visits, he can plug his laptop into your network and be assigned an IP address so that he can use your network. When he leaves, that IP address will eventually expire and be placed back into the pool for others to use. This way, IP addresses are not being wasted on systems that do not exist anymore.

Advantages of DHCP over Static IP Addresses

Depending on your situation, DHCP may have several advantages over simply assigning each system its own static IP addresses. These advantages include the following:

- **Ease of maintenance.** DHCP automatically keeps track of which IP addresses are in use and which ones are free. This prevents the system administrator from having to keep track of which IP addresses can be assigned to new clients, as well as having to remember to reclaim old IP addresses when clients are permanently removed from the network. All this is handled automatically with DHCP.

- **Ease of installing new clients.** When new clients are installed, you (or the user) do not have to worry about setting up the network information. You can simply ask the new client to obtain its information via DHCP, and all the networking information will be configured automatically.

- **Ease of use for travelers.** If your users travel to branch offices, DHCP makes their life a lot easier. With DHCP, they can simply plug their laptops into the network at the branch office and have all the network information configured for them automatically. At the next branch office they go to, they can do the same thing. This way, your users do not have to reconfigure their network settings at each office they visit. It also makes life easier for the network administrators because they do not have to worry about making IP addresses available for these traveling users.

- **It conserves IP addresses.** This is true, especially if you have traveling users who go to branch offices occasionally and plug their laptops into the network. DHCP allows these IP addresses to be automatically reclaimed after the traveling user leaves. This way, you don't have IP addresses wasted on systems that are rarely plugged in to the network anyway.

- **It eliminates problems caused by IP address conflicts.** It only takes one user to make one typing mistake when setting up a system to cause all kinds of problems on a network. The user might enter an IP address that conflicts with another system on the network, for example, or an address that conflicts with the IP address assigned to a server. DHCP eliminates these problems by assigning IP addresses automatically and keeping track of ones that are in use so that they do not get assigned to multiple systems.

Of course, if you are running a small network of only 10 or 15 systems and you rarely or never have visitors who need to plug into your network, these issues are not all that important. If that's the case, DHCP is probably not worth installing. DHCP is definitely worth considering, however, if you have several hundred or thousand clients on a network, or if you expect your small network to grow to a large number over time. If you anticipate this kind of growth, you may want to go with DHCP now, even if you currently have only 10 or 15 clients. It is much easier to configure DHCP when you still have only a small number of clients than it is to try to convert an existing network of several hundred systems over to DHCP.

Kernel Configuration for DHCP

In order to configure FreeBSD as a client on a DHCP network, you will need to have the Berkeley Packet Filter device installed in the kernel. This device is installed by default in the GENERIC kernel, so unless you built a custom kernel and removed it, you shouldn't have to do anything.

To verify that the Berkeley Packet Filter device is installed in the kernel, look for the following line in your kernel configuration file:

```
device bpf
```

If this line exists in your kernel configuration file, there is nothing you need to do here. If the line does not exist, you will need to add it and then rebuild your kernel. Complete instructions on kernel building can be found in Chapter 16, "Kernel Configuration."

> **CAUTION**
>
> There is a slight security risk involved with the Berkeley Packet Filter. The `bpf` device allows the root user to run packet sniffers on your network. Packet sniffers can be malicious because they can display passwords and such being sent across the network. Although only the root user can run the packet sniffers, this is still a concern in an environment in which security is absolutely critical. That being said, on a very large network, the benefits of DHCP probably outweigh the very slight risk involved with running `bpf`.

Enabling DHCP

Once you have made sure the kernel is configured for DHCP, you can enable it in one of two ways. The first is by going through the `sysinstall` program. The second is by manually editing the configuration files. The technique you use is one of personal preference; some people don't like messing with the config files directly. The following sections discuss both of these methods, beginning with the `sysinstall` program.

DHCP Through `sysinstall`

If you are installing FreeBSD for the first time, simply answer yes to the post-installation question when you are asked whether you want to try a DHCP configuration of the network. If you have already installed FreeBSD, perform the following steps to enable DHCP from `sysinstall`:

1. As the root user, type **sysinstall** at the command prompt to start the `sysinstall` program.

2. At the main menu, select the Configure option. Note that you cannot use the mouse in `sysinstall`. You must use the arrow keys and the Enter key to make selections.

3. At the Configuration menu, select the Networking option. This will bring up the Network Services Menu portion of `sysinstall` (see Figure 34.1).

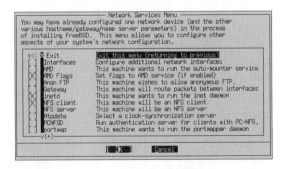

FIGURE 34.1   The Network Services Menu portion of `sysinstall`.

4. Select the Interfaces option by using the arrow keys to make sure it is highlighted and then pressing the spacebar.

5. Select the network interface that you want to configure from the next menu (see Figure 34.2).

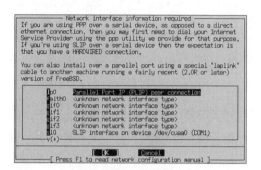

FIGURE 34.2   Selecting the network interface to configure. Many of the devices listed here are pseudo-devices, not real network devices.

6. Answer No to the question that asks whether you want to try an IPv6 configuration of the interface.

7. Answer Yes to the question that asks whether you want to try a DHCP configuration of the interface.

When you have answered Yes to the question about trying a DHCP configuration of the interface, the dhclient program will start and begin broadcasting a request for configuration information over the network. If it successfully receives configuration information back from a DHCP server, it will automatically fill in the values on the next screen that asks you to supply the network values. You can then select OK to accept the values that were supplied by DHCP.

If this is not a new installation (you are making changes to an existing installation), you will need to exit the sysinstall program and reboot the system before the new DHCP settings will take effect.

Manual Configuration of DHCP

You can also configure DHCP manually by editing the /etc/rc.conf file. To do so, you will need to add an ifconfig line to the file for the device that you want to configure with DHCP. For example, if your Ethernet device is ed0, the following line would be added to /etc/rc.conf:

```
ifconfig_ed0="DHCP"
```

If the network interface you want to configure with DHCP is not ed0, you will, of course, want to replace it with whatever the name of the device is that you want to configure. Another common network device name is fxp0.

If there is already an existing line in /etc/rc.conf for the device you want to configure and it contains something else, the device is probably currently set up to use static IP. In this case, either delete the existing line and replace it with the earlier line or comment out the existing line by placing a hash mark in front of it (#) and then add the line above.

After you have made this change to the /etc/rc.conf file, reboot the system for the new DHCP changes to take effect.

The dhclient **Program**

The dhclient program is the client portion of DHCP. It is run automatically at each system boot if you have any network interfaces that are configured to use DHCP.

If you need to modify the default behavior of dhclient, you can do so by supplying flags to it with an option in /etc/rc.conf.

If you do need to modify the default behavior of dhclient, the following line should be added to /etc/rc.conf below the ifconfig line where the DHCP interface is configured:

dhcp_flags="*flags*"

Here, *flags* is a list of options for dhclient. Table 34.1 shows the valid options that can be used.

TABLE 34.1   Valid Options for dhclient

Option	Action
-d	This option will force dhclient to stay in the foreground rather than move to the background after it gets its configuration information. This should be used only for debugging purposes and should probably never be used from /etc/rc.conf.
-cf *filename*	By default, dhclient reads its operating system–specific configuration information from the file /sbin/dhclient-script. The -cf option can be used to tell dhclient to read from a different configuration file, where *filename* is the name and path of that file.
-lf *filename*	By default, dhclient stores information on its leases in the file /var/db/dhclient.leases. The -lf option can be used to tell dhclient to use a different file for this, where *filename* is the name of the file and path where this information should be stored.
-pf *filename*	By default, dhclient stores its process ID (PID) information in /var/run/dhclient.pid. The -pf option can be used to change this. Here, *filename* is the name of the file that should be used to store this information.

TABLE 34.1   Continued

Option	Action
-q	This option tells dhclient to be quiet when it runs. In other words, dhclient will not be so verbose about the messages it prints.
-1	This option causes dhclient to try only once to get a lease on an IP address. If this fails, dhclient will exist with a status of 2. Note that this is the numeral 1 and not a lowercase letter *l*.

/sbin/dhclient-script

This is the operating system–specific configuration file for dhclient. You shouldn't need to make any changes to this file, and it is best left alone unless you are sure you know what you are doing.

/etc/dhclient.conf

This is the configuration file for dhclient in which you can control various options about its behavior. The file must exist for dhclient to run, although by default, the file contains nothing but comments. dhclient has reasonable default values that will work fine for most users, so most users will not have to worry about this file.

However, you should be aware of some of the options that can be controlled in this file. Table 34.2 lists some of them.

TABLE 34.2   Some dhclient.conf Options

Option	Action
timeout *n*	Here, *n* is the number of seconds dhclient should wait for a response when trying to contact a DHCP server before giving up and deciding the server is unavailable. By default, this is 60 seconds.
retry *n*	Here, *n* is the number of seconds dhclient should wait before trying to contact the DHCP server again if the first request timed out. By default, it will wait five minutes.
select-timeout *n*	Some networks may have more than one DHCP server on them. In this case, the client may receive multiple offers for configuration information. The first offer received is not always the best offer (for example, if the second offer received contains the same IP address the client has, it is preferable to an offer where the IP address is different). Here, *n* is the number of seconds dhclient should wait after receiving a first offer to see whether any other servers respond with offers.
reboot *n*	When dhclient starts, it will try to obtain the same IP address it had the last time. If it cannot get the same address, it will then accept a different one. Here, *n* is the number of seconds dhclient will wait before giving up and deciding it can't get the same IP address it had last time. The default is 10 seconds.

34

TABLE 34.2   Continued

Option	Action
request *option*	The client will request information for the specified options from the DHCP server. See the dhcp-options man page for information on the available options.
require *option*	The client will require information for the specified options from the DHCP server. If the required information is not provided, the client will reject the offer. See the dhcp-options man page for information on the available options.
default *option value*	If the DHCP server does not provide information for the specified option, then *value* will be used for that option. See the dhcp-options man page for information on the available options.
supersede *option value*	The specified option will always use *value*, even if the DHCP server sends a different value for that option. See the dhcp-options man page for information on the available options.
reject *address*	Any offers sent from the DHCP server with the IP address of *address* will be rejected.

Many more options can be used in the /etc/dhclient.conf configuration file. See the dhclient.conf man page for more information on options available in this file. Also, see the dhcp-options man page for more information about the DHCP options that can be requested or required from the DHCP server.

As mentioned previously, most users will not need to make any changes to /etc/dhclient.conf because the default dhclient values will usually work fine.

DHCP Server Daemon

FreeBSD does not come with the software required to run a DHCP server. However, free software is available in the FreeBSD ports collection for running a DHCP server. The port, called isc-dhcp3, is available in the net directory of the ports tree. See Chapter 14, "Installing Additional Software," for information on how to install ports.

In addition, a program called dhcpconf (also available in the FreeBSD ports collection under the net directory) helps you create the configuration files necessary to run a DHCP server on FreeBSD.

When isc-dhcp3 is installed, it will create a startup file in /usr/local/etc/rc.d called isc-dhcpd.sh.sample. The next time you restart your system, this file will cause the DHCP server to start automatically on system boot. The default startup file will work fine for a basic DHCP server configuration. See the dhcpd man page for the various options available to dhcpd.

You may want to rename the startup file in /usr/local/etc/rc.d to something that is easier to remember and type. For example, you might call it dhcpd. Assuming you rename it, you can now control the operation of the DHCP server by using the following commands as root.

This first command will start the DHCP server:

/usr/local/etc/rc.d/dhcpd start

This next command will stop a DHCP server that is currently running:

/usr/local/etc/rc.d/dhcpd stop

Finally, this command will stop and then restart a DHCP server that is currently running:

/usr/local/etc/rc.d/dhcp restart

Before you start the DHCP server for the first time, you will need to create a configuration file for it.

Configuring the dhcpd **Configuration File**

The configuration file for the DHCP server, named dhcp.conf, is located in /usr/local/etc. When you installed dhcpd, it placed a sample configuration file in the directory called dhcpd.conf.sample.

You can configure the dhcpd.conf file manually, or you can configure it with the dhcpconf program. If you have never configured dhcpd before, I recommend that you install and use the dhcpconf program. You can then look through the dhcp.conf file that dhcpconf creates to see how the file looks.

> **NOTE**
>
> The instructions presented in this section should get you up and running with a basic DHCP server setup. For more advanced configuration, see the man pages for dhcpd and also for dhcpd.conf, which contains all the options that can be configured in the dhcpd.conf configuration file.

Installing and Starting the dhcpconf **Program**

dhcpconf is a menu- and dialog-driven program that helps you set up a basic DHCP server configuration. Once you have it installed, you can start it by typing **dhcpconf** at the command prompt as root. You will get an About dialog that tells you a little about the program. Press Enter to continue on to the main screen. Figure 34.3 shows the main screen of dhcpconf.

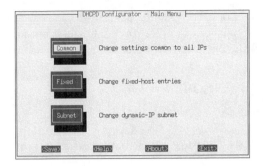

FIGURE 34.3   The main dhcpconf menu.

Note that the mouse cannot be used in this program. You will need to use the arrow keys, the Enter key, and the Tab key to navigate in the program.

The first menu option (Common) sets options that apply to all IP addresses assigned. This is the default configuration information that will be sent to clients. Press Enter to select it. Figure 34.4 shows the Common dialog.

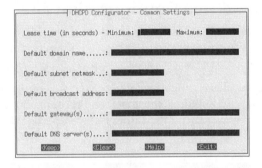

FIGURE 34.4   Here you set options common to all IP addresses, as well as default options.

Most of the options listed here are self-explanatory, with the exception of the first one, which defines the minimum and maximum lease periods.

The *minimum* lease is also the default lease period. This is the default time in seconds that a lease will be good for. The *maximum* time is the maximum amount of time the server will lease an IP address. The client can request a longer lease than the default defined in minimum, but the server will never lease an IP for longer than the value defined in maximum.

The default minimum lease period is 600 seconds (10 minutes), and the default maximum lease period is 7200 seconds (120 minutes). The client must renew its lease before the maximum lease period is up; otherwise, it will lose the lease, and the IP address it has will be placed back into the pool of available addresses.

Here are some considerations to think about if you want to change the default lease:

- Shorter lease times mean unused IP addresses will be placed back into the pool faster. What's more, configuration changes will be recognized faster. However, if a lease expires on a client and that client attempts to connect to the network when the DHCP server is unavailable, the client will not be able to use any network resources until the DHCP server comes back online.

- Longer lease times help protect against DHCP server outages. If the DHCP server is down, a client can still connect to the network as long as it has a valid lease on an IP address. However, configuration changes will not be recognized as quickly, and unused IP addresses will be tied up longer.

Once you have filled in all the values here, tab to the <Keep> button and press Enter. This will take you back to the main screen.

Configuring Fixed-Host Entries

In some situations, you might need to reserve static IP addresses (IP addresses that never change) for some systems, such as for systems that are acting as servers. This arrangement is called a *fixed host*. The second option, DHCP Configurator, allows you to reserve static addresses. Figure 34.5 shows the Fixed-Host Entries configuration dialog.

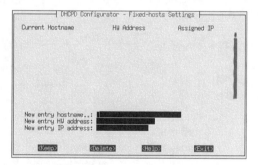

FIGURE 34.5   Configuring information for systems that require static IP addresses.

Table 34.3 shows the options in this dialog and what they do.

TABLE 34.3   Fixed-Host Configuration Options

Option	Description
New entry hostname	This is the hostname of the system that is being configured for static IP. You should provide only the hostname here, not the domain name, because the domain information was provided in the Common options.
New entry HW address	Enter the hardware address of the network card on the host that is being configured for static IP here.
New entry IP address	This is the static IP address that the host being configured for static IP will use.

Once you have finished entering the information, in the last field, press Enter to add the host to the list. You can then enter more hosts if you want, or you can tab down to <Keep> to return to the main menu. Note that you must press Enter after filling in the last entry. If you do not, and you simply tab to <Keep>, the entry will be lost.

Configuring Subnet Ranges

Finally, you need to configure the IP addresses ranges that are available on various subnets. Select the Subnet option from the main menu to do this. Figure 34.6 shows the Subnet configuration dialog.

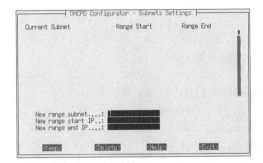

FIGURE 34.6   The Subnet dialog, which looks and behaves very much like the Fixed-Host Entries dialog discussed in the previous section.

Table 34.4 shows what these options do.

TABLE 34.4   Subnet Range Options

Option	Description
New range subnet	This is the subnet that this range of IP addresses will affect.
New range start IP	This is the first IP address that will be available to DHCP clients on this subnet that are receiving dynamic IP addresses.
New range end IP	This is the last IP address that will be available to DHCP clients on this subnet that are receiving dynamic IP addresses.

As with the Fixed-Host Configuration dialog, you must press Enter here after entering the range end IP address for the entry to be added to the list and for the changes to take effect. After you have done so, you can add more entries if you want.

If you want to have multiple IP address blocks available to a single subnet, simply create a new entry for the same subnet as an existing entry and include a different IP address range. Both of the entries will be valid, and both of the ranges of IP addresses will be available to the subnet.

Once you have finished creating all the entries you want, tab to <Keep> and press Enter to return to the main menu.

TIP

If you are unclear about some of the networking terminology in this chapter, such as *subnets*, and so on, see Chapter 21, "Networking with FreeBSD," for information on these various networking concepts.

Saving the Information and Quitting

From the main menu of DHCP Configurator, tab to the <Save> button and press Enter. The program will create the configuration file and then exit. The configuration file will be located in /etc/dhcpd.conf.

34

PART V

X-Windows

IN THIS PART

Advanced X-Windows Configuration

Chapter 4, "Your First Session with FreeBSD," Chapter 5, "Working with X-Windows," and Chapter 6, "Working with Applications," discussed some basics of the X-Windows system. X-Windows is a very powerful server framework, however, that can do much more than provide a basic desktop functionality. Other capabilities of X-Windows include the ability to display the output of graphical applications over a network. This chapter looks at these and other advanced features of X-Windows, starting with advanced configuration information of the basic X-Windows system.

Configuring X-Windows with the xf86config Script

The xf86config tool will ask you a series of questions and configure X-Windows based on the answers you provide.

CAUTION

Improper use of this tool when configuring video settings could actually cause physical damage to your hardware. Although most monitors have built-in protection circuits these days and will shut themselves down if you try to drive them with a refresh rate higher than they support, some monitors will try to display the screen at the given refresh rate, even if the monitor's hardware is not capable of handling it. The result could destroy your monitor.

CAUTION

The `xf86config` program will overwrite your existing `Xf86Config` file. If you have a working `XF86Config` file and you want to experiment with a new configuration, you should back up your existing file first. The file is located in `/etc/X11/XF86Config`. Make a copy of this file to `/etc/XF86Config.bak` (or some other name) before continuing. This way, you can restore your previous configuration easily if your new configuration does not work by simply copying the backup file back to `/etc/X11/XF86Config`.

You will need to be root to use this program. As the root user, type **xf86config** at the command prompt and press Enter. You will see a screen like the following:

```
This program will create a basic XF86Config file, based on menu selections you
make.

The XF86Config file usually resides in /usr/X11R6/etc/X11 or /etc/X11. A sample
XF86Config file is supplied with XFree86; it is configured for a standard
VGA card and monitor with 640x480 resolution. This program will ask for a
pathname when it is ready to write the file.

You can either take the sample XF86Config as a base and edit it for your
configuration, or let this program produce a base XF86Config file for your
configuration and fine-tune it.

Before continuing with this program, make sure you know what video card
you have, and preferably also the chipset it uses and the amount of video
memory on your video card. SuperProbe may be able to help with this.

Press enter to continue, or ctrl-c to abort.
```

Once you have read the information, simply press Enter to continue. The first thing you will be asked to configure is your mouse.

CAUTION

Double-check your typing when entering values in `xf86config`. The program is not very forgiving of mistakes and typos. If you accidentally make a wrong entry and don't catch it before you have pressed Enter, there is no way to back up and fix it. You will have to press Ctrl+C to exit the program and then start completely over again.

Configuring the Mouse

The mouse-configuration screen of `xf86config` looks like this:

```
First specify a mouse protocol type. Choose one from the following list:

1.   Microsoft compatible (2-button protocol)
2.   Mouse Systems (3-button protocol)
3.   Bus Mouse
4.   PS/2 Mouse
5.   Logitech Mouse (serial, old type, Logitech protocol)
6.   Logitech MouseMan (Microsoft compatible)
7.   MM Series
8.   MM HitTablet
9.   Microsoft IntelliMouse


If you have a two-button mouse, it is most likely of type 1, and if you have
a three-button mouse, it can probably support both protocol 1 and 2. There are
two main varieties of the latter type: mice with a switch to select the
protocol, and mice that default to 1 and require a button to be held at
boot-time to select protocol 2. Some mice can be convinced to do 2 by sending
a special sequence to the serial port (see the ClearDTR/ClearRTS options).

Enter a protocol number:
```

Simply enter the number representing the type of mouse you have and press Enter. Here are some guidelines for determining what type of mouse you have:

- If your mouse has a nine-pin, D-shaped connector where it plugs into your computer, it is a serial mouse. Use either 1, 2, 5, or 6. Note that most serial mice will work with either 1 or 2 and that all newer Logitech mice will use either 1 or 6. 5 is only for older Logitech mice.

- If your mouse has a small round connector where it plugs into your computer, it is a PS/2 mouse. Any PS/2 mouse should use 4. Even if you have a Microsoft mouse, you should use 4 if it has a PS/2 connector. The Microsoft mice listed are only for serial mice.

- If you are installing FreeBSD on a laptop or notebook computer, the built-in pointing device will probably work with 4 because it is most likely running on a PS/2 port. This includes touch-pads and touch-points.

After you have entered the type of mouse you have and pressed Enter, you will be asked the following:

```
If your mouse has only two buttons, it is recommended that you enable
Emulate3Buttons.

Please answer the following question with either 'y' or 'n'.
Do you want to enable Emulate3Buttons?
```

The first line of this message really should read "If your mouse has only two buttons, it is *required* (rather than *recommended*) that you enable Emulate3Buttons." X-Windows makes use of all three buttons on the mouse. If you have a two-button mouse, you need to answer Y here; doing so will cause clicking both mouse buttons at the same time to emulate clicking the middle button on a three-button mouse.

You will then be asked to give the name of the device the mouse is on:

```
Now give the full device name that the mouse is connected to, for example
/dev/tty00. Just pressing enter will use the default, /dev/mouse.

Mouse device:
```

Unless you have symlinked the actual device your mouse is on to /dev/mouse, you will need to enter the name of that device here. Table 35.1 shows guidelines on what you should enter, depending on what type of mouse you have.

TABLE 35.1   Device Names for Various Mouse Types

Mouse Type	Mouse Device
PS/2 mouse (or laptop)	/dev/psm0
Serial mouse on COM 1	/dev/cuaa0
Serial mouse on COM 2	/dev/cuaa1
Serial mouse on COM 3	/dev/cuaa2
Serial mouse on COM 4	/dev/cuaa3
Bus mouse	/dev/mse0

Enter the corresponding mouse device at the prompt and then press Enter.

Selecting the Keyboard

The next screen will ask you to select the type of keyboard you have:

```
Please select one of the following keyboard types that is the better
description of your keyboard. If nothing really matches,
choose 1 (Generic 101-key PC)
```

```
 1  Generic 101-key PC
 2  Generic 102-key (Intl) PC
 3  Generic 104-key PC
 4  Generic 105-key (Intl) PC
 5  Dell 101-key PC
 6  Everex STEPnote
 7  Keytronic FlexPro
 8  Microsoft Natural
 9  Northgate OmniKey 101
10  Winbook Model XP5
11  Japanese 106-key
12  PC-98xx Series
13  Brazilian ABNT2
14  HP Internet
15  Logitech iTouch
16  Logitech Cordless Desktop Pro
17  Compaq Internet
18  Microsoft Natural Pro

Enter a number to choose the keyboard.
```

35

> **TIP**
>
> On some systems, you might not be able to see the top part of the keyboard list. If this is the case, you will need to press Enter several times until you have cycled through the entire list and are back at the beginning.

Notice that the list of available keyboard layouts is too long to fit on one screen. Press Enter to see the next screenful of layouts. If you press Enter again at the end of the list, the display returns to the beginning of the list.

If you have a U.S. keyboard, select 1 here and press Enter. You will then be asked the following:

```
Please enter a variant name for 'us' layout. Or just press enter
for default variant
```

There is probably no reason for you to change the default here, so you can simply press Enter to continue on to the next question:

```
Please answer the following question with either 'y' or 'n'.
Do you want to select additional XKB options (group switcher,
group indicator, etc.)?
```

Select N here unless you want to remap some keys. If you do want to remap some keys (or you just want to see what is available), press Y. This action presents a couple of menus in which you can do various things, such as make the Caps Lock key into a Ctrl key (useful for Emacs gurus) or swap the Caps Lock key with the Ctrl key. Enter the number of an option you want to perform and then press Enter. If you want to exit the menu without doing anything, simply press Enter without selecting a number first.

Configuring the Monitor

In this section of the configuration program, you configure various aspects of your monitor, including the horizontal and vertical refresh rates. You first see this screen:

```
The next section you will be taken to will help you configure the refresh rates
for your monitor:
Now we want to set the specifications of the monitor. The two critical
parameters are the vertical refresh rate, which is the rate at which the
the whole screen is refreshed, and most importantly the horizontal sync rate,
which is the rate at which scanlines are displayed.

The valid range for horizontal sync and vertical sync should be documented
in the manual of your monitor. If in doubt, check the monitor database
/usr/X11R6/lib/X11/doc/Monitors to see if your monitor is there.

Press enter to continue, or ctrl-c to abort
```

Press Enter at this message to continue. You are then asked to set the horizontal sync range of your monitor:

```
You must indicate the horizontal sync range of your monitor. You can either
select one of the predefined ranges below that correspond to industry-
standard monitor types, or give a specific range.

It is VERY IMPORTANT that you do not specify a monitor type with a horizontal
sync range that is beyond the capabilities of your monitor. If in doubt,
choose a conservative setting.

    hsync in kHz; monitor type with characteristic modes
  1   31.5; Standard VGA, 640x480 @ 60 Hz
  2   31.5 - 35.1; Super VGA, 800x600 @ 56 Hz
  3   31.5, 35.5; 8514 Compatible, 1024x768 @ 87 Hz interlaced (no 800x600)
  4   31.5, 35.15, 35.5; Super VGA, 1024x768 @ 87 Hz interlaced, 800x600 @ 56 Hz
  5   31.5 - 37.9; Extended Super VGA, 800x600 @ 60 Hz, 640x480 @ 72 Hz
  6   31.5 - 48.5; Non-Interlaced SVGA, 1024x768 @ 60 Hz, 800x600 @ 72 Hz
  7   31.5 - 57.0; High Frequency SVGA, 1024x768 @ 70 Hz
```

```
8   31.5 - 64.3; Monitor that can do 1280x1024 @ 60 Hz
9   31.5 - 79.0; Monitor that can do 1280x1024 @ 74 Hz
10  31.5 - 82.0; Monitor that can do 1280x1024 @ 76 Hz
11  Enter your own horizontal sync range

Enter your choice (1-11):
```

> **CAUTION**
>
> The next few questions in the configuration are the parts that could potentially damage your monitor if you don't configure them correctly. Make sure you do not select frequency ranges higher than your monitor can support. Consult your monitor documentation for more information on the refresh rates that your monitor can support.

If you know the exact horizontal frequency range that your monitor can support, select 11 to enter the range manually. If you do not know the exact range, you might be able to find it in the file /usr/X11R6/lib/X11/doc/Monitors.

Unfortunately, this file is not in a readable format, but you can still find information in it if you look. Basically, the file contains the configuration for several types of monitors. The following is a sample entry from the file:

```
Section "Monitor"
    Identifier "ELSA GDM-17E40"
    VendorName "ELSA GmbH"
    ModelName "GDM-17E40"
    BandWidth 135
    HorizSync 29-82
    VertRefresh 50-150
    ModeLine "640x480" 25 640 664 760 800 480 491 493 525
    ModeLine "640x480" 31 640 664 704 832 480 489 492 520
    ModeLine "800x600x32" 45 800 820 904 964 600 601 604 621
    ModeLine "1024x768x16" 78.7 1024 1044 1140 1264 768 770 773 796
    ModeLine "1152x875" 135 1152 1416 1456 1664 875 875 877 906
    ModeLine "1152x900" 135 1152 1400 1440 1648  900 901 905 935
    ModeLine "1280x1024i" 80 1280 1296 1512 1568 1024 1025 1037 1165 interlace
    ModeLine "1280x1024" 110 1280 1328 1512 1712 1024 1025 1028 1054
    ModeLine "1280x1024" 135 1280 1312 1456 1712 1024 1027 1030 1064
EndSection
```

The lines that begin with Section and EndSection mark the beginning and end of a single monitor definition.

For now, you do not need to worry about what most of the lines in the section mean—you are concerned only with five lines.

35

The first three lines you are concerned about are the ones that begin with `Identifier`, `VendorName`, and `ModelName`. These lines identify the type of monitor this section is for. Look for the vendor name and model of your monitor in these lines.

The final two lines you are concerned with are the ones that begin with `HorizSync` and `VertRefresh`. If you find a section for your monitor, write down these two values for use in the configuration; then select 11 and enter the horizontal sync rate you wrote down.

If you can't find this information in your monitor's manual, and you can't find an entry in the `Monitors` file, select one of the predefined entries where the listed resolution and refresh rate does not exceed a refresh rate you know your monitor can handle.

> **TIP**
>
> Many hardware vendors are now making documentation and technical specifications for their products that are available online at their Web sites. If you can't find the printed documentation for your monitor, it might be worth a trip to the vendor's Web site to see whether it has documentation and technical specifications available online.

Once you have selected one of the predefined entries or entered your monitor's horizontal sync range, press Enter to move to the next screen, where you will be asked to set the vertical refresh rate:

```
You must indicate the vertical sync range of your monitor. You can either
select one of the predefined ranges below that correspond to industry-
standard monitor types, or give a specific range. For interlaced modes,
the number that counts is the high one (e.g. 87 Hz rather than 43 Hz).


1   50-70
2   50-90
3   50-100
4   40-150
5   Enter your own vertical sync range

Enter your choice:
```

Once again, it is very important that you do not select a refresh rate higher than your monitor can handle; otherwise, you may cause damage to your monitor. If you know the vertical refresh rate for your monitor, select 5 and then enter the refresh range for your monitor. Otherwise, you can select 1–4 for one of the predefined types. Press Enter after you have made your selection to continue on to the next screen:

```
You must now enter a few identification/description strings, namely an
identifier, a vendor name, and a model name. Just pressing enter will fill
in default names.

The strings are free-form, spaces are allowed.
Enter an identifier for your monitor definition:
```

This is the information that will show up in the XF86Config file that the program will generate after you have finished entering all the values. You can just press Enter here to accept the defaults.

Configuring the Video Card

Next, you will be given some information about configuring the video card. Press Enter after you have read the information to get to the card database. It will look like the following:

```
 0   2 the Max MAXColor S3 Trio64V+              S3 Trio64V+
 1   2-the-Max MAXColor 6000                     ET6000
 2   3DLabs Oxygen GMX                           PERMEDIA 2
 3   928Movie                                    S3 928
 4   AGX (generic)                               AGX-014/15/16
 5   ALG-5434(E)                                 CL-GD5434
 6   AOpen PA2010                                Voodo Banshee
 7   ASUS 3Dexplorer                             RIVA128
 8   ASUS PCI-AV264CT                            ati
 9   ASUS PCI-V264CT                             ati
10   ASUS Video Magic PCI V864                   S3 864
11   ASUS Video Magic PCI VT64                   S3 Trio64
12   AT25                                        Alliance AT3D
13   AT3D                                        Alliance AT3D
14   ATI 3D Pro Turbo                            ati
15   ATI 3D Pro Turbo PC2TV                      ati
16   ATI 3D Xpression                            ati
17   ATI 3D Xpression+                           ati

Enter a number to choose the corresponding card definition.
Press enter for the next page, q to continue configuration.
```

Once again, there are many more cards listed in the database than can fit on one screen. Press Enter to get to the next page. When you reach the end of the list, pressing Enter will start the list over at the first page.

35

If you can't find your video card in this list, simply press Q to quit. Don't select a model just because it looks similar, because this could cause problems. Models that have similar names do not necessarily have similar hardware.

If you do find the make and model of your video card in the list, enter its number and then press Enter. You will then receive information about the video card you selected. Here's an example:

```
Your selected card definition:

Identifier: Matrox Millennium G400
Chipset:   mgag400
Driver:    mga
Do NOT probe clocks or use any Clocks line.

Press enter to continue, or ctrl-c to abort.
```

Pressing Enter here will continue on to the next question. Pressing Ctrl+C will abort the entire program and cancel the configuration. If you do this, you will have to rerun xf86config and start over.

After you press Enter to continue, you are asked to give some more information about your video card, starting with the amount of RAM it contains:

```
Now you must give information about your video card. This will be used for
the "Device" section of your video card in XF86Config.

You must indicate how much video memory you have. It is probably a good
idea to use the same approximate amount as that detected by the server you
intend to use. If you encounter problems that are due to the used server
not supporting the amount of memory you have (e.g. ATI Mach64 is limited to
1024K with the SVGA server), specify the maximum amount supported by the
server.

How much video memory do you have on your video card:

1   256K
2   512K
3   1024K
4   2048K
5   4096K
6   Other

Enter your choice:
```

Unless you have a very old video card, you probably have more RAM than any of the default options here, so you will want to select 6 and then enter the amount of RAM manually.

If you do this, you will be asked to enter the amount of video RAM installed in the system in kilobytes. Remember that in binary math, a kilobyte is equal to 1,024 bytes, not 1,000 bytes. Table 35.2 shows the value to enter for various amounts of video RAM.

TABLE 35.2   Video RAM in Megabytes and the Corresponding Kilobyte Values

Video RAM in Megabytes	Amount of Memory in Kilobytes
8	8192
16	16384
32	32768
64	65536
128	131072

Enter the number under Amount of memory in Kbytes and then press Enter to continue on to the next screen:

```
You must now enter a few identification/description strings, namely an
identifier, a vendor name, and a model name. Just pressing enter will fill
in default names (possibly from a card definition).

Your card definition is Matrox Millennium G400.

The strings are free-form, spaces are allowed.
Enter an identifier for your video card definition:
```

If you selected a video card type from the card list, there will already be a suggested identification/description string listed here. I suggest that you accept the default that is given. If you can't find your card in the list, enter a description of your video card here and then press Enter.

Depending on whether or not you selected a card definition from the database, you will be presented with a different set of questions. Read the appropriate upcoming section, depending on whether you did or did not select a card definition from the database.

Selecting a Card from the Database and Saving the Configuration File

If you selected a card definition from the database list, you will be presented with a menu of currently configured video modes. The following shows an example of what this might look like:

35

For each depth, a list of modes (resolutions) is defined. The default
resolution that the server will start-up with will be the first listed
mode that can be supported by the monitor and card.
Currently it is set to:

```
"640x480" "800x600" "1024x768" "1280x1024" for 8-bit
"640x480" "800x600" "1024x768" "1280x1024" for 16-bit
"640x480" "800x600" "1024x768" "1280x1024" for 24-bit
```

Modes that cannot be supported due to monitor or clock constraints will
be automatically skipped by the server.

```
1   Change the modes for 8-bit (256 colors)
2   Change the modes for 16-bit (32K/64K colors)
3   Change the modes for 24-bit (24-bit color)
4   The modes are OK, continue.
```

Enter your choice:

You will probably want to make some changes here because, by default, X-Windows will
start up in a resolution of 640×480, which is virtually unusable. If you have a 17-inch
monitor, you will probably want to go with at least 1024×768, and you may want to go
even higher. If you have a 19- or 21-inch monitor, you can definitely go higher than
1024×768. If you have a 15-inch monitor, you might want to try 1024×768, but this might
be too small and you will have to go down to 800×600. If you have a 14-inch monitor,
1024×768 will likely be too small, and you will want to go down to 800×600 or possibly
even stay with 640×480.

Also, you will want to decide what color depth to use. As a general rule, the higher the
color depth, the better. If you have a small amount of video RAM, though, color depth
and resolution may be a tradeoff. In general, you will not notice a difference in most
applications between 16-bit and 24-bit color. However, there will be a big difference
between 8-bit color and 16-bit color. Although personal preference has to be the governing
factor, here are my recommendations:

- If the resolution you want to run does not allow more than 8-bit color (256 colors),
  it is probably better to reduce the resolution to a level that allows 16-bit color.
  However, if getting more than 256 colors requires you to reduce the resolution to a
  value lower than 1024×768, you may want to reconsider this.

- If the resolution you want to run does allow 16-bit color but does not allow 24-bit
  color, it is probably not worth reducing the resolution to allow 24-bit color. In most
  cases, unless you are doing something in which the number of colors is extremely
  important, you are not likely to notice a huge difference between 16-bit and 24-bit
  color.

Once you have decided on the default color depth you want to run, you will want to make changes to the mode line for that color depth (unless you plan on running 640×480 resolution by default, in which case you do not have to make any changes).

Select the number of the mode line you want to make changes to and then press Enter. For example, if you plan to run 24-bit color by default, you would select 3 in the sample screen given previously. This will take you to a screen similar to the following.

```
Select modes from the following list:

 1  "640x400"
 2  "640x480"
 3  "800x600"
 4  "1024x768"
 5  "1280x1024"
 6  "320x200"
 7  "320x240"
 8  "400x300"
 9  "1152x864"
 a  "1600x1200"
 b  "1800x1400"
 c  "512x384"


Please type the digits corresponding to the modes that you want to select.
For example, 432 selects "1024x768" "800x600" "640x480", with a
default mode of 1024x768.


Which modes?
```

Select the number corresponding to the default resolution that you want to use when X-Windows first starts up. For example, if you want X-Windows to start in 1024×768 resolution by default, select 4.

If you want to be able to switch between different resolutions, you can enter multiple numbers here. The first number will be the default resolution, and the numbers listed after that will be cycled through in the order they are listed when you issue the command to change the screen resolution. For example, if you want the default resolution to be 1024×768, the next resolution displayed when you cycle to be 800×600, and the final resolution displayed when cycling to be 640×480, you would enter **432** here.

Most people are not in the habit of changing the resolution on their screens at all once they have it initially set up. If you've never changed the screen resolution on your Windows or Macintosh system, chances are you won't in FreeBSD, either. Unless you anticipate having to flip back and forth between various resolutions for some reason, you can probably just set one resolution here.

35

When you have selected the resolution(s) that you want for this color depth, press Enter to continue. You will then be asked about virtual screens:

```
You can have a virtual screen (desktop), which is screen area that is larger
than the physical screen and which is panned by moving the mouse to the edge
of the screen. If you don't want virtual desktop at a certain resolution,
you cannot have modes listed that are larger. Each color depth can have a
differently-sized virtual screen

Please answer the following question with either 'y' or 'n'.
Do you want a virtual screen that is larger than the physical screen?
```

A virtual screen that is larger than the physical screen will cause parts of the desktop to be off the edge of the screen. To see the different parts of the desktop, you will need to scroll up, down, left, and right by dragging the mouse pointer off the end of the screen.

> **CAUTION**
>
> In my opinion, virtual screens are extremely annoying and difficult to work with. The only time they might make sense is if you are forced to use a very low resolution (640×480 or less). Even then, you will probably find the virtual screen intolerable and extremely difficult to work with. Because of this, I highly suggest that you select N here.

If you do decide that you want a virtual screen, you will be asked for the resolution you want the screen to be. Select the desired resolution and press Enter.

If you decide you do not want a virtual screen, you will be taken back to the mode line configuration screen shown earlier. Another sample screen is shown here:

```
For each depth, a list of modes (resolutions) is defined. The default
resolution that the server will start-up with will be the first listed
mode that can be supported by the monitor and card.
Currently it is set to:

"640x480" "800x600" "1024x768" "1280x1024" for 8-bit
"640x480" "800x600" "1024x768" "1280x1024" for 16-bit
"1024x768" for 24-bit

Modes that cannot be supported due to monitor or clock constraints will
be automatically skipped by the server.

1  Change the modes for 8-bit (256 colors)
2  Change the modes for 16-bit (32K/64K colors)
```

```
3  Change the modes for 24-bit (24-bit color)
4  The modes are OK, continue.
```

```
Enter your choice:
```

Notice that the mode lines for 24-bit color have changed. It now has only 1024×768 resolution.

Unless you plan to run multiple color depths, you can leave the other color depths alone. If you do plan to switch between color depths, simply select the number for the next color depth you want to configure and repeat the previous steps to configure the resolutions for that color.

When you have finished configuring all the modes you want to configure, select 4 (The modes are OK, continue) to move on to the next section.

You will then be asked to specify the default color depth you want to use:

```
Please specify which color depth you want to use by default:
```

```
1  1 bit (monochrome)
2  4 bits (16 colors)
3  8 bits (256 colors)
4  16 bits (65536 colors)
5  24 bits (16 million colors)
```

```
Enter a number to choose the default depth.
```

Simply select the number for the color depth you decided on earlier and then press Enter.

After you have selected the desired color depth, you will be asked whether you want to save the changes:

```
I am going to write the XF86Config file now. Make sure you don't accidentally
overwrite a previously configured one.
```

```
Shall I write it to /etc/X11/XF86Config?
```

Select Y to write a new XF86Config file. If you already have an XF86Config file, it will be overwritten with the new file.

Once you have selected Y here, xf86config will respond with the following:

```
File has been written. Take a look at it before running 'startx'. Note that
the XF86Config file must be in one of the directories searched by the server
(e.g. /etc/X11) in order to be used. Within the server press
```

35

```
ctrl, alt and '+' simultaneously to cycle video resolutions. Pressing ctrl,
alt and backspace simultaneously immediately exits the server (use if
the monitor doesn't sync for a particular mode).
```

```
For further configuration, refer to /usr/X11R6/lib/X11/doc/README.Config.
```

At this point, you will be returned to the command prompt. You can skip the next section and continue on with the section "Testing the X-Windows Setup," which follows.

Configuring a Card That Is Not in the Database and Saving the Configuration File

If you did not select one of the cards from the card list database, the first question you will be asked is what default color depth you want to use:

```
Please specify which color depth you want to use by default:
```

```
    1   1 bit (monochrome)
    2   4 bits (16 colors)
    3   8 bits (256 colors)
    4   16 bits (65536 colors)
    5   24 bits (16 million colors)
```

```
Enter a number to choose the default depth.
```

```
Please specify which color depth you want to use by default:
```

```
    1   1 bit (monochrome)
    2   4 bits (16 colors)
    3   8 bits (256 colors)
    4   16 bits (65536 colors)
    5   24 bits (16 million colors)
```

```
Enter a number to choose the default depth.
```

Select the number corresponding to the default color depth you want and press Enter.

You will then be asked whether you want to save the changes:

```
I am going to write the XF86Config file now. Make sure you don't accidentally
overwrite a previously configured one.
```

```
Shall I write it to /etc/X11/XF86Config?
```

Select Y here to write the configuration file. This will overwrite any existing configuration file you may have. Once you have written the changes, xf86config will respond with the following message and then exit:

```
File has been written. Take a look at it before running 'startx'. Note that
the XF86Config file must be in one of the directories searched by the server
(e.g. /etc/X11) in order to be used. Within the server press
ctrl, alt and '+' simultaneously to cycle video resolutions. Pressing ctrl,
alt and backspace simultaneously immediately exits the server (use if
the monitor doesn't sync for a particular mode).

For further configuration, refer to /usr/X11R6/lib/X11/doc/README.Config.
```

By default, X-Windows will start in 640×480 resolution. You will probably want to change this to a higher resolution. You will need to edit the XF86Config configuration file manually in order to do so. The XF86Config file is covered in the next section.

Understanding the XF86Config File

Like most other aspects of configuring FreeBSD, the X-Windows configuration is controlled by a configuration file that is in plain text. The primary X-Windows configuration file is located in /etc/X11 and is called XF86Config. This is the file that is created and/or modified by xf86cfg (the GUI interface for X-Windows configuration) and also by xf86config (the text-based interface for X-Windows configuration that was covered in the previous sections of this chapter). These configuration tools have made X-Windows configuration much easier than it used to be when the files had to be edited by hand.

However, there are still some situations in which you might need to make changes to the configuration file by hand. For example, if your video card was not listed in the card database, you may need to make changes to this file by hand. Another situation in which you may need to make changes by hand is if you configured X-Windows by using xf86config and you want to make changes to the mouse (such as the speed of the mouse). If you simply want to make one or two minor changes to X-Windows, it may be desirable to edit the file by hand rather than go through a complete configuration with xf86config.

To make changes to the XF86Config file, first make a backup copy of the file so that it will be easy to undo your changes if they cause problems. For example, you might want to copy /etc/X11/XF86Config to /etc/X11/XF86Config.bak. Once you have a backup copy, open the file /etc/X11/XF86Config in your favorite text editor (see Chapter 6 if you need information on how to use one of the text editors included with FreeBSD).

35

TIP

Remember that FreeBSD (and other Unix-like operating systems) are case sensitive. Do not confuse the text-based configuration program (xf86config) with the actual configuration file (XF86Config). Because of the case-sensitivity, they are two completely different files.

XF86Config **Syntax**

The XF86Config file is divided into several sections. Each section relates to a specific device or configuration issue. Each section begins with the keyword Section followed by the section name in quotes. Each section ends with the keyword EndSection. The body of the section is indented for readability purposes. Comments begin with a pound sign (#) and go to the end of the line. The following is an example of a section in the XF86Config file:

```
Section "Module"

# This loads the DBE extension module.

    Load        "dbe"   # Double buffer extension

# This loads the miscellaneous extensions module, and disables
# initialization of the XFree86-DGA extension within that module.
    SubSection  "extmod"
      Option    "omit xfree86-dga"   # don't initialize the DGA extension
    EndSubSection

# This loads the Type1 and FreeType font modules
    Load        "type1"
    Load        "freetype"

# This loads the GLX module
#    Load       "glx"

EndSection
```

The comments before this section are not shown, but in the XF86Config file, they explain what the section is for. In this case the Module section loads dynamic modules when the server starts to support various things. For example, the part of this example that begins with # This loads the Type1 and FreeType font modules loads dynamic modules to support various types of fonts. In this case, the first Load line loads a module that supports Adobe Type 1 fonts. The second Load module loads the freetype module, which is a freely available module that allows X-Windows to use TrueType fonts.

In addition to main sections, there are also subsections that can be embedded within the sections. These begin with the keyword SubSection followed by the name of the subsection in quotes. They end with the keyword EndSubSection. Like the main sections, they are also indented for readability purposes.

The following sections of this chapter take a look at the various sections and subsections in the XF86Config file.

Section "Module"

The Module section is where modules can be dynamically loaded to support things such as various font types. Dynamically loaded modules are not a part of the X binary; instead, these modules are loaded as needed when X-Windows starts. The advantage of dynamically loaded modules is that they are loaded only if they are needed. Modules that are not needed are not loaded and therefore do not waste memory and system resources. For example, if you don't have any TrueType fonts on your system, there is little point in having TrueType font support in X. You can comment out the Load "freetype" line.

Modules that are to be loaded begin with the keyword Load followed by the name of the module in quotes. For example, the following line loads the module that supports TrueType fonts:

```
Load "freetype"
```

Section "Files"

This section is similar to the X-Windows PATH environment variable. The Files section tells X-Windows where it can expect to find various files.

The only portion of this section you may ever want to modify is that which tells X-Windows where to look for fonts. Each one of the font directories begins with the keyword FontPath, followed by a directory enclosed in quotation marks. For example, the following line is where the Adobe Type 1 fonts are located:

```
FontPath    "/usr/X11R6/lib/X11/fonts/Type1/"
```

This is the directory in which you would install new Adobe Type 1 fonts that you may download or purchase. Details on X-Windows fonts will be covered later on in this chapter, in the section titled "Working with Fonts."

If you do add new font directories, the name of the directory is not really important. For example, there is nothing that says that Adobe Type 1 fonts have to be stored in a directory called Type1. This convention is just followed to make it easier for you to guess what types of fonts are in a directory.

Section "ServerFlags"

The ServerFlags section of the file contains some global options that control the behavior of X-Windows. Some of the available options are present in the configuration file generated by xf86config and include comments about what they do. All the options are commented out by default.

All the options in this section begin with the keyword Option, followed by the option in quotes. For example, the following line will disable the Ctrl+Alt+Backspace sequence that kills the X-Server immediately:

```
Option "DontZap"
```

35

(You definitely will not want to uncomment this option until you have tested your X-Windows system and are sure you have a working setup.)

The following subsections discuss some (though not all) of the options available in `ServerFlags` you're most likely to use.

Option "NoTrapSignals"

If this option is uncommented, X-Windows will not exit cleanly when there is a problem. Instead, it will write a core dump file. This can cause problems with the console not working correctly after X-Windows has terminated incorrectly.

You should probably leave this line commented out unless you are experiencing consistent X-Server crashes. In that case, uncommenting this option creates a core dump file that is invaluable for troubleshooting purposes. Even if you are not a programmer and cannot make heads or tails of the dump file, it will be invaluable if you want to file a bug report with the Xfree86 project.

Option "DontZap"

If this option is uncommented, you will not be able to kill the X-Server by using the Ctrl+Alt+Backspace key combination. You should definitely not uncomment this line until you have tested your X-Windows configuration and are sure it is working correctly. Even then, there is little reason to uncomment this line. About the only reason you would need to do so is if you have programs that run under X-Windows that use this key combination for some other function. Then, you might need to uncomment this line to prevent the X-Server from catching the combination and exiting.

Option "DontZoom"

If this option is uncommented, it will disable video mode switching using Ctrl+Alt+(keypad)+ and Ctrl+Alt+(keypad)-. By default, these key combinations will allow you to cycle between different video modes if you have configured multiple video resolutions.

About the only reason for uncommenting this would be if you have programs that require these key combinations for some other use. In this case, uncommenting this line will prevent the X-Server from intercepting the combination and causing the video modes to switch.

Option "DisableVidModeExtension"

If this option is uncommented, it will prevent the `xvidtune` program from making any changes to the video system. If this is a multiuser system, it may be a good idea to uncomment this line to prevent users from being able to use `xvidtune`, because the improper use of `xvidtune` can damage your monitor. Note that if the line is uncommented, `xvidtune` can still be loaded. But you will not be able to make any changes to the video system with it.

Most of the other options in this section that are present in the configuration file generated by xf86config should probably be left alone.

Other Options Not Present by Default for Section "ServerFlags"

Several other options may be of interest that are not present in the default configuration file generated by xf86config. We are not going to discuss all of them here, but many of the more useful ones are discussed. If you want to add any of these options, simply add the line in bold text to this section in XF86Config:

- **Option "AllowMouseOpenFail"**—By default, if the X-Server cannot open the mouse or other pointing device, the server will not start and will exit with an error. Adding this line will allow the server to start, even if the mouse or other pointing device cannot be accessed.

  Unless you are trying to use X-Windows without a mouse or other pointing device, there is probably no reason to change this option.

- **Option "BlankTime" "n"**—This option will cause the screen to go blank after the number of minutes represented by n. If this option is not present, the default is 10 minutes.

- **Option "StandbyTime" "n"**—This option will cause the monitor to go into standby mode after the number of minutes represented by n. If this option is not present, the default is 20 minutes.

  This option is not supported by all video drivers, and it only works with monitors that support DPMS. The Monitor section of XF86Config (discussed later in this chapter) must specifically specify that the monitor can support DPMS for this feature to apply.

- **Option "SuspendTime" "n"**—This option will cause the monitor to go into suspend mode after the number of minutes represented by n. If this option is not present, the default is 30 minutes.

  This option is not supported by all video drivers, and it only works with monitors that support DPMS. The Monitor section of XF86Config (discussed later in this chapter) must specifically specify that the monitor can support DPMS for this feature to apply.

- **Option "OffTime" "n"**—This option will turn the monitor off after the number of minutes represented by n. If this option is not present, the default is 40 minutes.

  This option is not supported by all video drivers, and it only works with monitors that support DPMS. The Monitor section of XF86Config (discussed later in this chapter) must specifically specify that the monitor can support DPMS for this feature to apply.

35

- **Option "NoPM"**—This option will disable some events that relate to power management. By default, power management is enabled on systems that can support it. You should need to add this option only if you are experiencing strange problems that seem to be related to power-management events.

A few other options can be included in this section, but they are less commonly used. If you are interested in some of the other options available, see the man page for `XF86Config`.

Section "InputDevice"

This section is where the input devices are configured. There can be multiple `InputDevice` sections in the configuration file. Usually there will be at least two: one for the keyboard and one for the mouse or other pointing device.

`InputDevice` sections have several keywords associated with them. The first is the `Identifier` keyword. It is followed by a name that identifies this device. X-Windows doesn't really care what you call the device, but it is best to use a descriptive name that defines the device.

The second is the `Driver` keyword. It is followed by the name of the driver for this device, in quotes. The most common drivers are `"keyboard"` and `"mouse"`, but there are a few others such as `"microtouch"` for a touch screen.

The final part of the `InputDevice` section consists of options for the device.

The following sections look at the two most common `InputDevice` sections—the keyboard and the mouse—and discuss some of the option lines available for configuring them.

Configuring the Keyboard Options

Here is an example of the first part of the `InputDevice` section for the keyboard:

```
Section "InputDevice"

    Identifier   "Keyboard1"
    Driver       "Keyboard"
```

You can choose from a number of available options for controlling keyboard behavior. Here are some of the most commonly used of these options:

- **Option "Protocol"**—If this option is omitted or commented out, the default value of `"standard"` will be used. There is probably no reason to change this.

- **Option "AutoRepeat" "x y"**—This option controls the repeat rate of the keys on the keyboard. The number represented by x is the delay in milliseconds before the key starts repeating. The number represented by y is the number of times the key will repeat each second.

The default is 500 milliseconds before the key starts to repeat, and 30 times per second that it will repeat.

- **Option** `"XkbRules"` `"xfree86"`—This option determines the way various aspects of the keyboard are interpreted. In most cases, you should leave this set to `"xfree86"` unless you have the Japanese PC-98 platform, in which case it should be `"xfree98"`.

- **Option** `"XkbModel"` `"pc104"`—If you have a 104-key Windows keyboard, this will be `"pc104"`. If you have a 101-key keyboard that does not have the Windows keys, it will be `"pc101"`. These values will also work for laptops. Even though laptops usually have fewer keys, they generally have ways of emulating the additional keys.

- **Option** `"XkbLayout"` `"us"`—This will usually be set to `"us"`. But if you are using the Japanese PC-98 platform, you will want to change it to `"nec/jp"`.

- **Option** `"XkbOptions"` `"ctrl:swapcaps"`—If this line is uncommented, it will cause the Caps Lock key to become a Ctrl key and the left Ctrl key to become a Caps Lock key. You may want to uncomment this line if you are an Emacs guru (Emacs relies heavily on the Ctrl key) or if you are used to a Unix keyboard layout in which the Ctrl key is placed in the position that the Caps Lock key is placed in on PC keyboards.

Configuring Mouse Options

Here is an example of the first part of the InputDevice section for the mouse:

```
Section "InputDevice"

# Identifier and driver

    Identifier  "Mouse1"
    Driver      "mouse"
```

The following subsections describe some of the most commonly used options.

Option "Protocol" "*protocol*"   In this option, *protocol* represents the type of mouse that your system has. This option is required, and the X-Server will not work if it is not present.

Many users will be able to get away with specifying Auto here to have the X-Server automatically attempt to determine the protocol the mouse uses. Several other options are available. Here are the valid protocol types: Auto, Microsoft, MouseSystems, MMSeries, Logitech, MouseMan, MMHitTab, GlidePoint, IntelliMouse, ThinkingMouse, AceCad, PS/2, ImPS/2, ExplorerPS/2, ThinkingMousePS/2, MouseManPlusPS/2, GlidePointPS/2, NetMousePS/2, NetScrollPS/2, BusMouse, SysMouse, WSMouse, USB, and Xqueue.

And here are some guidelines for choosing the correct protocol:

- The Logitech protocol is used only by older Logitech serial mice. If you have a newer Logitech serial mouse, use the Microsoft or MouseMan protocols.

- Use the PS/2 protocol for any PS/2 mouse, no matter who the manufacturer is. You have a PS/2 mouse if the mouse connector is a small round one.

- If you have a laptop or notebook system, the built-in pointing device (such as a track pad or track point) will probably work with the PS/2 protocol.

I suggest that you try using Auto first and then change it only if your mouse is not detected or is not working properly.

Option "Device" "*devicename*"   This option specifies what device the mouse is on. The option is required, and the X-Server will not work if this option is missing.

Table 35.3 lists some of the common device names where your mouse may be located.

TABLE 35.3   Device Names for Various Mouse Types

Mouse Type	Mouse Device
PS/2 mouse (or laptop)	/dev/psm0
Serial mouse on COM 1	/dev/cuaa0
Serial mouse on COM 2	/dev/cuaa1
Serial mouse on COM 3	/dev/cuaa2
Serial mouse on COM 4	/dev/cuaa3
Bus mouse	/dev/mse0

Note that *devicename* in this option should be replaced with the mouse device.

Option "Buttons" "*n*"   In most cases, the number of buttons on the mouse will be automatically detected. But if they are not, this option can be used to tell the X-Server how many buttons are on the mouse.

Here, *n* represents the number of buttons on the mouse. The most common values are 2 and 3, although numbers up to 5 are supported. If you happen to have a mouse with five buttons on it, go for it.

Option "Emulate3Buttons"   This line allows a two-button mouse to emulate a three-button mouse. If you have a two-button mouse, you will want to uncomment this line because X-Windows make extensive use of all three mouse buttons.

If you do uncomment this line, the middle mouse button is emulated by pressing the left and right mouse buttons at the same time.

Option "Emulate3Timeout" "*n*"   If the Emulate3Buttons option is set, this option will control the number of milliseconds that can elapse between clicking the left and right mouse buttons before X-Windows will no longer interpret the action to be a middle click.

In other words, both the left and right mouse buttons must be pushed within this time frame in order for the action to be interpreted as a middle click. Here, *n* is the number of milliseconds that can elapse.

If this line is not present and the Emulate3Buttons option is enabled, the default Emulate3Timeout value will be 50 milliseconds.

Section "Monitor"

This is where you configure the horizontal and vertical refresh rates for your monitor. It consists of the Identifier keyword followed by a name in quotes to identify this monitor. The name you choose is not very important.

Two other keywords are required to be present in this section: HorizSync and VertRefresh. You learn more about them in the following sections. A few other options can be used with the Monitor section, but they are not as common. For full details on all the available options, see the man page for XF86Config.

HorizSync

This is the horizontal sync rate in kilohertz that the monitor supports. It can be specified in several ways:

- **As a range**—This is normally the method used to configure multisync monitors (and virtually all monitors are multisync these days). For example, HorizSync 44-76 would be used for a monitor that can support horizontal refresh rates ranging from 44 to 76 kilohertz.

- **As a single value**—If you have a fixed frequency monitor that supports only one frequency, it is simply listed after HorizSync.

- **As a list of frequencies**—If your monitor supports several fixed frequencies, you can supply a list of the fixed frequencies that it supports, separated by commas (for example "HorizSync 31.5, 35.2").

- **As multiple ranges of frequencies**—If your monitor supports more then one range of frequencies but has a gap in the middle that it does not support, you can list multiple ranges (for example, "HorizSync 15-25, 30-50").

VertRefresh

This keyword lists the vertical refresh rate your monitor can support. It can take its value in any one of the formats that the HorizSync keyword can use.

> **CAUTION**
>
> Supplying values for HorizSync and VertRefresh that are outside the range of what your monitor can support can damage or destroy your monitor. Be extremely careful that you do not supply values outside the supported range. See your monitor's documentation or check the manufacturers Web site for technical specifications to find the values your monitor can support.

35

Section "Device"

This section is where you configure your graphics adapter. Like most other sections, it begins with the keyword `Identifier`, followed by a name in quotes to identify the device.

The `Driver` keyword is also required, followed by the name of the driver for your card in quotes. For example, if you have an NVIDIA TNT2, the line would look like this:

```
Driver "nv"
```

If you have a supported video card, it is much easier to go through `xf86config` (explained earlier in this chapter) to set up the graphics device than to do it manually in the `XF86Config` file. However, if for whatever reason you need to or want to do it manually, a full list of the supported cards, along with the driver that should be used to support each card, is available at `www.xfree86.org/current/Status.html`.

The other keyword that is most commonly used here is the `VideoRam` keyword to specify how much video RAM the video card has. For example, if your video card has 16MB of RAM, the line would look like this:

```
VideoRam 16384
```

As you learned earlier, the amount of video RAM is specified in kilobytes; in binary math, a kilobyte is actually 1,024 bytes. Table 35.4 repeats the list of Video RAM values you saw earlier in Table 35.2; these numbers should be entered here for various amounts of video RAM.

TABLE 35.4   Video RAM in Megabytes and the Corresponding Kilobyte Values

Video RAM in Megabytes	Amount of Memory in Kilobytes
8	8192
16	16384
32	32768
64	65536
128	131072

Some more options are available for graphics devices, but most of them will not be needed for most video cards. See the man page for `XF86Config` for full details on all the available options.

Also, you will probably want to have a look at the Web page located at `http://www.xfree86.org/4.0.2/index.html` to see whether there are any notes regarding your particular type of video card and any specific options you need to supply for it.

> **TIP**
>
> If you cannot find a driver for your video card, all may not be lost. You might be able to get the card working with the Vesa driver. The Vesa driver is a generic Super VGA specification that a lot of cards support to some extent. If you have to use this driver, the accelerated features of your card will not be fully supported. Also, the Vesa driver may not support all the resolutions and color depths that your video card can support. But it is better than nothing, and it may allow you to use a card for which there is no driver currently available for X-Windows. If you end up using this alternative, check the supported card database often because support for new cards is being added on a regular basis.

Section "Screen"

The Screen section is where a monitor is combined with a graphics card to make a display that will work with the X-Server. It starts with the Identifier keyword that contains a name enclosed in quotes, after which it gives this screen a name. There can be multiple screen sections present in the XF86Config file. The first one encountered will be the one that is used unless specified otherwise in the ServerLayout section.

After you have specified an identifier for the Screen section, you also must specify the "*devicename*", "*monitorname*", and DefaultDepth "*n*" keywords. Other available options are rarely used; see the man page for XF86Config for details on these options.

Device "*devicename*"

This is the name of the graphics device that should be used for this screen configuration. Here, *devicename* is whatever string appears in the Identifier section of the graphics device that should be used for this screen setting.

Monitor "*monitorname*"

This is the name of the monitor that should be used for this screen configuration. Here, *monitorname* is whatever string appears in the Identifier section of the monitor that should be used for this screen setting.

DefaultDepth "*n*"

This is the default color depth that should be used for this screen configuration. Valid values for *n* are 8, 16, and 24, assuming your video card supports all three color depths.

SubSection "Display"

After you have configured the Screen section, you will need to configure the Display subsection(s) for the screen. The Display subsection is where the resolutions and the order that they are cycled in are given for each color depth. There must be at least one Display subsection for the default color depth; otherwise, the X-Server will not start. However, there can be more then one Display subsection. There is one Display subsection for each color depth.

The first line in the subsection will be the keyword Depth followed by the color depth that this subsection is for. Here is an example of what the first two lines of this subsection might look like:

```
Subsection "Display"
    Depth       24
```

The third line that is required here is a mode line. It is simply the keyword Modes followed by a list of the resolutions you want to have supported. The first resolution listed will be the default. The resolutions listed after that will be cycled through when the Ctrl+Alt+(keypad)+ and Ctrl+Alt+(keypad)- key combinations are used. Note that this may not work on some systems.

Here is a sample mode line:

```
Modes "1024x768" "800x600" "640x480"
```

In this example, the default resolution will be 1024×768 for this color depth. Pressing Ctrl+Alt+(keypad)+ or Ctrl+Alt+(keypad)- will also allow the resolutions of 800×600 and 640×480 to be used.

X-Windows allows you to have a virtual screen that is larger than the resolution you have configured. For example, you can have your screen resolution set to 800×600 and have a virtual screen size of 1024×768. This was discussed in a previous section of this chapter when we talked about configuring X-Windows with the xf86config program.

If you decide that you want to use a virtual screen, you can use the "Virtual resolution" option to configure the resolution the virtual screen should be. For example, "Virtual 1024x768" will set the virtual screen size to 1024×768. If the actual screen resolution is lower than this, only part of the screen will be visible. To see the portions of the screen that are not visible, you will need to drag the mouse pointer off the edge of the screen. This will scroll the screen left, right, up, or down, depending on which edge of the screen you are interacting with.

Some other options are available here but are not commonly used. For a list of all the options available in the Display subsection, see the man page for XF86Config.

Section "ServerLayOut"

The ServerLayout section is optional. If it does not exist, the first screen listed and the first keyboard and mouse input devices listed will be used. If the ServerLayout section does exist, it is used to select the screen entry and the keyboard and mouse entries to be used for the X-Server.

The Identifier keyword is required, and it is followed by a string in quotes that gives this server layout a name. Here are some of the other items commonly used in the ServerLayout section:

- **Screen** *"screenname"*—This is the screen configuration that should be used for this device. Here, *screenname* is the name listed in the Identifier keyword for the Screen section that is to be used for this server layout.

- **InputDevice** *"keyboardname"* **"CoreKeyboard"**—This determines which keyboard entry should be used for this server layout. Here, *keyboardname* is the name listed in the Identifier keyword for the Keyboard section you want to use.

  The CoreKeyboard option that follows sets this keyboard to the default keyboard.

- **InputDevice** *"mousename"* **"CorePointer"**—This is like the Keyboard entry, except that it determines the mouse that should be used for this server layout. Once again, the CorePointer option that follows sets this mouse to the default mouse.

Option lines can also be included in the ServerLayout section. If they are included and they conflict with options listed in other sections, the options listed here will override the other options.

Other options are available for all aspects of the XF86Config file, but most of them are rarely used. Once again, see the man page for XF86Config for full details of all the available configuration options.

Testing the X-Windows Setup

Once you have finished with xf86config and/or hand-edited the XF86Config file and saved your changes, you are ready to test the X-Server.

Type **startx** at the command line to start the X-Windows system. If all goes well, your screen will go blank for a moment, and you should soon see a checkered background with a small × in the middle. The × is the mouse pointer. After a few more seconds, the window manager should come up, and you should be able to move the mouse around on the screen.

If you can't move the mouse or if X-Windows seems to start but then quits with an error message, double-check your XF86Config file to make sure you have everything configured properly.

> **CAUTION**
>
> If you start X-Windows and your screen appears to be garbled, and/or you hear a high-pitched whine coming from your monitor, *immediately* turn your monitor off and/or press Ctrl+Alt+Backspace to kill the X-Server. Either one of these symptoms indicates that you are probably driving the refresh rate of your monitor higher than it can tolerate, and the flyback transformer in your monitor is getting ready to fry. After you have killed the X-Server, reconfigure the sync rates and/or resolutions for your monitor in XF86Config or with the xf86config script and then try again.

If you type **startx** and your monitor goes blank and then seems to turn off or go into a suspend mode (the power light changes color, starts blinking, or you can hear the static on the monitor discharging), it probably means you have driven your monitor past the specs it can tolerate. Press Ctrl+Alt+Backspace to kill the X-Server. This should restore your screen and give you the command prompt back. Then, reconfigure your refresh rates and/or resolutions in XF86Config or with the xf86config script and then try again.

Once you have a working X-Windows setup, you may want to make some customizations to the way it works. The next section covers your personal .xinitrc file in your home directory.

Your Personal .xinitrc File

Changing the .xinitrc file in your home directory is the primary way of making changes to the basic X-Windows setup. One of the setup attributes controlled by this file is which window manager is used by X-Windows. You also can use this file to control which applications start automatically every time you run X-Windows, the background color of the screen, and the display of a background image. Each of these operations involves making changes to your personal .xinitrc file, as you learn in the sections that follow.

Changing the Window Managers

Many window managers are available in the x11-wm category of the FreeBSD ports tree. One popular window manager is Blackbox, which is shown in Figure 35.1. See Chapter 14, "Installing Additional Software," for information on how to work with the FreeBSD ports collection.

Blackbox is an ideal window manager for users who don't want the window manager to get in the way. It is also ideal for systems that are low on memory. Blackbox is a common window manager on servers.

Once you have installed a new window manager, you must edit your personal .xinitrc file to use it.

Open the .xinitrc file located in your home directory in your favorite text editor. If the file does not already exist, it will be created.

In this case, all you want to do is tell X-Windows what window manager to use, so you only need to add one line to the file.

For Blackbox, here's the line to add:

```
blackbox
```

Once you have added one of the correct lines to the .xinitrc file, save the file and exit the editor. The next time you start X-Windows, you will be placed in the new window manager.

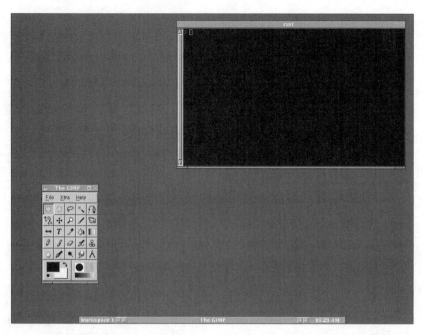

FIGURE 35.1   Blackbox is a very small and fast window manager. It contains few frills and takes up very few system resources.

Configuration of window managers is beyond the scope of this book. See the Web page for your chosen window manager for more information. (In the case of Blackbox, see http://blackbox.alug.org).

> **NOTE**
>
> Many other window managers are available for use with X-Windows. Many of them are available in the FreeBSD ports collection under the x11-wm directory.
>
> For more information, including screen shots of the more popular window managers, see www.xwinman.org.

Starting Applications Automatically

If you want to have applications start automatically each time you start the X-Windows system, you can add them to your .xinitrc file. Any applications that you want to start automatically should be added before the window manager and should end with an ampersand character (&). (Note that there should be a space before the ampersand.) This way, they start in the background. If you don't end them with an ampersand, they will start in the foreground, and the window manager will never get started.

Here is an example of an `.xinitrc` file that starts an X-terminal window and an X-clock along with the Blackbox window manager:

```
xterm &
xclock &
blackbox
```

Setting a Background Color or Background Image

Many window managers and desktop environments such as WindowMaker and Gnome have the built-in capability to set their own background colors or background images. However, some of the simpler window managers, such as FVWM and wm2, do not. You can set the background color or background image by calling external programs from the `.xinitrc` file, as explained in the following subsections.

Setting the Background Color

By default, X-Windows has a rather ugly checkered background that is hard on the eyes.

The program `xsetroot` allows you to set the background color to a solid color or to a tiled bitmap from an image. There is a text file that lists all the available colors located in `/usr/X11R6/lib/X11/rgb.txt`. Here is an example of how the background color can be set to a solid color:

```
xsetroot -solid ForestGreen
```

You can type this from an X-terminal window to set the background to forest green.

If you want this change to be permanent, you can add this command to your `.xinitrc` file before the window manager starts. For example, the following line will set the background color to forest green and then start the `twm` window manager:

```
xsetroot -solid ForestGreen &
twm
```

The color you use must be a valid color that is listed in the `rgb.txt` file, and if the color has a space in it, the name of the color must be enclosed in quotation marks.

In addition to setting the background color or pattern of the desktop, `xsetroot` can also change the appearance of the mouse pointer.

See the man page for `xsetroot` for details on how to configure bitmapped backgrounds and also change the mouse pointer to a different bitmap.

You can create your own bitmaps to use as the background and as the mouse pointers with the bitmap program. Figure 35.2 shows the bitmap program.

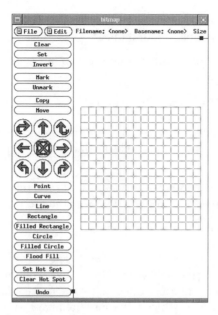

FIGURE 35.2 The bitmap program, which can be used to create bitmaps for use as background patterns and mouse pointers with xsetroot.

Configuring a Background Image

X-Windows does not come with any program that allows you to set a background image. However, there is a program available in the FreeBSD ports collection called xv that can handle this for you. xv is available in the ports collection under the graphics directory. Figure 35.3 shows xv running in interactive mode.

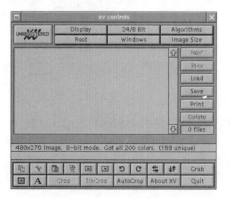

FIGURE 35.3 xv can do far more than just set the background image in X-Windows. It is also a full-featured image viewer that can be used interactively.

xv supports most common image formats, including GIF, JPEG, and BMP, and you can set any one of these formats as a background image.

The following command is an example of how xv can be used to load an image as a background image for X-Windows:

```
xv -root -quit /hone/foobar/images/myimage.jpg
```

This tells xv to load the image myimage.jpg onto the root window (which is the background of the window manager). It also tells xv that it should quit as soon as it has loaded the image.

In order to have this image loaded as the background each time you start X-Windows, you could do something like the following in your .xinitrc file:

```
xv -root -quit /home/foobar/images/myimage.jpg
twm
```

Some of the other options you may want to use with xv when using it to load background images include -max, which will cause the image to be resized and take up the entire available screen size, and -maxspect, which will cause the image to be resized to take up the entire available screen size within the limits of maintaining the proper aspect ratio of the image.

Working with Fonts

Sooner or later, you will probably want to install additional fonts in X-Windows for your applications (such as GIMP).

Although X-Windows supports several types of fonts, the most commonly installed are Adobe Type 1 and TrueType. Both are extremely popular because they are supported by Windows and Macintosh, as well as newer versions of Xfree86. Thousands of Type 1 and TrueType fonts are available free for download from various places on the Internet. Also, commercial fonts are available for purchase in both formats.

Because these are the most commonly used fonts, the following sections describe their use and configuration.

Checking the XF86Config File for Font Support

The first thing you will need to do is make sure the XF86Config file contains the proper modules to support the fonts you want to use. The XF86Config file was covered in detail under the section "Understanding the XF86Config File," earlier in this chapter. Basically, you need to check the file /etc/X11/XF86Config for the appropriate Load line under the Module section.

This line is necessary to support Adobe Type 1 fonts:

```
Load "type1"
```

This line is necessary to support TrueType fonts:

```
Load "freetype"
```

The preceding lines need to be located under the following heading in XF86Config:

```
Section "Modules"
```

You also need to make sure an appropriate font directory exists in the Files section to hold the new fonts.

Look for the lines in XF86Config that begin with FontPath. If you are installing a TrueType font, I suggest that you add the following line after the last FontPath statement in the file to hold all your TrueType fonts:

```
FontPath   "/usr/X11R6/lib/X11/fonts/TrueType/"
```

After you add this line, save the file and then exit the editor.

Creating the Directories and Installing the Fonts

Now, you must create the directory. As root, issue the following command:

```
mkdir /usr/X11R6/lib/X11/fonts/TrueType
```

That command creates the directory for the TrueType fonts.

When you have a directory for the fonts, copy the font files for the fonts you want to add into the appropriate directory. Type 1 fonts should be copied into /usr/X11R6/lib/X11/fonts/Type1, and TrueType fonts should be copied into /usr/X11R6/lib/X11/fonts/TrueType. The fonts only need read access, so you may want to change the permissions on the fonts so that they only have read access for everyone. You can do this with the following command:

```
chmod 444 fontname
```

Here, fontname is, of course, the name of the font you just installed. (Make sure you are currently in the right font directory. If you need help with basic shell commands and navigation through the directories, see Chapter 7, "Working with the Shell").

Next, you must run a couple of programs to set up the fonts correctly.

To set up TrueType fonts, you need the program ttmkfdir. It is available in the FreeBSD ports collection under the directory x11-fonts. To set up Adobe Type 1 fonts, you need the program type1inst, also available in the FreeBSD ports collection under the x11-fonts directory. See Chapter 14 for information on how to install software from the ports collection.

After you have copied the fonts to the appropriate directory, make sure you are in that directory and type one of the following commands at the command prompt.

For TrueType fonts:

```
ttmkfdir > fonts.scale
```

For Adobe Type 1 fonts:

```
type1inst > fonts.scale
```

You now must run just one more command; the `mkfontdir` command recognizes the new fonts and adds them to the font configuration file. To set up scalable fonts, such as Type 1 and TrueType, you need to run the command with the `-e` option. Once again, make sure you are in the directory to which you copied the fonts and then issue the following command from the prompt:

```
mkfontdir -e /usr/X11R6/lib/font/encodings
```

Next, restart X-Windows (if you are currently in it), and your new fonts should be available for use.

> **NOTE**
>
> Whenever you add new fonts to the system, you must repeat `ttmkfdir` or `type1inst`, followed by the `mkfontdir` procedure.

Using Remote X-Windows Clients

Because of the design of X-Windows, applications can be run on a host and have their output and input redirected to a remote host. Using a remote client can be useful, for example, if you have graphical applications on a server and you need to be able to control them from a workstation. In a way, this remote use is similar to simply using Telnet or SSH to log in to a remote system and then run a text-based application. The application is actually running on the server; the output and input are just being sent to your system. X-Windows extends this concept to graphical applications as well as text-based applications. However, this capability is disabled by default and needs to be enabled before it can be used.

The confusing aspect of using remote clients is that the terms *client* and *server* are reversed when dealing with X-Windows. In networking terminology, you think of a client as being a host that runs applications located on another system known as a server. In X-Windows, however, the server is running on the local system, and the client is located on a remote system. Basically, a client in X-Windows is any program that runs under the X-Windows system. To make things even more confusing, your X-Server may be running a client located on a remote system, which is actually a server. For example, you might load a graphical database administration client located on a remote system onto your X-Server. In this case, your client is located on a remote system, but the remote system is a database server.

In order for any of this to work, the system on which you want to display the output of and control the input of the remote X-Windows application must be running an X-Server. However, the X-Server does not have to be on the same type of system. The X-Server can be running on another FreeBSD system, a Linux system, a Solaris system, or a Mac OS X system. The system doesn't even have to be a Unix-based system. There are X-Servers available for Windows that can display remote X applications running on FreeBSD. Right now, the large majority of them are commercial. But Xfree86 is being ported to Windows, so soon a freely available X-Server will be available for Windows systems.

By default, your X-Server will not allow remote applications to be displayed on your screen. There are a few common ways to allow this. The most common, but also the least secure, is by using xhost.

Using xhost to Allow Remote Applications to Be Displayed

xhost will allow remote applications running on a different system to be displayed locally on your system and take their input from your system. To see the current xhost configuration settings, type **xhost** with no arguments. Here is what the default xhost configuration will return:

```
bash$ xhost
access control enabled, only authorized clients can connect
bash$
```

In this case, only applications being run on remote systems that appear in this system's authorization list will be allowed to be displayed on this system. Also, the list is currently empty, meaning that no clients are currently authorized to send their display to this system.

If you want to be able to run remote applications on the host named lion, you need to add it to the authorization list. To do this, you use the following command:

```
bash$ xhost +lion
lion being added to access control list
bash$
```

If you type **xhost** now without any arguments, the system responds with this:

```
access control enabled, only authorized clients can connect
INET:lion.samplenet.org
```

The remote host lion can now display its X-Windows applications on the local system.

The problem with this setup is that anyone who has an account on lion can send the display to your system. This can be a major security problem in an environment with untrusted users. Therefore, it is not a good idea to use xhost in these environments. Other methods are available that are more secure. These are discussed briefly later in this chapter.

Also, if you do use xhost, it is probably a good idea to authorize a host only just before you need it and then remove the authorization as soon as you are done working with the remote application. To revoke authorization from a host, you can use a command like the following:

```
bash$ xhost -lion
lion being removed from access control list
bash$
```

The remote host lion can no longer display applications on this system.

There is also a way to completely disable access control in xhost so that any clients can connect to the system. This is probably never a good idea because it is a serious security hazard. But if for some reason you want to do it, you can use the following command:

```
bash$ xhost +
access control disabled, clients can connect from any host
bash$
```

To enable access control again, type **xhost -**. The system responds with this:

```
access control enabled, only authorized clients can connect
```

> **CAUTION**
>
> Because of the security hazards involved with xhost, at a minimum you will want to have a firewall configured that blocks unauthorized users from outside the internal network from accessing the ports that xhost uses. xhost uses ports 6000 through 6063. See the "Configuring a Firewall" section of Chapter 29, "Network Security," for more information on configuring a firewall.

After you have configured the system to allow a remote application to display on it, you need to connect to the remote system and start the application. You can do this through Telnet, SSH, or rlogin, if the remote system supports rlogin from your system.

> **TIP**
>
> If you are connecting to the remote system by using an X-Server running on Windows, make sure you use the Telnet or SSH application included with your X-Server software. Because the Windows Telnet application knows nothing about the X-Server, it does not work correctly for the procedures described in the following sections.

Starting a Remote Application

To start an application on the remote host and have it display its output on the local system, you need to set the DISPLAY environment variable on the remote host to your local system. You can do this from the Telnet, SSH, or rlogin session. In your connection window to the remote host, you can usually use something like the following to start a remote application and display it on your system (this example assumes that your local host is named simba):

```
bash$ DISPLAY=simba:0; export DISPLAY
bash$ xcalc &
```

This code is for a Bourne-style shell (that is, bourne, korn, or bash). If you are using a C shell (or tcsh), replace the first line with the following:

```
% setenv DISPLAY simba:0
```

This code should start an xcalc on the remote host and display the output on your screen.

The DISPLAY environment variable has the following syntax:

```
DISPLAY=hostname:display#:screen#
```

Here, *display#* is almost always set to 0, and you can usually eliminate *screen#* unless you are on a system that has multiple screens attached to it.

> **TIP**
>
> Make sure you enter the information in the Telnet or SSH window that is connected to the remote host. Entering the information on a local xterm window will not have the desired effect.

Other Client Access Controls

There are other ways to control which hosts can display applications on the local host. Some of these ways are more secure than using the xhost method described previously. The other methods and their configuration are beyond the scope of this book. However, you might want to read the man page for Xsecurity to get you started. (Note that this is case-sensitive when you try to access the man page.)

Using the xdm **Graphical Login Manager**

xdm is a graphical login manager for the X-Windows system. When it is run, at system startup, it displays a graphical login prompt rather than the text-based login prompt at the console. The graphical login prompt is similar to a Windows NT/2000 login screen.

If you want to use xdm, you should edit a file called .xsession in your home directory. This file is the xdm equivalent of the .xinitrc file that the console login uses. It should contain the command to start your desired window manager, as well as the commands to start any applications you want to run automatically at boot time. All the commands in the .xsession file should end with an ampersand (&) so they start in the background. The following is what a sample .xsession file could look like:

```
wmaker &
xterm &
```

This would start the WindowMaker window manager and also start an xterm automatically after login.

Note that unlike the .xinitrc file, the .xsession file needs to be executable; otherwise, it will not work.

There are a couple of ways you can have xdm start automatically at each system boot. The method discussed here is the safest, because it allows you to access a text-based login prompt on another virtual terminal if you accidentally mess up your X-Windows configuration and end up with xdm not working correctly. The safest way to start xdm at system boot is to create a file that looks similar to the following in /usr/local/etc/rc.d:

```
#!/bin/sh
case "$1" in
    start)
        echo "**************************************************"
        echo "* Starting the XDM login manager. Please wait... *"
        echo "**************************************************"
        xdm
        ;;
    *)
        : #do nothing
        ;;
esac
```

Make the file executable and reboot the system. xdm should start automatically on the next system boot.

xdm is very configurable, and details of its configuration are beyond the scope of this book. See the man page for information on the various configuration files available to configure xdm.

PART VI

Appendixes

IN THIS PART

Command Reference and Configuration File Reference

This appendix contains a reference of common FreeBSD commands. The commands in this appendix are divided into sections based on those related to files and directories, system administration, and so on. Each entry gives a short description of the command along with the chapter in which more information can be found. This appendix also contains a list of some of the common FreeBSD configuration files.

> **TIP**
>
> For more information on any of the commands listed here, refer to the manual page for that command. Manual pages can be accessed by typing **man** *command*, where *command* is the name of the command you would like more information on.

Command Switches and Options

Most of the commands given in this appendix can take options, also known as *switches*. To supply an option to a command, follow the command name with a dash and then the letter of the option. For example, to display a directory listing in long format, the option to use is -l. Therefore, the command looks like this:

```
ls -l
```

If the option you are supplying requires more than one character, you must use a double dash before the option. If you don't, the letter options will be treated as separate arguments.

Note that because letters are treated as separate arguments if preceded by a single dash, you can supply multiple options to a command without typing multiple dashes. For example, to list all the files in the directory (including hidden files) as well as list the directory in the long format, you could use the following command:

```
ls -al
```

File- and Directory-Manipulation Commands

Command	Action
cd *dirname*	Used to change to the directory *dirname*. If the path is not specified, *dirname* is assumed to be relative to the current path. (See Chapter 7, "Working with the Shell.")
ls	Lists the contents of the current directory. Popular options include -1 to list the attributes of each entry, -a to list hidden files, and -F to help differentiate different types of files. (See Chapter 7.)
cp *oldfile newfile*	Copies *oldfile* to *newfile*. If no directory path is specified for either file, they are both assumed to be in the current directory. Common options include -r, to recursively copy a directory, and -i, to perform an interactive copy that prevents the clobbering of existing files. (See Chapter 7.)
mv *oldfile newfile*	Moves *oldfile* to *newfile*. If no directory is specified for either file, they are both assumed to be in the current directory. Common options include --i, to perform an interactive copy that prevents the clobbering of existing files. This command is also used to rename files and directories. (See Chapter 7.)
rmdir *dirname*	Removes the directory *dirname*, assuming that it is empty. (See Chapter 7.)
touch *filename*	Updates the access time on *filename*. If the file does not already exist, it is created. (See Chapter 7.)
mkdir *dirname*	Creates the directory *dirname*. (See Chapter 7.)
ln *file1 file2*	Creates a link named *file2* that points to *file1*, much like a shortcut in Windows. (See Chapter 7.)
mount *filesystem mountpoint*	Mounts the filesystem represented by *filesystem* on the directory represented by *mountpoint* to make it available for use. (See Chapter 8, "The FreeBSD Filesystem.")
umount *mountpoint*	Unmounts the filesystem mounted on the directory *mountpoint*, making it unavailable for use. (See Chapter 8.)

Security-Related Commands

Command	Action
chmod [permissions] *filename*	Changes the access permissions on *filename*. (See Chapter 9, "Users, Groups, and Permissions.")
chown *username filename*	Changes the ownership of *filename* to the user *username*. (See Chapter 9.)
chgrp *groupname filename*	Changes the group ownership of *filename* to the group *groupname*. (See Chapter 9.)
passwd	Used to change a login password. The root user can specify a name after passwd to change the password of a particular user. (See Chapter 9.)
adduser	Runs a script that adds a new user to the system. (See Chapter 9.)
rmuser	Runs a script that removes a user from the system. That user will no longer be able to log in to the system. (See Chapter 9.)
vipw	Allows you to edit the /etc/master.passwd file directly, and it updates the database when exiting. (See Chapter 9.)

Common Shell Commands

Command	Action
grep [pattern] *filename*	Searches the file *filename* for the specified pattern. (See Chapter 7.)
more *filename*	Views the contents of *filename* one screen at a time. (See Chapter 7.)
less *filename*	Views the contents of *filename* one screen at a time. This command is like more, but less actually has more features than more. (See Chapter 7.)
cat *filename*	Displays the contents of *filename*. cat is normally used with redirection or pipes. (See Chapter 7.)
wc *filename*	Displays the number of words, lines, and characters in *filename*. (See Chapter 7.)
diff *file1 file2*	Compares the contents of *file1* with the contents of *file2* and then displays the differences between these files. (See Chapter 7.)
fmt *filename*	Places *filename* in a format suitable for e-mailing. Output is sent to STDOUT by default. (See Chapter 7.)
cut [option] *filename*	Displays only a particular column or field from *filename*. Output is sent to STDOUT by default. (See Chapter 7.)
head *filename*	Displays the first 10 lines of *filename*. (See Chapter 7.)
tail *filename*	Displays the last 10 lines of *filename*. (See Chapter 7.)
sort *filename*	Sorts the contents of *filename* into alphabetical order. Output is sent to STDOUT by default. (See Chapter 7.)
cal	Displays a calendar for the current month. (See man page for more info.)

A

Command	Action
`date`	Displays the current date and time. The root user can also use this command to change the date and time. (See man page for more info.)
`man` *command*	Displays the manual page for *command*. (See Chapter 7.)
`vi`	Invokes the `vi` text editor. If a filename is specified, that file will be opened. (See Chapter 6, "Working with Applications.")
`ee`	Invokes the FreeBSD Easy Editor. If a filename is specified, that file will be opened. (See Chapter 6.)

System Utilities and Maintenance-Related Commands

Command	Action
`ps`	Displays the list of processes running on the system. Common options include `-l` for a detailed list, `-a` for all processes, and `-x` to display daemon processes as well. (See Chapter 13, "Performance Monitoring, Process Control, and Job Automation.")
`top`	Displays a list of processes and their resource usage statistics that is updated on a regular basis. (See Chapter 13.)
`kill` *n*	In this command, *n* is the process ID number you wish to kill. Options are available to send different signals to the process. (See Chapter 13.)
`killall` *pname*	In this command, *pname* is the name of the process to kill. All processes that match and belong to you will be killed. Options are available to send different signals to each process. (See Chapter 13.)
`at`	Schedules a job or command to run at a specified time. (See Chapter 13.)
`crontab` *filename*	Schedules jobs or commands to run on a regular basis. *filename* is the name of the `crontab` file you want to edit. (See Chapter 13.)
`shutdown`	Shuts down or reboots the system. (See Chapter 4, "Your First Session with FreeBSD.")
`halt`	Halts the system. (See Chapter 4.)
`reboot`	Reboots the system. (See Chapter 4.)

Printer-Related Commands

Command	Action
`lpr`	Sends a job to the printer. (See Chapter 15, "Printing.")
`lprm` *n*	In this command, *n* is a job number. This removes the job from the printer. Other options allow removing jobs for a particular user, and so on. (See Chapter 15.)
`lpq`	Displays the list of jobs currently in the printer queue. (See Chapter 15.)
`lpc`	Controls the printer queues and the print daemons. (See Chapter 15.)

Software Installation and Removal Commands

Command	Action
pkg_info	Displays a list of packages installed on the system, along with a short description of each package. (See Chapter 14, "Installing Additional Software.")
pkg_add *packagename*	Installs the software package *packagename* onto the system. (See Chapter 14.)
pkg_delete *packagename*	Removes the software package *packagename* from the system. (See Chapter 14.)
make	When issued from a port directory, this command obtains the port files and builds the port. (See Chapter 14.)
make install	When issued from a port directory, this command installs the port if it has already been built. If not, the command obtains the necessary files and builds the port first. (See Chapter 14.)
make deinstall	When issued from a port directory, this command removes the installed port from the system. It will also remove any dependencies that are not required by some other installed port or package. (See Chapter 14.)
make clean	When issued from a port directory, this command removes the work files and object files created when building the port, reclaiming the hard disk space used by them. (See Chapter 14.)
make distclean	When issued from a port directory, this command removes the work files and object files created when building the port as well as the source distribution files that were obtained, reclaiming the hard disk space used by them. (See Chapter 14.)

NOTE

This does not actually uninstall the port, nor does it remove the original archive file that was downloaded.

Common Configuration Files

Command	Action
.profile	The configuration file for Bourne-style shells (sh, ksh, and bash). (See Chapter 11, "Customizing the Shell.")
.login	The configuration file for C-style shells (csh and tcsh). (See Chapter 11.)
.cshrc	Contains configuration options for C-style shells (csh, tcsh) that affect subshells as well as login shells. (See Chapter 11.)
.bashrc	Contains configuration options for the bash shell that affect subshells as well as login shells. (See Chapter 11.)
/etc/csh.login	Contains default global configuration options for C-style shells (csh and tcsh) that affect all users. (See Chapter 11.)

Command	Action
/etc/profile	Contains default global configuration options for Bourne-style shells (sh, ksh, and bash) that affect all users. (See Chapter 11.)
.forward	Controls e-mail forwarding. (See Chapter 24, "Configuring E-mail Services.")
.xinitrc	Controls X-Windows options. (See Chapter 35, "Advanced X-Windows Configuration.")
/etc/rc.conf	The main system configuration file that controls startup options for FreeBSD. (See Chapter 10, "System Configuration and Startup Scripts.")
/etc/X11/XF86Config	The main configuration file for the X-Windows system. (See Chapter 33, "File and Print Sharing with Microsoft Windows.")

> **NOTE**
>
> In versions of X-Windows prior to 4.*x*, this file is /etc/XF86Config.

Hardware Compatibility Lists

This appendix lists some of the hardware that FreeBSD is known to work with, as well as the video cards that are supported by the X-Windows system. Note that this list only applies to FreeBSD running on *x*86 (Intel and compatible) hardware. Also, it is not intended to be a comprehensive list of all supported hardware but rather a general guide so that you can determine whether at least most of your system is compatible with FreeBSD before you install it. A comprehensive hardware compatibility list can be found on the FreeBSD Web site at www.freebsd.org. The list on the Web site can also be expected to be more up to date than this one.

System Requirements

Minimum requirements:

- Intel 386SX or compatible CPU
- 4MB of RAM

My recommended minimum configuration:

- Intel 486DX2/66 or compatible CPU.
- 32MB of RAM.
- At least 1GB of free disk space for a full install (with X-Windows), in which third-party applications will be added on a workstation. Servers may require much more space, depending on the number of users and the services the server is providing.

In addition, if you plan to run the X-Windows system, I recommend the following additional minimum system configuration:

- Monitor that can provide 1024×768 resolution (comfortably)
- Supported SVGA video card (see video card list) with at least 1MB of video RAM
- At least 64MB of RAM
- Three-button mouse

Supported Hardware

The following hardware is known to work with FreeBSD.

Disk Controllers (Non-SCSI)

Any generic MFM or RLL (WD1003)

Any generic IDE (WD1007)

ATA controllers

FreeBSD supports UDMA mode on EIDE controllers that can use it.

Disk Controllers (SCSI)

Note that some SCSI controllers (such as the SoundBlaster SCSI controllers) use a chipset from another manufacturer, such as Adaptec. If you don't find your actual card listed here, check to see what chipset it uses. In some cases, the chipset will be in the following list.

Adaptec:

174X series EISA SCSI controllers in standard and enhanced mode

274X/284X/2920C/294X/2950/3940/3950 (Narrow/Wide/Twin) series EISA/VLB/PCI SCSI controllers

AIC-7850, AIC-7860, AIC-7880, AIC-789X onboard SCSI controllers

1510 series ISA SCSI controllers (not for bootable devices)

152X series ISA SCSI controllers

AIC-6260- and AIC-6360-based boards, which include the AHA-152X and SoundBlaster SCSI cards

AdvanSys:

All AdvanSys SCSI controllers are supported.

AMI:

Any AMI FastDisk disk controller that is a true BusLogic MultiMaster clone

BusLogic:

MultiMaster "W" series host adapters, including BT-948, BT-958, and BT-9580

MultiMaster "C" series host adapters, including BT-946C, BT-956C, BT-956CD, BT-445C, BT-747C, BT-757C, BT-757CD, BT-545C, and BT-540CF

MultiMaster "S" series host adapters, including BT-445S, BT-747S, BT-747D, BT-757S, BT-757D, BT-545S, BT-542D, BT-742A, and BT-542B

MultiMaster "A" series host adapters, including BT-742A and BT-542B

Compaq:

Intelligent disk array controllers: IDA, IDA-2, IAES, SMART, SMART-2/E, Smart-2/P, SMART-2SL; Integrated Array; and Smart Arrays 3200, 3100ES, 221, 4200, 4200, and 4250ES

DPT:

SmartCACHE Plus, SmartCACHE III, SmartRAID III, SmartCACHE IV, and SmartRAID IV SCSI/RAID are supported. The DPT SmartRAID/CACHE V is not yet supported. The DPT PM3754U2-16M SCSI RAID controller is also supported.

DTC:

EISA SCSI controller in 1542 evaluation mode

SymBios (also NCR):

53C810, 53C810a, 53C815, 53C820, 53C825a, 53C860, 53C875, 53C875j, 53C885, and 53C896 PCI SCSI controllers, including ASUS SC-200; Data Technology DTC3130 (all variants); Diamond FirePort (all); NCR cards (all); SymBios cards (all); Tekram DC390W, 390U, and 390F; and Tyan S1365

QLogic:

1020, 1040, 1040B, and 2100 SCSI and fiber

B

> **NOTE**
>
> FreeBSD supports SCSI-I and SCSI-II devices. However, CD-RW and WORM devices are supported only in read-only mode by the driver included with FreeBSD. To get write access to these devices, install cdrecord from the FreeBSD ports tree.

CD-ROM Drives

Any ATAPI-compliant drive

SCSI-based drives

Matsushita/Panasonic (Creative Labs SoundBlaster) proprietary drives (562/563 models)

All Sony proprietary drives

Network Cards

This section lists the network cards supported by FreeBSD. Note that many generic cards, as well as many built-in network adapters, will use one of these chipsets. Therefore, if you don't find your specific card mentioned here, see if you can find out what chipset it uses. For example, many generic network cards have an NE 2000 compatible chipset, and many built-in adapters use the Intel EtherExpress chipset—both of which are supported by FreeBSD.

Adaptec:

Duralink PCI Fast Ethernet adapters based on the Adaptec AIC-6195 Fast Ethernet controller chip, including the following:

- ANA-62011 64-bit single-port 10/100BaseTX adapter

- ANA-62022 64-bit dual-port 10/100BaseTX adapter

- ANA-62044 64-bit quad-port 10/100BaseTX adapter

- ANA-69011 32-bit single-port 10/100BaseTX adapter

- ANA-62020 64-bit single-port 100BaseFX adapter

Allied-Telesyn:

AT1700 and RE2000

Alteon Networks:

Alteon Networks PCI Gigabit Ethernet NICs based on the Tigon 1 and Tigon 2 chipsets, including Alteon AceNIC (Tigon 1 and 2), 3Com 3c985-SX (Tigon 1 and 2), Netgear GA620 (Tigon 2), Silicon Graphics Gigabit Ethernet, DEC/Compaq EtherWORKS 1000, and NEC Gigabit Ethernet

AMD:

PCnet/PCI (79c970 and 53c974 or 79c974)

RealTek:

8129/8139 Fast Ethernet NICs, including the following:

- Allied-Telesyn AT2550
- Allied-Telesyn AT2500TX
- Genius GF100TXR (RTL8139)
- NDC Communications NE100TX-E
- OvisLink LEF-8129TX
- OvisLink LEF-8139TX
- Netronix Inc. EA-1210 NetEther 10/100
- KTX-9130TX 10/100 Fast Ethernet
- Accton "Cheetah" EN1207D (MPX 5030/5038; RealTek 8139 clone)
- SMC EZ Card 10/100 PCI 1211-TX

Lite-On:

98713, 98713A, 98715, and 98725 Fast Ethernet NICs, including the following:

- LinkSys EtherFast LNE100TX
- NetGear FA310-TX Rev. D1
- Matrox FastNIC 10/100
- Kingston KNE110TX

Macronix:

98713, 98713A, 98715, 98715A, and 98725 Fast Ethernet NICs, including the following:

- NDC Communications SFA100A (98713A)
- CNet Pro120A (98713 or 98713A)
- CNet Pro120B (98715)
- SVEC PN102TX (98713)

Macronix/Lite-On:

PNIC II LC82C115 Fast Ethernet NICs, including the LinkSys EtherFast LNE100TX, version 2

B

Winbond:

W89C840F Fast Ethernet NICs, including the Trendware TE100-PCIE

Via Technologies:

VT3043 "Rhine I" and VT86C100A "Rhine II" Fast Ethernet NICs, including the Hawking Technologies PN102TX and D-Link DFE-530TX

Silicon Integrated Systems:

SiS 900 and SiS 7016 PCI Fast Ethernet NICs

Sundance Technologies:

ST201 PCI Fast Ethernet NICs, including the D-Link DFE-550TX

SysKonnect:

SK-984x PCI Gigabit Ethernet cards, including the following:

- SK-9841 1000BaseLX (single-mode fiber, single port)

- SK-9842 1000BaseSX (multimode fiber, single port)

- SK-9843 1000BaseLX (single-mode fiber, dual port)

- SK-9844 1000BaseSX (multimode fiber, dual port)

Texas Instruments:

ThunderLAN PCI NICs, including the following:

- Compaq Netelligent 10, 10/100, 10/100 Proliant, 10/100 Dual-Port, 10/100 TX Embedded UTP, 10 T PCI UTP/Coax, and 10/100 TX UTP

- Compaq NetFlex 3P, 3P Integrated, and 3P with BNC

- Olicom OC-2135/2138, OC-2325, and OC-2326 10/100 TX UTP

- Racore 8165 10/100BaseTX and 8148 10BaseT/100BaseTX/100BaseFX multi-personality cards

ADMTek:

AL981-based and AN985-based PCI Fast Ethernet NICs

ASIX Electronics:

AX88140A PCI NICs, including the Alfa Inc. GFC2204 and CNet Pro110B

DEC:

EtherWORKS III NICs (DE203, DE204, and DE205)

EtherWORKS II NICs (DE200, DE201, DE202, and DE422)

DC21040-, DC21041-, or DC21140-based NICs (SMC Etherpower 8432T, DE245, and so on)

FDDI (DEFPA/DEFEA) NICs

Efficient:

ENI-155p ATM PCI

FORE:

PCA-200E ATM PCI

Fujitsu:

MB86960A/MB86965A

HP:

PC Lan+ cards (model numbers 27247B and 27252A)

Intel:

EtherExpress ISA (not recommended due to driver instability)

EtherExpress Pro/10

EtherExpress Pro/100B PCI Fast Ethernet

Isolan:

AT 4141-0 (16 bit)

Isolink:

4110 (8 bit)

Novell:

NE1000, NE2000, and NE2100

PCI network cards emulating the NE2000, including the following:

- RealTek 8029
- NetVin 5000
- Winbond W89C940
- Surecom NE-34
- VIA VT86C926

B

3Com:

3C501

3C503 Etherlink II

3C505 Etherlink/+

3C507 Etherlink 16/TP

3C509

3C579

3C589 (PCMCIA)

3C590/592/595/900/905/905B/905C PCI and EISA (Fast) Etherlink III/(Fast) Etherlink XL

3C980/3C980B Fast Etherlink XL server adapter

3CSOHO100-TX OfficeConnect adapter

Toshiba:

All Toshiba Ethernet cards

PCMCIA cards:

PCMCIA Ethernet cards from IBM and National Semiconductor

USB Devices

USB keyboards

USB mice

USB printers and USB-to–parallel printer conversion cables

USB hubs

Sound Devices

16550 UART (Midi). (Experimental; needs a trick in the hints file.)

Advance Asound 100, 110, and Logic ALS120.

Aureal Vortex1/Vortex2 and Vortex Advantage–based sound cards by a third-party driver.

Creative Labs SB16, SB32, SB AWE64 (including Gold), Vibra16, SB PCI (experimental), SB Live! (experimental), and most SoundBlaster-compatible cards.

Creative Labs SB Midi Port (experimental) and SB OPL3 Synthesizer (experimental).

Crystal Semiconductor CS461x/462x Audio Accelerator. (The support for the CS461x Midi port is experimental.)

Crystal Semiconductor CS428x audio controller.

CS4237, CS4236, CS4232, and CS4231 (ISA).

ENSONIQ AudioPCI ES1370/1371.

ESS ES1868, ES1869, ES1879, and ES1888.

Gravis UltraSound PnP and MAX.

NeoMagic 256AV/ZX (PCI).

OPTi931 (ISA).

OSS-compatible sequencer (Midi). (Experimental.)

Trident 4DWave DX/NX (PCI).

Yamaha OPL-SAx (ISA).

Miscellaneous Devices

AST 4-Port serial card using shared IRQ.

ARNET 8-Port serial card using shared IRQ.

ARNET (now Digiboard) Sync 570/i high-speed serial.

Boca BB1004 4-Port serial card (modems *not* supported).

Boca IOAT66 6-Port serial card (modems supported).

Boca BB1008 8-Port serial card (modems *not* supported).

Boca BB2016 16-Port serial card (modems supported).

Cyclades Cyclom-y serial board.

Moxa SmartIO CI-104J 4-Port serial card.

STB 4-Port card using shared IRQ.

SDL Communications RISCom/8 serial board.

SDL Communications RISCom/N2 and N2pci high-speed sync serial boards.

Specialix SI/XIO/SX multiport serial cards, with both the older SIHOST2.x and the new "enhanced" (transputer-based, a.k.a. JET) host cards. ISA, EISA, and PCI are supported.

Stallion multiport serial boards: EasyIO, EasyConnection 8/32 & 8/64, ONboard 4/16, and Brumby.

Connectix QuickCam.

Matrox Meteor Video frame grabber.

Creative Labs Video Spigot frame grabber.

Cortex1 frame grabber.

Various frame grabbers based on the Brooktree Bt848 and Bt878 chips.

HP4020, HP6020, Philips CDD2000/CDD2660, and Plasmon CD-R drives.

Bus mice.

PS/2 mice.

Standard PC joystick.

X-10 power controllers.

GPIB and transputer drives.

Genius and Mustek hand scanners.

Floppy tape drives (some rather old models only; driver is rather stale).

Lucent Technologies WaveLAN/IEEE 802.11 PCMCIA and ISA standard speed (2Mbps) and turbo-speed (6Mbps) wireless network adapters and workalikes (NCR WaveLAN/IEEE 802.11 and Cabletron RoamAbout 802.11 DS).

Video Cards Supported by X-Windows

The following is a list of the video cards that XFree86 currently supports. The list was taken from the XFree86 Project's Web site. If you cannot find an exact match for your card, see if you can find out what chipset your card uses and find a match there.

2 the Max MAXColor S3 Trio64V+

3DLabs Oxygen GMX

928Movie

AGX (generic)

ALG-5434(E)

ASUS 3Dexplorer

ASUS PCI-AV264CT

ASUS PCI-V264CT

ASUS Video Magic PCI V864

ASUS Video Magic PCI VT64

AT25

AT3D

ATI 3D Pro Turbo

ATI 3D Pro Turbo PC2TV

ATI 3D Xpression

ATI 3D Xpression+

ATI 3D Xpression+ PC2TV

ATI 8514 Ultra (no VGA)

ATI All-in-Wonder

ATI All-in-Wonder Pro

ATI Graphics Pro Turbo

ATI Graphics Pro Turbo 1600

ATI Graphics Pro Turbo with AT&T 20C408 RAMDAC

ATI Graphics Pro Turbo with ATI68860 RAMDAC

ATI Graphics Pro Turbo with ATI68860B RAMDAC

ATI Graphics Pro Turbo with ATI68860C RAMDAC

ATI Graphics Pro Turbo with ATI68875 RAMDAC

ATI Graphics Pro Turbo with CH8398 RAMDAC

ATI Graphics Pro Turbo with STG1702 RAMDAC

ATI Graphics Pro Turbo with STG1703 RAMDAC

ATI Graphics Pro Turbo with TLC34075 RAMDAC

ATI Graphics Ultra

ATI Graphics Ultra Pro

ATI Graphics Xpression

ATI Graphics Xpression with ATI68860 RAMDAC

ATI Graphics Xpression with ATI68860B RAMDAC

ATI Graphics Xpression with ATI68860C RAMDAC

ATI Graphics Xpression with ATI68875 RAMDAC

ATI Graphics Xpression with AT&T 20C408 RAMDAC

ATI Graphics Xpression with CH8398 RAMDAC

ATI Graphics Xpression with Mach64 CT (264CT)

ATI Graphics Xpression with STG1702 RAMDAC

ATI Graphics Xpression with STG1703 RAMDAC

ATI Graphics Xpression with TLC34075 RAMDAC

ATI Mach32

ATI Mach64

ATI Mach64 3D RAGE II

ATI Mach64 3D RAGE II+DVD

ATI Mach64 3D Rage IIC

ATI Mach64 3D Rage Pro

ATI Mach64 CT (264CT), internal RAMDAC

ATI Mach64 GT (264GT), a.k.a. 3D RAGE, internal RAMDAC

ATI Mach64 VT (264VT), internal RAMDAC

ATI Mach64 with AT&T 20C408 RAMDAC

ATI Mach64 with ATI68860 RAMDAC

ATI Mach64 with ATI68860B RAMDAC

ATI Mach64 with ATI68860C RAMDAC

ATI Mach64 with ATI68875 RAMDAC

ATI Mach64 with CH8398 RAMDAC

ATI Mach64 with IBM RGB514 RAMDAC

ATI Mach64 with internal RAMDAC

ATI Mach64 with STG1702 RAMDAC

ATI Mach64 with STG1703 RAMDAC

ATI Mach64 with TLC34075 RAMDAC

ATI Pro Turbo+PC2TV, 3D Rage II+DVD

ATI Ultra Plus

ATI Video Xpression

ATI Video Xpression+

ATI WinBoost

ATI WinBoost with AT&T 20C408 RAMDAC

ATI WinBoost with ATI68860 RAMDAC

ATI WinBoost with ATI68860B RAMDAC

ATI WinBoost with ATI68860C RAMDAC

ATI WinBoost with ATI68875 RAMDAC

ATI WinBoost with CH8398 RAMDAC

ATI WinBoost with Mach64 CT (264CT)

ATI WinBoost with STG1702 RAMDAC

ATI WinBoost with STG1703 RAMDAC

ATI WinBoost with TLC34075 RAMDAC

ATI WinCharger

ATI WinCharger with AT&T 20C408 RAMDAC

ATI WinCharger with ATI68860 RAMDAC

ATI WinCharger with ATI68860B RAMDAC

ATI WinCharger with ATI68860C RAMDAC

ATI WinCharger with ATI68875 RAMDAC

ATI WinCharger with CH8398 RAMDAC

ATI WinCharger with Mach64 CT (264CT)

ATI WinCharger with STG1702 RAMDAC

ATI WinCharger with STG1703 RAMDAC

ATI WinCharger with TLC34075 RAMDAC

ATI WinTurbo

ATI WinTurbo with AT&T 20C408 RAMDAC

ATI WinTurbo with ATI68860 RAMDAC

ATI WinTurbo with ATI68860B RAMDAC

ATI WinTurbo with ATI68860C RAMDAC

ATI WinTurbo with ATI68875 RAMDAC

ATI WinTurbo with CH8398 RAMDAC

ATI WinTurbo with Mach64 CT (264CT)

B

ATI WinTurbo with STG1702 RAMDAC

ATI WinTurbo with STG1703 RAMDAC

ATI WinTurbo with TLC34075 RAMDAC

ATI Wonder SVGA

ATI Xpert 98

ATI Xpert XL

ATI Xpert@Play PCI and AGP, 3D Rage Pro

ATI Xpert@Play 98

ATI Xpert@Work, 3D Rage Pro

ATI integrated on Intel Maui MU440EX motherboard

ATrend ATC-2165A

AccelStar Permedia II AGP

Actix GE32+ 2MB

Actix GE32i

Actix GE64

Actix ProStar

Actix ProStar 64

Actix Ultra

Acumos AVGA3

Alliance ProMotion 6422

Ark Logic ARK1000PV (generic)

Ark Logic ARK1000VL (generic)

Ark Logic ARK2000MT (generic)

Ark Logic ARK2000PV (generic)

Avance Logic 2101

Avance Logic 2228

Avance Logic 2301

Avance Logic 2302

Avance Logic 2308

Avance Logic 2401

Binar Graphics AnyView

Boca Vortex (Sierra RAMDAC)

COMPAQ Armada 7380DMT

COMPAQ Armada 7730MT

California Graphics SunTracer 6000

Canopus Co

Canopus Total-3D

Cardex Challenger (Pro)

Cardex Cobra

Cardex Trio64

Cardex Trio64Pro

Chips & Technologies CT64200

Chips & Technologies CT64300

Chips & Technologies CT65520

Chips & Technologies CT65525

Chips & Technologies CT65530

Chips & Technologies CT65535

Chips & Technologies CT65540

Chips & Technologies CT65545

Chips & Technologies CT65546

Chips & Technologies CT65548

Chips & Technologies CT65550

Chips & Technologies CT65554

Chips & Technologies CT65555

Chips & Technologies CT68554

Chips & Technologies CT69000

Cirrus Logic GD542x

Cirrus Logic GD543x

Cirrus Logic GD5446 (no-name card) 1MB upgrade

Cirrus Logic GD544x

Cirrus Logic GD5462

Cirrus Logic GD5464

Cirrus Logic GD5465

Cirrus Logic GD5480

Cirrus Logic GD62xx (laptop)

Cirrus Logic GD64xx (laptop)

Cirrus Logic GD754x (laptop)

Colorgraphic Dual Lightning

Creative Blaster Exxtreme

Creative Labs 3D Blaster PCI (Verite 1000)

Creative Labs Graphics Blaster 3D

Creative Labs Graphics Blaster Eclipse (OEM Model CT6510) XF86_SVGA

Creative Labs Graphics Blaster MA201

Creative Labs Graphics Blaster MA202

Creative Labs Graphics Blaster MA302

Creative Labs Graphics Blaster MA334

DFI-WG1000

DFI-WG5000

DFI-WG6000

DSV3325

DSV3326

DataExpert DSV3325

DataExpert DSV3365

Dell S3 805

Dell onboard ET4000

Diamond Edge 3D

Diamond Fire GL 1000

Diamond Fire GL 1000 PRO

Diamond Fire GL 3000

Diamond Multimedia Stealth 3D 2000

Diamond Multimedia Stealth 3D 2000 PRO

Diamond SpeedStar (Plus)

Diamond SpeedStar 24

Diamond SpeedStar 24X (not fully supported)

Diamond SpeedStar 64

Diamond SpeedStar A50

Diamond SpeedStar HiColor

Diamond SpeedStar Pro (not SE)

Diamond SpeedStar Pro 1100

Diamond SpeedStar Pro SE (CL-GD5430/5434)

Diamond SpeedStar64 Graphics 2000/2200

Diamond Stealth 24

Diamond Stealth 32

Diamond Stealth 3D 2000

Diamond Stealth 3D 2000 PRO

Diamond Stealth 3D 3000

Diamond Stealth 3D 4000

Diamond Stealth 64 DRAM SE

Diamond Stealth 64 DRAM with S3 SDAC

Diamond Stealth 64 DRAM with S3 Trio64

Diamond Stealth 64 VRAM

Diamond Stealth 64 Video VRAM (TI RAMDAC)

Diamond Stealth II S220

Diamond Stealth Pro

Diamond Stealth VRAM

Diamond Stealth Video 2500

B

Diamond Stealth Video DRAM

Diamond Stealth64 Graphics 2001 series

Diamond Stealth64 Graphics 2xx0 series (864 + SDAC)

Diamond Stealth64 Graphics 2xx0 series (Trio64)

Diamond Stealth64 Video 2001 series (2121/2201)

Diamond Stealth64 Video 2120/2200

Diamond Stealth64 Video 3200

Diamond Stealth64 Video 3240/3400 (IBM RAMDAC)

Diamond Stealth64 Video 3240/3400 (TI RAMDAC)

Diamond Viper 330

Diamond Viper 550

Diamond Viper PCI 2MB

Diamond Viper Pro Video

Diamond Viper VLB 2MB

Digital 24-plane TGA (ZLXp-E2)

Digital 24-plane+3D TGA (ZLXp-E3)

Digital 8-plane TGA (UDB/Multia)

Digital 8-plane TGA (ZLXp-E1)

EIZO (VRAM)

ELSA ERAZOR II

ELSA GLoria Synergy

ELSA GLoria-L

ELSA GLoria-L/MX

ELSA GLoria-S

ELSA GLoria-XL

ELSA GLoria-4

ELSA GLoria-8

ELSA Victory Erazor

ELSA Victory 3D

ELSA Victory 3DX

ELSA Winner 1000/T2D

ELSA Winner 1000 R3D

ELSA Winner 1000AVI (AT&T 20C409 version)

ELSA Winner 1000AVI (SDAC version)

ELSA Winner 1000ISA

ELSA Winner 1000PRO with S3 SDAC

ELSA Winner 1000PRO with STG1700 or AT&T RAMDAC

ELSA Winner 1000PRO/X

ELSA Winner 1000TRIO

ELSA Winner 1000TRIO/V

ELSA Winner 1000TwinBus

ELSA Winner 1000VL

ELSA Winner 2000

ELSA Winner 2000/Office

ELSA Winner 2000AVI

ELSA Winner 2000AVI/3D

ELSA Winner 2000PRO-2

ELSA Winner 2000PRO-4

ELSA Winner 2000PRO/X-2

ELSA Winner 2000PRO/X-4

ELSA Winner 2000PRO/X-8

ELSA Winner 3000

ELSA Winner 3000-L-42

ELSA Winner 3000-M-22

ELSA Winner 3000-S

EPSON CardPC (onboard)

ET3000 (generic)

ET4000 (generic)

ET4000 W32i and W32p (generic)

ET4000/W32 (generic)

ET6000 (generic)

ET6100 (generic)

ExpertColor DSV3325

ExpertColor DSV3365

Generic VGA compatible

Genoa 5400

Genoa 8500VL(-28)

Genoa 8900 Phantom 32i

Genoa Phantom 64i with S3 SDAC

Genoa VideoBlitz III AV

Hercules Dynamite

Hercules Dynamite 128/Video

Hercules Dynamite Power

Hercules Dynamite Pro

Hercules Graphite HG210

Hercules Graphite Power

Hercules Graphite Pro

Hercules Graphite Terminator 64

Hercules Graphite Terminator 64/DRAM

Hercules Graphite Terminator Pro 64

Hercules Stingray

Hercules Stingray 128 3D

Hercules Stingray 64/V with ICS5342

Hercules Stingray 64/V with ZoomDAC

Hercules Stingray Pro

Hercules Stingray Pro/V

Hercules Terminator 3D/DX

Hercules Terminator 64/3D

Hercules Terminator 64/Video

Hercules Thriller3D

Integral FlashPoint

Intel 5430

Interay PMC Viper

JAX 8241

Jaton Video-58P

Jaton Video-70P

Jazz Multimedia G-Force 128

LeadTek WinFast 3D S600

LeadTek WinFast 3D S680

LeadTek WinFast S200

LeadTek WinFast S430

LeadTek WinFast S510

LeadTek WinFast 2300

MELCO WGP-VG4S

MELCO WGP-VX8

MSI MS-4417

Matrox Comet

Matrox Marvel II

Matrox Millennium 2/4/8MB

Matrox Millennium (MGA)

Matrox Millennium G200 4/8/16MB

Matrox Millennium G200 SD 4/8/16MB

Matrox Millennium II 4/8/16MB

Matrox Millennium II AGP

Matrox Mystique

Matrox Mystique G200 4/8/16MB

B

Matrox Productiva G100 4/8MB

MediaGX

MediaVision Proaxcel 128

Mirage Z-128

Miro Crystal 10SD with GenDAC

Miro Crystal 12SD

Miro Crystal 16S

Miro Crystal 20SD PCI with S3 SDAC

Miro Crystal 20SD VLB with S3 SDAC (BIOS 3)

Miro Crystal 20SD with ICD2061A (BIOS 2)

Miro Crystal 20SD with ICS2494 (BIOS 1)

Miro Crystal 20SV

Miro Crystal 22SD

Miro Crystal 40SV

Miro Crystal 80SV

Miro Crystal 8S

Miro Crystal DVD

Miro miroCRYSTAL VRX

Miro miroMedia 3D

Miro miroVideo 20TD

Miro Video 20SV

Neomagic

Number Nine FX Motion 331

Number Nine FX Motion 332

Number Nine FX Motion 531

Number Nine FX Motion 771

Number Nine FX Vision 330

Number Nine GXE Level 10/11/12

Number Nine GXE Level 14/16

Number Nine GXE64

Number Nine GXE64 Pro

Number Nine GXE64 with S3 Trio64

Number Nine Imagine I-128 (2–8MB)

Number Nine Imagine I-128 Series 2 (2–4MB)

Number Nine Imagine-128-T2R

Number Nine Revolution 3D AGP (4–8MB SGRAM)

Number Nine Visual 9FX Reality 332

Oak 87 ISA (generic)

Oak 87 VLB (generic)

Oak ISA card (generic)

Ocean (Octek) VL-VGA-1000

Octek AVGA-20

Octek Combo-26

Octek Combo-28

Octek VL-VGA-26

Octek VL-VGA-28

Orchid Celsius (AT&T RAMDAC)

Orchid Celsius (Sierra RAMDAC)

Orchid Fahrenheit 1280

Orchid Fahrenheit VA

Orchid Fahrenheit-1280+

Orchid Kelvin 64

Orchid Kelvin 64 VLB Rev A

Orchid Kelvin 64 VLB Rev B

Orchid P9000 VLB

Orchid Technology Fahrenheit Video 3D

PC-Chips M567 mainboard

Paradise Accelerator Value

B

Paradise/WD 90CXX

PixelView Combo TV 3D AGP (Prolink)

PixelView Combo TV Pro (Prolink)

RIVA TNT

RIVA128

Rendition Verite 1000

Rendition Verite 2x00

Revolution 3D (T2R)

S3 801/805 (generic)

S3 801/805 with ATT20c490 RAMDAC

S3 801/805 with ATT20c490 RAMDAC and ICD2061A

S3 801/805 with Chrontel 8391

S3 801/805 with S3 GenDAC

S3 801/805 with SC1148{2,3,4} RAMDAC

S3 801/805 with SC1148{5,7,9} RAMDAC

S3 864 (generic)

S3 864 with ATT 20C498 or 21C498

S3 864 with SDAC (86C716)

S3 864 with STG1703

S3 868 (generic)

S3 868 with ATT 20C409

S3 868 with ATT 20C498 or 21C498

S3 868 with SDAC (86C716)

S3 86C260 (generic)

S3 86C280 (generic)

S3 86C325 (generic)

S3 86C357 (generic)

S3 86C365 (Trio3D)

S3 86C375 (generic)

S3 86C385 (generic)

S3 86C391 (Savage3D)

S3 86C764 (generic)

S3 86C765 (generic)

S3 86C775 (generic)

S3 86C785 (generic)

S3 86C801 (generic)

S3 86C805 (generic)

S3 86C864 (generic)

S3 86C868 (generic)

S3 86C911 (generic)

S3 86C924 (generic)

S3 86C928 (generic)

S3 86C964 (generic)

S3 86C968 (generic)

S3 86C988 (generic)

S3 86CM65

S3 911/924 (generic)

S3 924 with SC1148 DAC

S3 928 (generic)

S3 964 (generic)

S3 968 (generic)

S3 Aurora64V+ (generic)

S3 Savage3D

S3 Trio32 (generic)

S3 Trio3D

S3 Trio64 (generic)

S3 Trio64V+ (generic)

S3 Trio64V2 (generic)

B

S3 Trio64V2/DX (generic)

S3 Trio64V2/GX (generic)

S3 ViRGE (generic)

S3 ViRGE (old S3V server)

S3 ViRGE/DX (generic)

S3 ViRGE/GX (generic)

S3 ViRGE/GX2 (generic)

S3 ViRGE/MX (generic)

S3 ViRGE/MX+ (generic)

S3 ViRGE/VX (generic)

S3 Vision864 (generic)

S3 Vision868 (generic)

S3 Vision964 (generic)

S3 Vision968 (generic)

Sharp 9080

Sharp 9090

SNI PC5H W32

SNI Scenic W32

SPEA Mercury 64

SPEA Mirage

SPEA/V7 Mercury

SPEA/V7 Mirage P64

SPEA/V7 Mirage P64 with S3 Trio64

SPEA/V7 Mirage VEGA Plus

SPEA/V7 ShowTime Plus

STB Horizon

STB Horizon Video

STB LightSpeed

STB LightSpeed 128

STB MVP-2

STB MVP-2 PCI

STB MVP-2X

STB MVP-4 PCI

STB MVP-4X

STB Nitro (64)

STB Nitro 3D

STB Nitro 64 Video

STB Pegasus

STB Powergraph 64

STB Powergraph 64 Video

STB Powergraph X-24

STB Systems Powergraph 3D

STB Systems Velocity 3D

STB Velocity 128

STB Velocity 64 Video

STB NVIDIA 128

SiS 3D PRO AGP

SiS 5597

SiS 5598

SiS 6326

SiS SG86C201

SiS SG86C205

SiS SG86C215

SiS SG86C225

Sierra Screaming 3D

Sigma Concorde

Sigma Legend

Spider Black Widow

B

Spider Black Widow Plus

Spider Tarantula 64

Spider VLB Plus

TechWorks Thunderbolt

TechWorks Ultimate 3D

Toshiba Tecra 540CDT

Toshiba Tecra 550CDT

Toshiba Tecra 750CDT

Toshiba Tecra 750DVD

Trident 3DImage975 (generic)

Trident 3DImage975 AGP (generic)

Trident 3DImage985 (generic)

Trident 8900/9000 (generic)

Trident 8900D (generic)

Trident Cyber 9382 (generic)

Trident Cyber 9385 (generic)

Trident Cyber 9388 (generic)

Trident Cyber 9397 (generic)

Trident TGUI9400CXi (generic)

Trident TGUI9420DGi (generic)

Trident TGUI9430DGi (generic)

Trident TGUI9440 (generic)

Trident TGUI9660 (generic)

Trident TGUI9680 (generic)

Trident TGUI9682 (generic)

Trident TGUI9685 (generic)

Trident TVGA 8800BR

Trident TVGA 8800CS

Trident TVGA9200CXr (generic)

Unsupported VGA compatible

VI720

VL-41

VidTech FastMax P20

VideoLogic GrafixStar 300

VideoLogic GrafixStar 400

VideoLogic GrafixStar 500

VideoLogic GrafixStar 550

VideoLogic GrafixStar 560 (PCI/AGP)

VideoLogic GrafixStar 600

VideoLogic GrafixStar 700

ViewTop PCI

WD 90C24 (laptop)

WD 90C24A or 90C24A2 (laptop)

Weitek P9100 (generic)

WinFast 3D S600

WinFast 3D S600

WinFast S200

WinFast S430

WinFast S510

XGA-1 (ISA bus)

XGA-2 (ISA bus)

B

APPENDIX C

Troubleshooting Installation and Boot Problems

> **NOTE**
>
> This appendix is not a complete list of all the problems you could potentially encounter. Instead, it is designed to list the most common ones. Further information on troubleshooting problems can be found on the FreeBSD Web site at www.freebsd.org. The online handbook contains troubleshooting information for many common problems. If the handbook doesn't provide a solution, you can also post a detailed description of the problem to the FreeBSD Questions mailing list. More information on the FreeBSD mailing lists can be found in Appendix D, "Sources for More Information."

The first step toward resolving an installation or booting problem in FreeBSD is tracking down the problem's source. This appendix is designed to help you identify and solve some of the most common installation and booting problems. The first section covers installation problems, and the second section explains how to diagnose and resolve booting problems.

Installation Problems

This section of the appendix covers problems you might encounter following the installation of FreeBSD and possible solutions to these problems.

Booting from Floppy Causes System to Hang or Reboot

A few things can cause a system to hang or reboot when booting from a floppy, but a bad floppy is the most likely cause. Remember that the boot image is written to the floppy without checking the format and that the entire floppy is used. Even a single bad block on the floppy can cause problems. Try writing the boot disk to a new floppy and see if it fixes the problem.

If using a new floppy does not fix the problem, make sure you used binary mode and not ASCII mode to transfer the floppy in your FTP client.

Virus protection on the motherboard is another possible cause of this problem. You can disable this protection in the system's BIOS setup utility. Please refer to your system documentation for information on how to disable the virus protection on your motherboard.

Finally, make sure you created the floppy from DOS mode, not from a DOS prompt in Windows. The latter has been known to cause boot problems on occasion.

Boot Floppy Hangs at "Probing Devices"

The boot floppy sometimes gets confused by IDE Zip and Jaz drives. If you have one of these drives, try removing it and see if the system will boot. If it does, you can install FreeBSD and then reconnect the drive after the installation is complete.

System Boots from CD, but Installer Shows That CD-ROM Was Not Found

This problem is probably caused by an improperly configured CD-ROM drive. Some systems ship with the CD-ROM drive as a slave drive on the secondary controller and have no master drive on the secondary controller. To fix this, you will need to change your CD-ROM drive to the master if it is on the secondary controller. This can usually be done via a jumper on the back of the CD-ROM drive (you will need to go inside your case). When your system first starts up, it may display a list of disks it found, including CD-ROM drives, as well as information about whether they are configured as master or slave disks.

Hard Disk Geometry Is Not Detected Properly

If FreeBSD cannot detect your hard disk geometry correctly, there are two ways this can usually be fixed:

- You first might create a small DOS partition at the beginning of the disk. This partitioning will usually cause FreeBSD to see the right geometry.

- The second way is to use the pfdisk program included on the CD-ROM (located in the tools directory). pfdisk runs under DOS and will usually detect the proper geometry of the hard disk; you then can give the FreeBSD partition the proper geometry manually.

Micron and/or Other Systems Hang When Booting

Some Micron (and possibly other) systems have buggy PCI BIOS routines. This can cause PCI devices to be configured incorrectly when they are probed. You can work around this problem by disabling the plug-and-play operating support in the BIOS setup utility.

3Com PCI Network Card Doesn't Work with Micron System

This is related to the previous problem of the buggy PCI BIOS routines in Micron systems. Once again, disable plug-and-play operating system support in the BIOS to work around this problem.

HP Netserver SCSI Controller Is Not Detected

This problem has to do with an address conflict between the EISA SCSI controller and the PCI bus. The EISA SCSI controller with this system uses slot 11, which conflicts with PCI address space. To fix this problem, enter the plain command-line interface of UserConfig when prompted to do so during the installation. Note that the visual mode will not work. You will have to use the command-line interface. At the command prompt for UserConfig, enter the following commands:

```
eisa 12
quit
```

This should allow FreeBSD to detect the controller and install. After the installation is complete, you will also want to build a custom kernel with the following line:

```
options        EISA_SLOTS=12
```

This should take care of the problem.

Boot Problems and Other Non-installation Problems

This section covers problems related to booting as well as other non-installation-related problems that you might encounter after a successful install.

FreeBSD Says "Missing Operating System" When Trying to Boot

This message usually means that FreeBSD did not correctly detect your hard disk's geometry when it installed. There are two solutions to this problem:

- Create a small DOS partition at the beginning of the drive and install a bare minimum copy of DOS on it. This should cause FreeBSD to detect the right information for partitioning.

- Use the pfdisk.exe program found on the CD to detect the hard disk geometry and then set it manually in the FreeBSD partition editor.

Either way, you will have to reinstall FreeBSD to get things working.

FreeBSD's Boot Manager Hangs at "F?"

This problem is usually caused by FreeBSD not detecting your hard disk geometry properly. See the previous section for solutions to this problem.

FreeBSD's Boot Loader Says "Read Error" and Hangs

Once again, this is usually caused by FreeBSD not detecting the hard disk geometry correctly. See the previous two sections for solutions to this problem.

No Boot Manager; System Boots Right into Windows

Either the boot manager didn't get installed when you installed FreeBSD or something you did in Windows (`fdisk /mbr`, for example) clobbered the FreeBSD boot manager. Fortunately, it is relatively easy to restore.

Boot from the included CD or from the install disks you created. After you have gotten into the Sysinstall program, select Configure and then Fdisk (see Chapter 2, "Installing FreeBSD," if you need a refresher on Sysinstall). If you have multiple hard disks in your system, you will be prompted for which system you want to run `fdisk` on. Select the primary disk that your system boots from. Once you are in `fdisk`, simply select W to write the changes. You will be given a warning, telling you that this should be done only when making changes to an existing installation. Select Yes and press Enter. When the system asks about the boot loader, select Master Boot Record. Once you have completed this process, the boot manager should be back in operation.

FreeBSD Detects Less RAM Than Is Really in the System

FreeBSD can't always get the proper amount of memory in your system from the BIOS. Usually, this results in FreeBSD detecting only 64MB of RAM, even if you really have more.

To fix this problem, you will need to add the following option to the kernel configuration file:

```
options     "MAXMEM=n"
```

Here, n is the amount of memory you have in kilobytes. Remember that in binary math, a kilobyte is actually 1024 bytes instead of 1000 bytes. A megabyte is actually 1,048,576 bytes instead of 1,000,000 bytes. In binary math, there are 1024 kilobytes in a megabyte rather than 1000 kilobytes. So, you basically end up with

```
k = m * 1024
```

where k is the number of kilobytes and m is the number of megabytes. For example, if you have 128MB of RAM, the number you would enter here is `131072` (131,072 = 128 * 1024).

After you have made this change, you will need to rebuild the kernel (see Chapter 16, "Kernel Configuration," for detailed information on rebuilding the kernel).

FreeBSD Complains "Device Not Configured" While Trying to Mount a CD-ROM Drive

This problem can be caused by a few things, as follows:

- The CD-ROM drive might be empty; simply insert a CD and try again.

- The second possibility is that an ATAPI CD-ROM drive is configured as the slave drive on the secondary controller and there is no master drive on the controller. You will need to reconfigure your CD-ROM drive as the master if this is the case (you usually can do this reconfiguration from jumpers on the back of the CD-ROM).

- If you have a SCSI CD-ROM drive, the drive might not be getting enough time to answer the bus reset request when the kernel is started. If this is the case, find the options SCSI_DELAY line in the kernel configuration file and increase the time. (The time is given in milliseconds. By default, it is set to 15000, or 15 seconds. You might start by doubling it to a value of 30000.) You will then need to rebuild the kernel (see Chapter 16).

Programs Crash with Signal 11 Errors

This problem is somewhat like an illegal operation error in Windows. It basically means that a program tried to access memory that was not allocated to it. This could be the result of a bug in the program or, if it is occurring with utilities included with FreeBSD, a bug in FreeBSD itself.

A third potential cause of this problem is flaky hardware. If the problem occurs at random points while compiling software, you can be almost sure that flaky hardware is the culprit. Common hardware causes for such problems include defective RAM, a CPU that is over-heating (Is your CPU fan running? Are you overclocking?), defective cache memory, or a flaky power supply.

Strange Error Messages Occur When Running top, ps, and Other System Utilities

This type of error is almost always caused by your world and your kernel being out of sync. Often, the problem stems from using make world to build the system from source and then failing to build a new kernel. The reverse could also be true: You built a new kernel with sources that you downloaded but did not do a make world first.

Because it is much quicker to rebuild the kernel than to rebuild the world, the simplest solution is to try making a new kernel and rebooting first (see Chapter 16 for detailed information on rebuilding the kernel).

If rebuilding the kernel doesn't fix the problem, try rebuilding the world. (See Chapter 17, "Keeping Up to Date with FreeBSD," for details on doing a make world.)

Finally, if neither of these options solves the problem, getting the latest source (see Chapter 17), making the world, and then rebuilding the kernel should fix this problem.

Forgotten Root Password

If you have forgotten your root password, you can boot into single-user mode to recover it.

To get into single-user mode, press any key when you boot the system to see the countdown. Once you have pressed any key, the boot will be interrupted. You will get a prompt that simply says

```
Ok
```

At this prompt, type **boot -s**, which will boot the system into single-user mode. When you are asked which shell to use, simply press Enter for the default. You should then get a root user prompt that looks like this:

```
#
```

At the prompt, type **mount -u**/ and then press Enter to remount the root filesystem as read/write. Then, type **mount -a** to mount all the other filesystems. You can now type **passwd root** to change the password for the root account. You will not be asked for the old password. Simply enter the new password you would like to use, press Enter, confirm it, and press Enter again. Finally, reboot your system with shutdown -r now. When your system finishes rebooting, it should be back to normal.

Sources for More Information

FreeBSD has a large and growing community of users and developers. Many sources of information are available on FreeBSD and related products. This appendix lists some of those sources.

FreeBSD-Specific Resources

Web Sites

www.freebsd.org
This is the official Web site of the FreeBSD project. It is the place to go for news, updates, and information on ports and packages. It is also where the online handbook and various tutorials are located.

www.freebsddiary.org
This site is a gold mine of FAQS and how-to articles on a large number of subjects. It is also the home of some FreeBSD discussion forums, including the one and only "FreeBSD Pets" forum. Yes, it really is what the name says. Are you a FreeBSD user? Do you have a pet? Post a message here about your pet, along with a link to a picture of your pet for all other FreeBSD users to see.

www.freshports.org
The place to get the latest news regarding new and updated FreeBSD ports.

www.freebsdmall.com
The source for purchasing all things FreeBSD. Here, you can get CDs, T-shirts, jackets, mouse pads, coffee mugs, hats, books, and so on. You can also purchase professional support services for FreeBSD here.

Mailing Lists

Mailing lists are places where those in the FreeBSD community can share information and post questions that others subscribed to the list can view and respond to. There are several benefits to being subscribed to the various mailing lists, including being notified of problems with the source tree, security hazards, and so on.

All these mailing lists are official project mailing lists. To subscribe to any one of them, send an e-mail to `majordomo@freebsd.org` with the following in the body of the message:

```
subscribe list-name
```

In this case, `list-name` is the name of the list you want to subscribe to. You can unsubscribe to any of these lists by sending an e-mail to `majordomo@freebsd.org` with the following in the body of the message:

```
unsubscribe list-name
```

Many of the lists are high volume and will generate a lot of e-mail. To avoid this, you can subscribe to many of the lists in digest form. If you do this, you will only be sent an e-mail from each list you subscribe to when the number of messages posted has exceeded 100KB. All the messages will be sent in a single e-mail.

> **CAUTION**
>
> If you decide to unsubscribe from a list, make sure you post the message to `majordomo@freebsd.org`, not to the actual mailing list. Posting the unsubscribe message to the mailing list instead of to `majordomo` will have two undesirable effects: First, it won't unsubscribe you. Instead your unsubscribe message will be posted to the list for the whole world to see. Second, it will irritate people because you are sending junk to their e-mail address. Therefore, don't be surprised if you get a bunch of flames.

General Lists

Anyone can subscribe and participate in the general lists. However, you should read the list's guidelines (which will be sent to you when you subscribe) before posting to the list. Here are the general lists, along with a short description of what each one is used for.

freebsd-advocacy

A list for discussing the benefits of FreeBSD and different ways of promoting FreeBSD.

freebsd-announce

Important announcements regarding FreeBSD. This is a read-only list that is pretty low volume.

freebsd-arch

Discussions regarding architecture and design.

freebsd-bugs

Bug reports for FreeBSD. Note that you should not actually send bug reports to this list. Rather, you should submit a problem report into the GNATS database using the form located at `http://www.freebsd.org/send-pr.html`. Your submitted problem report will then be posted on the list for those subscribed to it to see.

freebsd-chat

A general, nontechnical discussion for the FreeBSD community.

cvs-all

Changes made to the FreeBSD source tree are posted to this list. This is a read-only list.

freebsd-config

A list for discussions regarding FreeBSD installation and configuration tools (such as new GUI installation tools that will probably eventually replace `sysinstall`). Mostly of interest to developers and programmers only.

freebsd-current

If you are tracking the CURRENT branch of FreeBSD, you *need* to be subscribed to this list. Among other things, reading this list can prevent you from "making world" when the source tree is broken and possibly rendering your system unusable. You should not be tracking CURRENT unless you are tech savvy and are willing to deal with problems like this. This means that you should not post general "how-to" questions to this list. Only technical questions regarding behavior in CURRENT should be posted to this list. For other types of questions, you will either not get a response at all or will likely be told to repost your question in `freebsd-questions`.

freebsd-isp

A discussion list for Internet service providers using FreeBSD. Note that this list is for providers, not users. In other words, if you are having problems getting FreeBSD to connect to your Internet service provider, this is *not* the place to post any questions.

freebsd-jobs

If you are a FreeBSD guru looking for a job, you can find job announcements on this list. If you are an employer and need a FreeBSD guru, you can post your "help wanted" ad to this list.

freebsd-newbies

A discussion list for users new to FreeBSD. Note that this is not a help list. Rather, it is a list for newbies to swap stories about their experiences with FreeBSD and such. Questions should be posted to `freebsd-questions`, not to `freebsd-newbies`.

freebsd-policy
Policy decisions made by the FreeBSD core team. This list is low volume and read-only.

freebsd-questions
The place to post technical questions about FreeBSD. If you post a question here, be specific. In other words, don't post a question that says "I can't get pppd to work. What am I doing wrong?" Such a question is not useful at all for troubleshooting. To get a useful answer, you will need to provide details, such as the contents of any error messages that are written to the logs, what kind of configuration you are trying to use, relevant sections of configuration files (.conf files), and so on. Also, be polite and don't flame the list if you don't get an answer right away. Remember, the people staffing this list are here on their own time and are entirely volunteers. Most of them have real jobs and are devoting part of their free time to reading and responding to this list. No one on this list gets paid to help you. Note that you do not need to be subscribed to this list in order to post to it. However, make sure you provide a valid e-mail address so that people have a place to send answers to your questions.

freebsd-stable
This list is for discussions regarding the FreeBSD STABLE tree. As with CURRENT, if you are tracking STABLE, you *need* to be subscribed to this list. Although serious problems that can break the distribution and can render a system unbootable are much more rare in STABLE than in CURRENT, they can and do occur. The FreeBSD developers and committers are only human, and like everyone else, they occasionally make mistakes. This list will tell you when there are problems with the tree and also let you know when it is safe to use the tree again. Note that general technical or how-to questions should not be posted to this list. Such questions should be posted to `freebsd-questions`.

freebsd-security-notifications
Although the FreeBSD project considers this a technical list, I am putting it here because everyone using FreeBSD in a production environment should subscribe to it. This is where notifications regarding FreeBSD security holes will be posted, as well as instructions for fixing the holes. Unless you don't mind having an insecure system, you should be subscribed to this list.

Technical Lists

There are many different technical lists for FreeBSD-related issues, such as porting to different platforms, porting various software to FreeBSD, using FreeBSD in embedded systems, and so on. Because these lists are not of interest to most people, I am not going to list them here. However, a full list of the technical lists can be obtained from `http://www.freebsd.org/doc/en_US.ISO_8859-1/books/handbook/ eresources.html#ERESOURCES-MAIL`.

As the category suggests, these lists are quite technical in nature. Do not post questions of a general nature to any lists considered "technical lists." Virtually all these lists have guidelines for the way they are to be used. Therefore, you should read the charter that is e-mailed to you when subscribing to any of these lists before posting to them.

> **CAUTION**
>
> The technical lists tend to be primarily only for advanced FreeBSD users. Posting how-to questions and such to this list will get you no answers at best and will get you flamed at worst.

> **NOTE**
>
> A list of all available mailing lists can be obtained at the following Web page address: `http://www.freebsd.org/doc/en_US.ISO8859-1/books/handbook/eresources.html`.

Usenet Newsgroups for FreeBSD

The following FreeBSD-related newsgroups are available on Usenet (contact your ISP to find out what news server you should be using to access Usenet):

- `comp.unix.bsd.freebsd.announce`

- `comp.unix.bsd.freebsd.misc`

IRC Channels

Several IRC channels are available for FreeBSD. I'm not going to list all of them here because some of them are general discussion channels in which the topics are rarely about FreeBSD. Here are the two in which you are likely to be able to get help for FreeBSD:

- On EFNet: `#freebsdhelp`

- On Undernet: `#freebsd`

Note that depending on the time of day you show up, these channels may have a lot of people in them and still be very quiet. Though it may look like people are ignoring you, that's probably not the case. Many people are working and are simply logged in to the channel as well. Also, during periods of high Net congestion, IRC can have very high lag times between when you post your message and when some people actually get it. Keep this in mind as well when you don't seem to be getting any responses (you might consider switching to a different server if it seems your lag time is very high).

D

Expect to be treated the way you treat others on IRC. If you are rude because you are not getting answers or are not getting the answers you want, expect people to ignore you or respond rudely to you (a channel operator might ban you from the channel, as well). Remember, like those on the `freebsd-questions` mailing list, no one here is paid to help you. People on IRC are helping you on their own free time, so keep that in mind before you get mad at them.

Other BSD-Related Resources

These resources are related to BSD in general but are not FreeBSD specific. Because FreeBSD is the most popular of the BSD-based operating systems, most of these resources cover FreeBSD extensively. You will find coverage of other BSD-related things here as well, though.

Web Sites

`www.freebsd.org`
This site is, of course, the official home page for the FreeBSD project. It is the first place to go for the latest information about FreeBSD releases, security advisories, and so on.

`www.daemonnews.org`
The premier site for news on all things BSD related. This site has forums and runs how-to articles. It is also home of the "Source Wars" comics.

`www.bsdtoday.com`
This is another Web site that contains daily updated news on items of BSD interest.

`www.maximumbsd.com`
Another site that contains news of BSD interest. This site also has some good archives and links to tutorials.

Other Internet Resources

This section covers other resources on the Internet that are somehow related to FreeBSD in a general sense. Included in this section are the home pages for some of the software used and described in this book.

Web Sites

`www.xfree86.org`
This is the home page for the XFree86 project, which is the free implementation of X-Windows included with FreeBSD. This is where you will find documentation and such related to the X-Windows system.

`www.gnu.org`

The home page for the GNU (a recursive acronym that stands for GNU's Not Unix) project. Many of the utilities included with FreeBSD—such as the GCC compiler, the GAWK pattern-matching language, the Emacs editor, and the f77 FORTRAN compiler—are from the GNU project. This site contains information on almost all the GNU project's software.

`www.gnome.org`

The home page for the Gnome Desktop Environment project. Gnome news, tutorials, and so on can be found here.

`www.kde.org`

The major competitor to Gnome. If you prefer KDE, this is your site.

`www.apache.org`

This is the home page for the Apache Web server project—the most popular Web server in the world. It is free and is the Web server of choice for FreeBSD. This site also contains information about projects that can be used to extend Apache's functionality, such as PHP, Perl, TCL, and more.

`www.mysql.com`

MySQL is the open-source SQL database of choice for FreeBSD. This site contains documentation, tutorials, and so on for the MySQL database software.

`www.postgresql.org`

The site for another open-source SQL database available for FreeBSD. PostgreSQL has more features than MySQL but is somewhat slower.

`www.php.net`

The home page of the embedded scripting language of choice for building Web-based applications. PHP is an open-source competitor to Active Server Pages (ASP). PHP is primarily used for linking Web sites to databases. It integrates well with MySQL and PostgreSQL.

`www.perl.com`

This site includes information and tutorials on the Perl programming language, which is included as a standard part of FreeBSD.

`www.python.org`

The home page for the Python programming language, which is a popular alternative to Perl.

D

`www.sendmail.org`

The home page of the Sendmail mail transfer agent, which is the default mail transfer agent included with FreeBSD.

`www.postfix.org`

The home page for a popular alternative mail transfer agent for Sendmail. Postfix is a drop-in replacement for Sendmail. It is my favorite mail transfer agent. New users will find it much easier to configure than Sendmail.

`www.osnews.com`

Although it is not FreeBSD specific, this news site often contains articles of general interest to FreeBSD users and sometimes runs FreeBSD specific articles.

Usenet Newsgroups

The following non-FreeBSD-specific newsgroups are available on Usenet (contact your ISP to find out what news server you should be using to access Usenet).

General Unix Newsgroups

These newsgroups cover topics that are not specific to FreeBSD but are of interest to Unix users in general. For example, they cover Unix administration practices, general Unix security issues, general Unix shell use, and so on.

- `comp.security.unix`
- `comp.sources.unix`
- `comp.unix.admin`
- `comp.unix.advocacy`
- `comp.unix.misc`
- `comp.unix.programmer`
- `comp.unix.questions`
- `comp.unix.shell`
- `comp.unix.user-friendly`

X-Windows Newsgroups

- `comp.emulators.ms-windows.wine`
- `comp.windows.x`
- `comp.windows.x.announce`
- `comp.windows.x.apps`

- comp.windows.x.i386unix
- comp.windows.x.intrinsics
- comp.windows.x.motif
- comp.windows.x.pex

Index

Symbol and Numbers

A

B

How can we make this index more useful? Email us at indexes@samspublishing.com

How can we make this index more useful? Email us at indexes@samspublishing.com

make clean command, 855

make command, 328, 855

make deinstall command, 855

make distclean command, 855

make install command, 855

make start command (Sendmail), 555

make world process

    buildworld process, 393

    considerations in, 384-385

    installworld process, 396-397

    kernel, upgrading

        CUSTOM, 395

        GENERIC, 394

    mergmaster utility, 397-399

    output log, starting, 392-393

    overview of, 383, 391-392

    pre-action tasks, 386

        merging /etc/group and /etc/passwd, 389-391

        merging /etc/make.conf, 391

        synchronizing source tree, 387-388

        UPDATING file, 389

    rebooting after, 400

    troubleshooting, 394-399

    /usr/obj, cleaning out, 392

makefiles, 550

man adduser, 192

man amd.conf, 775

man at pages, 308

man builtin pages, 245

man chmod, 199

man command

    -f option, 135

    -k option, 133-134

    -s option, 136

man command command, 854

man hier pages, 166

man mount msdos pages, 174

man mount nfs page, 773

man mount pages, 173

man ps pages, 300

man security page, 723

man sysctl page, 437

man syslogd pages, 228

man syslogd.conf pages, 228

man tunefs page, 437

man tuning page, 437

managing

    files and directories

        changing directories, 139-140

        copying, 140-141

        creating directories, 142

        deleting, 142

        filenames, 147-149

        finding files, 149-150

        links, creating, 143-145

        listing directory contents, 137-139

        meta-characters and wildcard operators, 146-147

        moving and renaming, 141

        pwd command, 140

        removing directories, 142

        touch command, 143

        universal command options, 145-146

    groups, 211

manual configuration and DHCP, 797

manual pages

    commands, 851

    searching for, 133-134

    sections of, 135-136

mapping

    names to IP addresses, 521

    Windows users, 787

N

operating systems. *See also* specific operating
systems (such as Windows)

  dual boot systems

    DOS, Windows 95, Windows 98, or
    Windows ME, 62

    limitations of, 61-62

    Linux, 62

  filesystems, 163

  keeping up-to-date, 379

  mounting and unmounting filesystems from

    Linux, 174

    overview of, 171-173

    Windows/MS-DOS, 173-174

  multiuser, 189-190

  partitions, 410

operators (Perl), 452-454

optimizing database performance

  cache tables, using, 676

  monitoring usage, 673-675

  temporary tables, creating, 675-676

options for commands, 851

OSI (Open Systems Interconnection) stack,
476-478

outer joins, 643

output log, starting, 392-393

output redirection, 156-157

overrides (Apache), 586-588

overwriting file contents, 141

P

package installation system, 48

Package menus, exiting, 320

package system

  installed packages, obtaining information on,
  316-318

  overview of, 314-315

  shared libraries and dependencies, 315

packages

  installing

    overview of, 318

    pkg add program, 321-323

    sysinstall program, 319-321

  installing shells from, 234

  Linux compared to FreeBSD, 426

  origins of, 322-323

  removing, 323

  updating, 323

Packages menu (sysinstall program), 319-320

packet forwarding, enabling, 625-626

packet sniffers, 488, 693-694

packets, misconfiguration of, 502

PAP authentication, 531-532

parallel ports

  configuring for printing, 339

  maintining configuration across reboots, 340

  printing and, 337-339

parsed HTML, 601

parsing files and memory, 602

Partition Editor, 27-30

Partition Magic, 56

partitioning, 168. *See also* partitions

  FIPS utility

    boot disk, creating, 58-59

    overview of, 57

    running Scandisk and defragmenter, 57

    starting, 58

    working with, 59-61

How can we make this index more useful? Email us at indexes@samspublishing.com

How can we make this index more useful? Email us at indexes@samspublishing.com

X

How can we make this index more useful? Email us at indexes@samspublishing.com

Your Guide to Computer Technology

www.informit.com

FreeBSD Installation Instructions

FreeBSD can be installed by booting directly from the CD-ROM or by booting from floppies. Other types of installations are covered in the INSTALL.TXT file on the top-level directory of the CD-ROM.

Start Installation with a Bootable CD-ROM

Insert the CD-ROM in your CD drive and restart your computer. Press the Del or the F2 key to access the BIOS setup utility while the computer is starting up. Once in the BIOS setup utility, look for a boot priority option. If your computer is capable of booting from a CD-ROM, your CD-ROM drive will be listed. Make sure the CD-ROM drive has a higher boot priority than your hard drive(s) to enable booting from a CD-ROM.

Start or reboot your machine with the disc in your CD-ROM drive. After a few moments, you should see the FreeBSD installation routine. For more details on the installation routine, please see the section, "Installation Quick Start Guide."

Create a Boot Diskette

To start the FreeBSD install process from a diskette, you will need two formatted 1.44MB 3.5" diskettes or one formatted 2.88MB 3.5" diskette. Label the two disks appropriately, such as BOOT and MFS ROOT, or label the one disk as BOOT.

1. Insert the FreeBSD 5.0 CD-ROM into your computer's CD-ROM drive. If you are using Unix without a volume manager, you will need to mount the disc.

2. Go to the command line.

3. Navigate to the TOOLS directory on the CD-ROM.

4. Insert one of the two formatted diskettes (BOOT) and type

   `fdimage ../floppies/kern.flp a:` [Enter]

   if using DOS or Windows or type

   `dd if=../floppies/kern.flp of=/dev/floppy` [Enter]

   if using Unix.

5. When the first image has been written, remove the first diskette and insert the second diskette (MFS ROOT). Use the same command as in Step 4, but this time use `mfsroot.flp`.

> **NOTE**
>
> If you formatted one 2.88MB 3.5" diskette, use the same command as in Step 4, but use the
> boot.flp image instead.

When you are through creating the boot diskette(s), leave the FreeBSD CD-ROM in your
CD-ROM drive and see the section, "Start Installation with a Boot Diskette."

Start Installation with a Boot Diskette

Insert the CD-ROM in your CD drive and the BOOT diskette in the floppy drive and
restart your computer. Press the Del or the F2 key to access the BIOS setup utility while the
computer is starting up. Once in the BIOS setup utility, look for a boot priority option.
Make sure the floppy drive has a higher boot priority than your hard drive(s) to enable
booting from the diskette.

Start or reboot your computer. If you are using the two-diskette option, you will be
prompted to insert the MFS Root diskette after a few moments to a few minutes. After a
few moments, you should see the FreeBSD installation routine. For more details on the
installation routine, please see the section, "Installation Quick Start Guide."

Installation Quick Start Guide

If everything went well, you will be presented with the FreeBSD Installation Main Menu
(called /stand/sysinstall Main Menu). The Usage menu option will describe the installation
options in detail, so you should read this guide before you do anything else.

Once you choose an installation option, follow the on-screen prompts to finish the installation.

NOTE

This CD-ROM uses long and mixed-case filenames requiring the use of a protected-mode CD-ROM Driver.